Best Places to Stay in the Mid-Atlantic States

The Best Places to Stay Series

Best Places to Stay in America's Cities
Kenneth Hale-Wehmann, Editor

Best Places to Stay in Asia
Jerome E. Klein

Best Places to Stay in California
Second Edition/Marilyn McFarlane

Best Places to Stay in the Caribbean
Second Edition/Bill Jamison and Cheryl Alters Jamison

Best Places to Stay in Florida
Christine Davidson

Best Places to Stay in Hawaii
Second Edition/Bill Jamison and Cheryl Alters Jamison

Best Places to Stay in Mexico
Bill Jamison and Cheryl Alters Jamison

Best Places to Stay in the Mid-Atlantic States
Dana Nadel

Best Places to Stay in the Midwest
John Monaghan

Best Places to Stay in New England
Fourth Edition/Christina Tree and Kimberly Grant

Best Places to Stay in the Pacific Northwest
Second Edition/Marilyn McFarlane

Best Places to Stay in the Rocky Mountain Region
Roger Cox

Best Places to Stay in the South
Carol Timblin

Best Places to Stay in the Southwest
Second Edition/Anne E. Wright and Gail Barber Rickey

Best Places to Stay in the Mid-Atlantic States

FIRST EDITION

Dana Nadel

Bruce Shaw, Editorial Director

Houghton Mifflin Company
Boston • New York • London

First Edition

ISSN: 1061-7353
ISBN: 0-395-58664-X

Printed in the United States of America

Illustrations by Chris Schuh
Maps by Charles Bahne
Design by Robert Overholtzer

This book was prepared in conjunction
with the Harvard Common Press.

VB 10 9 8 7 6 5 4 3 2 1

To Patrick, who made home my favorite vacation.

Acknowledgments

For their help in writing this book, I'd like to thank Paul Grimes, who introduced me to the world of travel with patience, objectivity, a rather strict code of ethics, and a rare spirit of generosity for which I am forever grateful; my mother, Robin Roush, who has been a remarkable and unconditional means of support, along with my siblings, Hannah and David; my father, Ethan Nadel, who takes credit (perhaps rightly so) for instilling in me the sense of adventure which accompanies travel; my grandparents, Ruth and Harry Nadel, who serve as constant reminders of what lies on that good road ahead.

I most certainly thank Bruce Shaw, the Editorial Director, and Dan Rosenberg, the Managing Editor, of Harvard Common Press for their confidence and encouragement during the last year; Barbara Flanagan, manuscript editor, for her insight; Marilyn Marlow, for her professional advice; and Margaret Foley for her professional friendship. Last, I owe a great deal to the hundreds of innkeepers and hoteliers who welcomed me during my travels, making my research a grand adventure.

Contents

Introduction

A vacation is a celebratory time, a skip in life's most regular beat. It might be a long-awaited romantic weekend, the knitting of schedules which unites friends separated by time and distance, that rare window when a family frees itself from school and work, or a well-deserved retreat from stresses of the job. Whatever the occasion, a vacation is an exciting, luxurious, unpredictable event. This book remembers quite sincerely every bit of hope, anticipation, and money that we put into our vacations—an ominous responsibility.

It's a familiar drama: well-wishes from co-workers, a final rush to the bank, stray phone calls, packing, making lists, losing lists, a vague feeling of butterflies as the taxicab meets traffic, picking out a magazine while watching the clock. Despite the recognizable emotions of travel, a vacation is often a blind act of faith. Will the weather hold up? Will this bed-and-breakfast be as charming as my twice-removed cousin's wife said it would (and now that I think of it, I never did like her taste)? What will we do at night? Will we make any friends?

Certainly, this book cannot guarantee a successful vacation, but it can alleviate some of those unsettling uncertainties. I have met nearly all the innkeepers you will meet, visited their homes, explored their rooms, their grounds, sometimes with their pets in tow. I've been to the hotels and resorts, seen that what they advertise as a tennis court is not a paved driveway, that their swimming pool doesn't double as a fishing pond (which they also advertise).

While taking notes, interviewing, exploring, and snooping, I tried to envision this place as the special place in which you have invested your hopes and finances. I tried to imagine you readers here for that long-awaited respite. Will you be happy here? What could go wrong? Why is this place in the woods better than another on the shore? How professional are the innkeepers, and how warm is this hotel staff? I tried to envision who would like it here: a businessman, a family, a businesswoman, an amorous couple, a sophisticated couple, a shy couple, an older couple, a single person—in hopes of finding the best places to stay for every person with every imaginable need.

It was a rewarding task: a beautiful hotel would warm my heart; a well-run inn would life my spirits.

After months of research and 12,000 miles driving in this unimaginably beautiful territory, having been hosted by hundreds of hoteliers and innkeepers, I was very taken with the concept of leisure. The eight Mid-Atlantic states comprise a fascinating gallery of Americana in a concentrated, accessible region smaller than Texas, home to more than fifty million people. Within its boundaries are some of the nation's most stunning geographical surprises, sophisticated culture, and the raw beginning of American history. I envy you your travels.

Please keep in mind:

For the purposes of this book, I have defined a bed-and-breakfast as an intimate hostelry that serves a morning meal. An inn is a bed-and-breakfast that serves dinner. Other lodging spots do not serve meals, unless otherwise stated, usually with the following terminology:

EP: European plan, includes no meals.

MAP: Modified American plan, includes breakfast and dinner.

AP: Full American plan, includes three meals.

Rates listed are double occupancy unless otherwise specified. Ask about single rates if you're traveling alone. Hotels and resorts have private baths unless otherwise specified.

While I am confident that the places in this book are wondrous and exceptional, there are several things which you as the traveler can do to make your stays more comfortable. Do be specific about your needs when you make reservations, especially in smaller establishments, which often have smaller rooms and which may be booked months ahead.

Do request an update on anything which may be of importance to you: smoking, rates, proximity to restaurants, views, fireplaces (gas or wood-burning), handicapped facilities, facilities for adults as well as for teenagers, children, and infants. Though I tried to be as accurate as possible in my research, policies, rates, and owners change.

Please (and I implore) do check in advance if you have a pet and wish for him or her to be as comfortable as you.

Happy travels.

Maps

Delaware

Lewes
New Devon Inn 59
Milford
The Towers 212
New Castle
The David Finney Inn 92
Wilmington
Christina House 315

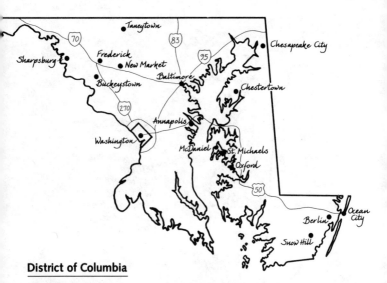

New Jersey

Absecon
Marriott's Seaview Golf
Resort 435
Bay Head
Conover's Bay Head Inn Bed
and Breakfast 163
Cape May
The Abbey 158
Captain Mey's Bed and
Breakfast Inn 160
Chalfonte Hotel 161
Colvmns by the Sea 218
John Wesley Inn 167
The Queen Victoria 170
The Mainstay Inn 220
The Virginia Hotel 173
Frenchtown
The Old Hunterdon House 68
Hope
Inn at Millrace Pond 100
Lambertville
Chimney Hill Farm 4
The Inn at Lambertville
Station 98

Milford
Chestnut Hill on the Delaware 66
Princeton
Peacock Inn 299
Short Hills
Hilton at Short Hills 380
South Belmar
Hollycroft 165
Spring Lake
Hewitt Wellington 164
The Normandy Inn 168
Sea Crest by the Sea 172
Stanhope
The Whistling Swan Inn 70
Stockton
The Stockton Inn
"Colligan's" 102
Woodbine
Henry Ludlam Inn 181

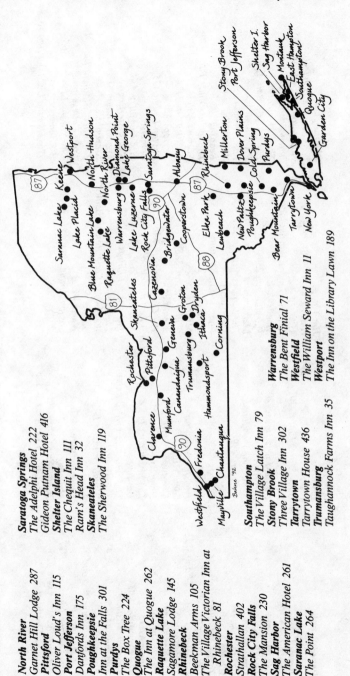

Baline '92.

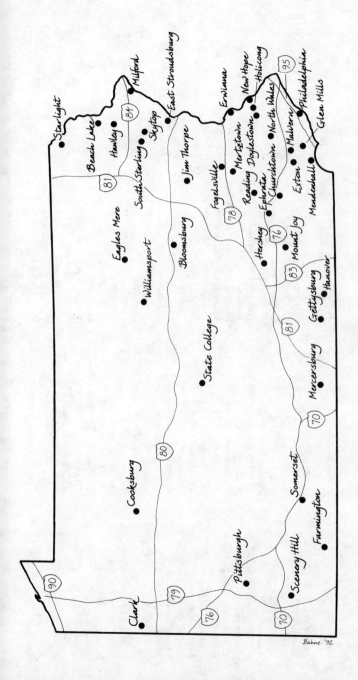

Bahne '92

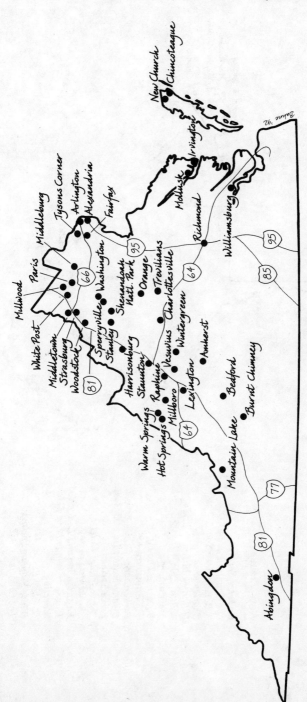

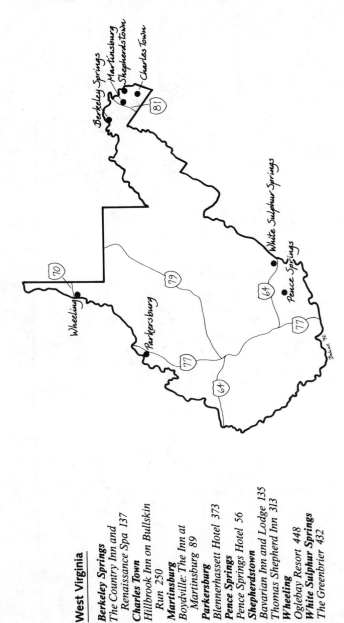

West Virginia

Berkeley Springs
The Country Inn and
Renaissance Spa 137
Charles Town
Hillbrook Inn on Bullskin
Run 250
Martinsburg
Boydville: The Inn at
Martinsburg 89
Parkersburg
Blennerhassett Hotel 373
Pence Springs
Pence Springs Hotel 56
Shepherdstown
Bavarian Inn and Lodge 135
Thomas Shepherd Inn 313
Wheeling
Oglebay Resort 448
White Sulphur Springs
The Greenbrier 432

Country Bed-and-Breakfasts

Maryland

Inn at Antietam
220 East Main Street, Box 119
Sharpsburg, Maryland 21782
301-432-6601

Proprietors: Betty and Cal Fairbourn
Accommodations: 4 suites, all with private bath
Rates: $95; $105 weekends and holidays
Included: Full breakfast
Minimum stay: Two nights on holidays and weekends
Added: $25 each additional guest; 8% tax
Payment: American Express
Children: Over 6 welcome
Pets: Not allowed
Smoking: Allowed in designated areas only
Open: Year-round except December 21–January 1

The Antietam National Battlefield marks the decisive point at which the Confederates failed in their effort to conquer the North. Eighty-seven thousand federal soldiers fought forty-one thousand southerners on this field in one of the bloodiest battles of the Civil War: on September 17, 1862, more than twenty thousand men were killed. On this twelve-square-mile setting, the National Park Service leads detailed tours and maintains a cemetery. After a day on the Battlefield, historians will appreciate a peaceful place to stay right on the property.

The Inn at Antietam is a serene, relaxing, pretty bed-and-breakfast with very generous and knowledgeable hosts, Cal and Betty Fairbourn. Bordering on historic property, the acreage of the Inn is very well-groomed, and the flowers around the property are quite lavish, tended to by the owner and his trowel. In

1983, the Fairbourns bought this white clapboard house, which was built in 1908 and served for years as a horse farm. They restored it over the course of a year and had it decorated professionally. The whole place mixes professional taste with sincere, personal touches by the owners.

Each of the four guest rooms is actually a unique two-room suite, with perfect antiques and traditional, lovely, spotless decor. A favorite room is the Smoke House, a masculine room with light blue plaid wing chairs and window treatments, wide-planked heart pine floors and walls, a cathedral open-beamed ceiling, and a huge brick fireplace. Up narrow stairs is the loft bedroom. At the front of the house is another first floor room, the Master Suite, which has an 1880 queen-size four-poster pineapple bed with a crown canopy, pink floral wallpaper matching the linens, and a lovely bay window permitting extra sunlight overlooking the front porch and sloping front lawn. Its sitting room is quite large. Above this on the second floor is the Blue Bird Suite, with a queen-size iron and brass bed; and across the hall is another favorite, the Queen Suite, done in pink and green, with a sun porch furnished in antique wicker. The preppy elegance of the decor came from the hand of Keith Knost, whose work can also be seen at the Greenbrier in West Virginia.

Guests are very pampered here, with good amenities and the excellent, professional hosting of the Fairbourns. They can spend time privately in their large rooms or gregariously in the three common spaces—the dining room, living room, and sun porch. Cal has the sociable air of a retired senator; and if she announced that her surname was Crocker, those who tried Betty's peanut butter cookies or large breakfasts wouldn't blink an eye.

Wades Point Inn on the Bay

Box 7, St. Michaels
McDaniel, Maryland 21663
410-745-2500

Proprietors: John and Betsy Feiler
Accommodations: 26 rooms, from rustic to elegant (3 rooms in Main House, 6 in Main House Summer Wing, 12 in Mildred T. Kemp house, 5 in cottage)
Rates: $69–$155; weekday discounts
Included: Expanded Continental
Minimum stay: 2 nights on weekends and holidays
Added: $10 each additional guest; 8% tax

Payment: Visa, MasterCard
Children: Welcome (under 12 free)
Pets: Not allowed
Smoking: Not allowed
Open: All year

Following bucolic Route 33 for five miles from St. Michaels toward the tip of the peninsula at Tilghman Island, an eastern shore visitor happens upon a sign for Wades Point Inn. A long, straight drive leads to the 1819 farmhouse, a graceful brick and white clapboard set on 120 acres of groomed, pastured fields. The waters of the Chesapeake Bay lap against the stone seawall surrounding the property.

Wades Point was named for Zachary Wade, who received a land grant for the property in 1657. The Main House was built a century and a half later, in 1819, by Baltimore shipwright Thomas Kemp, and the Summer Wing was added in 1890, completing the longer part of the T shape that stretches out to the waters on the Wades Point peninsula. The Kemp family operated the inn for nearly one hundred years before the Feilers arrived in 1984. Most recently, the Feilers added modern comforts in the 1990 Mildred T. Kemp wing, a two-story building with postmodern gingerbread.

The accommodations are quite varied at Wades Point. The six rooms in the Summer Wing were built for a growing Victorian family, with in-room sinks and two shared full baths. They are furnished with double beds, and the walls are painted a summery white with a pink hue warmed by diaphanous gauzy curtains, lending a glow to the breezy interior. On either side of a hall leading to a generous second-floor porch, all rooms have water views. Three additional guest rooms in the Main House are more traditionally appointed. Across the lawn is a white clapboard cottage with a rustic interior, set aside for families traveling together.

In the new Mildred T. Kemp wing, named for the estate's hostess of fifty-three years who retired at age ninety-one, the deluxe rooms have angled balconies overlooking the bay, the breakwater, and sweeping lawns and furnished with Adirondack chairs. The white clapboard exterior is trimmed in forest green and stained wood, with sky blue porch ceilings and off-white pink balconies. The twelve guest rooms in this wing have traditional reproduction furniture, with one or two queen-size beds, white spreads punctuated with colorful comforters, pink borders, and sparkling new baths with peach towels. Four rooms have kitchenettes.

Below the Summer Wing is the enchanting dining room, with three sides of windows providing water views. Below the windows, the walls are light with white wainscoting; and above, the walls become an airy mint-hued off-white. The tables and chairs are white wicker, set in three rows separated by two colonnades. Guests enjoy a Continental breakfast here of fresh-baked muffins, French rolls, cheese, and fruit. The formal dining room and common room are furnished traditionally with antiques and lead to screened porches on all sides of the house.

After exploring chic St. Michaels in one direction and wind-swept Tilghman Island in the other, guests can stroll the acreage at Wades Point or fish or crab in the Chesapeake waters off the inn's dock.

New Jersey

Chimney Hill Farm
Goat Hill Road, RD #3, Box 150
Lambertville, New Jersey 08530
609-397-1516

Proprietor: Kenneth M. Turi
Accommodations: 7 rooms, all with private bath, 2 with fireplace
Rates: $105–$150
Included: Full breakfast
Minimum stay: 2 nights on weekends
Added: 7% tax
Payment: Visa, MasterCard
Children: Not allowed
Pets: Not allowed
Smoking: Not allowed
Open: All year

Just before the Delaware River widens and congests toward its bay it serenely divides two charming towns: New Hope, Pennsylvania, and Lambertville, New Jersey. The former is a popular tourist spot, madly busy at certain times of the year, and the latter, just across a metal bridge, is often overlooked in the shadow of its Bucks County neighbor. Locked in the nineteenth century, Lambertville is a great place for antiquing as well as cycling along the flat scenic roads astride the Delaware.

Chimney Hill Farm is set atop steep Goat Hill, which hovers above Lambertville a half mile away. The ten acres of grounds are beautifully groomed, with lovely perennial gardens, old

Adirondack chairs, two huge and ancient holly trees, white and pink azaleas, and a boxwood maze.

The farmhouse was built in 1820, as a small two-story stone box. In 1927 an international attorney named Edgar Hunt bought the farmhouse as his summer retreat during the Bucks County Round Table days and contracted architect Margaret Spencer, MIT's first architecture grad, to put three stone wings onto the building, creating most of the structure as we see it today. The house lay vacant for a year and a half until the present owner bought and restored it, opening it as an inn in 1988.

Chimney Hill, highly and exactly decorated, borders on formal elegance. The federal living room has some exceptional antiques, including an 18th-century English secretary and a 17th-century William and Mary chest of drawers. Two steps down to the right is a great stone sun porch with flagstone floor, front and back views of the lawns through six wide-paned windows, and two floral wicker sofas. The dining room, in the 1820 section of the house, is lovely, with an embroidered rug over wide-planked floors, colonial tables, very low open-beamed ceiling, light green window seat, hunt placemats, and the owner's Blue Willow china collection. Full breakfast may include a specialty such as Grand Marnier french toast or pancakes with home-grown raspberries, which are highly acclaimed. The three common rooms have fireplaces, as do two of the guest rooms.

The only first-floor room has one of the two guest room fireplaces and a black and white toile ceiling canopy over the bed. There are five rooms on the second floor: one in red chintz with a queen-size canopy bed; a second room has the other guest fireplace and is decorated with a black rose duvet and linens; another room has unicorn tapestry fabric; and the fifth, exotic room has marbleized wainscoting and a bed entirely enclosed by curtains. Chimney Hill is a very romantic spot, with an overwhelming sense of elegance and privacy.

New York

Genesee Country Inn
948 George Street
Mumford, New York 14511
716-538-2500

Proprietor: Glenda Barcklow
Innkeepers: Glenda Barcklow and Kim Rasmussen
Accommodations: 9 rooms, all with private bath, 1 with
    fireplace
Rates: $80–$115
Included: Full breakfast, afternoon refreshments
Minimum stay: 2 nights on some weekends
Added: 7% state tax; 4% county tax
Payment: No credit cards
Children: Check with innkeepers
Pets: Not allowed
Smoking: Allowed
Open: All year

Where some bed-and-breakfasts stand out with one or two fine
details, Glenda Barcklow's has myriad memorable aspects.
Rochester is a half hour's drive and a world away. Not only is this
owner one of the more professional innkeepers in the business,
but she is infinitely warm-hearted, as is kindred soul Kim Rasmussen. The inn has a unique setting, built in 1833 as a plaster
mill right above Spring Creek (it was converted to an inn in
1982). The creek wends its way across a road to a waterfall that
empties at the inn's front lawn, a pleasant greeting for guests
checking in. Water flows audibly around and behind the inn,
calming on flat rocks to the delight of the family ducks. It's a
great spot for fly-fishing since the county fish hatchery is just
one town upstream from the little hamlet of Mumford.

   A stone house with two-and-a-half-foot-thick walls, the Genesee Country Inn looks smallish from the road—two stories
and six windows across—but there is another entire level from
the creek's eye view, totaling eighteen rooms. The cheery common room has a painted fire board and stenciling around the
walls, done by local artist Ruth Flowers from authentic 19th-
century patterns. Adjacent is the airy breakfast room, which is
very open with diagonal wood paneling under a pitched roof.
Breakfasts are ample and interesting, with entreés like cream
cheese–filled French toast, Cheddar egg bake, and pancakes
with cinnamon vanilla cream sauce.

   The Genesee Country Inn has a dual face. During the weekend, the inn is a romantic spot for couples retreating to the
countryside who love the New York Amish quilts and canopy
beds, the creative breakfasts, and six acres of wooded property
interrupted by a stream. On weekdays the inn marks a change
in pace, becoming a haven for businesspeople grateful for the
desk in every room, direct-dial phones, televisions hidden in

pine armoires, new private baths, oversize towels, and thoughtful amenities (such as razors and hair dryers in some rooms).

Though all rooms are charming and different, the three downstairs rooms are a bit newer and more spacious than the six upstairs rooms and each has a private entrance. Of these the Skivington is preferable, with a four-windowed view of Spring Creek and the back porch, the hilly back lawn, and ducks. The McGinnis has a gas fireplace and a little sun porch. Characteristically, this inn is extremely clean.

Those who venture out will want to visit the Genesee Country Museum and Nature Center, home to a 19th-century crafts village just down the road.

J. P. Morgan House Bed and Breakfast Inn

2920 Smith Road
Canandaigua, New York 14424
716-394-9232

Proprietors: John and Julie Sullivan
Accommodations: 7 rooms, 5 with private bath, including 1 suite
Rates: $85–$175
Included: Full breakfast
Minimum stay: 2 nights on weekends, May–November
Added: $20 each additional guest; $15 each child; 7% tax
Payment: MasterCard, Visa, Discover
Children: Welcome
Pets: Not allowed
Smoking: Not allowed
Open: All year

This J. P. Morgan was Judson Morgan, the true poor cousin to the better-known tycoon. Having recovered from the mild disappointment that it's not the magnate's mansion, a visitor quickly admits that this is a lovely home by any standards. Two miles from the tip of one of the westernmost Finger Lakes, Lake Canandaigua, and a short drive from its charming and surprisingly bustling town, this bed-and-breakfast has an extremely tranquil setting, removed from the country road junction by two long gravel driveways. The unusual stone and brick house was built in 1810 by a farmer, and present owners John and Julie Sullivan still retain 46 acres of lovely flat cornfields and hay fields.

The 1810 farmhouse was expanded in 1930 to become a long, narrow composite of two buildings, thick stone and brick, nearly submerged in ivy vines, with a kind of cottage-in-the-woods feeling. Guests enter through a brick foyer and either descend to the common rooms and several guest rooms or continue upstairs to the next two floors.

The Sullivans opened their bed-and-breakfast in January 1989, escaping a corporate environment and seeking a serene place for their young family. The rooms are on three floors. A favorite is the Antique Rose Room, furnished in a smashing, rare 19th-century five-piece bedroom set with green hand-painted wood and gold trim and offering two views of the farm fields. The master suite is very large, in muted white and beige, with a stunning 1749 serpentine French bedroom set and a room-size dressing area. A rope banister takes visitors to the third floor, with the charming Gothic Room and its pointed high windows, and to the spectacular Victorian Room, which has a barrel cathedral ceiling, a king-size bed fitted with dark and heavy tapestry linens, and floral trellised wallpaper. Some may think the bath the finest feature in the room: through the curved doorway one wall has been exposed to reveal the stone-work of the chimney, and green marble lines the floor and walls, leading to the Jacuzzi under the pitched ceiling. Some rooms have porches, and all have peaceful farm views. A great tennis court is framed by the stone foundation of an old barn.

Breakfasts are ample, served in the formal dining room or the enclosed slate porch overlooking the fields through enchanting wrought-iron doors. An outdoor slate patio sits amid the groomed gardens. Those who love the full breakfast — buckwheat pancakes, blackberry muffins, double cheese omelettes — will be pleased to know that John and Julie will cook dinners by prior arrangement.

Plumbush

Chautauqua-Stedman Road, Box 332, RD 2
Mayville, New York 14757
716-789-5309

Proprietors: Sandy and George Green
Accommodations: 4 rooms, all with private bath
Rates: $65–$85
Included: Buffet breakfast
Minimum stay: 2 and 3 nights in peak season and on some weekends
Added: 7% tax
Payment: MasterCard, Visa, American Express (add $2)
Children: Over 12 welcome
Pets: Not allowed

Smoking: Not allowed
Open: All year

The Chautauqua Institute, named for the lake on which it sits in southwestern New York, is a curious Victorian haven that becomes a cultural and artistic hub for nine weeks during the summer. Built in 1874 as a retreat for Methodist Sunday school teachers, the Chautauqua Institute is a panoply of Victorian architecture, narrow winding streets, and narrow teetering buildings tumbling toward the picturesque lakefront. Dance, music, theater, and lectures structure the aesthetes' days, and if one wants a more private or romantic place to stay than the famous and very busy Athenaeum, there is no better choice but Plumbush.

This glorious 1867 Italianate Victorian mansion is a minute's drive from the Chautauqua gates, painted in mauve and trimmed with plum, pale pink, and greens. Propped on a little hill, Plumbush is neat as a pin, and its four rooms are as pristine. The 125 acres of grounds are softly groomed. Only a turret pokes above the two stories of the house, with its arched windows, corner bays, a little corner porch where guests enter. To the left is the living room with a bay window, to the right a music room with a bay window, a piano, and an organ. The dining room has a spectacular cherry and hard maple floor in a striped inlay pattern, highly finished, with a handmade quilted tiger maple table. Past the kitchen is the sun porch, an addition to the old house, with brick flooring, large windows, and sliding doors to the lawns.

The walnut carved banister leads guests upstairs to the landing. A choice: to one's room or up the white iron spiral staircase that leads to the third-floor turret with four views of the property and the hovering maple trees outside.

The two larger of the four guest rooms, Pipestone and Bleufre, named for plums, face the front of the house. These rooms are preferable, with lovely antiques and cheery new baths generously supplied with Gilchrest and Soames amenities. Pipestone, to the right of the landing, has two large curved windows, a queen-size iron and brass bed, and two white wicker chairs with green chintz padding. Bleufre features an incredible double rope bed and a rare chest of tiger maple. Greengage down the hall is the smallest room, with a small Victorian pine dresser and a nice little bath. Bradshaw in the back of the house has two twin beds and the possibility of an attached small double room, only upon request.

Innkeepers Sandy and George are very knowledgeable about the area and are happy to offer advice over a buffet breakfast, served in the dining room or on the sun porch.

Toad Hall
Fly Creek, New York 13337
607-547-5774

Proprietors: Randy Van Syoc and Allen Ransome
Accommodations: 3 rooms, all with private bath
Rate: $70
Included: Full country breakfast
Minimum stay: None
Added: 8% tax
Payment: Major credit cards
Children: Not allowed
Pets: Not allowed
Smoking: Not allowed
Open: All year

Some people come to Cooperstown for baseball, while a sophisticated minority come just to pay homage to Toad Hall, a magnificent furniture and craft shop sitting modestly on a Cooperstown side street, a haven for antiques lovers. Devotees of this glorious shop, filled with the masterful work of furniture maker Allen Ransome as well as local crafts and folk art, will be thrilled to know that Toad Hall's talented owners operate a three-room bed-and-breakfast out of their home four miles from town.

That they chose an upstate New York location for their gallery is evidence that the owners of Toad Hall prefer understatement in everything they undertake—especially in the home they open up to guests. It's a very-low-profile place and visitors are invited to call ahead for reservations.

Before coming across the country from California to Cooperstown, Allen had a rich history in furniture and interior design, and Randy owned a fabric company. In 1985, they transplanted themselves and bought a near-to-falling-down 1820 stone farmhouse outside Cooperstown and undertook a three-year restoration effort. The house is a magnificent stone structure, with four large columns across shading a sweeping veranda. On their 80 acres of farmland, Randy keeps two horses and breeds Newfoundland dogs.

The common rooms are on the second floor, the three guest rooms on the third floor. The living room is decorated with American, 18th-century English, and 19th-century Japanese antiques. Displayed throughout the house is a gallery of interesting antiques, including pre-Columbian, Thai, and Cambodian pottery, folk art, and handmade quilts.

The guest rooms are generously sized, each with a private bath. Allen built the furniture, which includes a four-poster bed made of rare tiger maple in two rooms and a low-country queen-size and twin bed in the third. Handmade quilts adorn the beds, and artwork decorates the walls.

Guests enjoy a full country breakfast in the dining room, entirely representative of Allen's work, derivative of primitivism and folk art.

The William Seward Inn

South Portage Road, Route 394
Westfield, New York 14787
716-326-4151
800-338-4151

Proprietors: Jim and Debbie Dahlberg
Accommodations: 14 rooms, all with private bath
Rates: $80–$125
Included: Full breakfast
Minimum stay: 2 nights with some Saturday stays
Added: $15 each additional guest; 5-course dinners mid-
   September through mid-June, $35 per person; 7% tax
Payment: Visa, MasterCard
Children: Over 10 welcome
Pets: Not allowed
Smoking: Not allowed
Open: All year

This is an exciting property: In February 1991, Jim and Debbie Dahlberg bought the well-known but faded hostelry, which had been a bed-and-breakfast since 1983. Through devotion, hope, and much personal investment from Jim and Debbie, the William Seward Inn has markedly improved, from the decor to the grand breakfasts to the four deluxe rooms in a new addition.

Jim is a former a vice president of a Buffalo bank, and Debbie maintains her job as a fair-housing advocate in Buffalo. Jim does the cooking and the finances, and Debbie is redecorating with promising taste. The Dahlbergs refurbished the common rooms and have just finished a delightful four-room addition perpendicular to the main house, a clever architectural complement to the 1837 Greek Revival front, echoing the Palladian themes.

The two-story white clapboard, black-shuttered home has two faces: the original 1821 cottage front, built by Asa Farnsworth, which looks out to the side of the property, and the roadside Greek Revival face added in 1837. The later addition was built by William Seward, an agent of the Holland Land Company who took on the governorship of New York just a year later and eventually went on to serve as Abraham Lincoln's secretary of state. The grand Greek Revival front, three pillars across, four windows wide, with elegant Palladian arched windows, looks out over Route 394 and, in the distance, Lake Erie. In 1966, expansions at the nearby Welch Corporation had threatened the Seward home in its original location, and owner Lucille Owens moved the house to its present site, about three miles west of Westfield, on a hill with glorious views of Lake Erie.

Two front rooms in the main house (ask for one of the second-floor rooms with the porch) and all four rooms in the addition are blessed with lingering views of sunsets on Lake Erie. The latter rooms are truly the finest, featuring double Jacuzzis, floral paper, and queen-size canopy beds; the second-floor rooms have the additional advantages of vaulted ceilings and a shared porch. The rooms in the main house do need the work that Debbie is undertaking, but all have some lovely antiques.

The living room and library are charming, comfortable sitting areas. Debbie used creamy paint and yellow chintz fabrics to lighten the library, which is enhanced with long Palladian windows, original shelves, paneled walls, and a working coal fireplace.

Jim cooks a multicourse breakfast, featuring muffins such as apple-raisin-pecan, almond, kiwi-walnut, and blueberry-oatmeal as well as herbed eggs. The intriguing town of Chautauqua is a twenty-minute drive, and little Westfield on Lake Erie is a hub for antiquers and vintners.

Pennsylvania

Barley Sheaf Farm
Box 10, Route 202
Holicong, Pennsylvania 18928
215-794-5104

Proprietors: Don and Ann Mills and Don Mills, Jr.
Accommodations: 10 rooms, all with private bath, 1 with
    fireplace (7 rooms in the main house, 3 rooms in cottage)
Rates:
    July 4–October: Weekdays, $110–$155; weekends, $122–$175
    Low season: Weekdays, $90–$130; weekends, $110–$155
Included: Full farm breakfast; chocolate truffles; sales tax
Minimum stay: 2 nights on weekends, 3 nights on holidays
Added: $17 each additional person
Payment: American Express
Children: Over 8 welcome
Pets: Not allowed
Smoking: Allowed
Open: All year except Christmas week

Even before lyricist George Kaufman owned this stone farmhouse and entertained such notable guests as Lillian Hellman, S. J. Perelman, and the Marx Brothers from 1937 to 1954, Julianna Forge was the visible proprietress. An avid collector of Delaware Impressionists and first director of the Whitney Museum, Forge established an arts consciousness about the stone farmhouse, and it was she who built the early, elegant pool on the back lawns in 1927. There is a long tradition of creativity and entertaining at Barley Sheaf Farm which the Mills family gallantly continues today.

Truly, a visit to Barley Sheaf is a step into history, culturally and architecturally. There are two distinct parts to the house: the yellow stone part toward the back of the house was built in 1740, and the grander stone part from 1800. The guest cottage was built over the old ice house in 1910, and the 1820 barn was rebuilt after a fire in 1878.

During the thirty-one years that Don Mills worked in the perfume business, he and his family vacationed in Europe and England. They were inspired by their travels to open a bed-and-breakfast and in 1979 introduced the concept to Bucks County with Barley Sheaf Farm. Ann Mills decorated each room distinctly in English country elegance from her firsthand observations. A wonderful antique wallpaper called Aviary, a cream and rose pattern depicting different birds, enlivens the entrance hall and the second- and third-floor hallways. Up the private stairs from the library, Room 6 has cheery floral wallpaper and window treatments and a fully furnished dollhouse. The antique doll family, belonging to Ann, lives behind a glass cabinet in Room 2. Room 1 is a suite with a queen-size brass sleigh bed, from which one can look out a wrought-iron balcony toward the pool or enjoy the working fireplace in the sitting area. Room 4 has a bathroom as large as its sleeping area, with a glorious clawfoot tub as an island in the center, bordered by pine wainscoting. Baths are stocked with almond soaps and shampoos.

The cottage is a charming retreat, with three rooms centered around a common area with a large fireplace. The Hanora Coffee Room is named for its folk art wallpaper, though a favorite room is the Field of Flowers in a unique space under vaulted ceilings, brilliantly papered in a design of flowerets, suitable for those under six feet two.

In the morning, guests gather in the airy brick-floored breakfast room for a full home-cooked meal of fresh fruit, zucchini muffins, bacon, and blueberry pancakes. There is among the vast acreage a wonderfully shaped fishing pond stocked with catfish and wide-mouthed bass. Those who would cast their hooks in stores have Peddler's Village just down the road.

Churchtown Inn

Route 23, 2100 Main Street
Churchtown, Pennsylvania 17555
215-445-7794

Proprietors: Stuart W. and Hermine Smith and Jim Kent
Accommodations: 8 rooms, 6 with private bath, Honeymoon
   Carriage House
Rates: $49–$95; Carriage House, $125
Included: Five-course breakfast
Minimum stay: 2 nights on weekends, 3 nights on holidays
   and special weekends
Added: 6% tax
Payment: Visa, MasterCard
Children: Over 12 welcome
Pets: Not allowed
Smoking: Allowed in designated areas only
Open: All year except Christmas

Reclusives beware: the Churchtown Inn is an inescapably sociable place. Owner Stuart Smith was born to be an innkeeper. He simply loves his guests and loves his business. His wife Hermine and partner Jim Kent whisk around in the background like angels to his messenger. Summers are always busy with vacationers, and a creative time for the gregarious to visit is during Stuart's well-planned special-event weekends, from November through May. As a former choir director, Stuart has adopted music into the household: theme weekends may include a violin concert of Christmas music, a sock hop, a New Orleans jam session, or square dancing. Other weekends might feature a Victorian ball, California wine tasting, kite flying, or murder mysteries. Twice a year, Stuart accompanies guests to an Amish wedding feast; and each Saturday night, the innkeepers join guests for a dinner at a local Amish home.

Churchtown is a historic hamlet on a hill in rolling countryside about a half hour east of Lancaster. The fieldstone house is the town's cheerful center on a mossy green plot of land in Amish country. Built in 1735 by Welsh settlers, it was later owned by state legislator Edward Davies, who added a section in 1810. The innkeepers added the Carriage House and a glassed-in breakfast room in 1990. It's a very pretty place, and in fact the common rooms in front, the two parlors, are quite elegant. Intimacy is prevalent and can sometimes be intrusive, such as the signs on the beds directing guests to remove quilts and shams before retiring.

There are five rooms on the second floor, all with private bath, and three on the third floor that share two baths. Throughout are handmade pieces by Mennonites including flower baskets, quilts, lace doilies on lamps, and specially designed television cabinets. The lavish antique beds are cushy and feminine. Innkeeper Jim Kent created the huge crown canopy over an American Victorian sleigh bed in the David Jones Room.

On the third floor, as with any good garret, visitors must not be taller than six feet. The Henry Shirk Room has eaves that have bowed over time and an art deco walnut bed. Guests are given robes for the shared bath, which has only a tub and a European shower, but the rooms that share it are quite a value for $49 and $55. The Eleanor Fausset Room has a queen-size walnut Victorian high-back bed and a twin French sleigh bed as well, with skylights in a cathedral ceiling. The Carriage House is more contemporary than the senior rooms in the main house, though some may like the clean new lines, canopy bed, ballroom floor, and privacy. The heavy silk curtains were made from women's concert gowns after the Stuart W. Smith Singers performed at Carnegie Hall.

The garden breakfast room is contemporary in design, with a lovely view of the Welsh mountains and Stuart's English herb gardens in back. Stuart cooks breakfast elaborately, serving five courses, which may include Grand Marnier French toast or oatmeal-granola pancakes and local sausage and ham.

Clearview Farm Bed and Breakfast

355 Clearview Road
Ephrata, Pennsylvania 17522
717-733-6333

Proprietors: Glenn and Mildred Wissler
Accommodations: 5 rooms, 3 with private bath
Rates: $59–$79
Included: Full breakfast
Minimum stay: Some weekends
Added: $10 each additional guest; 6% tax
Payment: MasterCard, Visa
Children: Not allowed
Pets: Not allowed
Smoking: Not allowed
Open: All year

A bed-and-breakfast is about as easy to find as a horse and buggy in Lancaster County. Yet for a place fairly teeming with small establishments, there are relatively few good ones. Of these, Clearview Farm is one of the finest. Clearview was their beloved home for thirty-three years before the Wisslers transformed it into a bed-and-breakfast in October 1989. Glenn still runs his 200-acre farm, growing corn and soy, and for part of the year retains many heads of cattle. For fun, there are also four peacocks, two swans, and five cygnets.

The grounds are idyllic, with a picturesque holding pond separating the house from its vast farmland. The huge farmhouse, built in 1814, is of blanched stone with red shutters, and a sunny old porch on one side is decorated with wicker and white wrought-iron furniture. Inside, all the papering, linens, window treatments, and creative bathrooms are the result of the Wisslers' hard work. Glenn labored at exposing a lot of the two-foot-thick stone and brick, opening ceilings and exposing hand-pegged beams.

Guests enter through the sitting room adjacent to the kitchen. The common spaces are pleasant but old-fashioned, and Mildred concedes that she focused her talents on the guest rooms. The dining room is a display for her good china and crystal, which guests use when sitting down to elaborate breakfasts that might include ham and cheese soufflé in a jelly roll with hollandaise sauce.

The two third-floor rooms, Lincoln and Washington, are especially romantic. Here Glenn exposed the stone and brick walls and fireplaces and the hand-pegged beams in the ceilings. Both rooms have quilts draping four-poster pencil post beds; the Washington room has other quilts draped on a ladder leaning against the chimney. Glenn made the wardrobes from old shutters, which look like green French country decorator items. The random-width floorboards are as wide as 16 inches. The new baths seem old, with wainscoting, exposed beams, and unusual classic detail.

Each of the second-floor rooms is unique and beautifully decorated. The Garden is a bouquet of chintz, with a gilded crown canopy above a brass and iron bed; the Princess Room has a lace-covered curved canopy bed and two pink tufted Victorian chairs. Since these rooms share a bath, each has a basket filled with neatly rolled towels. The memorable chamber is the Royal Room, with an elaborately carved Victorian acorn bed and matching marble-top vanity. Red and gold tapestry curtains hang regally in the windows, heading toward an enchanting long and narrow bath with original clawfoot tub and a shower under a quirky sloped roof.

Once rejuvenated by this peaceful setting, guests may want to visit the Ephrata cloister or the charming antiquing town of Lititz on the way into Lancaster.

Highland Farms

70 East Road
Doylestown, Pennsylvania 18901
215-340-1354

Proprietors: Mary and John Schnitzer
Accommodations: 4 rooms, 2 with private bath
Rates: $98–$150
Included: Four-course breakfast, afternoon refreshments
Minimum stay: 2 nights on weekends, 3 nights on holidays
Added: $17.50 each additional person; 6% tax
Payment: Visa, MasterCard
Children: Over 12 welcome
Pets: Not allowed
Smoking: Permitted in the library
Open: All year

Musicians will adore Highland Farms. From 1941 to 1961, Oscar Hammerstein and his wife lived here, on the heels of the cultural migration to Bucks County from New York City. Stephen Sondheim and James Michener were among the many well-known guests. Under the grape arbor out back, Henry Fonda was married to Hammerstein's daughter.

The unusual 21-room house was built in 1840, three stories of gray stone and stucco, with a flat roof, black shutters, and white trim. The second-floor wrap porch is supported by straight columns, giving the house the look of a riverboat. The Schnitzers, interior designer and contractor, bought the home in 1986, and their thirteen months of renovations have placed the home on the National Register of Historic Places. While their own antiques contribute to the elegance, the house holds some lovely treasures—original leaded glass windows and chandeliers and a stunning Louis Koch limewood wall unit from 1740, taken from a castle in England. The glorious mantel in the living room is from the same period, found in an old house nearby. There is quite a bit of Hammerstein memorabilia here, including a good deal of sheet music (piano in living room) and records, which guests are free to use.

The four rooms, three on the third floor and one on the second, are named for Hammerstein productions. The Carousel room is large and playful, with wide-planked whitewashed floors and a large hand-painted pony in its private bath; Show Boat is smaller, its Tiffany lamp and shell shade sitting on an antique table near a 19th-century mahogany dresser; and Oklahoma is also smaller, with lace and linens more than one hundred years old. The King and I is most deluxe, with the only guest room fireplace and hand-painted paper in the private bath. The second-floor library is an informal alternative to the elegant living room, focusing on a working fireplace. The classic blue wallpaper is, of course, Highland plaid, with lots of books for guests to read in comfortable sofas.

In the formal dining room, Mary uses her Lenox goldware every day for her lavish four-course breakfasts, which may feature her highly lauded seven-layer crêpes.

On the five acres of hilltop grounds outside charming Doylestown, the landscape comes complete with a tennis court, a 60-foot swimming pool set in stone, and a refreshing view of the surrounding hills. Hammerstein's original outdoor speakers still pump appropriate music to the pool area. Even those underwater can appreciate "The Sound of Music," painted in fancy script on the pool's floor.

The Inn at Fordhook Farm
105 New Britain Road
Doylestown, Pennsylvania 18901
215-345-1766

Proprietors: Blanche Burpee Dohan and Jonathan Burpee
Innkeeper: Elizabeth Romanella
Accommodations: 5 rooms in the main house, 3 with private bath; 2 rooms in Carriage House with shared bath
Rates:
  Main house: $93–$126
  Carriage house: $163–$227
Included: Full farm breakfast, afternoon tea, Burpee seed packet
Minimum stay: 2 nights on weekends
Added: $20 each additional person; 6% tax
Payment: Visa, MasterCard
Children: Over 12 welcome
Pets: Not allowed
Smoking: Permitted only on terrace
Open: All year

W. Atlee Burpee was a teenage salesman of fancy poultry, but by 1876 he conceded that he was making more money on feed than he was on his birds. After several years, the young entrepreneur soon needed a plot of land for testing plants for his blossoming twelve-year-old mail order seed company based in Philadelphia. In 1888, he bought what is now the Inn at Fordhook Farm, and it was here that Burpee's seeds were first planted. His family built and summered in the Victorian cottage at the entrance to Fordhook Farm and renovated the 18th-century fieldstone farmhouse at the turn of the century. The property was the active home of the Burpees for three generations until 1985, when grandchildren Blanche Burpee Dohan and Jonathan Burpee decided to share their family wealth with others.

The present imposing stone structure, which is on the National Register of Historic Places, was built in three stages from east to west: the kitchen in the 1760s; the center portion of the house in the 1830s, a bit worse for wear having been a boys' school at one time; and the west wing during the Burpees' turn-of-the-century renovation. The separate Carriage House was erected in 1868. As one would expect from the country's first site of seed trial gardens, the 60 acres are lovely and well-groomed. The view from the terrace over the sloping lawns will take one's breath away almost as quickly as will a good game of badminton, the sport of choice for those not playing croquet.

The five guest rooms in the main house are all uniquely situated, some overlooking the endless front lawns, others with a shaded view of the seed building and Carriage House. Flower books are displayed in every room. The Burpee and Atlee rooms are especially grand, each with its own terrace and fireplace. The Simmons and Torrance rooms are a bit smaller but appointed with lovely antiques, and the third-floor Curtiss Room is a bit more modest than the others. Museum-quality Mercer tile decorates the fireplaces and foyers throughout the house.

The Carriage House is a short walk across the graveled drive; it is very private, with two rooms and a common room on the second floor. While the guest rooms are less impressive than those in the main house, the attraction is surely the privacy and the twenty-by-thirty-foot Great Room, with chestnut beams supporting a cathedral ceiling and Palladian windows overlooking the trial gardens.

In the sunny dining room, guests are served a full breakfast, which may consist of oatmeal buttermilk pancakes or an egg strata. In winter, afternoon tea is served in the living room, in the warmer months on the great stone terrace, which gazes upon the two-hundred-year-old linden trees. Nearby Doylestown and the Mercer Tile Museum are terrific options for a free afternoon.

Isaac Stover House
Box 68, Bucks Country
Erwinna, Pennsylvania 18920
215-294-8044

Proprietor: Sally Jessy Raphael
Innkeeper: Susan Tettemer
Accommodations: 7 rooms, 5 with private bath; 1 two-bedroom suite
Rates: With private bath, $175; with shared bath, $150; suite, $250
Included: Full gourmet breakfast, afternoon refreshments
Minimum stay: 2 nights; 3 nights on holidays
Added: 6% tax
Payment: American Express, MasterCard, Visa
Children: Over 12 welcome
Pets: Not allowed
Smoking: Only downstairs
Open: All year

There are two kinds of bed-and-breakfast: the great majority run by homeowners trying to make a living and those intriguing few owned by wealthy people who love entertaining and decorating. The Isaac Stover House is certainly the latter, a life-size dollhouse owned by talk show hostess Sally Jessy Raphael. It's a very pricey, very romantic place for those who want to be surrounded by expensively refinished antiques, lavish linens, and a decorator's dream of window and wall treatments—with lots of precious adorability and collectible Victoriana. The setting is ideal: across a towpath from the Delaware River in a very quiet setting, just 13 miles north of New Hope.

Raphael and her husband, Karl, bought the 1837 Federal brick mansion in February 1988. The only evidence of Victoriana on the outside is the gingerbread porch which extends the length of the wonderful building, and it is from this era that Raphael was inspired to decorate her inn. The Isaac Stover House opened after just three months of nonstop renovation, during which time one side of the sinking house was raised four inches, ceilings were torn down and rebuilt, and the extraordinary faux marble work was restored.

The strong arm of the decorator is quite evident: vibrant wall coverings in chintz or commanding patterns are interrupted by daring window treatments, often lace curtains framed by bold valances or balloon shades. Collectibles such as Scandinavian porcelain, 1920s *Vogue* covers, and quilted throw pillows are placed with a perfectionist's exacting touch in the right spots. Among the wondrous pieces are damask-covered slipper chairs adorned with antique antimacassars, tassels on doorknobs and stairways, a Victorian hat above a gilded French mirror, and tiny carved tables placed where guests won't trip. Of course, there are dolls from around the world, Indonesian shadow puppets, and the owner's favorite—stuffed animals.

The decorator often used puffs of draped material instead of moldings in the guest rooms, echoed above the headboards as a crown canopy. Each of the seven rooms has a very particular theme: Emerald City has Wizard of Oz memorabilia and stuffed animals in a cradle; Loyalty Royalty is done in splashes of red and blue, with a stuffed toy fox dressed for the hunt, a fireplace, and a chart of the kings and queens of England. The two-room bridal suite on the second floor has creative bows on the four corners of the room, a white iron double bed facing the fireplace with views of the Delaware, and dozens of Norman Rockwell prints on the wall.

The third floor has four smaller rooms: Shakespeare and Company displays prints depicting scenes from his plays; the Amore Room has a creative rose valance around the crown molding, with scenes of Italy and a mahogany bed; the intimate Secret Garden; and Cupid's Bower, with a bas relief of cherubim floating above the French bed on the pink floral wallpaper.

Innkeeper Sue Tettemer is a wonderful, natural addition to the Isaac Stover House, a great cook, fastidious housekeeper, and tasteful hostess who loves the home and respects her guests. There is much pampering, even down to the Caswell and Massey amenities with extras like shaving cream, emery boards, mouthwash, sewing kits, and a razor. Breakfasts are vast, including home-baked goods and an egg dish, and afternoon refreshments are always just out of the oven in an admirable variety. Be sure to book far in advance for dinner at neighboring Evermay-on-the-Delaware (Gourmet Getaways).

Longswamp Bed and Breakfast

RD 2, Box 26
Mertztown, Pennsylvania 19539
215-682-6197

Proprietors: Elsa and Dean Dimick
Accommodations: 6 rooms in main house, 3 rooms in cottage, 1 room in guest house
Rates: Main house, $70; guest house, $75; cottage, $150
Included: Full breakfast, refreshments on arrival
Minimum stay: None
Added: $30 each additional adult; 6% tax
Payment: MasterCard, Visa
Children: Welcome
Pets: Not allowed

Smoking: Not allowed in bedrooms
Open: All year

Near the small working-class village of Mertztown outside Allentown, Longswamp Bed and Breakfast is a huge 18th-century clapboard farmhouse accompanied by a barn and cottage, with walking trails throughout its five acres. After raising five children here, the Dimicks, a couple of excess energy, interest, and talent, decided to open a bed-and-breakfast in 1983. When Dean is not tending to his private medical practice, he is on call at the bed-and-breakfast. The ubiquitous presence, however, is Elsa: full-time innkeeper and a half-time practicing psychiatrist. More notable than her sophisticated skills as host are her talents as an innovative cook, to be sampled at breakfast.

The farmhouse, more than 200 years old and at one time the post office and general store, was creatively remodeled by the Dimicks with huge airy common rooms. The double-sized living room is a delightful space, with a fireplace, two plush couches, a sitting area in front of a picture window overlooking the fields, and three walls stacked with books accessible by a rolling library ladder. Even more extensive than their reading collection is their listening library: Dean is the classical connoisseur and Elsa the jazz enthusiast. Just across the hallway from the living room is the dining room, with lovely vistas to the fields. Elsa is quite adamant about having fresh flowers, vegetables, and fruits from gardens around the house.

Signs of a fastidious innkeeper are everywhere: only the best queen-size mattresses, ample reading lamps, lots of prop pillows and current magazines. Behind the scenes, Elsa stripped and refinished every piece of antique furniture in the house, as well as the highly polished hardwood floors. The two rooms on the second floor are the Colonel's, in yellows, named for Colonel Trexler, who built the house, and Rachel's large room, done in blues. The four third-floor rooms are named for seasons and share two baths; the largest of the rooms are over the living and dining rooms.

In addition to the main house is the cottage, the first structure on the property, formerly a stop on the Underground Railroad. The lower story, the Hideaway, is a private one-room guest house with a fireplace. The upper story, the Guest Cottage, is a magnificent space for families or couples traveling together: three rooms with an enormous open-beamed living room and stone fireplace, a private bedroom, and another bedroom under the eaves with a skylight and dressing area. The classic barn, built later, is inhabited by cats and has a full-size basketball court for guests to enjoy.

Allentown is just minutes away, antiquing is available nearby along the short route to Reading, and the Doe Mountain ski area is less than a five-minute drive.

Virginia

The Conyers House
Slate Mills Road, Route 1, Box 157
Sperryville, Virginia 22740
703-987-8025
Fax: 703-987-8709

Proprietors: Sandra and Norman Cartwright-Brown
Accommodations: 6 rooms in main house, 2 cottages
Rates: $100–$195
Included: Full breakfast
Minimum stay: 2 nights on autumn weekends and holidays
Added: 4.5% tax
Payment: No credit cards
Children: Check with innkeeper
Pets: Check with innkeeper
Smoking: On exterior porches only
Open: All year

Though American bed-and-breakfasting has been fashionable for a little less than a decade, the Conyers House shows no trace of such an influence. From the remote countryside at the eastern foothills of the Blue Ridge Mountains, this farmhouse seems lifted from the English countryside. It's a bed-and-breakfast in true European style: without bric-a-brac, solicitous hostmanship, matching chintzes, or marble baths — just Old World heirlooms and antiques. The only American thing about Conyers House is the price, which is quite steep for the area. But in true old-money fashion, no one speaks of such things here.

The Cartwright-Browns came to Sperryville, at the valley's north end in Rappahannock County, from Chevy Chase, Maryland. Their bed-and-breakfast is geared for their horsey tastes, or those of their former neighbors, the capital's elite in search of an unadorned country retreat. Sandra and British-born Norman bought the house as their own weekend retreat in 1979, installed plumbing, and opened it to guests in 1981. The oldest part of the house is the stone section, built by Hessian mercenaries around 1790, moved here and attached to Bartholomew Conyers' new house in 1810, when it became known as

Conyers' Old Store. Most notably, the house features ten working fireplaces.

Guests have to duck their heads descending the stairs en route to the Cellar Kitchen, with its huge fireplace, painted stone walls, exposed beams, and a waist-high antique double bed. The largest of the three second-floor rooms is Uncle Sim's Suite, with a long porch overlooking the narrow country road, an 1840 high canopy bed, an antique secretary, and a sitting room with a hanging French tapestry, and a television and VCR. Helen's Room also has a private porch, a fireside sitting area, and lots of windows; and the very cozy Grampie's Room has a fireplace also. Of the two attic rooms, one under the eaves has a clawfoot tub positioned in the middle of the room, either romantic or a nuisance; but either way the room has lovely views of the fields and horses. Choice though pricey accommodations are the cottages, romantic hideaways several paces up the hill from the house. The walk can be a bit muddy, but once arrived, guests may not want to leave since each cottage has a Franklin stove, television, VCR, and tape player, and a small, stocked refrigerator.

A satisfying full breakfast is served; with advance notice and a surcharge of $125 per couple, arrangements may be made for a six-course candlelight dinner. In addition, Sandra is an avid horsewoman and has five horses on the property. She will be quite happy to arrange for trail rides lasting several hours through beautiful scenery, for $35. Be sure to plan a meal at the nearby Inn at Little Washington (Gourmet Getaways).

Greenvale Manor
Route 354, Box 70
Mollusk, Virginia 22517
804-462-5995

Proprietors: Pam and Walt Smith
Accommodations: 9 rooms, 8 with private bath; 5 suites
Rates: $65–$95
Included: Full breakfast
Minimum stay: Some weekends
Added: 4.5% tax
Payment: No credit cards
Children: Not allowed
Pets: Not allowed
Smoking: Not allowed in guest rooms
Open: All year

The Northern Neck of Virginia is a rural refuge of flat, lush farmland, carved out like an incomplete puzzle with calm shores in nearly every direction. A peninsula bordered to the north by the Potomac and to the south by the Rappahannock, ending at the Chesapeake Bay, the Northern Neck isn't really on the way to anything but respite. Travelers might want to visit George Washington's birthplace at Wakefield or Robert E. Lee's at Stratford Hall. Ferries to Tangier Island and to Virginia and Maryland's eastern shores launch from the Northern Neck; and the famed Tides Inn and Tides Lodge, with some of the state's finest golf, are at its base in Irvington, across from the White Stone Bridge. Here, tucked in the soggy wetlands, is Greenvale Manor, an 1840 plantation home on 13 acres, including 3,400 feet of waterfront on the Rappahannock River and Greenvale Creek.

The mile-long gravel drive to the house is dressed with catalpas, cedars, and crepe myrtles and ends before the two-story white clapboard house at a circular drive planted with a little fountain. Originally from Connecticut, Pam and Walt Smith came to Virginia to buy this plantation home in 1987. Though its oldest part dates to 1840, when the house was built of cypress and oak joists, two wings and the outbuildings were added sensitively by the former owners in the 1960s. Among the original parts of the house are the dark-stained heart pine floors covered with Oriental rugs, the square winding staircase, the dining room mantel, and most of the millwork and molding. To the right of the foyer is the formal dining room, to the left the lovely parlor with antiques and formidable oil paintings by Walt's grandfather; and straight ahead, past a doorway to the wicker-filled veranda overlooking the vast groomed front lawn, is the Rappahannock River. Weather permitting, Walt takes guests out on his 27-foot fishing boat.

The finest accommodations are the two suites in the main house, Greenvale and Bluewater, reached by the terrific staircase. These have working fireplaces, quite large bedrooms, and sitting areas. The Greenvale Suite is preferable for its vast water views, though the Riverview and Chart rooms glimpse the shore as well. While the rooms in the manor house are furnished with antiques, quilts handmade by Pam's grandmother, and four-poster or canopy beds, the rooms in the outbuildings are done in a sparer country style. The Carriage House has two suites: the Waterview, with a kitchen, and the Rappahannock, with a sitting room and bedroom. The Creekside Guesthouse has a living room, kitchen, the River Room bedroom, and two additional bedrooms that share a bath and can be rented as a suite.

Pam cooks a large country breakfast, which may include strawberries and sweet cream, banana pancakes and country sausage, apple muffins, and cheese strata. Guests may pass the time by fishing, crabbing, playing badminton or croquet, or swimming in the pool. Those who want to play golf on the PGA Tides courses will surely pass the red brick Christ Church, built in 1735 and funded by tobacco baron Robert "King" Carter. For dinner, guests ought to venture to the nearby Inn at Levelfields. The owners are very happy with their home and its landscape, their way of life, and, consequently, their guests.

The Inn at Narrow Passage
Route 11 South
Woodstock, Virginia 22664
703-459-8000

Proprietors: Ed and Ellen Markel
Accommodations: 12 rooms, 10 with private bath, 7 with fireplace
Rates: $90 per couple
Included: Full breakfast
Minimum stay: 2 nights on autumn weekends and holidays
Added: 4.5% tax
Payment: Visa, MasterCard
Children: Welcome
Pets: Not allowed
Smoking: Not allowed in rooms
Open: All year

The Shenandoah Valley is replete with written and oral history dating back to colonial times. When Ed and Ellen Markel wanted to open a country inn with historic significance and undertake a restoration project, they were fortunate enough to find the Inn at Narrow Passage in 1982, two miles south of the town of Woodstock at the valley's northern end. After much restoration and construction, the Markels opened their inn in 1985 on a very lovely plot of land facing Massanutten Mountain and the north fork of the Shenandoah River, which is famous for its fly-fishing (lessons and classes are available from local Harry Murray).

The Inn was built in the 1740s as a refuge from raiding Indians and became a stagecoach inn for the great Valley Turnpike (now Route 11). Stonewall Jackson used it as his headquarters for the Valley Campaign in 1862 and 1864. Daisy Stover McGinnis later turned it into a girls' boarding school and summer resort.

The Markels' restoration was very involved because the Inn had been abandoned for a number of years and one of the original wings had been destroyed by fire nearly a century ago. The Markels breathed life back into the first structure, exposing much of the original logwork and hand-hewn beams of the older log cabin, and restored its five rooms to their colonial character. From independent research and oral histories from Woodstock natives, the Markels reconstructed the eastern wing as faithfully as possible, allowing all five rooms to open onto porches with mountain and river views.

The five rooms in the original building are on the second floor, including the Stonewall Jackson Room, simply furnished with reproduction colonial furniture, handmade queen-size pine beds, and standard comfortable baths. The 1880s wing and the new wing have pine furniture carved by a Pennsylvania woodworker in colonial simplicity. Most rooms throughout the property have working fireplaces.

The common room has a grand limestone fireplace, exposed original pine beams, and 1780s pumpkin pine flooring. Ellen makes a hearty breakfast, which guests enjoy by the dining room fireplace at colonial tables. Narrow Passage is not a fluffy place, bedecked with ruffles and trinkets; rather it's a hearty stopover, good for fishing, foliage, and country mountain air.

Oak Spring Farm and Vineyard
Route 1, Box 356
Raphine, Virginia 24472
703-377-2398

Proprietors: Pat and Jim Tichenor
Accommodations: 3 rooms, all with private bath
Rates: $55–$65
Included: Extensive Continental breakfast
Minimum stay: Some weekends
Added: 4.5% tax
Payment: Visa, MasterCard
Children: 16 and over welcome
Pets: Not allowed
Smoking: Not allowed
Open: All year

Seasoned bed-and-breakfasters will appreciate this idyllic, professionally run property. After twenty-six years in the army, sixteen of which were spent overseas, Jim and Pat Tichenor opened their first bed-and-breakfast, Fassifern, in Lexington, Virginia. A means of retirement for two very active, organized people, the bed-and-breakfast became a quick success. The Tichenors discovered that they wanted to spend more time with guests, sold Fassifern, and bought Oak Spring Farm, in the countryside halfway between Lexington and Staunton, in May 1989.

The original four-room white brick house was built in 1826 by a family called Fultz and their nine children. In 1840, the back ell was added onto the house. Today, the surrounding 40 acres of land remain nearly untouched but for the burros, dwarf cow, and Sheltand ponies from the Natural Bridge Petting Zoo, which leases part of the land.

The guests have their own living room with a working fireplace, and Pat has decorated the house with pretty period border papers, antiques, and beautiful Oriental rugs. Many of the artifacts around the house were collected from Pat and Jim's worldwide travels and years in Korea. Perhaps the most striking aspect of Oak Spring is its cleanliness, the result of Pat's standards, which are as high as the retired colonel's.

At the front of the house, the original 1826 section, are two larger guest rooms and a sitting area done in late Empire. The Art Deco Room has two twin rose-colored velvet tufted beds, a fireplace, beautiful Bukhara rug, and an old washstand made into a sink. The Victorian Room is notable, with an 1840 queen-size bed and a twin brass bed covered in an antique log cabin quilt. The bath is very large, with black and white parquet tiles and a double-size shower. The Regency Room in the back 1840 addition has two southern exposures and a small sitting area in the ell hallway. The Tichenors are very conscious about having good bed-and-breakfast touches such as current magazines, good reading lamps, drinking glasses, fresh flowers and plants, and soft towels. Though it should be a surprise, they offer the nice touch of chocolates on pillows.

They bake their own muffins, grow their own berries, pick their own flowers and fruit—apples, peaches, pears, plums, and cherries. The farm has been a vineyard for ten years, and in 1990 Jim harvested more than thirteen tons of grapes from the vines on five acres. Nearby is Natural Bridge, as well as the Virginia Horse Center.

The Shadows B&B

14291 Constitution Highway
Orange, Virginia 22960
703-672-5057

Proprietors: Barbara and Pat Loffredo
Accommodations: 4 rooms and 2 cottages, all with private bath
Rates: $70–$100
Included: Full breakfast, refreshments on arrival
Minimum stay: 2 nights in autumn and on special-event
  weekends
Added: $15 each additional guest; 4.5% tax
Payment: No credit cards
Children: Not allowed
Pets: Not allowed
Smoking: Not allowed
Open: All year

In the rolling hills of central Virginia are endearing incongrui-
ties at the Shadows that make it a memorable and lovely retreat.
Nestled among the Georgian and Federal mansions of Virginia's heartland, the Shadows is a stone and cedar shingle
farmhouse built in 1913 in rare and authentic Arts and Crafts
style. The generous Loffredos greet visitors warmly at the door,
not with lilting southern drawls but with a hint of New York
City: Pat was a Staten Island policeman, and Barbara worked
on Wall Street. They are touchingly thrilled with their life here,
with their unusual house (home to Virginia's first female lawyer), and with their lovely antiques and expansive grounds.
Their long search for a bed-and-breakfast ended with the Shadows, but their move was delayed for a year and a half. A friend
painted a picture of the Virginia countryside to sustain them
during the wait—and the Loffredos point fondly to this picture, which hangs in the hallway.

The house is embraced and shaded by two-hundred-year-old
cedar trees, part of the original grove that played a great role in
the naming of the house by its first owner, horseman Manley
Carter. Barbara and Pat spent a year restoring their home, and
where they had to replace old shingle they tried to match new
cedar as exactly as possible. The true impact of the Arts and
Crafts movement doesn't hit a visitor until he or she enters the
house at the common room, which runs the front length of the
house, with a grand stone fireplace at one end. A half staircase
leads to a landing where one can continue to the back half of the
house or up more right-angled steps to the four second-floor
rooms.

The rooms are spacious and tastefully done, with heart pine
wood floors in wonderful condition and private baths. The
most desirable room must be the Rose Room at the front of the
house; it's not too large, but it opens out to a grand front porch
along the length of the house. The Blue Room is the largest, the

bathroom of which Pat transformed from a room-size cedar closet. The Victorian and Peach rooms have views of the gazebo, fish pond, and Barbara's structured gardens. The Loffredos collected the wonderful antiques over the years, the grandest of which is the oversize fox hunt sideboard in the dining room.

The Loffredos are unusually sensitive hosts, and guests are afforded the utmost privacy. For those desirous of more than utmost, there are two cozy cottages that are original to the property. The Cottage and the Rocking Horse Cabin each have a full living room, bedroom, and sitting porch.

Pat cooks quite a full breakfast, beginning with fresh fruit garnished with flowers from the garden or pears poached in Grand Marnier, an entré, and always fresh eggs. Guests will surely venture on to Montpelier, the neighboring home of James and Dolley Madison, or further to Monticello and Charlottesville, the Skyline Drive, and local vineyards.

Country Inns

New York

Ram's Head Inn
Ram Island
Shelter Island Heights, New York 11965
516-749-0811

Proprietors: James and Linda Eklund
Manager: Brion Moorhead
Accommodations: 17 rooms, 4 with shared bath; 4 two-room
   suites
Rates:
   Shared bath: $85
   Private bath: $110
   Suite: $175
   Weekday discounts
Included: Buffet breakfast, sales tax
Minimum stay: 2 nights on weekends, 3 nights on holiday
   weekends
Added: $15 each additional person
Payment: MasterCard, Visa
Children: Welcome
Pets: Allowed
Smoking: Allowed only in lounge
Open: All year; restaurant has seasonal hours

First settled in 1652 by Quakers seeking refuge from persecution by the Puritans, Shelter Island today remains a peaceful retreat. Though only three hours by train from Manhattan, plus a five-minute ferry ride from Greenport, Shelter Island nevertheless seems very isolated. Even more remote is Ram Island, several miles from town and attached to its mother isle by a causeway. It is home to an idyllic, romantic country inn, often the setting for summer weddings.

Built in 1929, the Ram's Head Inn is a very traditional weathered-shingle building sitting on a grassy hill above the water. A long porch spans the length of the building, and third-floor dormer windows poke out from the green shingled roof. As very young newlyweds, natives James and Linda Eklund bought the inn in 1979 and invested a great deal of work over the years to get it to its current pristine condition. A cheerful, informal common room and bar sit to the right of the foyer. To the left is the lovely dining room, with bright floral wallpaper, light wood flooring, and pillars supporting the high ceiling.

The Eklunds and manager Brion Moorhead are quite proud of their creative chef, John Barton. His changing menu might include an appetizer of poached shrimp with sushi, tamari, and pickled ginger; seviche of scallops in vinaigrette over shoestring potatoes; or corn chowder with mussels. A choice of three salads could be grilled leeks with radicchio, tomato vinaigrette, and Gorgonzola. The entrées, ranging from $18 to $23, might include breast of chicken with cilantro and lime, sweet corn and black bean sauté, potato-crusted red snapper with roast tomatoes and garlic bread soufflé, or grilled yellowfin tuna brushed with wasabi and served with sesame scallion noodles. An artistic dessert chef makes a beautiful presentation of eight delicacies nightly.

While not luxurious, the guest rooms have the informal charm of a summer cottage, flanking a kelly green carpeted hallway. Each room is supplied with a new, firm mattress covered in soft cotton sheeting and white linens, a wing chair, white bureau, and endtables. The area carpets are simple and bright, as is the wallpaper and the new baths. The windows overlook sloping lawns, the tennis court, the little bay with a beach and moorings, the sandbox under the big oak tree, croquet, and volleyball.

The staff is extremely kind, relaxed, and happy at the Ram's Head Inn under the friendly leadership of the Eklunds. Guests are free to use the bicycles and boats—the 13-foot O'Day sloops, Sunfish, paddleboats, and kayaks. One third of Shelter Island is preserved as a wildlife refuge, a haven for bird watchers and naturalists.

The Redcoat's Return

Platte Clove Road
Elka Park, New York 12427
518-589-6379
518-589-9858

Proprietors: Tom and Peggy Wright
Accommodations: 14 rooms, 7 with private bath; 7 rooms
   share 4 baths

Rates: $80–$95
Included: Full breakfast
Minimum stay: Some holiday weekends
Added: $15 each additional guest; 7% tax
Children: Welcome
Pets: Not allowed
Smoking: Limited
Open: Closed April to mid-May

Halfway between Sugarloaf and Roundtop mountains in the heart of the Catskill Game Preserve is a British estuary. Tom Wright is the English half of the proprietary staff. He and his wife, Peggy, retreated to the Redcoat's Return in 1972, like most of their guests from Manhattan.

In 1910, potato farmer Willie Dale transformed his 1840 farmhouse into a summer boarding house called the Grenoble and built an addition. The result was a looming but elegant white clapboard structure, four stories high with a wrapping porch hanging over the first floor. A week's vacation at the Grenoble cost a Catskill vacationer $25 for three meals daily plus board. After World War II, the inn faded, closed, and reopened in 1955. Tom and Peggy Wright bought the place in 1972 with the intent of creating an English country retreat. The grand old house looks much as it did when the Dales hosted their hay rides at the turn of the century. The Wrights themselves seem a bit of that era, worldly, intelligent, and as if they just emerged from a thatch-roofed cottage in the Hebrides.

At 2,200 feet, enveloped by 18 acres laced with hiking trails, the house is decorated with cheerful plants hanging between columns of the wraparound porch. Guests enter through rickety doors. To the right are the dining rooms, to the left the wonderful antique mahogany bar, which Peggy and Tom found in an abandoned tavern. Couches are worn leather and rest in front of a large stone hearth. Decorated with lovely pieces of art, Redcoat's seems more like the home of particularly interesting people than a hostelry.

The fourteen guest rooms are split between the second and third floors and are decorated similarly in small floral print cotton comforters, oak dressers, wrought-iron double beds, rocking chairs, tiny flowered wallpaper in rust and green, and terra cotta–colored rugs. Though the rooms could use some repapering and relighting (the baths are harshly lit with fluorescent fixtures), this remains exactly what it was designed to be: a cozy country inn, a round-table refuge from the city.

Thoroughly British in every facet but his cooking, Tom is a wonderful chef. Those who have already been guests keep returning for entrées such as grilled quail with polenta and roasted peppers, breast of chicken stuffed with goat cheese and eggplant purée, and prime rib with Yorkshire pudding on Saturday nights. The menu is seasonal, and entrées range in price from $14.75 to $18.50. Guests dine in one of two rooms equipped with graceful Hitchcock chairs—a formidable library that looks like Oscar Wilde's study and an enclosed porch that leads out to the back lawns, home to an interesting sculpture of an empty suit that Peggy bought in Europe.

Woodstock is only a fifteen-minute drive, Schoharie Creek on the property is stocked aplenty with trout, and Hunter Mountain is a hop away for skiing.

Taughannock Farms Inn
2030 Gorge Road at Taughannock Falls State Park
Trumansburg, New York 14886
607-387-7711

Proprietors: Keith and Nancy Le Grand
Accommodations: 5 rooms with private bath; 2 two-bedroom guest houses
Rates: $75–$100; guest houses for four persons, $150–$175
Included: Expanded Continental breakfast
Minimum stay: Some college weekends
Added: 7% tax
Payment: Visa, MasterCard, American Express
Children: Welcome
Pets: Not allowed
Smoking: Not allowed
Open: Easter through Thanksgiving

Best known as a restaurant for the past half century, Taughannock Farms is a lovely country inn that teeters over Lake Cayuga's western shores on Point Goodwin, about eight miles north of Ithaca. The landscape is unbelievable, quite characteristic of the Finger Lakes, with precipitous cliffs and sweeping water views in the rolling landscape of wine country.

The rambling Victorian was built in 1873 by wealthy Philadelphian John Jones, who donated much of his 600-acre farm to New York State, creating Taughannock Falls State Park. In 1945 the Jones family sold the property to the Agards, who started the country inn. Since 1973 their granddaughter Nancy and her husband, Keith, have been maintaining the tradition. Pleasing details are everywhere: the first floor is covered by an overhanging porch, the third floor is hidden under gingerbread gables, a fourth-floor cupola pops out of the roof like a chef's hat.

The most memorable aspect of Taughannock Farms, aside from its setting, is the large dining room with spectacular views. Of the three discrete areas, the uppermost is the smallest, quite pretty, with a bay window and chandelier. Through a doorway is the two-tiered main dining room, which spills past dramatic square pillars to the lower level, where about twenty floor-to-ceiling windows look out across the front of the house to the Park and Lake.

Taughannock Farms has a reputation for hearty country dinners, ranging from $16.95 to $26.95, always including homemade rolls, relish, and a signature orange date bread. Specialties are roast loin of pork, sole stuffed with crabmeat, rack of lamb, and prime rib, served with brandied apples, minted apple jelly, or perhaps a pineapple raisin sauce served with hickory smoked ham. A daunting selection of fourteen desserts completes dinner: diners can choose from the likes of double chocolate mousse torte and bittersweet ice cream pie in almond crumb crust. The wine list is a creative blend of local vineyards' offerings.

The second floor has five quaint rooms—three with lake views, two with wood views, furnished in a tasteful mixture of antiques and an occasional reproduction. Perhaps the most sought-after room is the Garden Room at the end of the hall, with a curved fishnet canopy bed approached via old-fashioned steps, pretty period wallpaper, an antique desk and marble-top dresser. In a touch that is reminiscent of a summer boarding house, the rooms have slatted doors to welcome a hilltop breeze. The guest parlor has some great examples of Victorian antiques, such as an 1883 music box, most of which are original to the mansion.

The two guest cottages have rooms decorated more in family style than in high Victorian. The property's seven acres provide quick access to the park and falls. Keith and Nancy, lifelong natives, are informal, kind hosts who orchestrate this rare family environment.

The White House Berries Inn
Box 78, Route 8
Bridgewater, New York 13313
315-822-6558

Proprietors: Juanita and Crystal Bass
Manager: Ronald Bellamy

Accommodations: 3 rooms sharing 2 baths
Rates: $65
Included: Full breakfast
Minimum stay: None
Added: 7% tax
Payment: Visa, MasterCard
Children: Welcome
Pets: Not allowed
Smoking: Not allowed in rooms
Open: All year

Since it was built in the mid-19th century, the lavish Italianate house outside of Bridgewater has remained an elegant fixture, known simply as the White House, for its color. Several years ago, a sign appeared in front of the house advertising fruit from the owner's garden: "White House Berries," the sign said. When Juanita Bass bought the house in 1986, she restored the house and a bit of its lore as well, re-creating the sign for her country inn when it opened in January 1989. It's still vaguely a white house, somewhere under the green, mint, and mauve gingerbread.

Juanita Bass is so well loved by patrons and local residents that she is a bit of a legend. Bridgewater, about 12 miles north of Cooperstown, has been her home for generations: her father made history here when he became New York State's first black mayor in 1972. Juanita's experience as an antiques dealer is evident throughout. All is done with a fine collecting eye for Victoriana and a sense of humor. The Rest Room, for example, uses the huge clawfoot tub as a planter filled with greenery, with beautiful Wedgwood blue tiling. Her dining rooms are an eclectic mix of mismatched chairs and silver settings, interesting pieces individually that together create a beautiful ensemble. The wallpaper is a vivid red damask, a dramatic backdrop for her dinners, where the fun begins.

The left side of the menu reads, "Soul Food Dinners." Juanita is helped in the kitchen by her sisters Arlene and Deloris. Daughter Joyce's famous sauce is the reason so many come back to order the baby back ribs. Stuffed pork chops, fried catfish, southern fried chicken, and honey glazed ham are among the other choices, all served with black-eyed peas, macaroni and cheese, collard greens, and potato or rice.

These dinners make an interesting contrast to the right side of the menu, "Yankee Dinners," which include rosemary chicken, fresh fish, and strip steak, served with baked potato or rice and vegetables. All dinners are served with cornbread, hush puppies and hot syrup, and fresh-squeezed lemonade. A choice of five pies stymie the sweet-toothed: sweet potato, banana cream, pecan, peanut butter, and chocolate porch pie. Dinners range from $15.95 to $19.95 and are served daily except Monday.

The three guest rooms upstairs are showcases of Victoriana, sharing two very pretty baths. While the first two rooms are adorable, one with a three-piece teardrop oak bedroom set, the third is the prettiest, done in contrasting patterns of black and pink chintz, from the paper to the needlepoint rug to the lampshades, with a brass double bed. The common room for guests on the second floor has a television, viewed from the pretty settee.

Dinners are memorable, with next-day visits to expensive Cooperstown just a short drive away. Shoppers who don't want to venture far can sample Juanita's antiques shop in a little cabin behind the house, fortunate to spend more time with a delightful hostess.

Pennsylvania

The Cameron Estate Inn and Restaurant
RD #1, Box 305
Mount Joy, Pennsylvania 17552
717-653-1773

Proprietors: Abe and Betty Groff
Innkeeper: Janice Rote
Accommodations: 18 rooms, 16 with private bath, 7 with fireplace
Rates: $60–$110 seasonally
Included: Continental breakfast
Added: $10 each additional person; 6% tax
Payment: MasterCard, Visa, Discover, American Express
Children: Over 12 welcome
Pets: Not allowed
Smoking: Allowed
Open: All year

Eleven miles west of Lancaster and 13 miles from Hershey, the Cameron Estate Inn is a country haven with an air reminiscent of faded Federal elegance. It has the scale and grandeur of a southern plantation, set on 15 acres of groomed and wooded grounds. Visitors can take advantage of the many hiking paths carved throughout the grounds, as well as a stocked trout stream. The large three-story brick house is set apart from civilization by a series of straight, flat, often unmarked country roads. On your way down a lane toward the estate, you pass the historic landmark Donegal Church, built in 1721, which earned its way into history books through the Witness Tree made famous in the Revolutionary War.

The house was built in 1805 and was most importantly the home for Simon Cameron, Lincoln's first secretary of war. Owners Abe and Betty Groff bought the estate in August 1981, and it is now managed full-time by their daughter-in-law Janice Rote. Oriental scatter rugs and runners cover the hardwood floors. The rooms on the three floors reflect the traditional Federal decor in both antiques and reproductions. The size and grandeur of the rooms vary significantly throughout the house. The seven rooms with fireplaces, especially those at the front of the house, are significantly more regal than the others, which are cozy, often set under the eaves or dormers. Though the rooms are all comfortable, with restful views, leather wing-back chairs and ample reading lamps, writing desks, and interesting artwork, the baths need some updating.

One dining room is warmed by a fabulous fireplace; the other, in a glass-enclosed portico, is the setting for lunches, dinners, and Sunday champagne brunch. For dinner, an appetizer of crab-stuffed mushrooms may be or followed by chicken and shrimp Versailles, served with herbs and mushrooms in a light cream sauce over wild rice, or veal Cameron, rolled in grated cheese and bread crumbs, sautéed with white wine and lemon. Dinner entrées range in price from $15 to $21.50, and Sunday brunch is very reasonably priced, with entrees from $4 to $9.50, including seafood crêpes and French toast New Orleans, with Grand Marnier sauce.

While dinners at the inn are fine, guests should be sure to make a pilgrimage to the Groff Farm Restaurant, four miles away. In their 1756 stone farmhouse, their son Charlie prepares highly acclaimed American country food in two sittings Tuesday through Saturday. The meals are presented à la carte or family style, all you can eat, at one price per entrée, from $13.50 to $23.50 per table, and include local vegetables and fresh bread. Betty Groff, who has written several successful cookbooks, masterminded the country recipes for prime rib, home-cured ham, and chicken Stoltzfus, in which chunks of roaster chicken in cream sauce are served over flaky diamonds of butter pastry.

Duling-Kurtz House

146 South Whitford Road
Exton, Pennsylvania 19341
215-524-1830

Proprietors: The Carr Family
General Manager: John R. Faller
Accommodations: 12 rooms, all with private bath, 5 with
     fireplace
Rates: $80–$120 on weekends, $49.95–$69.95 on weekdays
Included: Continental breakfast
Added: $15 each additional guest; 6% tax
Payment: Major credit cards
Children: Welcome
Pets: Allowed
Smoking: Allowed
Open: All year

Sons are named after fathers; and country inns, in the case of the Duling-Kurtz House, are named for mothers. Owners Raymond Carr and David Knauer proudly passed on their mothers' maiden names to their pride and joy. In 1982, the business partners began to revive the 1830 clapboard farmhouse to its present state as a restaurant and also restored the neighboring plaster barn to house eighteen guest rooms. Some of the guest rooms were expanded to two-room suites and now number twelve.

The Duling-Kurtz House sits about halfway between Philadelphia and Lancaster, just off commercial Route 30. Once you turn off the busy road onto South Whitford Road, the setting abruptly changes to the serene 12 acres of manicured lawns, with a rose garden and gazebo and an audible brook. The inn is best known for its dining, with seven dining rooms in the original 1830 house, a curious working beehive oven open to public view, and seven Palladian fan windows across the back of the house that provide views of the gardens and fields. The bar and waiting area is a charming spot, with two tartan plaid couches before a huge fireplace. Where some dining rooms are decorated in simple period antiques, the second-floor bar and informal dining area is very sunny and preppy, with white wicker and green carpeting.

The Duling-Kurtz House solves a problem that many country inns encounter, providing distinct private space for overnight guests so they may not be disturbed by evening diners. Guests approach the barn via covered brick walkway. Throughout three floors, rooms have interesting configurations, with odd ell shapes and nooks and crannies where one finds an unexpected wing chair. Rooms are traditionally furnished in reproductions, in Williamsburg rusts and blues, and in English toile, with spotless new baths and personalized amenities. All rooms have televisions, five have fireplaces, and when the rooms are not two room suites, they are still generously sized.

Where some country inns have a homey feel, the Duling-Kurtz House is quite professional. General Manager John Faller is a nice link, having come from a corporate background from an upscale Florida property and his own bed-and-breakfast in Wisconsin.

French Manor
Huckleberry Road, Box 39
South Sterling, Pennsylvania 18460
717-676-3244
800-523-8200

Proprietors: Ronald T. and Mary Kay Logan
Innkeepers: Michael and Jennifer Logan
Accommodations: 5 rooms and 2 suites
Rates:
  Rooms: $170; $200 MAP
  Suites: $220; $250 MAP
Included: Breakfast and dinner with MAP
Minimum stay: 2 nights on most weekends
Added: $55 each additional guest; 15% gratuity; 6% tax
Payment: American Express, Visa, MasterCard, Discover
Children: Not allowed
Pets: Not allowed
Smoking: Allowed in common room
Open: All year

This beautiful stone house looks like a miniature fairy-tale castle. No wonder, as its beginnings are rather unearthly. The mini-château was built during the Depression by industrialist and art collector Joseph Hirshhorn as a country home — essentially for his art collection. Sixty artisans labored on the house, which was constructed outside with thousands of fieldstone blocks quarried on the original 600 acres and on the inside with oak, cedar, and pecky cypress woodwork. The two-story-high Spanish slate roof is interrupted by copper turrets inlaid with small panes of leaded glass and tiny dormers poking out at odd angles. The doorway is a dramatic terra cotta archway that leads either to the dining room to the left or upstairs to the guest rooms at the right.

The Manor was acquired in December 1990 by Ron and Mary Kay Logan, proprietors of the 54-room Sterling Inn down the road apace. As the Logans slowly make their mark on the house, some decor choices seem inconsistent; however, the owners are so kind and the property so sophisticated that it would be a shame to skip a visit just because the Versailles Room is done with Williamsburg prints. In an unspoiled part of the Poconos, near Lake Wallenpaupack and Tobyhanna State Park, the setting is glorious, with stunning views of Skytop Mountain from the Manor's 38 acres.

Aside from the aptly named Versailles Room, there are the descriptive Turret Suite, which includes a sitting room with couch and offers three views of the property's vistas, and the Venice, Monte Carlo, and Florence rooms, each with an extraordinary king-size bed. A small common room is a considerate addition. Throughout, the castle feeling remains as the ceiling folds and bends around one's head, and passageways reveal themselves just steps ahead of one's path. Recently, the Logans refurbished the neighboring Balish residence to add the deluxe San Remo and Geneva rooms.

The highly acclaimed chef, George Pelepko-Filak, is fortunate to have such a breathtaking dining room in which to serve his French cuisine. The two-story cathedral ceiling reveals oak beams, and the room is warmed by two enormous fireplaces at either end of the room. A cold first course may feature a sole mousse with cucumber and dill sauce, a warm one a wild mushroom crêpe with apples and hazelnuts. A choice of two soups may be followed by hearts of palm salad and fresh sorbet. Entrées, all more than $20, may include beef tenderloin with truffled demiglace; breast of chicken with morels, sundried tomatoes, and asparagus; or lobsterettes, scallops, and lobster in three-pepper sauce. Thursdays, a prix fixe eight-course meal is offered for $40. The wine list is quite versatile, as is the array of desserts.

The morning's breakfast ought to be taken on the large slate porch at the top of the hill, overlooking the mountains and the trees of the estate.

Glasbern
RD 1, Box 250
Fogelsville, Pennsylvania 18051-9743
215-285-4723
800-654-9296

Proprietors: Beth and Al Granger
Accommodations: 23 rooms, all with private bath, 11 with
   fireplace, including 13 suites with whirlpool tub
Rates: $95–$145 on weekdays; $100–$200 on holidays and
   weekends
Included: Full country breakfast
Minimum stay: 2 nights on weekends
Added: $15 each additional guest; 6% tax
Payment: American Express, Visa, MasterCard
Children: Check with innkeeper
Pets: Not allowed
Smoking: Allowed
Open: All year

Glasbern is a mecca for corporate retreats during the week, a
romantic retreat on weekends. Owners Beth and Al Granger hit
a chord. Among the many reasons to come are the gorgeous 100
acres in a valley setting ten miles west of industrial Allentown
and the French Continental cuisine.

Glasbern's foundation is an early-19th-century farm, but
guests today visit a country inn of contemporary comforts. The
Grangers bought the property in 1985, and it included the oversize barn, a tractor shed, and a farmhouse. They did a postmodern renovation of the barn and the shed (now the Carriage
House), combining the feeling of the old with the look of the
new, and restored the modest two-story farmhouse at the entrance of the property. The third building, the farmhouse with
three rooms, is the closest it gets at Glasbern to a typical country inn.

The exterior of the main barn is a rustic vertical clapboard,
reminiscent of a barn, but the interior is all contemporary sophistication. Half the building is a bilevel dining area, divided
in the middle by a stairway that leads to two levels of rooms on
the other half of the barn. On the outside, form follows the
function, and a white spire interrupts the plain wooden siding.
The dining room is modern open space, with a cathedral ceiling and plenty of windows and wood. The fourteen rooms here
are more modest than in the other two buildings, in informal
Victorian or traditional decor, with Gilchrest and Soames
amenities, some with whirlpool tubs, all with televisions and
VCRs, hair dryers, and phones—a far cry from clawfoot tubs,
double brass beds, and log cabin quilts. Six of the rooms have
outside entries.

The Carriage House has four rooms including two suites on
the first floor, all with fireplaces and whirlpools. These overlook the kidney-shaped swimming pool. Following the split rail

fence, one reaches the farmhouse, with three two-room suites set up in a duplex, all with fireplaces and whirlpool tubs.

Mark Shields is the chef who is given much free rein by the Grangers. Dinners are served Thursday through Saturday. Dinner appetizers might include carpaccio, thin slices of beef tenderloin, or escargot provençale, along with several soup and salad choices. Six entrées are presented on the menu, changing weekly: possibly Norwegian pink salmon poached in champagne court bouillon with fennel-lime cucumber dill salsa or roasted duckling stuffed with apples, pecans, and walnuts under a Grand Marnier and plum-cranberry glaze.

Glasbern has a bit of a formal atmosphere, owing in part to the large and important business clientele—who, although on vacation, expect a certain sophistication in their leisure.

Historic General Warren Inne

Old Lancaster Highway
Malvern, Pennsylvania 19355
215-296-3637

Proprietors: Jim and Endla Creed
Manager: Karlie Davies
Accommodations: 8 suites, all with private bath
Rates: $85–$135
Included: Continental breakfast
Minimum stay: None
Added: 6% tax
Payment: Major credit cards
Children: Not allowed
Pets: Not allowed
Smoking: Allowed
Open: All year

Built as an inn in 1745 to serve the stagecoach line from Lancaster to Philadelphia, the Historic General Warren Inne serves hearty food in colonial dining rooms and offers unusual two-room suites for overnight guests. It's an austere gray plaster building, two full stories under a third dormer story, all done in colonial simplicity, just off the hectic intersection of Routes 202 and 30 a short drive west of Philadelphia. First named the Admiral Vernon Inn after a British naval officer, the inn was purchased by William Penn's grandson John during the Revolution. Penn was a British sympathizer and the inn became a Tory watering hole. After the war, assuredly to gain a new clientele, Penn renamed the inn after Bunker Hill hero General Joseph Warren.

Hospitality continued over the years, and in 1981 Jim Creed and partners decided to revive the tradition. They restored the inn with the intention of making a restaurant. In 1985, the second- and third-floor rooms were renovated as guest rooms and a two-story addition housed a third dining room and more guest rooms. Though it was first conceived as a restaurant, the General Warren is now making a concerted effort to woo overnight guests. The rooms were redone in 1990, transformed into two-room suites.

There are five guest suites on the second floor and three on the third on a small, intimate scale. All rooms are done with Williamsburg reproductions. Stencil dances on the walls over period prints, and trim is painted in Williamsburg colors. Little steps lead up to beds, some with fishnet canopies and quilts. The more authentic rooms have dark stained floors with scatter Orientals rugs, and those in the new wing have muted wall-to-wall carpeting. The recent renovation afforded new baths in all the rooms, small but nicely appointed with Gilchrest and Soames amenities. Three suites have working fireplaces, and all have televisions, VCRs, and telephones.

The main dining room is in the recent addition, though it makes an effort to look as colonial as possible, with spindle-back chairs, square tables covered in modest white cloths, and scatter Oriental rugs over the darkly stained floor, warmed by an original fireplace. Dinners are nightly except Sundays and range from $16.96 to $24.50 with entrées such as beef Wellington and roast duckling. The General Warren features entertaining tableside preparation of its specialty dishes, such as Dover sole and, for two, rack of lamb and Châteaubriand served on a cutting board. Lunches, served weekdays, are reasonably priced under $10 and include broiled filet mignon with béarnaise sauce and the specialty, Wiener schnitzel General Warren. A lovely addition to the inn is the brick patios in the back of the house.

The Inn at Meadowbrook

Cherry Lane Road, RD 7, Box 7651
East Stroudsburg, Pennsylvania 18301
717-629-0296

Proprietors: Robert and Kathy Overman
Accommodations: 16 rooms (5 in Mill House, all with private bath; 11 in Manor House, 6 with private bath)
Rates: Manor House, $50–$85; Mill House, $70
Included: Full breakfast

Minimum stay: 2 nights on weekends
Added: 6% tax
Payment: Visa, MasterCard, American Express
Children: 12 and over welcome
Pets: Not allowed
Smoking: Allowed in common rooms
Open: All year

In the Poconos just west of the Delaware Water Gap is this pleasurable country inn, a welcome change from the clutter of hotels scattered through the area. The Inn at Meadowbrook looks like a New England farmhouse, built as such by a farmer in 1842 of white clapboard interrupted by small square panes of glass. And as every tireless patriarch dreams of doing, he later built an extension on the manor house for his grandchildren to visit.

The six original guest rooms in the main house are of average size; but the five for the grandchildren are rather small, with tiny sinks in each room and a shared hall bath (good for the budget-minded). There are lovely pieces of furniture: a brass bed, a leather tufted wing chair, oak washstands, and nice touches of original artwork. Kathy did the bold decor, with walls in surprising colors or vivid with floral paper. Across the narrow street is the Mill House, built as a gristmill in the 1930s, offering more interesting and more private accommodations. The rooms were all designed creatively by Kathy with interesting crown canopies and a fabulous painted log cabin room.

The Manor House's most elegant attribute is a 1930s addition, a wonderful space architecturally, which is now the dramatic setting for the dining room, overlooking the country, the stream, and Meadowbrook Pond. Three walls are forest green with windows to the countryside, and a fireplace rests along the fourth wall. There is a lovely area at the foot of the dining room facing Meadowbrook Pond, with two pillars separating three open archways in a classic, clean-lined setting, befitting a practice hall or a ballet studio. Bob Overman is the chef, and dinners range from $16 to $19, including salmon with mustard sauce, veal Valdastana, and cioppino.

The house has a nice common area for guests, with a fireplace, but if crowds at dinner are invasive there is a lounge downstairs, with two sitting areas, a closet of games, a television, and a mural of the homestead painted by Kathy.

A full equestrian facility is next door, and guests may take lessons and explore trails for a cost. An equestrian theme is carried out throughout the house, with riding hats, crops, boots in unexpected corners, and even a Polo-styled room. The 43 acres of Meadowbrook abut a tack shop, part of the equestrian facility. Other diversions at the Inn at Meadowbrook include two tennis courts, shuffleboard, a large sundeck, and a 20-by-40-foot pool.

The Inn at Phillips Mill

North River Road
New Hope, Pennsylvania 18938
215-862-2984
Restaurant: 215-862-9919

Proprietors: Joyce and Brooks Kaufman
Accommodations: 4 bedrooms, 1 suite, 1 cottage
Rates: $70, $80, $125, respectively
Included: Continental breakfast served in a basket
Minimum stay: 3 nights recommended during holiday
   weekends
Added: 6% tax
Payment: No credit cards
Children: No infants
Pets: Not allowed
Smoking: Allowed
Open: Closed in January

The town of New Hope offers a mystifying number of restaurants and bed-and-breakfasts. Combining the two into a successful vacation can be confounding. A clear-sighted answer to the dilemma is the Inn at Phillips Mill, a delightfully romantic place to stay with equally wonderful food.

Joyce and Brooks Kaufman bought the property in 1972 and undertook an extensive renovation, marrying their formidable talents—he, a renowned architect; she, with a classic eye for European interior design. The property itself is a captivating stone structure built in 1750 as a barn abutting Aaron Phillips' gristmill across the road, which operated as such under four generations of this prominent Bucks County family.

The early colonial structure has low ceilings, wide-planked floors, and cavernous fireplaces. The rooms are made airy by wide, mullioned windows and doors that Brooks designed in jade-colored iron. There are two halves to the ell-shaped building, reached by separate staircases. In one wing, two of the five rooms flank the second-floor dining area and are afforded privacy through castle-thick walls that bend away from the public spaces. One room has a darling green gingham bath with a clawfoot tub; another, above the main dining area, has a small sitting area in wicker and a rose-hued bedroom overlooking the back gardens. Room 3, an attic hideaway only for those under six foot five, has a cottage Victorian bed and Pierre Deux fabrics.

At the turn of the century when it was owned by one of the first Bryn Mawr graduates, a rickety old elevator was the alternate route upstairs to the other wing. Room 4, in shades of rose and Pierre Deux fabrics, is ingeniously cozy, with its bed tucked into the wall like a large window seat, separated from the room by drapery. Room 5 is a suite overlooking the backyard. Joyce Kaufman very modestly describes her taste as "old barn," but it seems the essence of country formal, and small cramped spaces have been transformed to private cozy havens.

A special treat is the cottage, just steps away from the main inn's patio. It looks like a hamlet from an English fairy tale, with modern touches: the rustic slate floors are heated, and the indigenous-looking massive fireplace was installed by Brooks during his renovations. The upstairs bedroom is lovely, with a monastic look.

A brick walkway laces around the back gardens and kidney-shaped pool, viewed from the back dining room. A brilliant feature is the wood-burning stone fireplace here that may be removed in the warmer months so guests can dine al fresco. The food is lovely. A sampling might include an appetizer of wild mushroom ravioli in a bechamel sauce, tender roast loin of pork in Calvados, and dessert of frozen blond mousse with bits of chocolate and nuts, Alsatian apple tart, or a heavenly Ilona torte, chocolate with a buttercream frosting.

Joseph Ambler Inn
1005 Horsham Road
North Wales, Pennsylvania 19454
215-362-7500

Proprietors: Richard Allman
Innkeepers: Steve and Terry Kratz
Accommodations: 28 rooms, all with private bath (12 in the Barn, 9 in the Farmhouse, 7 in Corybeck Cottage)
Rates:
  Barn: $110–$120
  Farmhouse: $95–$120
  Corybeck: $85–$95
Included: Full breakfast
Added: $15 each additional guest; 6% tax
Payment: Major credit cards
Children: Welcome

Pets: Not allowed
Smoking: Allowed
Open: All year

A half hour's drive north of downtown Philadelphia is the Joseph Ambler Inn, fairly lost in the 13 acres of its bucolic setting while being surprisingly close to urban sprawl. The inn was opened in 1983 as a fifteen-room bed-and-breakfast. Today, after renovations and the addition of the restaurant in 1989, the Joseph Ambler has evolved as well into a successful dining spot and corporate retreat.

There are two distinct faces to the Joseph Ambler Inn, for corporate guests and for casual weekenders. The Main House is more for the romantics, dating to 1734 with additions in 1820 and 1929. Its nine rooms have a distinct colonial feel, decorated with some period antiques and faithful reproductions. There are three common rooms downstairs in simple Williamsburg decor, including the 18th-century living room and the schoolroom with its walk-in fireplace. Of the four rooms on the second floor, the Penn Room is the earliest, with sloping ceilings, warped random-width floorboards, and tiny low windows overlooking the front fields. The Roberts Room is perhaps the nicest, with a straight yellow floral stripe canopy atop the queen-size bed, matching curtains and chairs, and a separate sitting area. The three charming rooms on the third floor have dormer windows set under the eaves and exposed beams and brickwork. Even the smallest, the Wright Room, is an adorable hideaway with soft floral Victorian wallpaper and upholstered window seats.

The Barn shares the same color scheme with the Main House, fieldstone offset with cheery butter yellow and barn red trim. The 1820 Barn was completely renovated in 1987, and the only testament to the past is its thick stone shell, which is nicely exposed on the interior in the guest and dining rooms. The restaurant, opened in March 1989, is decorated with colonial reproductions, handmade cherry tables, and Windsor chairs on random width floors. An airy wooden stairway leads to the twelve guest rooms on the second and third floors. Rooms here are more contemporary than in the Main House, furnished with useful reproductions, modern baths, televisions in highboys, desks, and telephones.

The tenant farmer's house was built in the 1920s and named Corybeck for the crows and blackbirds that migrated to the farm yearly. Its two floors of clapboard are painted a modest butter yellow. The seven rooms here are small and very cute, more traditionally done in the vein of the Main House, with canopy beds and stenciling. All rooms have access to the front porch or private patios. Here, like elsewhere, the baths are all new and fresh.

Dinners range from $16.95 to $23.95, with an emphasis on seafood and beef. The rack of lamb is the house specialty, served roasted, with Dijon mustard and bread crumbs or with apple and jam sauce.

The Thomas Lightfoot Inn
2887 South Reach Road
Williamsport, Pennsylvania 17701
717-326-6396

Proprietors: Jim and Rita Chilson
Accommodations: 5 rooms, 3 with private bath
Rates: $55 on weekdays, $60 on weekends
Included: Full breakfast
Minimum stay: On some weekends
Added: 6% tax
Payment: MasterCard, Visa
Children: Over 5 welcome
Pets: Not allowed
Smoking: Not allowed in rooms
Open: All year

A city of 33,000 on the Susquehanna River, halfway between Wilkes-Barre and State College, Williamsport is the door to Pennsylvania's north central mountain ranges and also home to the Little League World Series. Settled in the late 18th century by German Quakers who shared the community with valley Indians, Williamsburg became, a century later, one of the largest lumber centers of the world and home to a goodly number of millionaires.

Named for the town's surveyor and erected by his Quaker kinsman, the Thomas Lightfoot Inn was built in 1792 by the Updergraff brothers. The two-story brick and stone house rests right on the part of the Susquehanna that the Indians called the Long Reach, across busy highway 220 from downtown Williamsport and millionaire's mile, West Fourth Street. The 1783 log cabin, still standing across the street, was the granary for the Susquehanna canal, and the Updergraff house served as the inn for those loading from the granary. Descendants of the Updergraffs farmed the miles of surrounding acreage for 162 years. At one time, the house was an important stop on the Underground Railroad.

The Chilsons bought the badly faded historic property in 1986, restored it during eight months of labor, and opened it as an inn. It took a great deal of work to repair the plumbing and electricity, save the historic structure, and also get the building up to the standards of Jim Chilson, owner and town fire chief. The doors and first-floor shutters are done in Williamsburg blue, and the house is lifted up from the road by a flat lawn and a wet stone wall. The house is entirely original except for the back porch and dining room. The Chilsons saved the stone from the wall where they extended the house and used it to build a huge fireplace in the new dining room, consistent with the style of the house.

Four original rooms are at the front of the second floor, and a new room rests at the back. Three of the front rooms are quite large, with sitting areas, lots of lamps and tables adorned with fresh flowers, lovely period antiques, and some original colonial mantels — as well as televisions and phones. The linens are lovely, with down comforters and heavy sheeting.

Though the large dining room and English tap room downstairs are open on weekends, weekday dinner guests have the pleasure of eating in the cozy fireplace room. Samples of the fine food are a delicious corn and chicken chowder and an entrée of chicken and shrimp in champagne cream sauce over wild rice. The breakfasts are also generous, with a hot dish of choice accompanied by homemade biscuits.

Guests will leave remembering the lovely house, the fine food, but most of all cheerful and informative Rita Chilson, a woman of boundless energy and enthusiasm who sincerely loves her guests.

Virginia

Jordan Hollow Farm Inn
Route 2, Box 375
Stanley, Virginia 22851
703-778-2285, 703-778-2209

Proprietors: Marley and Jetze Beers
Accommodations: 21 rooms with private bath (1 Farm House suite, 16 rooms in Arbor View Lodge, 4 rooms in Mare Meadow Lodge)
Rates: $78–$130
Included: Full breakfast

Minimum stay: None
Added: 6.5% tax
Payment: Major credit cards except American Express
Children: Welcome
Pets: Not allowed
Smoking: Allowed
Open: All year

At Jordan Hollow Farm, twenty-five horses wait to be ridden, curry-combed, or simply observed against the backdrop of the Blue Ridge Mountains. Just west of the Skyline Drive near cavern-famous Luray, Jordan Hollow Farm is one of the few inns along the Shenandoah National Park possessing such a magnificent view from its 45 acres.

Marley and Jetze Beers met in West Africa. As newlyweds, they spent weekends renovating their 1790 weekend farmhouse with the intention of drawing conference groups to the country who wanted unique meeting facilities. On Memorial Day weekend 1981, the group that booked the entire property canceled hours before arrival. As the weekend's food was cooking on the stoves, the Beerses asked local hotels to send them their overflow. They had such fun that they geared their entire market toward individual travelers, many of whom return today.

Jordan Hollow Farm is a series of buildings. First is the 150-year-old stable; the Arbor View Lodge (built in 1984) and the Mare Meadow (finished in 1990) flank either side of the drive; and at the end is the old farmhouse, a blond two-story clapboard building with stacked porches. The latter is the main gathering spot, with one second-floor suite and four dining rooms serving breakfast and dinner. (Box lunches are provided on request).

The sixteen rooms in the Arbor View Lodge are on two floors and overlook the pasture, riding rings, meadows, goat houses, and Chinese chickens. Second-floor rooms have better views from the rocker-filled porch. These rooms are cozy and clean, country-decorated, with handmade furniture and interesting pieces like tapas from the South Pacific or Africa and Mennonite quilts.

Rooms are more deluxe in the Mare Meadow Lodge, with gas fireplaces, whirlpool tubs, and private porches overlooking the meadows. The furniture is handmade white cedar, with pretty quilts and throw pillows, decorated in quaint animal or country themes. Mare Meadow has its own common room, also with a fireplace.

The dining rooms offer unusual settings: the two 1790 log cabin rooms, the fox room with a hunt theme, and the exotic

African room with artwork from the Beerses' travels. Entrées range from $12.95 to $19.95 and are all served with soup, salad, vegetables, and fresh bread. Specialties are sautéed quail topped with white wine and cream sauce, served on wild rice or quinoa pilaf; rainbow trout amandine with crab stuffing; and calf's liver that promises to convert even the nonplussed.

The Beerses offer trail rides for all levels and pony rides for children. They are proud of their extremely rare Norwegian Fjord horses, one of the oldest breeds known, ridden and worked by the Vikings. For nonequestrians, there are trails for walking and carriage rides, swimming and fishing at Lake Arrowhead ten minutes away, nearby caverns, and skiing at Massanutten and Bryce resorts.

Maple Hall

Historic Country Inns of Lexington
Route 11 and Interstate 81
11 North Main Street
Lexington, Virginia 24450
703-463-2044

Proprietors: The Peter Meredith Family
Innkeeper: Don Fredenburg
Accommodations: 19 rooms with private bath, 10 with gas fireplace (12 rooms in Manor House; 3 rooms in Guesthouse; 4 rooms in Pond House)
Rates: $70–$115
Included: Continental breakfast
Minimum stay: 2 nights on some college weekends
Added: $15 each additional guest; 6.5% tax
Payment: Visa, MasterCard
Children: Welcome
Pets: Not allowed
Smoking: Not allowed in Pond House and Guesthouse
Open: All year

Maple Hall is one of the three Historic Country Inns of Lexington, a commendable restoration project undertaken by the Peter Meredith family of Norfolk in 1978. Two less formal properties are in the historic section of Lexington, while elegant Maple Hall is six miles north, just off the interstate. In 1984, the Merediths bought the distinguished Maple Hall from the descendants of John B. Gibson, who built the plantation house in 1850.

While within view of the interstate, the stunning three-story Georgian and Palladian brick structure is surprisingly removed on its 56 acres. The formal guest entrance is approached by a dual staircase in true Palladian fashion, leaving a separate ground-floor entrance underneath for the dining areas and two handicapped-accessible rooms. Large black-shuttered windows on two floors flank four white pillars.

The interior is decorated with period reproductions, Federal antiques, and Orientals rugs. Both the first and second floors have three queen bedrooms and one twin bedroom, each with a fireplace and television, four-poster reproduction bed with firm mattress, a desk, wing chairs, and a newly appointed bath. Each room features several good antiques. These rooms are much preferable to the two double-bedded rooms in a wing off the first floor. The common room is on the first floor, with a gas fireplace.

Maple Hall forms the third of a trio of brick buildings on the property set tidily around a courtyard of greenery. The middle building, just off the outdoor dining terrace, is the Guesthouse, the first on the property, built in 1828 by the Gibson family as it settled on the 257-acre plantation. Adjacent is the Pond House, completed in April 1990, a replica of its older cousin except for some modern details and porches. Both are two stories, decorated in Federal simplicity; some rooms have gas fireplaces and balconies overlooking the stocked fishing pond, the swimming pool, and the tennis court. There are several miles of trails maintained and mapped for active guests.

Dinner is served in three dining rooms, most pleasantly in the enclosed brick porch. The menu is specialized and seasonal, and entrées range from $14.50 to $18.95. A favorite appetizer is lobster bisque or angels on horseback—large gulf shrimp and oysters wrapped in bacon and broiled. The chef's offerings might include chicken Suzanne, a boneless breast sautéed with Virginia ham and topped with cheese sauce; filet mignon, wrapped in bacon with béarnaise sauce on the side; or grilled quail.

Innkeeper Don Fredenberg may be found at the McCampbell Inn in town, though the large Maple Hall staff is helpful and happy. Despite the genteel plantation atmosphere at Maple Hall, it is a busy place given its proximity to Washington and Lee University and the Virginia Military Institute.

Willow Grove Plantation
Route 15 North
Orange, Virginia 22960
703-672-5982
703-256-1976 in Washington, D.C.

Proprietor: Angela Mulloy
Accommodations: 2 suites, 3 rooms, some with fireplace
Rates: $95–$135
Included: Full southern farm breakfast
Added: 4.5% tax
Payment: Visa, MasterCard
Children: Welcome
Pets: Check with innkeeper
Smoking: Allowed
Open: All year

Willow Grove Inn, on the National Register of Historic Places and a Virginia Historic Landmark, is set on 37 acres of overgrown fields near Montpelier. The house, a sunny presidential yellow with black shutters and white trim, sits grandly at the end of a slightly winding drive, several miles from the bustling village of Orange. Several outbuildings remain in good standing on the plantation, including the first schoolhouse in Orange County. It's an informal sociable place, masterminded by friendly Angela Mulloy, a famous gathering spot for Sunday brunch.

The back part of the inn was built in the 1770s by Joseph Clark as a small Federal farmhouse. Clark's son William, a surveyor for nearby Montpelier, created the grand addition in 1830. The house is typical of Jefferson's classical revival style, with four white brick pillars two stories high supporting a third floor with a semicircular window carved into the cornice. As in a Palladian villa, stairs flank the formal first-floor entrance. Generals Wayne and Muhlenberg used the house as a camp during the Revolutionary War, and a Civil War cannonball was found in its eaves.

The rooms on the second floor and under the third-floor eaves are named for Virginia presidents born on the Constitution Trail and are decorated according to the period in which they reigned. Across the hall from the Madison Room and Taylor Monroe Suite is the Washington room, featuring a grand antique four-poster bed with an upholstered tester matching the swags above the windows and a working fireplace. This room has access to the front porch behind the columns, overlooking the acreage, with a twin at the University of Virginia. Here one notices the explicit Jeffersonian influence, as the huge brick pillars remain unattached to the porch front.

Under the eaves of the third floor, the Harrison Room has a small velvet child's fainting couch at the foot of the antique Jenny Lind bed, all in Empire style. The pretty two-bedroom Wilson Suite features two distinct rooms with wicker sitting areas, a pink quilt over an antique iron and brass bed in one room and two cottage twin beds in another in front of the semicircular Jefferson window.

Once the old root cellar, the ground floor is home to Clark's Tavern, an informal gathering spot with exposed hand-hewn beams. There are two full dining rooms on the first floor, with weekend piano and vocal entertainment. Dinners range from $17.95 to $19.95 and include hearty country food like beef tenderloin, loin lamb chops, medallions of Summerfield veal, and Rappahannock trout. The three-course Sunday brunch is a local tradition. A sampling might be smoked trout with dill mayonnaise followed by plantation toast royale with blackberry sauce and a meat or fish course of Virginia country ham baked with honey bourbon sauce served with fried tomatoes, and grits with cheddar cheese and creole sauce.

West Virginia

Pence Springs Hotel
Box 90
Pence Springs, West Virginia 24962
304-445-2606

General Manager: O. Ashby Berkley
Assistant Innkeeper: Rosa Lee Miller
Accommodations: 30 units, each with 2 bedrooms sharing a
   bath
Rates: $45–$65, suites $75–$150
Included: Breakfast

Minimum stay: None
Added: $15 each additional person, $10 for children under 12;
   9% tax
Payment: Major credit cards
Children: Welcome
Pets: Allowed in basement
Smoking: Allowed
Open: All year

Pence Springs Hotel, on the National Register of Historic Places, is most certainly worth a visit as one of the more unusual places in this book. It went from being a grand resort in the Roaring Twenties to a state prison for women as recently as 1983, with various incarnations in between. This incongruously elegant country Georgian structure is 20 miles from I-64 and 40 miles from I-77, along a beautiful stretch of Route 3 near Beckley, West Virginia. Rough mountains stretch up either side of the wild Greenbrier River, leading to an enormous mansion atop a hill in the hamlet of Pence Springs.

Built in 1918 as a resort, the 60-room hotel had a 9-hole golf course, mineral spa, and a staff of one hundred. At $6 a day for full American plan, it was a truly elegant place to be, almost a sister property to the nearby Greenbrier. The C&O Railroad would stop here fourteen times a day by 1926, and summers were booked to the capacity of 125. During Prohibition, several secret rooms reached by tunnel under the massive porch held stashes of alcohol. The Depression came, and the resort was turned into a girls' school, only to be shut down in the early forties. Soon after, it became a women's state prison until 1983, holding from 13 to 60 women at a time. It shut down again and remained abandoned until 1986. O. Ashby Berkley bought the place, put more than a million dollars into its renovation, and reopened in November 1988.

The main house has a three-story portico, four columns across, with two wings stretching off on either side. One enters the hotel from the back. The foyer abuts a lovely, large common room at the hotel's center portion. The room is eight-sided, with a piano, working fireplace, and many windows that open up to a generous porch overlooking the holly trees out front. The center halls have a pretty art deco runner. Downstairs is the Cider Press Lounge, whose gorgeous marble bar was in the movie *Matewan*.

Guest rooms on the second floor are small and boxy, with small windows, double beds, private phones, and spare, simple decor. There are also two rooms astride a bath with two double beds and connecting doors as well as two spacious suites. Baths, like the rooms, are clean and a bit barren.

Some may want to avoid the third floor, and others will certainly request to see it, but everyone ought to know about it. At the end of one guest wing, four of the original solitary-confinement cells remain. The locks were taken out when the jail closed, but the bars, the battleship gray floors, and even the inmates' graffiti remain. Without direct light, set in the center of the room with an exercise corridor around the perimeter, it's a haunting place, and innkeeper Rosa has some eerie stories about some of its infamous inmates.

The dining room looks like a ballroom, with hardwood floors and white walls and ceilings. The country-style restaurant serves three meals, including hearty suppers such as chicken with cornbread stuffing and gravy, old Virginia chicken and peanut pie, and baked ham with pineapple, ranging from $9 to $18. For fancier fare, guests should visit Mr. Berkley's Riverside Inn, a gourmet supper club about a mile down the road. Built by the late Governor Hatfield, a member of the infamous Hatfield-McCoy feud, it was at one time a state-sanctioned watering hole and was used by Pretty Boy Floyd as a summer retreat.

Village Bed-and-Breakfasts

Delaware

New Devon Inn
2nd and Market Streets
Lewes, Delaware 19958
302-645-6466

Proprietors: Dale Jenkins and Bernard Nash
General Manager: Barbara Lloyd
Accommodations: 24 rooms, 2 suites
Rates (vary seasonally): $60–$85; $80–$125; $95–$140
Included: Continental breakfast, nightly turndown
Minimum stay: 2 nights on summer holiday weekends
Added: $20 each additional guest; 8% tax
Payment: MasterCard, Visa, Diners Club, American Express
Children: Discouraged
Pets: Not allowed
Smoking: Not allowed in breakfast room
Open: All year

On the western shores of the Delaware Bay across from New Jersey's southern tip is the town of Lewes, Delaware, often and unfairly remembered as the "other end" of the Cape May ferry. This surprisingly lovely fishing village was founded by Dutch settlers in 1631 and has boundless charm and historic import. It's easy to miss Lewes (pronounced "Lewis") since the ferry access and Route 13 bypass the town by a quarter mile. However, it is certainly worth a detour if not a trip in itself to see this picturesque town and, on its fringes, Cape Henlopen State Park, which has some of the prettiest protected beachfront in the Delmarva peninsula.

The town looks like a movie set, and in the heart of it all is the New Devon Inn. The hotel sits on the corner of Market and 2nd streets, the town's main thoroughfare lined with gentle elm trees, quaint shops, and very good restaurants. The corner itself holds some historic merit, having been the homestead of John Rodney from 1725 to 1792; Rodney's cousin Caesar was one of the three Delaware signers of the Declaration of Independence, and his sons Caleb and Daniel each went on to govern the state.

The Caesar Rodney Hotel was built here in late 1927 and served as the town's hostelry over the years until it fell into disrepair during its tenure as a transient hotel. In 1987, Dale Jenkins, contractor and decorator, and her partner, Bernard Nash, bought the faded property, gutted the interior, and undertook a daunting renovation. The brick face and floors are the only testament to the original structure. In 1989, twenty-four rooms and two suites welcomed guests in sophistication and splendor; and today six retail shops enliven some of the lobby and the lower level. Owner Jenkins named the property rather touchingly for Devon Island, which disappeared in the Delaware Bay, an event chronicled by James Michener in his novel *Chesapeake*.

Guests enter from 2nd Street through wide welcoming doors to the fresh lobby, with slate tile floors and area Oriental rugs. Upstairs are two floors of sleeping rooms, and those overlooking 2nd Street are preferable. While the interior was entirely rebuilt, the room decor is made up of Victorian antiques. A Market Street third-floor room has a double-sized antique carved oak headboard, a petit point Victorian chair, marble-top dresser, and old-fashioned floral linens. Others have similar period antiques and beds in oxford stripe linens or masculine paisleys. The baths are new and sparkling, with black and white parquet linoleum, pedestal sinks with brass fixtures, thick towels, amenities from Scarborough and Company, cotton balls, and a hair dryer. Nightly turndown brings sherry on a silver platter, glasses, and a filled ice bucket. Oriental runners and scatter rugs add color to the light wood flooring.

There are two common rooms for guests: a downstairs television room and a ground-floor Victorian parlor with a grand piano where guests partake of a generous Continental breakfast of fresh baked goods, juice, yogurt, and fruit.

No one knows the charms of Lewes better than General Manager Barbara Lloyd, who must be sought out in the unlikely event that she has not greeted guests herself. A source of enthusiasm and historical knowledge, Barbara represents the best of the New Devon Inn service. Lewes is a great town for walking and viewing three centuries of architecture. In addition, 3,400-acre Cape Henlopen State Park is an incredible resource, with three miles of beachfront activities, including hiking, camping, a 9-hole Frisbee golf course, and the Seaside Nature Center.

Maryland

Chanceford Hall Inn
209 West Federal Street
Snow Hill, Maryland 21863
410-632-2231

Proprietors: Michael and Thelma Driscoll
Accommodations: 5 rooms, all with private bath, 4 with
   fireplace
Rates: $100–$115
Included: Full breakfast
Minimum stay: None
Added: $15 each additional guest; 8% tax
Payment: No credit cards
Children: Over 12 welcome
Pets: Not allowed
Smoking: Allowed
Open: All year

The small town of Snow Hill is one of Maryland's southernmost, on its eastern shore below Delaware and 12 miles north of Virginia's eastern peninsula and Chincoteague Bay. Owned by Thelma and Michael Driscoll, Chanceford Hall is truly memorable because of Michael's craftsmanship in furniture making. Anyone with an interest in woodwork ought to make a pilgrimage to this gallery of handmade furniture designed and created by the owner.

The house is an immaculate, elegant colonial of brick and white stucco with black shutters, built around 1759, with ten working fireplaces. It's set back from the residential street by a pretty lawn and a walkway lined with old English boxwoods, leading to a bright red front door. The Driscolls moved into the house in October 1986 and opened the inn after two years of restoration. Most of the color is applied in faithful Williamsburg hues—but some of the woodwork, like the stairs and gorgeously carved mantels, has been stripped and exposed throughout the house.

Guests enter at the side, where the large formal dining room is centered on a vivid antique Oriental rug. The gleaming dining room table is perhaps Michael's finest work, mahogany with ebony and holly inlay. It sits in front of a yellow pine dentil-carved mantel—complementing the carved crown moldings as do all the mantels throughout the house. The formal living room has a traditional sitting area in front of another fireplace and a tea table made by Michael that cleverly expands.

The Chanceford Room is the only first-floor guest room, with Williamsburg gold trim, crewel drapes, and a private bath. Directly above is the Chadwick Room, where Michael made the quilt rack (as he did in all rooms), the trestle schoolmaster desk, and the dark pencil-post queen-size bed. Tapestry swags —which Michael also made—cover the original windows. From the back stairway two more rooms are accessible: the Cliveden Room and the Carrington Suite, larger than the rest with a sitting area in front of a fireplace, three exposures, a dark-stained pencil-post bed, and an antique cannonball twin. All beds feature down comforters.

On the first floor, the wonderful kitchen, a nice gathering spot, was crafted entirely by Michael. At the back of the house is the only addition, built in 1970, an informal common room that runs the width of the house, with a turretlike ceiling and engulfing sofas from which guests can see the 200-year-old walnut tree that nearly touches the window and the acre and a half of groomed lawns on three sides of the house. In the backyard, under a covered trellis, is a small lap pool.

Thelma and Mike are extremely friendly and love their business. They moved to Maryland from Milwaukee in search of a perfect bed-and-breakfast and work tremendously hard to keep guests contented and returning. While the Driscolls are happy to prepare private gourmet dinners with advance notice, the in-town option is the Snow Hill Inn, for great seafood.

Inn at the Canal

104 Bohemia Avenue
Chesapeake City, Maryland 21915
410-885-5995

Proprietors: Al and Mary Ioppolo
Accommodations: 6 rooms, all with private bath
Rates: $70–$105 (lower rates in winter)
Included: Full breakfast, afternoon refreshments
Minimum stay: 2 nights on holiday weekends
Added: $25 each additional guest; 5% tax
Payment: MasterCard, Visa, American Express, Discover
Children: Over 10 welcome
Pets: Not allowed
Smoking: Allowed in the parlor only
Open: All year

The Chesapeake & Delaware Canal in essence makes an island out of the Delaware-Maryland-Virginia peninsula. An adorable tourist town teeming with antiques shops, Chesapeake City sits at the peninsula's western neck, under the arching narrow bridge that straddles the canal. Everything from oil tankers to pleasure boats passes slowly through the channel, which is 13 miles long, 35 feet deep, and 450 feet wide, originally completed in 1829.

The Inn at the Canal has a front-row seat to all the action, several houses from the end of the main street in town, its back lawn floating right on the water. The house was built in 1868 by the prominent Brady family, a reward of sorts when Mrs. Brady finally presented her husband with a son, their third child. In those days, houses were taxed by their width facing street, so the two-and-a-half-story front is quite modest while the house stretches forever toward the waterfront.

The owners of the bed-and-breakfast, Al and Mary Ioppolo, love the town's history and orientation. They bought the house in February 1989 and restored the fanciful creamy-white Victorian exterior, its celery-colored shutters, and the slate gable roof. The sweet gingerbread front porch with white wicker chairs unites the house to the busy street front.

The first-floor common rooms have looming 12-foot ceilings, with windows nearly as high. It's believed that Mrs. Brady herself hand-painted and stenciled the elaborate ceilings in the parlor and the breakfast room on either side of the foyer. They are being restored, along with the faux marble fireplaces. Al and Mary collect antiques—their shop is at the rear of the inn—and some of their best finds are on display throughout the house: antique door stops rest on every other step of the stairways; Peter Pan prints decorate the walls; and antique quilts are draped on an old sled on the second-floor landing.

Two rooms with water views rest in the back wing of the house. Mary made the black and pink quilt in the farthest room, which inspired the different black rose chintz patterns in the lampshade, two wing chairs, and the needlepoint rug. At the front of the house are four more rooms. An especially sweet room here features an antique white linen counterpane on a white brass and iron bed and diaphanous drapes. All rooms have small, unobtrusive televisions, often hidden in cabinets. The successful baths are the result of the renovation, with Mexican tile, wash sinks in old oak dressers, very fluffy towels, and Gilchrest and Soames amenities.

The kitchen features Al's extensive collection of antique cast-iron muffin pans. The great common porch at the back of the house overlooks the canal, and guests can sit in rockers, watch the boats, and listen to the sounds of the jazz band that plays in warmer months on Sunday evenings in a tiny old wooden band shell on the water.

National Pike Inn

9–11 West Main Street, Box 299
New Market, Maryland 21774
301-865-5055

Proprietors: Tom and Terry Rimel
Accommodations: 4 rooms, 2 with private bath
Rates: $75–$100
Included: Full breakfast
Minimum stay: 2 nights on some weekends in September and December
Added: 5% tax
Payment: MasterCard, Visa
Children: Over 10 welcome on weekdays
Pets: Not allowed
Smoking: Discouraged
Open: All year

New Market is an adorable little one-street town ten minutes from Frederick. It's about 40 miles north of Washington, D.C., and 30 miles west of Baltimore, a perfect weekend spot for urbanites who don't want to get lost in the country but who want a relaxed retreat. For weekend antiquers who are looking for a place of some historic merit without having to dust themselves off at every turn, the National Pike is just the place.

Named for the nation's first federally funded highway, the National Pike Inn was built at the turn of the 18th century, a few years after the town was founded. The house is two and a half stories of stucco over brick, painted brown with red shutters and ivory trim, with a cupola built into the center of the steep shingle rooftop. Tom and Terry Rimel lived in New Market for thirteen years before they bought the house in 1986 and restored it. The Rimels make good use of the two-family construction, using one side for their home and the other side for guests.

The Federal living room was built in 1802 and is furnished with period reproductions. Several steps toward the back of the house, what is now the dining room was built in 1796 and now contains some family heirlooms such as a 200-year-old tea cart, set on highly cared-for wide-planked original floors.

At the second-floor landing toward the back wing, two rooms share one bath. The wide planks of the floor are nearly hilly: one room has an antique oak bedroom set, the other has cherry furniture with cranberry trim and a brass bed. The pretty and simple Federal Room is in the middle of the house above the living room, with a small, nonworking fireplace, fireside bench, maroon steps up to the four-poster canopy bed, and a view of the 1820s smokehouse. Its hall bath is a creative black and white. The front Victorian Room has a four-poster spindle bed, a carved cherry dresser with a matching night-stand, and a new bath with a sit-shower.

The half acre of groomed backyard is quite pretty and socia-ble. From the brick patio guests enjoy the azalea gardens, a bird bath, and a fountain that trickles on the vast lawns—a grassy haven for a village bed-and-breakfast. Terry is the full-time inn-keeper, a warm hostess who is glad to welcome guests to her pretty home. As natives, both Terry and Tom have a lot of good advice about the goings-on of New Market and Frederick, home to Hood College.

Victoriana Inn

Box 449, 205 Cherry Street
St. Michaels, Maryland 21663
410-745-3368

Proprietors: Janet Bernstein
Accommodations: 5 rooms, 1 with private bath, 4 sharing two baths
Rates: $95–$135
Included: Full country breakfast
Minimum stay: 2 nights on weekends
Added: 8% tax
Payment: Visa, MasterCard
Children: Over 13 welcome
Pets: Not allowed
Smoking: Limited to the sun porch and parlor
Open: All year

Whether or not the octagonal Chesapeake Bay Maritime Mu-seum is the state's most recognizable piece of architecture is arguable; but surely the best place from which to ponder this thought is the porch at the Victoriana Inn, which stares right at the monument. This mansard roof two-story Victorian sits right on the channel and near the bay in St. Michaels. It was built by army officer Dr. Clay Dodson during the Civil War and underwent renovations in 1910 by a family who sold the house to present owner Janet Bernstein in 1988.

There are several particularly nice aspects about this bed-and-breakfast: private, but only a half block from the busy main

Talbot Street, with serene water views, lovely linens, and generous common space. Guests enter the house from the wide veranda; to the right is a living room with a fireplace leading to an enclosed sun porch. There is also a breakfast room where a full morning meal is served, always with two home-baked coffee cakes and a main dish such as strawberry pancakes, eggs Benedict, or creamed chipped beef.

The only guest room on the first floor is also the largest. The Tilghman Island Room has a wood-burning brick fireplace, pink-hued walls, a four-poster bed with a curved fishnet canopy, a daunting triple armoire, and windows with a view of the cove and the little bridge across the canal. Of the four second-floor rooms, Solomon Island is quite pretty, with a four-poster queen-size bed showing off a lovely presentation of triple Laura Ashley sheeting, ample pillows, and a tiny sachet placed on a pillow. The Poplar Island Room has an impressive French Victorian bedroom suite. Three of the rooms have water views. While they share two baths, the second-floor rooms each have a sink and vanity.

Janet is devoted to her home, a well-informed hostess. The little shops and restaurants of St. Michaels are all within walking distance; and back from a walk, guests have nothing better to do than sit on the wicker porch chairs or the Adirondack lawn chairs overlooking the little canal and the Maritime Museum.

New Jersey

Chestnut Hill on the Delaware
63 Church Street, P.O. Box N
Milford, New Jersey 08848
908-995-9761

Proprietors: Linda and Rob Castagna
Accommodations: 5 rooms and 1 bedroom cottage
Rates: Rooms, $75–$100; cottage, $130
Included: Full breakfast
Minimum stay: 2 nights on weekends
Added: 7% tax
Payment: No credit cards
Children: Check with innkeeper
Pets: Not allowed
Smoking: Not allowed
Open: All year

Thornton Wilder could well have been thinking of Milford when he wrote *Our Town*. In an area of the Delaware River Valley where much has been given over to the traveling public, Milford remains seemingly untouched by tourism. Chestnut Hill on the Delaware is nestled in this charming, near-to-minuscule town, just over the narrow metal bridge from Upper Black Eddy, Pennsylvania. It's about a half hour from New Hope and a world away but a short drive to Flemington's shopping outlets.

In honor of its first mill, which was destroyed by fire soon after it was built in 1760, what we know today as Milford began as a hamlet called Burnt Mills. The name was changed to Milford in 1820, and small, subtle changes have been made ever since: mandatory dog licensing in 1911, the purchase of its first town fire hose cart in 1912, laws against street ball in 1926, the paving of Bridge Street in 1929, and installation of a traffic light in 1954.

The bed-and-breakfast sits just across some rickety train tracks separating Chestnut Hill from the abrupt grassy banks of the Delaware. It's a neat old house, a white Victorian, with dark green wrought-iron pillars. The Castagnas have undertaken a laborious several-year project to remove twenty-five layers of paint and restore the original colors of the house: cranberry, gold leaf, and three shades of green. The Country Cottage just across the drive mimics the design of the house and shares the view of the river and the bridge. Anyone with a sense of romance will appreciate the porch rockers and the river views of both houses.

This is a very Victorian home. The common rooms are elegant, with lovely Victorian antiques such as a working pump organ, a mannequin with a satin wedding dress, reupholstered period settees, and Bradbury and Bradbury wallpaper.

As formal as are the common rooms, the guest rooms are playful and decorative, with some modern touches. The three rooms on the second floor are as pretty and sweet as their names denote: Bayberry, Peaches and Cream, and Pineapple. The third floor is called Teddy's Place, named for the 166 bears who live up here.

The Country Cottage has the advantage of independence without the cluttered hominess of the main house: it has a pine furniture set featuring an antique Norwegian armoire. It also has a generous kitchen, good for longer stays.

Breakfasts are full at a lovely dining table with a breathtaking sideboard. Specialties include German apple pancakes and home-baked muffins. As with long-standing bed-and-breakfasts, it's the owners who make this place memorable—proud, involved professionals who care about the needs of their guests.

The Old Hunterdon House

12 Bridge Street
Frenchtown, New Jersey 08825
908-996-3632

Proprietor: Tony Cappiello
Innkeeper: Larry Miller
Accommodations: 7 rooms with private bath, 2 with coal fireplace
Rates: $90–$115
Included: Full breakfast
Minimum stay: 2 nights with Saturday stay, 3 nights on some holidays
Added: 7% tax
Payment: All credit cards
Children: Infants not allowed
Pets: Not allowed
Smoking: Not allowed
Open: All year

Along the series of narrow metal bridges spanning the Delaware River connecting Pennsylvania and New Jersey is the latter state's Frenchtown. Named for a Swiss soldier who retreated here to escape death threats during the French Revolution in 1794, Frenchtown is a most charming stop along the Delaware's calmer banks, good for antiquing, cycling, and food. It's also home to the extremely romantic Old Hunterdon House, a stunning 1865 Italianate and Gothic brick mansion.

A stone's throw from the bridge, behind an elaborate wrought-iron gate, the formidable house is a trick-or-treater's dream: scary at night, evocative during the day. Its two stories are made of brown bricks with a third-story cupola crowning the flat roof. The facade, wrapped in a gingerbread porch, is punctuated with quirky floor-to-ceiling clerestory, arched, and round windows.

The breakfast and common rooms flank either side of the foyer, both with original faux marbling on their respective coal fireplaces. The rooms each have interesting period antiques and lavish floor-to-ceiling windows arched inches below the 14-foot crown moldings. One of the seven guest rooms is on the first floor, and despite its fireplace it is perhaps the least desirable, given its sociable setting and the comparative privacy of the other rooms.

Rooms are named for famous people who resided in the area. The jazzy Paul Whiteman Room has chiffon bows on its crocheted canopy bed, a tufted suede chair and ottoman, and three floor-to-ceiling windows. Even the baths are lovely, with paisley towels to match room colors, lace shower curtains, and Caswell and Massey amenities. The Daniel Bray Room, named for the Revolutionary War captain who ambushed the British at Trenton on Christmas night 1776, features a hand-carved burl bed, a wonderful tiled shower in a closet to the left of the door, and the rest of the bath in the closet to the right of the door. The Ruth Apgar Room has a huge carved mahogany Renaissance Revival headboard and a wainscoted bath with a marble-top sink, from which one sees the gingerbread through lace curtains.

Third-floor rooms are especially wonderful—the Lindbergh Room sits under pitched eaves with an enchanting clover-rosette window and a dormer skylight. The James Agee Room across the hall has a tartan couch and a burl bed under a tapestry spread. The beds are especially wonderful at the Hunterdon House, with thick sheets and pretty presentation.

Larry, new to innkeeping from the world of advertising, is thrilled with his work. Fresh juice and a newspaper are brought to the guest rooms while Larry prepares home-baked breads and muffins, fresh fruit, and hot entrées such as blueberry-apple pancakes, four types of quiche, and New York City bagels.

The adventurous must view the town from the cupola's mauve window seats. Make dinner plans ahead for the Frenchtown Inn for a memorable four-star dinner or at Evermay-on-the-Delaware (see Gourmet Getaways) across the bridge.

The Whistling Swan Inn

Box 791, 110 Main Street
Stanhope, New Jersey 07874
201-347-6369

Proprietors: Paula Williams and Joe Mulay
Accommodations: 10 rooms, including 1 suite, all with private bath
Rates: Rooms, $65–$85; suite, $95
Included: Full breakfast served buffet-style
Minimum stay: Some holidays
Added: 7% tax
Payment: Major credit cards
Children: Over 12 welcome
Pets: Not allowed
Smoking: Not allowed
Open: All year

The town of Stanhope is quite representative of the northwest New Jersey Skylands, characterized by old rolling mountains and a sprinkling of lakes and reservoirs, just a half hour east of the Delaware Water Gap. Several blocks from downtown Stanhope is the Whistling Swan Inn, a gray and white Queen Anne Victorian with black shutters and welcoming wrap porch, topped off in part by an octagonal turret.

The ten-bedroom house was built in 1900 by Stanhope's justice of the peace, Daniel Best, for his wife and seven children. Paula Williams and Joe Mulay bought the mansion in December 1985 and worked nonstop to open their six-room bed-and-breakfast on Memorial Day. They have since expanded to ten rooms, having recently completed the third-floor rooms quite successfully.

The innkeepers are creative scavengers. In nearby Hackettstown, Paula and Joe found the charming "Whistling Swan" sign that hangs out front, and the authentic brass bathroom fixtures were rescued from demolition at the great Essex-Sussex Hotel in Spring Lake.

Upon entering, a visitor will quickly become enamored of the old house. The first floor has rich tiger oak molding and fireplaces with vivid green Moravian tile in the foyer and a woody brown in the dining room. The thick carpeting and pink and red hues in the common rooms, however, mark a lapse in the traditional decor. The tiger oak continues up the stairs, in the boxy fashion of American shingle Victorians. While all rooms have new private baths, the original shared bath has been humorously transformed into Tubs for Two, with a pair of old clawfoot tubs painted a cheery cornflower blue (one tub is six feet long).

Highlights of the six second-floor guest rooms are the Harmony Room, with Oriental and Thai antiques collected by Paula's great-uncle; the Waterloo Village Room, with antiques from Paula's Oklahoma grandmother, including her great-grandmother's marriage license; and the Great Meadows Room, with an art deco theme, including a Lindbergh *Spirit of St. Louis* tapestry and Paula's grandmother's beautiful four-piece oak bedroom set (which she bought for $75).

The third-floor High Point Suite is the feature attraction of the house, its bedroom in the octagonal turret, which has an 18-foot ceiling and cedar wainscoting and is furnished with a three-piece carved oak bed, dresser, and washstand with a brass sink. Three windows at floorboard level welcome light. The sitting room is furnished in summery wicker, and the private bath, with a clawfoot tub, sits amusingly at a strange angle. Also striking is the 1940s Stillwater Room, set under steeply pitched gables, with a period bedroom suite.

The owners are generous people, very devoted to the concept of bed-and-breakfasting. They are extremely well informed and enthusiastic about the area, which is near Lake Hopatcong (the state's largest lake), ski areas, and historic Waterloo Village. In addition, Joe and Paula are good cooks, and the full breakfasts might include broccoli and cheese pie, farmhouse corn pancakes, frittatas, apple-cheese muffins, or cold fruit soup.

New York

The Bent Finial
194 Main Street
Warrensburg, New York 12885
518-623-3308

Proprietors: Pat and Paul Scully
Accommodations: 4 rooms, all with private bath, including 1 room with optional sleeping alcove
Rates: $85–$95
Included: Full breakfast

Added: 5% tax
Payment: No credit cards
Children: Check with innkeeper
Pets: Not allowed
Smoking: Limited
Open: All year

Bed-and-breakfasters disenchanted with the kitsch of Lake George and the expense of the impressive Omni Sagamore resort in Bolton Landing will want to stay at the Bent Finial in nearby Warrensburg, which opened in the fall of 1989. This lovely Queen Anne Victorian has a memorable 23 types of wood decorating the interior, mainly cherry on the first floor, in the form of paneling, wainscoting, coffered ceilings, and the elaborate Corinthian columns and carved stairs decorating the foyer and the stairwell.

Built in 1904 by wealthy cattle rancher Lewis Thomson, this house is three grand stories of white clapboard, with a stone portico that introduces the entrance and the curved wrap front porch. The gabled third floor ascends to a lovely candle-snuffer turret topped by a copper rod finial—bent, of course.

The vast front porch wraps to the left, and from this guests enter the foyer. To the right is the living room, with a fabulous alcove game room tucked into the turret space and elaborate Corinthian columns supporting the ceiling. There is a marvelous terra cotta fireplace here, one of many in the house. To the left is the dining room where guests have candlelight breakfast under birch-stained coffered ceilings. Pat cooks generously: soufflés, crêpes, and fresh baked goods are served on silver and crystal. Behind the dining room is a quaint glass-enclosed conservatory, oddly original to the house.

The rooms are done with antiques found by Pat at estate sales, nicely reupholstered, with a lovely variety within the Queen Anne and Victorian period, albeit a little sparse in the common rooms. Halfway up the magnificent stairs is a bench built into the landing overlooking the porte-cochere.

Turn-of-the-century family portraits decorate the second-floor landing. The incredible stained glass in the house is original and extremely colorful—there are 104 windows in all—used by Pat as the guidepost for decorating the rooms. The lovely Turret Chamber is to the left, easily the room of choice, with a sitting area in the turret and bright floral wallpaper. Its private bath is playful, designed by Pat to have all the gingerbread that this later Victorian is missing from its austere exterior. The Eastlake Chamber is named for its lovely bedroom set. The Master Chamber has another terra cotta fireplace, Schumacher border paper, in an odd brown and mauve color scheme that comes directly from its stained glass window.

Though there's not much to do in tiny Warrensburg but eat at the Merrill Magee House and fish in a narrow branch of the Hudson River, there is a lot to do nearby. Lake George is a short scenic drive away, and plentiful skiing and boating abounds in this area in the southeast corner of the Adirondacks.

Centennial House

13 Woods Lane
East Hampton, New York 11937
516-324-9414
Fax: 516-324-1986

Proprietors: David Oxford and Harry Chancey, Jr.
Accommodations: 6 rooms, all with private bath; 2-bedroom cottage
Rates:
  Low season: $150–$200
  Mid-season: $150–$225
  High season: $175–$250
  Cottage: $300–$375
Included: Full breakfast, not including cottage
Minimum stay: 4 nights on summer holidays, 3 nights on summer weekends, 2 nights on other weekends
Added: 7.5% tax
Payment: Visa, MasterCard
Children: Welcome in cottage
Pets: Not allowed
Smoking: Not allowed
Open: All year

For an island with the densest population in this country, there are surprisingly few places to stay on Long Island. The paucity is quickly felt in the beach communities: so exclusive that residents don't want or need tourism. However, a world of travel opened up in 1988 when attorney David Oxford and television executive Harry Chancey, Jr., unveiled their treasure, Centennial House, one of the most elegant bed-and-breakfasts in this book.

The house sits on the corner of Montauk Highway and East Hampton's Village Pond, half a mile from town or the gorgeous beach, in opposite directions. The owners opened their doors in 1988 on a fluke, when the well-known 1770 House (see Village Inns) down the street was overbooked. David and Harry, ever amenable, quite liked the experience and have welcomed over-nighters ever since.

The weathered shingle house was built in 1876 by Thomas E. Babcock, a celebrated local craftsman, and the owners spent nearly a year restoring the house from its worn state. They are avid antique-hunters and have fascinating stories about nearly every piece in the house. When neighbors are among the country's wealthiest, a yard sale can produce some treasures: brass sconces acquired at an auction at a millionaire's mansion; breakfast china bought for $85 because the owner paid "about that" for the set in the early part of the century; padded Schumacher wall fabric and Scalamandre silk in the dining room rescued from estate sales.

Like any moneyed East Hampton house, the rooms feel relaxed and rambling, but the individual pieces which populate them are extraordinarily valuable and lovely. The formal parlors have matching Czechoslovakian crystal chandeliers, a green marble hearth, and a four-windowed bay which permits a soft lighting on the stunning antiques, the chintz couches, and the grand piano. The formal dining room is the setting for bountiful meals of pancakes, French toast, and meat, while dishes like buttermilk pancakes and cheese grits reflect David's Alabama roots.

Of the four second-floor rooms, the Rose Room has a four-poster canopy corkscrew bed, hung with Waverly material that matches window treatments. The walls are a Schumacher floral. The baths are all beautifully decorated, and here a heavy tapestry serves as curtains to a clawfoot tub. A generous portion of Neutrogena products sits in all baths, including the thoughtful touch of sunblock. The Bay Room is David's favorite because of the size and its wonderful bathroom fitted with brass fixtures, off-white wainscoting, white clawfoot tub, and white pine washstand—a former pulpet found in England. The Lincoln Room has a beautiful Victorian bedroom set which David decorated, set against green walls with oval brass frames and handsome border paper. Its black and white marble bath is two steps down.

The Loft is the only third-floor room, for the nimble or the romantic, up impossibly steep stairs to a wonderful space under the eaves with thick pile rose carpeting, a king-size bed with a down duvet, and views through high, curved top windows. Its bath is cleverly placed under the roof's steep pitch. All rooms are provided with lush terry robes; as well, a split of wine and chocolate truffles are special treats in every room.

The three-bedroom Cottage in the backyard is tasteful and private, about a hundred years older than the house itself. The color tones are intriguingly fresh, the walls and wide floorboards a mint and ecru, lending a breezy, cottage feel. The Cottage features a kitchen, a gas fireplace, and a lovely front porch teeming with flower boxes.

A highlight at Centennial House is the acre and a quarter of groomed grounds, overseen by Harry. The 40-foot pool is set among pink and white rose bushes, near formal gardens, and a farther rambling English garden with rhododendrons. A legendary weeping birch and bench swing on another tree overlook the grounds.

David and Harry are elegant and gracious hosts, dissolving the mystique of East Hampton. Visitors here feel a magical combination of being invited weekend friends and guests at an elegant resort.

Pig Hill Bed and Breakfast

73 Main Street
Cold Spring on Hudson, New York 10516
914-265-9247

Proprietors: Wendy O'Brien
Accommodations: 8 rooms, 4 with private bath, 4 sharing 2 baths, 6 with fireplace
Rates: $85–$140, depending on day of week, bath, and fireplace
Included: Full breakfast
Added: $25 for cot or crib in room; 12.25% tax
Payment: Major credit cards
Children: Welcome
Pets: Not allowed
Smoking: Not allowed
Open: All year

Pig Hill Bed and Breakfast receives an unqualified recommendation, one of the prettier such properties along the far-reaching Hudson River. It's a very cosmopolitan place, with sophisticated, expensive decor, most of which is for sale through the ground-floor antiques shop. The house feels like a transplanted New York City brownstone, decorated by an expensive designer, in a humble version of Manhattan's SoHo, with antique shops and chic boutiques.

The bed-and-breakfast sits toward the bottom of Cold Spring's Main Street on a hill that barrels right through town, ending abruptly at a delightful gazebo that offers nonpareil views of the town marina, the Hudson River, and the precipitous facing banks. The three-story brownstone was built in the 1830s and became a Civil War foundry, a booming business in this town, which produced several thousand cannonballs for the Union. Wendy O'Brien, whose family summered in Cold Spring for decades, bought the run-down building in 1986, gutted and worked on it for six months, and opened it as a bed-and-breakfast that fall. The first floor houses an upscale antiques store, which also serves as a common area to guests—a bit disconcerting when weekend browsers are amid one's roost. Even the dining room table on which guests eat breakfast is for sale. A sweet back garden offers refuge, with flagstone steps and a brick patio—perfect for warm-weather breakfasting.

Pig Hill has eight guest rooms equally divided on the second and third floors, in a creative and intimate architectural space. The two outside rooms share the hall bath, and the two inner rooms have private baths. The decor will certainly change if guests want to bring their room home with them, but the level of luxury and design remains. All but two rooms at the front have colorful Franklin stoves, and the back rooms have nice views of the overgrown yard and patio.

The Adirondack Room has some enchanting examples of twig furniture, a bed and settee, and a pair of antlers above the fireplace. One of the private-bath rooms has a blue iron and brass bed, a blue Franklin stove, green damask wallpaper with a Victorian feather border, a lovely armoire, and lace curtains. The shared baths are clean and clever, one with a clawfoot tub enclosed in wainscoting, new sinks with brass or painted fixtures, and neoclassic keystone shelves. Plentiful original art decorates the walls, like Wendy's collection of old windows into which mirrors have been installed, making fascinating wall art. The bedding is especially lovely, with thick designer sheets and down-filled duvets.

Well known for breakfasts such as egg pot pie, spinach soufflé roll, and shirred eggs, Pig Hill is a very romantic spot. Be sure to eat at Hudson House, for the best water views along the Hudson, or at Wendy O'Brien's restaurant, Henry's, up the road apace.

Rosewood Inn
134 East First Street
Corning, New York 14830
607-962-3253

Proprietors: Dick and Winnie Peer
Accommodations: 7 rooms, all with private baths, including
  2 suites
Rates: $68–$100
Included: Full breakfast, afternoon tea
Minimum stay: None
Added: $15 each additional guest; 9% tax
Payment: Visa, MasterCard, Diners Club
Children: Welcome
Pets: Permitted in one suite
Smoking: Restricted
Open: All year

For those visiting one of New York State's largest tourist attractions, Corning offers a special place for die-hard bed-and-breakfasters in the Rosewood Inn. Winnie and Dick Peer introduced the concept to the Finger Lakes region in 1980 when they restored their home and invited guests inside. Winnie was a schoolteacher, Dick the former editor of the local newspaper who still retains a radio talk show and writes a daily newspaper column. They are consummate, intelligent hosts who have loved and lived in Corning since 1961 and are rich with enthusiasm for their town.

The house was originally built as a Greek Revival in 1853 and was given a Tudor face in 1917. Guests enter to the double-sized living room, which opens to a sun porch at the side of the house and, toward the back, to a elegant, family-style dining room. Around the dining room's oversized mahogany table, full breakfast is served each morning, beginning with Dick's home-baked goods, pineapple French toast, and oven-baked dishes such as strata and quiche so the Peers can socialize with guests.

The second floor has five rooms, each done in a theme. The Charles Dana Gibson Room has six prints of Gibson girls from the turn of the century, a lovely quilt on a Victorian faux wooded burl bed, part of a two piece Eastlake set. Other rooms include the Rockwell Gallery Room, with western art and a queen-size canopy bed; the Frederick Carder Room, named for the artisan who began the Steuben Glass works in 1903, which has a glass solarium and wicker furniture; the Herman Melville Room, which has whaling memorabilia in and about the walnut beds and marble-top dresser; and the Jenny Lind Room, whose bed was constructed shortly after the soprano's American tour in 1851. The second-floor landing is a makeshift informal common room, with a red rug, a television, and rockers.

For eighty years, the house was also a doctor's office. Winnie and Dick transformed the examining rooms into the two ground-floor suites. These have private entrances, phones, and televisions: the George Pullman Kitchen Suite, with a stocked kitchen, is simply furnished with a pair of twin pineapple single beds; and the Benjamin Patterson Parlour Suite has two rooms, a cherry queen-size canopy bed, and a sofa bed in the sitting room, which has a fireplace.

Guests receive a welcome basket with fruit, cheese, and crackers and as much interaction as they desire with their gregarious hosts. Nearby are vineyards at Hammondsport and its Lake Keuka, and auto racing at Watkins Glen. The Rosewood Inn is less than a mile's walk to the Corning Glass Museum and two blocks from the Rockwell Museum of Western Art.

Sarah's Dream

49 West Main Street
Dryden, New York 13053
607-844-4321

Proprietors: Judi Williams and Ken Morusty
Accommodations: 4 rooms and 2 two-room suites with
   fireplace
Rates:
   Rooms: $78–$110
   Suites: $120 on winter weekends (weekday discounts)
Included: Full breakfast
Minimum stay: Some weekends
Added: Afternoon tea on Tuesdays, Wednesdays, and
   Thursdays; dinner with advance notice; 7% tax
Payment: American Express, Visa, MasterCard
Children: Over 10 welcome
Pets: Not allowed
Smoking: Not allowed
Open: All year

A nine-mile drive east from Ithaca through rolling farmland brings one to Dryden, a small agricultural town in the valleys beyond the Finger Lakes. On the town's main street is Sarah's Dream, an 1828 Greek Revival home listed on the National Register of Historic Places, named for the owner's mother, who would always have wanted such a hospitable home.

While a charming bed-and-breakfast, Sarah's Dream is best known throughout the area as a refuge for high-tea takers. Three sittings daily during the middle of the week bring guests from all over to choose among nine kinds of tea that accompany the endless menu of scones, shortbread, walnut pie, lemon bars, gingerbread, cucumber sandwiches, quiche, Welsh rarebit, watercress sandwiches, chocolate torte, cream puffs, and madeleines. The delicacies are gorgeously presented on Judi's heirloom china, silver, and linens—truly the highlight of an area stay.

While most proprietors choose a house as a vehicle for inn-keeping, Judi and Ken always wanted this particular house. Both in real estate, they kept an eye on the house for years until it was put up for sale. They bought it in 1987 and the bed-and-breakfast followed, featuring Judi's wonderful cooking.

The three-story gray clapboard house sits on a groomed, village-sized plot of land on the corner of Main and Mill. Guests enter from the small portico. To the right they find the cozy, traditional living room, which opens into the dining room, with wooden tables and chairs and crewel drapes. Mirroring these are two guest rooms on the first floor, both to the left of the foyer: the Garden Room is simple and charming, with a brass bed under a crocheted spread and the quirky but successful touch of having its sink in a dresser in the closet. The Porch Suite faces the front of the house, with a brick wood-burning fireplace, a queen-size brass bed, a sitting area with a television and VCR, a wall full of books, and a private sitting porch.

The second floor consists of a pretty two-room suite with damask rose walls, a sitting area with a daybed and television, and a bedroom with a king-sized bed and adorable porcelain lamps that look like Staffordshire figurines. Of the others, the Rose Room is quite pretty, with a queen-size canopy bed in heavy carved oak and a wicker sitting area. The baths are new and extremely clean, and Judi's obsession is a fresh, full bar of soap for every guest. All the rooms have robes.

Those committed to afternoon activities who miss Judi's teas will be grateful for the opportunity to sample some of her elaborate cooking at breakfast. A perpetual baker, Judi serves fresh scones and muffins, casseroles, quiche, and fresh fruit in an old-fashioned presentation. This classic bed-and-breakfast is near Lake Cayuga and Lake Owasco, a hop from Greek Peak in Virgil for skiing and Ithaca's Sapsucker Woods for renowned bird-watching.

The Village Latch Inn
101 Hill Street
Southampton, New York 11968
516-283-2160
800-54-LATCH

Proprietors: Marta Byer and Martin White
General Manager: Chris Stanley
Accommodations: 25 rooms in the Latch, 12 rooms in the
   motel (6 duplexes and 6 singles), 3 rooms in the Potting
   Shed, 10 rooms in the Terry Cottage, 9 rooms in
   Homestead East, 6 rooms in Homestead West
Rates:
   Rooms: $95–$160 midweek (from $85 low season), $140–
      $195 weekends ($95–$125 low season)
   Suites and duplexes: $150–$250 midweek, $175–$300 week-
      ends (from $125 low season)
Included: Continental breakfast
Minimum stay: 3 nights in high season
Added: $50 each additional guest; 8% tax; 13% tax over $100;
   10% service charge
Payment: MasterCard, Visa, American Express
Children: Welcome
Pets: Not allowed
Smoking: Allowed
Open: All year

A small estate of five acres, the Village Latch Inn consists of five
buildings and just under seventy rooms, with wild variations in
style and decor. It's hard to call it a bed-and-breakfast, but it's
even harder to call it anything else. Some may find it a relaxing,
informal resort; others may find it a beachside cottage; still
others, a fitting place for corporate retreats and certainly for
weddings. If anything, the Village Latch is simply unique, a
dizzying combination of artifacts, playful decor, and architectural whimsy in one of New York's wealthiest towns.

   The eclectic set of buildings is the child of owners Marta Byer
and Martin White, she a former actress and theater director, he
a former fashion photographer. They travel several months a
year and send back oddities and necessities from faraway lands
like others send postcards. Just a half block or so from Southampton's main street, the Village Latch is set back from the
road by a lovely front lawn made private by a privet hedge. They
have a tennis court and a swimming pool and a little golf cart to
transport guests around the property.

   The three-story white clapboard Latch was the elegant annex
to a famous old landmark, the Irving Hotel, demolished a
quarter century ago on its prime spot across the street. This
main house therefore is a relic, as is the adjacent Terry Cottage,
also part of the complex. The main Inn has 25 rooms, some
comfortable and homey, some decisively decorated. Marta tries
to match the guests to the rooms—"typecasting" as she aptly

calls it. Room 60, for example, is a suite with windows on two sides, black chintz curtains, a fireplace and refrigerator, and a wicker sitting area. Nearby Room 52 is plain, with yellow walls and two twin beds. The third-floor rooms have interesting skylights that flood the rooms with color. Some have patios, some fireplaces. The common rooms for the property are in the Inn, and they teem with scary international dolls, throw pillows, mannequins, and artwork from the Whites' travels. A sunny porch breakfast room has green slatted chairs which lend a cottage feeling to the room.

The motel units across the parking lot are much more imaginative than their appellation would suggest. The six duplexes and six singles fit into a new two-story structure, all with private brick patio, nice, new private bath, and interesting decor with toile curtains, antique Oriental rugs, South American wall hangings, and Guatemalan pillows.

In the middle of the great lawn of the property, the Potting Shed is an ideal place for couples or families traveling together, with two bedrooms and a studio, which can also be rented singly. The living room has a huge A-frame ceiling of deep-hued woods, next to a full kitchen. The eclectic decor involves Indian pillows, Mexican painted pigskin chairs, a wood-burning fireplace, and a nine-foot carved stone statue.

The Homestead is the northernmost building, near the Potting Shed on the edge of the great lawn, and is made of weathered shingle. Consisting of two buildings with 15 bedrooms (the western one is Southampton's oldest), it is joined by a Victorian greenhouse that was moved onto the site. The western house has an Adirondack-type common area, woody and low-beamed, with old worn leather couches and chairs, heavy wood pillars, and a huge stone hearth. The eastern house has more of an arts and crafts feeling—geometric, with an open-beamed ceiling and brick fireplace. The connecting greenhouse is an enchanting painted iron with a hot tub in the center and porch furniture.

Try to seek out Marta and Martin, two fascinating people who seem like characters from a movie, cast as New York City expatriates who start an arts colony in a wealthy beach community—perfect for the part.

The Village Victorian Inn at Rhinebeck
31 Center Street
Rhinebeck, New York 12572
914-876-8345

Proprietor: Judy Kohler
Accommodations: 5 rooms, all with private bath
Rates: $175–$250
Included: Full breakfast, afternoon tea
Minimum stay: 2 nights on weekends
Added: $40 each additional guest; 12.25% tax
Payment: American Express
Children: Not allowed
Pets: Not allowed
Smoking: Not allowed
Open: All year

A picture-perfect bed-and-breakfast with luxury resort rates, the Village Victorian is a wonderful place for guests who care about romance and privacy but not a whit about finances. Rhinebeck is a wonderful weekending town just an hour from New York City, best known for its antiques and surrounding history and for being home to America's oldest inn, the Beekman Arms. It's a very walkable town with much to do, and within a short drive is Hyde Park, the Vanderbilt Mansions, and the Culinary Institute, for which one ought to make reservations months in advance.

The Village Victorian is just a block from the center of this bustling and charming town. There are some spectacular antiques here, which owner Judy Kohler has assiduously collected, refinished, and reupholstered with great precision. Not surprisingly, many of these pieces are for sale. The house is rather modest-looking on the outside, its facade painted a buttery yellow, with black shutters and white trim, sitting quietly behind a picket fence. Only two stories, the house has a sweet overhanging porch at its front entrance, furnished with white wicker settees. It was built around 1860, an early, none-too-ornate Victorian that Judy Kohler rejuvenated back to its pristine state in 1987, placing it on the National Register of Historic Places. Guests enter through the formal living room, with its wide-planked dark-stained floorboards, period Victorian furniture, and Oriental carpet. A precious table rests in the lace-covered bay window. This, the guests' common room, is also the setting for an ornate tea.

There is one guest room on the first floor, with two antique brass twin beds pushed together to make a king, a huge double armoire with two mirrors, and a settee positioned in the bay window. The four guest rooms on the second floor have elegant and formal antiques, such as brass or heavily carved Victorian headboards, fishnet canopy beds, delicate writing tables, formidable armoires, and slipper chairs and settees done in thick tapestries. The fireplace room has a curved fishnet canopy over a king-size bed, an antique fainting couch covered in tapestry, and a gilded oak French armoire. Perhaps the most lavish aspect of the inn aside from its breakfasts is the linens, with thick, high-thread-count sheets and duvets topped by myriad pillows. The wallpapers and curtains have equal attention to detail and pattern; the baths are simple, new, and clean.

Guests must remember that this is not a home stay but an elegant bed-and-breakfast, with a full-time professional innkeeper whose job is to pamper guests. It's a business, started by savvy Judy Kohler, a formal place for formal weekenders.

Pennsylvania

The Beechmont Inn
315 Broadway
Hanover, Pennsylvania 17331
717-632-3013

Proprietor: Terry and Monna Hormel
Accommodations: 7 rooms, all with private bath, 2 with fireplace
Rates: $70–$125
Included: Gourmet breakfast, afternoon tea
Minimum stay: 2 nights in Diller Room on winter weekends
Added: 6% tax
Payment: MasterCard, Visa, American Express
Children: Over 12 welcome
Pets: Not allowed
Smoking: Not allowed in guest rooms
Open: All year

The adorable town of Hanover in south central Pennsylvania is just nine miles from the Maryland border, midway between Harrisburg and Baltimore. Any street named Broadway would signify a certain amount of hubbub, and the Beechmont Inn certainly is in the thick of things. It's a period piece of 1834 Federal elegance, as is the entire town itself, which staged a battle during the War between the States. Today the town is a sleepy destination for weekend shoppers and antiquers heading to nearby New Oxford and Abbottstown.

The Hormels bought the Beechmont Inn in November 1985 with the intent of making it a full-time bed-and-breakfast. They restored the property, painted the brick barn red, the shutters black, and the trim white, planted window boxes and hung the flag, opening just three months later. Monna decorated with pieces from local antiques auctions, and Terry does the well-received cooking at breakfast. His granola has won prizes at York County fairs, and he serves it alongside a fruit, a meat, and an egg dish. A sample breakfast might be Amaretto baked pears, sausage crêpes, and shirred eggs.

Through the formal entrance from the Broadway sidewalk are three common rooms: the first a formal sitting area with Federal reproduction furniture and green swag windows treatments complementing a green Oriental rug, the second a game room that leads to a dining room with hints of the modern day in its parquet floor. The sideboard was built into the house in the 19th century, along with the grand corner cupboards.

The Diller suite is the largest accommodation, with a marble fireplace and a whirlpool bath. Toward the back of the house with a separate entrance is the Hershey Suite, featuring a fireplace. The grand wallpaper mural along the front stairway is from a Chinese silk motif. Among the prettier rooms upstairs are the Farnsworth with lovely reproduction Victorian wallpaper and views to the street; the tiny Stuart with a "marriage bed" for particularly close couples; and the Custer with a blue antique quilt as a decorative wall hanging. The Hampton Suite has a private porch and a full kitchen from its days as a private apartment.

The back gardens are lovely and tranquil, with a 200-year-old magnolia tree that blooms in full pink and hangs over the black wrought-iron furniture like an umbrella. On the slate patio sits a bench from which one can admire the restored trellis draped with an orange trumpet vine and the bird bath frequented by local doves.

The Brafferton Inn
44–46 York Street
Gettysburg, Pennsylvania 17325
717-337-3423

Proprietors: Mimi and Jim Agard
Accommodations: 11 rooms, 6 with private bath
Rates: $80–$95
Included: Full breakfast; afternoon tea; tax
Minimum stay: None
Added: $10 each additional person
Payment: MasterCard, Visa
Children: Welcome
Pets: Not allowed

Smoking: Allowed in Atrium and Garden area
Open: All year

Those visiting Gettysburg College and those exploring history
will love this eclectic bed-and-breakfast and its charitable hosts.
A hostelry in a town of such historic importance is somewhat
obliged to cater to the past, and the Brafferton does so easily.
Aside from its convincingly historic atmosphere, the Brafferton houses a Union bullet from the July 1, 1863, Gettysburg
battle in the mantel of a fireplace upstairs.

The present owners of this bed-and-breakfast, Jim and Mimi
Agard, speak with reverence about their role as keepers of this
historic house. Jim is the chairman of art at Gettysburg College,
and he and Mimi moved here with their five children in 1985.
They restored the 1787 brick structure during a year of nonstop
work, hoping to open a bed-and-breakfast when their children
went to college. However, when the adjacent house next door
went up for sale, they broke ground several years early and
placed their family there.

The Brafferton's stone facade looms over the sidewalk importantly, trimmed in Williamsburg blue. To the left of the
entrance is the living room, with an 1860 painting of Jim's great-
grandfather hanging over the original fireplace, a player piano,
and various top hats, part of a rather vast collection dispersed
throughout the house. Down a step is the breakfast room, an
addition built in the 1860s, exceptional for the four walls of
surrounding primitive mural painted by local artist Virginia
McGloughlan depicting eighteen historic Gettysburg landmarks and scenes. While guests sit in the middle of the scenery,
they are treated to a vast breakfast, which may include peaches
and cream French toast, strawberry pancakes, or eggs, all prepared by Mimi.

The main house has four rooms upstairs that share a bath
and a room in the back with a private bath. Of these, the Master
bedroom is the largest, at the front of the house, and the Child's
room is the smallest. These rooms are done in spare colonial
simplicity. A highlight is Jim's stencilwork, made by Mc-
Gloughlan from copies of 17th-century stencils, which Jim carefully reproduced and painted to complement the old plaster-
work of the walls.

The more luxurious rooms are the six downstairs behind the
Atrium, which connects the old stone house and its brick addition stretching off the back. These rooms all have private baths,
some antique brass beds, quilts, and Jim's stencilwork, and they
overlook the herb garden out back. Here, the Garden and New
rooms are most desirable, with a pretty view of the flowers and

garden herbs. The Atrium is a lovely common space for guests, with a greenhouse roof and exposed brick walls.

High tea is served to Brafferton guests and to the public three afternoons weekly and includes chocolates, scones, tarts, and finger sandwiches. Make plans for a memorable Pennsylvania Dutch meal at the family-style Hickory Bridge Inn nearby.

Wedgwood Collection of Historic Inns
111 West Bridge Street
New Hope, Pennsylvania 18938
215-862-2570

Proprietors: Nadine Silnutzer and Carl Glassman
Innkeepers:
   Wedgwood Inn: Arlene and Tim Stephan
   Umpleby House: Kirk and Tracy Wentzel
   Aaron Burr House: Mary Gerdes and Larry Weber
Accommodations: 18 rooms and suites, 6 in each house
Rates: $60–$85 with shared bath; $70–$160 with private bath
Included: Continental breakfast basket, afternoon tea
Minimum stay: 2 nights with Saturday reservation
Added: $20 each additional person; 6% tax
Payment: No credit cards
Children: Infants not allowed
Pets: Not allowed
Smoking: Not allowed
Open: All year

While many people retire to the industry of innkeeping, it was a first career for both Carl and Dinie Glassman. They started with the Wedgwood House in 1982 as young innkeepers and newlyweds, restoring the three-story 1870 Victorian clapboard guest house to a six-room bed-and-breakfast. They painted it Wedgwood blue with their large pottery collection in mind, and business took off. Fortunately, the neighboring house went up for sale in 1985. Carl and Dinie bought the 1833 Classical Revival stone house, and this time their restoration took only three months, resulting in the six-room Umpleby House. The trilogy was completed in 1990 with the acquisition of the Aaron Burr House across Bridge Street, several houses toward town. Built in 1854 by the same unknown author of the Wedgwood House, it was named for the vice president who sought refuge in Bucks County fresh from his duel with Alexander Hamilton. Today, all three houses retain that same feeling of a safe haven.

The main house has six guest rooms, four with private bath —a nice feature for those on a budget. The house is marked by a historic carriage on the front lawn painted the same Wedgwood blue, maroon, and white. Just steps away is the historic Victorian gazebo, the original wellhouse, a lovely setting for extensive weekend afternoon teas.

The adjacent Umpleby House is a cream-colored Federal plaster with maroon shutters and arguably offers the nicest accommodations. It's here that Dinie's antiques hunting is most evident in some of the spectacular pieces and old light fixtures.

Across the street and down the block, the Aaron Burr is the newest property, a yellow clapboard with arched Wedgwood blue shutters. Several of the six rooms have fireplaces, and two have king-size beds. The second-floor sitting area has lovely Empire furniture set on random-width black walnut floors, the focal point of which is a lavish fireplace. The third-floor rooms are particularly charming, set under the gables, but the others subtly lack the loved and lived-in elegance of the rooms in other houses that have been fussed to perfection by Dinie's antiquing eye.

No matter which house they might find themselves in, guests may expect a lovely breakfast basket with freshly baked muffins or danish, croissants, homemade jams, and fresh juice and fruit; afternoon refreshments; evening turndown; lovely Victorian common rooms and parlors centering around stoked fireplaces; fresh flowers and handmade quilts; original artwork, most by Dinie's great-aunt Sara Winston; and, of course, ubiquitous Wedgwood.

Service is extremely personal, never intrusive, with two innkeepers per home and the ever-present Glassmans overseeing new projects with zeal and knowledge. An added blessing is the proximity to a town sorely lacking in parking facilities—horse-drawn carriage rides are offered to town. The town park is across the street.

Virginia

Liberty Rose
1022 Jamestown Road
Williamsburg, Virginia 23185
804-253-1260
800-545-1825 for reservations

Proprietors: Sandra and Brad Hirz
Accommodations: 4 rooms, all with private bath, including 2
   suites
Rates: $95–$155
Included: Full breakfast, afternoon sweets
Minimum stay: Some weekends
Added: $40 each additional guest; 8.5% tax
Payment: MasterCard, Visa
Children: Welcome
Pets: Not allowed
Smoking: Not allowed
Open: All year

Liberty Rose is a beautiful, meticulously cared for bed-and-breakfast, a credit to the industry. A mile from historic Williamsburg, half that from the campus of William and Mary, Liberty Rose is outstanding for its gorgeous bedding and blissful owners, Sandra and Brad Hirz.

Though innkeepers' lives need not enter into a bed-and-breakfast, Sandra and Brad's history played a large role in the creation of this romantic hostelry. Friends for years, Sandra was a decorator in southern California and Brad was a farmer in Washington State. Brad had always encouraged Sandi to open a bed-and-breakfast. In 1986, when Sandi bought this 1920 Virginia house, Brad came along to help her with handiwork. They fell in love during the restoration, married on a Wednesday, and opened to a full house of guests that Friday. Somehow, the bed-and-breakfast substituted for a honeymoon, and the property is infused with that same romance. Liberty Rose is a product of their partnership: Sandra does the sewing and decorating and Brad cooks the full breakfast and afternoon sweets.

The simple exterior belies the lavish interior: a two-story white clapboard flanked by brick additions and topped by four dormers built into the pitched slate roof. The living room has several lovely pieces of furniture, some Victorian in lavish upholstery, a baby grand piano, and a fireplace. It opens through French doors onto the windowed breakfast wing seating eight people for Brad's breakfast, which may be something like French toast stuffed with cream cheese and marmalade or cinnamon bread with strawberries.

The Rose Victoria Room on the first floor is possibly the grandest, to the left of the foyer, a wing unto itself. The queen-size French canopy bed has elaborate tasseled curtains designed by Sandi which replicate 18th-century drapes encasing the Sheriden down duvet. A large cherry armoire sits in a corner across from a tapestry couch, all under a pressed tin ceiling.

The bathroom here is exquisite; one wall is hidden by a row-house oak closet front from 1890. Romantics will use the claw-foot tub, and the practical will use the red poured-marble free-standing glass-enclosed shower.

The three bedrooms upstairs are also appointed with lavish and thick bedding in silk and tapestry. Magnolias Peach has a rice bed with a fishnet canopy, draped in silk and down bedding, and a cherry armoire. Its private bath has black marble; and an adjunct is the Blossom Room, tucked into the dormer, with an antique mahogany twin bed framed by a Regency red swag to match its coverlet. Suite Williamsburg has a wood-burning fireplace, yet another lavish four-poster canopy bed draped in copies of hundred-year-old fabrics, and a lavish bath. All the guest rooms have televisions, VCRs, and access to a library of movies.

In a town dominated by the industry of Colonial Williamsburg, Liberty Rose is a refreshing and luxurious alternative.

West Virginia

Boydville: The Inn at Martinsburg
601 South Queen Street
Martinsburg, West Virginia 25401
304-263-1448

Proprietors: Owen Sullivan and Ripley Hotch
Accommodations: 6 rooms, all with private bath, 2 with fireplaces
Rates: $100–$125
Included: Full breakfast
Minimum stay: 2 nights on weekends in May and October
Added: $25 each additional guest; 9% tax
Payment: MasterCard, Visa
Children: Over 12 welcome
Pets: Not allowed
Smoking: Not allowed
Open: All year

A plaque on Martinsburg's Queen Street describes the historic house that belonged to General Elisha Boyd, hero of the War of 1812. A turn here will head a visitor down a beautifully mani-cured drive flanked by gorgeous trees introducing the manor house at the end. Its generous two stories are built of native limestone, in some cases five feet thick, covered in stucco, now painted white with green shutters. It is a truly elegant southern plantation house, a place for American royalty. It's also a fitting place for innkeeper Owen Sullivan, who will tell his guests in a soft-spoken lilting accent about his family, which came from Confederate military heights and generations of plantation life. In 1987, he and partner Ripley Hotch restored the magnificent house and opened their bed-and-breakfast.

Owen is an interior designer, an art collector, and a capital district refugee. He is both reservedly proud and charmingly involved in his eclectic collections, which include Imari china, soapstone, American Indian notables, Staffordshire figures, and paintings from notable American and female artists.

The house is a gallery not just for Owen's wide-reaching, refined tastes but for its own architectural merit: the foyer is an incredible display of faux graining, made in France in 1811, which is carried up the stairs to the second-floor hallway. The paint on paper successfully mimics elaborate inlays of burl, walnut, and tiger mahogany in huge panels. In addition, all the brass and Waterford chandeliers, interior woodwork, and window glass, including the English fan Palladians, are original to the house. The five rooms of inlaid flooring and bronze ormolu chandeliers were brought from Europe to the house by General Boyd's daughter, whose husband was minister to France. (Their grandson went on to become a United States senator.)

As with any grand mansion, the common rooms are wide, airy, and bountiful. There is a music room, a formal living room, and dining room. All the mantels are original and hand-carved. The house is furnished in English and American period antiques, and some treasure-like heirlooms. In addition, a huge, sprawling sun porch stretches off the back of the house with an engulfing stone fireplace and library of books. Guests may stroll the 14 acres and explore the original outbuildings or simply survey the property from the elegant veranda that stretches along the entire front of the house, furnished in original rockers and swings.

Each of the two first-floor guest rooms has a working fireplace. The elegant General Adam Stephen Room features a mural of scenic America that was hand-painted in France in the 19th century and a solid African mahogany bookshelf from floor to ceiling, which holds, among other first-edition leather books, the rare Robert E. Lee biographies by Douglas Freeman. The neighboring Adirondack Room has twig tables and chairs, a 1920s Navajo rug, and a bird's-eye maple dresser.

Four rooms on the second floor are more traditionally formal. The Senator Charles Faulkner Room has a four-poster bed and 1840 coverlet; the Stonewall Jackson Room has a great

1920s Kohler bath; the General Elisha Boyd Room has an 1800s cherry cannonball bed and an 18th-century mahogany four-poster; and the Belle Boyd Room is named for the infamous Confederate spy. Even the baths are unusual, clean with Old World charm, some oversized fixtures and old octagonal tiling, with considerate amenities.

Breakfasts are full at Boydville, with fresh fruits and sauces, apple pancakes, soufflés, or frittatas, and home-baked breads. Owen is simply delightful, modest, and fascinating; he enjoys his guests and his house like a newfound gift.

Village Inns

Delaware

The David Finney Inn
216 Delaware Street
New Castle, Delaware 19720
302-322-6367
800-334-6640

Innkeeper: Judith S. Piser
Accommodations: 17 rooms, all with private bath
Rates: Rooms, $75–$90; suites, $120
Included: Continental breakfast
Minimum stay: 2 nights on special weekends
Added: 8% tax
Payment: Major credit cards
Children: Welcome
Pets: Not allowed
Smoking: Allowed in tavern only
Open: All year

It seems unlikely, during a particularly uninspired seven-mile drive south of Wilmington, that anything as pure as historic New Castle exists so close to the Delaware Memorial Bridge. Thankfully, it does, and it comes upon a traveler so suddenly that there's a certain joy in finding this town. It was purchased from Indians by Peter Stuyvesant for Dutch settlers in 1651, but it was the English who named it New Castle in 1664.

Rent was a bushel of wheat per year on the land which Renere Vandercoolen bought in 1683 to build an inn where today the David Finney stands. Some of the handmade bricks in the inn date back to two separate buildings on the site in 1713. Militia officer and attorney David Finney is noted to have joined the two buildings in 1757. The brick building is a handsome colonial: two large mullioned windows flank the Willliamsburg blue door on the first floor; five windows span the second floor; and three dormers cut into the saltbox shingled roof.

The seven second-floor rooms and ten third-floor rooms are decorated very simply in a combination of modest antiques and colonial reproductions. The trim is done in Williamsburg blue. Like the guest rooms, the baths are clean and sparely appointed, though all is clean and hospitable. Televisions and phones are available on request. Guests are welcomed with a basket that includes a split of wine and cheese and crackers.

More than for the comfort of its rooms, the David Finney is known for its atmosphere and food. Dinner entrées range from $15.95 to $24.95. Guests start with a choice of appetizers and salad; the shellfish bisque with cream chantilly is a favorite. The roast rack of lamb is served with boursin cheese crust and Madeira wine; another specialty is the veal Oscar David Finney, served with lump crabmeat, asparagus, and hollandaise sauce. The dining room decor is done in simple colonial spindle-back chairs, but guests love the outdoor patio, an extensive area that stretches to the backyard and is furnished with wrought-iron chairs and tables. Common rooms, shared by dinner and overnight guests, have Williamsburg reproduction furniture.

Five museums in town re-create Dutch and English colonial life. With more than fifty buildings from the early 18th and 19th centuries, New Castle is a walker's delight. The town maintains a grassy, groomed park on the Delaware waterfront, bordered by the cobblestone Strand and the village commons, often enlivened by weekend activities.

Maryland

Atlantic Hotel Inn and Restaurant
2 North Main Street
Berlin, Maryland 21811
410-641-3589

Proprietors: Atlantic Hotel Partnership
General Manager: Stephen Jacques
Accommodations: 16 rooms, all with private bath
Rates: $55 and up; July and August: $65 and up
Included: Continental breakfast
Added: 8% tax
Payment: Visa, MasterCard
Children: Welcome
Pets: Not allowed

Smoking: Allowed
Open: All year

The din of Ocean City will quickly fade into memory at the Atlantic Hotel, seven miles west of the beach in Berlin amid the lush flat fields of eastern shore farmland. The hotel sits on an odd intersection of three streets in the middle of town, slightly askew on the sidewalk with a pretty, tiny park as its front lawn.

For years, this tidy Rockwellian working-class town was subjected to the prominent sight of the crumbling 1895 Atlantic Hotel, exacerbated by a lousy 1946 addition. A group of local businessmen rescued the property from demolition in 1986. The ugly addition was the first thing to go, but workers said it was holding up the old building. After stabilizing the older structure, they tore down the addition, and, as their journal cites, "the swan arose." The Atlantic Hotel opened in August 1988, a faithful period restoration.

The front porch of the Atlantic stretches along its entire facade, supported by a row of pillars. Guests enter an elegant foyer decorated with sepia-toned photographs of the hotel and antiques, wallpapers, and rugs lifted from the Victorian era. To the right is a highly polished lounge and elegant period bar. Green wainscoting complements maroon stools and handsome upholstery, all warmed by a carved mahogany fireplace.

To the left of the foyer is the dining room, which has received excellent reviews. Appetizers might be coconut shrimp, wild mushrooms in pastry, or crab bisque en croûte. Entrées range from $18 to $24 for unusual dishes such as locally raised quail stuffed with cornbread, crab, shrimp, and tomato finished with garlic glaze or chicken and scallops with orange almond cream. The meals are presented in a sophisticated setting of two rooms divided by a wide archway, blue wallpaper, and striped Victorian portieres. Victorian prints and details from *Gody's Lady's* book decorate the walls.

An Oriental runner guides guests up a wide set of stairs. At the landing is an extremely elegant sitting area for overnight guests, with nicely restored antiques and a detailed journal that chronicles the hotel's restoration. The rooms on the upper two floors vary in shape and size, all generous but for two budget rooms. The beautiful rugs are all Victorian reproduction patterns of latticework and floral swirls. The rooms display eclectic, high-quality antiques, including brass lamps and unmatched end tables, and full carved wood and marble bedroom suites. The corner rooms are particularly nice, with bay windows and tasseled drapery. The bathrooms are surprisingly tasteful for a renovation, with old fixtures or brass reproductions and Lord and Mayfair amenities.

For all its elegance, the Atlantic Hotel is a friendly place with a happy, helpful staff. A long list of local activities keeps guests forever busy if they decide to leave their romantic rooms.

The Inn at Buckeystown
3521 Buckeystown Pike
Buckeystown, Maryland 21717
301-874-5755

Proprietor and Partner: Daniel R. Pelz and Chase Barnett
General Manager: Rebecca E. Shipman-Smith
Accommodations: 9 rooms, 5 with private bath, 1 room in St. John's Cottage
Rates:
   Rooms: $188–$230 MAP; discounts on weekdays
   Cottage: $272 MAP
Included: Dinner and breakfast; tax; gratuities
Minimum stay: Two nights in October and on some holiday weekends
Added: 5% tax; $10 service charge per room
Payment: MasterCard, Visa, American Express
Children: Over 16 welcome
Pets: Not allowed
Smoking: Allowed only in parlors
Open: All year

An evening at the Inn at Buckeystown is like an evening reuniting with old friends. Innkeepers Dan Pelz and Chase Barnett are unusually warmhearted and take great pride in their dinners. The M.A.P. rates remind guests that the food is an integral part of a stay at the inn, the real highlight of the occasion.

Buckeystown was named for John Buckey, village tavern-keeper during the late 18th century. More a hamlet than a village, Buckeystown has changed little since then, but for the additions of some wonderful buildings here and there— among them, a magnificent 18-room Italianate white clapboard structure that sits on the main Pike. This is the inn at Buckeystown, with its large wrap porch, slate gable roof, white clapboard, and black shutters, built in 1897 by the influential Keller family.

Inside, the house has a very large scale, with 12-foot ceilings on the first floor, 10- and 8-foot ceilings on the remaining floors. The woodwork is chestnut and golden oak with cherry-stained heart pine floors. The two parlors have fireplaces, and the two dining rooms are large and airy. Dan and Chase have filled the house with their eclectic collections: Dan's pictures and figurines of clowns, antique china and glass, and American art pottery and Chase's toy collection.

The four second-floor rooms have private baths and fine antiques. The Love Room has a cottage Victorian bedroom suite, its appellation woven humorously into the carpet's pile. Fresh flowers and sherry are provided in every room. All rooms have crystal chandeliers, and the Winter Suite has a fireplace with a Victorian oak bedroom suite. The third-floor rooms are smaller, snug under the eaves, and share one large bath down a bright green carpeted hall.

For special occasions, remember the St. John's Cottage down the Pike a quarter of a mile. In 1985, then partners Dan Pelz and Marty Martinez bought the 1884 brick Georgian structure, the tiny St. John's Reformed Church, which they converted for guests. This wonderful space is great for romantics seeking seclusion; it has magnificent pointed vitrine windows on three sides, a kitchenette, a piano, high cathedral ceilings, and a redwood hot tub on the private porch.

Dinners are served at 7:30 on fine china, antique lace, and crisp linens, in formal family style. Specific meals are set daily, but a typical Thursday meal might be white navy bean soup, salad, London broil with béarnaise sauce and garlic potatoes, and fresh strawberries with ice cream and whipped cream and pound cake.

Robert Morris Inn

Morris Street on the Tred Avon River, Box 70
Oxford, Maryland 21654
410-226-5111

Proprietors: Wendy and Ken Gibson
Innkeeper: Jay Gibson
Accommodations: 34 rooms, all with private bath (14 rooms in main inn, other rooms in Sandaway Lodge, Sandaway Hideaway, River Rooms, River House)
Rates: $70–$160
Included: Continental breakfast in mid-winter
Minimum stay: 2 nights on high-season weekends
Added: 8% tax
Payment: Visa, MasterCard
Children: Over 10 welcome
Pets: Not allowed

Smoking: Allowed in some rooms
Open: All year; restaurant closes in mid-winter

The puzzle-pieced shoreline and low-lying farmland of tawny Talbot County is filled in by strands of the Chesapeake from all directions. The sleepy 18th-century port of Oxford is where the Tred Avon and Choptank rivers meet and float imperceptibly to the Chesapeake. At the ferry crossing from Oxford to Belle-vue is the Robert Morris Inn, the kind of contemplative place where people come to fall back in love. It's the setting which is most conducive to romance: long walks, vivid sunsets on the rippling waters of the Tred Avon River, and dining over candle-light at the inn's restaurant, famous for its fresh seafood.

Ken and Wendy Gibson bought the Robert Morris Inn in 1971 when they began their family. Today, Ken's brother Jay is the hospitable innkeeper. The Gibsons are sociable, effortless hosts who love their inn and enjoy seeing others captivated by its restful and romantic setting.

The inn is two stories of sunny yellow clapboard with white trim, topped by a third story of weathered shingle with dormer windows peeking out of a mansard roof. An overhanging porch spans its length. The main inn was built by ship carpenters in the early 1700s with wooden pegged paneling, ship nails, and hand-hewn beams. The original Georgia white pine lines the second-floor hall. The building was bought in 1730 by an English trading company for its Oxford representative, Robert Morris. His son Robert Morris, Jr., invested wisely and financed the American Revolution; became fast friends with George Washington, for whom he served as superintendent of finance; and went on to sign the Declaration of Independence, the Articles of Confederation, and the Constitution.

The 14 rooms on two floors in the main inn (as well as the 2 in the adjacent River Cottage) are simply furnished in reproductions and some period antiques. Though they are quite interesting for their place in history, far more desirable and private rooms are located down the block on the brief peninsula that juts into the Tred Avon.

The Sandaway Lodge is a rambling Victorian built in 1875, a cream-colored clapboard with black trim and wrap porches. The rooms here have been newly redecorated, with floral papers and lovely tiled baths. Adjacent are two new structures hidden in the foliage, home to the four River Rooms. These are capacious, with large screened porches, picture-perfect views of the river, king-size beds, sitting areas, and large wainscoted baths with clawfoot tubs in the middle of wood floors, showers, separate vanity areas, and Lord and Mayfair amenities. Farther down the shore is the contemporary River House. And at the sunset-facing riverfront is the Sandaway Hideaway, a romantic cabin with a king-sized waterbed and television.

Evocative fishing and nautical scenes by local artist John Moll are displayed throughout the public spaces. The wallpaper murals in the dining room are identical to those chosen by Jacqueline Kennedy for her redecoration of the White House in 1962, made in France in the early 19th century and depicting indigenous American scenes: West Point, Winnipeg Indian Village, Natural Bridge of Virginia, and Boston Harbor.

The dinner menu ($14 to $20) offers a generous selection of seafood, including expert ideas with crab: crab Norfolk, with butter and sherry; crab imperial, in a seasoned white sauce; and varieties of the crabcakes of which even James Michener, king of the Chesapeake, has spoken highly.

New Jersey

The Inn at Lambertville Station
11 Bridge Street
Lambertville, New Jersey 08530
609-397-4400
800-524-1091 out of state

Proprietor: Dan Whitaker
General Mananger: Michael Ring
Accommodations: 45 rooms, including 8 suites, all with
    private bath
Rates:
    Rooms: $75–$110
    Suites: $150
Included: Continental breakfast
Minimum stay: Surcharge for most Saturday-only stays
Added: $15 each additional guest; 7% tax
Payment: Major credit cards
Children: Welcome (12 and under free)
Pets: Not allowed
Smoking: Allowed
Open: All year

The Inn at Lambertville Station rests on the calmer banks of
the Delaware River across from bustling New Hope, Pennsylvania, via a narrow two-lane bridge. It is one of the few places in
Bucks County (Pennsylvania) and Hunterdon County (New
Jersey) that enjoys a Delaware River location, with water views
from some rooms and an unobstructed view from the breakfast
room.

Unlike most area properties, the Inn at Lambertville Station
is new, completed in August 1985. It's certainly not an intimate
bed-and-breakfast, which may be a relief to some sated by the
quaintness of Bucks County. Rather, it is trying to be a small
luxury hotel, with formal, discreet service. There are two unfortunate aspects to this otherwise ideal spot: the blacktop
landscape of a parking lot separating the inn from Lambertville Station and the town, and the placement of the rectangular building with its shorter side on the river. Of its 45 rooms,
only four suites take advantage of this beautiful view, which
others may see obliquely.

With the look of a contemporary barn, the inn has brown
siding with white trim. The lobby is three stories of dramatic
open beams with some interesting antiques, a huge fireplace,
and one wall filled with lovely and unusual old paintings. Past
the fireplace, through French doors, is a shaded deck over a
babbling brook that spills into the Delaware.

There are 15 rooms on each of three floors, named for cities
around the world with representative decor: the Miami Room
has light wood furniture; the Salzburg Suite has European antiques. The standard rooms are more spacious than elaborate,
with either queen-size or two twin beds, telephones and televi-

sions, separate vanity areas next to the new baths, with Gilchrest and Soames amenities. The London Suite is one of four overlooking the Delaware, and quite representative of the eight suites, with a dark wood headboard on a king-size bed, a large sitting area with antique marble-top tables, and a gas fireplace. Guests have breakfast in the Riverside Room, graced with glorious river and bridge views through arched windows.

A great draw for the inn is its affiliation with the renowned restaurant at Lambertville Station, a restored 19th-century train depot. Dinners range from $12 to $20, and among the grilled swordfish and shrimp amandine are also famed exotic meats: alligator, wild boar, and buffalo. On Sundays, the Black River and Western Railroad train leaves from the front doors of Lambertville Station for a ride through the countryside. There is a leisurely ride or a direct ride to Ringoes, where shoppers can catch a train to the Flemington clothing outlets.

Inn at Millrace Pond

Route 519
Hope, New Jersey 07844
908-459-4884

Proprietors: Richard Gooding and Gloria Carrigan
Accommodations: 17 rooms, all with private bath (9 in
    Gristmill, 2 in Wheelwright's Cottage, 6 in Millrace House)
Rates: $80–$115
Included: Hearty Continental breakfast
Minimum stay: 2 nights on weekends
Added: 8% tax
Payment: Visa, MasterCard, American Express
Children: Welcome (limited availability)
Pets: Not allowed
Smoking: Nonsmoking rooms available
Open: All year

The town of Hope is about ten miles east of Delaware Water Gap. The building which now houses the Inn at Millrace Pond was the groundstone for the Moravian village founded here in 1769, one of the country's first planned communities. About twenty of the original buildings are still standing in Hope. During its heyday in 1774, the town peaked at a prosperous 147, but it quickly shrunk to 84 people by 1799, was finally abandoned in 1807, and was sold a year later in 1808 for $48,000.

Today, the Inn at Millrace Pond is again a keystone for its community. During a two-year project that began in 1985,

Richard Gooding and Gloria Carrigan bought this abandoned mill, restored the exterior and interior, incorporated the adjacent miller's house and wheelwright's cottage, and groomed the 23 acres of grounds, part of which contains a thousand-foot millrace which the Moravians carved by hand through slate.

The inn is a huge fieldstone block resting heavily at the bottom of a hill in Hope. The restaurant on the ground floor of the mill has colonial Windsor chairs, hardwood flooring, and minty green cloths accented by candlelight. Hearty entrées range from $15 to $19 and might include trout in parchment, roast duckling with raspberry balsamic vinaigrette, or New York sirloin with bourbon sauce. After dinner, guests can venture downstairs, past the trickling millrace and the wine cellar, to the tavern room. Cooled by brick flooring, heated by a brick fireplace, the tavern is filled with relics of the working mill: a 15-foot wood drill, and the original grain chute.

Rooms in the Gristmill are on the second and third floors, decorated successfully in spare Shaker and colonial style with reproduction queen-size pencil post beds, televisions hidden in William Draper antique reproduction armoires, Williamsburg colors on the walls, and all with new, simple private baths, some with whirlpool tubs. All rooms have wing chairs, telephones, clock radios, dried flower arrangements, and some original exposed wood from the old mill. Some upper rooms have cathedral ceilings with sleeping lofts tucked under eaves.

Across a brick patio from the dining room is the Millrace House, built in the late 1700s. Its six rooms are more decorative than those in the Gristmill, featuring formal Queen Anne, Chippendale, and Sheriden antiques and Oriental rugs. The first floor has a nice common room with books and sitting areas in period decor. The Wheelwright's Cottage next door is a good place for families or couples traveling together. It's configured in a duplex, which can be separate or joined by a central staircase. The adorable building has some lovely pre-1835 antiques, such as a Hepplewhite dresser, original wide-planked floors, and charming and deep dormer windows on three sides of the upstairs suite.

The grounds are lovely, often the setting for weddings. The lawns behind the inn are mildly hilly and rambling, leading from the millrace to a tennis court, Beaver Brook, and a pond. A hearty Continental breakfast is served in the main dining room, and throughout the day the owners are always about, happy to chat about the inn's restoration.

The Stockton Inn, "Colligan's"
One Main Street, Route 29
Stockton, New Jersey 08559
609-397-1250

Proprietor: Andy McDermott
Accommodations: 11 rooms with 8 fireplaces, including 8 suites (in the Main, Carriage, Wagon, Federal, and Smith Houses)
Rates: $60–$105, weekdays; $80–$145, weekends
Included: Continental breakfast
Minimum stay: 2 nights on weekends, 3 nights on some holidays
Added: 8% tax
Payment: No credit cards
Children: Limited facilities
Pets: Not allowed
Smoking: Allowed
Open: All years except Christmas Day

Though hospitality was founded at the Stockton Inn around 1796, the place became a cultural mecca in the 1930s and 1940s. Words from the Rodgers and Hart musical *On Your Toes* were inspired at the Stockton Inn: "There's a small hotel with a wishing well. I wish that we were there . . . together." Secret meetings during the Lindbergh trial were held here in 1935. Bandleader Paul Whiteman signed off his radio show by saying that he was going to the Stockton Inn for dinner. Other regulars included F. Scott Fitzgerald, Clark Gable, Helen Hayes, Dorothy Parker, George S. Kaufman, and S. J. Perelman.

Today, what started as a three-story stone hostelry is now a complex of five buildings in a charming town on the banks of the Delaware. One of the most outstanding features of this inn is its hospitable dining rooms. Three of the six share magnificent, brightly-colored primitive murals depicting colonial scenes of a courtship, a fox hunt, a Flemington fair, and a Stockton schoolhouse. These were painted by three artists in the 1930s in exchange for room and board; one of the artists went on to illustrate the book *Bambi*. A fourth room in the 1930s addition is done in clubby, masculine plaids, with an intimate alcove curtained off in paisley tapestries. At the back of the inn is a slate garden room with a wood trellis and piano, used for weekend entertainment; the room extends into a modest private dining area. In the warmer months, people dine outside on the slate patio to the sounds of the waterfalls set into the landscape.

Dinners range from $14 to $24; offerings might include veal with lemon, sundried tomatoes, and capers; shrimp and "blue" mussels in chardonnay with fresh dill cream sauce over sweet red pepper fettucini; or roasted rack of lamb crusted with Dijon and herbed bread crumbs with minted apricot chutney.

The two suites in the main house have wide-planked, creaky floors and fireplaces, and two have access to the front porch which runs the length of the building, looking straight ahead into town to Centre Bridge. The furnishings are comfortable and traditional, in colonial simplicity. The adorable 1832 Carriage House is steps from the slate porch dining room, which has parquet flooring and dramatic black and pink chintz decor. Just beyond are two loft suites in the stone Wagon House. Across the street is the recently redecorated Federal House, built in 1860, which has a fresh, crisp feel about its rooms. Three suites have wood-burning fireplaces and access to a charming garden in the back with wrought-iron outdoor furniture. The Victorian Smith House just south of the inn is currently being restored.

Innkeeper Andy McDermott adopted the property in 1989. His primary concern as a former restaurant manager was to renew its reputation as a fine dining establishment, and he has also added a formidable wine list. He deserves much credit for redecorating and refreshing the Stockton Inn's accommodations. He and his staff are extremely kind and proud of the way they are have rejuvenated this historic property.

New York

Asa Ransom House
10529 Main Street
Clarence, New York 14031-1684
716-759-2315

Proprietors: Robert and Judith Lenz
Accommodations: 9 rooms, including 2 suites, all private bath, 7 with fireplace
Rates: $85–$135; $160–$200 MAP on Saturdays
Included: Full breakfast; breakfast and dinner with MAP
Minimum stay: None
Added: $15 each additional guest; 11% tax; 13% over $100
Payment: MasterCard, Visa, Discover
Children: Welcome
Pets: Not allowed

Smoking: Not allowed
Open: All year except January to early February; restaurant
  closed Fridays

The area surrounding Buffalo and Niagara Falls was settled as late as the turn of the 19th century. The oldest town in Erie County is Clarence, founded in 1803. Several years before this, in 1799, the Holland Land Company offered plots of land ten miles apart to anyone who would build a tavern for the area. Asa Ransom, a Lake Erie fur trader, was the first to take up the offer. He built a log cabin and tavern on the site which now bears his name, as well as Erie County's first gristmill in 1803. Parts of today's Asa Ransom House, the library, Tap Room, and gift shop, date to 1853.

The rest of the inn, including the two large dining rooms and two of the guest rooms, was built by Robert Lenz in 1975. It's beige clapboard with red trim, to complement the historic brick home. An addition with five guest rooms was built in 1991. Lenz and his wife, Judy, opened the Asa Ransom House in 1976 as young newlyweds and have been attracting a large dinner crowd from Buffalo ever since.

A large brick fireplace warms two dining rooms: one is traditional and overlooks the street through bay windows; the second has views of the woods behind the house. This latter room is walled with bookshelves, interspersed with wonderful maps from an 1875 atlas of Erie County marked with all the towns and original family tracts. The original section contains the common room, furnished with antiques in cozy sitting areas, a gift shop, and the convivial Tap Room, papered with an impressive collection of wine bottle labels.

The two rooms on the second floor of the 1853 house have a distinctly older feel. Of these, the Green and Lavender Room has an unusual Chippendale broken arch king-size bed that matches an antique armoire. Two much larger rooms are of note in the 1975 wing: the Gold Room has one wall entirely of exposed brick, the exterior of the original house, and a queen-size iron and brass bed with a fireplace; the Green Room is a favorite, as dentil molding around the fireplace is echoed in crown canopy treatments over two double pine beds draped in green plaid. The new wing has five rooms which equal or better this large scale, four with gas fireplaces. Gilchrest and Soames amenities including mouthwash are offered in the baths.

Breakfasts are generous at the Asa Ransom House, with a choice of two hot entrées: perhaps a soufflé, a breakfast pie, quiche, or crêpes with berries. A three-course afternoon tea is served on Thursdays, and otherwise a full lunch is served. Ex-

cept for Fridays and Saturdays, dinners (from $11 to $20) are
served nightly, specializing in New York farmland hearty fare,
including smoked corned beef with apple raisin or horseradish
sauce or salmon pie with tomato and vegetables, topped with
cheese pastry. From greetings to good-byes, Bob and Judy are
ever the good neighbors, kind hosts, and informed area guides.

Beekman Arms

Route 9
Rhinebeck, New York 12572
914-876-7077

Proprietors: Charles LaForge
Manager: George Shattuck, III
Accommodations: 59 rooms (13 in main building, 46 in nine
   outbuildings), 22 with fireplace
Rates: $55–$99, seasonally
Included: Continental breakfast
Minimum stay: None
Added: $10 each additional guest; 10.25% tax
Payment: Major credit cards
Children: Welcome
Pets: Not allowed
Smoking: Nonsmoking rooms available
Open: All year

Reputed to be the country's oldest continuous inn since 1766,
the Beekman Arms is a composite of ten buildings, with history concentrated in the main inn. Rhinebeck was settled in
the early 18th century by German religious refugees, named for
their beloved Rhine, which looked so like the Hudson River.
Halfway between Albany and New York City, Rhinebeck became a major commercial center. In 1766 Arent Traphagen
constructed an inn—two stories tall, with three-foot-thick
stone walls, 8-by-12-inch oak beams, and 14-inch-wide floor
planks—as a stagecoach stop. The Bogardus Tavern, as it was
then known, was quickly caught in the throng of the Revolutionary War and often served as a meeting spot for generals and
soldiers. In 1777, the entire town of Rhinebeck sought refuge in
the tavern when given word of an impending British attack—
which later proved to be false.

A gathering spot for dignitaries over the years ever since, the
Beekman Arms is a living piece of history. The common rooms
and five dining areas in the main house are filled with lore,
colonial pewter collections, a 1795 deed, Civil War muskets, a
1760 tavern table, and an 18th-century Hudson Valley corner

cupboard. Adjacent to the reception area is a Federal addition, with a library furnished in comfortable couches and wing chairs. Old pictures of inn and area decorate the walls, including an ancient ferry ticket from Fishkill to Newburgh across the Hudson (fare for a man and a horse: 2 shillings).

There are five separate dining areas: the main room a sunny brick-floored atrium with green and white awnings; a small, primitive room; a wooded Tap Room with high-backed banquettes; and two colonial rooms. The inn is open daily for lunch and dinner, and a lavish brunch is served on Sundays. Dinner entrées range from $12 for vegetarian lasagna to $20 for filet mignon, with hearty dishes like New England chicken pot pie with a biscuit crust and, the house specialty, prime rib with natural juice.

The second-floor rooms in the main house vary in size, from smallish to pretty large, with traditional furnishings, antiques, and Lord and Mayfair amenities in modest private baths. The variety of other accommodations have telephones and televisions, and most are decorated with traditional reproduction pine furnishings. The prettiest is the 1844 Gothic Revival Delamater House, two stories of vertical cream clapboard, with much gingerbread and dozens of diamond-paned Tudor windows (of the seven rooms, choose the first-floor south room with a settee in the three-sided diamond-paned bay). The Delamater House heads a grassy commons around which sit the similarly decorated courtyard buildings flanking the Federal Germand House. The single-story Carriage House with five very deluxe rooms for business travelers was built on the site a century earlier, across the lawn from the new patio. Behind the inn adjacent to the Rhinebeck Antiques Center are the Fire House, built in the 1800s, and the Guest House for the budget-minded.

For a large property, the staff is extremely kind and helpful. It's quite an unusual place, with the intimacy of bed-and-breakfast, the comforts of a modern hotel, and the history of a museum.

Benn Conger Inn
206 West Cortland Street
Groton, New York 13073
607-898-5817

Proprietors: Peter and Alison van der Meulen
Accommodations: 3 suites, 1 room (6 junior suites planned)
Rates: $75–$125; fireplace suite, $150

Included: Full breakfast
Minimum stay: 3 nights on holidays and university weekends
Added: $25 each additional guest; 10% tax; 15% tax over $100
Payment: Major credit cards
Children: Check with innkeeper
Pets: Will consider
Smoking: Allowed in common room and library
Open: All year

This transitional property in the heart of the Finger Lakes is extremely exciting. Peter and Alison van der Meulen bought the twelve-year-old, well-reputed country inn in 1990 with grand ambitions. A young cosmopolitan pair from the downstate city, Peter is a former operations producer for "Nightline" and "World News Tonight,' and Alison worked in magazines and fashion for years. During their tenure in New York City, they restored several brownstones to period status, which led to their desire to buy a country inn to display Alison's flair for decorating and Peter's skills as a trained chef.

The Greek Revival house is a magnificent structure which was built in 1921 by industrialist Benn Conger, a founder of Smith Corona who later became a state senator. The two-story facade of white clapboard and green shutters is introduced by a portico of equal height, topped by a mansard roof with dormers, all vaguely reminiscent of the White House. Scandalously, Conger's proper political family had a twenty-year friendship with mobster Dutch Schultz, who maintained a room at the mansion. The inn sits on a hill on 18 acres, a short walk to the adorable town of Groton.

At present, the inn is best known for its extensive, award-winning wine list and Peter's Mediterranean-inspired cuisine, ranging from $14 to $22. Guests await dinner in the library to the left of the foyer, with a cherry bar and working fireplace, one of three originals in the house with marble mantels. The common areas and three dining rooms have recently been re-done by Alison, with beautiful results. Most spectacular is the small Conservatory dining room with green tile and trim and three sides of floor-to-ceiling Palladian windows, its linens done in Pierre Deux. The seasonal menu might include entreés like Cornish game hens with apricot–Grand Marnier stuffing, served with Dijon mustard cream sauce, or medallions of pork de la Touraine served with a red wine demiglace.

There are four rooms on the second floor of the main house and six rooms to come in an addition behind. Alison has decorated all accommodations in the height of elegance, with the quality and style of the finest country inn, including

350-thread-count designer linens and decorator wallpapers in bold but traditional colors and patterns. The small Cornell Suite has a Perry Ellis delft comforter and a balcony over the porte-cochère opening through French doors. The Dutch Schultz Suite is a massive 16-by-30-foot room, with a balcony over the Conservatory. Its sleigh bed sits grandly in the middle of the room, and notable is the huge Old World tiled bath with a walk-in closet. The four rooms encircle a private hot tub. The six guest rooms in the addition will each have a private veranda that looks out to the pergola and groomed acreage.

Unusual for a full-service country inn are the elaborate breakfasts, prepared by Alison, where one might expect a pancake ball stuffed with glazed apple, eggs Benedict, frittata, or soufflé.

Brae Loch Inn
5 Albany Street, Route 20
Cazenovia, New York 13035
315-655-3431
800-722-0674

Proprietors: Grey and Jim Barr
Accommodations: 14 rooms, 12 with private bath
Rates: $75–$95; luxury rooms, $125
Included: Continental breakfast
Minimum stay: Some weekends
Added: $15 each additional guest $15; 7% tax; 12% tax over $100
Children: Welcome (under 12 free)
Pets: Not allowed
Smoking: Allowed
Open: All year

Owned by the same family most impressively since 1946, the Brae Loch is one of the few in this book with a theme. The Barr family is of Scottish descent, and their ancestry is heralded throughout the rambling home as if pumped in by bagpipes. A gift shop on the first floor sells Scottish items such as wools, kilts, and crystal; and the family is always there to greet guests with convivial, proud smiles. All guests are Scottish under this friendly roof.

Best known as a large family-style restaurant, the Brae Loch has an extensive dinner menu, which ranges from $12 to $18. In addition to tournedos of lamb Athena, wrapped in phyllo pastry in a Madeira herb sauce or mustard fried Delta catfish with Cajun mayonnaise, there are Scotch steak and kidney pie in Edinburgh tradition; the royal Scot, a mixed grill of veal, lamb, beef, and pork; and the house specialty of prime rib minister served in natural juices. From September through Father's Day, the restaurant offers an extensive Sunday brunch. A tartan rug escorts guests throughout most of the dining rooms, which ramble through the first and the ground floors, these dug out by Grey and his brother more than forty years ago.

Much to their credit, the Barr family is constantly updating the inn. The original house on the site was built in 1805, and there are four rooms in this section around a center stairwell, done in a respectful Victorian style. Room 11 has a beautiful striped cherry and pine floor, Oriental rug, and marble sink top, and it's the only room with the Scottish themes echoed in its tartan rug and chair. Room 12 is the prettiest in the old section, with a king-size fishnet canopy, unusual purple tiling with a religious theme on the fireplace, and a large window seat flanked by carved wood columns. The fireplace in Room 13 also has fancy tilework.

Four rooms in the back addition are deluxe, with king-size canopy beds, traditional reproduction furniture, large new baths, and a complimentary bottle of wine. Those who don't mind sharing a small but elegant marble bath may want one of the two third-floor rooms, with high ceilings which open to a skylight, exposed brick walls, and a brick fireplace. There are also two rooms on a private stairwell above the gift shop, good for families, with two three-quarter-size beds and new baths with marble tiling under a pitched roof. All rooms have televisions, phones, and coffee makers.

Brae Loch sits across the street from Lake Cazenovia and it's a parklike setting. A half a block in the other direction is the charming town. Chittenango Falls State Park is a short drive away, and within a half hour's drive are several colleges, including Colgate, Hamilton, Syracuse, and Cazenovia College.

The Brewster Inn

6 Ledyard Avenue
Cazenovia, New York 13035
315-655-9232

Proprietors: Dick and Cathy Hubbard
Accommodations: 9 rooms, all with private bath, including 1 four-room suite
Rates: Rooms, $55–$140; suite, $225
Included: Continental breakfast
Added: $10 each additional guest; 7% tax; 12% tax over $100

Payment: Major credit cards except American Express
Children: Welcome
Pets: Not allowed
Smoking: Not allowed in dining rooms
Open: All year

One of three unique and complementary lodging spots in the charming town of Cazenovia, the Brewster Inn is the only one to sit right on the village lake. Guests enter at the back driveway but look forward to a lovely two and a half acres of groomed front lawn which drinks in the beauty of glass-surfaced Lake Cazenovia, five miles long.

The 1890 stone mansion was designed in the Richardson style by New York architect Robert Stevenson, built for his cousin William Brewster, who was a descendent of pilgrims and one of the country's wealthiest men, partial owner of Standard Oil. Brewster called his house Scrooby, after the English ancestral home that his relative Elder William Brewster relinquished when he sought refuge in the New World in 1620 and which was resultantly destroyed by Charles I. When Dick and Cathy Hubbard bought the mansion in 1984, they passed up the sentimental name Scrooby for the more dignified family name of Brewster.

The Hubbards have spent the last years redecorating the nine guest rooms and restoring and maintaining the grande dame. Dick is the proud host who cares particularly about his seafood, which is flown in daily from Foley's in Boston. Some specialties include fillet of blackened seabass, scallops Mornay in white wine with cream and Gruyère served with artichoke hearts. Other dishes such as sweetbreads or veal Atlantis with lobster and béarnaise sauce range quite reasonably from $13 to $17. The wine list is admirable. The three dining rooms have spartan, uninspired decor but lovely architecture: two rather traditional spots in the original house have coffered ceilings of mahogany and working fireplaces. One room glimpses the lake through a five-windowed bay; another is set in a rounded glass atrium overlooking the water.

The rooms are exceptionally large, as befitting a millionaire's home, some with outdoor decks and porches. The master bedroom is one of several decorated in antiques, this with a stunning three-piece 1890 Eastlake bedroom set with a particularly grand headboard of carved wood, the remainder upholstered in boudoir red and carpeted with Orientals. The bath features a three-and-a-half-foot-wide pedestal sink, adorned with Gilchrest and Soames soaps. Its porch has three exposures and descends to the front lawn. Two third-floor rooms with lovely views need some attention.

Other rooms are done exclusively in reproductions, like the Harden Room, with a four-poster cherry queen-size fishnet canopy bed, a modern bath, and a large deck through a sliding glass door. The third-floor Stickley Suite is more than one thousand square feet, with semicircular window views to the lake. Its fabulous bath is walled with light blue tiles, and a sunken Jacuzzi overlooks the lake.

Original blueprints of the mansion are displayed in some of the halls. The second-floor landing features a lovely Horace Waters square piano from around 1870 with mother-of-pearl inlay from the prior owner. The elegant entry has an impressive coffered ceiling, quartered oak walls, and a gilded mirror over the mantel of a working fireplace.

The Chequit Inn
Grand Avenue
Shelter Island, New York 11965
516-749-0018

Proprietors: Alice Klaris, Guy Gorelik, Mindy Goodfriend-Chernoff, Harry Chernoff
Accommodations: 32 rooms (12 in Main House, 12 in Cedar, 8 in Cottage)
Rates: $75–$150
Included: Continental breakfast
Minimum stay: 2 nights on weekends
Added: $20 each additional guest
Payment: Visa, MasterCard, American Express
Children: Welcome
Pets: Not allowed
Smoking: Not allowed
Open: May 15 to October 31

In January 1990, two creative couples bought the long-standing, neglected Chequit's on Shelter Island. They knew not to compete with the two nonpareil local properties, the Ram's Head Inn and Sag Harbor's American Hotel. Instead, the owners have made Chequit's a spare, clean, postmodern inn, a place for art directors, architects, and designers. While some may find it lacking in warmth and character, others will enjoy the stark, bold furnishings and cottage-white floors.

One hundred miles east of New York City, wedged between Long Island's north and south forks, Chequit's is a landmark in Shelter Island's village, up a steep hill from the ferry dock. It was built around 1870, roughly the same time as the rest of the island's architecture. Of the three buildings that constitute the inn, the Main House offers the most rooms and activity. Dining is on the wide wrap porches and outdoor patio, as well as indoors in a lovely dining room reminiscent of a SoHo warehouse loft, its tin ceiling supported by rows of seven pillars, painted an airy pink and white.

The menu is hastily written in freehand, with entrées ranging from $13 to $21. Dinners are artistic and eclectic, including roast Muscovy duck breast with raspberry-rhubarb relish and warm rice salad and grilled New York shell steak with potato, leek, and onion pancake and warm tomato salad. The appetizers are interesting also: a seared yellowfin tuna salad on cold noodles with sesame dressing, crabcakes with corn and tomato relish. Downstairs is a local hangout, with a pool table and bar.

The guest rooms are decorated sparely as if by a New England Georgia O'Keeffe: the walls and floors serve as a white canvas to offset dramatic colors. A tiny night table is checkered with red and yellow; the beds are done in blue chambray; a piece of driftwood holds a reading lamp. Fresh flowers and original art enliven the spareness. Each piece was decidedly placed by owner Alice Klaris.

Service is understated and casual, like most of Shelter Island. More than one third of Shelter Island is set aside as the Mashomack Nature Preserve, which provides a full range of activities, from hiking to bird-watching.

Lincklaen House

79 Albany Street
Cazenovia, New York 13035
315-655-3461

Proprietors: The Tobin Family
General Manager: Howard M. Kaler
Accommodations: 21 rooms, all with private bath
Rates: $70–$130
Included: Continental breakfast, afternoon tea
Minimum stay: Some college weekends
Added: $8 each additional guest; 7% tax; 12% tax over $100
Payment: Visa, MasterCard
Children: Welcome
Pets: Allowed
Smoking: Allowed
Open: All year

An exciting property on Cazenovia's main corner is the Lincklaen House, an unusually sophisticated small hotel which underwent a much needed renewal starting in 1988. It's said to be the oldest continuously operating hotel in New York, having kept it doors open since 1835, even when fire marred its walls in the early 1900s.

The lobby was recently restored, resulting in a stunningly elegant formal entrance with diagonal black and white parquet tiling. The house sits on the corner, so two entrances converge in front of the old reception desk. Some of the elaborate wood paneling was reproduced, painted over with thick white paint. A waiting area has lovely formal Federal antiques, high coffered white ceilings, and an elaborate carved mantel warmed by a gas fireplace. Through French doors away from the reception area is a formal double parlor with traditional couches and chairs. Cheerful but elegant floral swags decorate the huge windows. The lines throughout are clean and white, with a formal air about the entire place.

The serenely beautiful dining room is reached through French doors in the other direction from the reception area, the floors done in a light wood parquet. Four columns support the coffered ceiling, each a slender cluster of Corinthian elegance cordoning off three rows of tables. At the end of the room an elaborate fireplace warmly lights the soft white walls. The tables are decorated in white linen, with Windsor chairs. Ahead of the fireplace is a brick patio, where receptions are often held. The Tap Room in the lower level of Lincklaen House is a woody Ivy League enclave whose walls bear witness to visitors of the last century and a half.

The renovations married some of the smaller rooms, bringing the number down from 28 to 21 on two floors. Though the remaining twin rooms are very small (unless you're traveling alone, try to avoid these), the larger rooms are wonderful, with Hitchcock furniture, a Martha Washington chair, a writing desk, a reproduction highboy, and lovely wallpapers and window treatments—some in chintz, some more masculine. There is some clean and spare stencilwork in and around the borders and bathrooms, usually of flowers and vines. All rooms have televisions and phones. The bathrooms are the most recent beneficiary of the improvements, with ceramic faux marble black and white tiling and clean new fixtures.

Innkeeper Howard Kaler is sure to greet guests, a devoted host. His staff is warm and enthusiastic about the recent changes in the Lincklaen House. There is an elegant gentility about this place, a bit of nobility in a charming small town. Be sure to visit Lake Cazenovia at the end of the street and Chittenango Falls State Park. Local colleges are Colgate, Hamilton, and Syracuse.

Maidstone Arms

207 Main Street
East Hampton, New York 11937
516-324-5006

Proprietor: Gordon Campbell-Gray
Manager: Donna Cullum
Accommodations: 16 rooms in inn, including 4 suites; 3
   cottages
Room Rates:
   Off-season and midweek: $95–$150
   Weekends: $295–$515 (3 days, 2 nights); $345–$570 (3 days,
      3 nights)
Cottage Rates: $1,460–$1,530 per week
Included: Continental breakfast
Minimum stay: 2 nights on summer weekends
Added: $10 each additional guest; 13% tax
Payment: Visa, MasterCard, American Express
Children: Welcome
Pets: Not allowed
Smoking: Allowed
Open: All year

East Hampton is the most exclusive of the Hamptons on Long
Island, and the most exclusive place to stay has been a reliable fixture for years, the Maidstone Arms. Devotees will be
thrilled and newcomers will be rapt with the new and improved Maidstone Arms, which made its society debut on Memorial Day 1992. British innkeeper Gordon Campbell-Gray
bought the impressive property in the fall of 1991 and invested
the off-season to the inn's entire refurbishment. The result is
exactly what one would hope a beachside inn would be—
sophisticated yet unpretentious.

With the seasoned experiences of world travel and having
owned several properties in London, Oxfordshire, and Holland, Mr. Campbell-Gray is making a much-needed contribution to Long Island. He envisioned a sunny, beachy atmosphere
during the summer, with lots of blue and yellow stripes and a
light, willowy feel. When the summer season comes to a close,
the interior furnishing are slipcovered for a wintry, cozy atmosphere, in plaids, reds, and rusts.

The white clapboard inn is shaded by blue and white striped
awnings and blue shutters and sits across from the Town Pond
and Village Green on the sleepy corner of Routes 114 and 27.
The building was erected between 1800 and 1830 and is in
pristine condition. While the exterior is much as it was, the

interior has been entirely redecorated, most strikingly in the guest rooms. The furnishings are mostly American antiques and wicker, with nautical themes. The airy blue and yellow stripe wallcoverings and fabrics are Brunschwig & Fils or Quadrille, complemented by a low nap beige carpet. There are novels and coffee table books in every room, brightened by fresh flowers. The baths have been entirely renovated, in bright white tile with a bold colored border, offering upscale amenities.

The cottages offer wonderful, albeit expensive, accommodations for families or couples traveling together. They are cute clapboard reiterations of the main inn with similar decor, complete with immaculate, stocked kitchenettes.

Most impressive is Mr. Campbell-Gray's desire to welcome local residents. Open all year, the inn's restaurant serves three bountiful meals daily, orchestrated by Christophe Bergen and chef Matthew Tivey, both formerly of Blantyre, the Relais et Château property in the Berkshires. In the airy dining room, with yellow and blue themes softened by roman shades, chef Tivey serves real American food with a magic touch— afternoon tea is the only English thing about the Maidstone Arms. Guests may take either a Continental or a full breakfast on a bright, wicker-filled sun porch with age-old sloped wooden floors overlooking the pond through a wall of mullioned windows, or they can dine in the floral courtyard. Dinners are quite reasonably priced, from $15 to $25.

The beach is a 15-minute walk, and the inn thoughtfully provides bicycles, beach passes, and towels for guests and will make picnic lunches on request. Winter months see a lot of activity at the Maidstone Arms, with flower arranging classes, lecturers from Sothebys, and painting classes among the interesting events.

Oliver Loud's Inn
Bushnell's Basin
Pittsford, New York 14534
716-248-5200

Proprietor: Vivienne Tellier
Accommodations: 8 rooms, all with private bath
Rates: $157
Included: Breakfast basket and welcome basket; tax
Added: $10 each additional guest
Payment: Major credit cards
Children: Over 12 welcome

Pets: Not allowed
Smoking: 4 nonsmoking rooms
Open: All year

The group of buildings at Bushnell's Basin, ten miles east of Rochester, is a restoration of an 1820s hamlet including Richardson's Canal House Restaurant, Oliver Loud's Inn, and several shops. In 1978, Vivienne Tellier and her husband, Andrew Wolfe, happened upon a historic building destined for demolition. Dating to 1818, it was the oldest tavern on the 373-mile-long Erie Canal, which reached the Rochester area in 1821. The tavern served as a stagecoach stop between Rochester and Canandaigua for nearly a century, survived various other incarnations including tenure as a nudist colony in the 1930s, but had been abandoned since 1968. The couple bought the building and undertook a full restoration, resulting in the highly acclaimed Richardson's Canal House Restaurant, which has consistently earned four stars from the *Mobil Guide.*

As the restaurant prospered, the couple saved yet another abandoned building from demolition in 1985, a formidable inn which belonged to Oliver Loud, dating from 1812. The Wolfes moved it four miles to Bushnell's Basin. The inn is a two-story mustard yellow clapboard with black shutters and trim. It sits on a nice grassy plot of land with views of the canal, across a parking lot from Richardson's Canal House. The first-floor porch extends like a hat brim beyond the house and wraps around the entire structure, supported by square pillars, and has lots of hanging flower baskets and wicker furniture with floral pillows.

Vivienne documented the interior design to remain faithful to her 1820s restoration. The brick-face hall paper was a common theme, as were the ornate borders, their subjects the names for the guest rooms: Feathers, Boxwood, Garland, St. Cloud. The original moldings to the inn were reproduced, and an artist was hired to do the faux mahogany graining on all the doors. The common room features a silver service from 1825, Wedgwood china, and a wonderful mantel done in elaborate faux marble and gold leaf panels. The guest rooms, four on each floor, are furnished in Stickley reproductions, immaculate and generously sized, with creative swags and window treatments. About half the rooms have views of the canal. While romantics enjoy the canopy beds and antique quilts, business travelers appreciate the modern baths and private telephones—especially since Rochester is lacking in interesting accommodations.

Guests are greeted by a bountiful display of refreshments upon arrival: a split of champagne, spring water, crackers, cheese, fruit, and cookies on a pretty European tray. A breakfast basket is presented in the mornings like a country picnic, with fresh baked muffins, an egg, and fruit. Lists of local activities, from shopping to museums, are provided in the inn's common room.

Richardson's Canal House remains easily accessible but independent. It's an extremely popular restaurant with a series of small, intimate dining rooms. The captivating colonial and folk art interior is decorated with stencilwork by Ruth Flowers and primitive murals by Edith Lunt Small. Dinners are a fixed price of $32 for four courses, which might start with dill-cured gravlax with brown bread and dill mustard sauce. After salad, guests have a choice of nine entrées: perhaps roast tenderloin of beef with wild mushroom sauce, duckling with rhubarb-raspberry glaze, or Cajun broiled sea scallops with avocado and serrano pepper relish.

The 1770 House

143 Main Street
East Hampton, New York 11937
516-324-1770

Proprietors: Sid and Miriam Perle
Accommodations: 7 rooms, including private cottage; 3 rooms in Philip Taylor House
Rates: $105–$225; $195 at Philip Taylor
Included: Expanded Continental breakfast
Minimum stay: 4 nights on July and August weekends
Added: $50 each additional guest; 13% tax
Payment: MasterCard, Visa
Children: 12 and over allowed
Pets: Not allowed
Smoking: Allowed
Open: All year

A traveler will be hard-pressed to find a kinder host than Sid Perle. One would surely think the same of his wife, Miriam, if she stood still, but she is too busy planning breakfasts and elaborate dinners at the 1770 House. They have passed on their generosity and hospitality to their two children, Wendy and Adam, who are ever-present at the inn.

In this exclusive community, the 1770 House has been a welcome fixture since 1977 when the Perles first opened their doors. In 1985, they introduced three rooms in the Philip Taylor

House several doors down the street, their magnificent Tudor family home which is named for their grandchildren. While the Hamptons have the uncanny ability to make visitors feel like outsiders, the Perles welcome guests like family.

The white clapboard home with black shutters sits modestly on Main Street, Route 27, just past the East Hampton village pond. Once through the old front door, guests immediately understand the appeal of this home. A 16th-century English grandfather clock greets guests in the foyer, its face coincidentally declaring "Hampton" long before its New World analog was discovered. Among the impressive antiques collected by the Perles over the years are hundreds of timepieces amassed by Sid: large grandfather clocks, mantel clocks, wall clocks, in carved wood, metal, and porcelain from all over Europe. Like those in the shop downstairs, all the antiques in the 1770 House are for sale. The Tap Room was formerly the town's watering hole, a wonderful cozy grotto with a 1740 beehive oven.

The dining room is to the left of the foyer behind a toile screen. In these two intimate rooms, curiosities abound: Sid's clocks, a wonderful mantelpiece, treasurelike paintings, all with a story attached. To the right of the foyer is the ancient paneled library, dating from 1740, where guests gather before dinner.

Upstairs are four guest rooms filled with an eclectic collection of antiques, most with canopy beds. Guests sensitive to street noise may want to request rooms away from Main Street. Two rooms downstairs have private entrances, the Junior Suite with a fireplace, and the other (Room 12) with a garden view.

The Philip Taylor House is a short walk toward the village pond, a glorious regal Elizabethan manor whose foundation was built in 1650 and greatly expanded in 1911. There are an impossible 2,405 panes of glass here, yet the house's finest feature remains a secret until one is invited inside: the formal maze of boxwood gardens behind the house, with a hundred-year-old wisteria arborvitae and statues of the four seasons. The Perles' real treasures are housed inside, from statues to furniture to artwork to the incredible architecture of this home. The Wisteria, Boxwood, and Peartree rooms are lavishly romantic and capacious, with working fireplaces and English and French furniture that seems transplanted from overseas palaces.

Dinner is an intimate affair, for a fixed price of $32, with a choice of appetizer, entrée with vegetable, and dessert with coffee or tea, all tailored by Miriam and executed by daughter and chef Wendy Van Deusen.

The Sherwood Inn
26 West Genesee Street
Skaneateles, New York 13152
315-685-3405

Proprietors: Bill and Joanne Eberhardt
Innkeeper: Chris Shields
Accommodations: 17 rooms, including 5 suites, all with
    private baths
Rates: $70–$120
Included: Continental breakfast
Added: 12% tax
Payment: Major credit cards
Children: Welcome
Pets: Allowed
Smoking: Discouraged
Open: All year except Christmas Eve and Christmas Day

The classic Sherwood Inn sits in the heart of one of the Finger
Lakes' prettiest towns at the north end of Lake Skaneateles.
Isaac Sherwood, a successful stagecoach businessman, built
this inn and tavern in 1807 and it's been run nearly continuously as such ever since. The only thing that has changed is its
name, which has had seven incarnations.

The Sherwood Inn is a beautiful slate-blue shingle building,
three stories high, with regal black trim. The first floor is enclosed by a porch, lined with about 50 windows, that wraps
around the sides and front of the building overlooking the lake,
a breezy memorable place in warmer months, a quaint and
cozy enclave in the winter. Visitors enter at the center, to a
traditional Williamsburg foyer, with neutral paneling, a generous hearth, and a piano. To the left are formal and informal
dining; to the right, a tap room.

Upstairs are two floors of rooms that remain as they were
when the Sherwood Inn was built. It's up here that the history of
the place seems to emerge with the feeling of a colonial refuge.
The halls are unusually wide with light random-width plank-
ing. Rooms are in three wings: a short hall progresses straight
ahead from the stairs to the back of the inn, a long hall extends
to the left, and a shorter wing to the right, introduced by curved
plaster walls. The wallpapers are traditional and varied
throughout the guest rooms: sometimes a floral or heavy chintz
or a stencil print, sometimes a stripe. There is some variety in
the size of rooms, but none is too cozy, and the suites are quite
roomy. Each room features some nice antiques, including ar-

moires, highboys, and marble-top tables and vanities and is done in Williamsburg, masculine Stickley, or sometimes, like the Red Room, number 31, a playful Victorian with a red fringed chandelier and brass bed. About half the rooms have lake views, and these are highly preferable. All have nice, clean, modest baths, with a tub and shower combination.

Meals are a great event here, quite reasonably priced from $11 to $17. Guests might try sea scallops in red pepper and caper cream sauce over linguine, crabmeat au gratin in white wine cream sauce over rice, or pork loin medallions in a mustard cream sauce.

The warmer months are a great time to visit, with lakeside band concerts, sailing regattas, and polo; and the fall is especially picturesque. The Finger Lakes have an easy hospitality, their beauty still relatively undiscovered, and the staff at the Sherwood Inn is always immensely helpful and proud.

Simmons Way Village Inn

Route 44 East, Box 965
Millerton, New York 12546
518-789-6235

Owners and Innkeepers: Richard and Nancy Carter
Accommodations: 10 rooms, all with private bath
Rates: $115–$150
Included: Full breakfast, tea, wine; gratuities
Minimum stay: 2 nights on weekends April–November, 3 nights on holidays
Added: $25 each additional guest; 10.25% tax
Payment: American Express, Visa, MasterCard
Children: Welcome
Pets: Not allowed
Smoking: Restricted
Open: All year

Millerton is closer to Connecticut than to its nearest New York neighbor, south of the Taconic State Park near the Berkshire foothills. This small lumber town is nearly level with Rhinebeck on a map, in a narrow valley of scenic Route 22 that is rarely traveled farmland. Simmons Way Village Inn is a wonderful attraction in this area, offering congenial dinners and lovely overnight accommodations.

The rambling white clapboard building sits on a sweeping hill overlooking Millerton's main street. Eddie Collins, the exonerated ninth man of the Chicago Black Sox, was born here. It was built by industrialist E. W. Simmons in 1854 and Victorianized in 1888 with its present array of gingerbread and porches. Ninety years later, the house was transformed into a country inn, eventually bought in 1987 by its present owners, Richard and Nancy Carter. This warm, interesting couple has traveled all over the world, lived in Vienna for years during Dick's tenure with the United Nations, and happily decided to settle in Millerton.

The three stories undulate in gabled peaks which render the interior spaces interesting and unpredictable. Guests enter a common room to the left, which opens onto the guests' breakfast room, illuminated by a large bay window. Throughout are some fascinating pieces from the Carters' travels, including the handmade breakfast table where guests enjoy homemade granola and goat's milk yogurt from nearby Coach Farm.

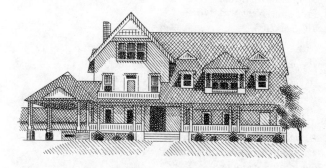

To the right of the foyer is a tea room and veranda of white wicker where the Carters host high tea on summer Saturdays. At the back of the house is the dining room, a rather contemporary addition with large gabled skylights that allow moonlight to reflect off the oil lamps and antique silver chargers. Chef Michael Myers might prepare a meal of smoked salmon terrine with dill sauce and red caviar for an appetizer, followed by a main dish of seafood ragout with miniature vegetables in goat's milk yogurt cream, or sautéed quail with bitter orange and currant sauce, and ending with white chocolate mousse cake. Entrées range from $14 to $23. The wine list is selective but chosen with much attention to particular items on the menu.

The carved and paneled oak staircase leads to ten rooms on two upper floors. Some, like Nos. 2 and 4, are unusually large, with private porches through which guests can appreciate some of the original stained glass. While some rooms are feminine, with circular crown canopies, some, like room 7 on the third floor, with king-size duck comforter, are more masculine.

Room 3 is a particularly lovely room with an off-pink Italian linen damask coverlet draped on a pine four-poster queen-size bed under a two-sided pink canopy, with a sitting area tucked under a gabled window. The baths are newly appointed with generous amenities but retain an Old World elegance with antique sinks and tubs, Old World octagonal tiling, and brass fixtures. All beds are antiques lengthened for modern sleepers, and all the rooms maintain an unusual cleanliness.

The Housatonic River and Appalachian Trail are four miles away in Connecticut, near twin lakes Wononpakook and Wononskopomuc by Salisbury. Nearby Hotchkiss offers tennis, great cross-country skiing, and local trout fishing.

The White Inn

52 East Main Street
Fredonia, New York 14063
716-672-2103
Fax: 716-672-2107

Proprietors: The Palmers and the Bryants
Accommodations: 23 rooms, all with private bath
Rates: $49–$159
Included: Full breakfast
Minimum stay: None
Added: $5–$10 service charge; 7% tax; 12% tax over $100
Payment: Major credit cards
Children: Welcome
Pets: Not allowed
Smoking: Nonsmoking rooms available
Open: All year

Halfway between Buffalo and Erie just south of Great Lake is the town of Fredonia. Passersby can't miss the White Inn, an imposing structure on Fredonia's Main Street. The massive three-story plaster over brick is painted white, so named coincidentally for the family who built it in 1811, some of the county's first settlers. The house was expanded to its present mansion parameters in 1868. The huge Greek Revival facade was added in 1919 and greatly dresses up the rectangular structure, with a two-story portico supported by six looming pillars, flanked by a single-story porch, making the veranda an endless hundred feet in length. The White Inn was one of the country's first motor inns, transformed into an overnight hostelry with forty rooms in 1919, and it remained such until 1980. It was reviewed in the 1930s by a frequent traveler who wrote the nation's first lodging and dining books, Duncan Hines.

Underfoot in the grand foyer is a pretty green and pink trellis rug which leads into a huge wood-paneled bar to the left and into the dining rooms to the right and to the back of the inn. Guest rooms are on the second and third floors, in a T shape. They are all decorated differently, some furnished with traditional reproductions, others with Victorian antiques. The baths are all new and sparkling.

While the rooms are large and comfortable, people flock from all over for the food at the White Inn. Entrées range from $12.50 to $18.95 on a large and creative menu. Gingered pork tenderloin with apples and apple brandy finished in cream; loin of lamb Wyoming stuffed with almonds, spinach, garlic and shallots; and venison with port wine and cranberries are among some of the interesting choices.

There is a festive quality about the White Inn, with informal friendly service in a formal atmosphere. The owners are two academic couples who love their town and the property. There is a busy gift shop in a barn at the back of the lot, full of local products, artwork, and crafts. Chautauqua Institute is a half-hour drive, and Lake Erie is a hop away. Fredonia is a busy working community, with some history, said to be the country's first town to be lit by natural gas.

Pennsylvania

The Beach Lake Hotel
Box 144
Beach Lake, Pennsylvania 18405
717-729-8239

Proprietors: Roy and Erika Miller
Accommodations: 6 rooms, all with private bath
Rates: $95; $75 per night for 3 weeknights
Included: Full breakfast
Minimum stay: 2 nights on holidays and on weekends May–October
Added: 6% tax
Payment: MasterCard, Visa, American Express
Children: Not allowed
Pets: Not allowed
Smoking: Not allowed in rooms
Open: All year

The village of Beach Lake, in an understated part of the Poconos, is separated from New York by only several miles and the Delaware River. The modest exterior of the Beach Lake Hotel sits in the heart of town—consisting of several buildings and a post office—and announces itself with a quaint sign. It's a quiet area in Pennsylvania's lake district, with its own lake for which the town was named, several miles uphill from the magnificent Lake Wallenpaupack in Wayne County.

Built in the 1830s as a hotel, the three-story clapboard house was christened during the Civil War as the Beach Lake Hotel. Throughout its many lifetimes, the house served as a tavern, a general store, and finally a post office from 1879 to 1936. Roy and Erika Miller resurrected the property in 1987 and rejuvenated the beauty of the wainscoted walls and ceilings.

In keeping with their respect for history, the Millers have filled the house with antiques, which are all for sale. Antiques dealers in previous careers, the Millers are avid collectors and have made the house a living gallery. Not only are the guest rooms and dining rooms filled with wonderful furniture and artwork from the 18th and 19th centuries, but part of the inn serves as an antique gallery. The Millers close for dinner on Tuesdays and Wednesdays to replenish their troves. Among the treasures throughout the house are an 1840 English cabaret piano with mahogany inlay, a set of delft plates, an art deco leather screen, an 18th-century Sheraton field bed, and—unusually—several art dioramas from a taxidermy artist whose work is displayed at the Museum of Natural History in New York and the Smithsonian Institution in Washington, D.C.

With Victorian reproduction patterns from Schumacher as background, the rooms recede into history with antique full beds and lavish fabric treatments and canopies designed by Erika. Armoires, marble tables, writing desks, and chairs complete the picture—yet the decor is ever-changing as guests leave with a painting, a pillow, a lamp, or even their bed. The two third-floor rooms are charming, set under the eaves, with pretty yellow pine floors. A great asset is the common porch at the front of the house on the second floor.

There are two dining areas, one with wicker chairs at seven tables covered in florals, the other with several couches and banquettes, enlivened by chintz balloon curtains. The dinner menu, prepared by Erika, is varied, eclectic, and creative. Entrées may include fettucini d'hotel with lobster, scallops, cream sauce, and prosciutto; quail in brandy sauce; sea scallops in bourbon mustard; or fettucini Alfredo with chicken, tomato, and pistachio sauce. Overnight guests enjoy a full breakfast of several courses, including possibly eggs Benedict, a baked dish, pancakes, and home-baked goods.

Future plans at the Beach Lake include seven additional guest rooms in the neighboring Greek Revival house, decorated in Williamsburg and Shaker simplicity.

The Golden Plough Inn
Peddler's Village, Route 202 and State Street
Lahaska, Pennsylvania 18931
215-794-4004

Proprietors: Earl Jamison
Manager: Robert Cassidy
Accommodations: 47 rooms (22 in main building, 13 in Merchants Row, 8 in Wagon House, 2 in Mill View, 2 in Carriage House)
Rates: $85–$200
Included: Continental breakfast
Minimum stay: None
Added: $15 each additional guest; 6% tax
Payment: All credit cards
Children: Welcome
Pets: Not allowed
Smoking: Allowed
Open: All year

Everything about Bucks County suggests history, from its colonial settling days, to the Victorian gingerbreaded bed-and-breakfasts, to the Algonquin Round Tablers who frequented the area in the 1930s. Those who enjoy history by day but prefer contemporary comforts by night may want to stay at the Golden Plough Inn. The setting is thirty-year-old Peddler's Village in Lahaska, several miles from New Hope, where more than seventy shops and restaurants and an upscale inn were added by local developer Earl Jamison in 1989. Though the construction is nearly all new, Peddler's Village has an old feel: dinners in a colonial kitchen, quilt competitions, light tavern fare in an easily walkable setting.

The atmosphere at the Golden Plough is that of a luxury hotel, with discreet and formal service. Guest rooms are scattered throughout the complex, about half in the hotel, the rest in small numbers throughout the historic-looking complex, lending a bed-and-breakfast feel. The rooms are impressively decorated with Henredon reproductions and quite lovely Waverly fabrics. The upholstering is noticeably nice, from the settees to wing chairs and even headboards and bedding with creative draped canopies, often matching window treatments.

Surprising for a larger property is the attention to wall art at the Golden Plough, with folk art and crafts, primitive cupboards, decoys, and dried flower wreaths and arrangements that make the rooms seems intimate and personable. All rooms have televisions hidden in armoires, refrigerators hidden in closets, one-third have fireplaces, and some have Jacuzzis.

Guests are offered an overwhelming selection of dining possibilities: the Cock 'n' Bull, with family-style American colonial cooking, ranging in price from $11 to $22 for dinner; Jenny's for country elegance with a French influence; and informal pub fare at the Spotted Hog, Peddler's Pub, and Hart's Tavern. Of course, for those who manage to explore the area, there are endless activities in New Hope, Doylestown, and Bucks County, as well as ongoing seasonal activities at Peddler's Village.

The Guesthouse and The 1777 House at Doneckers

318–324 North State Street
301 West Main Street
Ephrata, Pennsylvania 17522
717-733-8696

Proprietor: Bill Donecker and family
Manager and Innkeeper: Jan Grobengieser
Accommodations: 19 rooms in Guesthouse, all but 2 with private bath; 12 rooms in 1777 House, all with private bath
Rates: $59–$115; suites, $135–$175
Included: Extensive Continental breakfast
Minimum stay: None
Added: $10 for rollaway; $8 for crib; 6% tax
Payment: Major credit cards
Children: Welcome
Pets: Not allowed
Smoking: Allowed
Open: All year; restaurant closed Wednesdays

In the charming town of Ephrata near Lancaster, famous for its odd 19th-century cloister, the Donecker family opened a clothing store about thirty years ago. Patrons came from all over to spend the day shopping. Eventually, Bill Donecker answered more of their needs by providing a restaurant, overnight accommodations, and a complex of art galleries and studios.

Today, the Doneckers community rather dominates the commercial aspects of Ephrata, yet in a sensitive and complementary way. The overnight accommodations at the Guesthouse are in several connecting buildings: a restored Queen Anne Victorian and three residential brick houses. The 1777 House is a colonial several blocks away. The well-received French restaurant is across the street from the Guesthouse, on the edge of town near Artworks, a gallery for local artisans located in a renovated 1920s shoe factory warehouse.

Each room is unique. At the Guesthouse, some roomy suites are in large parlors, and other cozy rooms are tucked away in gabled attics. A favorite is the luxurious Wheatland Suite in the house's former foyer, with original inlaid floors, stained glass windows, lovely bay windows, a satin-draped crown canopy bed divided from a sitting area by supporting pillars, leading to a Jacuzzi. The rooms are decorated with lovely and varied antiques and reproductions, with primitive detailing and stenciling. All have cute marble washstands and separate baths, except two rooms which share one bath.

While the Guesthouse feels like a larger inn, the 1777 House seems like a bed-and-breakfast. It was built by clockmaker Jacob Gorgas for his family and adjacent shop. Gorgas was a member of the Ephrata cloister, and rooms are named for some notable members. The entry is done in turn-of-the-century Mercer tiles, as are some of the working fireplaces—though the one in the Gorgas Suite is done in original green marble. All the rooms have Alsatian armoires or German kasses and are decorated in antiques from several centuries. The Conrad Biessel Suite has a 19th-century tiger's-eye maple table, the Prioress Maria Suite has an 1828 dower chest. Quite outstanding are the two suites in the Carriage House, triplexes, with bedrooms and fireplaces on the first floor, stepping up to a whirlpool, then a sitting area on the third floor.

Certainly, the Restaurant at Doneckers is a large part of a visit. Chef Jean-Marie Jugé has presided over the food since its opening in 1984, with much success. There are several dining areas, from garden to formal, and the romantic Chateau. Dinner entrées are rather expensive though highly lauded, ranging from $19 to $27, with an entirely French menu. Specialties include Dover sole served in strawberry butter sauce; pheasant served with vegetables, foie gras, and a truffle dumpling; or Châteaubriand for two served with béarnaise sauce. A full menu of appetizers is astounding, as are the soups and desserts. A lighter supper menu is also available nightly, from $9.

The Logan
Ten West Ferry Street
New Hope, Pennsylvania 18938
215-862-2300

Innkeeper: Gwen Davis
Accommodations: 16 rooms, all with private bath
Rates: $95–$125
Included: Full breakfast
Minimum stay: 2 nights on weekends, April–November, 3
   nights on holidays
Added: $17 each additional person; 6% tax
Payment: American Express, Visa, MasterCard
Children: Welcome
Pets: Not allowed
Smoking: Allowed
Open: All year

In a county abounding with bed-and-breakfasts, the Logan is a diverting change of pace. The only downtown hostelry, the Logan is set right in the middle of New Hope on its busiest street and enjoys all the bustle of its popular town. With sixteen rooms, the Logan seems more like a hotel than an inn, especially because of its busy dining traffic. However, an extensive renovation completed in 1988 provided lovely antiques and thorough colonial decor in most rooms, so guests cannot help but feel pampered in a way that only country inns might prompt.

Built in 1727, the Logan is New Hope's oldest building and looks every bit its age, albeit preserved in time. The first of its three stories is exposed fieldstone bordered by an overhanging green porch. Its next two stories are plaster over fieldstone, trimmed with green with the convincing result of an old stagecoach stop, one of the first between Philadelphia and New York on the Shore Swift Line and one of the five oldest inns in the country.

A recommendation of the rooms must be accompanied with a warning about front and back rooms—the former being much more spacious, the latter being small and uninspired (Nos. 1, 2, 12, and 14), furnished with antique brass beds. Of the front rooms, however, much good can be said: Gwen Davis, the manager since the renovation and a member of the New Hope Chamber of Commerce, has set consistently high standards for her guest rooms: all-cotton sheets, down quilts, fresh flowers in warmer months replaced by plants in winter, Lord and Mayfair amenities, remote televisions hidden in cabinets, and telephones. Each room has a different Williamsburg color trim to match its new and clean bathroom tiling, complementing a low-nap carpet. Rosemont reproduction pencil post queen-size canopy beds are reached by wooden steps, and some rooms have old and valuable antiques—especially Room 6, which features a Victorian armoire from the 1890s and a carved mahogany bed. The interesting prints on the wall are for sale, antiques and work by local artists, lending a gallery aspect to the Logan.

The tavern, set in the oldest part of the inn, has an imposing stone fireplace and fascinating murals painted in the 1930s and restored by a local artist, with a true colonial feel of heavy ceilings and thick walls. There are two dining rooms, a formal Gallery Room and an enclosed glass atrium where guests take a full breakfast, the latter featuring a stained glass wall made by local artist Val Sigstedt. The tented patio opens in warmer months for outdoor dining with pretty wrought-iron furniture in a slate setting.

Virginia

The Belle Grae Inn
515 West Frederick Street
Staunton, Virginia 24401
703-886-5151

Proprietor: Michael Organ
Accommodations: 8 rooms in main house, 4 suites in Jefferson House, 3 rooms and 1 suite in Townhouse, 2 suites in Bishop's Suite, 3 rooms in Bungalow
Rates: $55–$90, suites from $95–$150
Included: Full breakfast
Added: $2 per person daily service; 7.5% tax
Payment: Major credit cards
Children: Well-behaved children welcome
Pets: Not allowed
Smoking: Limited
Open: All year

This inn is a successful compilation of many aspects of hospitality, the result of the inexhaustible efforts of owner Michael Organ. He bought the Belle Grae in 1983 and has been hard at work continuously, expanding, restoring, decorating, antiquing. In addition, he is a consummate host, providing a thorough library of local history and activities for guests, the author of a brochure of day trips from the inn and a flyer detailing Staunton's ten formidable restaurants (including his own). Daily from 5 to 6 P.M., he hosts an innkeeper's social in the parlor where he meets his guests; and he is always present at breakfast. He is paternally close with his staff, who happily and busily roam about this mansion like family members—an aspect of innkeeping which guests notice only when it is absent.

Staunton is a beautiful town which has been successfully restored during the last several years, a Virginian San Francisco with Victorian architecture on hilly streets. Mary Baldwin College and the Woodrow Wilson birthplace are among the many sights. The Belle Grae Inn sits atop a hill in the Newtown Historic District, an elegant three-story Federal brick house built in 1873, expanded in the latter part of the century to 19 rooms with an Italianate wrap porch. Eight rooms are on two floors of the main house, with wonderful antique spool, brass, and sleigh beds and lovely Victoriana. The Bistro, serving Continental food, offers spectacular views of Staunton through large picture windows. The full breakfast is served in the Bistro. Light-fare dining is available on the sunny patio behind the Bistro.

The four satellite houses vary in decor. The Bishop's House was built in the 1880s for the Episcopalian bishop of the diocese and is now home to two suites, adjacent to the registration office and decorated in period antiques. Built in the 1880s for workers at the local pajama factory, the Jefferson House is the newest property to be restored and has the most daring, romantic decor, mixing traditional Victoriana and lovely antiques with creative patterns, colors, and crown canopies. The Townhouse is at the front of the Belle Grae and connects to the Bistro by a footbridge. It was built in the 1860s as a traditional valley home and has three rooms good for business travelers, with desks, televisions, and phones, and one contemporary suite. The Bungalow has three bedrooms suitable for families.

An hour's drive provides dozens of local activities: to the west, Hot and Warm Springs in the Allegheny Mountains and the Homestead; to the south, Natural Bridge and historic Lexington, with the Virginia Military Institute and Washington and Lee University; to the north, James Madison University in Harrisonburg and Endless Caverns in New Market; or a drive across the Skyline Drive east to Charlottesville and Monticello.

The Inn at Gristmill Square
Box 359
Warm Springs, Virginia 24484
703-839-2231

Proprietors: The McWilliams Family
Accommodations: 16 rooms, all with private bath, 8 with
  fireplace
Rates: $90 per couple; $141 MAP per couple
Included: Continental breakfast in room
Added: $10 each additional person; $32.50 each additional
  person MAP
Payment: Visa, MasterCard
Children: Welcome
Pets: Not allowed
Smoking: Allowed
Open: All year

Warm Springs was named for its curative sources of hundred-degree natural pools, reputed to have been built by Thomas Jefferson himself. The hamlet is only several miles north of Hot Springs, home to the legendary Homestead Resort. Both Springs sit on Route 220, the westernmost road along this mountainous stretch, which rides along the valley of the Jackson River through breathtakingly beautiful farmland overlooking the lush thicket of the Washington National Forest.

The village of Warm Springs consists of a post office, several municipal buildings, a church, and the Inn at Gristmill Square. The Square is a lovely composition of five preserved 19th-century buildings centered around a gristmill that served as the town's main industry for more than two hundred years. The present mill was built in 1900 and functioned until 1970, when it was transformed into the Waterwheel Restaurant. This forms a triad across a white gravel walkway with the old blacksmith shop (now the Country Store and Office) and the old hardware store, which today houses six guest rooms. Adjacent is the Miller's House, which has four guest rooms; and across the narrow street that spans Warm Springs Mill Stream sits the elegant Steel House with four guest rooms.

The kind-hearted McWilliams family has been a proud fixture in Warm Springs since 1981, when they bought the inn from Phil Hirsch, who restored Gristmill in 1972 (he now owns the nearby Meadow Lane Lodge—see Wilderness). All the rooms are completely different, some with a sense of independence, like the outer rooms in the Steel House and Miller's

House, and some with a sense of community, like those in the old hardware store. The Steel House rooms are lovely and traditional, furnished with antiques, all with telephones, televisions, and refrigerators. The Jenny Payne Room is especially pretty, with a queen-size bed, a working fireplace, and a separate room with a tub overlooking the mountains. The Quilt Room has four antique quilts on an antique rack with a spinning wheel tucked into the corner.

Favorite rooms in the Square are the Silo Room and the Tower Apartment, with entirely round walls in their common rooms, giving it a feeling of being in the interior of a barrel. Bedrooms in each radiate off the circular living rooms, and the Tower Apartment has the advantage of a tin-roofed turret that is much fun in the rain.

The Waterwheel Restaurant is a popular attraction. The wheel was a working part of this gristmill for more than half a century and today is a functioning part of the restaurant, used to display more than 96 varieties of wine, which rest in its gears and picks. Guests trudge ritualistically down steps to select their wines. The dining rooms are intimate, dimly lit, with open-beam ceilings. Entrées range from $15 to $20 for roast duckling with oranges, tenderloin en croûte with Marsala served in a pastry shell. The smoked mountain trout is an area specialty, smoked over hickory chips and served with horseradish cream. After dinner, the impossibly small and charming Simon Kenon Pub lures the gregarious.

Hotel Strasburg

201 Holliday Street
Strasburg, Virginia 22657
703-465-9191

Proprietor: Gary Rutherford
Accommodations: 27 rooms, 4 suites in Taylor House, all with private bath
Rates: Rooms, $69–$99; suites, $149
Included: Continental breakfast on weekdays, full breakfast on weekends
Added: $10 each additional guest; 4.5% tax
Payment: Visa, MasterCard, American Express
Children: Welcome
Pets: Check with innkeeper
Smoking: Nonsmoking rooms available
Open: All year

In the northwest corner of Virginia at the top of the George Washington National Forest, the town of Strasburg is the oldest settlement in the Shenandoah Valley, a fitting place for the state's largest antiques emporium. It's a strategic tourist spot in an untouched historic town, near the Skyline Drive and Luray Caverns. Seeing a growing need for Strasburg accommodations, Leo Bernstein, owner of the historic Wayside Inn in nearby Middletown, decided to buy and restore the four-story Queen Anne Victorian in 1977. The property was recently upgraded and reopened in July 1990, still somewhat of a sleeper deserving of much attention.

The four-story white clapboard, black-shuttered building is a rectangular box on a main corner in the center of town. Columns support a second-story wrap porch. It was built in 1895 as a hospital and took on its present role as a place of dining and lodging in 1915, with many incarnations during this century. The hotel serves as a working display for the Strasburg Emporium antiques. All the formidable antique furnishings throughout the common and guest rooms are for sale, collected by the Bernstein family with care and expertise.

The guest rooms are on the second and third floors and in the adjacent colonial Taylor House, which was acquired in 1990. Each room has a list of the furnishings for sale and a description and history of the pieces. There is a wide variety of carved wood and brass beds, Victorian fringed lamps, gilded mirrors, tufted slipper chairs, now and again a stunning piece. The wallpapers and borders and colors are done in bold, heavy Victorian patterns under ten-foot ceilings. Though the rooms are roughly the same size, the third-floor rooms are set under eaves rendering a particular coziness. Half the rooms have televisions, and six suites have Jacuzzis, including the four at the Taylor House. The latter rooms are particularly interesting, with baths overlooking the stunning Shenandoah Mountains and large sitting rooms and highly decorated bedrooms.

Lunch and dinner are served daily, the latter ranging in price from $10 for chicken breast in lemon beurre blanc to $17 for tournedos zinfandel. The dining rooms are rather rustic and informal, a friendly, bustling spot with colonial spindle chairs and bare wooden flooring.

Morrison House
116 South Alfred Street
Old Town, Alexandria 22314
703-838-8000
800-367-0800
800-533-1808 in Virginia

Proprietors: Robert and Rosemary Morrison
Accommodations: 45 rooms, including 3 suites
Rates: $165–$195; suites from $250
Included: Continental breakfast, afternoon tea
Minimum stay: None
Added: $20 each additional guest; 9.5% tax
Payment: Major credit cards
Children: Welcome
Pets: Not allowed
Smoking: Nonsmoking rooms available
Open: All year

The deluxe Morrison House is an impressive undertaking for a private venture. Robert and Rosemary Morrison, longtime Washington residents, wanted to open an inn after years in real estate development and chose their site in Old Town Alexandria, five blocks from the waterfront. In 1983, they presented quite a challenge to James M. Goode, curator of architectural history at the Smithsonian, when they asked him to oversee the design that would replicate a Federal manor house. It would nestle between carefully preserved 18th-century buildings, and any inconsistencies in style would be simply out of place.

The result is quite convincing, a five-story brick house with a beautiful marble portico supported by four pillars, accessible by two curved stairways a half story above the ground. A fountain encircles a marble sculpture by local artist Miles Stanford Rolph—the only modern touch. The house sits regally behind a gold-tipped black wrought-iron fence and brick courtyard. Palladian windows and dentil cornice molding are among the convincing details.

The faithful Federal design continues throughout the interior. Guests enter the foyer of grey and white polished marble. Dentil crown molding runs throughout the house, echoed in fireplace mantels. The formal parlor has Chippendale detailing above the threshold and fireplace, lit by a crystal chandlier and sconces. The clubby library has luxurious mahogany paneling and plush red damask window treatments. Reproduction Federal furniture, hall tables, sofas, and chairs are perfectly placed in front of a backdrop of gray-green and off-white.

Upstairs are eleven rooms and a suite on each of three floors, decorated with lovely floral arrangements. The smallest are the red and rose–themed Federal rooms; the Alexandria rooms have a small sitting area, four-poster king-size bed, and nonworking fireplace. All rooms, including the suites, have mahogany armoires with terry robes, remote televisions, and telephones. The opulent baths are tiled in imported Italian marble, with double vanities and hair dryers, and nicely presented amenity baskets. Rooms are serviced with nightly turndown and chocolates, newspaper in the morning, and 24-hour room service.

The Grill is much like an English club, with red leather chairs, mahogany tables, Brazilian cherry floors, and original art. Entrées, under $20, have a hint of Tidewater influence, including Carpetbagger steak; tenderloin stuffed with Chesapeake Bay oysters wrapped in Amish bacon with an oyster cream sauce; and Powtowmack paella with game sausage, Virginia ham, lobster, fish, mussels, oysters, shrimp, and scallops in saffron rice and peas.

The staff works very hard to maintain the superb service which brought excellent ratings from Mobil and AAA. Outside is the wonderful living exhibit of 18th-century Old Town Alexandria; and at the waterfront is the Torpedo Factory, which houses a gallery of studios of more than two hundred working artists and craftspeople, as well as the laboratory of urban archaeology.

West Virginia

Bavarian Inn and Lodge
Route 1, Box 30
Shepherdstown, West Virginia 25443
304-876-2551

Proprietors: Erwin and Carol Asam
Accommodations: 42 rooms, all with balcony and private
   bath (3 in main lodge, 39 in 4 chalets)
Rates: $65–$100 weekdays; $80–$125 holidays and weekends
Minimum stay: 2 nights on some holidays
Added: $10 each additional guest; 9% tax
Payment: Major credit cards
Children: Welcome
Pets: Not allowed
Smoking: Some nonsmoking rooms
Open: All year

Those seeking an old restored house with creaky floors and well-used antiques and a Robert Frost communion with nature ought to look elsewhere. This is a place for couples who want privacy, fireplaces, deluxe accommodations, a river view from a private balcony, and hearty German food.

Owners Erwin and Carol Asam moved to the area from Washington, D.C., in 1977 with the intent of opening a small country restaurant. Four years later, they expanded their services to include overnight accommodations, which stand in the form of four chalets built, as Erwin Asam describes, in a Bavarian Alpine motif on the steep cliffs of the Potomac. The inn has received four diamonds from AAA and four stars from Mobil every year since 1984, much to the credit of the innkeepers and their staff.

Separated from Maryland by the scenic Potomac River, Shepherdstown is located in West Virginia's eastern panhandle, a lovely historic place and a college town with more than four thousand students. It was originally founded as Mecklenburg and was home to the state's oldest settlement, in 1730, comprising mostly Germans. This influence is rekindled at the Bavarian Inn, which sits on 11 acres just outside of town.

The old building, built in 1930, serves as the restaurant and is also home to three guest rooms. It is a charming fieldstone house with a steeply pitched roof etched with three dormer windows. The restaurant is fairly bustling, a great place for groups. The three-meal daily menu is extensive, specializing in Bavarian dishes as well as American and Continental cuisine. Dinners range from $11 to $20, the pride of which are offerings like sauerbraten marinated for a week with vinegar and spice brine, served with red wine ginger sauce; geschmorte rindsroulade, a roll of roast beef stuffed with bacon, onions, and pickles; and wiener, paprika, or jaeger schnitzel. Two dining rooms are sociable and expansive like a beer garden; and one is quaint with Bavarian memorabilia and history decorating the walls, colored by firelight.

The upstairs rooms are decorated quaintly with feminine linens and pretty antiques. Across the parking lot are the four chalets, each in a light stucco with dark beams revealed and dressed with Bavarian stenciling and artwork. With nine rooms per house, there is ample privacy. Each has a large bath (some have a Jacuzzi) and a private balcony overlooking the Potomac and the C&O Canal National Historic Park in Maryland. The furnishings are traditional, hotellike, with reproduction canopy beds, good lighting, hidden televisions, sitting areas, and some fireplaces. Guests are sure to find rooms spotless.

On the grounds is a pool, a tennis court, and putting green. The Nen Cress Creek Golf Course is within walking distance, and the C&O Canal has scenic paths for walkers and joggers.

The Country Inn and Renaissance Spa
Berkeley Springs, West Virginia 25411
304-258-2210
800-822-6630

Proprietors: Jack and Adele Barker
General Manager: Jim Kell
Accommodations: 66 rooms, including 3 suites, some with
 shared baths (30 rooms in old building, 36 rooms in new
 building)
Rates: $35–$105
Added: $10 each additional guest; 9% tax
Payment: Major credit cards
Children: Welcome
Pets: Not allowed
Smoking: Allowed, nonsmoking rooms available
Open: All year

The town of Berkeley Springs is located in the eastern panhandle of the state, six miles from Hancock, Maryland. Its mineral springs have summoned the healthy and wealthy for centuries. George Washington is noted to have bathed in the springs in 1748, and he returned to plant an elm tree that remains standing today. Present-day visitors can enjoy these same waters with some modern conveniences, found at the Country Inn and Renaissance Spa.

The regal main building of the Country Inn was built in 1932, a colonial design of red brick and black trim whose entrance rests under a two-story portico six columns across. Jack and Adele Barker bought the property in 1972, after he retired from his position as teacher of a boys' school and director at a boys' camp. The energetic couple made vast improvements over the years—to everyone's delight.

Quite wonderfully, the first-floor common room also serves as an art gallery. Here the work of local artists is displayed, and one can view them, in true salon form, from many comfortable couches and chairs. A fellow visitor might know how to play the 18th-century melodoon, fixed like a museum piece near the center of the room, while the less accomplished tinker on the baby grand.

The rooms on the second and third floors of the main inn are all different. The hallways are emboldened by bright red carpeting, and some of the rooms adopt the dash of color in wallpapers and upholstery, resulting in a preppy good taste. The majority of rooms have been recently redecorated to include traditional reproduction furnishings. The annex behind the main inn is a new three-story building with large hotellike rooms with color cable televisions, roomy baths, uniformly decorated with locally made oak furnishings.

Cut into the hillside behind the inn is the pride of the property, the Renaissance Spa, completed in 1987. Echoing the rotunda of the dining room, the spa hovers above the property like a glass and stone flying saucer—albeit an inconspicuous one. Inside, guests will find stress relief in three whirlpool tubs, as many massage rooms, and a beauty salon, all decorated with marble tiles in high-tech cleanliness.

The round dining room, completed in December 1990 to the left of the reception area, made way for an unusual tradition at the Country Inn: seasonal pasta dishes prepared tableside, such as fettucini Alfredo or seafood primavera, ranging from $14 to $16. Other main dishes include Continental fare such as blackened prime rib or a specialty of crabcakes. Locals love the Country Inn, a telling aspect of its hospitality, which hosts entertainment and dancing on weekends. A preamble to dining is found in an intimate lounge which looks like a speakeasy, its booths gleaming in highly lacquered wood.

Nearby Cacapon State Park has a lovely 18-hole golf course designed by Robert Trent Jones, as well as tennis, hiking, and horseback riding. A short hike up the mountain is Berkeley Castle, which bills itself as the only English Norman Castle in this country.

Historic Stops

Maryland

Historic Inns of Annapolis
16 Church Circle
Annapolis, Maryland 21401
410-263-2641
800-847-8882

Management: Grand Heritage Hotel Group
Accommodations: 138 rooms, all with private bath (44 in
    Maryland Inn, 29 in Robert Johnson House, 9 in State
    House Inn, 56 in Governor Calvert House
Rates: $100–$165, $135–$260 (seasonal)
Included: Continental breakfast (except at Maryland Inn)
Minimum stay: None
Added: $10 each additional guest; 11% tax
Payment: Major credit cards
Children: Welcome
Pets: Not allowed
Smoking: Limited
Open: All year

For a town with such a rich past, Annapolis has appropriately
historic accommodations. The Historic Inns of Annapolis are a
wonderful concept, offering the amenities of a larger hotel in
four properties within walking distance set in historic houses.

Of the four, the Maryland Inn is the most recognizable, for its
facade, which looks like a colonial version of the Flatiron
Building, and for the popular Treaty of Paris Restaurant. Built
in 1776 in a panoply of brickwork, the Maryland Inn sits on the
angular corner of Main and Duke of Gloucester streets on
Church Circle. As the two streets come together, the building
narrows to a five-sided turret on the corner. Porches and windows protrude at odd angles, and the dark-tiled mansard roof is
topped by a Victorian cupola. Guests enter a parquet marble
foyer to the hotel or through a separate entrance below to the
renowned Treaty of Paris Restaurant, the King's Wine Cellar,

and the original 1784 King of France Tavern for well-loved jazz. The four stories of sleeping rooms are undergoing a much-needed, several-million-dollar renovation.

The remaining three buildings are a block away on State Circle, the finest of which is the Governor Calvert House, built in 1727. There are 56 rooms here, most of which are in a newly built, unseen annex in the back that houses a conference center. If possible, request one of the historic front rooms, with highly polished original flooring, attenuated windows looking out to the Capitol. Guests enter at ground level, ignoring the formal entry up the grand stairway and Victorian portico to the second story. All rooms are different, with much antique furniture, Victorian curtains, armoires, and reproduction rice beds or Queen Anne headboards.

Across State Circle from the Calvert House, the 1820 State House Inn has nine rooms on three floors, above La Piccola Roma Restaurant. From State Circle, the house looks like a three-story early Federal, with a Victorianized porch at the ground level. Guests may descend a narrow set of stairs beside the house to Main Street and the Maryland Inn to view the four-story back of the building.

The Robert Johnston House, built in 1765, sits on the corner of School Street, which connects State and Church circles, with views of the Governor's Mansion and gardens from most rooms. The regal brick four-story building has a flat roof, its facade making a convex curve aligning with State Circle.

All guests enjoy full turndown service, morning newspaper, and, except at the Maryland Inn, a generous Continental breakfast of muffins, cereals, and fresh fruit. The staff is noticeably happy, helpful, and enthusiastic about their beautiful town.

The White Swan Tavern
231 High Street
Chestertown, Maryland 21620
410-778-2300

Proprietors: The Havemeyers
Innkeeper: Mary Susan Maisel
Accommodations: 2 suites, 4 rooms, all with private bath
Rates: $85–$135
Included: Continental breakfast
Minimum stay: On college weekends
Added: $25 each additional guest; 5% tax
Payment: No credit cards
Children: Welcome
Pets: Not allowed
Smoking: Allowed
Open: All year

This museum-quality restoration of a 1733 house has its own museum about the restoration process itself, which took place from April 1978 through September 1979. The two-story brick structure with a sweeping overhanging first-floor porch was originally built as a private home but served as a tavern from 1760 through the 1850s. The restoration brings the house back to these days of hospitality, roughly 1795.

There were seven thousand shards in the White Swan's restoration, making it one of the most interesting archaeological finds in colonial Maryland. Among the relics were pieces of 1790 square graywacke sandstone pavement and pre-1750 treasures such as iron fire tongs from England, a triangular clock key, a horse bit, a glass decanter stopper, a pipe bow with the seal of royal arms, and a large ale glass.

After a perusal of history, guests may either be exhausted or excited but either way will want to stay overnight in the six admirable bed-and-breakfast accommodations, all pristine, decorated with beautiful and noteworthy antiques. The White Swan is a cartologist's treasure trove, with maps of Maryland

and the eastern shore dating from the mid-18th century. At the entrance, common rooms flank the foyer. To the left is the living room, with primitive colonial tables, a 1797 map of Maryland, and maroon Federal swags over the windows; to the right is the breakfast room, formerly a game room for the tavern. This room features an incredible reproduction of an Evans desk made in colonial Williamsburg, a William and Mary walnut secretary from the 1600s, as well as fascinating maps and prints on the walls.

With a private entrance at the back of the house on the ground floor is the Thomas Lovegrove Kitchen—named for a shoemaker who worked on the site in a tannery that predated the house. The room was used as the colonial kitchen of the original tavern, has brick floooring, an open-beam ceiling with thick plaster walls, and a five-foot-wide fireplace. Antique rope double and twin beds decorate the sleeping area, along with an ancient pew table and chairs.

The romantic Sterling Suite is at the front of the house on the first floor. The bedroom is the first room, with white floral linens over a queen-size bed and a wonderful canopy matching a dressing table skirt and upholstered chair. Through double red doors is the living room, with a wing chair and huge windows overlooking Chestertown's High Street.

The Bordley and Wilmer rooms in front on the second floor are decorated in spare colonial furnishings, the latter with a 1755 French map of Maryland. At the back is the smallest, the Peacock Room, with a wonderful curved fishnet canopy bed nestled perfectly under the eaves. Last, the Eliason Suite has a hint of Victorian decor in two rooms.

Innkeeper Mary Susan Maisel is highly enthusiastic about the inn and serves a wonderful afternoon tea open to the public. Afterward, guests will want to stroll the wonderful brick sidewalks of Chestertown, visit the river, and surely dine at the Imperial Hotel (see Gourmet Getaways) across the street, known for its exceptional food and epic wine list.

New York

Athenaeum Hotel
Box 66, Chautauqua Institution
Chautauqua, New York 14722
800-821-1881

Proprietor: W. Thomas Smith
Accommodations: 160 rooms, all with private bath (48 in new
    annex, 112 in main building)
Rates: $86–$120 per person, double occupancy, AP
Included: Three meals daily
Minimum stay: None
Added: $25–$29 for Chautauqua gate ticket; 7% tax; 12% over
    $100
Payment: No credit cards
Children: Welcome
Pets: Allowed
Smoking: Not allowed in public areas
Open: Mid-June through August

Squeezed into the southwest corner of New York's 47,400 square
miles sits Lake Chautauqua and the cultural enclave which
bears its name, a sleepy community of less than five hundred
which swells to thousands during the summer. Methodist Sunday school teachers first sought intellectual refuge here in 1874,
and the tradition of cultural enrichment continues today from
late June through August with programs at the Chautauqua
Institution. The village is cluttered with teetering, gingerbreaded, brightly colored houses on narrow streets meant more
for strolling than for driving.

It is fitting that the place to stay here is the grandest piece of
Victorian architecture within the Chautauqua gates, the palatial Athenaeum Hotel, built in 1881 and commendably restored
in 1984 by the present manager, W. Thomas Smith. The exterior
is one of the grandest in this book. From the lakefront, the
lawns sweep up to a double staircase embracing a fountain,
which reaches a two-storied portico spanning the length of the
grand building, outfitted with green wicker rockers. At the
center above the third floor is an immense mansard-roofed
cupola with floor-to-ceiling Palladian windows on four sides,
topped by a flag. The centerpiece Chautauqua amphitheater is
just steps behind the hotel.

The lobby is two stories high, lit by Victorian brass chandeliers with etched globes, diagonal wainscoted wood, and rich
exposed flooring. The ballroom-size common room is full of
creamy wicker furniture, with double floor-to-ceiling windows
shaded in lace overlooking the lake, all complemented by a
latticework floral Victorian area carpet. The dining room is
brightened by grandmotherly floral paper with white linen
cloths covering tables, Queen Anne chairs, and polished
wooden floors. At the Athenaeum, everyone is on the full

American plan and is treated to its hallmark of two desserts with lunch and dinner.

The second- and third-floor rooms all have very high ceilings, twin beds, Victorian antiques and wallpapers, and, just recently, private baths. They are simple and tidy, with different accommodations for families, doubles, and singles. The rooms are configured in a square, in the center of which is an outdoor patio on the second floor, with wicker furniture, slatted flooring, latticework, and a gazebo, decorated with an abundance of plants.

There is an overwhelming insider feeling here, as most of the staff and guests are Chautauqua veterans, happy and relaxed. No visit is complete without a visit to the institution's bookstore.

Old Drovers Inn
Dover Plains, New York 12522
914-832-9311

Proprietors: Alice Pitcher and Kemper Peacock
Accommodations: 4 rooms, all with private bath, 3 with
    fireplace
Rates: Week nights: $90–$150; weekends: $110–$170
Included: Full breakfast
Minimum stay: 2 nights on holidays, in October, and on May
    weekends
Added: $25 each additional guest; 12.25% tax
Payment: Visa, MasterCard, Diners Club
Children: Welcome
Pets: Allowed (dogs by prior arrangement)
Smoking: Allowed
Open: All year

Old Drovers Inn is due east of Poughkeepsie, shouldering Kent, Connecticut, and the Berkshire foothills. It sits on 12 acres neighboring Old Route 22, which at one time was the main thoroughfare between Bennington, Vermont, and New York City. The inn was named for its clientele, rowdy drovers who herded cattle and swine down the main thoroughfare to sell downstate.

Restored as an inn as early as 1937 by Olin Chester Potter, Old Drovers has enjoyed great fluctuations in reputation. Its latest incarnation is the finest in years, under the guidance of Alice Pitcher and Kemper Peacock, summoned by the charms of the 260-year-old house from Nantucket and Westport, Connecticut, in 1989. As innkeepers, they are consummate emissaries of history.

The dining room on the ground floor of the inn is a most enchanting spot. The ceiling of the dark Tap Room is made of exposed logs, the walls of original stone. Two rooms are separated by a huge hearth with brass guards, one room with chairs in aristocratic tooled leather, the other with elegant banquettes. Charlie Wilbur has stooped in the six-foot space for twenty-six years as the host of the restaurant, which serves lunch and dinner. The latter menu changes every six weeks but always includes the Inn's famous Cheddar cheese soup and possibly lobster and corn chowder or lamb and parmesan sausage with wilted greens and sherry vinaigrette. Entrées range from $15 to $27 for double cut rack lamb chops with Charlie's tomato chutney. Other dishes might include pepper-crusted sirloin with potato blue cheese gratin or sautéed paillards of duck with fresh mango and red onion jam.

Upstairs, the inn's floors are endearingly buckled with age. The main sitting room has a marble and stone fireplace over which hangs an old musket. A second common room has Lafayette green paneling; and the library has three walls filled with volumes of wonderful reading and accommodating down chairs and sofas. An original inset shell cabinet, which mirrored another in the second common room, is now on display at the Metropolitan Museum of Art.

Three of the four guest rooms upstairs have working fireplaces. The Meeting Room, which functioned as such for the town until 1840, is memorable, with an incredible barrel-vaulted ceiling arching high over two double beds, a fireplace, charming chintz-covered wing chairs, and dark wide-plank flooring. The Sleigh and the Cherry rooms have authentic colonial paneling, fireplaces, and clawfoot tubs.

Guests take breakfast in the fabulous Federal Room on the first floor surrounded by four walls of hand-painted murals done in 1941 by Edward Paine, depicting Old Drovers, West Point, Hyde Park, and a Dover Plains barn. There is also a patio with wrought-iron furniture for outdoor dining.

Sagamore Lodge
Sagamore Road
Raquette Lake, New York 13436
315-354-5311

Proprietor: Sagamore Institute, Beverly Bridger, director
Accommodations: 45 rooms in 29 buildings for 60–75 guests
Rates: $68–$85 per person AP; weekend programs, $195 per
  person AP
Included: Three meals daily
Minimum stay: For some weekend packages
Payment: Visa, MasterCard
Children: Welcome
Pets: Not allowed
Smoking: Not allowed
Open: Summer through Thanksgiving

Sagamore is an Indian word for "wise chief," a fitting name for
a place which has, since 1973, served as a unique intellectual
retreat. Propped on the resortlike setting of Raquette Lake in
the western part of the Adirondack Forest Preserve, the Sagamore Lodge is one of the few remaining Great Camps built at
the turn of the century by William West Durant—one of an
even smaller few accessible to the public. Not to be confused
with the Sagamore Resort owned by Omni Hotels in Lake
George, this Sagamore was built in 1897 for the Vanderbilt
family, a recreational home for upscale "roughing it."

Raquette Lake rests halfway between Old Forge, the westernmost access into the Adirondack Forest Preserve (and
famous for its wonderful hardware store), and Blue Mountain
Lake, home to the renowned Adirondack Museum. A four mile
dirt road from main Adirondack Route 28 brings a visitor to
Sagamore Lodge. Its vast acreage is comprised of 27 original
buildings which were erected from 1897–1930. Sagamore is set
up like a northern plantation with every building serving a
single purpose: a blacksmith shop, a woodshed, an icehouse, a
school house, a men's chalet, and even a bowling alley. Nearly
half the land is devoted to service buildings and servant quarters, a sizeable amount except when one discovers that ser-
vants outnumbered guests six to one.

A Sagamore weekend is spent in accomplishment: guests
enrol in specific programs, like the Adirondack weekend,
mountain biking, Adirondack geology, north country wildflowers, fly fishing, or llama trekking. There are craft programs, like tapestry weaving, blacksmithing, and wood carving. There are storytelling and landscape photography on
weekends. Especially pertinent are the Adirondack history
weekends, including a great estates tour. Weekends include
three meals daily in the beautiful woody dining hall, as well as
full use of the Sagamore facilities.

The classic Adirondack architecture is characterized by

rough-looking logs still clothed in bark, bent-twig railings and support beams, wide, low-pitched roofs sturdy enough to hold heavy amounts of snow, and fireplaces of large, quarried stone. There are no great creature comforts here except in the intellectual satisfaction of residing in unaltered history and aesthetic beauty. Accommodations are authentic but rustic, in several lodges. The rooms are furnished with original Adirondack furniture, twin beds covered with thick plaid wool blankets, and shared hall baths.

Tours are conducted twice daily (except Wednesdays) in summers, weekends only through Columbus Day. A good number of craftspeople reside at Sagamore, including rustic furniture maker Jackson Smith and blacksmith John Breed. Twenty miles of carved skiing and hiking trails lace through the property, and canoeing and fishing are offered on Raquette Lake.

Pennsylvania

Century Inn
Route 40
Scenery Hill, Pennsylvania 15360
412-945-6600
412-945-5180

Proprietors: Megin and Gordon Harrington
Accommodations: 7 rooms
Rates: $75–$125
Included: Breakfast
Added: 6% tax
Payment: No credit cards
Children: Welcome
Pets: Not allowed
Smoking: Allowed
Open: Mid-March to mid-December

A nice stop between Pittsburgh and Morgantown, Scenery Hill is a minuscule hamlet on top of a hill outside Washington, Pennsylvania. The fieldstone brick house, on the National Register of Historic Places, was built in 1794 on the Nemacolin Indian Trail, which was traversed by a pre-presidential George Washington and his militia during the French and Indian Wars. The road became better known as the National Pike (today's U.S. 40), which joined the eastern seaboard to the open western frontier. It still feels as such here in the Monongahela Valley, hardy and untrodden, with glimpses of villages every 20 miles or so.

The stone inn looks blanched by winds over the years, the first floor protected by an overhanging porch supported by six pillars. Five small colonial windows peek out from the second floor under three dormer windows cut into the slate roof. Guests enter the foyer into three dining rooms: an intimate room by the foyer with a fireplace hung with ancient kitchen utensils, a cozy main dining room decorated in warm maroons and flowers with exposed fieldstone walls, and a back porch protected by a green awning with vistas to hilly backyards. Breakfast is available to guests, but lunch and dinner are served daily, with latter entrees ranging from $10 to $24. An appetizer might be a famous peanut soup, and a sampling of entrées include chicken croquettes, turkey Devonshire, Virginia ham with raisin sauce, and chicken Jackson, a breast stuffed with scallops and lobster.

While waiting for a table, be sure to visit the parlor to the right of the foyer in which is displayed a flag from the Whiskey Rebellion as well as Monongahela glasswork. The walls throughout the inn have become a canvas for tracings designed by Moses Eaton, one of the first recognized stencilers of the early 19th century.

The seven rooms upstairs are very charming, decorated in colonial simplicity, with memorably papered walls and a variety of antiques from different periods collected over the years by Dr. and Mrs. Gordon Harrington, who bought the inn in 1945 and are the parents-in-law of owner Megin Harrington. Tom the Tinker is an especially charming room with two impossibly small twin beds covered in different blue-patterned antique quilts, floweret paper above the chair rail and Williamsburg prints on the walls. The Dolley Madison Room is always open to public view, seemingly a guest room but rather a museum to children, teeming with dolls and their furniture, antique toys and carriages.

Noted guests aside from present visitors were Andrew Jackson in 1824 and again two years later en route to his inaugural, and General LaFayette, who breakfasted here in 1825.

Virginia

Colonial Houses & Taverns
Post Office Box C
Williamsburg, Virginia 23187
1-800-HISTORY

Proprietors: Colonial Williamsburg Foundation
Accommodations: 84 rooms in 26 buildings, from 1 to 4
  bedrooms
Rates:
  Low season: $99–$139
  High season: $197–$296
  2–4 bedrooms: $242–$458
Added: 8.5% tax
Payment: Major credit cards
Children: Welcome
Pets: Not allowed
Smoking: Nonsmoking rooms available
Open: All year

There is nothing like Colonial Williamsburg, an unreal mixture of historically accurate 17th-century and corporate 20th-century America. More than a million visitors each year travel to this magical place and peruse the 800 acres of history. Its varying accommodations total more than 250 rooms from a budgetary $29 to upwards of $197 for five-star treatment. The most authentic place to stay in Williamsburg are the Colonial Houses and Taverns. The 84 rooms in 26 buildings around the historic complex successfully imitate a bed-and-breakfast environment in the restored and reconstructed houses of Colonial Williamsburg.

Despite its endless attention to historic accuracy, Williamsburg is a mastery of artifice. The graveled drives, the one hundred men and women who ply more than thirty trades here—from blacksmith to tanner—all look convincingly old but suspiciously new. Either a wand was waved over a town asleep for three hundred years or you were transported backward in time. However, just as a visitor begins to believe the magic, it's back to the hotel room, with remote television, king-size beds, room service, and showers.

The colonial houses contain these modern amenities, but in the context of the historic houses themselves—cottages with wide-planked flooring, canopy beds, fireplaces, traditional furniture, and decor—so the feeling of colonial life is somewhat continued into the evening. The houses range in size to accommodate from two to twelve people in rather enchanting properties mixed into the historic setting. Some are two-story adorable suites for two, some larger taverns, some with fireplaces and full kitchens. All are decorated meticulously, with antiques and faithful Williamsburg reproductions. Interestingly, a piece of reproduction furniture is not taken from an Ethan Allen warehouse: it is hand-crafted by a historically trained artisan, upholstered by another, placed in a room with paint matched to the history books and wallpaper designed after its ancient cousin.

Of course, guests can enjoy all the wonders of Williamsburg: the two golf courses, one designed by Robert Trent Jones, one completed in 1991, the acclaimed food, tennis, pool, exercise equipment, and the endless perks of resort living.

Martha Washington Inn
150 West Main Street
Abingdon, Virginia 24210
703-628-3161
800-533-1014

Proprietors: United Company, Jim McGlothlin, president
General Manager: Deborah Bourne
Accommodations: 61 rooms, 11 suites
Rates:
   Regular: $75–$85
   Deluxe: $105–$125
   Suites: $145–$250
Added: $10 each additional guest; 4.5% tax
Payment: Major credit cards
Children: Welcome
Pets: Not allowed
Smoking: Nonsmoking rooms available
Open: All year

People come to Abingdon rather continuously from April through December to see performances at the famous Barter Theater, the country's longest-running Equity theater. It is so named because during the Depression, when the theater was founded, the price of a ticket was "35 cents or the equivalent in produce." When people come to the Barter Theater, they can stay at the historic Martha Washington Inn, conveniently across the street.

It's quite fascinating to find this bastion of culture here in Virginia's southwest corner, 14 miles from North Carolina off Interstate 81, 9 miles from Emory University in Atlanta. Abingdon is nestled in a narrow but lofty valley with an elevation of 2,000 feet, between the Appalachian and Blue Ridge mountains.

The inn was built in 1832 as a lavish private residence. In 1858 Martha Washington College bought the building, which doubled as a hospital during the Civil War. The Depression took its toll and the college was closed in 1932, but the building was reopened as a hotel three years later, given the new popularity of the Barter Theater. More recently, the hotel underwent a nine-million-dollar renovation, received with rave reviews in 1986.

A grand single-story veranda runs the length of the brick facade, supported by pillars, draped with flags, topped by a green shingled mansard roof. Flanking the main inn are two Greek Revival wings four pillars wide, which were built when the hotel first opened to resemble the Barter Theater.

The interior is as elegant as the exterior promises, especially, if you can get in, the private Presidents Club and Epicurean Club. The First Lady's Dining Room is a stupendous space, its pressed tin ceiling supported by faux wood-grain columns. The wooden bar is gorgeous, set off by the green Queen Anne chairs. The treasurelike silver dining table in the center is fifty years old, found in a box during the 1986 restoration. There are twelve Waterford crystal chandeliers, bought originally for $11 each. The murals in the grand foyer are replicas of those used by Jacqueline Kennedy when she redecorated the White House, painted in France and made into wallpaper, depicting scenes of colonial America and national sights including nearby Natural Bridge.

While all the rooms are configured differently, they have a unique and very pleasing decor for a luxury hotel: the beds are dressed with plain duvets with printed skirts matching curtains, with a distant Chinese influence. The furniture is a mixture of reproductions and excellent antiques, and the baths are beautifully appointed with green marble. Luxury amenities include nightly turndown and room service.

Nearby outdoor activities are found in Mount Rogers National Recreation Area (which peaks at 5,700 feet), nearby Holston Lake, or the ubiquitous Appalachian Trail nine miles south. The Virginia Creeper Trail, once a railway between Abingdon and Whitetop Mountain, is now a 34-mile-long scenic pathway, good for hiking, biking, and skiing.

The Red Fox Inn and Mosby's Tavern

2 East Washington Street, P.O. Box 385
Middleburg, Virginia 22117
703-687-6301
703-478-1808 in Washington, D.C.
800-223-1728 outside Virginia

Proprietor: Turner Reuter, Jr.
Accommodations: 19 rooms (6 in main inn, 8 in Stray Fox, 5 in McConnell House)

Rates: $125–$225
Included: Continental breakfast served in room
Added: $25 for a cot; $10 for a crib; 6.5% tax
Payment: Major credit cards
Children: Welcome
Pets: Not allowed
Smoking: Allowed
Open: All year

This favorite retreat for Washingtonians, an hour's drive west, is best known for its wonderful food. Built by Joseph Chinn in 1728, the Red Fox is one of the oldest original inns in the country. It was a convenient stopping point between Alexandria and Winchester, and such a valuable and strategic plot of land that it was sold to the town for $2.50 an acre in the late 18th century. While always an inn, what was then called the Beveridge House served as temporary headquarters for the Confederates during the Civil War, as well as a hospital. The pine service bar used today was made from a field operating table in General Stuart's cavalry.

The inn comprises three buildings, as well as the new Mosby's Tavern for groups and functions. The main building is an important-looking blanched four-story fieldstone. Two mullioned bay windows overlook the street, astride a porticoed entrance. The fourth floor has four dormer windows cut into a tin roof. Behind the Red Fox, the Stray Fox was built in the early 1800s as an inn—familiarly referred to as the Stray Shot for the time during the Civil War when an errant cannonball hit its foundation. Across the path, the McConnell House is a robin's egg blue pill box home, built for a dentist at the early part of this century and adopted into the Red Fox complex in 1985.

Rooms in the Red Fox are decorated in a spare colonial style. While all have televisions, telephones, and private baths, most have working original fireplaces and four-poster canopy beds. The original flooring is charmingly warped. Preferable are rooms in the Stray Fox, for their decor and lack of street noise. Here the walls and floors are stenciled and the rooms have more of a country feel. The McConnell House rooms are even a little larger, as the house is more contemporary, three of the five rooms having fireplaces and canopy beds. A majority of the rooms have hand-held showers.

There are seven dining rooms throughout the Red Fox, two on the ground level and five on the second floor. Deep and original stone fireplaces contain ongoing roaring fires. The exposed hand-hewn beams on the ceiling, thick plaster walls, and spindle-back chairs contribute to the authentic colonial atmosphere. Lunch and dinner are served daily, the latter a festive and bustling affair. Entrées range from $15 to $23 for hearty colonial meals, including grilled medallions of elk with fresh pear sauce and foie gras, grilled venison loin with cinnamon cream sauce and wild rice pancakes, or, for a change of pace, Louisiana bayou gumbo. Guests must try the Red Fox peanut soup, a Virginia tradition, or the pub Cheddar soup.

The former Stray Fox stables were rebuilt in 1983 to serve as the Red Fox Fine Art Gallery, which displays 19th-century paintings and sculpture, some of which are on permanent display on the dining room walls in the inn. Outside the charming town is horse country, so try to slate a stay at the Red Fox during race season.

Wayside Inn
7783 Main Street
Middletown, Virginia 22645
703-869-1797

Proprietor: Richard Bernstein
Manager: Maggie Edwards
Accommodations: 22 rooms, all with private bath, including 6 deluxe rooms
Rates: $70–$125
Added: $10 each additional guest; 6.5% tax
Payment: All credit cards except Discover
Children: Welcome (under 16 free)
Pets: Not allowed
Smoking: Allowed
Open: All year

One can't help be reminded of the Red Fox at the Wayside Inn—even the names of the towns are similar. Here, Larrick's Tavern dates to 1724, though most of the inn was built in 1740, finally opening as a stop on the stagecoach route from Winchester down the Shenandoah Valley in 1797. Like the Red Fox, the Wayside served as a hospital during the Civil War, though it sided contrarily with Union troops and served as Union headquarters in 1862 and 1864. Here the differences begin.

The Bernsteins, who bought the property in 1960, are avid antiques collectors. They also own the Strasburg Emporium of Antiques, the state's largest antiques market. Their wide-ranging taste is displayed throughout the Wayside Inn, and resultingly most pieces are available for purchase. The inn's decor is an eclectic mixture of colonial, Chippendale, Victorian, and European pieces with a museum of results, all set on Oriental carpets.

The guest rooms are accessible from two different stairways, on the second and third floors. Some are smaller and cozy, while some of the state rooms and suites are expansive and decorator-designed. Whatever the size, they all have lovely antiques from different periods: a neoclassic French armoire and bedroom set with Egyptian influences; another with Queen Anne chairs in pink damask; four-poster colonial beds as well as king-size reproductions, with Victorian and art deco lamps. Amid all the antiques, each room has a remote television and private phone. The baths are pretty, with floral curtains.

The three dining rooms are wonderful, open spaces. A favorite room is the low-ceilinged slave quarters, chock full of colonial utensils and relics from the inn's early days around the stone hearth. Lunch and dinner are served daily from a faithful country Virginia menu, with ham, peanut soup, and game in informal family style.

The staff is very personable and welcoming at the Wayside. Just being a short distance from Washington is enough to slow down the pace impressively. Several miles away is Front Royal, the gateway to the Skyline Drive and the Shenandoah Valley. Farther south are the Luray Caverns and the George Washington National Forest, with endless hiking and skiing activities. A short drive east to Strasburg off I-81 will please any antiques buff.

Woodstock Hall

Route 3, Box 40 (located on Route 637)
Charlottesville, Virginia 22901
804-293-8977

Proprietors: Jean Wheby and Mary Ann Elder
Innkeeper: Joe and Adrian Consylman
Accommodations: 4 rooms, all with private bath and fireplace
Rates: $95–$130, $15 less on January weekdays
Included: Gourmet breakfast and afternoon tea
Minimum stay: Some weekends
Added: $25 each additional guest; 6.5% tax
Payment: None
Children: 8 and over welcome
Pets: Not allowed
Smoking: Not allowed
Open: Year-round except during Christmas week

Woodstock Hall sits on a hill overlooking untouched rolling fields, as does its neighbor, Monticello, Thomas Jefferson's home, on a much larger scale. In fact, regal foreign dignitaries in Jefferson's day would spend several days at Monticello, make the carriage ride several miles across Charlottesville, and rest overnight at Mr. Woods's tavern before embarking on a tour of the Shenandoah Valley.

This faithful restoration sits two miles into the countryside off I-64. The house is really two houses, a 1757 section built by local surveyor Richard Woods, who ran an overnight hostelry, and an 1808 Federal half, which made the building a regal homestead. The house is known for being the least altered, oldest extant structure in Ablemarle County (including Charlottesville). Ninety percent of the glass in the house is original; all else is entirely preserved, from the flooring to sashes to mantels to hardware and stairs.

The Elder family, proprietors of Woodstock Hall, also own the 1740 House antiques shop in Charlottesville and are internationally recognized for the quality of their collections. As a result, Woodstock Hall is treated much like a museum, a gallery for the finest antiques in two distinct periods. The 1808 front of the house looks out on present Route 637; the colonial facade in the back looks onto where the main road used to be. The Federal section houses the award-winning parlor, which is furnished and decorated entirely in period antiques, with beautiful window treatments, furniture, and every detail. Guests take afternoon tea here, a thorough presentation prepared by innkeeper Joe Consylman. The Federal Room rests on the second floor above the parlor and is decorated similarly in flawless period detail.

The colonial section at the back of the house has an entirely different look, more primitive than formal. The blue check parquet floor in the dining room was the former tavern and would have been appropriate to the period. Here, guests take a full gourmet breakfast in the morning. Joe is a wonderful cook and a typical meal is shirred eggs with hollandaise and home-baked danish. Upstairs are two colonial rooms: the Richard Woods Room, whose bath has gorgeous views of the two-hundred-year-old sycamores in the backyard, and the Duc Liancourt Room, named after a notable who raved about Mr. Woods's tavern in 1796 after a stay at Monticello.

The kitchen quarters, built in 1808, rest in a detached brick building next to the house, a low two-story structure among Joe's gardens, overlooking the pastures. Though Federal, the kitchen is decorated in more of a country primitive style, with a sitting room and a bedroom—a very romantic hideaway with a fireplace. From the backyard, guests survey the six acres of land, the footbridge and gazebo, and beautiful farmland flecked with cows.

Seaside Stops

Maryland

Coconut Malorie
60th Street in the Bay
Ocean City, Maryland 21842
410-723-6100
Reservations: 800-767-6060

Proprietors: John and Denise Fager
General Manager: Angela Reynolds
Accommodations: 84 suites
Rates:
   1-bedroom and studio suites: $79–$179
   Penthouse suites: $149–$199
   Presidential suites: $180–$350
Minimum stay: 2 nights on weekends, 3 nights on holidays
Added: $15 each additional guest, including children; 8% tax
Payment: Major credit cards
Children: Welcome
Pets: Not allowed
Smoking: Allowed
Open: All year

The Coconut Malorie, the sister property of the Lighthouse Club (see Romantic Retreats), is the premier hotel in Ocean City, a nine-mile peninsula of beach on Maryland's brief Atlantic shore, sandwiched between Delaware to the north and Virginia to the south. Due west several hundred yards from the Atlantic are the Isle of Wight and Assawoman bays and it is here, perched on these calm shores, that the Coconut Malorie sits, on a bit of marshland developed by John and Denise Fager. It's the closest thing to a Caribbean vacation west of the Caribbean.

The Coconut Malorie is a rectangular baby blue building, on the outside identified tersely by the word "Hotel," a grave understatement in this town teeming with undistinguished properties. This 84-suite luxury hotel was modeled after the Grand Hyatt in the Cayman Islands, with a definite Caribbean feel. The owners have invested much research, care, and finances in the extensive collection of Haitian art which thoroughly decorates the hotel.

Though the outside looks a bit garish, the hotel's interior is in luxuriously good taste, filled with impressive original art, cool, contemporary decor, and wonderful marble. The two-story lobby has a terraced fountain, and hand-quarried Greek blond and green marble offers fine acoustics for the grand piano played nightly. A pair of 18th-century Manchurian wall specimens loiter on stairs, which lead up to the great deck and pool overlooking the bay. Elevators are especially lovely, with green marble and mahogany walls.

There are five floors of studios and one-bedroom suites, all with portallike observation terraces, some with views of the ocean, most of the bay. The decor, as at the Lighthouse Club, was specially designed for the hotel to give a sandy beachy Caribbean feel, fresh, clean, neutral colors for linens and drapes and either light or dark rattan furniture and clean white-tiled floors. All rooms have televisions, wet bars, microwaves and kitchens, telephones, and luxurious marbled baths with phones, hair dryers, full amenities from Saks Fifth Avenue, plush terry robes, and Jacuzzis. The cathedral-ceiling penthouse rooms offer all this plus nightly turndown, Continental breakfast, and newspapers. Room service is available from Fager's Restaurant.

Be sure to ask about the configuration of the rooms: the upper-floor rooms have a thorough view of Ocean City, one side the ocean, the other the bay. As the hotel gets wider at its base, the first-room floors have only a bay view from the living room and an oddly placed window to the hallway in the bedroom. New tower additions of the library and art gallery provide wonderful views of the city and ocean.

New Jersey

The Abbey
Columbia Avenue and Gurney Street
Cape May, New Jersey 08204
609-884-4506

Proprietors: Jay and Marianne Schatz
Accommodations: 14 rooms (7 in Villa, 7 in Cottage), all with
   private bath
Rates: $80–$175
Included: Full breakfast, afternoon refreshments
Minimum stay: 3 or 4 nights June–September and most
   weekends
Added: 7% tax
Payment: Visa, MasterCard, American Express
Children: Over 12 welcome
Pets: Not allowed
Smoking: Not allowed
Open: Mid-April to mid-December

Cape May, on New Jersey's southern tip, is a glorious seaside
town with the largest concentration of Victorian architecture in
the Mid-Atlantic outside Chautauqua, New York. One of the
more whimsical buildings here is the Abbey, a mint-colored,
three-story Gothic Revival structure decorated profusely with
gingerbread and clerestory windows, rarefied by a four-story,
60-foot tower at its corner entrance. It was built in 1869 for a
wealthy Philadelphia coal baron named John McCreary.

   The Abbey main house, or Villa, was bought in 1979 by Jay
and Marianne Schatz when they retired from careers in chem-
istry to start a bed-and-breakfast. In 1986, the Schatzes acquired
the adjacent property, the Cottage, built in 1873 by McCreary's
son George as a neighboring family summer home. The narrow
Second Empire house, with a convex red mansard roof on its
third story, doubled the seven rooms of the Villa, echoing its
colors.

   Jay and Marianne have collected beautiful antiques over the
years and have displayed them throughout the two houses. In
addition to antiques, the owners found ornate and impressive
period reproduction wallpapers from Bradbury and Bradbury
which hang like artwork on the walls and even the ceilings of
the formal parlors and dining room. Some of the plaster medallions are original to the house, and the brass gasoliers and
fixtures are from the period. Around the front parlor is a Herter
Brothers–style three-piece parlor set from 1860, of gilded rosewood of the same period as the walnut secretary. Musicians will
appreciate the square mahogany grand piano from 1850 and
the Swiss harp. In the back parlor is a set of freestanding bookshelves from 1870, viewed from a Renaissance Revival parlor
set, inlaid in highly crafted satinwood and fruitwood.

The guest rooms, on the second and third floor of the Villa and throughout three floors of the Cottage, are named for cities. The rooms are all vastly different, yet throughout is an impressive continuity of showroom antiques. The bathrooms are nicely sized for a Victorian house: some nearly rooms unto themselves, others cleverly created from tiny closets. The second floor of the tower has a charming nook of a room, two sides of tall, double arched windows. Those wishing for extra privacy might like one of the Cottage rooms, a favorite being the Nantucket Room under the third-floor eaves with a many-sided bathroom with a shower and clawfoot tub.

Afternoon tea is a grand tradition in Cape May, during which time Jay and Marianne are happy to chat with guests. Their long tenure in Cape May has made them well versed in all areas of this town, from history to local events. Breakfasts are full, over the 1862 banquet table. The town center is just two blocks away, the beach a block in the other direction.

Captain Mey's Bed and Breakfast Inn

202 Ocean Street
Cape May, New Jersey 08204
609-884-7793

Proprietors: Carin Feddermann and Milly LaCanfora
Manager: Robin Feddermann
Accommodations: 9 rooms, 6 with private bath
Rates: $75–$155
Included: Full breakfast
Minimum stay: 3 or 4 nights May–October
Added: $25 each additional guest; 7% tax
Payment: MasterCard, Visa
Children: Over 10 welcome
Pets: Not allowed
Smoking: Not allowed
Open: All year

The town of Cape May was so named for the Dutch West India representative who discovered its shores in 1621, Captain Cornelius J. Mey. A charming bed-and-breakfast several houses from town is more directly named for this explorer, a tribute to the Victorian times in which the town first flourished and to its early Dutch history. Innkeeper Carin Feddermann and her daughter Robin are quite proud of their own Dutch heritage, which is prominently and creatively displayed throughout the inn. Carin and partner Millie LaCanfora have owned the inn since 1979 and are the inspiration for one of the busiest, most festive weekends of the year, the Cape May Tulip Festival, during which the town explodes in color like a New World Holland.

The three-story American shingle Victorian was built in 1890, its clapboard painted a neutral ecru set off by teal and maroon trim. The third floor has four dormers set into its roof facing four directions. As deceptively regular as the house seems from its exterior, the interior is a whimsical collage of Victorian and Dutch influences. Carin and Millie's delft blue china collection is quite impressive, from elaborate figures to porcelain to the tiling in the fireplaces. In faithful Dutch custom, Persian rugs lie on the dining room table and are draped on stair rails to keep out drafts.

The nine guest rooms are named for Dutch rulers such as Queen Beatrix, poet William the Silent, and Prince William of Orange. Each quite busy, the rooms have Schumacher wallpaper everywhere, on walls and ceilings, in large floral prints. The windows are dressed with bold material often matching linens or bed skirting, paneled in Dutch imported lace. Mannequins dressed in Victorian finery secure hallways and landings. Though three rooms share one third-floor bath, it is a great room, with an 1870 wicker pram and a nursery full of Victorian toys. There is even a wicker sitting area in the bath under wainscoted walls. It is a plentiful, busy atmosphere, feminine, and very clean.

The common room is cozy, decorated with a set of Victorian chairs and settee. Around the room is the original parlor glass double doors, leading to the chestnut oak Eastlake paneling in the dining room, where full country breakfasts are served featuring Holland cheeses. Millie and Carin are great ambassadors for Cape May, extremely active in their community, and guests are treated like welcome dignitaries.

The Chalfonte Hotel

301 Howard Street
Cape May, New Jersey 08204
609-884-8409

Proprietors: Anne LeDuc and Judy Bartella
Accommodations: 103 rooms, most with shared baths
Rates: $73–145 per couple MAP
Included: Full breakfast, full southern dinner
Minimum stay: 2 nights on weekends
Added: $25 each additional guest; $3–$15 each child in room
    with parents; 7% tax; $6 gratuity

Payment: Visa, MasterCard
Children: Welcome
Pets: Not allowed
Smoking: Allowed in public rooms
Open: Memorial Day to Columbus Day

The Chalfonte is renowned for two reasons: it's the best deal in Cape May and the meals are legendary. Don't expect the glamour of the other Cape May bed-and-breakfasts. The Chalfonte is bare bones boarding, with shared baths along long hallways, sparely decorated rooms with a double bed or two, an in-room sink, with very little in chintz or lace. Though it may seem rather uncharacteristic for a Cape May hostelry not to have museum-quality antiques, Chalfonte fixture Eldred Morris explains thoughtfully that when the Victorians came to the shore, their customs were closer to the Chalfonte way than to the luxurious elegance of the local bed-and-breakfasts. The elegant furniture and ceiling wallpapers belonged in their Philadelphia and New York City homes; their vacation houses were spare and functional.

From the outside, the Chalfonte looks as regal as do its Cape May neighbors. Colonel Henry Sawyer, Civil War hero, built the Chalfonte in 1876 and oversaw its daily activities for seventeen years. The hotel was bought by Virginian Susan Satterfield in 1910 and remained in her family until 1980, when the present owners took over. Its three stories of white clapboard are shuttered in green, with its first two levels covered in elaborate gingerbreaded porches and verandas. It even has an accessible cupola with four views from arched windows looking to town and to the ocean. Inside, the Chalfonte is spare, simple wood and home to the oft-visited King Edward Bar.

For more than seventy years until 1990, the meals were orchestrated by the saintly Helen Dickerson, who proudly presided over the Chalfonte's kitchen. Her daughters Dorothy and Lucille have inherited her silver spoon, and Helen's spirit lives on through their cooking and the large, bustling dining room which came into its own during her reign. Included in the rates are a huge Virginia breakfast of spoonbread, biscuits, muffins, eggs, fish, and fruit and a hearty southern dinner with a choice of three entrées. The four-course dinner is accompanied by homemade relishes, soups, rolls, vegetables, salads, fruit compotes, and desserts. The menu changes with the day of the week: Monday's menu may include turkey with Virginia ham and oyster dressing or fried scallops with cornmeal breading; Tuesday is herbed roast leg of lamb with mint sauce or deviled crab à la Chalfonte; Thursday could include seafood Newburg or roast pork with apple dressing. In a solution that satisfies all parties, children six and under eat in their own supervised dining room.

The Chalfonte hosts a wonderful tradition each year, volunteer work weekends in exchange for room and board, at the beginning and end of the season. Other in-season themes have prevailed over the years, including quilting, rug hooking, and watercolor workshops, two weeks in July and August devoted to children's activities, a mystery weekend, and a Gilbert and Sullivan weekend. There is a lighthearted friendliness about the Chalfonte, like a college reunion or similar convivial event. Those who warm to the rustic informality of the Chalfonte return for generations.

Conover's Bay Head Inn Bed and Breakfast

646 Main Avenue
Bay Head, New Jersey 08742
908-892-4664

Proprietors: Carl, Beverly, and Tim Conover
Accommodations: 12 rooms, all with private bath
Rates: $75–$110 low season; $80–$165 summer
Included: Full breakfast
Minimum stay: 2 nights on weekends, 3 nights on holidays
Added: $30 each additional guest; 7% tax
Payment: Visa, MasterCard, American Express
Children: Check with innkeepers
Pets: Not allowed
Smoking: Not allowed
Open: All year

One of the oldest bed-and-breakfasts on the Jersey shore looks like its newest thanks to the perpetual work of its proprietors, the Conover family, who opened their home to the public way back in 1970. Having recently installed gleaming private baths into the six third-floor rooms and replaced the common room rugs with a beautiful Victorian carpet, Conover's seems as if it opened its doors for the first time.

Beverly is responsible for the splendor of the 12 guest rooms. The antique beds here look like they are from a decorator's showroom, their matching and complementary linens from Ralph Lauren, Laura Ashley, Mario Buatta, and Jennifer Moore all hand-ironed. Balloon shades and window treatments match the skirting or comforters of the beds, echoed in a window seat or throw pillow. Lovely antiques decorate the rooms with different results: a matching oak bedroom set in one, pineapple twins in another, a dominating armoire in a third, light summery wicker in yet another. Beverly's choice in wallpapers is traditional yet bold, with hunt paper in one room, soft tulip paper on neighboring walls. Third-floor rooms are particularly sweet with deep dormers inset with odd-shaped triangular windows, and the rooms only accent these charming eccentricities. The new baths are spotless, fit cleverly into small spaces, with Gilchrest and Soames amenities. Above all else, the rooms are immaculate.

Bay Head is just south of Spring Lake, a calm village of summering families. Like most things in Bay Head, Conover's was built at the turn of the century, a three-story weathered shingle with white trim, two blocks from the town beach. While the common room space is limited to one room, it is charming, with a cut stone fireplace and generous chintz sofas surrounded by walls of books. The dining room is lit by two sets of three-quarter mullioned windows six panes high, three wide. Beverly serves a very full breakfast in this room, always different, but usually featuring an egg casserole and home-baked breads and lemon muffins. Afternoon tea is served in the colder months.

Bay Head is a relaxing retreat, without the tourist frenzy of neighboring Spring Lake or southern Cape May, yet within a short drive of both.

Hewitt Wellington
200 Monmouth Avenue
Spring Lake, New Jersey 07762
908-974-1212

Proprietors: Hewitt Wellington Condo-Hotel Association
Manager: Patrick Barber
Accommodations: 29 rooms, including 17 suites
Rates:
   Low season: $70–$120 weekdays; $90–$150 weekends
   High season: $110–$190 weekdays; $130–$220 weekends
Minimum stay: Most weekends
Added: $10 each additional guest; 7% tax
Payment: Visa, MasterCard, American Express
Children: Welcome (under 6 free)
Pets: Not allowed
Smoking: Limited
Open: April 1 to October

The Hewitt Wellington Hotel, recently facelifted in 1988 for four million dollars, is a great example of the Old World wealth which has defined Spring Lake for the last century. In 1875, a development group called the Spring Lake Beach Improvement Company set out to build some grand hotels. The Hewitt Wellington was built several years later as a result, at the south end of the lake from which the town took its name. In fact, there are a great number of grand hotels around town as a result of these turn-of-the-century development plans, most of which have gone bankrupt over the years, palatial mansions faded like Tara after the Civil War. Fortunately for the Hewitt Wellington, CT Investments, Inc. bought the property in 1987 and saved it from demise.

The hotel is a marriage of two houses connected by a newly constructed breezeway, one facing east, another facing south, both done in fresh white clapboard in the Queen Anne style, of turrets, wrap porches, and subtle gingerbread, topped by a green shingled roof. The hotel was built by the same man who constructed St. Catherine's Roman Catholic Church a block away, modeled after St. Peter's in Rome.

The restoration work of 1988 left the hotel with an elegant and pristine atmosphere, much like a country club, the service formal and elite. In fact, the property is a condominium hotel, though transient guests make up a large percentage of the hotel's business. The rooms are decorated with Drexel Heritage reproduction furnishings, with four-poster beds and wing chairs in traditional dark woods, with televisions, telephones, and luxurious marble baths. Some rooms have balconies overlooking the lake or the ocean. The Hewitt Wellington has the elegance of a large hotel, but the intimacy of a country inn, as there are only from four to six rooms per floor.

Its restaurant, Whispers, is open seasonally, with entrées ranging from $15 for tomato basil spinach linguine to $22 for tournedos of beef with béarnaise and bordelaise sauces. The dining room has a rose-hued marble floor, with Louis XV chairs upholstered in striped silk.

Aside from beach activities, Spring Lake is a historic town worthy of an extended stay, its Victorian railroad depot recently restored and used by the Jersey Shore Coast Lines. Nearby is the Garden State Arts Center for music, Monmouth Park and Freehold racetracks, several golf courses and public tennis courts, as well as Great Adventure amusement park and Allaire State Park.

Hollycroft
506 North Boulevard
South Belmar, New Jersey 07719
908-681-2254

Proprietors: Linda and Mark Fessler
Accommodations: 6 rooms, all with private bath
Rates: $85–$95, June–September; $65–$75, rest of year
Included: Expanded Continental breakfast
Minimum stay: 2 nights on weekends, 3 nights on holidays
Added: 7% tax
Payment: American Express
Children: Over 12 welcome
Pets: Not allowed
Smoking: Not allowed in rooms
Open: All year

The New Jersey coastline is full of pleasant surprises. Here, on the cusp of South Belmar and Spring Lake, still above Atlantic City, is a wonderful bed-and-breakfast called Hollycroft. Several blocks from the lovely beach on an inlet called Lake Como, Hollycroft is an enchanting piece of architecture, built in 1908 as a log cabin in the Arts and Crafts style.

While the towns along the Jersey shore sit amid flat, scrubby beach growth, Hollycroft's is a wooded setting of bramble, bushes, and trees. Its first floor is tightly stacked ironstone, and the second story is Tudor. The building bends at odd angles, finally at ninety degrees with a porch where guests enter.

It seems fitting that a rare Arts and Crafts house would belong to an architect, but Mark Fessler was lucky. The house was built in the turn of the century by the Ripleys as a summer retreat and remained a family member over the years until Linda and Mark Fessler bought it in 1985. The wood used to built the house is cedar and pine, revealed in ceiling beams, creating a rustic Adirondack feel. The remainder of the house is ironstone, quarried from what is now neighboring Allaire State Park, home of the first Fulton steamship. The interior space is a fascinating collection of low-ceilinged transitional areas, separated by open-beam thresholds, with the particular intimacy of a mountain log cabin.

The common room is an enclosed slate patio with pretty green velvet couches and chintz chairs with full views of the woods outside. The austere dining room is a concert hall of cedar and pine. The mantel of the large stone fireplace is adorned with an enormous English porcelain delft bowl which was on display at the Philadelphia Exhibition in 1876. Two mirroring stairways embrace the fireplace and meet above on a landing. One side of the second-floor hallway overlooks the stairs like a balcony; the other side leads to four guest rooms.

The rooms were given English names, contributing to the feel of an English country house. The Ambleside, Windsor

Rose, and Pomeroy have breezy porches. All rooms have antique beds—some canopied—with pretty linens, lovely European lace window treatments, and several important antiques as focal points. Linda made a lot of the crafts in the house: the quilts, the stenciled washstands, and throw pillows. The baths are immaculate and lovely, with Crabtree and Evelyn soaps, and rooms are sweetened by chocolates and graced with a gift of Perrier and sherry.

Linda, a former New York City copywriter, loves her job as an innkeeper. In or out of beach season, there are other activities besides the shore: nearby Englishtown has the largest flea market on the East Coast; and for the less acquisitive, Great Adventure amusement park is a short drive away.

John Wesley Inn
30 Gurney Street
Cape May, New Jersey 08204
609-884-1012

Proprietors: The Tice Family
Accommodations: 6 rooms, 4 with private bath, 2 suites with kitchen off-season
Rates: $75–$125
Included: Full breakfast
Minimum stay: 2 nights on weekends, 3 nights on weekends in season
Added: 7% tax
Payment: No credit cards
Children: Over 10 welcome
Pets: Not allowed
Smoking: Not allowed
Open: All year

The John Wesley Inn is not a traditional Cape May bed-and-breakfast. While most try faithfully to replicate Victorian decor, the John Wesley goes one step beyond, combining turn-of-the-century flair with elegance from other eras, for beauty's sake. The result is a kind of postmodern Victoriana which looks more like a decorator's showcase than anything historic.

Neighboring the famed Abbey, the John Wesley Inn is a pretty three-story Victorian several houses from the beach. The exterior is architecturally similar to many others in town, built in 1869, with red shingled dormers protruding from the rooftop. A wide double-story portico laced with almond gingerbread covers the olive-colored facade. John and Rita Tice bought the

John Wesley in 1983, restored it, and opened as a bed-and-breakfast in July 1987.

The wallpapers here are glorious. The parlor paper is the same as that in the Cooper Hewitt Museum in New York City, from a pattern dated 1870. While the hall and stairwell wood was refinished, the Tices added the deep walnut paneled wainscoting. Upstairs, rooms have interesting crown canopies in lovely thick Waverly fabrics with antique tassels. There is one second-floor room at the back of the house, separated by a red velvet portiere. This, the Lafayette Room, is decorated in French Empire with 17th-century French paper that simulates drapery. The front room is especially grand, with a private veranda from which guests have an oblique view of the ocean. Wild Schumacher paper covers the walls. A lovely mural of a Franklin stove was painted on the underside of a Murphy bed, which can easily be lowered if guests need one in addition to the 1870 Renaissance Revival bed. Adjacent to this front room is a cozy, elegant room with a crown canopy which mimics the same over a dresser.

The third-floor front room has 15th-century Egyptian paper called lotus blossom, a crown canopy over its bed, a Bukhara rug on the floor, and a burl armoire in the corner. Other rooms have equally unusual pieces and elaborate window treatments and bedding. Baths are quite playful, with clawfoot tubs encircled in heavy tasseled drapery. The sitting room is also on this floor, a vast, airy addition to the back of the house, with large postmodern windows overlooking the rooftops of Cape May.

For high Victoriana and socializing, visitors to Cape May have many choices. For creative decorating, the John Wesley is an interesting alternative, with its romantic bedding, baths, and window treatments.

The Normandy Inn

21 Tuttle Avenue
Spring Lake, New Jersey 07762
908-449-7172

Proprietors: Michael and Susan Ingino
Innkeeper: Mary Clare Beaulieu
Accommodations: 17 rooms, all with private bath
Rates: $92–132, mid-May–September; $75–$100, rest of year
Included: Full breakfast
Minimum stay: 2 nights in May, June, September; 4 nights on weekends, 2 nights on weekdays in July and August

Added: $20 each additional adult guest; children under 12, $1
    per year of age; 7% tax
Payment: American Express
Children: Welcome
Pets: Not allowed
Smoking: Limited
Open: All year

While most of the large houses in elegant Spring Lake are of the
conservative grand Queen Anne style, with wide calm porches,
a turret or two, done in cool white clapboard, one in particular
makes a stunning contrast, as if swept from the southern shores
of High Victorian Cape May. The Normandy Inn is a three-
story olive clapboard with a square wrap porch on the first
floor, another inset porch on the second floor, and a series of
grand, puzzling, round and arched windows punctuating its
exterior, culminating in a fourth-story square cupola. The two
porches and many levels to the house give a large role to the red
shingled rooftop which reappears at different stories.

The Normandy Inn was built before 1889 and moved to its
present location near the beach around 1906, shortly before it
became a guest house. The tradition continued, albeit informally, for more than seventy years, until Michael and Susan
Ingino bought the property in 1982 to satisfy two loves: for
innkeeping and for antiques. Over the years, they have continued to add to their vast collection, searching for period wallpaper, furniture, light fixtures, and decorative pieces — right
down to the Victorian urn on the front lawn. The only reproductions found at the Normandy Inn are the period wallpapers
from Schumacher and the lovely flowered rug which traipses
through the halls.

Michael and Susan redo about three rooms every year. There
are eight rooms each on the second and third floors, with a
wonderful, creative tower room in the cupola. While those at
the front are larger than those in the back, all the guest rooms
have unusual pieces: Room 101 has an 1850 four-poster canopy
bed in southern style with a gathered silk canopy; Room 102 has
a four-piece 1870 Renaissance Revival bedroom set including a
nine-foot headboard of walnut and burl; Room 109 has two
brass French twins, with a German regulator clock; Room 209
has a pair of Eastlake twins made into a king-size bed.
Throughout, every room has a lavish Victorian chandelier or
globed lamps or sconces. The wallpapers are deep paisleys and
patterns or boldly bordered in complementary patterns. Com-

mendably, the baths are large and useful, difficult in an old Victorian.

Breakfasts are just great at the Normandy Inn and are open to the public, with reservations. In the large, convivial dining room, several full courses are served on Villeroy and Boch china within sight of an 1886 Chickering piano. Of the two common rooms, the front parlor is decorated with a rare six-piece 1870 Renaissance Revival set in the Jeliffe style, surrounded by artifacts, sculpture, clocks, and curios. Guests relax here or on the sweeping, wicker-filled wrap porches. Michael and Susan are gregarious professionals who correspond with return guests by a frequent newsletter, which also provides ample information about activities in Spring Lake.

The Queen Victoria

102 Ocean Street
Cape May, New Jersey 08204
609-884-8702

Proprietors: Dane and Joan Wells
Accommodations: 22 rooms in Queen Victoria and Prince Albert Hall, 3 cottages, all with private bath
Rates: $65–$140; $110–$235, luxury suites
Included: Full breakfast, full afternoon tea
Minimum stay: 2 or 3 nights on holidays and weekends
Added: $20 each additional guest; 7% tax
Payment: Visa, MasterCard
Children: Welcome
Pets: Not allowed
Smoking: Allowed on porches
Open: All year

The Queen Victoria is one of the prettiest and most professional of Cape May's bed-and-breakfasts. It stands out among its colleagues for two reasons: it welcomes children and is open all year. While filled with precious antiques, the Queen Victoria is not a velvet-rope property. Here, modern convenience meets Victorian splendor, where whirlpool baths, in-room refrigerators, and electric blankets happily co-exist with 19th-century oak bedroom sets, marble-top dressers, and rare Stickley mission furniture.

Dane and Joan worked in Philadelphia as manager of the Main Street revitalization program and executive director of the Victorian Society of America, respectively, jobs which more than prepared them for restoring and running a bed-and-breakfast. Their gregarious, warm-hearted natures further qualified them for their new life, which they began in 1980 in Cape May.

One of the main buildings was completed in 1882 for $4,000 on a site one block from the beach that cost $3,500; the other was built six months later. In addition to these, the Queen Victoria and Prince Albert Hall, are three satellite cottages, a surprisingly large property that retains the intimacy of a much smaller bed-and-breakfast.

The Queen Victoria is a light jade, with a cedar shingle red mansard roof. Two double-story bay windows flank the entrance, nearly undulating with windows across the facade, trimmed in maroon. Alongside the house, the porch displays some of the inn's fifty trademark green rockers with yellow caning, leading to adjacent Prince Albert Hall, a buttery yellow with jade and red accents. On its third floor roof at the back of the house, a generous sun deck provides great views of the town and ocean.

All the rooms have traditional bed-and-breakfast decor, like handmade Mennonite quilts, Oriental rugs, canopy beds, decorative Victorian antiques including a tufted slipper chair or an Eastlake settee. At the same time, the rooms are serviced twice daily with turndown and custom-made chocolates, electric blankets in the winter, refrigerators and whirlpool tubs in some, all the new baths with Queen Victoria amenities presented in a cute miniature bathtub. Pantries in the two guesthouses provide a bottomless supply of popcorn, ice, snacks, and drinks.

Of all the activities at the Queen Victoria, Dane and Joan are proudest of the breakfasts over which they preside, the setting where guests gather and chat about Cape May, their visit, and their plans. The meal can go on for hours in each of two houses around the expansive antique dining tables. Unfinished stories will continue at afternoon tea where home-baked sweets and savories are served. To work off the meal, guests may borrow bicycles at no charge.

Sea Crest by the Sea
19 Tuttle Avenue
Spring Lake, New Jersey 07762
908-449-9031

Proprietors: John and Carol Kirby
Accommodations: 12 rooms, all with private bath
Rates: $100–$140, May–September; $80–$112, rest of year
Included: Full breakfast
Minimum stay: 2 nights in July and August; 2 nights on low-season weekends; 3 nights on holidays
Added: 7% tax
Payment: Visa, MasterCard
Children: Not allowed
Pets: Not allowed
Smoking: Not allowed
Open: All year

Though Spring Lake's two finest bed-and-breakfasts are neighbors, the Normandy Inn and Sea Crest by the Sea really don't overlap. While the former is a more formal setting for seasoned bed-and-breakfasters and antiques lovers, Sea Crest has a pampered intimacy. Most of the rooms have themes, like Casablanca with a rattan bedroom set and a curtain of beads at the doorway, Mardi Gras with masks decorating the walls, and Yankee Clipper, a tribute to the owner's days in the Merchant Marines. Though theme rooms may represent a certain cutesy in the industry, here it means a thoughtful decor. All is done in the finest of taste: exceptionally memorable bedding, with chocolates at turndown, and, throughout, interesting family heirlooms and lovely Victorian French and English antiques.

The Kirbys were determined to make bed-and-breakfasting a second career and searched along the Jersey shore for the perfect place. They found the Sea Crest, a well-worn 35-room hostelry of fifty years, several houses from the two-mile-long boardwalk on Spring Lake's beachfront. This 1885 Victorian house was perfect, and they bought it on Valentine's Day 1990, investing much work in its restoration. It was built next to the Hewitt Wellington and eventually moved near the beach as the owners grew wealthier. Today, it stands as a white clapboard with peach shutters, three stories topped in a center turret flanked by two cozy dormers, with a festive blue and white striped awning shading the length of the first-floor porch.

A comfortable library is complemented by a formal living room, with elegant tapestry chairs warmed by a gas fireplace, where afternoon tea is served to the tunes of a player piano. The dining room, where guests have a full breakfast, is centered on an 1870s French table. The menu changes daily but may include fresh fruit and homemade granola, buttermilk scones with marmalade and clotted cream, banana bread, cinnamon raisin bread, baked honey walnut French toast, and special Sea Crest coffee.

The seven guest rooms on the second floor and five on the third have private baths and the highest-quality Simmons queen-size beds draped in Scandia Down quilts with 400-thread-count duvet covers. Tiny televisions are hidden in each guest room. The Victorian Rose and the Sleighride have gas fireplaces, the former with an 1880s American walnut bed. Baskets with fluffy towels and Caswell and Massey amenities make a nice bath presentation. Family heirlooms throughout the house include John's family deed from West Virginia in the George Washington Room, a window in which is draped with a flag swag.

The Kirbys are joyous owners, enamored of Spring Lake and their newfound duties as innkeepers.

The Virginia Hotel
25 Jackson Street
Cape May, New Jersey 08204
609-884-5700

Proprietors: The Chamberlain Hospitality Group
General Managers: Curtis Bashaw and Margie Rovira
Accommodations: 24 rooms, all with private bath
Rates: $85–$165, standard; $105–$235, premium
Included: Continental breakfast
Minimum stay: 2–4 nights on weekends and some holidays
Added: $20 each additional guest; 7% tax
Payment: Visa, MasterCard, Diners Club, American Express
Children: Welcome
Pets: Not allowed
Smoking: Allowed
Open: Year-round except January

For those who love the adorability of Cape May but not the intimacy of bed-and-breakfast travel, the Virginia is a wonderful solution. Though its 24 guest rooms make it the size of some of the larger bed-and-breakfasts, the Virginia is a small luxury hotel, with cosmopolitan service. In addition, its Ebbitt Room is one of the finest restaurants in this seaside resort town.

The Virginia even looks like a Victorian bed-and-breakfast. A flat-roofed, three-story structure in white clapboard, it boasts a magnificent double-story veranda covered in gingerbread. Built in 1879 by Alfred and Ellen Ebbitt as a hotel, this property was Cape May's first to be open year-round with steam heat, a half block from town, a block the other direction to the beach. It remained an active hotel until the 1980s, when it lay vacant for seven years.

Curtis Bashaw bought the dilapidated building in 1988 and undertook an extensive restoration. The 1950s had stripped all the artwork of history from the hotel's exterior, and Bashaw and his architect pieced it back together, reconstructing the lattice and gingerbread from a 1912 postcard of the hotel. The original 112-year-old stained glass casts a colorful light on the interior stairwell. Three of the baths are original to the hotel, on stilts at the side of the building, and renovated to modern standards. The Virginia reopened in June 1989, its exterior faithfully recalled to its 19th-century days, its interior an elegant full-service hotel.

The guest rooms are all slightly different, decorated in chic postmodern cleanliness. The walls are a sedate beige, often papered in a faithful Bradbury and Bradbury Victorian reproduction sponge print in similar soothing hues of beiges and creams. The beds, custom-made in cherry, are covered in down comforters with raw silk duvets and thick cotton sheeting. The armoires, housing televisions and even VCRs, are a sand-washed light wood. Terry robes are provided in gleaming compact baths with gray, off-gray, and white geometric tiling. The standard rooms have queen-size beds and the larger, better-located premium rooms have kings, three of which open onto the graceful veranda. Room service and nightly turndown are available.

Dinner in the Ebbitt Room is an elegant affair offering regional American cuisine around $20 a plate. A dinner might include an appetizer of shrimp seviche over grilled jalapeño corn cake with black bean sauce and roasted tomato salsa, followed by a Belgian endive and radicchio salad with chevre crouton in pear vinaigrette. Entrées might include champagne scampi in champagne cream sauce over rainbow fettucine; cioppino, a California shellfish stew in spicy tomato broth served with lemon garlic aioli; or roast Cornish game hen marinated in lemon, thyme, garlic, and juniper berries served on a bed of caramelized vegetables.

New York

Danfords Inn
25 East Broadway
Port Jefferson, New York 11777
516-928-5200
800-332-6367 outside New York

Proprietor: James McNamara
General Manager: Kathy Pass
Accommodations: 85 rooms in 7 buildings
Rates: Rooms, $123–$135; $140–$160 with water view; suites, $180–$280
Included: Buffet breakfast on weekdays
Added: $10 each additional guest, 13% tax
Payment: Major credit cards
Children: Welcome
Pets: Not allowed
Smoking: Nonsmoking rooms available
Open: All year

Port Jefferson is very much a working fishing town and also the terminus for the Bridgeport ferry, halfway out on Long Island's north shore. This old port and historic whaling town is rather dominated by the phenomenon of Danfords Inn, an over-whelmingly large property in the heart of town. Though its seven sweeping white clapboard buildings were completed only in 1983 (with a new fitness center and 40 more rooms in 1992), Danfords looks convincingly seasoned. In addition to housing a large number of lovely guest rooms, Danfords is home to numerous gift shops and a reputable restaurant beloved by locals and travelers alike for its extensive seafood selections.

Five of the seven buildings are three-story white clapboard with red trim lining the harborfront. But for the main building, these are attached along a brick walkway decorated with urns, from which hang potted geraniums in front of first-floor shops. Their facade is a medley of second- and third-floor balconies, dormers, and porches which seem like a haphazard collection of New England home fronts. Two without water views include one brick building behind the main inn and another around the corner with a historic stone facade.

The success of the interior spaces is due largely to owner James McNamara's passion for art and antiques. The main building has a great lobby, its knotty pine wide-planked floor made especially for Danfords, covered with antique Orientals. Worn leather wing chairs and sofas comfortably fill the room, decorated with a wondrous eclectic collection of Victoriana, colonial Americana, and seafaring memorabilia. Of the five dining rooms, some have great water views, others are ensconced in greenery, and the sail loft is tucked in the A-frame of the second floor. Three meals are served daily in bustling, friendly service. Dinner entrées range from $18 to $27 for twin rock lobster tails, Alaskan king crabmeat, and fresh capellini abruzzi with bacon, mushrooms, and peas in light pink cream, and roast Long Island duck in Grand Marnier.

Even the lowest of the eight-room categories are impressive, with a minimum of four hundred square feet. They are each decorated differently, and while most have reproduction furniture, the more deluxe rooms have glorious antique treasures like a mission period bookcase, imposing armoires, or perhaps a tufted fainting couch. Mahogany television cabinets were handmade for the inn. The bed treatments might be a gathered chintz crown canopy or a two-poster bed with linens matching curtains framing a harbor view. Chippendale chairs sit attentively behind desks, and Queen Anne settees are decorated in plush damask. The new baths have Gilchrest and Soames amenities including a thoughtful toothbrush and mending kit. Lovely artwork decorates the walls in hunt or nautical themes.

Danfords is a luxurious but friendly and informal place. Visible owner James McNamara is wholeheartedly involved in the inn's daily activities. His happy and helpful staff seems to enjoy his attention and accessibility.

Gurney's Inn Resort & Spa
Old Montauk Highway
Montauk, New York 11954
516-668-2345
800-445-8062

Proprietors: Lola and Nick Monte
General Manager: Paul Monte
Accommodations: 109 time-sharing units, including 5 cottages
Rates: $240–$320; cottages, $320 and up
Included: Breakfast and $23 credit toward dinner
Minimum stay: 2 nights on summer weekends
Added: $65 each additional guest; 15% gratuities; 13% tax

Payment: Major credit cards
Children: Welcome; cribs available
Pets: Not allowed
Smoking: Nonsmoking dining area
Open: All year

The main access to Montauk, Long Island's easternmost town, is Route 27, though it digresses at one point as the scenic Old Montauk Highway, laid out in the 1700s. The landscape is quite unusual here: scrubby, windswept dunes, rough undulating rock with stubborn, thick shrubbery low to the ground. Along this well-beaten, at times desolate road which ventures beachside, 2.6 miles west of Montauk's town center, is Gurney's Inn Resort and Spa, the only marinotherapeutic spa in North America.

Without the modest sign at the entrance, Gurney's could go unnoticed, its many buildings terraced into the hill which tumbles from the historic road to the beachfront. Gurney's is one of the few Long Island properties open to the public right on the south shore's glorious beach.

The resort was built in 1926 by early developer Carl Fisher, who wanted to make Montauk the Miami of the North. The original parts of the inn remain today, an unobtrusive row of weathered shingled buildings. Nick and Joyce Monte bought Gurney's in 1956, lending a warm-hearted generosity to this place over the years. Unlike the nearby Montauk Yacht Club, which is a new, luxurious corporate venture, Gurney's is a retreat for generations of repeat guests and families. The staff is very much a part of the continuity here, friendly and enthusiastic.

Anticipating a boom in fitness and health consciousness as early as the 1970s, Nick Monte decided that Gurney's needed a spa. To make it unique and complementary to his beloved seaside setting, he decided the spa should concentrate on marinotherapeutic treatment, using seawater and seaweed extracts available only in Europe. After much research, the spa opened in February 1979, the only one of its kind on the North American continent. Unique to the spa is an indoor heated saltwater pool (84 degrees), less saline than the ocean, and massage rooms, fango packs, seaweed wraps, Thalasso tubs, Swiss showers, and a beauty salon.

The premises are uniquely tiered, carved into the hillside, with no structure above the tree line. Wooden walkways connect the six guest houses and four cottages to the ample public spaces, resulting in an ever-changing perspective on the waterfront. Among the public space are two dining rooms, an outdoor dining area, an entertainment lounge, and an outdoor walking track above the spa.

Montauk stands fast by its dune preservation laws. The guest houses abut the dune growth without disruption, though over the years several noticeably new buildings have been added to Gurney's. Included in these are the deluxe sand-colored Forward Watch, guests of which have only to step off porches to touch sand. Four cottages line the near beachfront by the prominent Foredeck, with 20 rooms. Guest rooms all have balconies, some at beach level, some teetering above with the higher views, and even the less desirable rooms behind the parking lot have water views: the Chart House, the Flying Bridge, the Promenade Deck, and the Forecastle. Decorated in contemporary style, all rooms have televisions, private phones in the room and the bath, with full Royal Orchard amenities from France. From studios to two-bedrooms, rooms are done in summery pastel colors, each with a sitting area and queen-size sofabed, divided by modern wall units that close with curtains around the sleeping area, with modern slatted mirror headboards, covered in floral shell pattern spreads.

Be sure to visit Hither Hills and Montauk State Parks and the historic lighthouse erected in the 1790s.

Montauk Yacht Club Resort and Marina
Star Island
Montauk, New York 11954
516-668-3100
800-832-4200

Proprietors: Brock Associates Management
General Manager: Bruno Brunner
Accommodations: 107 rooms, including 4 suites and 22 rooms in 5 villas
Rates: Low season, $119–$150; mid-season, $179–$205; high season, $249–$285
Included: Continental buffet breakfast
Minimum stay: 2–4 nights on weekends
Added: $25–$50 each additional guest; 18% service charge; 13% tax
Payment: Major credit cards
Children: Welcome
Pets: Not allowed
Smoking: Allowed
Open: Closed January to mid-March

Just north of town on Star Island in the northern bite of Montauk Bay is a glimpse into the days of Jay Gatsby at the Montauk Yacht Club. The marina resort was bought, in faded condition, by Brock Associates in 1988 and renovated through 1990. Its impressive history was conceived during the roaring twenties, built as a private club with founding members like J. P. Morgan, Marshall Field, Vincent Astor, William K. Vanderbilt, Jr., John Wanamaker, and Harry Payne Whitney. The Yacht Club bordered on the Ziegfeld estate, which is now incorporated at the northern end of the property.

The Yacht Club centers around the original 1929 hexagonal lighthouse, a symbolic structure of whitewashed concrete, which now serves as the Lighthouse Bar, overlooking the 247-slip marina. The shingled saltbox buildings to the south of the lighthouse are original; those to the north, including Ziegfeld's Restaurant and adjacent buildings, are additions designed to replicate the old architecture. The original lobby adjacent to the lighthouse has floors of darkly stained wood, with a compass underfoot six feet in diameter. An elaborate model of the 1883 *Atalanta* yacht sits nearby encased in glass, one of many nautical treasures which decorate the club.

Most rooms have a water view obliquely or directly on the marina's boardwalk, but all have balconies decorated with flower barrels. The saltbox buildings provide two floors of rooms along a vertically paneled wooden hallway, up or down a half flight of steps. The rooms are finished in several different decor schemes in summery pastels, some with wicker headboards and bedroom sets, some with a rose toile spread, some with a beautiful crown canopy in a weedy print complemented by a plaid inlay and bed skirting. The remote television and refrigerator are hidden in a blanched wood corner cupboard, topped by a handmade decoy or a cherubic weathervane. Bathrooms are large and contemporary with a separate vanity area, pedestal sink, generous amenities, and plentiful closet space.

Guests who don't mind a mild walk to the main hotel may prefer the 22 rooms in the five Ziegfeld Villas, all individually decorated. The stucco, green-shuttered villas at the north edge of Star Island look like fairy-tale Tudor cottages set around a little commons made fanciful by four trampolines gracing the lawns. There are some nice art deco antiques in these rooms, amid the original architecture of nonworking marble fireplaces and heavy square-paned leaded Tudor windows with a whimsical triangular portal now and again. The darkly stained walls and floor have the feeling of an old library on a north shore estate.

Throughout the acreage are two outdoor pools, waterskiing, horseback riding, boat rentals, golf at nearby Montauk Downs, and an indoor pool with a fitness area and sauna. Dinners at Ziegfeld's range from $17 to $26, with fresh fish cooked on an outdoor grill. A short drive away is the Montauk State Park and the historic lighthouse, constructed by word of George Washington in the 1790s.

Lakeside Stops

New Jersey

The Henry Ludlam Inn
1336 Route 47, Dennisville
Woodbine, New Jersey 08270
609-861-5847

Proprietors: Marty and Ann Thurlow
Accommodations: 5 rooms, 3 with private bath
Rates: $75–$95
Included: Full breakfast, wine and sherry on arrival
Minimum stay: 2 nights July and August
Added: $20 each additional guest; 7% tax
Payment: MasterCard, Visa, American Express
Children: Over 12 welcome
Pets: Not allowed
Smoking: Not allowed
Open: All year

Here, five miles inland between Atlantic City and Cape May, is a quaint, romantic bed-and-breakfast characterized by creative cooking and antique beds dressed in featherbeds and hand-made quilts. Though set on well-trafficked Route 47, the Henry Ludlam Inn is rooted in the countryside, with its lovely groomed grounds, Adirondack chairs, proprietary geese, and a gazebo looking over 56 acres Henry Ludlam Lake. Parts of this sweet old house were built in 1740 and still display the original wide-planked flooring. The traditional Federal three-story front was added in 1800, and today the house is a smart-looking gray with maroon trim.

Ann and Marty Thurlow bought the house in 1983, realizing their lifelong dream of opening a bed-and-breakfast. They restored the house and decorated everything themselves, naming the property after an area lawyer who was one of the social founders of Cape May County. Victoriana was left in nearby Cape May as this bed-and-breakfast leans more toward Pennsylvania country colonial. The common room is in the charming 18th-century part of the house, used as a sitting room with wooden banquettes. In the Federal part of the house is a very pretty breakfast area where black and pink chintz cloths cover wooden colonial tables, warmed by one of the original fireplaces.

While most travelers neglect New Jersey's coastline in the colder months, the Henry Ludlam seems highly desirable during this time of year, especially for guests including Ann's six-course gourmet dinners on autumn and winter Saturday nights ($37 per person). Featherbeds adorn antique beds, and three of the five guest rooms have wood-burning fireplaces, including first-floor Wicker Room and, on the second, the Pine and Oak rooms, with lovely views. Though without fireplaces and sharing a small bath, the cozy third-floor rooms are adorable, set under the eaves, their walls of exposed brick from the fireplaces downstairs. The pitched ceiling in the Linden Room is of pickled pine; its window seat overlooks the lake with the help of a telescope, also used for bird-watching.

Upon arrival, guests are greeted with a tray of two splits of wine and glasses. Marty also makes picnic baskets for $25, filled with wine, sandwiches, cheese, fruits, and dessert—a romantic idea when taken in a canoe on Ludlam Lake or fireside in winter.

Nearby are many activities: the beach in Sea Isle City or Avalon; Victorian walks in Cape May, its County Zoo, Historical Society, and the Physick Estate; nearby 50-acre Leamings Run, an arborial sanctuary, bird-watching in Stone Harbor's Sanctuary and Wetlands Institute; historic sights in Cold Spring Village and Bridgeton; Belle Plain State Park; and Wheaton Village for a history of glassmaking.

New York

Blushing Rosé
11 William Street
Hammondsport, New York 14840
607-569-3402
607-569-3483

Proprietors: Ellen and Bucky Laufersweiler
Accommodations: 4 rooms, all with private bath
Rates: $75–$85

Included: Full breakfast
Minimum stay: 2 nights on holiday and special-event weekends
Added: $15 each additional guest; 9% tax
Payment: No credit cards
Children: Will consider; $10 additional
Pets: Not allowed
Smoking: Not allowed
Open: All year

Lake Keuka is one of the westernmost Finger Lakes, and Hammondsport is the endearing town at its southern shores. The old town is a good base for viewing the Finger Lakes, auto racing in nearby Watkins Glen, the tourist mecca of Corning, and especially the wine country, with Taylor vineyards just minutes away. This is the heart of wine country—even back in 1843, when grape growers built a sweet two-story house at the end of William Street, known today as the Blushing Rosé.

With only four rooms, the Blushing Rosé is reserved for those who love the bed-and-breakfast concept. Ellen and Buck are gregarious hosts who moved here from the Catskills in 1986, restored the house, and opened for bed-and-breakfast business. The pretty pink clapboard house with maroon trim, topped by a tiny cupola, is a cozy place. Full breakfasts made by Ellen are sociable events where guests linger over zucchini quiche and Belgian waffles. Buck built a wing in the back of the house which contributed two lovely new rooms.

The living room is a busy lived-in place, full with the lives of its owners. Upstairs, two rooms in the original section of the house are called Magnificent Walnut, for the bed it features, and Moonbeams, for its skylight. Ellen made the pink and mauve quilt to cover the Magnificent Walnut. Buck did the charming stencil in Moonbeams, a preferable room set under the eaves with a blue iron and brass bed covered in white eyelet linens, with a clever slim bathroom with a lace shower curtain.

The two new rooms are the large Burgundy, with a king-size bed covered with a log cabin quilt and a lace canopy, a wicker sitting area, and dried eucalyptus wreaths on the walls. Buck skillfully refinished the floors to look like pine. The Four Poster Room is more feminine, with a curved fishnet canopy atop a dark Bennington bed. Given her guests' penchant for early fishing on Lake Keuka, Ellen has considerately put a coffeemaker in each room.

The boat launch is half a block away, and the lovely town square of Hammondsport, offering wonderful shops and walking, is half a block in the other direction.

Canoe Island Lodge
Box 144
Diamond Point, New York 12824
518-668-5592

Proprietors: William and Jane Busch

Accommodations: 65 rooms with 7 two-room suites, in 15 buildings, including chalets and log cabins

Rates: $72–$134, MAP (AP spring and fall) per person; special weekly rates;

Included: Breakfast and dinner (three meals spring and fall); extensive boating facilities, tennis

Minimum stay: 3 nights

Added: 7% tax; three-quarters of full rate for each additional adult; children: 2 and under, $12; age 3–6, $24; age 7–12, $36

Payment: No credit cards

Children: Welcome

Pets: Not allowed

Smoking: Discouraged

Open: Mid-May to mid-October

For a classic lake setting, one can hardly do better than Canoe Island Lodge, which sits on 16 acres on the southern part of 32-mile-long Lake George. The legendary owners are Jane and Bill Busch, who have made Canoe Island Lodge their home and livelihood for more than forty years, some of the kindest and proudest innkeepers in this book.

Mr. Busch bought the property in 1946 and two years later his new bride joined him in his endeavors. By carving out the steep, rocky landscape on Lake George's shores and doing his own logging, Mr. Busch built every one of the 15 buildings on the property, including four real log cabins, some small houses, and chalets. The property also consists of Canoe Island, which floats four acres across Lake George, named for the American Canoe Federation, which was founded in a log cabin on the island in 1882 (ask Mrs. Busch to see pictures). Several weekly events are planned on Canoe Island, including Thursday barbecues, Tuesday breakfasts, and sandcastle building contests.

From Route 9N, the buildings of Canoe Island Lodge tumble down the tiers of slate to the sandy beach on Lake George. The Main Lodge has an enchanting lobby, made of dark pine logs all cut on the property. Several sitting areas prompt cozy chats by a huge stone fireplace. Many items have sentimental significance, including a pair of clarinet lamps atop a piano made by a frequent guest and the braided oval rugs handmade for the Busches thirty years ago by a local friend. Steps from the main common area is the woody oak bar with views of Lake George through a picture window.

Views from the dining room are spectacular, looking to the lake from the 40-foot height of the lodge down the slate hill. The Busches are extremely proud of their food, all of which is served family style, homemade and hearty, with entrées like beef Stroganoff, roast beef, sautéed chicken breast, and sea scallops, combined with steamed vegetables from their own garden. Their baker makes breads and desserts daily. Finally, the ground level is also the dancing and activities room, built right on the ledge rock.

Throughout the property is an astounding variety of accommodations—in luxurious chalets, rustic log cabins, traditional lodge rooms, and family houses. All guest rooms have a patio or deck as well as a wood-burning fireplace, and most have lake views. Rooms vary in extent of luxury: most deluxe rooms are in Chalet Erika, the mini-chalets, and Chalet Edelweiss, with its bright stencil colors and decor and large patios. Some of the cabins are more rustic; the upper log cabin, for instance, has a huge cathedral ceiling and stone fireplace, a little patio, and a picture window onto Lake George. The staff is treated like extended family at Canoe Island Lodge, happy to help, lighthearted, and enamored of the beautiful environment.

Below Chalet Edelweiss is a common area covered in green all-weather carpeting, where guests indulge on light fare and watch the lake's activities. The boating facilities are exceptional, among them four 31-foot sailboats, two cruise boats, plenty of rowboats, a Ski-Nautique for waterskiing, and the *Ark*, a 40-foot passenger boat which takes guests on cruises. Those with sights elsewhere might enjoy the three tennis courts, a great hiking route to a high vantage point called the Ledges, and the obligatory visit to the nearby magnificent Omni Sagamore for high tea (see Grand Old Resorts).

The Hedges
Blue Mountain Lake, New York 12812
518-352-7325
518-352-7672

Proprietors: Dick and Cathy van Yperen
Accommodations: 6 rooms in Stone Lodge; 4 rooms in Main Lodge; 14 cottages (1 to 4 bedrooms)
Rates: $58–$70 per person, MAP; seasonal and midweek discounts
Included: Two meals, use of all boats and facilities

Minimum stay: One week, July and August
Added: $40 each additional adult; $20–$30 each additional
child; 7% tax
Payment: No credit cards
Children: Welcome
Pets: Not allowed
Smoking: Allowed in rooms only
Open: June 14–Columbus Day

Set on the lapping shores of Blue Mountain Lake, the Hedges is
a pristine, rather formal family retreat. The elegant architecture
of the Main Lodge and dining room is thoroughly faithful to an
Adirondack Great Camp, and the lakeside cottages are picture-
perfect log cabins. The Hedges sits at eye level with Blue Mountain Lake, with a tiny beach and 1,500 feet of grassy lakefront.
The 12 acres of grounds are very well groomed, consistent with
the air of formal rusticity.

The Hedges has an interesting history. The Main Lodge was
built as a retreat for Colonel Hiriam B. Duryea, who after a
highly successful career in the Civil War made his fortune as
president of the National Starch Company, with the help of his
brilliant son Chester, who invented cornstarch. Duryea had
this upstate estate built by 1892 and several years later added
the Stone Lodge for another son who was paralyzed, with the
several buildings costing about $80,000. In a frightening exit,
Duryea was murdered by his son Chester.

In 1920, the estate was sold for $22,000 at auction to Richard
Collins, a caretaker for the Vanderbilt family at their nearby
Great Camp, the Sagamore in Raquette Lake (see Historic
Stops). Mr. Collins built the dining room in 1924 for his overnight guests, and the cottages followed in the 1930s. The Hedges
remained in the Collins family until 1972, when the van Yper-
ens began their long and successful tenure here.

The Stone House, made from hand-cut stone, topped with a
roof of imported cypress shingle, has beautiful interior woodwork, coffered light wood ceilings, and several working terra
cotta fireplaces. The first floor is home to an unusual three-
room suite with a private porch. Upstairs are five guest rooms,
two with wonderful water views.

The Main Lodge is an enchanting, rambling Adirondack
camp structure, a masterful gallery of woodwork. Its large wrap
porch is characteristic of the architecture, with unfinished pillars supporting the heavy second floor, the rail wrapped in its
original bark just feet away from the lake and curved lawns
which undulate around its banks flecked with white Adirondack chairs. The first floor is lined with cherry and oak, inlaid

with yellow pine. The large library has a ceiling finished to look like a rolltop desk, walls lined with shelves of books, and original furniture warmed by a terra cotta fireplace. Upstairs, the grandest of the four lovely rooms is the Colonel Duryea Room, with a stunning original window seat nestled into carved woodwork in a bay window.

The cabins that line the lakefront are charming: the first three are cut log; the following two are knotty pine; the last three are shingle with sleeping lofts, two bedrooms, and a living area and are situated around a little beach.

The dining room is a wonderful structure in itself, consisting of two large rooms with tin walls, a ten-foot tin ceiling, and a polished wood floor underfoot, all warmed by a huge stone fireplace. One entrée is served nightly, in formal service, with waitresses and white linens. On view is the original oak breakfast table and a 19th-century Adirondack guide boat strapped to the wall.

Guests who tire of the large number of canoes and boats may use the clay tennis court on the property. Nearby is the Adirondack Museum, an upstate cultural mecca, and 60 miles of trails including a hike up 3,800-foot Blue Mountain. Daily tours are led through Sagamore, a short lovely drive away through countryside.

Hemlock Hall

Blue Mountain Lake, New York 12812
518-352-7706
518-359-9065

Proprietors: Paul and Susan Provost
Accommodations: 8 rooms in Main House, 5 with private bath; 14 cottage and motel units
Rates: June 16–September: $93–$123 per couple, MAP; rest of year: $80–$111 per couple
Included: Breakfast and dinner, use of boats
Minimum stay:
Added: $30 each additional adult; $20 each additional child age 2–8; 7% tax
Payment: No credit cards
Children: Welcome
Pets: Not allowed
Smoking: Limited
Open: May 15–October 15

Where the Hedges, across Blue Mountain Lake, is somewhat formal in its rusticity, Hemlock Hall is entirely without pretension—a place where kids let loose and parents don't worry. This informal setting is ideal for small children and active families. The tone of the Adirondack lodge is camp, set by owner Paul Provost, a self-admitted overgrown child, who loves life, his family, and this property.

Paul had vacationed at Hemlock Hall under its prior ownership with his family from age three and had always wanted to own the place. In 1986, he and his wife, Susan, were able to buy this Adirondack camp, which had been welcoming guests since 1949. Paul is simply thrilled, expressing glee at times with his loon call, reportedly one of the best in the area.

The meals are very indicative of life at Hemlock Hall. Dinners are announced by a big outdoor bell, and because every kid gets a chance to ring the bell, the process may go on for five minutes. Guests eat family style on Blue Willow china, sitting on twig chairs at one round table in the older part of the house and around five tables in the 1960 wooden addition, which overlooks the backyard streams to the lakefront. Freshly baked bread accompanies the evening's single entrée: lamb on Monday, roast pork on Tuesday, chicken and biscuits on Wednesday, corned beef on Thursday, cured ham with haddock fillet on Friday, a Thanksgiving turkey dinner on Saturday, and a big roast beef on Sunday afternoon. There is no alcohol at Hemlock Hall.

The Adirondack Victorian Main House was built in 1890, and from the original twig rockers on the sociable wrap porch, guests look out over the property, which descends through carved paths and green lawns to Blue Mountain Lake. Inside are two lovely common rooms, with wainscoted cedar walls and clear pine wainscoting laid in patterns on the ceiling. Pretty window seats are tucked in several bay windows. The granite fireplace is the house's center, opening in three directions: to the round table in the dining room, to the entry foyer, and to the sitting room—containing its only working hearth.

The upstairs rooms work well for couples. The guest rooms have the original French diamond-paned leaded windows, some of which open to the noises of the brook beside the house. Set under lovely gables and pitched eaves, each room is different, cheerful, and rustic, some with canoe canvas for walls painted in artistic pastels, like lavender and creamy yellow.

The cabins scattered throughout the property are fun and informal, from one to several bedrooms, some with fireplaces. Those nearer the lakefront seem more desirable and best suited to families. The lakefront offers a pretty, narrow beach, with many canoes, rowboats, and sailboats and a swimming dock.

Fishing is highly rewarding at Blue Mountain Lake, excellent for large- and smallmouth bass and rainbow and brown trout. Sixty miles of hiking trails are etched throughout the area, including an exciting walk to Blue Mountain's 3,800-foot summit. Well worth a visit is the Adirondack Museum, within a short walk of Hemlock Hall, sure to take up the entirety of a rainy day.

The Inn on the Library Lawn
One Washington Street
Westport, New York 12993
518-962-8666

Proprietors: Bernard and Christine DeLisle
Accommodations: 20 rooms, all with private bath
Rates: High season: $55–$85;low season: $45–$65
Included: Continental breakfast
Minimum stay: None
Added: $10 each additional guest; 7% tax
Payment: Visa, MasterCard, American Express
Children: Welcome
Pets: Not allowed
Smoking: Not allowed in rooms
Open: Inn, all year; Gables, May–November

A charming place for an overnight, food, and children's books, the Inn on the Library Lawn sits at the corner of Westport's commons teetering on the eastern edge of New York State between mountains and lakefront. The lake is called Champlain, a long and looming body of water that stretches from above Lake George all the way to Quebec, separating New York and its Adirondacks from Vermont and its Green Mountains.

Twelve miles north at Essex, the states connect via a ferry to Charlotte, just south of Burlington, Vermont.

Westport's first building was erected in 1800, and by 1850 its population had grown to 2,350. Most of the town's landmarks were built around this time through the Victorian era, including the Inn on the Library Lawn, comprising two buildings, the Inn and the Gables, from 1870. These were annexes to the famed Westport Inn, an elite gathering spot during the late 19th-century of such import that it commanded its own column in the *New York Times* and Boston newspapers titled "Social Notes from the Westport Inn." The Westport Inn was torn down in 1966, and despite the historic loss its absence provides a pretty public park called Ballard with wonderful views of Lake Champlain. Westport hospitality, however, lived on through its annexes. The Inn on the Library Lawn opened to guests in 1979 and was bought and upgraded to its present state by Bernie and Christine DeLisle in 1987.

Bernie came from Martha's Vineyard, and the Inn on the Library Lawn is very derivative of that island's summery cottage feel—an unusual departure in decor in the land of twig and bare bark furniture. The main building is an elegant two-story, square-topped yellow Italianate. Inside, a cheerful dining room with wide-planked pine flooring is furnished with spare oak tables and chairs and tapestry banquettes, with two huge picture bay windows to the lake and a third to the lawn. Breakfast is served here daily for guests in both houses. Lunch and dinner are also served daily, the latter ranging from $13 to $17 for baked chicken with prosciutto and provolone in light tomato sauce, or perhaps shrimp and scallops in puff pastry with tarragon Pernod sauce.

Upstairs, the ceilings of the ten guest rooms are extremely high, and, in fact, some rooms seem higher than wide, with three-quarter-height Italianate windows. Christine, a decorative artist, painted the walls above the picture rails in charming little vines. Do request a lake view in the Inn. Though these rooms are charming, decorated with interesting Victorian antiques, the rooms in the next-door Gables building are preferable.

Also built around 1870, the Gables is a huge white clapboard house with a curved mansard roof trimmed in black, sitting behind a white picket fence and pretty green lawn. Its Victorian common room opens to a lovely porch, dressed with wicker furniture, that steps down to the lawn. Six of the ten guest rooms have working fireplaces. Here, the Martha's Vineyard influence is quite noticeable: the floors are whitewashed, and the abundant wainscoting is a clean, creamy white, like that of a summer cottage. The house's original French windows open outward. The rooms are clean and spare, and the baths are new and immaculate, with lovely chintz curtains.

In warmer months, guests enjoy the public 18-hole PGA golf course at the Westport Country Club, the town's summer stock theater, and ample boating opportunities on Lake Champlain. Bibliophiles will love the Inn on the Library Lawn for its wonderful children's bookstore and gift shop, managed by Christine. Her selections are very creative, full of hardcover classics.

Lake Placid Manor
Whiteface Inn Road
Lake Placid, New York 12946
518-523-2573

Proprietors: Bob Hardy and Carolyn Hardy
Accommodations: 13 rooms in Main Lodge, 22 rooms in 5 cottages
Rates: High season, $40–$140; low season, $32–$112; MAP rates also available
Minimum stay: 2 nights on winter weekends
Added: $10 each additional guest; $4–$8 for each child; 7% tax; 12% tax over $100
Payment: Major credit cards
Children: Welcome
Pets: Check with innkeeper
Smoking: Not allowed in dining room
Open: All year; weekends only in April and November

Though a recommendation of Lake Placid Manor ought to come with reservations about some of the lesser guest accommodations, this family-owned Old World resort is so unusual that it cannot be neglected. This classic Adirondack camp sits on Lake Placid staring up at Whiteface Mountain. Guests must drive through the public PGA golf course at neighboring Whiteface Mountain Resort to get to the lodge.

Lake Placid Manor feels like a country retreat. The property consists of an Adirondack-style main lodge and five satellite cottages carved into a precipitous landscape that tumbles to the lakefront. Built in 1895, the Main Lodge is an enchanting place. The brown clapboard building has yellow trim, original diamond-paned leaded windows, and bare bark railings on its long porch, which loftily overlooks the lake. The tap room is a warm, wooded Adirondack room with green and white striped wicker furniture. It is adjacent to the gorgeous common living room, with exposed yellow birch and wainscoting, warmed by a huge stone fireplace over which hangs a moose under a cathedral ceiling. The foyer is cheerful and clean, with a yellow birch banister leading upstairs to the Main Lodge rooms. The atmosphere changes abruptly to the light-floored dining room, covered with scatter Orientals, at the other end of the lodge. It offers two water views and leads out to an array of steps that climb the hill to cottages and descend to the beachfront.

When booking a room, ask for a redecorated room, preferably with a lake view. In the Main Lodge, at the top of the yellow pine stairs with its Oriental runner, the second floor has charmingly rustic rooms with a kind of summer cottage feel, with those on the lakeside being a bit more deluxe. Though less traditional, the rooms on the floor below reception have been recently renovated with new baths, some interesting Adirondack furniture, and exterior patios.

The Swiss and Lake cottages claim the finest views: the former quite nice and newly redone, the latter in need of refurbishment. The Pine cottages, above the Main Lodge, also have lovely views.

Diners in the more contemporary light wood dining room feast on lake views and Continental fare. After an interesting selection of appetizers, such as lime and lager prawns, entrées range from $15 to $22 for dishes like pork tenderloin with mustard and cassis sauce and grilled yellowfin tuna with a ragout of tomatoes and olives.

Jane Reeder bought Lake Placid Manor in 1987, having always wanted to run a historic inn. Today, her son and daughter run Lake Placid Manor in a personable, kind-hearted style, lending a rare aspect of family and generosity to this rather cosmopolitan area. Their staff is happily able to help guests with the myriad activities in the immediate area.

The Lamplight Inn Bed & Breakfast

2129 Lake Avenue, Box 70
Lake Luzerne, New York 12846-0070
518-696-5294
800-262-4668

Proprietors: Gene and Linda Merlino
Accommodations: 10 rooms, all with private bath
Rates: $70–$140 (seasonal)
Included: Full breakfast
Minimum stay: 2 nights on weekends
Added: 7% tax; 12% tax over $100

Payment: All credit cards
Children: Over 12 welcome
Pets: Not allowed
Smoking: Not allowed in bedrooms or dining area
Open: All year

Eleven miles south of Lake George, across the street from the azure, still Lake Luzerne is the Lamplight Inn, the highest point in town. Inngoers will be hard pressed to find a more devoted and hardworking couple than Linda and Gene Merlino, who bought this large Victorian in 1984 and opened on Memorial Day 1985 after laborious restorations, including winterizing. Though their work for the inn seems exhaustive, it energizes this friendly couple. Linda decorated the rooms and made the curtains and coverings for the beds, while Gene built the new sun porch and four rooms above with utmost respect for the grandeur and craftsmanship of the original 1890 Victorian. He also cooks breakfast for the inn's guests while Linda serves.

The Lamplight Inn is a cheerful and rambling wooden house, yellow with blue and white trim, with an extensive wrap porch, lots of hanging flower baskets, and groomed hilly lawns. It was built in 1890 by an eligible bachelor named Howard Conkling as a summer party house. He was in the lumber business and imported all the chestnut molding and elaborate wainscoting from England, as well as the wonderfully unique carved keyhole staircase. (When Gene built the sun porch in 1989, he made sure to match the windows and wood to the original moldings and framing downstairs.) The house remained with bachelor Conkling until the 1920s, when it was bought by the Ketchum family, who owned it until the 1980s.

Guests enter to a double parlor, each room with a fireplace of carved chestnut inlaid with colorful tiling. The first parlor has two Victorian sitting areas and wainscoted walls; the second parlor is less formal, with the air of a game room. These lead to the back sun porch where guests take breakfast, with almost a double-height ceiling, its windows overlooking the sloping lawns.

The ten guest rooms are on the second floor, five of which have gas fireplaces; of these, three are in the new wing over the sun porch. Rooms not furnished with Victorian antiques have convincing reproductions. Two original rooms at the front of the house are exceptionally pretty, the mahogany bedded Canopy and Rose rooms with brass beds and unusually tiled fireplaces. Four smaller rooms in the adjacent wing lead to the larger new rooms with fireplaces. Of these, the Victoria Room is especially lovely, with a lace-covered Henredon canopy bed and art deco bedroom suite. Bathrooms are tidy and small, with personalized amenities including a shower cap. Linda is immaculate as well as creative and has equipped each room with dried flower baskets and the thoughtful gift of a mending kit.

With equestrian influences from Saratoga Springs (20 miles south), Lake Luzerne is home to one of the oldest rodeos in the country, and trail rides abound in the area. In addition, it is the summer home of a music camp for gifted students run by the Philadelphia Philharmonic.

Mirror Lake Inn

35 Mirror Lake Drive
Lake Placid, New York 12946
518-523-2544

Proprietors: Ed and Lisa Weibrecht
Accommodations: 128 rooms in five buildings (52 rooms in Mountain View, 36 rooms in Terrace Building, 5 rooms in Colonial Cottage, 8 rooms in Lake Cottage)
Rates: High season, $72–$258; low season: $92–$326
Minimum stay: 2 nights on winter weekends
Added: $34 for MAP; 7% tax; 12% tax over $100
Payment: Major credit cards
Children: Welcome
Pets: Not allowed
Smoking: Nonsmoking rooms available
Open: All year

On Mirror Lake, just yards south of Lake Placid, the Mirror Lake Inn looks like one of the grand old hotels that occupied this resort town in the early part of the century; and until 1988 it was. Destroyed by fire, the hotel was immediately reconstructed as closely as possible to its original state through the grand efforts of its current owners, Ed and Lisa Weibrecht. Today it looks much as it did in 1926, when Rufus Wikoff, better known as the Fuller Brush Man, expanded a grand lakeside home and opened its doors as a grand hotel and shortly thereafter winterized it for the 1932 Olympics. Historic pictures reproduced from the original plates depict the hotel and its guests from these days and are displayed on the public walls and in guest rooms. Though tied to history, the Mirror Lake Inn offers sophisticated accommodations and the amenities of a luxury hotel.

The white clapboard mansion sits on eight acres above Mirror Lake, wedged into a steep hill. Up the front stairs, the lobby very successfully imitates its ancestor, with deep mahogany paneling, traditional sitting areas in front of a stunning green marble hearth, and a 1902 Knabe piano. It abuts a clubby library, with vertical and horizontal wainscoting lined with shelves of books, a huge buck above the grand stone hearth, opening to a porch permitting wonderful breezes from the lake. At the other end of the building, across from the reception area, is the dining room, along an entire windowed wing overlooking Mirror Lake. Front porches with lakefront views decorate the inn, for quiet reading or sociable gathering.

There are five types of rooms, nearly all with a balcony and water view, throughout the inn, which expands up the hill to a newer section and across the street in the Colonial and Lake cottages on the banks of the lake. Most preferable are those in the Mountain View; those in the Terrace Building are more generic. All are generously sized, decorated with reproduction furniture, some with cathedral ceilings and modern conveniences like televisions and phones. The new bathrooms are spotless and spacious. For a bed-and-breakfast feel, some guests may prefer the Colonial and Lake cottages. The Lake Cottage has four rooms on each of two floors, each room with a large balcony right on the lake—be sure to ask for the front rooms for the best view. The Colonial Cottage has no balconies and is decorated in English country style.

The charming Cottage Café neighbors the Lake Cottage, with wonderful light fare on an outdoor porch and informal indoor setting. On the ground floor of the Main Inn is Mirror Lake's fitness center, with an indoor pool, hair salon, and exercise equipment, whirlpool, and sauna. Service is cosmopolitan though friendly. The abundance of outdoor activities—winter and summer—is exhilarating, and the staff is happy to provide information.

Pennsylvania

The Inn at Starlight Lake
Starlight, Pennsylvania 18461
717-798-2519

Proprietors: Jack and Judy McMahon
Accommodations: 26 rooms, all but 3 with private bath (14 in main inn, 12 in 4 outbuildings, including 1 suite)
Rates (MAP):
  Rooms: $110–$140 per couple
  Suite: $185 per couple
  Summer: Additional 10%

Included: Breakfast and dinner
Minimum stay: 2 nights in high season, 3 nights on holiday
   weekends
Added: $49 each additional adult; $37 each additional child
   age 7–12; 6% tax
Payment: Visa, MasterCard
Children: Welcome; under 7, free
Pets: Not allowed
Smoking: Not allowed in dining room
Open: Closed first two weeks of April

In the very northeast corner of Pennsylvania, neighboring New York, the Inn at Starlight Lake rests in the lovely unspoiled Appalachians. While certainly removed from civilization, the inn does not seem remote. Its intelligent, personable, professional innkeepers have honed an air of comfort and sophistication about this place during their tenure since 1975. They raised a family here and remain very visible fixtures, greeting and socializing with guests and offering interesting local lore.

The inn was built in 1909, encouraged no doubt by the now abandoned railroad depot several hundred feet away, which made this undiscovered area suddenly accessible to New Yorkers. The main building is a green clapboard introduced by a welcoming front porch; an adjacent tennis court forms a kind of courtyard for the three outbuildings. The inn offers canoes, sailboats, and rowboats for guests to enjoy the 45 spring-fed acres of Starlight Lake, one of more than one hundred lakes in this area, referred to as Pennsylvania Lake Country.

The large lobby of the Main Inn is immediately welcoming, its heart pine walls and floors highly varnished, with scatter Orientals underfoot, leading to an enormous stone hearth housing a wood-burning stove that casts warmth onto Mission furnishings. Through French doors, guests find the informal Stovepipe Bar; beyond are the two dining rooms, one of which is an enclosed section of the inn's front porch from which guests view the lakefront. Dinner is a combination of elegant and rustic, ranging from $10 to $24 for Continental entrées such as beef Stroganoff-tenderloin or lamb chops in light brandy sauce, always with home-baked bread. Pasta night is once weekly.

Upstairs in the Main Inn are 14 guest rooms, cozy and comfortable, some with brand-new baths and recently refurbished cheery decor, all with silk flowers, plants, and a commendable reading library. Prints, ink drawings of American primitives, and Victorian art decorate the walls, and occasional period antiques serve as pleasant surprises. Be sure to request a room with a lake view, as the rates in the Main Inn are all the same.

Two of the three units in the unfairly named "motel" have great cathedral ceilings. Adjacent are a two-unit cottage and a three-room house on two floors, offering the inn's most elegant accommodation, a two-room suite with a whirlpool bath. Above is an unusual room with two sleeping alcoves on the porch. The family house has three guest rooms, its bottom floor with a capacious bunk room.

The Inn at Starlight Lake is a great place for families as well as for couples seeking a romantic retreat. Golf and horseback riding are within close range, and fishing is optimal at the Upper Delaware trout fishery five miles away. As well, the McMahons have forged 18 miles of cross-country trails in the surrounding area. Downhill skiers venture only 15 minutes away to Mt. Tone, 30 to Elk Mountain, the state's largest.

Woodloch Pines

RD1, Box 280
Hawley, Pennsylvania 18428
717-685-7121

Proprietors: John Kiesendahl and Russell Kranich
Accommodations: 160 rooms in 4 main buildings and smaller houses
Rates: $60–$150 per person AP (seasonally)
Included: 3 meals a day, all activites
Minimum stay: 3 nights during the summer
Added: Children age 13–19, half adult rate; age 7–12, $45; age 3–6, $23; 6% tax
Payment: Visa, MasterCard
Children: Welcome, under 3 free
Pets: Not allowed
Smoking: Allowed
Open: Closed Christmas week

This family resort, set on Lake Teedyuskung in the Poconos, is a secret, rarely advertised. Difficult to find on a map, it's nine miles east of Hawley and Lake Wallenpaupack, Pennsylvania's largest recreational lake. Its original structures were built as a summer estate in 1918 by the wealthy Lochwood family and were bought in 1946 by Olga and George Svenningsen, who expanded and maintained the property as a Scandinavian boardinghouse until 1958.

At that time, two young couples, a foursome of friends—Harry and Mary Kiesendahl and Don and Margie Kranich—

decided to open a business together. They found an ad for the estate, which was known from the days of its first owners as Woodloch, on the lake where Mary had fond memories from childhood summers. A new generation of Kiesendahl and Kranich families runs Woodloch Pines today, in the spirit of their watchful elders, with love and respect for their lake, its tradition, and their generations of returning guests. The staff is an extension of their families, a wholesome, dependable, happy bunch, numbering about four hundred for just as many guests in warmer months—most of whom were introduced to Woodloch Pines by their families.

Woodloch Pines borders the southern end of Lake Teedyuskung, fed by underground springs and named for a majestic Indian chief known as the King of the Delawares. With a 65-acre surface, the lake is a mile and a half long and a half mile wide, with an average depth of 15 to 20 feet. As it hovers 1,500 feet above sea level, the lake offers magnificent winter activities such as tobogganing, skating, ice fishing, skiing, and sleigh riding; in addition, warmer months offer the usual day's fill of waterskiing, boating, and swimming.

The architecture centers around the original shingled house, surrounded by rambling cottages and several contemporary lodges. While some buildings may be new and not necessarily beautiful, they remain hidden in the foliage and natural landscape. In addition to the resort characteristics of well-appointed rooms in the larger buildings, Woodloch Pines can also feel like a camp, with smaller cabins tucked off pathways, areas for go-carts, volleyball, basketball, handball, and horseshoes.

The rooms are decorated with a clean American country feeling, in traditional light pine or reproduction cherry or in contemporary furnishings. Meals are served family style in the large dining rooms, with no limit to consumption of the wholesome, hearty food made fresh in the Woodloch kitchens. They even make their own ice cream.

Joey Ranner and Randy Barnes mastermind a dizzying number of activities for every imaginable group, from toddlers to senior citizens. In addition to lakeside activities, there is an outdoor pool, a new fitness complex with an indoor pool, and, a mile from the resort, an 18-hole golf course which opened in 1992.

Virginia

The Manor at Taylor's Store
Smith Mountain Lake, Route 1, Box 533
Wirtz, Virginia 24184
703-721-3951

Proprietors: Mary Lynn and Lee Tucker
Accommodations: 6 rooms and 3-bedroom Christmas Cottage
Rates: $70–$100
Included: Full breakfast
Minimum stay: Selected weekends
Added: 6.5% tax
Payment: MasterCard, Visa
Children: Welcome in the Christmas Cottage
Pets: Not allowed
Smoking: Limited
Open: All year

The Manor at Taylor's Store is three miles from wondrous Smith Mountain Lake, an active boating and state recreation center in Virginia's southwestern frontier. The 20,000-acre lake has 500 miles of shoreline, is about 40 miles long, and is well loved by fishermen looking for landlocked striped and large-mouth bass. The lake's overwhelming beauty is best—and uniquely—appreciated from the basket of a hot-air balloon, an undertaking that innkeepers Lee and Mary Lynn Tucker will be most happy to arrange.

Fifteen miles east of Roanoke and the Blue Ridge Mountains, the Manor at Taylor's Store is named for a famous merchandise trading post established on this site in 1799 by Skelton Taylor, an introduction to the unexplored West on the Old Warwick Road. Most of what stands today is an elegant three-story white clapboard manor house set back from Route 122 by lovely lawns, built in the early 19th century as part of a tobacco plantation, rebuilt in the 1890s, and restored by its current owners over two years starting in 1986 when they were new-lyweds. Lee, a pathologist, and Mary Lynn, a former nurse, are consummate hosts with contagious enthusiasm for their home and surroundings.

Over the years, the Tuckers have carefully collected some beautiful antiques, including the formal Victorian living room set with several velvet tufted chairs and a mirror-back couch. The imposing tall case clock in the corner was designed in 1903 by Stanford White for a wealthy Long Island family. Through a threshold are the dining room and enclosed sun porch with views to some of the 120 acres, home to two Newfoundlands, several horses, and six spring-fed ponds, which are wonderful for fishing, swimming, and canoeing; the largest has two swimming docks.

Lee and Mary Lynn devoted much space for guests' common use: the lower level Great Room has a slate floor with a big-screen television and a fitness room with rowing and cross-country ski machines, an exercise bike, and weights. Adjacent to this is an enclosed hot tub and a kitchen for guest use. The cozy Garden Room shares the ground floor, with a private entrance and sun porch.

A favorite is the first-floor Plantation Suite, with a working fireplace and two antique handmade double beds in rich carved walnut, under canopies whose linens match bedskirts and window treatments. Among the preferred second-floor rooms are the Colonial Room, past the well-stocked hall library, with a queen-size fishnet canopy bed and a private balcony; the Toy Room, with antique quilts and toys, opening through French doors to a dramatic view of the back pastures; and the Castle Suite, with a queen-size canopy bed, mountain views, and a new bath featuring a sunken tub. Mary Lynn prefers the comfort of flannel sheets year-round and is meticulous about her rooms.

The Booker T. Washington National Monument stands proudly four miles away on the route to Smith Mountain Lake.

Mountainside Stops

Pennsylvania

The Crestmont
Eagles Mere, Pennsylvania 17731
717-525-3519

Proprietors: Kathleen and Robert Oliver
Accommodations: 16 rooms and 4 suites
Rates: $62.50 per person, MAP
Included: Full country breakfast and four-course dinner;
    country club facilities, tennis, golf, use of boats
Minimum stay: 2 nights on weekends
Added: 10% gratuity; 6% tax
Payment: No credit cards
Children: Six and over welcome
Pets: Not allowed
Smoking: Nonsmoking rooms available
Open: May–October, winter weekends

About halfway between Williamsport and Scranton, the tiny town of Eagles Mere is a turn-of-the-century resort for local Pennsylvanians. At 2,354 feet, Eagles Mere is the highest point in Sullivan County and home to a spring-fed, picture-perfect, crater-made lake with a sandy beach. The northern part of Pennsylvania is quite mountainous and wooded, with towns few and far between, and Eagles Mere displays all the virtues of this topography.

Owned since 1982 by the Oliver family, Crestmont is a short drive heavenward from the charming main street of Eagles Mere. The ten-acre property consists of the Olivers' home, several condominium townhouses, and the inn and its restaurant, all situated around a circular drive. While the rooms are modestly decorated, guests are treated rather royally at Crestmont.

On the property is a pool and six Har-Tru tennis courts, with a full-time pro during the summer, the setting for several tournaments. In addition, guests have country club privileges which entitle them to use the scenic golf course as well as full lake privileges. Sailing is a big activity at Eagles Mere Lake, which hosts many a summertime regatta, and guests may rent boats nearby.

Four-course candlelight dinners in the cherry Garden Room are an elegant affair, included in the overnight rate, with a choice of 12 Continental entrées. Kathleen, of Irish descent, is the inspiration for the menu, the sauces, jams, breads, and lavish homemade desserts, such as English trifle.

The rooms at Crestmont are on the first and second floors of a turn-of-the-century light blue clapboard building at the corner of the property. Twenty rooms span two floors, small and comfortable, with Victorian reproduction wallpaper, modest antiques, and clean, renovated private baths.

The virtues of Eagles Mere have been celebrated by locals for nearly a century, and those virtues consist of a love of the mountain air and the azure lake. Overnighting here means a good, clean room in which to get a good rest on fine mattresses for the next day's outdoor activities. The Olivers are an elegant, gracious couple who love the comforts of their perch on Eagles Mere. Winter skiing is enjoyed at Picture Rocks, a 30-minute drive south; nearby Lake Mokoma is a short drive east, as is Ricketts Glen State Park; and Worlds End State Park is a jump northward.

Virginia

Irish Gap Inns
Route 1, Box 40
Vesuvius, Virginia 24483
804-922-7701

Proprietor: Dillard Saunders
Innkeepers: Lucie Garland, Martha Shewey, Dillard Saunders
Accommodations: 4 rooms in Bee Skep Inn, all with private bath; 3 rooms in Gate House, 2 with private bath
Rates: $68–$98; April–October, $68–$108
Included: Full breakfast
Minimum stay: 2 nights on May and October weekends
Added: $20 each additional guest; 6.5% tax
Payment: MasterCard, Visa

Children: 12 and over allowed in Bee Skep; all ages allowed
   in Gate House
Pets: Not allowed
Smoking: Allowed
Open: All year

Just south of Waynesboro, the pay-to-enter Skyline Drive turns
into the Blue Ridge Parkway, offering views just as breathtaking without cost. The Irish Gap Inns, on the northernmost
stretch of the Blue Ridge Parkway, are one of the few overnight
hostelries on this scenic drive. In this dramatic mountain setting, guests are as pampered as they are removed from civilization.

   The Blue Ridge Parkway feels like the frontier, seldom offering a structure of any kind — much less a luxurious hostelry —
on its cloud-level roads. Vaguely set between mileposts 37 and
38, separated from the parkway by a dirt road, the Irish Gap
Inns comprise two buildings, built in 1986 and 1987 by Dillard
Saunders, her mother, and her sister. Via a winding dirt road,
guests first pass the Victorian-style Gate House before approaching the Bee Skep Inn, a traditional timber-frame building with four guest rooms overlooking three ponds and mountain views.

   The Bee Skep has enormous 300-year-old Palladian windows in its expansive common room, which overlooks Dillard's
farmhouse and horses, two fishing ponds, one frog pond, two
llamas, seven dogs, horses, goats, chickens, turkeys, and of
course the famous rabbits — French, English, and Holland lop
— who greet guests at the entrance. Dillard brings to her innkeeping a career's worth of experience as an interior designer,
creating an eclectic mix of rare antiques with the color and
patterns of modern design. The common room has a beamed
ceiling, with clean, light wood and spare, colorful furniture,
progressing into the dining room with its fabulous high-backed
chairs.

   There are two guest rooms per floor, each with a generous
balcony. The Fox Hunter and Heart rooms have wonderful
views of the pond and mountain, the latter room on the second
floor used as a honeymoon suite with a queen-size four-poster
bed. The other two rooms overlook the rabbit garden. The
first-floor room, named accordingly, is decorated with rabbit
themes and has a reproduction German armoire and two double beds. Above, the Woodland decor is a Cloisters unicorn
tapestry complemented by maroon linens and unicorn wallpaper in the bath.

Set away from the inn, the Gate House is a remote, pretty place, perfect for families or couples traveling together, with stunning views east down Pedlar Valley. The Stripe Room and a common area occupy the first floor. The second floor has two bedrooms including the Butterfly Room with a four-poster queen-size bed, breathtaking views from its window seat, and a whirlpool bath.

Dillard and fellow innkeepers Lucie and Martha work hard to create an intensely relaxing experience at Irish Gap. In addition to a marvelous country breakfast, they will make elaborate dinners with advance notice. For activities, guests travel 18 miles down the mountain to Lexington, home of the Virginia Horse Center; farther south to wondrous Natural Bridge; north to Victorian Staunton; or east to skiing at Wintergreen.

Mountain Lake

Mountain Lake, Virginia 24136
703-626-7121
800-346-3334

Proprietor: Mary Moody Northen Foundation
General Manager: Buzz Scanland
Accommodations: 92 units (45 in main lodge, 16 in Chestnut
    Lodge, 31 in 19 cottages)
Rates (MAP):
    Room: $150–$160
    Suites: $185–$240
    Family suites: $255–$265
    Chestnut Lodge: $175
    1-to-3-bedroom cottages: From $125–$340
Included: Breakfast and dinner
Minimum stay: 2 nights on weekends
Added: $35 each additional guest; children age 5–12, $20
    (under 5 free); 6.5% tax; $5.50 service charge per person daily
Payment: Major credit cards
Children: Allowed
Pets: Not allowed
Smoking: Nonsmoking rooms available
Open: All year

Mountain Lake is one of the more remote resorts in this book, wedged in the Potts Mountains of Jefferson National Forest on the lower border of the Virginias. A winding, narrow seven-mile drive up Salt Pond Mountain offers spectacular, ever-changing perspectives on the mountainous setting. At the summit, just under 4,000 feet, is the beautiful stone lodge, a series of log cabins, and the stunning vista of sparkling Mountain Lake, one of only two natural freshwater lakes in Virginia. The resort remains a well-kept secret, and its 2,600 acres and 15 miles of trails a rare treat for naturalists. If the place looks rather familiar, it's because *Dirty Dancing* was filmed here in 1986.

There are three faces to Mountain Lake: the elegant stone manor house, with nicely appointed rooms, some with Jacuzzis; the less formal, contemporary Chestnut Lodge, in which rooms have fireplaces and balconies; and the very rustic cottages. Resort days at Mountain Lake date to 1857 and a white wooden boarding house, which became vastly popular at the turn of the century. William Lewis Moody from Galveston, Texas bought the property in the early 1930s and erected the grand lodge in 1936 using native stone. Eventually, his daughter Mary took over, and though she died in 1986, her presence lives on in the generous, happy traditions of Mountain Lake.

Couples may want to spend time in the main lodge or Chestnut Lodge, the former with 45 rooms on two floors furnished in deluxe, traditional reproduction furniture, the latter in a more contemporary style, built in 1985, with 16 rooms. Families tend to gather in the many informal log cabin cottages scattered around the property. The main lodge remains the focal point of a stay at Mountain Lake. The public rooms on the first and ground levels seem rather fortresslike, with thick stone walls, low ceilings, cozy, library-inspired sitting areas leading to tranquil porches overlooking the lake. The dining room is wonderful, with romantic fireside and lake views, its ceiling supported by stone pillars.

Though couples will love long walks, the fireplaces, carriage rides, golf, tennis, and cross-country skiing, families with children will be overwhelmed by the dozens of activities organized daily by a full-time staff. Cookouts, clambakes, steak fries, storytelling, dancing, and other events take place in the recreation barn and loft. Mountain Lake is stocked with trout, largemouth bass, blue gill, and sunfish. For above-water pleasure, there are canoes, paddleboats, and rowboats. An electric pontoon boat takes daily rides to the Boat House at the end of the lake. There is an Old World elegance about Mountain Lake that remains casual, and while hosting all activities of a large resort, the management maintains a small, intimate scale. The staff seems like a large family, helpful and genuinely happy to be in this setting and part of a great hospitality tradition.

Peaks of Otter Lodge
Box 489
Bedford, Virginia 24523
703-586-1081

General Manager: Don Humphreys
Accommodations: 62 rooms, with 3 suites in main Lodge
Rates: Winter: rooms, $75; suites, $85; rest of year, $65 (no meals)
Included: Weekday dinner and breakfast; weekend dinner only
Added: $4 each additional adult; 6.5% tax
Payment: MasterCard, Visa
Children: Welcome
Pets: Not allowed
Smoking: Allowed
Open: All year

The Peaks of Otter Lodge is propped up on the Blue Ridge Parkway, halfway between Roanoke and Lynchburg. The magnificent mountainside, lakeside property is leased from the National Park Service; and the Lodge, built in 1964, is privately owned. Accommodations, therefore, are a tad fancier than average National Park fare, at extremely reasonable rates.

The Peaks of Otter are two neighboring mountains providing majestic views: Flat Top, just over 4,000 feet, and Sharp Top at 3,875 feet. Three theories have evolved around the naming of this scenic place: the appellation could have derived from the Indian word *ottari*, meaning "high places"; the peaks might have been named by Scottish settlers after a mountain in their homeland which resembles Sharp Top, called Ben Otter; or they may have been directly named for nearby Otter River.

The Lodge hovers at a lowly 2,560 feet, dominated by a busy public restaurant which serves three meals daily, as well as a famous Sunday buffet. Overnight units are set apart from the Lodge in a contemporary two-story structure. Yet most important, the Peaks of Otter rest around the one-mile perimeter of manmade Abbott Lake, 24 acres of crystal waters stocked with smallmouth bass.

Each room is furnished in motel-style simplicity, quite clean, with two double beds covered with white spreads and sensible furniture including a writing desk and ample reading lamps, all looking toward a picture window with an expansive lake view. The baths are new, clean, and spare. Happily, all the rooms at Peaks of Otter have balconies or patios overlooking Abbott Lake and Sharp Top Mountain.

Most commendable are the reasonable rates for this groomed lakeside property with mountain views. Dinner entrées range from $8 to $14 in the sociable dining hall. The Peaks of Otter is an active recreational hub for appreciative visitors to the Blue Ridge Park. Guests have the double pleasure of the Lodge, which is fairly bustling during high season, and the privacy of clean, comfortable rooms with mountain-view balconies.

Skyland Lodge
Big Meadows Lodge
Skyline Drive
Shenandoah National Park, Virginia
703-999-2211
800-999-4714

Proprietors: ARA Virginia Sky-Line Co., Inc., Box 727, Luray, Virginia 22835
Accommodations: 186 rooms in motel units and cabins in Skyland Lodge; 100 rooms in Big Meadows Lodge (25 in Lodge, others in cabins with fireplaces)
Rates: $38–$122 (highest on weekends and in October)
Minimum stay: None
Added: 6.5% tax
Payment: Major credit cards
Children: Welcome
Pets: Not allowed
Smoking: Allowed
Open: Skyland: Early April through November; Big Meadows: Mid-May through October

Ten miles apart on the Skyline Drive, just outside of Stanley, Skyland and Big Meadows are the only two lodging facilities on the 105-mile-long scenic mountain pass. Owned by the ARA Sky-Line company, which runs the concessions along the drive, these two lodging spots combine the rustic excitement of camping and the comfort of a hotel in one of the country's most beautiful National Parks.

The Skyland Lodge is the northern property at milepost 41.7, considered slightly more private than Big Meadows. At 3,703 feet, Skyland is the highest point on the drive, offering inspirational views. The property consists of 186 rooms shared among 28 buildings, from contemporary two-room suites to motel units to rustic two-room cabins. All rooms have balconies looking westward to the glorious landscape of the Shenandoah Valley. The large dining room, which shares its menu with Big Meadows, serves hearty mountain food and Virginia cooking, like steak and quail, shepherd's pie, country cured ham served with spiced apples, or southern fried chicken served with corn fritters and local honey. The specialty dessert is blackberry ice cream pie, enhanced with blackberry syrup and meringue.

Big Meadows offers a little more beauty in its architecture. Its main lodge, built in 1939, is introduced by a flagstone patio looking 3,640 feet down the Shenandoah Valley. While the grand dining room shares this view, it is in itself a most glorious sight, with a cathedral ceiling of open-beamed wormy chestnut. Some rustic guest rooms are in the lodge, others are spread throughout cabins with fireplaces.

Each property hosts its own nightly entertainment. As the accommodations are furnished sparely with average decor, the consensus at Big Meadows and Skyland is that the splendor rests in the outdoors.

A visitors center at Big Meadows details the dizzying amount of outdoor activities in the park: more than 500 miles of marked hiking trails, including a 95-mile segment of the Appalachian Trail, horseback riding, wagon rides, bird-watching of more than 200 species in the park, family camping, and dozens of naturalist programs.

Trillium House
Wintergreen, Box 280
Nellysford, Virginia 22958
804-325-9126

Proprietors: Betty and Ed Dinwiddie
Accommodations: 12 rooms and 2 suites, all private bath
Rates: Rooms, $65–$95; suites, $120–$150
Included: Full buffet breakfast
Minimum stay: 2 nights on most weekends, 3 nights on some holidays
Added: $35 for additional guest in appropriate room; 6.5% tax
Payment: MasterCard, Visa
Children: Well-behaved children welcome
Pets: Not allowed

Smoking: Not allowed in dining room
Open: Closed Christmas Eve and Christmas Day

For those who love the modern conveniences of resort life and a traditional country inn atmosphere, Trillium is a great find, on the peak of Wintergreen resort at 3,800 feet. The resort, though rather contemporary in design, is unusually appreciative of its 11,000 acres of wilderness, set into the Blue Ridge Mountains just south of Waynesboro, 43 miles southwest of Charlottesville. Trillium guests have access to the best of Wintergreen: extensive naturalist programs, admirable snow-making facilities for downhill skiing, two award-winning golf courses, 20 miles of marked hiking trails, horseback riding, spa, and tennis courts.

The weathered gray clapboard house was built on the 17th hole of Wintergreen's mountaintop Devil's Knob golf course by Ed and Betty Dinwiddie in 1983. The house is an interesting combination of traditional two-story, dormer-windowed saltbox and contemporary structure with Palladium windows, set at oblique angles. Quite generous with its common space, Trillium House is blessed with a large center section with a cathedral ceiling, into which was built a library loft filled with four walls of books. Below, a comfortable sitting area surrounds a Vermont stove. Around the center chimney is a sunny porch, looking out to the golf course. The walls are a clean white, and the trim, poplar moldings, and floors are finished in dark oak and covered in Orientals.

Single-entrée dinners, prepared by chef Ellen English, are served at a 7:30 seating in the dining room on Friday and Saturday nights only, a sociable, informal event. The first floor of the inn has eight rooms; the second floor has four. These are furnished sparely, with occasional antiques, done in simple winter resort style with little clutter.

The Dinwiddies are kind, family people, with a great passion for their unique location at Wintergreen and their profession as innkeepers. Try to visit Wintergreen's nature center, staffed with highly informed professionals who impart a great appreciation for the environment in this mountain resort.

Wintergreen
Box 706
Wintergreen, Virginia 22958
804-325-2200
800-325-2200

Proprietors: Wintergreen Partners Inc.; Dana Percival, C.O.O.
General Manager: Gunther Muller, C.E.O.

Accommodations: 350 mountain villas (including studio to
   4-bedroom condominiums)
Rates: Studios, $95–$135; 4-bedroom, $270–$380 (seasonally)
Minimum stay: 2 nights on weekends
Added: 4.5% tax
Payment: American Express, Visa, MasterCard
Children: Welcome
Pets: Not allowed
Smoking: Allowed
Open: All year

It would be easy to say that the most special aspect of Wintergreen is its location, 3,800 feet high in the Blue Ridge Mountains, a mile from the scenic Blue Ridge Parkway; but there are
so many other features of life at Wintergreen that make it a
wonderful, unique, and commendable new resort. Even more
important than its two golf courses, 25 tennis courts, six swimming pools, and indoor spa, even better than its ski facilities,
Virginia's best, which offer snow making for a mountain with a
1,000-foot vertical drop, most notably Wintergreen has a great
environmental conscience, with one of the finest nature de-
partments of resorts in this book.

Wintergreen is privately owned by its shareholders. The
property comprises condominiums, homes, and hotel units,
with a great architectural range of more than 20 communities,
all built below tree level and approved by an architectural re-
view board, so as not to disrupt the landscape. If this sounds
busy, accommodations at Wintergreen are spread over 11,000
acres—so even if the resort is booked to its capacity of 1,300,
each guest has about 9 acres to himself or herself. The interior
decor is contemporary, deluxe, and quite varied.

There are six restaurants throughout Wintergreen, ranging
from snack shops to country cooking to formal dining; two
lounges; nightly entertainment; and a gallery of shops. The
Wintergarden Spa has a great indoor lap pool, three hot tubs,
saunas, and an exercise room.

The resort has set aside 6,700 acres as undisturbed forestland, overseen by naturalist Doug Coleman, a full-time em-
ployee. He and his staff of five conduct guided field trips, maintain more than 25 miles of marked trails, and give lectures
about the area's natural history—from 8,000-year-old artifacts
to the 400 species of wildflowers to wildlife at Wintergreen.

Wintergreen's children's programs are nationally acclaimed.
Four-day children's summer camps focus around scientific
study of ecology, botany, archaeology, and animals. Teen camps
are designed with a more adventurous spirit, offering canoeing

down the rapids, ropes courses, horseback riding, hiking, and scuba diving at Lake Monocan. Youngsters are watched at the fully staffed Treehouse. Nighttime activities as well as ski season activities are thoroughly planned.

Wintergreen is home to two award-winning golf courses: uppermost Devil's Knob, the highest in the state at 3,800 feet with 50-mile vistas, and Stoney Creek in the foothills, providing incredible views over two very different foliage seasons, given their different altitudes. In fact, since Stoney Creek is kept open year-round, guests may move from the links in the morning to the slopes in the afternoon. Its new golf school, introduced in 1991, boasts a four-to-one student-teacher ratio.

The Skyline Pavilion was completed in 1990 for $3.5 million, the base for the state's best ski facilities and rental equipment with 1,800 pairs of skis. Of the ten ski slopes with runs up to 4,500 feet, five are lit for night skiing and improved by advanced snow making. The Wintergreen Ski School offers beginning through advanced instruction, as well as racing facilities at Diamond Hill.

Romantic Retreats

Delaware

The Towers
101 Northwest Front Street
Milford, Delaware 19963
302-422-3814
302-424-0321
Reservations: 800-366-3814

Proprietors: Michael Real and Mark Springer
Accommodations: 6 rooms, 4 with private bath, including 2
    suites
Rates: $85–$125
Included: Full breakfast
Minimum stay: Some weekends
Added: 8% tax
Payment: MasterCard, Visa
Children: Not allowed
Pets: Not allowed
Smoking: Not allowed
Open: All year

The Towers is an incredibly beautiful bed-and-breakfast in the
fairly uninspired working-class town of Milford, several miles
inland from the Delaware Bay. The twelve shades of mauve,
lavender, yellow, purple, blue, pink, and mint on the exterior
were inspired by the colors of the original and extravagant
stained glass windows found in the house. Almost fantasy, this
house goes on forever, with turrets, towers, and ten different
kinds of gingerbread in a carnival of colors. The fabulous exterior is only a preamble to the lavish interior decorating done by
owner Michael Real, who concentrates on French antiques.

Oddly, the house was built far before any of this fanciful
architecture was even invented, in 1783, four years before Milford was founded. Dr. John Wallace was the proprietor; his

stepson John Lofland, born here, became a poet of notable fame known as the Milford Bard, whose friend and colleague Edgar Allan Poe often visited. In 1840, the house was bought by Delaware governor William Burton who, fifty years later, gave the house to his granddaughter Rhoda Roudebush, and she spent $42,000 on a complete Victorianization in 1895. Roudebush imported a master craftsman from Italy who supervised the installation of the lavish stained glass in every window of the house.

In 1985, Michael Real and partner Mark Springer were swept away by this property on their way to look at another in Lewes. Their restoration took two and a half years and included stripping plywood off walls to find traces of gold leaf. The music room, to the right of the foyer, several steps down, has a coffered ceiling in light sycamore, extinct from blight by 1900. The parlor across the hall has cherry paneling; the mirroring dining room combines cherry with chestnut; and upstairs, the wainscoting combines these woods with walnut.

The music room has a grand piano, carved mantel, rose couches, and two lion-headed gilded French chairs from the turn of the 18th century. The room is separated from the hallway by thinly carved sycamore spindles that permit music to waft throughout the house. The formal living room displays some of Michael's French treasures — notably, a Second Empire cylinder desk gilded in bronze, with green marble top, from Napoleon III, with Egyptian influences.

Surely the third-floor Rapunzel Suite is the most magnificent, with a twelve-foot ceiling, named because of its access to the turret tower in a screened porch under the eaves. The bed is a Louis XVI with linens from Scalamandre, and its crown canopy falls from a gilded Louis XV mantel. A Sun King double armoire lingers in the corner of the room, as do other treasures, like an onyx statue, an elegant settee, and a sitting suite near the bath. Across the hall is the Victorian Bird's Nest Room, with a nine-foot carved walnut headboard.

The four second-floor rooms are all very different, equal only in elegance. The Tower Room, under the Rapunzel Suite, has a little window seat in the turret as well as a French Tiffany mantel clock and a statue of David on a marble-top table. The bed of the Louis XVI Garden Room has a lovely gathered and puckered white linen coverlet. The shared bath here is wonderful, with dark wainscoting, a canopy over the bath up two steps, and separate washroom with stained glass. There are six fireplaces in the house, some marble, some carved in garlands, two of which are in the guest rooms.

The back gardens are highly groomed, with swirly extensive high-backed white iron furniture, very similar to that in the film version of *The Great Gatsby*. There are statues, a fountain, and a gazebo where guest may take breakfast. Toward the back of the property, up several steps to a deck is a swimming pool.

Maryland

Antrim 1844
30 Trevanion Road
Taneytown, Maryland 21787
410-756-6812

Proprietors: Richard and Dorothy Mollett
General Manager and Chef: Michael Sell
Accommodations: 12 rooms, all with private bath, most with fireplace
Rates: Weekends, $150–$250; weekdays, $125–$200
Included: Full breakfast
Minimum stay: 2 nights on weekends and holidays
Added: 5% tax
Payment: Visa, MasterCard
Children: Allowed
Pets: Not allowed
Smoking: Allowed
Open: All year

Antrim is quite an exciting property, set on 25 acres of rural farmland about 40 minutes north of Washington, D.C., and 12 miles south of Gettysburg. The mansion is genteel and impressive, from its preserved architecture to its 11 fireplaces, its lovely accommodations and luxurious baths, and the gourmet dinners and stunning collection of antiques. In 1988, Dort and Richard Mollett rescued this brick plantation home from fifty years of vacancy and undertook an extensive, year-long restoration which included installing electricity.

Antrim was built in 1844 by Andrew Ege, a wealthy Irish immigrant who fondly named his home after the county in which he was born. In 1860, Antrim was bought by George Washington Clabaugh, expanded to 2,800 acres, and remained in the family until 1965. It was used at one time by Union General Meade during the Civil War, who observed Confederate troops from the widow's walk.

The house, a unique composite of Greek Revival, Federal, and Italianate architecture, has a single-story veranda running the length of the facade and wrapping around one side. The other side of the building, covered in striped awnings, faces the structured gardens, a fountain anchored in a fishpond, and graveled walkways illuminated by lanterns leading to the clay tennis court, the competition-style croquet lawn, and the bowling lawn. Past the yellow clapboard Ice House (with one luxurious guest room) is the black-bottom swimming pool and, farther, the green barn, containing two guest rooms.

Visitors enter from the veranda to a magnificent foyer on whose heart pine floors is laid a great Oriental carpet and a Scottish case clock from 1830. To the right is a double parlor with grand pocket windows at either end of each room, vertically opening French doors which disappear into the wall above the threshold. Among the vast treasures here are two marble mantels carved by sculptor William Rinehart, an 1880 Knabe piano, a Queen Anne highboy from 1780, and an 1840 Chinese Chippendale settee with a tapestried base. All the plaster moldings are original, including the magnificent rose medallions from which hang a pair of brass chandeliers.

Opposite the parlors across the foyer is the blue-walled formal dining room, where a breakfast might include Belgian waffles, fried tomatoes, grilled scrapple and bacon, and poached pears. Adjacent is the Hunt Room den, with a pair of tufted leather sofas, a full stereo system, and polished granite working fireplace.

Four rooms fill each of the following two floors above, decorated by Dort, a former interior designer. Most notable are the museum-quality canopy beds. The Clabaugh Room has a 19th-century rosewood half-tester bed covered in tapestry linens, with the original gas sconces attached on the headboard, now electrified for night reading. Across the hall is the chintz-papered Boyd Room, named for the colonel who owned the magnificent 1790 canopy bed. The Meade Room has access to the side balcony through a weighted window in its marble bath. Its 1820 canopy bed is Honduras mahogany, and the walls are done in a masculine blue and white stripe.

Among the other accommodations are the four third-floor rooms, the Room with a View from its veranda on the back wing of the second floor, the roadside cottage, the luxury Ice House room, and two rooms in the green barn. Guests are treated to port and chocolates at nightly turndown.

A new feature at Antrim is its dining room in the former Summer Kitchen and Smokehouse adjacent to the mansion. This romantic brick-floored place has been open to the public for a short time, featuring dinners by chef Michael Sell Thursdays through Sundays. Guests sit in soft wool plaid wing chairs, of Ralph Lauren derivation and dine fireside by a stone hearth on distinctive gold-trimmed Antrim china.

Brampton Bed and Breakfast
Route 20, RR2, Box 107
Chestertown, Maryland 21620
410-778-1860

Proprietors: Michael and Danielle Hanscom
Accommodations: 6 rooms, including 1 suite, all with private
  bath, 4 with fireplace
Rates: $90–$110
Included: Full breakfast
Minimum stay: 2 nights on weekends, 3 nights on holidays
Added: $25 each additional guest; 5% tax
Payment: MasterCard, Visa
Children: Alowed in suite only
Pets: Not allowed
Smoking: Allowed only in television room
Open: All year

This is one of the more beautiful homes along the back roads noted in this book, a regal Greek Revival built in 1860 of classic red brick, three stories high and five black-shuttered windows wide, complete with a pair of porch swings on the white-trimmed portico. Even the grounds are welcoming: a short mile drive from the charming, ageless village of Chestertown brings one to the circular drive, bordered by bushes and groomed lawns and flowers throughout the 35 acres.

The Hanscoms, a refreshing, young couple, opened Brampton as a bed-and-breakfast in December 1987. Built in 1860 by peach farmer Henry Ward Carville, the house has inspired generations of care and love, having originally been restored in 1937. Brampton is now on the National Register of Historic Places and was at one time a stop on the Underground Railroad. The walnut woodwork on the doors, trim, and stairway is all original, as are the old slate mantels, plaster walls, and grand ceiling medallions. The interior is majestic on a large scale—ceilings 12 feet high on the first floor, 11 feet on the second floor, and 9 on the third floor. Upon entry, at right is the living room with a fire blazing most months of the year and immense floor-to-ceiling windows on three sides of the room. To the left of the entry hall is the dining room, featuring a 1930s Waterford crystal chandelier and wonderful wide-planked floors. The Hanscoms cook full breakfasts served by a blazing fire, with several courses and a choice of two entrées.

The Hanscoms are quite adamant about bed-and-breakfasting: an ample breakfast, a formal and informal common area for guests, queen-size beds (a rare compromise with the modern world), down duvets, good reading chairs, Caswell and Massey amenities, and very fluffy towels. The choice rooms are in the front of the house. The two second-floor rooms, Yellow and Blue, have old fireplaces; and the two third-floor rooms have Franklin stoves on marble platforms. Michael put in the new bathrooms on the third floor. Across from the Red Room, the third-floor Green Room has a fishnet canopy with Martha Washington chairs and displays some of Danielle's grandfather's sophisticated artwork. Throughout are some wonderful antiques from Danielle's family in Switzerland.

This is an unusually involved couple matched to an architecturally exquisite home. Be sure to have dinner at the magnificent Imperial Hotel in Chestertown (see Gourmet Getaways).

Lighthouse Club Hotel
56th Street in the Bay
Ocean City, Maryland 21842
410-524-5400
Reservations: 800-767-6060

Proprietor: John Fager
General Manager: Angela Reynolds
Accommodations: 23 rooms with decks, including 8 suites
Rates: Rooms, $90–$169; suites, $150–$209
Included: Continental breakfast
Minimum stay: 2 nights on weekends and on holidays in season
Added: $15 each additional guest; 5% tax
Payment: Major credit cards
Children: Welcome
Pets: Not allowed
Smoking: Allowed
Open: All year

Eastern Maryland has a short, 30-mile stretch of gorgeous beach along the Atlantic Ocean, below Delaware and above Virginia, most of which is the pristine Assateague Island National Seashore, home of the wild ponies. Just north of this is nine miles of similar beachfront open to the public, which ends busily at Ocean City. Configured like a sandbar, the stretch in

Ocean City is about five miles long and several hundred yards wide, flanked on one side by the Isle of Wight and Assawoman bays and on the other by the Atlantic Ocean. The city looks more like Miami Beach than the Maryland shore, a four-lane, five-mile highway sandwiched between walls of motels.

There are two extremely deluxe properties here amid all the clamor, both on the Isle of Wight Bay on a spit of wetland owned by John Fager: the Lighthouse Club and Coconut Malorie (see Seaside Stops), separated by the well-attended Fager's Island Restaurant. Though surf people might be discouraged, the bay itself is absolutely lovely and serene, a retreat from the bustle of the city, with sunsets spilling picturesquely onto calm and marshy waters.

The Lighthouse Club is the intimate, romantic spot, a 23-room luxury inn built in 1989 to replicate the historic octagonal lighthouse in St. Michaels on Maryland's eastern shore. Its three stories of white clapboard have a cheerful red roof topped by a cupola in true lighthouse fashion. The lobby is the first floor; 15 studio suites radiate around the second floor of the octagon like pieces of a pie, each with semiprivate decks and whirlpool tubs; and the third floor has 8 deluxe one-bedroom suites twice the size of the second-floor rooms, with entirely private balconies and heart-shaped double Jacuzzis. If it sounds a little kitschy, rest assured that the inside is all luxury, with interesting angles to all the rooms.

The unique and fresh decor is the same in both sister properties. Lawrence Peabody designed all the contemporary furniture for the Lighthouse Club and Coconut Malorie to give the clean beachy feeling of light and air: rattan headboards on beds with cool off-white linens, modern rattan armoires, which hold a television and wet bar (with coffeemaker, ice maker and fridge), nightly turndown, sitting area and low white rug, with the great view of the bay. Baths have Saks Fifth Avenue amenities, hair dryers, phones, and fluffy terrycloth robes.

Room service is available from 11 A.M. to 10 P.M. from Fager's Island Restaurant.

New Jersey

Colvmns by the Sea
1513 Beach Drive
Cape May, New Jersey 08204
609-884-2228

Proprietors: Barry and Cathy Rein
Accommodations: 11 rooms, all with private bath
Rates: $105–$155
Included: Full breakfast, afternoon refreshments
Minimum stay: 3 nights on weekends in season
Added: 7% tax
Payment: No credit cards
Children: Over 12 allowed
Pets: Not allowed
Smoking: Allowed on veranda only
Open: Mid-April through December

During summer weekends, Cape May is fairly teeming with people. For those who come to escape crowds, Colvmns by the Sea is clearly the choice, set about a mile from town on Beach Drive, which parallels the boardwalk. Oddly, it is one of the very few bed-and-breakfasts in this seaside town with a waterside location. While surf lovers adored Colvmns by the Sea in past years, they have a new reason to visit. A major beach restoration completed in 1991 returned the sand to Cape May's badly eroded shores. Visitors once again can hear the sound of the surf on the sand at Colvmns by the Sea.

The house was built in 1905 by Charles Davis, the Philadelphia dermatologist who invented calamine lotion. The first floor is a whitewashed plaster, two sides of which form a recessed wrap porch. Above, supported by Ionic columns, are two stories of weathered shingle, with red shutters and white trim, topped by a flat roof. Barry and Cathy Rein bought the house to open a bed-and-breakfast in 1985, he with much experience in restoration and contracting, and she a New York City businesswoman. The house is a showplace for their museum-quality collections of Victoriana, which include stunning furniture sets reupholstered to period perfection, artwork, light fixtures, and table-sized treasures which keep a guest enchanted.

Guests enter a large formal parlor with an intricate coffered ceiling and carved paneling. Several sitting areas, including a tufted Jeliffe parlor set, invite guests to relax while admiring the display of antiques and collections of ivory, porcelain, and Victorian curios. An informal parlor is bordered with several elegant sideboards filled with delicate tea sets, candlesticks, and china. During his gourmet breakfasts (his specialty is spinach and kale soufflé), Barry might conduct a Victoriana quiz with items from a breakfront drawer: something which resembles a pepper mill was used as a hearing aid, something which looks like a lingerie bag was used to keep flies off the heads of carriage horses. Those with no answers may look preoccupied by counting the number of oyster plates in the extensive collection on the dining room's plate rail.

The upper two floors offer 11 guest rooms, each floor with an antique-filled front parlor. The most spectacular room is number 7, with a Renaissance Revival bedroom suite (with an eight-foot carved burl headboard) built in 1876 for Blair House, the vice president's residence, and believed to have been part of the Smithsonian's bicentennial celebration. Some baths have original plumbing, brass fixtures, and marble sinks, yet all have modern comforts. Each room has a written introduction to some aspect of Victoriana displayed therein, as well as a description of some of the finer antiques and customs of the day. In one room on the third floor is an essay on Mission furniture and the American Craft movement. Others hold more traditional Eastlake or Renaissance Revival furniture, lit by amber cut glass lanterns dressed with tasseled lampshades and walls decorated with Victorian wall pockets and paintings. The elaborate cotton bedding is removed and transformed at turndown. Through traditional wood slat blinds, one can hear the lullaby of the surf.

The Mainstay Inn
635 Columbia Avenue
Cape May, New Jersey 08204
609-884-8690

Proprietors: Tom and Sue Carroll
Accommodations: 12 rooms (6 in main house and 6 in Cottage)
Rates: $90–$165
Included: Full breakfast, afternoon tea
Minimum stay: 3 nights in season and on spring and fall
    weekends
Added: 7% tax
Payment: No credit cards
Children: Not allowed
Pets: Not allowed
Smoking: Not allowed
Open: Mid-March to mid-December

The most elegant bed-and-breakfast in a most elegant town, the Mainstay is a legendary place. Its beauty starts with the magnificent architecture of Stephen Decatur Button. Built in 1872 as an exclusive entertainment and gambling club for men, the house was designed to represent the height of the era's luxury. Above the two stories of butter yellow clapboard, a cupola crowns the flat rooftop. The first-floor windows are nearly as high as the 14-foot interior ceilings, shuttered in forest green with white trim. A deep, lavish single-story porch wraps around three sides of the building, supported by gingerbread pillars, in true Italianate elegance. Inside, the glory continues, with wide plaster moldings, crystal chandeliers, marble mantels, and 12-foot mirrors all designed for the house. Some of the majestic original furnishings are still here, but owners Tom and Sue Carroll have contributed their own findings to this palatial interior in appropriate splendor.

As some of the first people to open a bed-and-breakfast in Cape May in the 1970s, the Carrolls are true professionals. Despite their seasoned ways, they are young, creative, sophisticated, and quite gregarious. It's therefore necessary to take a tour of the house to understand the thoroughness of Tom and Sue's endeavor, from the elaborate wallpapering to the choice of antiques and upholstery to the carefully chosen relics around the house. While the ceiling decorations are a composite of 19 period papers, the walls are hand-painted in a period stencil motif.

To the left is the elegant front parlor filled with Tom and Sue's antiques, lit by the original brass-plated chandelier; and to the right is the formal drawing room. The wallpapering was designed specially by Bradbury and Bradbury, a collage of ten different period papers. Many original pieces are displayed throughout the room, including the mirror above the mantel, which matches that in the dining room; a marble-top table and desk; and several sitting pieces. The 1886 Chickering and Sons grand piano is in working order, as is the turn-of-the-century mahogany grandfather clock, which belonged to Tom's grandfather—one of the most recent pieces in the house.

Across the hallway is the dining room, a gathering spot for formal breakfast and afternoon tea. Its large pieces are original, like the 300-pound mirror which hangs above the 500-pound marble-top buffet illuminated by a solid brass Cornelius and Baker chandelier.

Upstairs, the General Grant and Stonewall Jackson suites rest at the back of the house. Of the four front rooms, the Cardinal Gibbons is the most often requested, with an original walnut bedroom suite. The nimble should climb the steep set of stairs to the cupola for a view of the town and sea.

Fortunately, there is more to the Mainstay. The Carrolls bought the neighboring Cottage in 1980, built a century earlier by the same architect who built the main house. The tall, narrow three-story villa has a double-story porch running the width of the building. The yellow clapboard echoes its sister property, but the maroon shutters and celery trim differentiate it just a bit. A parlor features wicker furniture and period magazine drawings of Cape May. Several of the six guest rooms have porches.

The food is as elegant as the decor at the Mainstay, with endless cookies and cakes at teatime and beautifully prepared full breakfasts. Tom and Sue are some of the more gracious and intelligent hosts in the business. Be sure to plan months ahead for perfect sojourn here.

New York

The Adelphi Hotel
365 Broadway
Saratoga Springs, New York 12866
518-587-4688

Proprietors: Gregg Siekfer and Sheila Parkert
Accommodations: 36 rooms, all with private bath
Rates: Low season, $65–$115; high season, $155–$285
Included: Continental breakfast in room or on veranda
Minimum stay: 3 nights on racing weekends, 2 nights on
    some other weekends
Added: 11% tax; 16% tax over $100
Payment: MasterCard, Visa
Children: Allowed
Pets: Not allowed
Smoking: Allowed
Open: May weekends, June through October

Visiting the Adelphi is like following Alice through Wonderland. At every turn, there is something magical, otherworldly, and illusory. The Adelphi, built in 1877 and restored to its former glory, stands as a reminder of Victorian opulence and the lavish beginnings of Saratoga Springs. The landmark hotel is the quintessence of sophistication during the exuberant summer months of horseracing season and cultural events at the Performing Arts Center. However, the Adelphi leaps beyond a simple period restoration with boundless creativity and humor within its three stories and behind its brick walls.

Owners Gregg Siekfer and Sheila Parkert bought the Adelphi in 1979 after it had been abandoned for ten years. Sheila is a painter and interior designer and Gregg is an artistic carpenter: their marriage has produced a wondrous work in progress which attests to their inspired talents. They are true collectors, finding pieces at local antiques shows and trips abroad. Furniture is reupholstered to fit a room or a mood, mirrors are regilded, lamps refringed, old photographs rematted and framed—and all eclectic pieces come together in a cohesive room. Gregg and Sheila opened with four overnight rooms. By crafting and tailoring two or three rooms yearly, they have arrived at the present 36: individual, unique worlds in themselves.

More important than the innumerable treasures within the hotel is the sensory rapture a guest feels at the Adelphi. Standing out as one of Broadway's most elegant, the three-story brown brick building has creamy yellow trim and maroon highlights, with wooden columns climbing the full height, adorned with gingerbread. Through the doors, guests enter an imaginary world. Eclectic Victorian parlor sets huddle together amid lush greenery, separated by faux marble pillars supporting the coffered ceiling. The walls are colorfully handpainted by famed stenciler Larry Boyce from Victorian patterns. Underfoot, the floors are stained dark and covered with scatter Orientals. A straight walk brings a guest to the Café Adelphi, decorated with tasseled drapery, upholstered banquettes, wall murals, and pillars, lending the air of a European hotel or even a movie set. The outdoor gardens sit through French doors, with fountains, trellises, and wrought-iron furniture, shaded by awnings.

A Victorian trellis-patterned carpet leads a guest upstairs to two floors of rooms, and, for common use, a formally appointed double parlor leading to a wicker-filled sun porch overlooking Broadway where guests take breakfast and watch the crowds. Sheila designed each room around a specific era, piece of furniture, or carpet. The Neoclassic Suite has faux granitework painted on the walls, faux black marble pillars, a gold and white silk Empire couch, and murals on the living room walls depicting a Roman landscape. With the same attention to detail and trompe l'oeil brushwork, other rooms successfully take on sweeping generalizations: the French Room, the Hungarian Room, the Adirondack Room, the Victorian Room, the Dorothy Draper Room. Smaller rooms might not create these overwhelming effects, but they still have gorgeous wallpaper with playful borders, Sheila's handmade crown canopies, window treatments, and crocheted bedding. The baths are new and clean, sometimes wedged into confounding spaces, with generous Gilchrest and Soames amenities, including a mending kit and toothpaste. Rooms all have phones, televisions, and air conditioning. Breakfasts are a treat, brought to the room in a basket with home-baked muffins and fruit.

For all their whimsical creativity, Gregg and Sheila are surprisingly friendly and accessible, and their staff is extremely enthusiastic.

The Box Tree
Route 22 & Route 116
Purdys, New York 10578
914-277-3677

Proprietor: Augustin V. Paege
Manager: Alain Pirony
Innkeeper: David Bennett
Accommodations: 3 suites, all with private bath, 2 with fireplace
Rates: Weekends: $180–$220; weekdays, $120–$140
Included: Full breakfast
Minimum stay: None
Added: 12% tax
Payment: American Express
Children: Not allowed
Pets: Not allowed
Smoking: Limited
Open: All year

The romance at the Box Tree, which recently celebrated its twentieth anniversary, is due to the lavish work of decorator Heinz Simon, who has draped and swagged luxurious Waverly fabrics around museum-quality French and English antiques. Also responsible for the amorous experience is chef Ken Lindh, whose French cuisine is served in three intimate candlelit rooms fitted with muted tapestry chairs, crystal, and china.

A weekend at the Box Tree is transporting. The 48-mile drive from Manhattan into upstate New York's horse country brings a couple to a 1775 colonial house, two and a half stories high, set in front of pastures and ponies. The white clapboard building is introduced by an enclosed porch across its facade, walled in mullioned windows.

The restaurant is preceded by a small waiting area, with hand-painted tiles graced by the brush of Heinz Simon. The three rooms look like colonial refuges, decorated in plush French and English antiques. The Aubusson tapestry chairs are reproduction Louis XIII with rococo legs, surrounding gleaming wood tables. Entrées from the French menu range from $22 to $29, and a dinner might proceed as follows: an appetizer of timbale of pasta, herbs, and ragout of lobster, shrimp, and scallops, or perhaps snails gratiné in Pernod butter; followed by roasted duck in ginger and pinot noir sauce, or bobwhite quail filled with wild rice and truffled sauce, or sautéed sea scallops with red pepper beurre blanc in caviar sauce. To end the meal is a selection of seven desserts which may feature a terrine of dark chocolate with hazelnut cream or apples in pastry with mango coulis. The wine list is admirable.

Two of the three guest suites rest above the dining room, and a third has a private porch on the ground level at the back of the house. David Bennett is the conscientious innkeeper who serves as full-time butler. The finest room is the François Premier Room, with a stunning carved canopy bed from 1665, draped elaborately in black chintz. This room also has the finest bath, done in black and white parquet, with plush towels and terry robes, a bidet, and hair dryer. King Ludwig's Room has a carved Renaissance Revival suite, with olive-painted walls. The Florentine Suite at the back has a stunning canopy bed, its four posters gilded and interestingly gnarled. Here the bath is done in pink marble. The guest's lounge between the two second-floor rooms has a green silk-covered Regency parlor set against a backdrop of peach moiré walls, linked by Waverly chintz drapes. Elaborate gilt ormolu candelabras are used as wall sconces.

The high level of luxury is intriguing in this modest colonial house. Service is quite solicitous, while guests are left very much to themselves.

Geneva on the Lake

1001 Lochland Road, P.O. Box 929
Geneva, New York 14456
315-789-7190
800-3-GENEVA

Proprietor: Norbert R. Schickel, Jr.
Accommodations: 29 suites (studios and one and two bedrooms)
Rates: Summer, $178–$338; winter, $158–$318
Included: Bottle of wine, fresh fruit, Continental breakfast
Minimum stay: 2 nights May through October, with Saturday stay
Added: Additional guests: age 4–9, $17; age 10–15, $29; adults, $52; 12% tax
Payment: Major credit cards
Children: Allowed
Pets: Not allowed
Smoking: Not allowed in public rooms
Open: All year

The hilly wine country around the Finger Lakes reminds a traveler of Europe. In fact, on the shores of Seneca Lake, a bit of Italy exists in an inn called Geneva on the Lake. A replica of the Villa Lancellotti in Frascati, near Rome, this palatial white stucco building, with a red Mediterranean tiled roof, immediately transports a visitor to Italian shores. Throughout the ten acres, formal gardens are connected with walkways peopled with Greek and Roman sculptures. Near the hill that descends steeply to Seneca Lake, gilded Italian urns border a 70-foot swimming pool which contributes the azure of the Mediterranean.

The mansion was built as a private home for the Nester family from 1910 to 1914 and served as a Capuchin monastery from 1949 to 1974, relics of which remain throughout the inn. In 1979, Norbert Schickel bought the property, which had been vacant for five years, and performed extensive restoration as well as renovations with apartments in mind. Involved in the project were some of his 13 children as well as his brother, a prominent designer and artist. As the phoenix rose from the ashes, the family decided that the mansion was better suited to resort living.

The suites show traces of the short-lived apartment idea, equipped with full kitchens and refrigerators stocked with a chilled bottle of Finger Lake wine for guests upon arrival. All but two have lake views. There are six groups of suites, set around vertical hallways, furnished with reproductions, decorated with traditional chintz curtains and area carpeting, and equipped with new baths. While some rooms have a traditional yet contemporary feeling as a result of the renovations, others, like the Classic Suite and the Library, retain the original plaster moldings, medallions, wall paneling, and outward-opening French windows.

The common rooms and grounds are truly exceptional. Mr. Schickel commissioned reproductions of significant sculptures to decorate the grounds. The two intimate original dining rooms are breathtaking, tiled in marble, overlooking the formal gardens through French doors. Some of the rare antiques include a 17th-century Bible box, a tiled Portuguese 18th-century planter, Italian Renaissance church candlesticks, and gold carved panels from an 18th-century French carriage.

Mrs. Schickel hosts a wine and cheese party every Friday on the outdoor piazza. Dinner is served on weekends only, in a careful presentation of five entrées ranging from $18 for chicken Jacqueline with port wine cream sauce, sliced apples, and almonds to $32 for Australian lobster tail with brandy cream sauce. Elaborate desserts may include baked Alaska or strawberries Romanoff in Grand Marnier. A pianist and singer enhance the romance of the setting. Sunday brunch is a popular event here.

A strong sense of family unites the staff and creates a pleasant warmth throughout the formal property. Among the activities on the immaculate grounds are croquet, swimming, and sailing. Only a short drive away is the public Seneca Lake country club and tours of the magnificent wine country.

Inn at Belhurst Castle

Lochland Road, Box 609
Geneva, New York 14456
315-781-0201

Proprietors: Robert and Nancy Golden and Cathy Golden
Accommodations: 12 rooms, including 2 suites, all with
  private bath
Rates: Rooms, $90–$125; suites, $175 and $225; rates lower in
  winter
Included: Continental breakfast in low season
Added: $15 each additional guest; 7% tax; 12% tax over $100
Payment: MasterCard, Visa
Children: Welcome (under 8 free)
Pets: Not allowed
Smoking: Allowed
Open: All year

Without reminders of the modern world or evidence of place, a visitor would assume that Belhurst Castle was rooted in the Loire Valley, home to royalty, the subject of fairy tales. It was built, however, high on the northern banks of Finger Lake Seneca over four years beginning in 1885 for Carrie Harron Collins, daughter of the founder of Dun and Bradstreet. Her picture painted in porcelain greets guests at the foyer. History notes that fifty men built the castle with materials imported from Europe, for an overwhelming cost of $475,000, with red Medina stone in the Richardson Romanesque style of heavy masonry, small windows, and witch-hat turrets wrapped in ivy.

The castle was owned by Cornelius Dwyer for half a century, run largely as a gambling house and speakeasy. In 1975, the Golden family bought Belhurst Castle for their family home until 1985, when they opened 12 guest rooms and what has become a successful restaurant. The interior of Belhurst Castle is an impressive display of carved and highly varnished wood paneling and coffered ceilings of cherry, golden oak, and mahogany. To the right of the foyer is a masculine library, walled in deep mahogany.

The elegant restaurant comprises two pretty rooms in cherry wood and a porch dining room on the first floor. Dinners begin with the Belhurst appetizer tray of pâté, cheese, marinated vegetables, and Gulf shrimp; following is a choice of soup and salad. Entrées range from $13 to $24 for roast pheasant Amaretto, veal Quebec with Canadian bacon and brie, or scallop thermidor with mustard and cream. A dessert tray completes the evening.

Because of the busy nature of Belhurst's restaurant, guests may not receive intimate attention from the innkeeper and hosts. Romantics might not care, however, once shown to their grand guest room. The formidable carved stairway in golden oak leads the second- and third-floor rooms. Some are lit by original stained glass, with toile and damask wallpaper, offering elaborately carved mantels, four of which have working fireplaces. The furniture is mostly reproduction, but the focus of the rooms rests in the high ceilings, with is odd pitched angles, and the patterned wainscoted walls and alcoves tucked into turrets. The finest room is the Tower Suite, with little stairs leading to the tower turret, including a huge wainscoted bathroom with a double Jacuzzi.

As the hub of New York's wine country, the Finger Lakes offer wonderful day trips for romantics. The public Seneca Country Club is a mile away, as are Hobart and William Smith colleges.

J. P. Sill House

63 Chestnut Street
Cooperstown, New York 13326
607-547-2633

Proprietors: Laura and Angelo Zucotti
Accommodations: 5 rooms, all with private bath
Rates: $70–$95; $5 less, October through May
Included: Full breakfast
Minimum stay: Selected weekends
Added: 8% tax
Payment: American Express, Visa, MasterCard
Children: Teenagers welcome
Pets: Not allowed
Smoking: Not allowed
Open: All year

Baseball is a wonderfully romantic sport: full of nostalgia, long afternoons in the park, loyalty, heroism, celebration, and heartbreak. Cooperstown is home to the Baseball Hall of Fame, and those who know the poetry of the sport might want to complete the romance at the J. P. Sill House, an elegant, sophisticated bed-and-breakfast in the heart of town.

Painted a warm yellow with deep maroon trim, the J. P. Sill House is a pristine Victorian restoration on the National Register of Historic Places, set back from the road by a groomed lawn and colorful flowers. Sill was the wealthy president of a Cooperstown bank who had this house built between 1862 and 1864 to mirror his own residence across the street. It sold for $1,200.

Although the former owners of this bed-and-breakfast did much of the restoration work in the 1980s, the Zucottis have made the property a first-class bed-and-breakfast since they bought it in 1990. Former owners of El Morocco Club in Manhattan, from Italy and England, the couple are worldly, gracious hosts. Laura insists on three dressings for every bed: a light European matteless woven cotton, and summer and winter weight comforters which match the elaborate window treatments.

The walls are covered in Victorian reproduction wallpapers designed by William Morris and Audsley Brothers of London. The doors are faux grained pine; and the ceiling moldings are done in elaborate tiger oak. Through the foyer, the formal parlor sits to the left, the setting for afternoon tea. Laura's china collection is housed in shelves. The original carved window valances are echoed in the mirror above the working fireplace. A television is thoughtfully hidden in a cabinet, a dollhouse replica of the Sill House made by local artisans at Toad Hall, a Cooperstown craft and antique shop.

Across the hall is the Bridal Room, the only first-floor accommodation, and the most luxurious. The valuable brass and white wrought-iron bed is from the Roebling estate. In the corner of the room is a large Jacuzzi and bath area that was photographed for the Laura Ashley catalog, furnished with British Florid and Yardley amenities. Linen robes are provided for summer and terry robes for winter. The armoire holds a television, VCR, and stereo. Lace curtains fall from ceiling to floor, covered in Scalamandre silk balloon curtains. A private front porch enjoys views of the gardens and Chestnut Street. The original brass door poles, used to deter drafts, hover over the doors hung with heavy damask Chinese silk, continued throughout the house.

Four rooms rest upstairs, all with equally lovely and varied displays of Laura Ashley linens, elegant window treatments, and Victorian wallpapers. Rooms are graced with magnificent antique armoires fragranced by small sachets. All rooms have private baths, one of which has a pewter tub in oak casing.

Guests take breakfast on the sun porch or in the formal dining room, framed by Scalamandre silk curtains and bordered in golf leaf paper. Tea is served from a silver samovar from the Ottoman Empire, and the full meal is served on antique china and silver accompanied by antique linens. Breakfast may feature a soufflé or egg custard, with chocolate or lemon bread.

The Mansion
Route 29, Box 77
Rock City Falls–Saratoga Springs, New York 12863
518-885-1607

Proprietors: Alan Churchill and Tom Clark
Accommodations: 5 rooms, including 1 suite, all with private bath
Rates: $85; $95 in July; $150 in August; suite $15 extra
Included: Five-course gourmet breakfast
Minimum stay: On selected weekends and in high season
Added: 12% tax
Payment: No credit cards
Children: Teenagers welcome
Pets: Not allowed
Smoking: Allowed
Open: All year, except two days at Christmas

Saratoga Springs comes alive in the summer with events at the Performing Arts Center and its horseracing season. Seven miles west, the Mansion is a beautiful bed-and-breakfast that retains all the finery of Saratoga Springs without the traffic, crowds, and unreasonable rates.

In 1866, George West, best known as a philanthropist and the inventor of the folding paper bag, built a Venetian-style villa across from his paper mill in Rock City Falls for use as a summer home. The Italianate house was bought in 1986 by Tom Clark, who spent months restoring it to its former grandeur. The three-story peach-colored clapboard house was built with chestnut, trimmed in white, topped by a cupola, and framed by a half dozen tiger tail spruce trees which tower above the house often higher than one can see. Nearly all of the house is original: from the brass and copper chandeliers with Waterford shades found in nearly every room, to the carved brass hardware and doorknobs, to the parquet flooring and chestnut and walnut moldings, to the six elaborately carved wood and marble fireplaces. Even the wooden shutters in the long, narrow windows are particular to the era.

To the left of the foyer is an informal library, lined with ample reading material in a comfortable setting. Two floor-to-ceiling windows look out to the front lawn, and in a three-windowed bay facing west stands a 300-pound sculpture of St. Francis carved of solid mahogany. To the right of the foyer are two parlors separated by arched pocket doors. The first is done in Empire furniture, with a black marble mantel and a carved wood mirror 13 feet high. The second parlor has Eastlake furniture with a white marble fireplace and a hand pump organ.

At the back of the house sits the dining room, with five intimate tables. Alan is quite proud of his breakfasts of French toast, omelettes with fresh herbs, or maybe eggs Benedict, served fireside with a special blend of coffee and fresh fruit breads. Just outside, Dutchman's pipe vine clings to the 60-foot porch, decorated with wicker furniture and flower boxes.

Of the five bedrooms, the first-floor suite has a little sitting room brightened by a pink marble fireplace and the original parquet flooring of oak, maple, and rosewood. A set of Currier and Ives horseracing prints appropriately decorates the walls. Some of the antiques which fill the four second-floor rooms include a bird's-eye maple chest, a chestnut and walnut Renaissance Revival bedroom suite, and original faux marble fireplaces in green and black. Here, the plant-filled sitting room features six Winslow Homer wood engravings and Bentwood rockers which look to the front lawns and river through arched windows. Before strolling the four acres, scan the grounds from the cupola.

Resident innkeeper Alan Churchill strives to immerse his guests in luxury and elegance. Many activities are just a short drive away, including day trips to the Hudson River and Adirondacks.

Rose Inn
813 Auburn Road, Route 34 North
Box 6576, Ithaca, New York 14851-6576
607-533-7905

Proprietors: Sherry and Charles Rosemann
Accommodations: 15 rooms, including 4 suites, all private
   bath, 3 with Jacuzzi, 2 with working fireplace
Rates: Rooms, $100–$150; suite, $175–$250

Included: Full breakfast
Minimum stay: 3 nights on holidays and some university
  weekends
Added: Dinner by prior arrangement, $50 per person; 12% tax
Payment: American Express, Visa, MasterCard
Children: With prior consent
Pets: Not allowed
Smoking: Not allowed
Open: All year

The Rose Inn is the only country inn in New York to have been
awarded four stars from Mobil and four diamonds from AAA
for several years running, owing to a decade's hard work from
owners Charles and Sherry Rosemann. Guests enjoy exceptionally decorated rooms and, with prior reservations,
gorgeous meals in a rare, romantic setting. What's more, the
Rose Inn is architecturally magnificent, an 1840s Italianate
mansion painted a subtle pink with dark green shutters and
white trim, with a stunning spiral staircase made of Honduras
mahogany, which ascends three floors to a cupola from which
one can view the countryside.

In the early 1980s, Charles, a German hotelier, and Sherry, a
Dallas native, agreed that their skills were well suited to innkeeping. They realized a lifelong dream when they bought this
house on Lake Cayuga's eastern shores, ten miles north of Ithaca in the heart of the Finger Lakes. After months of restoration, they opened the inn in 1983 with five rooms and four
baths. With quick success, they were able to expand with a
first-floor addition in 1986 and a second in 1988, a commendably sensitive structure which Sherry designed. They are a rare

breed: Sherry, one of those few creative souls who has found her calling, and Charles, a true romantic who has found his muse.

The house, high on a hill, sits on 20 parklike acres of groomed gardens, distinguished trees, and, in part, a walkable apple orchard in the back fields. Though the majority of the five first-floor and ten second-floor rooms are in the new part of the house, guests really don't notice. When Sherry designed the addition, she insisted on classic molding and wall paneling to match the original structure, as well as matching windows and exterior cornice molding. The Honeymoon Suite, for example, looks out back through three Palladian windows to the orchards from a solarium with a Jacuzzi sunken in marble flooring. The bedroom is Neoclassic in design with clean lines in strong taupes, blacks, and creams. The Perry Ellis linens complement an upholstered gilded headboard; and ornate brass sconces are set into the paneled walls aside Victorian prints.

Each room is as thoroughly decorated and different as the next, with Schumacher wallpapers in lush damasks with impeccable French and 19th-century American antiques throughout. The baths are sophisticated, with beautiful amenities, some with parquet tiling in classic patterns. Sherry insists on the finest quality bedding, down comforters, 250-thread-count designer linens, and oversize bath sheets; and she executes an elegant evening turndown. Two rooms have wood-burning fireplaces, yet all are romantic boudoirs in themselves.

Guests dine intimately at separate tables in the living room, library, dining room, and the base of the circular stairway, which feels like a conservatory. At the time of reservation, guests may choose to dine here and are wise to do so. It's quite a romantic experience which lasts several hours. Sherry selects the wines and tailors the meal to the desires of guests. Appetizers might be smoked oysters in beurre blanc, artichoke heart strudel on puréed tomato with fresh dill, or stuffed ravioli quartet of lobster, Gorgonzola, salmon, and mushrooms. A hearts of palm salad dressed in edible flowers might follow. Entrées might include Châteaubriand with béarnaise sauce, rack of lamb with herb marinade, veal chasseur with a creamy Madeira sauce, or scampi Mediterranean, shrimp flambéed in brandy with tomato, curry, and cream. As if one could think about breakfast, a several-course meal is elegantly presented.

From here, guests may enjoy a day trip to local wineries, or a ten-mile drive south to Ithaca College and Cornell University.

Pennsylvania

Fairville Inn
Route 52, Kennett Pike, Box 219
Mendenhall, Pennsylvania 19357
215-388-5900

Proprietors: Patricia and Ole Retlev
Accommodations: 15 rooms, all with private bath, 7 with fireplace (5 rooms in Main House, 4 rooms in Barn, 6 rooms in Carriage House)
Rates: $95–$165
Included: Afternoon tea, Continental breakfast
Minimum stay: 2 nights on most weekends
Added: 6% tax
Payment: Major credit cards
Children: Over 10 welcome
Pets: Not allowed
Smoking: Allowed
Open: All year

However daunting the sprawl and congestion may be between suburban Philadelphia and Wilmington, the Fairville Inn has escaped it all. Set back like a country estate from wooded Route 52 near Chadds Ford, the Fairville Inn is a picturesque stone and clapboard manor house, with a Barn and Carriage House behind, 10 minutes north of Wilmington and about 30 minutes west of Philadelphia in the heart of the Brandywine Valley. Longwood Gardens, Winterthur, and the Brandywine River Museum are nearby, as well as horseracing events. It is a tasteful retreat, immaculate, quiet, and very private. Above all, there is an overwhelming sense of comfort here in the large rooms, most with fireplaces, balconies, telephones, televisions hidden in highboys, and large and elegant baths.

After owning an inn in Vermont and working as ski instructors, Patricia and Ole Retlev wanted a property that would keep them busy all year. They fell in love with the hamlet of Fairville, its proximity to the two major cities and wonderful museums, and the wonderful 1820s manor house. In 1986, they restored the butter-colored stone farmhouse, with its five guest rooms, a large common living room, and comfortable breakfast area. As well, they built the Carriage House and redid the Barn behind to provide ten additional guest rooms, which some may prefer for added space and privacy. Ole commissioned a local artist to do the oil paintings hung throughout the inn. These copies of Dutch master prints are on loan and are all for sale.

The rooms are done in reproduction Queen Anne furniture, with traditional color schemes varying from room to room. Patricia is always redecorating, with perfect detailing which has the effect of a showroom: the bedskirt matches the drapes, which complement the wallpaper, and colors are picked up in the upholstered wing chair.

Preferable rooms are in the two charming outbuildings, white vertical clapboard with dark green trim, with serene views through paned windows of the dale behind the property and trees framing a pond set into gently sloping grass. The two-story Carriage House is more elegant: all six rooms have balconies, three have fireplaces, some have cathedral ceilings, exposed beams, and canopy beds, with an emphasis on very large bathrooms, copper fixtures, and separate wash areas. The Barn has four extremely large rooms in two stories, with two-poster king- or queen-size beds, fireplaces, and ample sitting areas.

Tea is nearly elaborate at Fairville, with cold and hot drinks and plates of little homemade cakes and cookies in the breakfast room, very cheery and sociable. Ole and Patricia are almost always present with helpful details of where to dine and what museums to see. Breakfast is a freshly baked Continental affair, featuring Patricia's truly memorable muffins, with the expectation that guests are health-conscious businesspeople or couples who want to get on with their museum-going in the area.

Harry Packer Mansion
Box 458, Packer Hill
Jim Thorpe, Pennsylvania 18229
717-325-8566

Proprietors: Pat and Robert Handwerk
Accommodations: 13 rooms, including 1 suite (7 rooms in main house, all but 2 with private bath; 6 rooms in Carriage House, all with private bath)
Rates: $75–$95; suite, $110; Murder Mysteries almost every weekend, $320–$410 per couple
Included: Full breakfast
Minimum stay: 2 nights on weekends
Added: 6% tax
Payment: MasterCard, Visa

Children: Not allowed
Pets: Not allowed
Smoking: Not allowed in guest rooms
Open: All year

The Harry Packer Mansion was built in 1874 by Harry's father, Asa Packer, at the time the third wealthiest man in the country, who made his fortune as the founder of the Lehigh Valley Railroad. Asa built the mansion next to his own (now a museum) as a wedding gift for son Harry, who died several years later from kidney failure at the young age of 34. Much to his father's dismay, he left no heirs but an illegitimate daughter. As a result, the mansion was incorporated into the Packer estate.

The town of Jim Thorpe, named for the Olympic track star born here, sits on the Lehigh River in the western hills of the Poconos. On an impossibly steep cliff above town, the salmon-colored three-story brick house rests next to Asa Packer's regal mansion. Gothic in style, the first-floor porch is framed in a colonnade of carved sandstone laced with ivy. Third-floor dormer windows poke out from the undulating lines of the mansard roof, which follows the bayed exterior. Bought by the seventh and present owners in 1984, the house was elaborately restored. The Tiffany windows, English Minton tiles, brass and bronze chandeliers, carved wood mantels, a few antique furnishings, and hand-painted ceilings are all original.

Guests wanting special privacy ought to know two things: tours are conducted Sunday through Thursday and some Saturdays. The house is also the scene for a well-written murder mystery which involves the Packer family and fortune. Less structured guests ought to inquire ahead about murder plans or may want to request a midweek stay.

To appreciate the enormity of scale at the mansion, know that the exterior doors are 500 pounds, and the interior doors before the foyer with hand-etched glass are a mere 400. The first-floor ceilings are 15 feet high, with gilded mirrors soaring to the ceilings. There is a ladies' and a gentlemen's parlor, the latter's walls papered in a reproduction of the original pattern. The Library has mahogany paneled walls interspersed with the original blue silk wallcovering, images of Shakespeare and Byron in the stained glass windows, and 18-karat gold paint on globes of the chandelier.

When overnighting, you will feel remarkably like you just removed a velvet rope while visiting a museum, undressed, and retired to bed, especially in the seven rooms of the main house. The six rooms in the Carriage House avoid this feeling of time travel. The present owners have made these rooms traditional and cheery, on the smallish side, with queen-size beds, reproduction Queen Anne furniture, tufted wing chairs, settees, and clean new baths, in a hunt theme.

The must-see Asa Packer Museum next door is open during the spring, summer, and fall. To have the full Packer experience, one ought to ride the trains. A short drive away is the Hickory Run State Park, and several ski mountains.

Historic Smithton
900 West Main Street
Ephrata, Pennsylvania 17522
717-733-6094

Proprietors: Dorothy Graybill and Allan Smith
Innkeeper: Dorothy Graybill
Accommodations: 7 rooms and 1 four-room suite, all with
    private bath
Rates: Rooms, $65–$115; suite, $140–$170
Included: Full breakfast
Minimum stay: Two nights with Saturday and holiday stay
Added: $35 each additional guest; $20 each additional child;
    6% tax
Payment: MasterCard, Visa, American Express
Children: Well-behaved children welcome by prior
    arrangement
Pets: Will consider
Smoking: Not allowed
Open: All year

The town of Ephrata in northern Lancaster County is famous for its Cloister, comprising medieval German buildings, the home of an 18th-century Protestant monastic society who called themselves Seventh Day Baptists, led by iron-fisted Conrad Beissel. One of the Cloister's ardent members was Henry Miller, who, despite his involvement with the sect, invited the wrath of Beissel and was barred from worship. Miller, however, maintained his allegiance to the sect and in 1762 built a fieldstone house overlooking the monastery. A year later he opened an inn and tavern for visitors to the Cloister. Descendants of Henry Miller owned this large stone house until the 1970s, when they sold it to Dorothy Graybill and Allan Smith. Dorothy and Allan labored over the years and opened the Historic Smithton Inn in 1983, a pristine bed-and-breakfast filled with beautiful crafts and artwork from the Pennsylvania Dutch.

The inn sits just above the Cloister Museum, on the edge of Ephrata's main street, the old main road to Scranton. Despite its congested location, the inn is a peaceful refuge and wonderful place in which to immerse oneself in Lancaster lore. Dorothy is a charming, accomplished historian of the Amish and Mennonites, as well as of the Ephrata Cloister. Guests approach the Inn from a stone walkway and enter through a single-story white columned portico. The breakfast room is to the left, decorated with red tablecloths, red velvet curtains, and Amish and Mennonite quilts hanging on the walls. To the right is the common room, often lit by a welcoming fire; behind it is a cluttered library, comfortable for cozy reading. Nearly all the house is original to 1763, immaculate, with wonderful wide-planked floors.

The furniture which Allan did not make was handmade by local craftspeople. The step-up trundle beds and four-poster upholstered canopies are dressed with down pillows, feather beds upon request, and Mennonite quilts. Rooms have ample lighting, with handcrafted lampshades and pewter sconces. Hand-painted blanket chests, leather wing chairs, and sofas adorn the rooms, and the Shaker tables astride the bed control classical music which is piped into the rooms. Rooms are named for the decor color, and two matching nightshirts, flannel in winter and cotton in summer, are available upon request. Dorothy has stocked every room with classics and short stories. Favorite rooms are the first-floor Gold Room and the third floor, with four skylights and a Franklin stove. The separate suite is a wonderful space, with a traditional leather-furnished living room and working fireplace, a snack area, a new bath with a whirlpool tub and shower, and, upstairs, a blue crown canopy bed and tree of life quilt.

Breakfasts are very much a part of the romance at Smithton. In the plush breakfast room, guests eat a full gourmet meal by candlelight.

The Mercersburg Inn
405 South Main Street
Mercersburg, Pennsylvania 17236
717-328-5231

Proprietor: Fran Wolfe
Accommodations: 15 rooms, all with private bath
Rates: $105–$175
Included: Breakfast
Minimum stay: For fireplace rooms in winter

Added: $25 each additional person; 6% tax
Payment: Major credit cards
Children: Welcome
Pets: Not allowed
Smoking: Allowed on porches
Open: All year

The Tuscarora Mountains bisect the confluence of Maryland, Pennsylvania, and West Virginia, old rolling hills which remain fairly unpopulated and quite rural. Mercersburg, Pennsylvania, is nearby, toward Chambersburg, best known as the birthplace of President Buchanan. There is a fine boys' preparatory academy here in this charming town nestled in the hills, on the National Register of Historic Places. As well, atop a hill is a regal house called the Mercersburg Inn.

In 1909, a tanner named Harry Byron built a grand brick Georgian Revival house for his wife and three sons. From Mercersburg's main street in the valley, the four-columned double-story portico of the inn is quite visible. When asked about the size of her 20,000-square-foot house, Mrs. Byron is noted to have said, "I don't know how many rooms we have, but I have 40 closets."

Fran Wolfe bought the mansion in December 1986 and opened it as an inn nearly a year later after massive restorations. The intriguing brochure for the inn was taken from a real estate advertisement in 1948 which describes the house shortly after Mr. Byron's death. Guests enter at the drive behind the house. The overwhelming foyer is formalized by elaborate faux marble pillars. The highly polished original floor is white oak with walnut inlay. On one side is the formal ballroom with a large brick fireplace, adjacent to the Arts and Crafts style Billiard Room, which opens through French doors to a single-story wrap porch overlooking the Tuscarora range.

Mirroring this section of the house to the other side are several dining rooms: one paneled with rich mahogany that complements the coffered ceilings, their gleaming surfaces warmed by a green marble fireplace, another in an enclosed porch facing the academy. Fixed-price six-course dinners are served here Wednesday through Sunday. Dinner might begin with an appetizer of crab, escargot, and caviar in pastry shell. Entrée choices might include roasted lamb with juniper berries and spaetzle or lobster tail wrapped in pastry with saffron beurre blanc.

The double staircase embraces the foyer leading to the gleaming maple parquet flooring of the second floor. Guest rooms line the L-shaped hall on two upper floors. Several second-floor rooms have porches with glorious mountain views, and some have working fireplaces. A smaller favorite is Room 2 at the top of the stairs overlooking town, the mountains in the background. All the beds have reproduction king-size canopy beds. Private baths, when not original with monumental fixtures and elaborate tiling, have been cleverly transformed from the ample closet space. As elaborate as is the architecture of the house, the rooms are nicely but sparely furnished. The only noise heard from the guest rooms is actually quite loud, but no visitor would object to the 43-bell carillon which calls out from Mercersburg Academy.

Sweetwater Farm

50 Sweetwater Road
Glen Mills, Pennsylvania 19342
215-459-4711

Proprietors: Michael Gretz and Jonathan Propper
Innkeepers: Guillermo A. Pernot and Lucia D. Menocal
Accommodations: 13 rooms, 6 with private bath (4 rooms in 2 cottages, 9 rooms in main house)
Rates: $85–$145 weekdays; $110–$165 Friday–Sunday
Included: Full breakfast
Minimum stay: Some weekends
Added: Saturday dinner with advance notice; 8% tax
Payment: Visa, MasterCard, American Express
Children: Welcome
Pets: Small pets allowed
Smoking: Allowed outside
Open: All year

Like a Wyeth painting, Sweetwater Farm captures the untouched nature of the Brandywine River Valley and the warmth of the homestead, looking more like a memory from one's past than a picture from the present. Incongruously, this 1734 fieldstone structure is just 35 minutes from Philadelphia and 20 from its airport and Wilmington, Delaware. From the rural wooded 50-acre setting, to the gracious innkeepers, to the colonial and Federal architecture and the elegant, Old World rooms, this is truly one of the classic bed-and-breakfast properties in the Mid-Atlantic.

The circular drive from the wooded country road is a majestic introduction to Sweetwater Farm. Early spring prompts magenta and bright pink azaleas to frame the drive and embrace the fieldstone manor house with its white trim and red shutters (slate blue in the back of the house).

Guests enter through the 1815 Federal half of the manor. The halls and rooms are wide and grand, and all wood and plaster work is original, Federally austere. To the right is a large double-parlor living room with some elegant antiques and dentil-carved fireplace (one of nine in the house); to the left is an informal library with an enormous collection of books and a hidden television for viewing old movies; and then the dining room, with a formidable china collection and an 1865 hunt print on the wall. Here is the setting for Guillermo's elaborate, careful cuisine: breakfasts may be chocolate waffles or an egg dish. Dinners, with advance notice, are five courses, a recent meal having been leek soup, salad, redfish on peppers, black beans and corn vinaigrette, an entrée of rack of lamb, and napoleons for dessert.

The four second-floor rooms each have fireplaces and candles on the mantels: the Georgian, the Nursery, the Master Bedroom, and the masculine Calabrese (with private bath). The Nursery is typically lovely, with butter-yellow walls and tulip stenciling, white embroidered antique linens and coverlet, a settee in front of the fireplace, over which hangs a Wyeth print. The beds are all gorgeously prepared, if not with antique linens, then with Laura Ashley prints and patterns. A vibrant pie quilt about 80 years old hangs from the third-floor landing. The two quirky rooms here include the favorite Fan Window Suite, with plaster walls in a pinkish hue, a view through the dormer fan window through the trees to the fields, and a charming, cute bath tucked under the eaves, with a half clawfoot tub and view of the back grounds. The Loft Room is a bit more rustic.

The original three-story half was built by Quaker farmers in 1734, a smaller, low-ceilinged version of its Federal partner, home to the convivial kitchen with hanging baskets and an early American primitive table. The second floor has the enchanting Garden Room with a curtained four-poster bed, three Williamsburg windows looking to the back fields, and a huge bath. The wonderful third-floor Dormer Room stretches the entire width of the house, with wide-planked floors, exposed brick, fireplace, white linens on a queen-size and a twin bed, a dormer skylight, and a huge bath under the eaves at the front of the house.

The four cottage rooms are all vastly different, good for families, and very private. The Window Box has a practical bent, with kitchenette, washer, and dryer. The Greenhouse has a glass atrium ceiling with two bedrooms. The Gardener's Cottage is intimate and lovely, with a sitting room, corner stone fireplace, and a pretty floral bedroom. Attached by a front porch is the Herb Room, tiny, cute, with an adorable little bath.

In warmer months there is an airy sense about this house; a generous back porch with white wicker furniture overlooks the big oval pool, one of the cottages, and the groomed grounds. Nine horses are boarded on the property in several pastures.

Tara — A Country Inn
3665 Valley View Road
Clark, Pennsylvania 16113
412-962-3535
800-782-2803

Proprietors: Jim and Donna Winner
General Manager: Deborah DeCapua
Accommodations: 27 rooms, all with private bath
Rates: $198–$318 MAP; 20% less on weekdays
Included: Breakfast, dinner, and afternoon tea; use of spa
  facilities
Minimum stay: None
Added: 6% tax
Payment: Visa, MasterCard, Discover
Children: Not allowed
Pets: Not allowed
Smoking: Limited
Open: All year

After the novel comes the movie, then the sequel . . . then the inn! True romantics erring on the side of fantasy will love Tara. Few places in this book have a theme, but even fewer execute their ideas as tastefully as does Tara, an elegant country inn in northwest Pennsylvania that is done in the style of Scarlett O'Hara's family plantation. Jim and Donna Winner have owned this 1854 mansion since June 1986. They recently completed an addition with 14 rooms and spa facilities with mineral baths, investing more than two million dollars. A second four-diamond award from AAA proves that their hopes for Tara have not "gone with the wind."

The two-story white brick house has a double-story portico supported by six Ionic columns. Two wings stretch out on either side of the Tara centerpiece. The many common rooms have the generous scale of a plantation house, furnished with Civil War–era antiques. To complete the antebellum illusion, the women are dressed in floral hoop skirts. All is genteel, chivalrous, and elegant. Guests are greeted with smiles and in their rooms by a basket of wine and cheese.

Named either for characters from the book or Civil War themes, the guest rooms at Tara are thoroughly and beautifully decorated. Donna has seen *Gone With the Wind* at least twenty times, vows her niece and sales director Laura Shaffer, simply to garner more ideas for the inn. Throughout are precious antiques, majestic armoires, and lovely bed and window treatments in sweeping silks and tapestries. Gas fireplaces add to the romance in many rooms. In addition, unique for an older home, there is an abundance of whirlpool baths for which bath grains are provided. Many rooms have exceptional decor, including the Victorian, with a lace-draped canopy; Master Gerald's room, done in dominating and regal reds; Rhett's Room, with an intriguing gathered canopy; and Belle's Room, a lovely, feminine boudoir with a white satin canopy bed. To complete the romance of an overnight stay, breakfast is brought to one's room on a tray, with home-baked banana bread, a coffee cake muffin, coffee, juice, and a fruit cup with raspberry sauce.

As thoroughly designed and executed as are the rooms, the dining experience at Tara is lavish. A piano player sets the formal tone for Ashley's Gourmet Dining Room, a stunning setting for a six-course meal prepared tableside with white glove service. The Old South Restaurant serves family style. Stonewall's Tavern serves semiformal Continental cuisine in a fabulous cozy grottolike setting of the thick stone walls of Tara's foundation. Notably, the wine list is one of Pennsylvania's largest, with more than 150 bottles in the award-winning cellar.

The spa facility is an exciting addition to Tara, and to the area as a whole. The Winners discovered that the well underneath their property has a mineral content nearly as high as that of White Sulphur Springs. The impeccable staff is anticipatorily attentive. Everyone seems tickled—and proud—to be living the fantasy of *Gone With the Wind*. The Winners are extremely enthusiastic and manage to keep an intimacy about this emerging property.

Virginia

The Bailiwick Inn
4023 Chain Bridge Road
Fairfax, Virginia 22030
703-691-2266
800-366-7666

Proprietors: Anne and Ray Smith
Accommodations: 14 rooms, all with private bath, 5 with
   fireplace
Rates: $95–$145
Included: Full breakfast, afternoon tea
Minimum stay: None
Added: 6.5% tax
Payment: Visa, MasterCard
Children: Welcome
Pets: Not allowed
Smoking: Not allowed
Open: All year

One of the lovelier and newest bed-and-breakfasts in this book, the Bailiwick opened in January 1990 after a three-million-dollar restoration by owners Anne and Ray Smith and the efforts of a handful of creative decorators. This three-story Federal brick house was built in the early 1800s by county sheriff Joshua Coffer Gunnell, across the street from the courthouse of the same period. It was expanded in 1832 and used as a hospital during the Civil War.

The Oliver family bought the house from Gunnell's descendants in 1899 for $2,500, and after a series of owners, it was placed on the National Register of Historic Places in 1987. Many of the original Federal architectural details are present: side and transom lights around the solid front door, since refinished in faux graining by an English expert; fireplaces with Federal and Greek Revival mantels; architraves over doorways and windows; and a single-story portico with a second-floor porch.

The rooms are named for famous Virginians and decorated according to the period in which they lived: the first-floor Thomas Jefferson Room is a replica of his Monticello chamber, with exact gold-trimmed tassels on the canopy and the drapes, echoed in the bathroom shower curtain. The Lord Fairfax Room is named for the 18th-century English absentee landlord who owned more than five million acres in Virginia, decorated in the Charles II style of Leeds Castle, his English home. The James Madison Room echoes themes in the Montpelier mansion, and the front corner George Mason Room derives from his original Gunston Hall mansion, where he drafted the Bill of Rights.

Whatever the period of the room, the antiques are quite lavish and exact, and even some of the rugs were custom-made using specific colors and patterns. The window treatments are done with thick, lovely material, complementing borders and mantels and often matching curtains in baths as well. Four rooms have fireplaces, and several have whirlpool baths.

The common rooms, including the double parlors, are decorated in the height of Federal elegance, with boldly colored walls, inset curio cabinets, and original moldings. A large 1984 addition built onto the back of the house has since been gutted and made into a sunny, two-tiered breakfast area. The several-course breakfast is quite lavish and prettily prepared. Guests may also eat in their rooms or on the brick patio out back, fountainside, decorated with white wrought-iron furniture.

The luxurious air of the Bailiwick is carried throughout by the innkeepers, who are quick to offer discreet, sophisticated service. This restful, pampered retreat is just 15 miles west of Washington, D.C., near the Metro and the Capital Beltway.

Brookside Bed and Breakfast

Millwood, Virginia 22646
703-837-1780

Proprietors: Gary and Carol Konkel
Accommodations: 3 rooms, 1 cabin, all with private bath and fireplace
Rates: $95–$125
Included: Full breakfast
Minimum stay: Selected weekends
Added: 6.5% tax
Payment: Visa, MasterCard
Children: Not allowed
Pets: Not allowed
Smoking: Not allowed
Open: All year

Those inclined to bed-and-breakfast travel will love Brookside, about 90 minutes west of Washington D.C., in the softly rolling hills of Virginia's horse country. Brookside has an abundance of virtues, a rarity in bed-and-breakfasts, which often require a certain flexibility from their guests. Gary and Carol Konkel are intelligent, friendly, discreet hosts; the canopy beds are handmade reproductions, down-covered with elaborate and rare featherbedding and hand-ironed, starched sheets. All rooms have working wood-burning fireplaces; the furnishings are consistently beautiful antiques from the 18th and 19th centuries; and nearby are three highly acclaimed restaurants—the convivial Ashby Inn, the four-star L'Auberge Provencale, and the colonial Red Fox Tavern.

Millwood is a nearly forgotten working mill town transformed in recent years to an informal gallery of antiques shops. Though Brookside sits in the village just feet from the old Burwell-Morgan Mill which founded the township, the bed-and-breakfast is set on five quite rural acres abutting the millrace and a trickling tributary from the nearby Shenandoah River. The three-story cream-colored clapboard house was built in 1780 by Nathaniel Burwell, the grandson of Robert "King" Carter, a famous colonial Virginian. The Konkels, veteran Washingtonians, retired early from administration jobs and bought Brookside in 1985, opening the bed-and-breakfast two years later. As well, the Konkels have made a forum for their interests in antiques in an outbuilding on the property, which houses beautiful furniture and an impressive print collection. Resultingly, most of the formidable pieces in the house are for sale.

The house is a study in American country and primitive furniture, art, and crafts. Though the second-floor rooms, the Cranberry and Blue rooms, are lovely, most guests prefer the third-floor Garret Room, the Burwell children's nursery. A subtle theme of childhood plays throughout the room. Displayed are curiosities like a tiny linen nightgown, an antique doll bed and quilt, an antique toy sleigh, intriguing children's games, and a painting above the fireplace of a Victorian child. The large bathroom, set under the eaves, one wall of which is exposed stone from a chimney, has a clawfoot tub, a restored washstand, and a ladder for a towel rack. Most prized about Brookside are the down-covered canopied featherbeds: a Sheraton field bed under a fishnet canopy in one room, a structured crewel canopy in another. A generous, romantic touch is the welcome basket with a nightcap and fresh fruit that greets guests in their specially prepared rooms. The log cabin is a particularly romantic retreat.

Guests will need a lot of activity after the large gourmet breakfasts made by Gary and Carol. The mill actually chugs away from May to November, and visitors may buy fresh-ground flour and cornmeal. Nearby are wonderful bike routes; hiking and fishing at Sky Meadow State Park; and some of Virginia's finer vineyards.

Clifton, The Country Inn
Route 13, Box 26
Charlottesville, Virginia 22901
804-971-1800

Proprietors: Mitch and Emily Willey

Innkeepers: Steven and Donna Boehmfeldt

Accommodations: 13 rooms, all with private bath (5 rooms in main house, 3 in Carriage House, 2 in Law Office, 3 in Cottage)

Rates: $138–$188

Included: Full breakfast

Minimum stay: 2 nights September to mid-November

Added: $15 each additional guest; 4- and 5-course dinner on weekends; 6.5% tax

Payment: MasterCard, Visa

Children: Welcome (under 12 free)

Pets: Not allowed

Smoking: Not allowed in house

Open: All year

The way of life around Charlottesville is a continuing tribute to the vivid presence of Thomas Jefferson. A wonderful way to visit the area and still be immersed in history is with a stay at Clifton. This graceful plantation house is the quintessence of antebellum southern elegance, built in 1799 on a portion of Jefferson's Shadwell estate. It was home to his daughter Martha and son-in-law Thomas Mann Randolph, an early governor of Virginia.

The entrance to Clifton by way of a graceful circular drive bordered by flowers and tall trees is most authentically approached by carriage or horseback. Six tall columns stretch up two stories to support the overhanging red rooftop shading the elegant facade. The shutters are painted a formal black. What was once a tobacco plantation is now home to 45 wooded acres soaring above the Rivanna River. While Martha spent much time as her father's hostess at nearby Monticello, her husband was a rather reclusive lawyer who would retreat for weeks in his books at Clifton—an activity which has a great appeal today.

Despite its formidable appearance and role in history, Clifton remains an informal country retreat. The heart pine floors, paneled walls, and fireplaces in every room are original to the manor house. Six of the eight guest rooms are suites, these with wood-burning fireplaces and interesting, large baths with colonial painted parquet floors and sometimes large tubs. Several rooms have wonderfully designed canopies which fall grandly from ceiling moldings.

Though the bilevel Carriage House was built in 1985 when the owners bought the property, the floors, windows, and banister were taken from the neighboring Merriwether Lewis house, a contemporary of Clifton. The whitewashed walls and cathedral ceiling lend the feel of a summer cottage, as do the French doors which open at either side of the living room. The Law Office, with two rooms, is even more wonderful as the original building on the premises. The Cottage is original to the property, recently restored to house three suites with Jacuzzis and lovely views of the lake.

Steven is an award-winning chef who makes good use of his industrial kitchen, with four-course dinners Wednesday–Friday and five-course dinners with a Jeffersonian harpist/historian on Saturday. Guests may ask for a gourmet platter of homemade hors d'oeuvres to start or may sit down to a multicourse gourmet dinner ranging from $30 to $40. Such a meal might begin with onion soup with saffron and sherry with four different cheeses over puff pastry. A sorbet intermezzo is followed by a tenderloin au poivre or canardeau with an orange sauce and liqueurs. Dessert soufflés are a great house specialty, as is baked Alaska flambé in raspberry Chambord. Rest assured that breakfasts are quite full as well, with delicacies like homemade muffins, fruit smoothees, Belgian waffles, Canadian bacon, and stradas.

The grounds at Clifton are beautifully landscaped as would befit a governor, with gravel paths, a sundial, gardens, sculptures, croquet pitches, and unexplored woods. Mountain bikes are available for local touring, with several walking trails as well. The innkeepers are extremely professional, enthusiastic, and quite knowledgeable about local history and activities.

Prospect Hill, The Virginia Plantation Inn

Route 3, Box 340
Trevilians, Virginia 23093
703-967-0844
800-277-0844

Proprietors: Bill and Mireille Sheehan
Innkeeper: Mike Sheehan
Accommodations: 5 rooms in main house, 8 rooms in 7 cottages
Rates: $180–$260 per couple, MAP
Included: Full breakfast and dinner, afternoon tea
Minimum stay: Two nights on weekends
Added: $35 each additional guest; 4.5% tax
Payment: Visa, MasterCard
Children: Check with innkeeper
Pets: Not allowed

Smoking: Allowed
Open: All year except Christmas Eve and Christmas Day

Prospect Hill is one of the more unusual accommodations in the Mid-Atlantic. Fifteen miles east of Charlottesville toward Richmond, this country inn is set on ten acres of a resurrected southern plantation. Guests stay in several rooms in the warm manor house and in seven outbuildings, including the slave quarters, a log cabin (built in 1699), the overseer's house, a summer kitchen, a smokehouse, a carriage house, and the groom's quarters. While guests share the social warmth of a country inn, they have the unique advantage of the romance of private cottages.

In 1977, Bill Sheehan introduced Prospect Hill to an untried public. At the time, country inns were an unusual concept in overnight travel, especially in the South—yet even more interesting was the idea of using individual cottages to create a country inn experience.

The manor house is a beautiful, pristine yellow clapboard with white trim and black shutters, completed in 1732 by Roger Thompson. Slaves were brought over as early as 1796, and the other buildings were erected under the ownership of Richard Terrill. Years later, the plantation was owned by William Overton, who returned from the Civil War like Scarlett to Tara only to find ruin and despair. The Overtons began taking in guests, expanded the manor house, and renovated the slave quarters. Sheehan expanded on Overton's hospitality ideas, bringing to the plantation a sense of sophistication, luxury, and romance.

A great part of Prospect Hill's appeal rests in the elegant dining experience. Guests gather in the colonial common rooms by fireside for a drink and sit down to dinner at the signal of a bell. The meal is a four- or five-course French Provençale meal, the menu of which changes nightly. A sample might be a potage (fermier cream and potato soup), a house salad, suprèmes de volailles Beaugency with artichokes, and a Genoise chiffon cake, chocolate with mocha buttercream. Guests dine intimately by candlelight, with occasional storytelling by host Bill Sheehan, who is quite proud of his well-stocked wine cellar.

The groomed drive stretches grandly toward the picturesque manor house, the drive flanked by adorable cottages, each quite different, connected by smoothed walkways covered with white trellises, bordered by trimmed bushes, picket fences—the overall picture is simply charming. The Overseers, the Little Boys, and Uncle Guy's cabins rest on one side of the drive; on the other, two cottages: the Kitchen and the Carriage House above the Groom's Quarters. Most luxurious are the Carriage House and Sanco Pansy's cottage, a short walk behind the manor house. The former has a tiled floor, sweeping Palladian windows, a full sitting area, with an 1840s cherry four-poster bed. The cottages are furnished with antiques, and all have working wood-burning fireplaces, refrigerators, stereos, sometimes whirlpool baths, private porches, and views of the rolling countryside. Guests are welcomed by a bottle of wine, fruit and cheese basket, and homemade cookies.

Rooms in the manor house are decorated in traditional Williamsburg, authenticated by sloping original flooring, window sashes, doors, and mantels.

Service at Prospect Hill is discreet, pampered, and genteel. Full breakfasts are brought to one's room in a charming presentation on a silver tray. Guests may pass time with an idle walk in the fields to pet the horses or a swim in the pool.

West Virginia

Hillbrook Inn on Bullskin Run
Route 2, Box 152
Charles Town, West Virginia 25414
304-725-4223

Proprietor: Gretchen Carroll
Assistant Innkeeper: Nadia Hill
Accommodations: 5 rooms, including 1 suite, 2 rooms with fireplace
Rates: $120–$190; $35 additional on Saturdays and holidays
Included: Full breakfast
Minimum stay: 2 nights on weekends
Added: 9% tax; 15% gratuity; 7-course dinner, $55 with wine
Payment: MasterCard, Visa
Children: Welcome
Pets: Not allowed
Smoking: Limited
Open: Year-round; dinner served Thursdays through Sundays

In the green, flat farmland of West Virginia's eastern panhandle, six miles from Harper's Ferry National Historic Park where Maryland and Virginia meet, an exquisitely beautiful country inn decorates the outskirts of Charles Town. Hillbrook nestles in a dreamlike setting on 17 acres of undulating hills divided by a spring-fed stream and Chinese footbridge, speckled with 40 ducks who have the run of the place.

Most captivating is the architecture of this 1922 Tudor-style manor. While only one room wide—about 20 feet—the half-timbered home is quite long, descending the hill on which it is built with the sensitivity of Frank Lloyd Wright's Falling Water. The gabled peaks of the second story punctuate the skyline like treetops, rising and falling while following the decrescendoed slope of the setting. The dark wood beams and white plaster exterior make a striking contrast to the bright flowers which decorate the grounds.

The beauty of the interior quite matches that of the exterior. There are 15 fireplaces throughout the house. Incredibly, there are more than 2,000 panes of leaded glass in the mullioned windows, 360 alone in the living room. Several rooms rest in loft areas in the gabled second floor, while others are found in nooks along narrow passages on the first floor. Facing west, the house has spectacular sunlight which filters through the tiny panes. The wallpapers, sometimes a dark paisley, sometimes a gilded pattern, either absorb or reflect the light with ever-changing results.

This stunning piece of architecture is made complete by the impeccable taste of its innkeeper. Gretchen Carroll has owned Hillbrook since 1985, opening in the spring after months of restoration. An extremely enthusiastic woman of sophisticated, creative taste, Gretchen came to Hillbrook after a lifetime of international travel. Her experience fills the rooms figuratively and literally: precious antiquities such as South Pacific tapas, Mayan sculpture, a Thai spirit house, and a Scottish teapot. Antique scatter Oriental rugs decorate the original flooring. While some furnishings may be Victorian, the flavor is uniquely European and eclectic. The Locke's Nest, the Lookout, the Point, the Bamford Suite, and the Cottage have designer linens on antique beds, some with fireplaces or patios. Chocolates at turndown and fresh flowers add to the pampered luxury of Hillbrook — though the baths are surprisingly spare. Guests enjoy a full gourmet breakfast in the beautiful dining room, perhaps of pecan pancakes with ginger butter.

The seven-course European dinner changes with the whims of the talented chef at Hillbrook. Twenty-five guests sit in the magical setting of the dining room at intimate tables during the several hours of this romantic interlude. The woody Bull-Skin Tavern rests quite separately at the bottom portion of the Tudor building, the setting for live music on the weekends.

Gretchen is planning a major expansion with a separate building of Mediterranean flavor.

classic wing that parallels Eleventh Street. The custom-designed furniture in the neoclassic wing is quite intriguing, with clean, masculine, modern lines, Roman shades, and complementary artwork anointing the walls. Service is exceptional, with nightly turndown, twice-daily maid service, morning newspaper, room service, and in-room movie rentals.

The common rooms and dining rooms at the Morrison Clark are simply beautiful. The foyer is a parquet marble, with a huge floral centerpiece on a precious round table, set off by deep rust-colored walls. Daunting, heavy mahogany doors lead to the breakfast room and bar, one of five dining areas, with floor-to-ceiling windows, and carved marble fireplace mantel. An intimate dining room follows, with a circular banquette, high ceilings, and enormous windows covered in diaphanous white curtains, lending a soft light to the room. Other dining areas are in the exterior courtyard between the wings of the houses, on the Chinese veranda, and in the sunny solarium.

Dinners in this eclectic and elegant setting are orchestrated by Susan Lindeborg, a noted pastry chef whose talents have expanded to great acclaim. Her vegetables and side dishes are called sensational, memorable, and luscious by local reviewers. A dinner might begin with an appetizer of goat cheese and roast garlic flan with tart tomato fondue, or stuffed quail with grilled polenta and ancho chili sauce. Warm leek salad with pommery mustard and honey dressing might follow; or perhaps a salmon chowder with tomato and ginger. Entrées are quite reasonably priced for the capital, under $20. Among the baffling choices are beef tenderloin with two-mustard laphroaig Scotch sauce; tuna steak with grilled vegetables and semolina gnocchi; grilled salmon with green lentils, applewood bacon, and horseradish; or grilled lamb leg with coriander sauce and couscous. The setting is a lovely backdrop to the gorgeous meal.

Preservationist Massoni also owns the Imperial Hotel in Chestertown, across the Bay Bridge on Maryland's eastern shore, which is listed in this chapter.

The Watergate Hotel
2650 Virginia Avenue, N.W.
Washington, D.C. 20037
202-965-2300
800-424-2736

Proprietors: Trustehouse Forte and Cunard Hotel Group
Managing Director: Ibrahim Fahmy
Accommodations: 235 rooms, half of which are suites

Rates: $240–$350 suites from $450; weekends $145–$185, suites from $225
Included: Use of health club facilities
Minimum stay: None
Added: $25 each additional guest; 11% tax; $1.50 room tax
Payment: Major credit cards
Children: Welcome, under 14 in room free
Pets: Allowed
Smoking: Nonsmoking rooms available, no smoking in restaurant
Open: All year

Everyone would recognize the Watergate Hotel, but perhaps not from the newest face it puts forward. Though the exterior looks the same—still a modern collection of scalloped buildings trimmed with balconies overlooking the Potomac—the interior is impressively improved. The Trustehouse Forte Hotel Group acquired the landmark hotel in the spring of 1990 and redecorated all the guest rooms to their current state of elegance. In addition, the hotel was given a fantastic new health club, one of the few and certainly plushest in Washington hotels. Most exciting is its two-star Michelin chef Jean-Louis Palladin, Washington's only chef to have earned five stars from the Mobil guide for his culinary mastery.

The Watergate has quite an international clientele, with half of its guests from overseas. The staff prides itself on its linguistic versatility. The lobby is a glistening display of polished marble, the setting for afternoon high tea. Guest rooms hover above, and about half have balconies and views of the Potomac River on whose banks the hotel sits, next to the Kennedy Center. Not including the deluxe suites, there are three tiers of regular guest rooms at the Watergate in several types of traditional decor. The rooms are furnished with dark wood reproduction furniture, and chintz fabrics in light colors, rusts, or blues decorate the windows and beds. Period reproduction highboys contain remote televisions, videos, and tape decks, and all rooms have stocked mini-bars. The baths are appointed in light marble, with dryers and a basket of Gilchrest and Soames amenities.

In a fairly glamourous marbled setting, the health club offers several rooms equipped with a Nautilus gym, a 25-by-30-foot lap pool, a whirlpool, and saunas. The lockers are done in light oak, and adjacent rooms offer massages.

Jean-Louis's dining room is an incredible spot, with only twelve tables in a mystical, dim setting, lit obliquely behind swatches of silk which hang from the walls under a smokily mirrored ceiling. The menu is boldly handwritten in flourishes by the chef in French, with a typed English translation, and it changes like the palette of a working artist. Jean-Louis offers two fixed price selections at $85 or $95. The experience might proceed as follows: a crab soup with small crabcakes and quenelles; a salad of fresh seaweed, macerated with sesame, smoked salmon, and ginger; roasted saddle of rabbit with herbs and marrow flan, a julienne of celery root and truffles; followed by tiramisu with coffee coulis and cacao ice cream.

The plusher menu offers six courses, which proceed as follows: celery root soup with rabbit sausage, truffle quenelle, and fresh truffle; Santa Barbara abalone with enoki mushrooms; fresh American duck foie gras with rhubarb; fresh salmon wrappped with a leaf, concassée of tomato and black olives, butter of epazote; followed by mignon of Pittsburgh lamb with cheese ravioli and spices; finishing with a symphony of pears.

Maryland

Imperial Hotel
208 High Street
Chestertown, Maryland 21620
410-778-5000

Proprietors: Albert and Carla Massoni
Accommodations: 11 rooms, including 2 suites, all with
    private baths
Rates:
    Rooms: $88 weekdays, $110 weekends
    Parlor suite: $160 weekdays, $200 weekends
    Carriage House: $200 weekdays, $250 weekends
Included: Continental breakfast
Minimum stay: 2 nights on holiday weekends
Added: 5% tax
Payment: MasterCard, Visa
Children: Welcome
Pets: Not allowed
Smoking: Allowed
Open: All year

The Massonis are people of passion. They love food, wine, art, and a great old building in need of revival. They were welcomed into elite Washington food circles with the Morrison Clark Inn, applauded by travelers insightful enough to stay there. Next, in the fall of 1990, the Massonis turned their energies to their beloved eastern shore home of Chestertown and the neglected town hotel.

Historic Chestertown is north of the Chesapeake Bay Bridge in Kent County, on the Chester River—an ideal weekend destination. On charming High Street near the river, the Imperial Hotel is a three-story brick building with a generous white gingerbread porch to match its height. Built in 1903 by Wilbur W. Hubbard to reign the town, it was placed on the National Register of Historic Places in 1984 and then fully restored. Al Massoni found a picture of the hotel from 1910 and had the sign reproduced as exactly as possible, so look for the "Hotel Imperial" when in Chestertown.

An impressive Audubon print collection is displayed on the first floor, as well as some of the original elevations of Hotel Imperial. The Victorian beauty of the restaurant lounge is equaled only by that on the second-floor guest lounge, which opens onto the wide porch overlooking town. Of two floors of guest rooms, the Parlor Suite is the hotel's loveliest: two rooms dressed in high Victorian antiques and a porch, taking up the third-story front of the building. Other rooms have similar levels of elegance on a smaller scale, appointed with bold wallcoverings and curtains, antique end tables and armoires holding televisions, and reproduction king-size brass beds. The bathrooms are new and spotless, with attention to fabrics and amenities. Interesting prints and antique quilts decorate the walls.

Though an overnight stay is highly recommended, a meal is mandatory. The Massonis wanted to make the Victorian restoration of the Imperial Hotel a backdrop to a restaurant of highest repute, with the talents of chef Daniel Turgeon. Their extensive wine list has already received the Award of Excellence from *Wine Spectator* magazine. Their monthly winemaker dinners match the talents of the finest vintners to those of their chef—to the delight of guests lucky enough to get a reservation.

Chef Daniel Turgeon is awarded free rein and boundless respect, his gallery in two intimate, elegant dining rooms on the first floor to the left and right of the entrance. The darkly lit tartan room has the feel of an English supper club, with eight tables in two rooms, green tufted Queen Anne chairs, candle lamps and fresh flowers on the tables, and hunt scenes on the walls. The Leighton Room, named for Carla's uncle (a New York restaurateur) is more decorative, with black and claret chintz, and on the nine tables silver chargers and fringe lamps.

The award-winning crab bisque is worth the trip (from no matter where); and an entrée of crabcakes is nonpareil, served with watercress, mustard, and tomato cream. Other master-pieces include an appetizer of smoked salmon, shrimp and bay scallops with cucumber salad in fresh dill, horseradish, and mustard cream, and entrées of grilled lamb chops with parsley, orange rind, and lemon and lime jus; grilled breast of chicken with corn custard, roasted tomatoes, onions, and cilantro jus; or roasted semiboneless quails stuffed with wild mushrooms, sage, and mustard in shallot butter.

A separate light-fare menu is offered in warmer months in the back garden, amid wooden Jefferson furniture and umbrella tables. It faces the Geddes-Piper House, built in the 18th century, recently restored with perfection, often the location for receptions hosted by the Imperial Hotel. A sleek new conference center is an added attraction.

Back on High Street, visitors ought to trudge down to the Cellar. This wonderful shop is based on the Massonis' love of art and wine. Every bottle is an individual work of art, and here is the gallery: an eclectic shop of wines, local artists, potters, vinegars, crafts—in celebration of true art.

The Inn at Perry Cabin

308 Watkins Lane, on the Miles River
St. Michaels, Maryland 21663
410-745-2200
800-722-3427

Proprietor: Sir Bernard Ashley
General Manager: Ian Fleming
Accommodations: 41 rooms, all with private bath
Rates: $195–$450
Included: Breakfast, afternoon tea
Minimum stay: None
Added: 8% tax
Payment: All credit cards
Children: Not allowed
Pets: Not allowed
Smoking: Allowed
Open: All year

The British have again touched ground on American shores, more specifically on Maryland's eastern shore, via the Chesapeake Bay. With the Inn at Perry Cabin, Sir Bernard Ashley has created a tribute to his late wife Laura, the fabric designer of legendary repute. He sought to replicate the genteel life of the English country house using Laura Ashley wallpapers, fabrics, and furniture, in the form of a country inn. Not only is Perry Cabin a thoroughly elegant and romantic experience, it is an exciting setting for the culinary creations of chef Scott Hoyland.

During his extensive travels, Sir Bernard found international accommodations a bit lacking. As a result, he sought to realize his own ideas of hospitality in the United Kingdom (Wales) and the United States. Perry Cabin is the first of several planned American inns—the next is Keswick, on the outskirts of Charlottesville, to open in late 1992.

Sir Bernard searched for a suitable property of historic merit and found exactly that in tony St. Michaels, part of Maryland's wealthy Talbot County. Just outside the charming township, Perry Cabin sits tranquilly at the end of a formal drive, a three-story white clapboard Federal house built in 1820. The front of the house, with its two-story Greek Revival portico supported by four Ionic columns, faces the Miles River. The grounds are immaculate and elegant and include one of Maryland's largest holly trees. The work of the full-time gardening staff is very much evident throughout the 25 acres.

While the main house dates to 1820 and contains the four common rooms and three dining rooms, Sir Bernard added two complementary wings with guest rooms stretching out from either side. The new architecture displays carefully crafted wainscoting, wide arched doorways, chair rails, and moldings to match those in the original house. Yet the new influences add an interesting depth to the classic aspects, with some duplex guest rooms with hand-carved jointed spiral stairs in odd angular spaces.

The rooms were elegantly designed in consistent Laura Ashley style, overseen by Nick Ashley, Sir Bernard's son. Most rooms have an outdoor patio through French doors with an oblique or direct view of the water. Antiques, unusual artwork of England or the eastern shore, lots of books, and fresh flowers lend an elegant but personal touch to each room. The baths are traditional but quite luxurious, with lavish scented Penhaligon amenities from London, a towel warmer, fluffy bath sheets, and creative curtains and tiebacks.

Guests may take an elaborate, traditional afternoon tea in the many public rooms that open airily to the front patio and grassy lawns. Sir Bernard's extensive art collection decorates the halls and walls. Every aspect is at the height of elegance, setting the tone for the exquisite meals at Perry Cabin. The prix fixe menu is $50 for four or five courses and changes seasonally.

A sample menu might include an appetizer of tartare of local oysters or house-made fromage blanc with pesto aspic and marinated artichoke bottoms; a consommé between courses; an entrée of tempura fried soft-shell crab with creamed corn and braised leeks, or Atlantic salmon fillet in potato crust with foie gras and clear tomato broth. The creativity and presentation are overwhelmingly artistic, served on Ashley china by Spode. Service, as with every aspect of life at Perry Cabin, is discreet, elegant, and simply flawless.

New York

The American Hotel
Main Street
Sag Harbor, New York 11963
516-725-3535

Proprietor: Ted Conklin
Accommodations: 8 rooms, all with private bath
Rates: $75–$130 per person (rates vary seasonally)
Included: Continental breakfast
Minimum stay: 2 nights on weekends, 3 nights on holiday
  weekends
Added: 8% tax
Payment: Major credit cards
Children: Not allowed
Pets: Not allowed
Smoking: Restricted
Open: All year

The port of Sag Harbor reached its populous peak in the early to mid-19th century when whaling was its mainstay. Today, the charming streets are less populated than they were in Melville's day, though doubtless as charming, with Federal and Victorian houses flanking narrow streets which join at Shelter Island Harbor. This is the one tony Hampton resort town without surf, a refuge for the rich and famous who don't want to be seen. This understated wealth is best typified by a Sag Harbor landmark, the oft-mentioned American Hotel.

Built in 1846 as a hotel during the Sag Harbor heyday, the three-story brick edifice was bought by its present owner, Ted Conklin, in 1972. Over the years, the hotel had served businessmen as a boarding house with rather nonluxurious quarters, small and boxy. During his renovations, Ted Conklin broke through walls and expanded the rooms to their present large state. The 8 guest rooms today spread throughout what once stood as 20 rooms, expanding into odd corners and ells. The beds represent the different periods: simple sleighs, rare twin brass beds, deep wood pre-Victorian headboards, and even an art deco suite. Some walls are papered in paisleys and stripes in masculine colors, others in light peach or floral patterns. The antiques and wonderful prints are the result of Ted Conklin's twenty years of collecting.

From the sunny street to the wicker-filled porch lined with abundant flower boxes, guests enter to a living room foyer with a working fireplace and Empire couches under the original pressed tin ceiling. A double parlor dining room is to the left, with pretty floral paper over wood wainscoting. Ahead is a smaller dining room with café tables and the magnificent original bar with its deep wood wainscoting and enormous moose head hovering above. A pretty light-filled atrium dining area is a last alternative, to the right of the bar. Oriental rugs lend color to the deep wood floors of the foyer, while the bar has old-style octagonal tiling.

While the French menu changes, entrées range from $16.50 for shepherd's pie to $28.50 for tournedos Rossini. Other entrées might include exotic sautéed sweetbreads à la meunière, baby pheasant with fresh black truffles, antelope paillard au poivre vert, or brace of quail Véronique. The creative chef also offers appetizers like terrine de lapin au porto, sautéed foie gras with grilled fennel, or saumon frais marine a l'Aneth. The wine list is quite extensive and well researched.

The American Hotel is one of Long Island's more sophisticated experiences and, except for the tans and the easy smiles, could easily be mistaken for a Midtown Manhattan gathering spot for the chic-elite.

The Inn at Quogue

Quogue
Long Island, New York 11959
516-653-6560
800-628-6166

Manager: Cathy McCabe
Accommodations: 70 rooms, including suites and cottages
Rates (depending on day of week):
    June 15–Labor Day: Rooms, $117–$140; suites, $170–$225
    Off-season: Rooms, $95–$110; $139–$149
Minimum stay: 3 or 4 nights on weekends in high season; 2 nights off-season

Added: $25 each additional person; 13% tax
Payment: American Express
Children: Allowed
Pets: Allowed
Smoking: Allowed
Open: All year; restaurant closed during the winter

While the Hamptons bustle in the summer like Wall Street in the bear market or Bloomingdale's at Christmas, the hamlet of Quogue has escaped all signs of tourist intrusion. A visit here reveals the unspoiled, historic Hamptons before the crowds discovered the island, with regal clapboard and weathered shingle houses used as summer retreats for the country's wealthiest and most influential, hidden on shady lanes a short, barefoot walk from the east's most beautiful beaches.

The Inn at Quogue is the town's only licensed establishment for food, drink, and board. While such a monopoly might suggest indifference, the result is quite the opposite—as if the inn auditioned for the privilege of representing Quogue. Its restaurant, with a new and revered chef from Canova in Manhattan, has received a daunting two stars from the *New York Times*, certainly designed to please weekend patrons who dine during the week at Le Cirque and Le Bernardin.

The Inn is a 200-year-old white clapboard paragon of Hamptons sophistication, understated, set on groomed grounds sprinkled with flowers attended to by an exacting gardener. In addition to the classic old building are the Civil War–era Weathervane and private cottages from this century. Recently redecorated by the skilled hand of Marsha Fox-Martin, the rooms are quite cheery and comfortable, airy and immaculate, befitting a summer cottage of impeccable taste. The rooms vary from small to quite spacious, some with fireplaces and original wide-planked floors. Characteristic are bright chintz linens falling from windows, matching bedskirts, and upholstered headboards. On the beds is a light cotton comforter. In the vein of a true summer cottage, where the precious furniture is saved for the city house, the Inn at Quogue has spare, clean furnishings mixed and matched in perfect taste. There are ample reading lamps, fresh flowers and plants, and a freshly swept look reminiscent of summertime.

The Inn has a 20-by-40-foot outdoor pool, but for those who prefer the gorgeous surf here, beach passes are provided to the village's private beach, a mile's walk. As well, guests may use the facilities at the Quogue Racquet Club and Hampton Athletic Club, offering tennis, racquetball, aerobics, Nautilus, as well as an outdoor pool and spa. Facials and massages are also available. The best way to explore Quogue is on bicycles provided by the Inn.

As recently as the summer of 1991, the restaurant was graced with the presence of Chef Ali Fathalla, whose work may be appreciated in the winter months at Canova restaurant in Manhattan. His efforts produced rave reviews in national publications. The Egyptian chef was French trained, though his cuisine is best described as a blend of Mediterranean and Italian influences. His prix fixe menus are $37.50 for three courses, and his specialties, among others, are in seafood and lamb. His presence is an exciting addition to Long Island's finest resorts.

The Point

Saranac Lake, New York 12983
518-891-5678
800-255-3530

Proprietors: David and Christie Garrett
Innkeepers: Bill and Claudia McNamee
Accommodations: 11 rooms, all with fireplace and private
　　bath (4 rooms in Main Lodge; 3 rooms in Eagles Nest; 3
　　rooms in the Guest House; the Boathouse)
Rates: $625–$775 per couple, AP
Included: Three meals daily with wine and open bar
Minimum stay: 2 nights on weekends, 3 nights on holidays
Added: 15% service, 12% tax
Payment: American Express
Children: Welcome, with prior notice
Pets: Allowed, with prior notice
Smoking: Allowed
Open: Closed April

The Point is the embodiment of Old World sophistication, and its introduction will take us back several generations. In 1932, William Avery Rockefeller, nephew of John D., commissioned notable architect William Distin to built a Great Camp on Upper Saranac Lake in the untrodden reaches of the six-million-acre Adirondack wilderness. Camp Wonundra has since been renamed the Point, the only Great Camp standing today that sustains the extraordinary level of luxury from the period in which it was built. Guests of the Point experience one of the most thoroughly romantic and elegant vacations a traveler can have in this country: from the food overseen by three-star Michelin chef Albert Roux and executive chef and innkeeper Bill McNamee, to the unusually beautiful rooms which seem lifted from the pages of *Architectural Digest*, to the non-pareil Great Camp Adirondack architecture, to the breathtaking remote lakeside setting, to the etiquette-perfect service orchestrated by innkeeper Claudia McNamee.

The Point was sold in 1980 by the Rockefeller estate to Ted Carter, who began the tradition of elegant hostmanship, and subsequently went to the present owners David and Christie Garrett in 1986. To upgrade the food to national renown, the Garretts asked Bill and Claudia McNamee to join them at the Point in 1987 as innkeepers. While Claudia lends a tasteful touch to the design and manages the administrative aspects, Bill brings to the Point his experience as an accomplished chef, who received accolades for his work at Le Pavillon in Washington, D.C., Le Chardon d'Or at the Morrison House in Alexandria, and Le Gavroche in London under chef Albert Roux.

The resort consists of nine buildings on a ten-acre peninsula called Whitney Point. The architecture is intriguingly endemic to the Adirondacks, a varied collection of luxurious Canadian pine log cabins with the original slate roofs and Queen Anne gables. The rich wooden interiors have open-beamed cathedral ceilings, formidable stone hearths, and traditional twig furniture and museum-quality antiques. The walls are enlivened by beautiful original art. The decor of the common and guest rooms is a successful, eclectic combination of Ralph Lauren ease and sophistication; colorful Aztec and Indian patterns on wall hangings, heavy draperies and bedding; and hunting and wilderness themes, evidenced by lumberjack plaids and moose heads, antlers, and zebra and bearskin rugs. The king-size beds are triple-sheeted and turned down nightly, and several have inventive canopy treatments, like the diaphanous scarf wrapped around the bed in the Boathouse. The baths are of a grand old scale, large and traditionally luxurious, with Crabtree and Evelyn amenities, terribly thick terry robes, and hair dryer.

Set around a groomed drive are the three main buildings for guests: the Guesthouse with three rooms; the Eagles Nest, with three rooms and a Pub, a pool table, and a common room; and the Main Lodge, with two guest rooms in each wing, astride the Great Hall, where guests dine and socialize around two enormous fireplaces. A great slate porch rests outside, facing Upper Saranac Lake. Down a path is the Boathouse, with a second-floor guest room above the dock and a small fleet of boats for guests' use. These include a 30-foot launch for nightly predinner excursions, a ski boat, smaller outboard motorboats, sailboats, canoes, and a vintage mahogany touring boat which cost more than the nice Porsche that brought you here.

The three meals served daily are gorgeously presented, if on a silver tray to one's room, in a picnic basket taken to an island, or around the polished round wooden tables gleaming with candlelight in the Great Hall. Under the guidance of Albert Roux, Adam Votaw is the chef who works with Bill McNamee, organizing the elaborate kitchen staffed with protégés of the master chef from London. The dinners are especially memorable under the dramatic 25-foot ceilings of the Great Hall, flanked by blazing fires. The four-course meal might proceed as follows: a terrine of pheasant with wild mushrooms and truffle sauce; salad of goat cheese and walnuts; roasted fillet of salmon on coulis of leek with pommes fondants and bouquets of spinach and carrots in champagne butter sauce; ending with chocolate truffle cake served with rum crème anglaise. Wines are presented with each course, and after dinner appropriate liqueurs are introduced.

Claudia and Bill are ever-present when needed, invisible when privacy is preferred. Every whim and fancy is answered, from fishing to golf to tours of the Great Camps of Saranac Lake on the Hacker boat, led by Bill with utmost acuity. Every aspect of a stay is the height of elegance and sophistication, as the Rockefellers or the Vanderbilts or the Whitneys intended life to be in the Adirondacks.

Troutbeck

Leedsville Road, Box 26
Amenia, New York 12501
914-373-9681

President and Innkeeper: Jim Flaherty
General Manager: Kathy Robinson
Accommodations: 34 rooms, all with private bath
Rates: $575–$790 per couple per weekend, AP
Included: Six meals daily, all drinks
Minimum stay: 2 nights in season
Added: 12% gratuity; 7.25% tax
Payment: American Express
Children: Over 12 welcome
Pets: Not allowed
Smoking: Allowed in public rooms only
Open: All year

Due to Troutbeck's success with corporate groups, couples are limited to weekend visits at this 422-acre estate. But it's a very full weekend, with an indoor pool, tennis courts, fishing, walking, and six meals daily—the real attraction at Troutbeck.

A weekend here is more like a stay at an English lord's manor house than at a country inn two hours from Manhattan. Since the 1920s, Troutbeck has been a gathering spot for literati and intellectuals, who, among other great ideas, conceived the NAACP within the walls of this grand fieldstone Tudor mansion. Owners Jim Flaherty and Bob Skibsted encourage this exciting, sophisticated atmosphere today in their private corporate meetings and couples weekends.

Most of the indoor activity at Troutbeck takes place in the Tudor house. Guests wander through the rambling mansion as room spills into room, from the formal to the informal living rooms, to the oak-paneled library, to the dark woody conference room, and finally to the Winter Garden dining rooms with an entire wall of small-paned glass overlooking the brook for which the estate was named. The decor is befitting an English country house: the traditional wing chairs and camelback sofas are suitable for novels and intimate conversations, chintz curtains decorate the small lead-paned windows, walls are boldly painted, covered with shelves of books or intriguing prints and maps.

The rooms are comfortable, filled with antiques and curios that are both valuable and well worn, as in the New England house of a wealthy Mayflower-descended aunt. Some rooms have sleeping porches, others are set cozily under pitched roofs, some are grander, and others more modest. An additional 18 guest rooms are in the robin's egg blue clapboard Guesthouse which sits at the beginning of the Troutbeck drive, part of which was built in the mid-18th century, with a recent addition erected in a complementary fashion. The Guesthouse affords a bit more privacy than the main house, with several large, airy common rooms and two wings of guest rooms, four of which have working fireplaces.

Meals are lengthy and glorious events at Troutbeck, created by Chef Jonathan Rosenbloom and team. A five-course spring menu might consist of an appetizer of fried baby artichokes Roman-Jewish style, followed by a salad of mixed wild greens from the gardens, with smoked tomato vinaigrette and celery root remoulade. White Italian peach sorbet prepares one for an entrée of grilled swordfish on mango shallot vinaigrette and corn pudding with citrus-ginger cream; or Norwegian salmon en croûte with arugula, raspberries, and black chanterelle champagne sauce. A choice of six desserts concludes the ceremonious meal—among them chocolate checkerboard mousse cake with Amaretto crème anglaise.

The object of this kind of estate living, while strolling these overgrown or highly groomed grounds, is to work up an appetite for the next culinary creation.

Pennsylvania

Evermay on-the-Delaware
River Road
Erwinna, Pennsylvania 18920
215-294-9100

Proprietors: Ronald Strouse and Fred Cresson
Accommodations: 16 rooms, all with private bath, including 1 suite (11 rooms in main house, 4 in Carriage House, 1 in Cottage)
Rates: Rooms $80–$145; suite $175; weekday discounts
Included: Continental breakfast, afternoon tea
Minimum stay: 2 nights with Saturday stay, 3 nights on some holidays
Added: 6% tax
Payment: MasterCard, Visa
Children: Not allowed
Pets: Not allowed
Smoking: Not allowed in dining rooms
Open: Year-round; for dinner Fridays, Saturdays, Sundays, and holidays

Of the dizzying number of country inns in Bucks County, the Evermay on-the-Delaware is the easy choice for those in search of formal Victorian elegance and the finest of dining. Owners Ronald Strouse and Fred Cresson made extensive renovations on the manor house in 1981, and after two years of success with their rooms introduced their fine restaurant in 1983.

The hamlet of Erwinna sits just across a narrow metal bridge from Frenchtown, one of New Jersey's more charming antiquing villages; as well, Erwinna is a memorable 13-mile drive north of New Hope on winding River Road, which shoulders the Delaware. No matter what the approach, Evermay on-the-Delaware rests in rural seclusion peeking at the Delaware through trees and past a towpath that attracts a good number of walkers, with proximity to the river, which few overnight hostelries in the area can claim.

The Evermay was built in the 18th century and significantly remodeled in 1871. Listed on the National Register of Historic Places, it stands today behind a row of trimmed hedges and a circular drive, a regal, cream-colored building, six windows across trimmed with Tudor brown shutters. The first of its three stories is shaded by a Victorian porch which runs along the facade. The main house is the setting for 11 guest rooms and the dining area, but two outbuildings contain more guest rooms for added privacy.

Rooms names read like a Round Table guest list, for noted figures who lived in the area: Edward Hicks, Josephine Herbst, Henry Stover, James Michener, Oscar Hammerstein, S. J. Pereleman, Dorothy Parker. The owners decorated the rooms with lovely antiques, refinished and reupholstered with luxurious results. Victorian floral wallpaper is a background to carved headboards, marble-top dressers, and converted kerosene lamps on pretty mismatched end tables. It is wise to invest in a larger room, since these have significantly more space. Though the outbuildings are beautifully decorated in Victoriana, guest rooms in the main house are more authentic.

Guests relax in one of two beautifully decorated Victorian parlors, preparing for dinner with a glass of champagne or brandy. The six-course prix fixe dinner is served on the enclosed back porch in one seating, and while the menu changes nightly, a guest might expect the following: hors d'oeuvres with smoked trout salad, sun-dried tomato crostini, and country pâté with green peppercorns; cioppino with saffron croutons; a Mediterranean vegetable tart; a salad of Boston and mache with violets and toasted walnuts with balsamic vinaigrette; grilled yellowfin tuna with lime-caper hollandaise served with poached asparagus and gingered baby carrots; cheeses followed by dessert and coffee.

The Settler's Inn at Bingham Park
4 Main Avenue
Hawley, Pennsylvania 18428
717-226-2993
800-833-8527

Proprietors: Grant and Jeanne Genzlinger and Marcia
  Dunsmore
Accommodations: 18 rooms, all with private bath

Rates: $60–$75; weekends, $65–$80
Included: Full breakfast
Added: 6% tax
Payment: Major credit cards
Children: Welcome
Pets: Not allowed
Smoking: Restricted
Open: All year

Settler's Inn is a great gathering and dining spot in the pretty Victorian town of Hawley, on the shores of manmade Lake Wallenpaupack in the Poconos. At most of the properties in this chapter, the exceptional food is matched to the quality of the accommodations. Though the rooms at Settler's are sweetly decorated, the emphasis is clearly on the dining experience. However, the informality of the guest rooms adds to the general ambience of sociability, good cheer, and familial friendliness created by Settler's owners. Grant Genzlinger is the talented chef; his wife, Jeanne, is a member of the Chamber of Commerce; and family friend Marcia Dunsmore is the notable baker.

The large three-story Tudor building is a creamy plaster trimmed in dark chestnut, with lead-paned mullioned windows, which rambles on at different angles at the corner of town. Across the street is Hawley's town park, with basketball and tennis courts, a mile and a half from beautiful Lake Wallenpaupack. Settler's was begun in 1927 but not completed until after World War II, serving as a hotel, a boys' school, a nightclub, and a senior citizens' home.

The owners bought the property in 1980 as a forum for Grant's culinary skills, an unusual blend of Asian and German cooking. Grant and Jeanne are touchingly and loyally tied to their community: their cheese comes from neighboring Amish farms, their meats are all cured and smoked in-house, and their produce is grown locally, if not on the property. The menu is hearty and interesting, providing suggestions from the large list of Pennsylvania wines and beers. Appetizers might include applewood smoked trout with apple horseradish cream or wild mushrooms and walnuts in armagnac sweet cream. Entrées could include roast chicken breast stuffed with cornbread and bauern schinken (German country ham); or scallops, shrimp, and flounder in Asian sauces. The desserts are extensive, all made fresh each day by Marcia, and might include apple cobbler or maple crème brulée. In addition, she bakes four to five breads for dinner, for which a garlic boursin cheese is provided. Entrées range from $12 to $20. Sunday brunch is a famous event, summoning hungry charges from all over for full meals from $9 to $11.

Comfortable queen-size beds with fresh linens, wicker furniture, antique dressers, and clean baths flank a long hall of second-floor rooms. These are clean, cheery, and old-fashioned.

Guests ought to consult Jeanne for advice about numerous local activities, including boat tours, train excursions from Honesdale (the birthplace of the American railroad), hiking, bird-watching, or museumgoing.

Virginia

The Ashby Inn & Restaurant
Route 1, Box 2/A
Paris, Virginia 22130
703-592-3900

Proprietors: John and Roma Sherman
Manager: Beryl Pearmund
Accommodations: 6 rooms, 4 with private bath in Inn; 4 suites in Old SchoolHouse
Rates: $80–$175
Included: Full breakfast
Minimum stay: $20 extra for Saturday-only stay in 4 rooms
Added: $20 each aditional guest; 4% tax
Payment: Visa, MasterCard, American Express
Children: Over 10 welcome
Pets: Not allowed
Smoking: Allowed in Tap Room and library only
Open: All year

There are two magnificent gourmet country inns in the northeast part of Virginia: the Ashby Inn and L'Auberge Provençale (see next listing). Quite unusual is the personable nature of the Ashby Inn: the service is natural and friendly, the food is wonderful, the accommodations are understated and lovely. Set breathtakingly in the foothills of the Skyline Drive, right on the Appalachian Trail, the Ashby Inn is a white colonial three-story stucco farmhouse with green shutters. The hamlet of Paris is an hour's drive west of Washington, D.C., in the rolling hills of horse country. It's an understated but sophisticated gathering spot for Washington elite as well as for locals with boots muddied from the horse races—surely the place to go in the area.

John is a speechwriter, Roma is an excellent chef, and their staff, headed by Beryl, is a happy, interesting group devoted to this convivial refuge. The active, intelligent Shermans came here in November 1984 to share Roma's wonderful cooking with the world, offering rooms for enthusiastic guests who simply would not leave.

The guest rooms at the Ashby's main inn are elegantly spare, dressed in primitive, Shaker decor. Most desirable is the Fan Room, with stunning views of the Blue Ridge foothills in the distance, seen through French doors and the porch. The East Dormer Room shares this view on the third floor from two double beds tucked into the attic and across from the vaulted ceilinged West Dormer by a colonial painted pine floor. Roma and John have collected wonderful artwork displayed throughout the inn (some for sale), including antique decoy prints in the New England Room, with its gorgeous green star quilt and painted furniture and beautiful fireboard painted with a primitive mural. The four new suites in the SchoolHouse are quite deluxe while in period decor.

After a drink in the library, with its roaring fire, guests enjoy meals in one of four dining rooms. The enclosed porch has mountain views through mullioned windows, another room has wooden banquettes and booths, upstairs across from the library. Most gregarious is the fabulous Tap Room on the lower level, with a grottolike coziness. There is a bit of the hunt theme in several stuffed animal dioramas, well enough above plate level to be of interest.

Eric Stamer's creative menu changes daily and is reasonably priced from $13 to $21. An autumn menu might begin with a soup purée of roasted butternut squash with pecan butter followed by an appetizer of warm white bean salad with roasted red peppers, oregano, olive oil, and spinach pesto. Entrées could include a choice of roasted pork loin with garlic mashed potatoes, braised red cabbage, and apple chutney; Ashby Inn jumbo lump crabcakes with lemon-caper mayonnaise served with fried potato ribbons; or roasted rack of Colorado lamb with sun-dried cherries, Warres port, and rice pilaf. John takes great care in selecting a small but varied wine list.

L'Auberge Provençale
Box 119
White Post, Virginia 22663
703-837-1375

Proprietors: Alain and Céleste Borel
Accommodations: 10 rooms, 5 with fireplace (1 suite and 2
    rooms in Manor House; 4 rooms in La Petite Auberge; 3
    rooms with fireplace in Les Chambres des Amis
Rates: $115–$165
Included: Full breakfast
Minimum stay: None
Added: $25 for Saturday and holiday stay; 4% tax
Payment: MasterCard, Visa
Children: Well-behaved children over 10 welcome
Pets: Not allowed
Smoking: Restricted
Open: All year except January; restaurant closed Mondays
    and Tuesdays

In the foothills of the northernmost part of the Blue Ridge
Mountains, north of Front Royal, is some of Virginia's finest
French cuisine at L'Auberge Provençale. The owners, Alain
and Céleste Borel, are quite young, energetic, and enterprising
—much like their good neighbors at the Ashby Inn. Their accommodations resulted from Alain's formidable skills as a
chef, which beckoned crowds from a good distance away. L'Auberge Provençale, however, is a thoroughly country French experience, from the magnificent menu to the charming rooms.

Alain and Céleste came to the countryside outside White
Post in 1981 to buy a 1753 stone farmhouse on eight acres of
rolling fields. Two years later, after Alain's restaurant received
rave reviews, they introduced guest rooms. Part of the house
was expanded in 1890, and again by the Borels a century later, in
low single-story units to one side of the stone house.

The several rooms in the main house above the dining rooms
are large and sunny, offering views of the surrounding fields,
furnished with interesting antiques provided by Alain's father, a
dealer from Avignon, France. The rooms in the addition are
reached by a walkway bordering Alain's herb garden. They have
unique Italian chandeliers, accented with pineapples, daisies,
or lemons; the fireplaces are lined with traditional country
French tiles, and the baths are enlivened by wonderful Mexican
tile. Wrought-iron beds, wicker furniture, and varied antiques
fill the rooms, which are bright with sunshine and valley views.

The main house has three dining areas, two of which are
done in simple country French decor, and the Peach Room,
with five French doors in a semicircular addition at the side of
the house, filled with interesting curios from Europe. Alain's
menu changes monthly, and his entrées range from $19 to $24.

He and chef Albert Leach offer a legendary bouillabaisse as well as filet mignon with Roquefort sauce and mixed nuts, noisettes of lamb with black olive sauce and julienne vegetables, or roasted squab with woodland sauce and wild mushroom tarte. Appetizers might include duck breast with pasta and port sauce, lobster and chicken sausage with spring onion purée, or foie gras wrapped in Norwegian salmon with sherry and crème fraîche or sautéed with fresh mango and ginger. Alain and Céleste have established a commendable wine list to complement the menu. Naturally, desserts are quite wondrous, including white chocolate mousse cake with dark chocolate glaze and raspberry brown butter tart with sabayon.

Unusually, Alain also prepares breakfast for his guests, a lavish, full event which begins with homemade croissants and jams, café au lait and fresh juice, followed by a sumptuous egg dish. He and Céleste are quite proud of their home and enamored of the surrounding countryside, which offers antiquing, fox hunts, and visits to the Skyline Drive and local vineyards.

Channel Bass Inn

100 Church Street
Chincoteague, Virginia 23336
804-336-6148

Proprietor: James S. Hanretta
Accommodations: 8 rooms, including 2 suites, all with
    private bath
Rates: $108–$217
Included: Virginia tax
Minimum stay: 2 nights on weekends, 3 nights on holidays
Payment: Major credit cards
Children: Not allowed
Pets: Not allowed
Smoking: Allowed in public rooms only
Open: Year-round except December 1 to mid-January

Chincoteague is Virginia's easternmost town at the top of the eastern shore peninsula, a busy fishing and beach community comprising mostly fishermen's houses and summer cottages. It sits in the Chincoteague Bay, alee of Assateague Island, the national park famous for its packs of wild ponies and miles of beautiful beach lining the Atlantic Ocean. The drive out to Chincoteague takes a visitor past a NASA facility to a causeway over marshy waters about seven miles long. Once on the island, a guest soon approaches the Channel Bass Inn, a fixture and culinary mecca since 1972, run by chef and owner James

Hanretta. Mr. Hanretta is an extreme perfectionist and master chef. Those who come to his inn come from all over for the food regardless of cost.

The three-story yellow clapboard house was built in the late 1870s as a private home, expanded during the 1920s for touring guests, and still retains a private understated facade. Guests enter through a single-story mullioned side porch to the charming check-in area, trimmed in Williamsburg colors and furnished with wing chairs and a beautiful Victorian tapestry couch. The dining room is straight ahead at the back of the inn, quite a simple room with only seven tables dressed in austere white linens.

The food is marvelous and painstakingly prepared, though the prices are fairly daunting. Dinner entrées range upwards of $30, for broiled seafood espagnol with shrimp, lobster, clams, oysters, chorizo sausage, bacon, onion, and Parmesan cheese, in sauce espagnol ($39); or prime beef tenderloin en brochette with a secret Peruvian marinade. The chef's specialty, backfin crab soufflé for two, made with Parmesan cheese, herbs, and lump crabmeat, is priced at $95. Mr. Hanretta prepares only twelve dinners each night between six and nine o'clock, with utmost fastidiousness and creativity. Service is quite formal, with the staff in black tie and the meals served on Wedgwood china and crystal.

There are four second-floor guest rooms and two on the third floor. Each is extremely quiet, with plush pile carpeting, furnished with reproduction Queen Anne furniture in the vein of a fine hotel. Neutrogena amenities are presented in the clean, simple baths.

Breakfast is not included in the rate and is quite pricey (the Continental breakfast of juice, coffee or tea, and croissants is $15). Guests ought to try the omelettes or famed breakfast soufflés, which range from $15 to $24, made from whisked egg whites, fresh cream, eggs, flour, vanilla, and three liqueurs, served with maple syrup and butter, plain, with strawberries and cream, with pecans, or with the chef's own hollandaise.

Those who respect his art might want to inquire about Mr. Hanretta's three-day cooking school.

The Garden and the Sea Inn
Box 275
New Church, Virginia 23415
804-824-0672

Proprietors: Victoria Olian and Jack Betz
Accommodations: 2 rooms with private bath (3 rooms to come in Garden House, with private bath)
Rates: $75–$95 (seasonally)
Included: Fresh-baked Continental breakfast
Minimum stay: 2 nights on weekends from Memorial Day to Columbus Day
Added: $15 each additional guest; local and state taxes
Payment: All credit cards
Children: Welcome
Pets: Not allowed
Smoking: Allowed downstairs only
Open: April–October

Virginia's eastern shore floats like a tail underneath eastern Maryland and Delaware. Approaching the peninsula from the north, the first town one hits is New Church, home to a new and sophisticated culinary refuge called the Garden and the Sea, which opened in the spring of 1989.

After traveling extensively throughout Europe and having been inspired by accommodations and Provencale food, Victoria Olian and Jack Betz made plans to buy an inn. They were quite familiar with Virginia's eastern shore, having summered for years in Chincoteague. In 1988, they discovered that what had been known as Bloxom's Tavern was up for sale. The three-story 1802 clapboard building had been Victorianized in the early 1900s to its present shape with twin gables and a long single-story front porch. Victoria and Jack spent months restoring the inn, which would be a focal point for Victoria's culinary skills.

Though the Garden and the Sea has only two guest rooms, Victoria and Jack plan to open three more deluxe rooms in the neighboring Garden House—the oldest house in New Church—with a tea room and library/music room. The existing rooms are magnificent and romantic, on the second floor flanking the center staircase. Victoria and Jack tried to give their large baths an air of European luxury, with skylights, bidets, a pair of sinks, with plush terry robes, and towels.

The French Garden Room has a fabulous rare bedroom suite of Victorian wrought-iron furniture painted green: the suite includes a large bed with a richly patterned canopy (a testament to Victoria's prior experience as a decorator), matching a vanity and stool, two end tables, and an armoire. Victoria's window treatments are luxurious and inventive. Across the hall is the Chantilly Room, dominated by a French wicker sleigh bed with accents in teal green and pink, with a Louis XV–style dresser in stenciled pine. Both have sitting areas tucked into three-windowed bays.

The dining room is the antithesis of Victoriana. Light pine chairs are covered in salmon-colored cloth, and the fireplace is painted a minty color with a flowered tile, with blond walls as the background. Victoria, whose French country menus feature only fresh local seafood and produce, wanted an atmosphere derivative of the garden and the sea, in natural, sandy beach tones. Guests may enjoy meals à la carte or at fixed prices of $25 or $30 for four courses. Choices might include a cream of cauliflower soup with shrimp and entrées like boneless chicken breast stuffed with goat cheese, roasted peppers, toasted pine nuts, and cumin butter sauce; Chincoteague oysters sautéed with leeks, shiitake mushrooms, spinach, and seasoned cream; or grilled Norwegian salmon with apple cranberry chutney.

Victoria and Jack are great promoters of local art, crafts, and music. Once a month on Sundays, they host a dinner concert with eastern shore musicians. As well, crafts, sculpture, art, and jewelry are on display.

The Inn at Little Washington
Middle and Main Streets, Box 300
Washington, Virginia 22747
703-675-3800
Fax 703-675-3100

Proprietors: Patrick O'Connell and Reinhardt Lynch
Accommodations: 9 rooms, 3 suites, all with private bath
Rates: $240–$500
Included: Continental breakfast
Minimum stay: None
Added: $40 each additional guest; 7% tax
Payment: MasterCard, Visa
Children: Not allowed
Pets: Not allowed
Smoking: Allowed
Open: All year

Of all the superlatives associated with this property since its inception in 1978, none is too strong and none is quite adequate. The Inn at Little Washington, 67 miles west of the capital nearing the Shenandoah National Park, has been lauded for years by the most esteemed critics as a place of absolute perfection. In 1991, the Inn was the first American property in the history of the Mobil guide to receive a five-star rating for both food and accommodations. With only nine rooms and three suites, and only 65 dining tables, the Inn at Little Washington requires its guests to plan long in advance and pay a good deal for the honor of a meal and a room. However, regardless of cost or personal sacrifice, a lifetime of luxury is not complete without an experience at the Inn at Little Washington.

Perhaps what makes the inn such an inspiring accomplishment is that owners Patrick O'Connell and Reinhardt Lynch built the property from scratch, with $5,000 and undaunted determination. The two met in 1970 in Washington, D.C., where Patrick worked as a chef and Reinhardt at a hospital. Two years later, they were able to buy a 100-acre farm in Rappahannock County in the foothills of the northern stretch of the Blue Ridge Mountains, where they started a catering business. After six years, they established a faithful following who pledged frequent countryside pilgrimages, and Reinhardt and Patrick confidently but tentatively opened a restaurant. They rented a garage for $200 a month in the rural farming community of Washington, Virginia, transformed the mechanic's pit to Patrick's kitchen, and slowly refurbished the premises. In January 1978, they served their first dinners to seventy thrilled guests. By 1984, they provided eight oft-requested guest rooms and, several years later, two duplex suites. Today, amid deafening accolades, the Inn at Little Washington is one of only 19 independent American properties in the elite and prestigious Relais et Châteaux, a European organization with 377 properties worldwide.

While much has been written about Patrick O'Connell's brilliant, artistic French-inspired cuisine, less has been written about the stunning guest rooms, which were designed by English stage set designer Joyce Conwy-Evans. She is quite famous for her use of rich fabrics and combinations of lavish patterns —all beautifully displayed throughout the guest rooms and dining areas. Her early sketches are framed and hung in the inn's reception area. The antiques, fabrics, and wallpapers were shipped from England; and the extensive faux wood graining and marbling throughout the inn was done to her specifications by artist Malcolm Robson. Of the nine guest rooms, each is thoroughly insulated and a world unto itself: one is a cozy alcove dressed in floral wallpaper; another is a successful hurricane of patterns, with a blackberry wood headboard crowned by a yellow floral canopy with a reverse in rose floral material, over a plaid spread; yet another has a Chinese influence with a pagoda-style canopy over a rosewood headboard. The two third-floor duplex suites are identically furnished with regal baths with Jacuzzis, separate showers, heated towel racks, and

Greek marble countertops (the only real marble in the inn). These each have two balconies with mountain views.

The staff of 55 at The Inn is highly polished and trained, the definition of discreet and solicitous service. Guests enter a wood-paneled reception area whose stained glass ceiling is a collage of five thousand hand-drawn gilded and painted blocks. The dining areas are to the right, so thoroughly draped, festooned, swagged, and tapestried as to conjure images of the inside of a genie's bottle: cushioned, exotic, lavish, and plush.

While no short description may do justice to the depth of the chef's offerings, a sampling follows: guests are tantalized by an introductory sesame pastry filled with shiitake mushrooms, Jarlsberg, and leeks; a steaming puff of French poppy bread; a taste of marinated oyster mushrooms; or a bite of trout smoked over applewood with horseradish. Such a prelude might be followed by a creamy fresh fennel bisque or asparagus vinaigrette with raspberry cream sauce presented as if sprinkled by New Year's confetti. The appetizer of three fishcakes of crab, tuna, salmon, with seasoned mayonnaises in a shoestring potato presentation always receives rave reviews. This course is followed by a tart lemon sherbet sculpted into a frozen lemon, with crystals of sugar frosted over the plate. The entrée is most certainly astounding, with equally artistic accompaniments. While the desserts present baffling choices, a fine solution is to request the Seven Deadly Sins, a sampling of seven of the offerings, presented in a Mondrian design of dripped sauces on the canvas of the plate.

Breakfast is prepared with similar elegance in European understatement, a medley of freshly made croissants, muffins, picture-perfect fruits, coffee, and juices, and homemade lemon curd and raspberry jam. Weather permitting, guests might like to dine in the brick patterned garden filled with rattan chairs and tables, lattice and trelliswork, gazebos, fountains, and sculptures.

A visitor to the Inn at Little Washington will be surprised and rather honored to meet these gracious hosts who seem unusually accessible and elated with a honeymooners' glow about the success of their endeavor.

Wilderness, Fishing, Skiing, and Golf

New York

The Bark Eater
Alstead Mill Road
Keene, New York 12924
518-576-2221

Proprietor: Joe Pete Wilson
Manager: Jodi Downs
Accommodations: 7 rooms in main house, 6 share 2 baths; 4
  rooms, all with private bath, in Carriage House; 2 three-
  room suites, 2 rooms, both with private bath, in Log Cabin
Rates: $45–$55 per person; 5-day MAP and B&B packages
  available
Included: Full breakfast; breakfast and 5-course gourmet
  dinner with MAP
Minimum stay: 2 nights on weekends
Added: $22–$28 each additional adult; children, $6.50 each;
  13% gratuity; 7% tax
Payment: Major credit cards
Children: Welcome
Pets: Not allowed
Smoking: Not allowed
Open: All year

The Adirondacks are literally defined in a country inn called
the Bark Eater, in Keene, halfway between Lakes Placid and
Champlain. The Bark Eater, or Adirondack, was the pejorative
epithet given to the Algonquin Indians by their Mohawk neighbors. The white surveyors, having often heard the term, began

referring to the wilderness area by this name as early as the 1830s. Around the same time, a 1780 farmhouse in the town of Keene was transformed into a stagecoach stop. The family of the present owner, Joe Pete Wilson, bought the farmhouse/inn in the 1930s, and they adopted the name Bark Eater as a tribute to the first tenants of the land.

The two-story white clapboard house is an architectural collage of additions, from 1780 to the present. It encompasses the neighboring 1890 spruce clapboard Carriage House, renovated in 1985 to provide four guest rooms, and, reached by a five-minute walk into the woods, a fairly luxurious Log Cabin with two rooms and two suites. Only one of the seven guest rooms in the main house has a private bath; the other six share two baths. The guest rooms bespeak a comfortable informality, decorated with eclectic well-worn antiques.

For deluxe and more private accommodations, guests might prefer the Carriage House, with cut pine interior walls, new private baths, and more contemporary sitting areas. Even more deluxe are the recently redecorated rooms and suites in the nearby Log Cabin, some with fireplaces, with a huge wrap deck set into the woods.

The Bark Eater is a place for the informal and the active, reflecting the varied outdoor interests of owner Joe Pete, a former Olympic Nordic skier. In addition to its bed-and-breakfast rates, the Bark Eater offers special instructional packages for cross-country skiing, horseback riding, Hudson River Gorge whitewater rafting, and Adirondack climbing. Guests explore the 200 acres of Bark Eater land on horseback or on cross-country skis, rented on premises. The 55 stabled horses are trained in English and western saddles. The adventurous might like to try their hand at polo, played seasonally on the grand fieldlike front lawn.

Yet another appreciated aspect of the Bark Eater is the cooking of chef Peter Varnes. Guests eat at a long table in the low-ceilinged colonial dining room. His five-course dinner might begin with Asian carrot or tomato garlic soup, followed by an appetizer or salad, and an entrée of leg of lamb or grilled swordfish, possibly finished with a Sacher torte. The next morning, guests eat a full breakfast introduced by Peter's trademark Morning Glory muffins, at the same table or in the pretty, informal sun porch in the front of the house.

Bear Mountain Inn
Bear Mountain, New York 10911
914-786-2731

Proprietors: ARA Leisure Services
Accommodations: 60 rooms (12 in Main Lodge, 24 in
   Overlook Lodge, 24 in four Stone Lodges)
Rates: $59 weekdays, $84 weekends and holidays
Added: $10 each additional guest; 7% tax
Payment: Visa, MasterCard, American Express
Children: Welcome
Pets: Not allowed
Smoking: Allowed
Open: All year

The 38-mile Palisades Parkway serves as a great and scenic driveway from the George Washington Bridge to Bear Mountain's front door. The state park comprises 5,067 acres and is most unusual for its winter offerings, including a skating rink, sledding, and ski jumping competition hosted during Winter Carnival. The land was formally incorporated as Bear Mountain State Park in 1908–1910 when construction of Sing Sing Prison threatened the environs.

The magnificent Adirondack inn was built in 1916, three stories hand-crafted from native rock and chestnut. Most spectacular is the enormous common room, two stories high with an open-beamed mansard ceiling and a vast stone fireplace that flickers off the highly varnished, rich wood, revealing two views of the park. Guests may have a formal dinner in quaint Wildflowers or a lavish Sunday brunch in the larger dining hall overlooking the playing fields.

ARA Leisure Services, which also runs the concessions on the Skyline Drive, has managed the historic inn since the mid-1970s. While the 12 rooms above the Inn are comfortable, those across Hessian Lake are preferable simply for their setting. Of these, the Stone Cottages are the more charming, built in the 1940s, with 6 rooms in each of the four-square single-story structures. Each cottage has a common room with a large stone fireplace. Off this are 6 private rooms, decorated in modest "French country" found in the inn rooms, with pine furniture, thick pile blue carpets complementing blue chintz drapes and spreads on queen-size beds. The rooms in the Overlook Lodge are quite contemporary and dormlike, though the magnificent locale, on the rocky, steep banks above Hessian Lake, is quick to distract.

Traditional square dancing is an unusual and extremely popular activity at Bear Mountain. Hessian Lake, 200 feet deep, offers pedal and row boats and is one of seven area lakes which host fishermen, who also may try their lines in the Hudson River. The park maintains more than 30 trails, measuring more than 200 miles. The Trailside Museum and Zoo was founded in 1927 under the sponsorship of John D. Rockefeller, Jr., and the American Museum of Natural History, visited today by more than half a million people annually. On a series of planned walks and treks, visitors learn about geology, zoology, history, and botany of and around Bear Mountain.

The inn is an informal place, especially wonderful for families, who no doubt will love the 94-by-224-foot pool.

Beaverkill Valley Inn
Lew Beach, New York 12753
914-439-4844

Proprietor: Laurance Rockefeller
Manager: Christina L. Dennis
Accommodations: 20 rooms, 10 with private bath, 10 with shared baths
Rates: $140 or $165 per person per day, full American plan
Included: Three meals a day, afternoon tea, gratuities
Minimum stay: 2 nights on weekends
Added: 7% tax
Payment: Visa, MasterCard, American Express
Children: Welcome
Pets: Not allowed
Smoking: Allowed in Card Room and outdoors
Open: Daily in May and June; weekends the rest of the year; closed August and November

Teddy Roosevelt missed the Catskills when he deemed part of upstate New York State "forever wild." Larry Rockefeller, however, did not. In 1978, this environmental lawyer bought up parcels of land which he thought to be perilously close to development in the historic Beaverkill Valley in the 50-mile-wide Catskill Forest Preserve. One of the most precious resources of this area is the Beaverkill Valley River, known to those who practice the art as the home of American fly-fishing, born here around 1865.

The former Bonnie View Inn was built in 1893 to house the increasing number of fly-fishermen, one of the earliest boarding houses on the Beaverkill River, outside the hamlet of Lew Beach. When Larry Rockefeller bought the inn in 1983, it was barely standing. Renovation and restoration have established this boarding house as an informally elegant, privileged retreat for anglers and moguls alike who want to relax and fish in the wilderness.

The Rockefellers are well represented by Christina Dennis, the young and hardworking innkeeper who maintains the Beaverkill Valley Inn somewhere between an exclusive private retreat and a country inn. The house and its 60 surrounding acres are quite far removed from civilization, about ten miles from the nearest town, Livingston Manor. The inn looks rather like a grand Newport cottage, a square three-story clapboard painted white with green shutters and trim and dormer windows peeking out from a red shingled roof. A white porch wraps around the perimeter, filled with green-painted swings and wicker furniture looking out from three sides onto a lawn groomed casually for croquet. Inside, the cherry staircase, oak millwork, and hardware are original, though the rest of the house is the result of recent renovation. Comfortable, traditional chairs and sofas decorate the large parlor to the right of the foyer; clubby leather furnishings fill the informal Card Room to the left. Downstairs are pool and Ping-Pong tables and tabletop soccer in three rooms with rich wainscoted walls, decoy lamps, wing chairs, and settle benches. Throughout, Larry Rockefeller has selected wonderful original artwork of nature, wildlife, and Catskills geography, most by watercolorist David Armstrong.

On the second floor are ten guest rooms, each with a private bath, and ten rooms around the perimeter of the third floor share five baths in the center. Simply decorated as if by the hand of a fisherman with ample funds and fine taste, the rooms have replaced designer fabrics with handmade quilts, and precious antiques with useful dressers, and comfortable wing chairs in earth-tone upholstery. Half the rooms have queen-size beds, half have twins. The clean, new bathrooms have Mexican tiled flooring and framed maps of the Beaverkill for reference. Reading is a major activity here, and the rooms are stocked amply with books and current wildlife and outdoor magazines, good reading chairs and lights.

Despite its rather informal decor of square oaken tables, the dining room is the setting for elegant American regional cuisine. A day is introduced here with a full buffet breakfast. Guests have about two entrée selections for lunch and again at dinner, a four-course meal prepared by chef and innkeeper Christina. By using local products, Christina might serve the following meal: a green pea and mint soup, a cherry tomato and artichoke heart salad, perhaps filet of beef with bleu cheese sauce or poached Norwegian salmon with ginger lime beurre blanc, and a dessert of chocolate Kahlua mousse with hazelnuts.

Inn guests have private access to three miles of the Beaverkill River and many more miles of ten-foot-wide cross-country ski trails laid out by Rockefeller himself. Several tennis courts are carved in a plot above the inn. Behind, in the former dairy barn, is a conference center which doubles as a square-dance hall, an indoor pool with an atrium ceiling and Mexican tiles, and a lighthearted self-serve ice cream bar.

Elk Lake Lodge

North Hudson, New York 12855
518-532-7616

Proprietors: Elk Lake Lodge, Inc.
Innkeeper: Peter Sanders
Accommodations: 12 rooms (6 in Main Lodge, 6 in Emerson Lodge), 6 one-to-four-bedroom cottages
Rates: $90, $95, $100 per person per day, full American plan
Included: Three meals a day, full use of all canoes and boats
Minimum stay: 2 days
Added: 15% gratuity; 7% tax
Payment: No credit cards
Children: Welcome
Pets: Not allowed
Smoking: Allowed
Open: Early May through mid-November

Off the lonely North Hudson exit on the Northway, with the highest Adirondack peak Mt. Marcy looming in the distance at 5,300 feet, a visitor travels five miles toward the heart of the wilderness, then five miles on a private road which shortly becomes unpaved. Only when one feels undoubtedly lost do the gates of Elk Lake Lodge appear. Within the 6 million acres of the protected Adirondack Forest, Elk Lake Lodge is part of a private 12,000-acre forest preserve within which lie two lakes: Elk Lake, dotted with islands and comprising 600 acres of inlets, bays, and open water, and Clear Pond, a 95-foot-deep glacial pond covering 200 acres.

Hopeful fishermen come for landlocked salmon, lake trout, and a special strain of speckled trout which Elk Lake Lodge has worked to develop since 1971 with Cornell University. Elk Lake empties into the Branch River, a favorite haunt for fly-fishing. While a limited game hunting season occurs in early November, most come simply to enjoy the tranquillity of the magnificent wilderness at Elk Lake Lodge, its 40 miles of walking trails, and five mountain views of the High Peaks area which surround the lodge. Naturalists delight in the variety of wildflowers, birds, and the occasional black bear.

The two-story weathered shingle main lodge was built in 1904 by a logging company in the Adirondack and Arts and Crafts style. The rustic interior shows off exposed logs and knotty pine paneling. The common room has a huge stone fireplace surrounded by Adirondack twig and leather Mission-style furniture, the blanched corner hutches built by a man in Schroon Lake.

Hearty country meals are taken family-style in the dining addition to one side of the lodge, with frames supporting a cathedral ceiling. A free-standing round stone fireplace serves as the room's centerpiece, with one wall devoted to picture windows providing breathtaking lake and mountain views.

The Elk Lake dam creates an audible and pleasant waterfall between the Main Lodge and three cottages, and between Emerson Lodge and three other cottages. The cottages, with one to four bedrooms, have views of the lake from porches outfitted with rockers, all painted a neutral gray. The interior furnishings are rustic, with starburst quilts, simple, tidy decor, some with fireplaces and comfortable sitting rooms.

Adirondack chairs sprinkle the front lawn overlooking the little docks lining the lakefront. Available for guest use are eight canoes and about twenty rowboats. Mr. Sanders has been the innkeeper since 1975, following in his father's footsteps. He and his staff are true pioneers of the area, used to the ways of the wilderness.

Garnet Hill Lodge
13th Lake Road
North River, New York 12856
518-251-2444

Proprietors: George and Mary Heim
General Manager: Peter Fitting
Accommodations: 29 rooms in 4 buildings (16 rooms in Log
    House, 4 in Birches, 2 in Tea House, 7 in Big Shanty, the
    old manor house)
Rates: $55–$80 per person MAP; 4- and 7-night packages
    available
Included: Gratuities and sales tax
Minimum stay: Some weekends
Added: $40 each additional guest, MAP; $28 each child
    under 10, MAP
Payment: No credit cards
Children: Welcome
Pets: Not allowed
Smoking: Limited
Open: All year

Garnet Hill Lodge is a sophisticated Adirondack refuge for
trout fishing on Thirteenth Lake, Hudson River fly-fishing,
cross-country skiing on Garnet Hill's 35 miles of groomed
trails, and downhill skiing on nearby Gore Mountain, with an
elevation of 3,600 feet. George and Mary Heim have happily
presided over their 600 acres since 1977.

The two-story Adirondack lodge, built in 1936, is tucked on a
scenic plateau a mile's hike above Thirteenth Lake, four miles
through an intricate web of dirt roads from North River. Since
1879, garnet mining has been the mainstay of this tiny mountain community which once produced the world's greatest supply of garnets, the ruby of the Adirondacks. The Log House was
built by mining magnate Frank Hooper in 1936, in which he
and his son-in-law Charles Tibbits opened a guest house and
restaurant. Today, the Heims carry on their tradition in this and
several buildings, including Frank Hooper's original classic
Adirondack mansion, Big Shanty.

The Log House is a long two-story building of dark-stained
wood trimmed in traditional red, its first floor finished in
stacked logs, the second in rough-hewn clapboard with an overhanging balcony railed in unfinished logs. Inside, the first floor
consists of an impressive common area, dark with varnished,
exposed wood, supported by bark-clad yellow birch pillars and

beams. Classic Mission couches rest around the enormous stone fireplace, which sparkles, not surprisingly, with hunks of garnets dredged from local rock. The rectangular room opens to an enclosed porch where people dine overlooking the groomed front lawn and the wonderful sunsets provided by the western view.

Upstairs, the guest rooms retain the richness of exposed wood. The rooms facing the back have pine walls and ceilings, though the front rooms are preferable for their larger size and furnished balconies, which peer over the trees to the lake at the bottom of the hill. The rooms are furnished in rustic comfort, with new baths and personalized amenities. Down the hill, groups enjoy the Big Shanty's informal, rustic accommodations, wonderful Adirondack living room, and great front porch with a large front lawn. The Birches and Tea House have more contemporary furnishings.

Meals at Garnet Hill are hearty and plentiful, always accompanied by fresh breads and pastries by Mary Jane Freeburn, who has been at Garnet Hill since before the Heims. As well, guests ought to visit Highwinds Country Inn for a spectacular view, intimate setting, and French food prepared by Scott Aronson at the Barton family house.

Garnet Hill Lodge offers guests mountain bikes, canoes, sailboats, cross-country ski equipment, and two tennis courts. Its kind, warm staff is headed by innkeeper Peter Fitting, who offers knowledgeable and enthusiastic advice about all these activities and more.

Pennsylvania

Cliff Park Inn
Milford, Pennsylvania 18337
717-296-6491
800-225-6535 outside Pennsylvania

Proprietors: Harry Buchanan and family
Manager: Patricia O'Connor
Accommodations: 10 rooms in main house, 8 rooms in private cottages
Rates:
European Plan: $85–$$120
B&B: $100–$135
MAP: $140–$185
Included: Half the greens fees on 9-hole golf course

Minimum stay: Some weekends
Added: $20 each additional guest; 6% tax
Payment: All major credit cards
Children: Welcome
Pets: Not allowed
Smoking: Allowed
Open: All year

The joys of Cliff Park are golf, good food, and Scotland. Here, on the upper reaches of the Delaware River, across from New Jersey's northwest corner, George Buchanan built a regal three-story farmhouse in 1820 on the fields outside Milford. The house remained solely a family property until the new century, when Annie Buchanan, wife of the patriarch's grandson, decided to open a small summer hotel. In 1913, a family friend, who happened to be a golf course architect, offered to transform some of the surrounding fields into a 9-hole golf course, observed from high-backed rockers on the vast front veranda. The tradition of golf and hospitality remains today at the fifth-generation Buchanan estate, which encompasses 560 acres encircled by the Delaware River National Recreation Area.

The spacious old farmhouse is a testament to history, with rambling common rooms and sloping original wide-planked floorboards. Original mantels rest atop blazing fires, which shed a further warmth onto the heirlooms throughout the house. Narrow and worn stairs lead to the second- and third-floor guest rooms, which are furnished with family antiques. The guest rooms, while not luxurious, are heartwarmingly comfortable, quaint, and clean, some with wonderful sun porches overlooking the links at different angles.

The Garden and Club cottages are more daringly furnished, the latter with a high cathedral ceiling and fieldstone fireplace; and the Augusta House is decorated as a classic Scottish golf cottage.

Scotland is celebrated in the Grill Room, one of two Cliff Park dining rooms. The wallpaper, tablecloths, curtains, and even the rugs are cheerily done in the pattern of the Buchanan family tartan. The other dining area is quaintly decorated in the style of a traditional country inn, with lace tablecloths, wooden chairs, peach walls, and a crackling fire. The chef, a member of the Chaîne des Rôtisseurs, is well loved and prepares three meals daily, with dinner entrées ranging from $15 to $19. A prelude to dinner might be hickory smoked salmon gravlox with capers, onions, and cream cheese, or perhaps snapper turtle soup with sherry. Entrée choices might include rabbit and spring vegetable fricassee; charred baby lamb chops with eggplant and leeks; roast filet of beef Wellington with bordelaise sauce; or baked game pie, with venison, pheasant, grouse, wild boar sausage, mushrooms in red wine sauce, and puff pastry.

In-season, guests pay half price for greens fees on the 9-hole course and enjoy seven miles of walking trails in and around the glorious palisades bordering the Delaware River. The golf course and trails become a mecca for cross-country skiers in the winter.

Gateway Lodge and Cabins
Cook Forest, Box 125, Route 36
Cooksburg, Pennsylvania 16217
814-744-8017
800-843-6862 in Pennsylvania

Proprietors: Joe and Linda Burney
Accommodations: 8 rooms in lodge, 3 with private bath; 8 one-to-four-bedroom cabins, all with fireplace and kitchen
Rates: Rooms $65–$79; cabins $80–$110, weekly $392–$539
Included: Use of lap pool for lodge guests only
Minimum stay: 2 or 3 nights in cabins
Added: 6% tax
Payment: MasterCard, Visa, American Express
Children: Over 8 welcome in the lodge; all ages welcome in cabins
Pets: Permitted; $15 per day
Smoking: Allowed
Open: All year except several days around Thanksgiving and Christmas

The rustic Gateway Lodge looks more like an Adirondack cabin than a northwestern Pennsylvania country inn. The lodge and its cabins sit just a quarter of a mile north of the Clarion River and the 6,500 acres of the surrounding Cook Forest State Park.

This charming lodge was built in 1934 of hemlock and pine logs, with walls and trim in wormy chestnut and oak flooring. Guests enter from the fabulous rough-hewn front porch, with exposed beams and debarked railing, decorated with a handmade rope swing and wicker chairs. The lounge is so picturesque that it looks like a movie-set version of a log cabin. The walls are made of chinking sandwiched between the heavy pine and hemlock logs, the enormous weathered stone fireplace crackles and snaps at readers lounging in country plaid sofas, and weighty wood beams support the low exposed-log ceiling.

Through a low threshold, the dining room perpetuates the picture-perfect log cabin motif with the chinking and log walls, a wagon wheel chandelier, dark random-width floorboards, and tables dressed in country gingham for breakfast and reset with formal pewter and lit by kerosene lanterns at dinner.

The eight lodge rooms are quite small, but charmingly cozy. They are furnished with hand-hewn wormy chestnut or brass double beds covered with calico-printed or Amish antique quilts, quaint antique furnishings, and braided oval rugs which contribute to the early American feel. The cabins are extremely simple and rustic, and guests bring their own towels, linens, and kitchen supplies.

Abundant dinners are served à la carte or in four courses, with soup or salad, two relishes, a loaf of homemade bread and honey butter, mashed potatoes and vegetables, and ice cream or sherbet. For the four-course dinner, a guest chooses from hearty country recipes like pork chops with bread stuffing, rock Cornish game hens with sausage stuffing, chicken cordon bleu, or baked trout filled with crabmeat, ranging from $14 to $20. Homemade gourmet pies are among the desserts. Afterward, guests visit the sociable old Tap Room.

When Joe and Linda Burney bought the Gateway Lodge and Cabins in 1980, they added an indoor swimming pool at the back of the lodge, four feet deep heated at 92 degrees. They also added a country store, which sells some crafts displayed throughout the inn, including Amish quilts and rope swings. They and their staff are very kind and ever-present at this unpretentious woodsy retreat. Seventeen miles of cross-country ski trails are maintained through the Cook Forest State Park; visitors may rent skis, skates, and show shoes at the Lodge. Among other park activities along the Clarion River are fishing, tubing, canoeing, and horseback riding.

Virginia

Fort Lewis Lodge
Millboro, Virginia 24460
703-925-2314

Proprietors: John and Caryl Cowden
Accommodations: 15 rooms, 8 with private bath, with 3 silo rooms
Rates: $110–$125 MAP; 2-bedroom family suite, $135; Bunk Room, $100; hunting packages available

Included: Breakfast and dinner
Minimum stay: 2 nights
Added: $25 each additional guest; $15 each child age 5–12;
   4.5% tax
Payment: Visa, MasterCard
Children: Welcome, under 5 free
Pets: Not allowed
Smoking: Not allowed
Open: Closed January through March; seasonal hunting

Fort Lewis Lodge and little else rests in a 3,200-acre dell in the Allegheny Mountains and lower reaches of the George Washington National Forest, along a five-mile stretch of the Cowpasture River. The mountain farm had been known for two centuries as Fort Lewis Plantation, named for Colonel Charles Lewis, who built a stockade on this land in 1754 to protect his family from the Indians. Today, the five square miles of untouched wilderness belong to John and Caryl Cowden, who transformed their crop and cattle farm into an overnight lodging place in 1986.

John built the lodge as a modern testament to the traditional structures of barn and silo. The lodge is sided with three stories of western red cedar, incorporating a 40-foot stone silo at one end which houses three guest rooms with fabulous mountain vistas in every direction. John then restored the 1850s gristmill, two floors of open-beamed wooden ceilings and walls, with a dining room, common area, and gift shop. Outside is a swimming hole, a dammed section of the old millrace.

The lodge has a great cathedral-ceilinged common room trimmed in wood beams, with plaid couches and comfortable traditional rockers and wing chairs warmed by a brick fireplace. The wallpaper borders are country patterns of animals and a great *Field and Stream* magazine cover motif. The skills of a local taxidermist display the white-tailed deer, bobcat, turkey, and other creatures of the wild frozen in time. The 15 guest rooms are decorated in Virginia Shaker simplicity. The furniture was made by local craftswoman Beth Brokaw from such diverse woods as locust, butternut, walnut, cherry, and white and red oak. The yellow pine floors are covered in woven rugs, and the beds are draped with red and black plaid blankets in the winter and quilts in the warmer months.

Fort Lewis Lodge is a mecca for hunting and fishing in the spring and late fall, and in the months between for leisure guests. The springtime brings trout and bass fishermen to the Cowpasture River, and wild turkey hunters from mid-April through mid-May. The hunting resumes from mid-October through December, when wild turkey, pheasant, and deer are hunted with bow, rifle, or black powder. Leisure guests come less intrusively from mid-May through mid-October's foliage season.

Rates include a full country breakfast of home-baked muffins, egg and sausage casseroles, and oatmeal pancakes, and Caryl's bountiful dinners, signaled by the ringing of a bell across the fields. The family-style buffets include hearty dishes like barbecued chicken and ribs, harvest roast, and Cowpasture River trout, all served with garden vegetables. On the vast acreage, guests enjoy exploring wildflowers, bird-watching, tubing, swimming, trout and bass fishing, and 18 miles of hiking trails.

Meadow Lane Lodge

Star Route A, Box 110
Warm Springs, Virginia 24484
703-839-5959

Proprietor: The Hirsh Family
Innkeeper: Cheryl Hooley
Accommodations: 9 rooms
Rates: $90–$130 (depending on room, season, and day of the week)
Included: Full breakfast
Minimum stay: 2 nights on weekends May–October
Added: $15 each additional guest; 4.5% tax
Payment: Visa, MasterCard, American Express
Children: Over 6 welcome
Pets: Not allowed without prior approval
Smoking: Allowed in rooms only
Open: All year

Meadow Lane Lodge is secluded on 1,600 acres of protected farmland, four miles west of historic Warm Springs in the dells of the Allegheny Mountains. Visitors fish for trout along two private miles of Jackson River, hike, splash in a six-foot swimming hole, or simply bask in the peaceful nature of this glorious retreat.

The rich land of Meadow Lane dates to 1750, when William Warwick bought the plot from Charles Lewis, who had received it as a land grant from King George III. The impending threat of the French and Indian Wars prompted Warwick to build a stockade-type fort on this property in 1754, known as Fort Dinwiddie, named for the state's governor. The second building on the property was built by Warwick's son Jacob in

1805. The only standing historic building is the Slave Cabin, dating from the late 18th or early 19th century.

The lodge and its satellite cottages were built in the 1920s by Mr. Hirsh's father, who bred thoroughbred horses at Meadow Lane. Phil Hirsh acquired the land in 1951, twenty years before he and his wife, Catherine, opened the Inn at Gristmill Square in Warm Springs (see Village Inns). In 1981, the Hirshes returned to Meadow Lane for full-time innkeeping. Today, octogenarian Mr. Hirsh cooks historic southern breakfasts every morning during the season and is famous for his soufflé-like batter bread, grits, and greens.

Lodge accommodations are antique-filled, with porches and fireplaces. The lodge's Great Room is a fine gathering spot with twin stone fireplaces over a country plaid rug; and the Breakfast Room features a 1710 oak sideboard. Contemporary accommodations are also in the Ice House, Craig's Cottage, and the Car Barn, formerly the Carriage House. In the Warm Springs Historic District, the Francisco Cottage is a two-bedroom cabin built in 1820 of hand-hewn square logs, furnished with antiques, a modern kitchen, and a shady porch.

Wonderful activities abound at Meadow Lane. Seven trails, from one to three miles, provide not only magnificent views but sightings of bald eagles, osprey, fox, mink, bobcat, deer, and an occasional bear. A favorite walk is only an eighth of a mile to the Deck, with spectacular views of the verdant plateau against the backdrop of the Alleghenies. Inhabitants of the barns are Nubian goats, donkeys, peacocks, ducks, geese, Chinese chickens, and peacocks.

The Jackson River divides the acreage. While its natural inhabitants include smallmouth and rock bass, blue gill, pickerel, and fall fish, the river is stocked with rainbow and brown trout for recreational fly-fishing. In addition, guests may use the Dynaturf tennis court, the pool, and the Homestead's Upper and Lower Cascades golf courses.

Meadow Lane is a member of the United States Croquet Association, with an official court for six-wicket croquet. For equally posh diversions, visit the Warm Springs thermal pools, reputed to have been designed by Mr. Jefferson himself, which retain a constant 98 degrees year round.

College Towns

Maryland

The Inn at the Colonnade
4 West University Parkway
Baltimore, Maryland 21218
410-235-5400
800-456-3396

Managing Partners: Howard and Richard Rymland
Director of Sales: Antony M. Gross
Accommodations: 125 rooms, including 36 suites
Rates: Rooms $115–$125; suites $160–$460
Minimum stay: None
Added: $10 each additional guest; 12% tax
Payment: Major credit cards
Children: Welcome
Pets: Allowed
Smoking: Nonsmoking rooms available
Open: All year

For convenience to Johns Hopkins University with Inner Harbor elegance, Baltimore visitors stay at the Inn at the Colonnade. This new property opened in early 1990 and has already received a Four Diamond Award from AAA. A tall brick condominium building with two floors used to accommodate hotel guests, the Inn devotes special attention to overnighters, given the personable nature of the property.

Across the street from John Hopkins's lacrosse field, the Inn sits behind a surprisingly elegant portico supported by two-story cement pillars, introducing the colonnade concept echoed throughout the property. The colonnade covers the porte-cochere, a semicircular drive which is a grand introduction to the property. The main sitting room is lovely, octagonal with formal paneled walls made of satinwood from Sri Lanka, and a round mural overhead hand-painted by local artist Janet Pope, suggesting the feel of an open-air rotunda and a Greek architectural influence. Underneath, the octagonal carpet, handmade in a neoclassic pattern, follows the lines of the walls. The floor is mahogany inlaid with redwood, and the columns that support the rotunda and the subsequent hallway are a burnished maple with painted capitals. To one side of the rotunda are several gift shops, a salon, and the Polo Grill. Down the hall is reception and the neoclassic elevators.

The unique and tasteful 18th-century Beidermier-inspired furnishings of the guest rooms result in a commanding, masculine decor. The headboards of the beds look like pediments trimmed in black, flanked by bedstands supporting interesting neoclassic lamps in three varieties. Televisions and VCRs are tucked into Beidermier armoires, and each room has two telephones, with a third in the bath. Luxury services include nightly turndown, room service until 1 A.M., and same-day valet. The baths are grandly appointed with floor-to-ceiling light-colored marble, brass fixtures, Estuary amenities, and some with Jacuzzis, with separate vanities outside the baths. Beautiful original artwork and architectural drawings are a highpoint of the decor.

In the back courtyard is the glass-domed poolhouse, with deep Italian marble walls interrupted by picture windows, sparkling Tivoli lights, and two hot tubs. Below, guests may use exercise equipment and rowing machines in a newly appointed fitness room walled in pink marble.

The favorably reviewed Polo Grill offers eclectic American cuisine from Chef Harold Marmulstein in an intimate setting. Entrées range from $14 to $29 and may include interesting dishes like pan-fried Mississippi farm-raised catfish in cornmeal crust with chili beurre blanc; grilled moularde duck breast with glazed apples, oyster mushrooms, and tangerine sauce; or medallions of buffalo on potato cake, creamy wild mushrooms, amd Italian mustard fruit on peppered red wine sauce.

Prince George Inn
232 Prince George Street
Annapolis, Maryland 21401
410-263-6418

Proprietors: Bill and Norma Grovermann
Accommodations: 4 rooms, with 3 baths
Rates: $75–$85
Included: Full breakfast
Minimum stay: 2 nights on special-event weekends

Payment: Visa, MasterCard
Children: Over 12 welcome
Pets: Not allowed
Smoking: Allowed on first floor and in courtyard
Open: Mid-April through December

Annapolis is full of history and students. The town was named for Princess Anne (who later reigned as queen) in 1694. The following year, Francis Nicholson laid out the British-named city streets. Yet another year later, in 1696, St. John's College was founded, a beautiful introverted place of architectural purity where students study only the classics. The United States Naval Academy was founded in 1845, on 300 acres on the banks of the Severn River. For a complete history lesson, however, one must turn to the host and hostess of the Prince George Inn, Annapolitans for a quarter of a century. Their charming bed-and-breakfast is steps from the shady lawns of St. John's College and two blocks from the Naval Academy.

Norma and Bill Grovermann opened Annapolis's first bed-and-breakfast in 1983. Prior to that, Norma was the president of the Tourism Council for the City and County for eight years, started the tour service for the Historic Annapolis Foundation, and cofounded Three Centuries Tours, a group which conducts city tours in authentic colonial dress. Bill was involved in historic preservation throughout Maryland, including that of the nearby 37-room William Paca House, built in 1763.

The Grovermanns' own house is a meticulously restored narrow brick Italianate built in 1884. Once through the Texas tiled foyer, guests may be lured upstairs by fascinating relics found during the Grovermanns' restoration and now displayed on the wall. Instead, a right turn takes a visitor to the common areas and to the breakfast porches added in 1910. The living room is papered in a rust-colored William Morris pattern around which Norma designed the room. A grand wall mirror belonged to Bill's grandfather, the jeweler for the McKinley administration who so admired the piece that the president gave it to him at the end of his tenure. Other artifacts from the Grovermanns' extensive travels fill the room: tapestry on the mantel, original paintings, interesting prints, and sculpture.

There are four guest rooms on two subsequent floors, plushly decorated. The beautiful antique beds might be in brass, Gothic Revival, or Victorian carved wood, and the linens complement the deep tones of the decor. The back second-floor room has a narrow Victorian armoire, a crewel chair, its bath papered in black and white nautical designs, introduced by a model of the *Mayflower* made by Norma's father. The third-floor back room has a Persian theme, with wonderful tapestries, a ceiling fan, and on the wall a fascinating Indian mosque decoration of carved wood. The front room has a Gothic Revival bed, an armoire, and a dresser that Norma painted in green sponge-work with the effect of tooled leather.

The Grovermanns are wonderful people whose love for their city and home is quite evident and easily shared.

Tyler Spite House

112 West Church Street
Frederick, Maryland 21701
301-831-4455

Proprietors: Andrea and Bill Myer
Accommodations: 6 rooms, 4 with private bath
Rates: $80; $100 Friday–Sunday and holidays
Included: Full breakfast, high tea
Minimum stay: Most weekends
Added: 10% gratuity; tax
Payment: Visa, MasterCard
Children: Not allowed
Pets: Not allowed
Smoking: Limited; not allowed in rooms
Open: All year

Hood College was born about a hundred years ago, by the time most of Frederick had been well established. In the heart of Frederick's 33-block historic district, the Tyler Spite House is a fine representative of the town's rich history. The Federal mansion was built in 1814 by Dr. John Tyler in an overnight plan to "spite" the town zoning commission, which planned to extend Record Street into a thoroughfare. To prevent the traffic, Dr. Tyler built a foundation for his house on the spot slated for construction. Today, the whitewashed three-story mansion stubbornly sits like an exclamation point at the end of Record Street.

Bill and Andrea Myer bought the Spite House in 1989, and after a year of restoration they opened their second bed-and-breakfast — their first was the Castle in Mt. Savage. Three stories high, and three green-shuttered windows across, the Tyler Spite House is quite grand on the inside. The first floor has soaring 13-foot ceilings, Georgia pine woodwork with raised paneling, and the original plaster moldings. Many of the mantels of the eight working fireplaces are the original imported marble. Five chandeliers hang throughout the house, the grandest set in its original medallion in the center of the three-story winding staircase. Among the large-scale common rooms are the formal music and dining rooms and a library. An addition was built onto the back of the house in 1850, providing a wall of privacy for the outdoor garden paved in patterned brick — and the pool — where guests dine around wrought-iron tables and chairs in warmer months.

Of the four rooms on the second floor and two on the third, most have working fireplaces. The decor is dressy though uncluttered. The third-floor Parsons Room has a wicker sleigh bed and a pair of Philippine mahogany rockers inlaid with mother-of-pearl. The Thomas Johnson Room, named for Maryland's first governor, has two wing chairs and a queen-size bed with a maroon canopy. The Page Room overlooks the pool through tall windows framed in yellow Federal swags. The floors are covered with Oriental rugs, and if the furnishings are not antiques they are fine-quality reproductions. Beds are covered in down comforters and white cotton linens. Guests are greeted with fresh flowers and sherry upon arrival.

Bill's high tea is equaled in lavishness only by his breakfasts, which might feature Belgian waffles, chipped beef, and always a hot fruit compote like baked apples. Conveniently, the Tyler Spite House is the only bed-and-breakfast in the historic district — a blessing given the town's dearth of parking. The inn offers, for $10, horse-drawn carriage rides for guests who want to forget their car entirely.

New Jersey

Peacock Inn
20 Bayard Lane
Princeton, New Jersey 08540
609-924-1707

Proprietors: Michael Walker and Candy Lindsay
General Manager: Michael Walker
Accommodations: 17 rooms, 15 with private bath
Rates: $105–$125
Included: Continental breakfast
Minimum stay: None
Added: $15 each additional person; 7% tax
Payment: American Express, Visa, MasterCard
Children: Welcome
Pets: Allowed

Smoking: Allowed
Open: All year

Princeton parents, alumni, and friends have a nice alternative to the sprawling, uninspired Nassau Inn. The Peacock Inn has been a sophisticated hostelry since 1912, having hosted guests of such repute as F. Scott Fitzgerald, Albert Einstein, and Bertrand Russell. In addition to its 17 guest rooms decorated quaintly in antiques, the inn has a fine French Restaurant called Le Plumet Royal, which serves lunch, dinner, and Sunday brunch.

The white fieldstone mansion dates to 1775, built for John Deare—not the tractor-maker but a Princeton scholar. The three stories are topped by a gambrel roof punctuated by three dormers and two chimneys. A single-story porch spans the front of the house, supported by six pillars. Inside, the first floor is dominated by Le Plumet Royal, which consists of several separate dining areas warmed by peach walls, green carpeting, and Queen Anne chairs with chintz upholstered seats. Several choice dining spots rest near the many bay windows of the house or in the enclosed sun-filled back porch. Guests may choose from an à la carte menu ($20–$27) or a special four-course $20 prix fixe menu, written in French and English. A meal might include an appetizer of sautéed raviolis filled with duck confit and caramelized onions in green onion and balsamic vinegar; a lobster bisque with cream and brandy; and a salad, a timbale of smoked chicken, radicchio, pancetta, and fontina cheese on a bed of greens with bacon and sherry vinaigrette. An entrée may be a choice of sautéed medallions of tuna, wrapped with smoked salmon, served atop a soy-accented beurre blanc; or sautéed medallions of venison on wild rice and green onion pancakes, finished with grand veneur sauce and lingonberries. The wine list is extensive.

There are ten guest rooms on the second floor and seven on the third under the eaves, of varying luxury and decor. The sloping floors hint at the great age of the house, as do the moldings. Some rooms have televisions or fireplaces, but all have some pretty French, American, or English antiques, and always an image of a peacock in some fashion. Room 5 has a wonderful art deco bedroom suite, with an inlaid wood dresser, half sleigh bed, and matching end tables. The antique brass bed in Room 8 rests in a five-windowed bay, with a tufted blue wing chair nearby. While not dressed in formal elegance, the Peacock Inn is comfortably decorated as might be the homes of well-to-do Princeton parents.

Guests are treated to a Continental breakfast in the sunny dining rooms. A large common room downstairs is an informal gathering spot, as is the old-fashioned bar on the first floor.

New York

Inn at the Falls
50 Red Oaks Mill Road
Poughkeepsie, New York 12603
914-462-5770
800-344-1466

Proprietors: Arnold and Barbara Sheer
Manager: David Wiley
Accommodations: 36 rooms, all with private bath (22 rooms, 2 mini-suites, 12 large suites)
Rates: $107–$137; one suite is $150
Included: Continental breakfast
Minimum stay: None
Added: State and local taxes
Payment: Major credit cards
Children: Welcome
Pets: Not allowed
Smoking: Nonsmoking rooms available
Open: All year

The Inn at the Falls is a unique property on the outskirts of Poughkeepsie, several miles from Vassar College. It's not quite an inn since no dinners are served; it's not quite a bed-and-breakfast, since it has the amenities, decor, and service of a small luxury hotel; and it's certainly not historic, having been built in 1985 for $2.5 million by Arnold and Barbara Sheer, a hardworking, sincere couple whose most recent endeavor is a cumulative effort of their several decades in the hotel industry.

The Inn at the Falls is a wonderful place for excellent service and comfort in an area which sorely lacks fine and unusual accommodations. Arnold Sheer wanted to built an intimate property devoted to excellent service—so much so that he avoided adding a restaurant for fear that it would detract from the emphasis on overnight guests.

Just alee of a terribly congested traffic area, the inn is set on three and a half acres of relative countryside. The contemporary brick building sits on the banks of some busy little rapids, called Wappinger Creek, which spill over at the foot of Red

Oaks Mill Road to a tiny waterfall at the entrance to the inn. Half of the ell-shaped inn borders the creek, takes a left, and spans the driveway like a bridge. Guests enter to a marble foyer which leads to a sunny common area overlooking the creek through two stories of mullioned windows.

The guest rooms on the first- and second-floor wings flare out from the center point at reception; half the rooms have views of the creek's rapids. Rooms have private phones and televisions, and the suites have mini-refrigerators. Arnold conceived of four decorating schemes hoping to please as many guests as possible, with contemporary, English, country, and Oriental designs. Original artwork was commissioned for the inn. The English rooms have fishnet canopy beds and chintz window treatments; the contemporary rooms have sectional couches, mauve textured walls, and black lacquer furniture; the country rooms have wicker headboards and caned chairs. All have fluffy monogrammed robes in large, luxurious baths with a tray of amenities including Sassoon shampoo and conditioner, toothpaste and mouthwash, two soaps, as well as telephones and hair dryers; some baths have whirlpool tubs. There's always a little gift at night, which might be something like gourmet chocolates or port wine.

The full Continental breakfast may be taken in the common room or delivered on a silver tray with a pot of coffee, juice, home-baked muffins and breads, and little jams. This ought to sustain a visitor through a day at Vassar or touring the mansions of the Hudson, until it's time for dinner at the Culinary Institute of America, a short drive away.

Three Village Inn
150 Main Street
Stony Brook, New York 11790
516-751-0555

Proprietors: Jim and Lou Miaritis
Accommodations: 27 rooms (6 in original house, 3 in annex, 18 in 6 cottages)
Rates: $95–$110
Minimum stay: None
Added: $10 each additional guest; $20 for cot; 8–15% added tax
Payment: Major credit cards
Children: Welcome, under 16 free
Pets: Not allowed
Smoking: Allowed
Open: All year

After immigrating from Greece as a young man, Jimmy Miaritis worked for thirty years in the hotel business on Long Island. In 1989, he and his son Lou took over the lease of a historic landmark called the Three Village Inn, about halfway out on Long Island's north shore in Stony Brook. One of the kinder souls to set foot in the house since it was built in 1751, Jimmy has his staff smiling and his guests leaving with the promise that they will see him again on their next visit.

Three Village Inn was saved from disrepair by Jennie Melville in 1921. During the 1920s, the Old Homestead became a popular place for tea and later welcomed its first overnight guests in 1939. Ward Melville inherited his mother's love for this town and sought to rebuild its colonial history. The Museums at Stony Brook were the result of his efforts, comprising varied exhibits which include the country's largest display of horse-drawn vehicles as well as several restored 19th-century buildings. A branch of the New York State University system found its home here in 1951.

The inn sits at the base of Stony Brook in the back of a sweeping lawn shaded by trees and dotted with flowers. The rambling, comfortable hostelry is a composite of the original two-story colonial clapboard house, with additions over the years reaching out like branches from a family tree. Behind the main house and its many dining rooms, six cottages welcome guests, built at the turn-of-the-century by a Presbyterian retreat group.

While the cottages are great for privacy, fireplaces, and porches which scan the Harbor over tidy lawns, the six rooms in the main house are wonderful for ambience and romance. Laura Ashley decorators recently redid the rooms, reached by slanted stairs and narrow passageways, tucked under the low-ceilinged eaves. Floral wallpapers cover the thick stone walls, and Williamsburg trim frames the old-paned windows covered with lace curtains.

The dining rooms are attended by a staff dressed in colonial attire. Jenny Melville's antique sugar bowl collection is displayed in a case for guests to admire before being seated in the sunny Old Field, Setauket, and Stony Brook dining rooms, or the colonial tavern. To the right of the old foyer, in the original house, common rooms reveal the pre-Revolutionary beams, hearth, and wood paneling, trimmed in Williamsburg colors.

Lunch and dinner are served daily, with dinner entrées priced from $20 to $30. Guests might start with cold plum soup, followed by old-fashioned Yankee pot roast with potato pancake; individual baked lobster pie; or roast prime rib with popovers. The dessert menu is extensive, which the staff bakes daily. In keeping with its celebratory nature, the Three Village Inn hosts Thanksgiving every Sunday, with native turkey, cornbread and sausage stuffing, gravy, and cranberries, for $19.95.

Pennsylvania

The Inn at Turkey Hill
991 Central Road (I-80 at Exit 35)
Bloomsburg, Pennsylvania 17815
717-387-1500

Proprietor: Babs Pruden
Innkeeper: Andrew B. Pruden
Accommodations: 18 rooms, including 2 suites (2 in main house, 16 in newer section)
Rates: Rooms, $68, $82; suites, $140
Included: Continental breakfast
Minimum stay:
Added: $15 each additional person; 6% tax
Payment: All credit cards
Children: Welcome
Pets: Allowed
Smoking: Not allowed in main house
Open: All year

Bloomsburg State College was founded in 1839, the same year that a family farm went up on the edge of town. Progress was kind to Bloomsburg as the university expanded to about six thousand students, and the family farm on Turkey Hill became a popular country inn on an idyllic hill just before the entrance to I-80. Babs Pruden is the owner of the Inn at Turkey Hill, quite devoted to the property which her parents bought in 1942. Her son Andrew is the innkeeper, an unusual asset to Turkey Hill as a young and enthusiastic third-generation influence.

In 1983, Babs Pruden decided to transform her childhood home to a country inn as a tribute to her father. A greenhouse was added to the back of the white clapboard farmhouse providing one of three dining areas, which looks up to the stars at night and to the groomed back lawns, a duck pond framed in daffodils, and a trellised gazebo by day. A single-story clapboard wing was built perpendicular to the farmhouse, which contains 16 new guest rooms.

The entrance foyer at the side of the farmhouse is elegantly and traditionally furnished in the style of a library with wing chairs and sofas, a fireplace, and a tiny nook where guests may buy bath goods and powders from a Bloomsburg shop. Around the inn is lovely original artwork as well as some furniture painted by local artist Fran De Ballas.

Two of the three dining areas are the Mural Room and the Stencil Room, lined with ivy above the chair rail and pineapple designs between windows, painted with Williamsburg trim in the old section of the house. The Mural Room had a magnificent mural painted by De Ballas, which was destroyed in a fire and is being slowly re-created by a local artist. The greenhouse dining room is brighter and more contemporary. Dinner and Sunday brunch are served at the inn, priced reasonably under $20. Among some of the chef's specialties are appetizers like lobster ravioli and Lightstreet clams and entrées like Kahlua chicken and salmon in puff pastry.

While the two guest rooms in the main house are pretty, guests might prefer the newer units for privacy and comfort, with duck pond and gazebo views. The traditional country furnishings are reproductions from Habersham in Georgia. Four-poster king-size beds in rich wood are covered in duvets of either blue or forest green. De Ballas's paintings hang in every room, which are enlivened by plants and flowers and spindle, wing, or club chairs. All rooms have phones, televisions, and roomy private baths with Gilbert & Soames amenities including nice touches like shoe cloths and a razor. Guests enjoy a Continental breakfast in their rooms, the garden, or the greenhouse.

The Nittany Lion Inn

North Atherton Street on Penn State Campus
State College, Pennsylvania 16803
814-231-7500
800-233-7505

Proprietor: University of Pennsylvania
General Manager: Richard Benefield
Accommodations: 275 rooms
Rates: $65–$160
Minimum stay: None
Added: $10 each additional guest
Payment: Major credit cards
Children: Welcome

Pets: Not allowed
Smoking: Nonsmoking rooms available
Open: All year

As one approaches the two-story portico of the Nittany Lion, a visitor immediately conjures up images of football weekends, tailgates, and fall foliage; or perhaps tasseled caps and black gowns flowing animatedly against a background of late-spring blossoms. The regal old inn looks like a country club, a place befitting the distinguished and gregarious alumni who return to Penn State. Built in 1931, eighty years after the university was founded, the Nittany Lion completed an exciting and massive renovation in January 1992.

State College is a thriving community in a beautiful setting overlooking the Seven Mountains of wooded central Pennsylvania. The Nittany Lion sits like a mascot in the heart of town, conveniently in the middle of the Penn State Campus. The three-story whitewashed brick building has the air of a colonial mansion, topped with a gambrel roof studded with dormer windows. Rows of small-paned windows are stacked two stories high, trimmed with black shutters. Several wings radiate from the long center portion of the inn, lined with single-story porches with lattice railings. The landscaping is fastidious and colorful, a big part of the atmosphere at the Nittany Lion, which continues on the walkways throughout the property and the garden areas on the interior.

The grand two-story lobby is bordered by an eight-sided balcony and centered around an enormous chandelier. Additions to the Nittany Lion include an Alumni Ballroom which will easily accommodate 500 people, opening to a skylit area and garden courtyard; the Pavilion Lounge, which overlooks the courtyard; ample meeting space; and a new health club and Jacuzzi room. The common areas are generous at the Nittany Lion, including two galleries where guests may read at fireside. Alternatives to the formal dining room include several lounges.

The three floors of guest rooms were entirely redecorated in a new version of their traditional colonial design. Rooms have either two-poster king-size beds or two doubles, with televisions, telephones, and bright new baths. The furnishings are a reproduction Williamsburg design, with wallpaper appropriate to the period.

There is a sprightly new air about the Nittany Lion which is quite evident in the staff, who seem thrilled with their new environment. Recreational facilities abound, not just in the Nittany Lion's fitness center, but at the two championship golf courses within walking distance, indoor and outdoor tennis, and swimming pool, used by guests of the inn.

Virginia

Dulwich Manor Inn
Route 5, Box 173A
Amherst, Virginia 24521
804-946-7207

Proprietors: Bob and Judy Reilly
Accommodations: 6 rooms, 4 with private bath, 2 with
shared bath
Rates: $65–$85
Included: Full breakfast
Minimum stay: Some college weekends
Payment: No credit cards
Children: Welcome
Pets: Not allowed
Smoking: Restricted
Open: All year

A half-hour drive east of the Blue Ridge Parkway and north of Lynchburg brings a visitor to the doors of Dulwich Manor, a grand three-story brick mansion in the countryside just three miles from Sweet Briar College. Sweet Briar was founded in 1901, several years after Dulwich Manor had been completed. The house belonged to a single family for sixty years, built on more than 1,000 acres of farmland. It was used as a boarding school from 1965 to 1980 and was purchased by Bob and Judy Reilly in 1988. The Reillys are quite thrilled with their relatively new endeavor, settling on 5 acres of rural bliss after years in New York City, during Bob's career as an actor and Judy's as a theater public relations officer.

Despite its proximity to Sweet Briar, Dulwich Manor seems lost in rural farmland, reached by a winding quarter mile of gravel drive. A 300-year-old oak tree and new privet hedges line a brick walkway which leads to the majestic entrance. The front porch is shaded by a double-story portico with four massive Ionic columns holding up a triangular third-floor pediment. Oversized picture windows with Palladian treatments flank the entrance, allowing light to filter into the library and parlor on either side of the foyer.

Traditional furnishings, both antiques and reproductions, fill the original library, which has a fireplace, the double parlor with pocket doors, and the formal dining room. The second floor has five large guest rooms named for British counties and furnished with pretty antique beds lengthened to queen size. A third-floor room was recently added, with beautiful exposed wood floors, lovely views through a triad of dormer windows, tucked under the eaves of the high rooftop. There are five working gas fireplaces throughout the house, three of which are in guest rooms. The Scarborough Room has a whirlpool bath as well as a reproduction curved fishnet canopy bed and a beautiful mirror-back Victorian settee. The Coventry Room has a graceful Victorian bedroom suite in pine and walnut. Guest rooms are freshened with flowers and potpourri, though the baths are rather plain, with travel-sized generic amenities. Robes are provided in each room so guests may use the outdoor hot tub in the gazebo.

Judy cooks a very full breakfast, served in the formal dining room or on the long veranda, consisting of fresh muffins and breads, a hot entrée, and country sausage or bacon. A day's activity apart from a visit to Sweet Briar or the seven colleges surrounding Lynchburg might consist of a trip north to Wintergreen for four seasons of activities, or a trip across the Blue Ridge Parkway to Lexington, the Virginia Horse Center, and Natural Bridge.

Joshua Wilton House

412 South Main Street
Harrisonburg, Virginia 22801
703-434-4464

Proprietors: Roberta and Craig Moore
Accommodations: 5 rooms, all with private bath, 2 with
    working fireplace
Rates: $85–$95
Included: Full gourmet breakfast
Minimum stay: None
Added: $25 each additional guest; 6.5% tax
Payment: American Express, MasterCard, Visa
Children: Over 10 welcome
Pets: Not allowed
Smoking: Not allowed
Open: All year

Harrisonburg, a bustling town west of the Shenandoah National Park, is home to two large student populations, at James Madison University, established in 1908, and at Eastern Mennonite University, founded nine years later. A visitor driving down Main Street will undoubtedly notice an impeccably restored Victorian house, brightly painted in roses and mauves, called the Joshua Wilton House. This fancy Victorian is home not only to five lovely guest rooms but also to great dinners served in a formal, elegant setting.

Craig Moore was a well-established Harrisonburg chef before he and his wife Roberta opened their own inn in May 1988. The goal for this young and creative couple was to create the town's most elegant dining spot, a luxurious setting with beautiful food complemented by a full wine list. After restoring the house to its pristine original condition of 1883, the Moores had the Joshua Wilton House placed on the National Register of Historic Places.

The first floor is devoted to the elegant dining experience. Guests enter the magnificent foyer, where the light falls on the floor in a spectrum of color fractured by the elaborate beveled glass around the front door. Before dinner, guests await their table in a mahogany-paneled lounge, with tufted leather chairs and banquettes, in front of an antique oak and carved soapstone bar. Of the four dining areas, one has a bay window, another a turret, another is a cozy and private nook, and the last is an enclosed sun room. The front two dining rooms have working fireplaces with original mantels of faux art carved oak. Guests also dine outdoors under kiss-shaped umbrellas on the patterned brick patio.

Upstairs, each of the five rooms was decorated by a different member of the Moore family, in Victorian elegance with varied design, some feminine, others reserved and dignified. Roberta and Craig parted from heavy Victorian colors and lightened the walls and window treatments. The pleasing art on the walls is for sale, a gallery for the Shenandoah Watercolor Society. Room 2 has a working fireplace, a brass and white iron bed, an armoire with a mirror, and a pair of ladies' slipper chairs. Room 3 is the smallest, featuring a lovely rosewood rocker, with a window seat nestled in a four-windowed bay. Room 5 has the other working fireplace with, marble inlay, and a four-poster pencil post bed. The antique pieces, including the beds, are lovely, in the finest taste, and the chairs are reupholstered in precious silk and damask.

It is no surprise that a full breakfast is integral to a stay at the Joshua Wilton House, with specialties of jumbo lump crabmeat asparagus omelettes or poached eggs with smoked salmon or smoked duck.

Silver Thatch Inn
3001 Hollymead Drive
Charlottesville, Virginia 22901
804-978-4686

Proprietors: Joe and Mickey Geller
Accommodations: 7 rooms, all with private bath (3 in main house, 4 in Cottage)
Rates: $105–$125
Included: Expanded Continental breakfast
Minimum stay: 2 nights on some spring and fall weekends
Added: 6.5% state tax
Payment: Visa, MasterCard
Children: 5 and over welcome
Pets: Not allowed
Smoking: Not allowed
Open: All year except Christmas Eve, Christmas Day, New Year's Eve, New Year's Day; restaurant closed first two weeks of August, two weeks at Christmastime

Silver Thatch Inn is a classic country inn several miles north of the University of Virginia on a rolling country road just off horrific Route 29. Though the inn has been a strong town presence for years, the property has been nicely revived since its new and hospitable owners, Mickey and Joe Geller, took the helm in 1988. The addition of chef Janet Henry greatly improved the standing of the restaurant, which has received wonderful reviews and awards for its wine list.

The common room is the original part of the house, one of the county's oldest structures, having been built in 1780 by Hessian soldiers imprisoned on the plot during the Revolutionary War. Various additions elaborated on the white clapboard and black shutter theme, in 1820 and again in 1920–30, creating a panoply of undulating weathered shingle rooftops which range from one to three stories. A Carriage House borders one side of the U-shaped structure, with a manicured courtyard, an enormous holly tree befriended by magnolias and dogwoods, and a brick walkway in the middle.

Each of the three dining rooms has a very different feel. The colonial tavern room is dressed in early American primitives; the middle room is more elegant, with plush maroon chairs, floral wallpaper, and wine-colored trim, spilling down to the third dining room, a large enclosed porch with a more contemporary, though traditional setting. Janet Henry's American light eclectic menu changes monthly to make the best use of local produce, and entrées range from $14 to $23. Interesting appetizers might include a twice-baked chevre soufflé with sun-dried tomato sauce. Entrées are international, like Mediterranean seafood lasagna, with shrimp and lobster in tomato fennel sauce and saffron bechamel; or Moroccan chicken stew with pumpkin, chick peas, carrots, and turnips seasoned with harissa sauce served over couscous; or a grilled filet mignon served on a mustard crouton with mushroom, onion, and beer sauce.

The Gellers redecorated the guest rooms in early American antiques and reproductions, with authentic Williamsburg trim, stenciling, and playful country wallpaper borders, all spotlessly maintained. As a result of the varied height of the rooftops, the rooms all have surprising eaves, clever window seats, shelves, or desks built into the pitch. The James Madison Room in the main house has a wallpaper border of melons echoed in several pictures, an antique school bench, and a log cabin quilt over crisp white linens on a pencil post canopy bed with matching skirting. The bathrooms have a generous variety of Caswell and Massey amenities. Homemade treats or cookies greet guests, and all rooms have fresh plants.

The Gellers are extremely kind people, happy to share their knowledge of the area and love for the Silver Thatch. The inn has a swimming pool and tennis courts, as well as hiking and biking trails nearby.

200 South Street: A Virginia Inn
Charlottesville, Virginia 22901
804-979-0200

Innkeeper: Brendan Clancy
Accommodations: 20 rooms, all with private bath, 9 with
   fireplace (11 rooms in mansion, 9 in Cottage)
Rates: $85–$160
Included: Continental breakfast
Minimum stay: Special college weekends
Added: $20 each additional person; 8.5% tax
Payment: Visa, MasterCard, American Express
Children: Welcome
Pets: Not allowed
Smoking: Allowed
Open: All year

In 1985, a group of five investors, devoted alumni of the University of Virginia, bought a pair of houses in Charlottesville's historic district with the intent of opening a bed-and-breakfast for visitors of refined tastes. The two adjacent houses—the mansion and the Cottage—are lemon-colored, trimmed in white, both three stories, but quite different architecturally. The mansion was built in 1856 for Thomas Jefferson Wertenbaker, son of the first librarian at the University of Virginia, a close friend of its brilliant founder and president. The adjacent Cottage is an early Victorian that recedes from the street in four sections like an accordion, with a broad front porch.

While the restoration was completed in April 1986, the matter of furnishings had to be settled. Two of the owners traveled to Europe to consult with British art dealer Keith Bycroft, who helped procure the glorious English and Belgian antiques which fill the guest and common rooms, as well as the paintings and antique Turkish rugs.

The square brick mansion is the main gathering spot for guests, with dormer windows facing four different directions from the mansard roof. A neoclassic veranda wraps around three sides of the house, and descends in the back to a brick breakfast patio. The interior of the mansion is formal and grand, with beautiful Oriental and Turkish rugs covering wood floors. The walls are hung with paintings by Virginia artists as well as with historic Holsinger photographs of Charlottesville. The wicker-filled Library is the congregating spot for guests, rather small for a bed-and-breakfast of 20 rooms. A plentiful Continental breakfast is served here or on the outdoor patio.

Every room has its own book describing the furnishings and artwork found therein. Most pieces date from the 18th and 19th centuries, like an armoire from Northern France circa 1800, a 1789 armoire from Austria, or a beautiful painting of an elephant dating from about 1865. In addition to the artwork and furnishings, the beds are quite stunning, with rails extended to accommodate queen-size mattresses. Of the four rooms with twins, one features two rare tiger maple sleighs. Other beds might be canopied with lace or draw curtains, Victorian or Eastlake with elaborately inlaid or carved wood, or perhaps with an upholstered headboard. Some rooms have whirlpool baths, and nine have working gas fireplaces.

Memory and Company, the restaurant, rests on the other side of the mansion, with distinctive new American cuisine peppered with influences from southern France, embellished by a small but representative wine list.

Though the inn is only one mile from the campus, the neighborhood is a bit transitional. Veteran innkeeper Donna Deibert is extremely professional and provides guests with all the local advice and information needed.

West Virginia

Thomas Shepherd Inn
Corner of German and Duke Streets, Box 1162
Shepherdstown, West Virginia 25443
304-876-3715

Proprietor: Margaret Perry
Accommodations: 6 rooms, all with private bath
Rates: $75–$95
Included: Full breakfast
Minimum stay: 2 nights on holidays and weekends
Added: Surcharge for credit cards
Payment: Major credit cards
Children: 12 and over welcome
Pets: Not allowed
Smoking: Not allowed
Open: All year

Shepherdstown is its state's oldest community, settled more than a hundred years before West Virginia was deemed a state in the Union in 1863. A literal stone's throw from Maryland and the Antietam Battlefield (site of the Civil War's bloodiest fight),

Shepherdstown rests on the western banks of the Potomac River. It is home to a college which shares its name, founded in 1871. The historic town looks more like a refined New England outpost than a part of wild and wonderful West Virginia, with its main street a gallery of Federal and Victorian architecture. The Thomas Shepherd Inn greets visitors at the town's main junction, an introduction to charming Main Street and a block's walk to the college.

Built in 1868 as a Lutheran parsonage, the inn was transformed from a private residence to a bed-and-breakfast in 1984. The owners restored the inn to its original pristine Federal condition, a two-and-a-half-story whitewashed brick, with a modest single-story portico. Margaret Perry came from New England seeking a suitable bed-and-breakfast and found her ideal property here in September 1989. She is quite devoted to her innkeeping tasks, enthusiastically hosting tea every afternoon, cooking large morning breakfasts, gardening, and packaging soaps and potpourri for the guests.

The scale of the inn is intimate. To the right of the foyer is the double parlor, with a working fireplace, furnished with reproduction and antique Federal pieces, the trim in colonial colors. The two dining rooms are similarly decorated in meticulous Federal style, where Margaret serves her full breakfasts which include fresh muffins and a hot dish like sour cream pancakes with Vermont maple syrup, topped with an edible flower to complete the presentation.

The three guest rooms in the front section of the house are preferable to those in the back, which are less formal. The most deluxe room is at the front of the house, with a Pierre Deux crown canopy, maroon wing chairs, and an antique hope chest. A pencil post canopy sits across the hall and a sleigh bed in a room behind, topped with an elaborate antique quilt. Guests use the library at the back of the house, which overlooks the gardens and yard beyond. Beyond Shepherd College is Harper's Ferry National Historic Park; and within sight on the Maryland banks of the Potomac is the C&O Canal and Towpath for hiking and biking enthusiasts.

Intimate City Stops

Delaware

Christina House—Continental Suites Hotel
707 King Street
Wilmington, Delaware 19801
302-656-9300
800-543-9106

General Manager: Denise L. McCool
Accommodations: 35 two-room suites, 4 large studio suites
Rates: $125; weekends $75
Included: Continental breakfast
Minimum stay: None
Added: 8% tax
Payment: Major credit cards
Children: Welcome
Pets: Not allowed
Smoking: Nonsmoking rooms available
Open: All year

While the gorgeous beaux-arts Hotel DuPont is under renovation until 1993, the place to stay in Wilmington is undoubtedly the Christina House—and some guests may prefer its intimate scale, personal service, reasonable rates, and large, contemporary rooms even after the DuPont is resurrected. The two-room suites are configured with the business traveler in mind, with separate work and sleep areas and mini- and wet bars.

The Christina House sits just around the corner from the Hotel DuPont. As with any good piece of postmodern architecture, the space was developed from two existing brownstones—formerly Braunstein's Department Store—connected and elaborated with a glass atrium and concrete additions. It opened in 1987 spanning the full block between King Street to the pedestrian mall behind called Market Street.

Guests enter a rather traditional reception area in one brownstone and proceed to the triple-story atrium in the center of the Christina House. Like a greenhouse, the room is flooded with light that spills onto white walls and blond wood floors covered with cushy Oriental rugs and filled with contemporary living room furnishings. Plants bask in the sunlight, and a fireplace is stoked at night.

While the atrium serves as a centerpiece, the guest rooms border the perimeter on three upper floors. The two-room suites number 35, appointed in deluxe hotel fashion, each configured a bit differently with similar decor and a dark green low nap rug. The unusually spacious suites feature two televisions hidden in contemporary or reproduction armoires, traditional wing chairs and camelback sofas in colorful complementary upholstery, and enormous closets. The queen-size beds are covered with spreads matching window treatments. The baths are luxurious, with a third telephone, hair dryer, and full amenities. The service is prompt and friendly, and the only blameless drawback is the dearth of views from most of the guest rooms.

The Atrium Dining Room offers a reasonably priced lunch and dinner daily in a private, contemporary fireside setting. Entrées like veal saltimbocca or chicken Christina served over spinach fettucini with shallot and watercress cream sauce range from $8.50 to $16.95. The business district is a short walk away. The staff will happily advise about local museums and activities in hardworking Wilmington.

Maryland

Admiral Fell Inn
Fell's Point, 888 South Broadway
Baltimore, Maryland 21231
410-522-7377
800-292-INNS
Fax 522-0707

General Manager: Dominik Eckenstein
Accommodations: 38 rooms, 4 with Jacuzzi
Rates: $105–$125
Included: Continental breakfast, free off-street parking
Minimum stay: None
Added: $10 each additional guest

Payment: Visa, MasterCard, American Express
Children: Welcome
Pets: Not allowed
Smoking: Nonsmoking rooms available
Open: All year

With the intimacy and originality of a bed-and-breakfast and the sophistication of a luxury hotel, the Admiral Fell Inn is a unique property that epitomizes the rich history of its Fell's Point neighborhood. The inn sits on the oblique corner of South Broadway and Thames Street, with an unobstructed view of the historic waterfront docks. In a microcosm of its eclectic neighborhood, the Admiral Fell comprises four joined buildings, built between 1720 and 1910: the northernmost is the oldest, the former home to Baltimore's first mayor; the second is a three-story red brick building with a cast-iron Victorian facade; and the middle two are four tall stories with Georgian detailing in red brick. In former lives, part of the property was known as the Anchorage Hotel, a YMCA, and a vinegar bottling plant. The buildings remained vacant between the mid-1970s and 1984 when the property was bought with the intent of creating a deluxe country inn.

Decorated with period reproductions and occasional antiques, the rooms are an intriguing array of shapes and sizes, so be sure to inquire thoroughly. Some are large with harbor views; others are small or have odd, intriguing angles. The double beds have fishnet canopies on four-poster rice beds; king-size beds have crown canopies that fall from ceiling moldings. There are always two telephones and a writing desk, ample lighting, and often a television hidden in an armoire. Either the walls or trim is painted in traditional Williamsburg rusts, yellows, or greens, decorated with floral or period prints which pick up the tones of the carpet.

Guests entering from the corner find a pleasant foyer with seating areas on either side. To the right is a reception desk and a lovely forest green paneled fireplace, with faux marble, which reaches to the crown molding. Comfortable sofas and chairs gather by hunting and sailing prints on the walls. Visitors relax here, in the atrium, the brick courtyard in the quiet back of the inn, or in the heart pine–floored library, where they have Continental breakfast mornings.

Guests will be grateful for the proximity of the fine restaurant on the lower level and for its separate entrance. The several rooms include a cozy pub with a tartan rug, a dining room with exposed brick walls, and another with exposed stone walls. The low ceiling lends a romance to the setting. Lunch and dinner are served daily, brunch on Sundays. The dinner entrées range from $15 to $21, and a sample meal might come as follows: crab, corn, and jalapeño bisque; an appetizer of baby crabcakes; and an entrée of pork tenderloin, rack of New Zealand baby lamb, or swordfish tropique served with pineapple-mango salsa; all followed by a long list of desserts.

The Admiral Fell is a busy place in the heart of a busy neighborhood—which gets quite lively on weekends—with surprisingly friendly service.

Ann Street Bed and Breakfast

804 South Street
Baltimore, Maryland 21231
410-342-5883

Proprietors: Joanne and Andrew Mazurek
Accommodations: 3 rooms, including 1 suite, all with private
  bath, 2 with fireplace
Rates: $75–$85
Included: Full breakfast
Minimum stay: None
Added: $15 each additional guest; 12% tax
Payment: No credit cards
Children: Check with innkeeper
Pets: Not allowed
Smoking: Not allowed
Open: All year

For those ardent bed-and-breakfasters who have come as far as Baltimore's Fell's Point for a taste of history, the Ann Street Bed and Breakfast will authenticate the experience. Just around the corner from harborfront Thames Street is the Mazurek home, opened to overnight guests in 1988. Theirs is a beautiful marriage of two colonial houses, mirror images in brick, four windows across, with dormer windows peeking out from the fourth-floor rooftop, centered with a tall chimney that services an incredible 12 working fireplaces.

The houses were built in the 1790s, and Joanne and Andrew have decorated faithfully, using Williamsburg trim, pewter light fixtures, dried wreaths, candles on the windowsills, and 18th-century reproduction furniture where they could not find antiques. What cannot be seen from the street is the charming backyard, a small garden with patio furniture accessible to guests.

The left house is devoted entirely to guests. The dining room is the fireside setting for the large breakfasts, which include a hot entrée. The common room is furnished in primitive country decor and also is warmed by the fireplace. The accommodations are on the second floor. The suite has a sitting room including a blue-checked sofa bed and blue wing chairs, and the wall is enlivened by an antique quilt. The trim is traditional green and maroon. The other guest room is furnished with a crewel wing chair and a four-poster fishnet curved canopy bed.

The right house, which is also the Mazureks' home, has one large guest room which is quite notable not for its antique rope bed but for the impressive bath, with a working cast-iron fireplace and whitewashed brick walls. Most striking is the cleanliness of the place, including the wide-planked original pine floors and the original mantels in deep Williamsburg colors. Flannel sheets and antique quilts dress up the beds.

While the accommodations in the Mazurek home might seem intimate, the other house offers a great deal of independence. The young couple is ever-present to answer questions and recommend activities, yet they are respectful of their guests' privacy. Theirs is a wonderful home for bed-and-breakfast enthusiasts: historic, immaculate, and very pretty.

Celie's Waterfront Bed & Breakfast

1714 Thames Street
Baltimore, Maryland 21231
410-522-2323

Proprietors: Celie Ives
Accommodations: 7 rooms, all with private baths, 4 with whirlpools, 2 with fireplace
Rates: $95–$140; handicapped-accessible room, $85
Included: Continental breakfast
Minimum stay: 2 nights in some rooms on weekends
Added: 12% tax
Payment: Visa, MasterCard, Discover, American Express
Children: Age 10 and over welcome
Pets: Not allowed
Smoking: Not allowed indoors
Open: All year

Celie Ives opened a single room in her private home to overnight guests several years ago and liked the bed-and-breakfast business so much that she decided to expand. Around the corner from her Fell's Point home, she built an old-looking new Federal rowhouse on cobblestoned Thames Street, which would be right across from the water but for the Fells Point Recreation Center, which sits just opposite. Her three-story inn, opened in February 1990, is gray brick with wine-colored trim and old detailing, quite a complementary addition to its historic neighbors.

Where many a bed-and-breakfast is characterized by old moldings, Victoriana, and slanted wood floors, Celie's is a fresh haven of clean lines, cream-colored walls, low nap carpeting, and traditional antiques and furnishings. There is some historic detailing, like three wood-burning fireplaces, built-in bookshelves, mullioned windows, French doors, and window seats, but these are done crisply and tidily in contemporary comfort.

The first floor comprises the neat-as-a-pin living room and a tiled breakfast room where guests enjoy a Continental breakfast of freshly squeezed orange juice and several baked goods. In warmer months, the French doors of the breakfast room open to the brick-patterned patio, furnished with wrought-iron café tables and walled-in weathered wood. A handicapped-accessible room is also on the first floor, with three rooms on each of the two upper floors.

Celie is adamant about down comforters, cotton linens, full bath sheets (not towels), and fresh flowers. The finest room is the third-floor king suite, with a fireplace and whirlpool bath, which overlooks the harbor from three large mullioned windows topped by chintz swags and underscored by a long window seat filled with cushions. The king-size bed has a crown canopy. The room directly below shares the same view; two rooms have views of the back gardens, and two more rooms look into the atrium in the middle of the house. All these guest rooms are decorated in light colors, with soft-bordered beige duvets, a single-color trim, alcoves with refrigerators and coffee makers, and sparkling new baths.

Celie is a gregarious hostess who heartily enjoys her guests and sharing her knowledge of Baltimore and the historic neighborhood of Fell's Point.

Inn at Government House

1125 North Calvert Street
Baltimore, Maryland
410-539-0566
Fax 410-539-0567

Proprietor: Baltimore International Culinary College
Managing Director: Mariana Palacios, assisted by Meg Daly
Rates: $100–$125
Included: Continental breakfast, high tea
Minimum stay: None

Added: 12% tax
Payment: MasterCard, Visa, American Express
Children: Welcome
Pets: Check with manager
Smoking: Not allowed
Open: All year

The Inn at Government House, for years the leading property in the Society Hill Hotels, is now home to the Baltimore International Culinary College, which has another branch in Ireland, founded in 1991. Not only do guests have the privilege of staying at this magnificent house, they are also treated to fresh-baked croissants and sticky buns cooked each morning by the students, as well as an elaborate high tea.

The Government House is composed of three connecting townhouses in the elite Mount Vernon district. Dating to the 1880s, the grand corner Government House with its three-story turret was built for William Painter, the inventor of the bottle cap. Today, the Government House is where political royalty often stay or entertain. In addition to being furnished with beautiful period antiques, the house has been impeccably restored, with faux wood graining on original wood and millwork, and wood flooring patterns unique to each room. The Anglo-Japanese sitting room has a Renaissance Revival parlor set and such treasures as Ming Dynasty temple jars on bookcases. The dining room has a stunning Renaissance Revival chandelier, an electrified gasolier from 1843 with original glass shades. The ceiling paper is typical Victorian elaborate découpage in seventeen patterns. Guests may explore the Edwardian library with its unusual paneling, original marble fireplace, and stained glass windows.

The guest rooms, accessible with a ride from a luscious wood elevator or a walk up a light-filled atrium staircase, are blessed with original stained glass, woodwork, molding, some marble mantels, and unusual spaces. Certainly, two of the finer ones rest in the turret. Unusual is the lush quality of the fabrics and window treatments framing lace panels. Reproduction patterns of Victorian wallpaper decorate each room in interesting patterns. The baths are nicely updated, with bonuses like hair dryers and personalized bath grains. The Government House is notably stocked with a beautiful collection of original lithographs.

Mariana and Meg are consummate, gracious hostesses who revere this wonderful building. Guests receive a museum-type tour of the house upon check-in. As well, the innkeepers are quite enthusiastic about the school and its sister property, the Park Hotel in County Cavin, 50 miles northwest of Dublin.

The Inn at Henderson's Wharf
1000 Fell Street
Baltimore, Maryland 21231
410-522-7777
800-522-2088

Proprietor: Linda Lowe
Accommodations: 39 rooms, including 1 suite
Rates: $115–$125
Included: Continental breakfast, evening reception
Minimum stay: None
Added: $15 each additional guest; 12% tax
Payment: Major credit cards
Children: Welcome
Pets: Not allowed
Smoking: Not allowed
Open: All year

Nestled into Baltimore's Harbor, Fell's Point is a curving bite of shoreline lined with historic brick-faced buildings that date to the early 18th century. However nautical this district may be, no property in Fell's Point has water views like Henderson's Wharf. Half of the 39 guest rooms look out over the water to the planked boardwalk that scurries around the harborfront. Belying its history, which is over a century old, Henderson's Wharf opened as an inn quite recently, in the summer of 1991.

The end of cobblestoned Fell Street looks like it might tip right into the harbor, as a huge and heavy brick building sits at its peninsular tip. This is Henderson's Wharf, a seven-story pentagonal brick structure trimmed with light blue wooden-plank shutters. Built as a tobacco warehouse in the 19th century by the Baltimore and Ohio Railroad, Henderson's Wharf was restored in 1990–91 and placed on the National Register of Historic Places.

There are two faces to its entrance, and three more sides complete the pentagon. Visitors enter a large, long, traditionally appointed lobby dressed in French furnishings, with Oriental rugs thrown over the highly polished wooden floors. One entire side is walled with mullioned French doors overlooking the formal English garden and brick patio, allowing light to sweep into the long, narrow lobby.

The guest rooms radiate from the center corridor of the lobby in several wings. Half rest around the perimeter, with views of the water through sliding doors behind floor-to-ceiling plantation shutters, custom-made and set into a brick archway; and the other half have views of the English garden or of cobblestoned Fell Street. Decorated in two different nonhistoric schemes of formal and country, the rooms have low nap blue or seafoam carpeting, and all have televisions hidden in single armoires in pine or mahogany. The beds are brass and black wrought-iron or oak spindle sleighs, and the wing chairs complement the spreads, in tapestries or in black chintz; some rooms have blanket chests and dressers painted with historic murals. The baths are elegant, with ceramic tiles, brass fixtures, and Dickens-Hawthorne amenities including mouthwash.

Guests take a Continental breakfast to their rooms or eat in the lobby or gardens. Service is that of a deluxe hotel, discreet and formal. Because the property is largely a condominium, Henderson's Wharf overnight guests have a feeling of independence and privacy. Active guests may use the exercise studio. There is a 200-slip marina, and plans are under way for a dockside pool. Courtesy van or water shuttle service to the business district is provided.

New York

The Box Tree
250 East 49th Street
New York, New York 10017
212-593-9810

Proprietor: Augustin V. Paege
General Manager: Nina Fuenmayor
Accommodations: 12 suites, all with private bath
Rates: $270–$300, including $100 credit toward dinner
Included: Continental breakfast
Minimum stay: None
Payment: American Express
Children: Allowed
Pets: Allowed
Smoking: Not allowed in rooms
Open: All year

Manhattanites have been preparing for the urban Box Tree for years. Its 20-year-old upstate relative in Purdys, 40 miles north, is a romantic guest house and culinary refuge (see Romantic Retreats). Since 1982, the Box Tree Restaurant has prepared wondrous dinners, but it began welcoming guests only in 1989.

However much one readies for the Box Tree experience, it is nevertheless quite a stunning surprise: romantic, fantastic, whimsical.

Guest pick out the nattiest brownstone on East 49th Street, between Second and Third Avenues, marked by a verdigris marquee and a scripted sign adorned in literal gold leaves. Inside is an interior landscape created by Mr. Paege, the result of a lifetime of collecting and impeccable, eclectic, wondrous taste. Guests enter a patterned brick foyer. Among the curiosities are a Louis XIII tufted leather wing chair with a back that evolves into a hood. Two 18th-century Italian porcelain figures support a mantel designed specifically for the setting.

A series of intimate dining rooms on the lower two floors adds to the sense of evolution at the Box Tree, each scene capturing the imagination, proceeding quickly into another realm. The Music dining room has reproduction Louis XIII chairs covered in Aubusson muted tapestry, backlit by a turn-of-the-century stained glass window. Here, the magnificent fireplace mantel is supported by wide terra cotta columns inset with colored glass. Yet another dining room, the Marie Antoinette, looks lifted from Versailles, with lavish gilded millwork and molding, as well as candelabras and chandelier. Most masterful is the Gaudi-inspired staircase, sculpted by collaborator David Mills, which connects the two levels of dining rooms.

Each of the twelve suites on several floors above and in the adjacent brownstone is a private boudoir, a world unto itself, derivative of different countries, diminutive versions of palaces in China, Egypt, or France. The trompe l'oeil painted doors reflect their respective interior decor, painted by decorative artist Heinz Simon, who crafted much of the Purdys Box Tree. Each has a sitting area facing a working gas fireplace. The uppermost high-ceilinged suite has a malachite fireplace. The Chinese Suite has lacquered tables and chairs accented with Chinese porcelain filled with plants or atop tables. The Japanese Suite has Mackintosh English antiques. The King Boris of Bulgaria Room is filled with Louis XVI gilt. Horizontal gilded millwork decorates the walls in the Consulate Suite, with a green marble fireplace. The Irish linens have a 600-thread count. The amenities are by Guerlain.

Guests may either focus on the precious individual treasures and antiquities which decorate the inn or revel in the whirlwind, atmospheric changes from room to room. It's a wondrous, magical place. Be sure to come back from shopping for high tea, a tradition seemingly invented for this setting, with fresh-baked delicacies made to be eaten in this lavish setting.

Hotel Wales
1295 Madison Avenue
New York, New York 10128
212-876-6000

Proprietor and Manager: Henry Kallan
Accommodations: 92 rooms, including 50 suites and 1
    penthouse suite
Rates: Rooms, $145; suites, $175, $225; penthouse, $375
Included: Continental breakfast
Minimum stay: None
Added: 19.25% tax; $2 occupancy tax
Payment: Major credit cards
Children: Welcome
Pets: Not allowed
Smoking: Allowed
Open: All year

As daunting and impersonal as New York City can be for an
out-of-towner, the Hotel Wales is just as comforting and
friendly. This oasis on Manhattan's Upper East Side is as much
a country inn as a city hotel, with refreshingly rural rates.

The Hotel Wales is located on Madison Avenue between
92nd and 93rd streets, miles from the bustle of midtown. To
know the area is to know the relative peacefulness of that part of
town, which is referred to by New Yorkers as old-moneyed
Carnegie Hill, named for the famed industrialist who built a
modest home on Fifth Avenue and 89th Street (today, the fortresslike Cooper-Hewitt Museum). This high up on Madison
Avenue, fashionable boutiques are outnumbered by posh private schools, as close as you'll get in Manhattan to suburbia.

The Wales was built in 1901 as a lovely brownstone hotel,
designed as a leisurely place of respite for busy travelers who
would stay for weeks at a time. Many of the suites have kitchenettes. The configuration is beneficial for nearly every room
(except the smallest of singles): the suites are on the corners of
the building, looking either southwest or west, but with a guar-
anteed view of glorious Central Park and the lakelike reservoir
at 90th Street. Even if the pastoral setting is slightly obscured by
the block between Madison and Fifth avenues, such oblique-
ness is a luxury: this is the highest-rent view in the city.

In early 1990, the hotel underwent a $6 million renovation
that revealed ubiquitous oak woodwork: transoms, molding,
trim, French doors, and mantels have been stripped of decades
of paint and the original richness restored. The rooms are furnished with English antiques or credible reproductions in ma-

hogany and oak, all excellent choices, often matched with original artwork. Each room is different, more in the style of a turn-of-the-century mansion than a hotel: a fine writing desk, a fireplace, or a canopy bed are pleasant surprises in some of the rooms. The bathrooms are nearly sparkling thanks to the renovation, with touches of marble here and there, and any native would say they are bigger than a city studio.

A word of advice: Make sure a crowded weekend does not leave you with one of the smaller singles, which are small even by city standards. Conversely, the penthouse is quite magnificent, a full one-bedroom apartment attached to 1,000 square feet of terrace overlooking Central Park.

Although there is no room service at the Hotel Wales, adjacent is handsome Busby's and one of the chic-elite brunch locales in the city, the immensely popular Sarabeth's Kitchen, which boasts a 45-minute wait on weekends without hope of reservations. Service at the hotel is hushed, reverent, and near to invisible. Continental breakfast is served in the recently finished salon, 1,600 square feet of grandeur, also the pleasant setting for Friday night classical concerts.

Mansion Hill Inn

115 Philip Street at Park Avenue
Albany, New York 12202
518-465-2038
518-427-7358
800-477-8171

Proprietors: Steve and Maryellen Stofelano
Accommodations: 12 rooms, including 3 with kitchens (2
    above restaurant, 5 at 45 Park Avenue, 5 on Philip Street)
Rates: $105–$145
Included: Full breakfast, depending on rate
Minimum stay: None
Added: $10 each additional guest; 7% tax
Payment: Major credit cards
Children: Welcome, under 12 free
Pets: Check with manager
Smoking: Allowed
Open: All year

The Albany Hilton sits several blocks below the capitol building, the Albany Marriott a short hop from the airport—plush, contemporary, and unsurprising. City travelers who prefer a smaller scale along bed-and-breakfast lines will be glad for a relative newcomer in a town with a sad paucity of alternatives.

Mansion Hill Inn sits south of Empire State Plaza and the Governor's Mansion. In addition to housing seven comfortable rooms, the inn has a pleasant, bistro-style restaurant that serves three good meals daily.

The Mansion Hill Inn toes the neighborhood line between trendy, restored Victorian brick rowhouses and those in need of a little attention. Steve and Maryellen Stofelano bought a condemned three-story clapboard townhouse in 1983 in the Mansion neighborhood and worked for nearly a year restoring its 1861 frame. Here, two rooms hover above the small restaurant. The Stofelanos rescued the adjoining property on Park Avenue, providing five more guest rooms. The five additional rooms in the Philip Street rowhouse are the newest, connected to the Mansion Hill Inn by outdoor garden dining.

The guest rooms vary in size, providing comfort to a transient guest as well as for those who plan a longer tenure in Albany. All rooms are furnished with dark wood Queen Anne reproduction furniture including queen-size beds, private telephones, remote cable televisions tucked in cabinets, and serviceable desks. Two suites have a living room and a den, a fully stocked kitchen, bedroom, and a terrace. A smaller third suite has a stocked kitchen. The remaining rooms have unusual alcoves providing separate work areas, some with stained glass windows, and bright new baths with pedestal sinks, fluffy towels, and a second telephone. Fresh flowers and Saratoga water greet arriving guests.

The dining room, which dresses up for dinner or down for breakfast, is a small, friendly spot with an exposed brick woodburning fireplace, mint green wainscoting, and blue floral paper above the chair rail. David K. Martin is the dinner chef, whose entrées range from $12 to $21 for various pasta dishes, shrimp Madagascar with Pernod cream sauce, or perhaps veal sauté with smoked Canadian bacon, avocado, and tomato.

The Stofelanos and other staff are friendly, informal, and helpful about Albany activities.

Morgans

237 Madison Avenue
New York, New York 10016
212-686-0300
800-334-3408
Fax: 212-779-8352

General Manager: David Baldwin
Accommodations: 113 rooms, including 29 suites

Rates: Rooms, $205–$235; suites, $275–$400 (lower rates on weekends)
Included: Continental breakfast, morning newspaper
Minimum stay: None
Added: 19.25% tax
Payment: Major credit cards
Children: Welcome
Pets: Not allowed
Smoking: 3 nonsmoking floors
Open: All year

The first of Ian Schrager's three New York City hotel creations, Morgans is an ultracool, postmodern, high-tech place of supreme calm and style. Today, those who want to be seen go to the Royalton. Those who don't particularly want to be seen will go to Morgans.

The hotel, with a sophisticated three-column stone exterior with 20 floors of brickwork above, has a wonderful location on 38th and Madison, just a block north of the J. P. Morgan library and residence, for which the hotel was named. It was built in 1929 as the Duane Hotel and was entirely redone in 1983 by Ian Schrager, Steve Rubell, and Phil Pilevsky.

There are few hotels in the low-key residential neighborhood of Murray Hill, despite the fact that Grand Central Station is only four blocks away. Guests might pass by the doorway of Morgans, marked subtly by bellhops who look like models on a break from a shoot, dressed in double-breasted black suits and white shirts. The lobby is striking and impersonal, marked by a trompe l'oeuil black and white parquet rug, with glass and bronze wall panels soaring two stories. It's not a comfortable place, but rather encourages guests to their rooms, reiterating the theme of privacy that prevails at the hotel.

Morgans created quite a stir when it opened as the city's first modern boutique hotel in 1984. French designer Andree Putman designed the interior: from the low-profile beds, to soothing window seats under wooden slat blinds, to the fabulous baths, with poured granite floors, stainless steel surgical sinks, and floor-to-ceiling glass-enclosed showers (made from bus-stop enclosures), bordered in black and white parquet tiling. Robert Mapplethorpe was commissioned to do a series of black and white photographs for every room, justifiably the only artwork other than the fresh flowers.

With only about ten rooms per floor, each landing feels private and quiet. The halls are carpeted in soft gray, bordered in the ubiquitous black and white parquet. The guest rooms are carpeted in gray, with low beds covered in Oxford blue duvets from Brooks Brothers, topped by black and white wool blankets. The surfaces are stark, clean, and spare. A cassette player, VCR, and remote television sit in every room, attended to by 24-hour room service. Morgans has a library of more than 200 videos, any one of which may be brought up to one's room with hot popcorn. Unusually, most rooms have good sunlight and sometimes two exposures.

A special treat is Continental breakfast served in a sunny, cool breakfast room overlooking Madison Avenue and a chic bistro across the street. The staff is low-key, personal, and extremely attentive.

Pennsylvania

Independence Park Inn
235 Chestnut Street
Philadelphia, Pennsylvania 19106
215-922-4443
800-624-2988

Proprietors: Inns of Distinction
General Manager: Thierry Bompard
Accommodations: 36 rooms, all with private bath
Rates: $120–$135, with lower weekend and corporate rates
Included: Continental breakfast, afternoon tea
Minimum stay: None
Added: $5 each additional guest over agee6; 12% tax
Payment: Major credit cards
Children: Welcome
Pets: Not allowed
Smoking: 2 of 4 floors nonsmoking
Open: All year

Business travelers on a budget or who prefer a more intimate, informal environment will adore the Independence Park Inn. Weekend visitors will appreciate the personal service and proximity to Philadelphia's Independence Mall.

The elegant granite building was built in 1856 as a dry goods store for a wealthy merchant named John Elliott, designed by architect Joseph C. Hoxie to reflect the grandeur of the owner's accomplishments. For decades during this century, the building served as a baby furniture warehouse before it was bought and restored in 1988 by the present owners, whose efforts put the building on the National Register of Historic Places.

The exterior is five attenuated stories tall, with high and narrow double-arched windows which span five across the front of the six-columned exterior. Just inside, the lobby is lovely, with three grand floor-to-ceiling windows and tufted leather couches facing one another in front of a working fireplace. Exposed wood floors are covered with a large Oriental rug. Guests are treated to quite a lavish afternoon tea in this elegant setting. Toward the back of the lobby, past reception, is a long, narrow, sunny atrium between buildings where guests have Continental breakfast.

There are nine rooms on each of the upper four floors, decorated slightly differently. Preferable are the front queen and king parlor rooms, which have beautiful views of Independence Park through long three-quarter windows hung with traditional heavy striped curtains tucked behind round brass tiebacks. All rooms are furnished with two-poster beds and reproduction Chippendale furniture. The rugs are a bright green, and the walls are hung with historic Philadelphia prints. Televisions are hidden in large armoires, and two telephones are provided in each room. The baths are nice, but not exceptional. The smaller rooms that overlook the atrium are good for the budget-minded and offer a fair sacrifice for the very friendly service at the Independence Park Inn.

This is a friendly, casual place, pretty and sunny in an exceptional piece of architecture. While the innkeeper may be dressed in a rather formal tie during the business week, the inn relaxes quite nicely during the weekend to a leisurely pace. Convenient to historic sites, the Independence Park has the professional virtues of the many luxury hotels nearby on an intimate, friendly scale.

The Inn at Centre Park
730 Centre Avenue
Reading, Pennsylvania 19601
215-374-8557

Proprietors: Andrea and Michael Smith
Accommodations: 5 rooms, including 1 suite, all with private bath
Rates: $130–$190
Included: Full breakfast; basket of fruit on arrival
Added: 6% tax
Payment: MasterCard, Visa
Children: Check with innkeeper
Pets: Not allowed

Smoking: Not allowed
Open: All year

The Inn at Centre Park is the rare kind of place that could not be built today — not only would costs be prohibitive, but much of the rare materials simply cannot be found. Andrea and Michael Smith, natives of Reading, had their eye on the old Wilhelm mansion for years — and in early 1989 the property went up for sale. Five months of restoration transformed this three-story mansard-roofed stone house from a spooky mansion to one of the grandest properties in this book.

The city's only original Gothic mansion was built in 1877 across from Centre Park by the Smith family (not related to the present owners) and was appropriated by the Wilhelm family, who embellished upon its finery during their reign from 1886 to 1936. Some of the unbelievably beautiful original artistry includes ornate plaster ceilings and elaborate crown moldings laden with cherubim wrapped in vines and designs; vibrant stained glass on most of the windows; a two-story curved bay addition in copper; quarter-sawn oak floors (only several boards per tree) and sideboards built into the formal dining room with a vaulted ceiling; eight fireplaces (five working) with faux grained or real marble mantels, including one seven feet high; and unusual designs of Mercer tile decorating the entire back of the exterior first floor.

The drama begins with a step into the foyer, finished in Bradbury and Bradbury wallpapers in the elaborate design of Cape May's finest Victorian mansions. To the left is a sitting room with beautiful Victorian antiques, above which hover some of the plaster angels in the moldings. To the right are an informal dining area and a living room with overstuffed couches on a Bukhara rug. Straight ahead is the magnificent dining room with an enormous sideboard built into a wall made from quarter-sawn oak under a barrel-vaulted ceiling.

Guests are greeted with a basket of fruit, and every room has a stocked refrigerator. The Green Room has a sitting area, separated from the bedroom by a wide archway above which is a transom of elaborate leaded and stained glass. A little sitting area in the bedroom rests within the copper bay addition, with three floor-to-ceiling windows. At the foot of the bed is a working fireplace, above which hangs a huge carved mirror. The grand and rare Old World bath has geometric tiles, the original clawfoot tub with a new shower, and an arched beveled window that allows light in from a hallway. Terry robes are provided so guests may step out onto the balcony accessible from the bath, which also rests over the copper addition.

The most magnificent room rests in the back of the mansion. The sitting room hosts a carved wood fireplace seven feet high inset with a mantel of red Austrian marble. A hallway is trimmed with more carved wood, with an archway decorated with wooden cherub faces supported by wooden columns. The bedroom has a white wood sleigh bed, teal plaster trim, and, most rare, a Mercer tiled fireplace and ceiling. The bath is again a beautiful Old World room with star-shaped tiles and a marble sink, all with Caswell and Massey amenities, made comfortable by a window seat with wooden shutters.

The stone Carriage House behind the mansion was built in 1890 for the drivers and horses, larger than many a house. The second floor reveals itself in several dormer windows, the rooftop interrupted with a Mediterranean tiled tower and chimney. The rooms here include a two-bedroom suite and a single room with stained glass dormer windows.

Andrea cooks a sumptuous morning breakfast, a finishing touch for a fantasy-filled stay. The inn is in the heart of Reading, within a short walk to restaurants and sights, as well as across the street from delightful Centre Park.

The Priory — A City Inn
614 Pressly Street
Pittsburgh, Pennsylvania 15212
412-231-3338

Proprietors: Maryann and Edward Graf
Innkeeper: Tracy Callison
Accommodations: 24 rooms, including 2 suites, all with private bath
Rates: $82–$135
Included: Continental breakfast
Minimum stay: None
Added: $7 each additional person; $10 for a rollaway; 11% tax
Payment: Major credit cards
Children: Welcome
Pets: Not allowed
Smoking: Allowed
Open: All year

Across the Ninth Street Bridge, which spans the Allegheny River, a small hotel of supreme elegance and refinement overlooks the city of Pittsburgh from its half-mile distance. The Priory was built in 1888, a refuge for Benedictine priests and brothers serving the adjacent St. Mary's Parish, built in 1852 by Swiss and German Catholics and one of the few examples of

Italian classical architecture in Pittsburgh. The luxurious Austrian stained glass windows were added to St. Mary's in 1912 once the property was safe from anti-Catholic sentiments of a group called the "Know-Nothings."

Less than a century later, in 1981, the life of the church was again threatened, this time for secular reasons as the Transportation Department planned to traverse through the site with a new part of the interstate. At the last minute, however, the highway was moved back 40 yards and the Priory was rescued and put up for sale. The Graf family bought the church and Priory and completed a restoration effort of the latter in 1986. What stands today is a monumental brick structure, with three stories of attenuated arched windows and an air of otherworldly beauty.

Those interested in architecture will be fascinated with the elevation drawings on the walls of the Priory detailing its construction. The building centers on a stunning octagonal staircase, around which radiate common rooms and several guest rooms on the first floor and the more deluxe guest rooms of the second and third floors. Like the church's nave, a long wing stretches back from the center section, housing a beautiful marbled elevator and the large kitchen, breakfast rooms, and additional guest rooms on the upper floors. Mrs. Graf procured the sophisticated artwork and plates of Pittsburgh landmarks which adorn the walls of this European-style hotel.

The guest rooms are each furnished differently but share the consistent themes of high, narrow windows trimmed simply in lace, original deep oak moldings, and stunning Victorian antiques and furnishings. Each room has a television and private phone and a brand-new bath with personalized amenities and impressively fluffy towels. While the rooms in the front of the Priory are quite grand, with tapestried Victorian chairs, precious writing desks, original faux marble mantels inset with fire screens, and antique brass, wood, or iron beds, the cozy rooms are just as nicely appointed on a small scale, adding to the breadth of the accommodations. Victorian lamps rest on wooden end tables; and all is most quiet.

During the evening, guests are welcome to relax and enjoy a drink in one of two Victorian parlors, each with a working fireplace. The Continental breakfast is served in two informal breakfast rooms where guests enjoy muffins and coffeecake baked in the Priory's beautiful original kitchen, which exudes baking smells as a wake-up call. There is even a wrought-iron courtyard at the back of the Priory where guests may gather in warmer months.

Most impressive is the warmth of the staff, who are friendly and helpful in this rather formal environment, happy to advise about dining, museums, and local events.

Virginia

Linden Row
First and Franklin Streets
Richmond, Virginia 23219
804-783-7000
800-348-7424

Proprietors: Winthrop Hotels and Resorts
General Manager: Jeannette Weir
Accommodations: 73 rooms, including 7 parlor suites, all
   with private bath
Rates: $99–$119
Included: Continental breakfast; wine and cheese reception
Minimum stay: None
Added: $10 each additional guest; 9.5% tax
Payment: Major credit cards
Children: Welcome
Pets: Not allowed
Smoking: Nonsmoking rooms avaliable
Open: All year

There are two reasons why a stay at Linden Row is unavoidable: no one can walk by the magnificent row of architecture on East Franklin Street, between First and Second, without peeking inside—and once inside, no one can resist the charm of its hostess, Jeannette Weir. In this strikingly proud southern town, nearly everyone but a native will feel like an outsider—except for French-born Miss Weir, and everyone on whom she smiles.

   The row of seven Greek Revival townhouses is the finest example of its kind in the nation. Thanks to the preservation efforts of noted local architect and oral historian Mary Wingfield Scott and the Historic Richmond Foundation, the buildings were saved from destruction and kept alive. Thanks to the 1988 restoration efforts of Winthrop Hotels and Resorts, visitors may stay overnight in lovely accommodations in the architectural marvel. And thanks to the legendary hospitality of Jeannette Weir, guests will extend their visits and return again and again. It's not an understatement. Miss Weir has left a trail of admirers around the world, most recently in Washington, D.C., as the manager of the Embassy Row Hotel. Her staff is quite smitten, as guests can tell the moment they walk in the door and for a memorable while after they leave.

The antebellum address of Linden Row was Richmond's most exclusive. Built between 1847 and 1857 in the height of Georgian elegance as private homes, the rowhouses numbered ten altogether. Two of the rowhouses were razed in 1922, and the remaining eight were threatened in 1950 when Mary Wingfield Scott bought up the land. The 1988 restoration was greatly aided by the Historic Richmond Foundation, which painstakingly researched period details such as furniture, wall coverings, and carpeting.

Seven of the eight original townhouses belong to Linden Row, containing 38 guest rooms with seven extremely large parlor suites. Every room has a writing desk, a queen-size or two double beds, some interesting period antiques, remote televisions, and telephones. The baths are quite large, with elegant old tiling.

Behind the facade is a lovely brick courtyard with café tables, umbrellas, and manicured gardens—as well as three two-story brick buildings which served as the original kitchen and carriage houses to the antebellum townhouses. Along the brick paths and pretty gardens, the Garden Quarters have 35 smaller rooms decorated in French country with furniture commissioned for Linden Row, double beds covered with wedding ring quilts, and private phones and televisions.

Miss Weir greets guests each evening in a rather extensive wine and cheese party, with a fireside presentation of appetizers in the original parlor. Guests have only to walk several steps to the dining room, in an intimate boutique setting. Lunch and dinner are served daily, with latter entrées ranging from $9 $18 for coquilles St. Jacques, sea scallops encased in duchess potatoes, Chesapeake crabcakes, or steak au poivre served with French mustard and white wine. The ambience transforms from romance to a sunlit breakfast area in the morning, with a convivial, bottomless Continental breakfast consisting of hot oatmeal, cereals, and fresh muffins and fruit.

With its courteous, likable staff and exceptional hostess, Linden Row feels like a European boutique hotel. The service is that of an attentive full-service property with bed-and-breakfast friendliness.

The William Catlin House

2304 East Broad Street
Richmond, Virginia 23223
804-780-3746

Proprietors: Robert and Josephine Martin
Accommodations: 5 rooms, 3 with private bath, 4 with fireplace
Rates: $70–$90
Included: Virginia tax and room tax; full breakfast; gratuities
Minimum stay: None
Payment: Visa, MasterCard
Children: Welcome
Pets: Not allowed
Smoking: Allowed
Open: All year

Among the most significant of Richmond's many landmarks is the church where Patrick Henry requested liberty or death, St. John's atop the Historic Church Hill District. Weary patriots will find refuge right across the street at the William Catlin House. After two years of preparation, Robert and Josephine Martin left careers in newspaper photography and the police force to open a bed-and-breakfast. They took with them some pretty antiques, a strong work ethic, and great hopes for their property.

In 1990, the Martins bought this established bed-and-breakfast, changed its recognizable name from Catlin Abbott to the William Catlin House, after its contractor William Catlin, who erected the three-story brick house in 1845. The masonry was done by his servant William Mitchell, the father of the country's first black bank president and founder of the first black-owned bank—who was also a woman.

The house is nearly twice as deep as it is wide. After the Civil War, during which more than eight hundred Richmond homes were burned, an addition was built to house some of the recently homeless. The Martins live in the addition, which shares lovely porches with the original section of the house, overlooking the old Carriage House and gardens.

The traditional double parlor is decorated nicely in high Victorian and late Empire antiques collected by the Martins over the years, with a working fireplace. The two guest rooms on the second floor have working fireplaces and queen-size canopy beds, with traditional furniture, wing chairs, and lovely bedding. The unusual third-floor room is quite large, tucked under the eaves, with two very deep dormer windows and a quilt rack in an odd alcove—the only room without a fireplace. The English basement has two cozy rooms, each with a fireplace, good for families as they share one bath. The room features a separate front entrance as well as a back porch and garden and also has a full kitchen.

Guests enjoy a full breakfast in a rather formal setting around the reproduction Chippendale dining table, with hot meats, eggs, and pancakes, as well as fresh fruit and juice. The meal provides sustenance for a leisurely drive to see the plantations along the James River on Route 5 toward Williamsburg. Robert and Josephine are hard-working, sincere professionals, who love their change of life.

Classic City Hotels

District of Columbia

The Hay-Adams Hotel
One Lafayette Square
Washington, D.C. 20006
202-638-6600
800-424-5054

Proprietor: David H. Murdock
General Manager: William N. Trimble
Accommodations: 143 rooms, including 18 suites
Rates: Rooms, $150–$375; suites, from $475
Minimum stay: None
Added: $25 each additional guest; 11% tax; $1.50 room tax
Payment: Major credit cards
Children: Welcome
Pets: Not allowed
Smoking: Nonsmoking rooms available
Open: All year

Arguably Washington's most beautiful hotel, the Hay-Adams certainly has the city's best location, facing the White House and Lafayette Square. Although this grand old building looks as if it has held a position of prominence since it was built in 1928, its glory days have been recent, since June 1983 when David H. Murdock undertook a massive restoration and renovation of the formerly mediocre hotel. With the help of his wife, Gabriele, who did a magnificent job of interior design, Murdock opened the Hay-Adams to a vastly appreciative Washington audience in 1985.

The history of the hotel predates the building and rests on this landmark site. In 1885, world-renowned architect Henry Hobson Richardson designed adjoining homes on a lot across from the White House for John Hay and his longtime friend and Harvard classmate Henry Adams. Adams, the direct descendant of two presidents, and Hay, a millionaire who had been at one time the private secretary to President Lincoln, were great friends and certainly the hub of Washington's inner circle. Their houses were done in a classic, heavy Richardson Romanesque style and served as the gathering spot for the country's most important guests, including President Roosevelt, who would often stop by for lunch.

After the houses' heyday, they were purchased by Washington developer Harry Wardman in 1927 for $600,000. With an additional $900,000 investment, Wardman erected an eight-story 200-room hotel. Turkish architect Mirhan Mesrobian designed the building after the river elevation of the Farnese Palace in Rome. Faced in Indiana white limestone, the hotel featured intricate plaster moldings on nearly every ceiling and balconies accessible through French doors, and it made tribute to John Hay by copying the Tudor detailing and coffered paneling from the foyer of his home.

Like a quick-burning flame, the hotel fell into the lurches of the Great Depression, and after only four years of prosperity, the Hay-Adams was sold at public auction. The Manger Hotel Company owned the property for nearly forty years, operating it as a transient hotel, followed by several other owners, until David Murdock came along in 1983. The result of the Murdocks' work is a breathtakingly beautiful, fully restored interior introduced by a new porte-cochère supported by four polished columns approached by a circular drive. The rich walnut paneling of the lobby is adorned by gilded pilasters, above which are light-hued molded arches and an elaborately coffered ceiling with 16th-century motifs, from which hang several brass chandeliers. A 17th-century Medici tapestry adorns one wall at the entry, complemented by tasseled royal red velvet club chairs and varied precious antiquities.

Up a half flight of stairs, guests have breakfast and lunch in the sunny Henry Adams Room, or afternoon tea and dinner in the several sections of the John Hay Room. The latter is one of the most magnificent public rooms in this book, with heavy carved walnut paneling, brightened by a gilded and light plaster coffered ceiling. Archways are hung with heavy red patterned drapery tied back with tasseled cords, revealing lavish floral bouquets. While one area is done in casual couches and Martha Washington chairs, the other formal dining area has patterned tapestry chairs around tables covered in white linen, dressed with delft pottery holding flowers. Brass sconces decorate walls, echoed in large chandeliers hanging from ceiling medallions. Tea is a beautiful event here, a must on any Washington visit. Tea master Chow, a fixture at the Hay-Adams for years, presents an array of delicacies and teas in the height of etiquette.

All the guest rooms are unique, and nearly all, no matter what floor, have intricate plaster moldings and ceiling designs. Gabriele Murdock intended the rooms to have more the feeling of a lavish private residence than a hotel and decorated all individually. While window treatments are done in the same patterns as the bedding, they are all unique, in light florals or geometric patterns. The chairs, some wing, others bergères, are upholstered beautifully in silk prints or cotton chintz. The reproduction furnishings vary from room to room—some Queen Anne, some Chippendale—with an occasional antique chair or mirror. Some have structured canopy beds reached by wood steps. Rooms facing the White House have the best views in the city, some of which feature balconies through French doors, some carved mantels. Guests are greeted with bottled water and fruit, and are provided with rich terry robes.

The service is formal, discreet, and high quality, and the excellent concierge service rises to every challenge. The Eagle Grill Bar is a relatively new offering, downstairs from the lobby, a fabulous clubby setting of dark leather chairs and leaded glass under a carved wood ceiling. Nooks under arches are filled with bookshelves, and tables are candlelit.

The Henley Park Hotel

926 Massachusetts Avenue, N.W.
Washington, D.C. 20001
202-638-5200
800-222-8474

Proprietor: RB Associates
General Manager: Michael Rawson
Accommodations: 96 rooms, including 17 suites, all with private bath
Rates: Rooms, $145–$225; suites, from $325
Added: 11% tax; $1.50 room tax
Payment: Major credit cards
Children: Welcome
Pets: Not allowed
Smoking: Nonsmoking rooms available
Open: All year

The Henley Park is Washington's small European Hotel: understated, scaled down, with intimate public space that includes a romantic restaurant, Coeur de Lion. While 16th Street serves as the gallery for grand old Washington hotels, the Henley Park sits apart like a quiet foreigner at a party, in a rather wanting area near the Convention Center, brightened by the Morrison Clark across the street.

The Henley Park underwent restorations in 1982 that returned the original elements of its 1918 Tudor architecture, including some 119 gargoyles. A pretty patterned brick courtyard welcomes guests, a white awning stretched overhead forming a carport. While the eight-story brick and limestone building has a rather straightforward neo-Gothic exterior, the Tudor features greet a guest in the low-ceilinged, Mercer-tiled foyer.

The Wilkes Room, to the right of the foyer, is used as a common room and library. Guests lounge in leather wing chairs and tapestried sofas. Neutral drapes fall from crown moldings, covering floor-to-ceiling French windows.

Through an archway is ell-shaped Marley's, where the afternoon sun filters through thick leaded glass windows while guests take high tea of eight varieties, complemented by scones and clotted cream, finger sandwiches, sweets, ports, and sherries. Nighttime jazz and cocktails are enjoyed at the marble-top bar or in tapestried banquettes and chairs.

The Coeur de Lion is reputed to have one of Washington's more romantic dining rooms, named for Richard the Lionhearted, whose crest hangs above the threshold. The dining rooms are three separate spaces which begin in the Atrium, with exposed brick and a gathered beamed glass ceiling centered in a crystal chandelier, laced in greenery. French doors open to a bilevel dining area with stained glass windows and mirrored pillars, lavish crystal sconces on gray walls, a background to the strong mauve upholstered chairs. Chef Joseph Nguyen's French cuisine is peppered with Asian influences. Entrées range reasonably from $13.50 to $17.50. In addition to medallions of beef, escalope of veal, and duck, the seafood offerings are quite strong, including perhaps Florida red snapper, Norwegian or baby coho salmon, or a specialty of baby lump crabmeat cakes with smoked sweet peppers in lemon butter sauce.

On the upper floors, the guest rooms retain the feeling of apartments, with about 12 rooms per floor along a winding corridor. The suites have interesting configurations, and some have kitchens. Rooms are furnished very traditionally, with reproduction Queen Anne and Chippendale furniture, linens and window treatments in soft chintz, with a light color borrowed for the walls. Among the niceties are Lord and Mayfair amenities, nightly turndown, complimentary newspaper, and a stocked mini-bar. Service is quiet and helpful, like every aspect of the Henley Park.

Hotel Washington

15th Street and Pennsylvania Avenue
Washington. D.C. 20004
202-638-5900
800-424-9540

Proprietor: Gal-Tex Corporation
General Manager: Muneer Deen
Accommodations: 350 rooms, including 16 suites, all with private bath
Rates: $157–$197; $69 family plan offered seasonally and weekends
Minimum stay: None
Added: $18 each additional guest; 11% tax; $1.50 room tax
Payment: Major credit cards
Children: Welcome
Pets: Allowed
Smoking: 2 of 10 floors nonsmoking
Open: All year

Among the attractive aspects of the Hotel Washington are its location overlooking the White House, its relatively low rates, and the wonderful eleventh-story rooftop café, one of the best places from which to view this planned city.

The Hotel Washington was built in 1918 and has been owned for the last half century by the Gal-Tex Corporation. Maintaining its reputation as the oldest continually operating hotel in the city, the Washington remained open during its two-year $12 million renovation, completed in time for its seventieth anniversary celebration. One of the most costly projects was the restoration of the colored facade, one of the few example of Italian sgrafitto in North America. An Austrian artisan painstakingly restored the arabesque sgrafitto designs around the perimeter and between the upper windows, medallion portraits of Washington, Jefferson, and Lincoln, emblazoned in bold red and white on the brick and limestone exterior, at a cost of $300,000.

The two-story lobby features fabulous arched floor-to-ceiling windows which run the entire length of the building, decorated with white Roman shades and framed by dressy pink tasseled drapes. Lit by lavish chandeliers, the wooden molding is richly carved with friezes, columns, and capitals, its themes reproduced in the authentic Corner Bar of the lobby. The furnishings are upholstered in busy chintz and thick fabrics, separated by lots of plants and a set of nine marble urns from the late 19th century.

The Two Continents restaurant on the lobby floor is a lovely room of historic merit. Murals above the windows feature not-so-pithy quotes from George Washington that once served as incentive when the room was used as the Bache Stock Exchange: "Timely disbursements to prepare for danger frequently prevent much greater disturbances to repel it." The Empire chairs and geometric carpeting are formalized by the lush Corinthian columns supporting the ceiling.

Any Washington visitor ought to whisk up to the eleventh floor to have a bite or a drink on the Sky Terrace, which runs the length of the building. From period reproduction wicker chairs, guests can gaze at the lovely city panorama. Ceilings in the Sky Room are 15 feet high, under which enormous windows display views across the Potomac. Three wallpaper panels decorate the walls, by Jardin d'Armide, painted in the mid-19th century.

The guest rooms retain their original doorbells and are now decorated with 18th-century reproduction mahogany furnishings. Behind muslin curtains are old-fashioned lace panels, and cranberry carpeting and light wallcoverings contribute to the traditional feel. The pretty baths are appointed in Italian marble, and amenities include a sewing kit.

The Washington Hotel offers quite special packages for families.

The Jefferson

Sixteenth and M Streets, N.W.
Washington, D.C. 20036-3295
202-347-2200
800-368-5966

Proprietor: Lancaster Group Hotels
Managing Director: Elmer Coppoolse
Accommodations: 100 rooms, including 32 suites
Rates: Rooms, $245; suites, from $275; weekends $145, $180
Added: $25 each additional guest; 11% tax; $1.50 room tax
Payment: Major credit cards
Children: Allowed
Pets: Small pets allowed
Smoking: Nonsmoking rooms available
Open: All year

The Jefferson is most certainly a candidate for Gourmet Getaways, with the new Virginia cuisine of its extremely young award-winning chef Will Greenwood; and it is just as convincingly in the running for the Romantic Retreats chapter, with its plush, individually decorated rooms and intimate, nearly residential scale. However, its standing as one of Washington's great grand old hotels is so compelling that it must be represented as such in a town with this country's finest examples.

Four blocks from the White House, next to the National Geographic Society, the Jefferson is the height of Washington sophistication imbued with European grace. Originally built as a residence in 1923, the U-shaped beaux-arts building is eight stories of light stone. The subtle entrance is marked by wood doors under a single-story portico of intricately carved stone, topped by a Palladian fan window and wrought-iron detailing. The understated reception desk introduces the Atrium Court, one of the more beautiful reception halls in Washington. The long single-story barrel-vaulted corridor, the open part of the U shape, looks rather like a lost wing of the National Gallery. This main breezeway is flanked by two small atriums with fountains, where guests may have breakfast in a cool, shaded light. The elaborate plaster moldings and trim, from the Doric columns to the arched vaulting, are painted a soothing ecru, contrasting well with the light cream walls. Three formal Federal parlor sets divide the Atrium Court into separate areas, with brushed velvet sofas, attenuated wing chairs, linked by classic benches along the wall. The back of the Atrium Court is marked by a faux marble fireplace flanked by green faux marble Ionic columns under a portrait of Lafayette. The blond marble floors are covered with area Orientals.

The hallways on the guest floors are graced with beautiful lithographs and architectural drawings. Each of the 100 guest rooms is decorated in surprisingly different and boldly successful colors and patterns, all with unusual antiques, classic reproductions, and creative window and bed treatments. While Room 810 is decorated in soft champagne tones, Room 811 is done in a splashy but classic orange plaid, with a fitted crown canopy over the king-size bed. Some beds have upholstered headboards matching their linens, and others have rich wood sleigh beds. Some have French doors leading to bedrooms, others have working fireplaces or whirlpool baths. While televisions and VCRs are in each room, the suites are furnished with armoires housing mini-bars and compact disc players. Among the amenities are robes and hair dryers in the baths, which have charming flowered porcelain fixtures. Guests are greeted with a half bottle of red wine, and rooms are serviced with nightly turndown.

The Jefferson Lounge, to the right of the Atrium Court, is a clubby place, with leather chairs, red walls, and a fireplace under a nautical oil painting. The intimate, L-shaped restaurant is quite striking, with wood floors and tufted leather banquettes. The wall rounds slightly between the classic white crown moldings, textured in an interesting faux burl finish and graced with historic 18th-century prints, some of which hung in the White House and Blair House at one time.

Will Greenwood's menu changes daily. A choice of appetizers might include plantation corncake with smoked salmon and chive cream, wild rice and pheasant cakes with shiitake mushroom essence, or crab hush puppies with red pepper marmalade. Entrées, all below $20, could include venison escalops with lingonberry sauce and chestnut spoonbread or smoked pork chop roasted with cider honey glaze served with sweet potato hotcakes. The desserts are highly acclaimed, as is the extensive wine list.

Service is impeccable. Beyond the formality, the staff is genuinely friendly, personable, and solicitous.

The Mayflower — A Stouffer Hotel
1129 Connecticut Avenue, N.W.
Washington, D.C. 20036
202-347-3000
800-468-3571

Proprietor: Stouffer Hotels
General Manager: Bernard Awenenti
Accommodations: 680 rooms, including 68 suites
Rates:
    Weekdays: Rooms, $210; suites, $375
    Weekends: Rooms, $135; suites, $185
Included: Coffee and newspaper with wake-up call
Added: 11% tax; $1.50 room tax
Payment: Major credit cards
Children: Welcome
Pets: Small pets allowed
Smoking: 1 of 9 floors nonsmoking
Open: All year

Two weeks after its opening, the Mayflower hosted 6,000 guests at Calvin Coolidge's inaugural ball, on March 4, 1925. This event exemplifies the enormity of scale and richness of history that The Mayflower represents in Washington. This historic property completed its most recent, $10 million renovation in 1991, focusing on accommodations.

The troublesome construction of the hotel was delayed three years as a result of such unplanned obstacles as fossilized tree stumps, quicksand, and an underground stream. In 1925, at a cost of $12 million, the block-long neoclassic Mayflower opened with 1,057 guest rooms, furnished with 25,000 pieces of furniture that took three months to install. The ten-story brick building was designed by Warren and Wetmore of New York, who also designed Grand Central Station. A promenade one-tenth of a mile long served as a public hallway between blocks, with Oriental rugs, sculpture, and more gold leaf than any building in the country outside the Library of Congress. Upholstery and carpentry shops were instituted in the hotel, as well as a medical clinic for its one thousand employees.

The 1950s ushered the Mayflower into a self-conscious era during which it down-scaled its glories to appeal to the masses: the 24-karat detailing was covered by paint, wood paneling replaced the lobby's marble pillars, the chandeliers were stored, and the bronze doors were traded for stainless steel and glass.

A caring group of Washingtonians bought the underappreciated Mayflower in 1965 and invested $65 million in its resurrection. By 1985, the hotel was once again the grande dame it was born to be. The reproduction trim and crown moldings measured more than 50 miles. Bathrooms received 46,800 square feet of marble. The capitals and ceiling glimmered in gold once again. Most recently, Stouffer Hotels bought the Mayflower and completed its most recent refurbishments.

On Connecticut Avenue taking up the entire block between L and M streets in the center of businesses and shops, the Mayflower seems to urge guests not to leave. Its famous promenade holds an arcade of shops, as well as the formal Nicholas restaurant offering new American and Mid-Atlantic cuisine, the informal Café Promenade, the Town & Country Lounge for entertainment, and the Lobby Lounge. The two-story lobby has the grandeur of a ballroom, with marble flooring, plaster pillars topped by gilded capitals and crown molding, observed from a second-floor balcony that wraps around the room.

The guest rooms needed a face lift and are quite lovely today, with custom-made Henredon reproduction furnishings and upholstery and fabrics consistent with the Federal period. For such a large property, service is surprisingly available at every turn.

The Ritz-Carlton
2100 Massachusetts Avenue, N.W.
Washington, D.C. 20008
202-293-2100
800-241-3333

Proprietor: The Ritz-Carlton Hotel Company
General Manager: Marcos Bekhit
Accommodations: 230 rooms, including 23 suites
Rates: Rooms, $195–$380; suites, from $500
Added: $30 each additional guest; 11% tax; $1.50 room tax
Payment: Major credit cards
Children: Welcome
Pets: Not allowed
Smoking: Nonsmoking rooms available
Open: All year

Inspired by the legendary service and taste of the London Ritz Hotel, the Old World sophistication of the Ritz-Carlton Hotel Company first landed on America shores as recently as 1983. The Washington property was adopted, transformed from the grande dame Fairfax Hotel. Appropriately, the lovely Fairfax had been a sophisticated Washington fixture since it was built in 1927 and home to the famous Jockey Club restaurant for more than 20 years.

The two-story portico on the corner of 21st Street and Massachusetts Avenue rests on a brick drive, separated from traffic by a sculpted hedge. Six columns support the flat stone facade, part of a pentagon, and guests enter under a white awning, repeated in domed forms across the ground floor windows. Sister Parish was brought in from Great Britain to redecorate the entire property as an English country manor house, with dark wooded librarylike parlors, formal Federal hallways, and bright yellow and blue accommodations decorated in chintz. The extensive art collection begs a guest to meander through the hallways gazing at the 18th- and 19th-century oil paintings. In true Anglophile fashion, the themes are often nautical or equestrian—of the races, the hunt, or portraits of beloved hunting dogs poised at attention.

At any Ritz-Carlton, the reception desk is warm and understated, here leading to elevator banks and the Fairfax Bar at the back of the hotel. This wonderful lounge and gathering spot is the setting for afternoon high tea. Sweets and scones, salmon, and cucumber and tomato sandwiches are served in front of the wood-burning fireplaces. Decorative shadow boxes rest in the neighboring Potomac Room, plush with tapestried pillows, banquettes, and leather wing chairs.

Since it opened in 1961 on the eve of President Kennedy's inauguration, the familiar Jockey Club has been an insider's restaurant. It has the atmosphere of an English tap room, with dark paneled walls, sporting art, and white and red linens. Recently, the sophisticated menu was appended to accommodate children in the form of a coloring book featuring Carlton the lion, and offering suitable choices like peanut butter and marshmallow, spaghetti and meatballs, and banana splits.

The guest rooms are done in the height of British good taste, with bright chintz fabric covering club chairs, floor-to-ceiling drapes, and bedding, with two-poster custom-designed beds in dark wood matching end tables and writing desks. The walls are either a buttery yellow or robin's egg blue. Guests can expect such luxuries as 24-hour room service, nightly turndown, and terry robes. The top two floors denote the Ritz-Carlton Club, with special concierge service, use of the Federal parlor, and five complimentary food presentations, including Continental breakfast, a midday snack, tea, cocktails and hors d'oeuvres, and chocolate and cordials.

The staff is reliably professional and highly trained in Ritz-Carlton etiquette at this classic property.

The Sheraton Carlton
923 16th Street at K Street, N.W.
Washington, D.C. 20006
202-638-2626
800-325-3535

Proprietor: The Sheraton Corporation
General Manager: Michel J. Ducamp
Accommodations: 197 rooms, including 13 suites
Rates: Rooms, $210–$240; suites, $340–$875
Included: Complimentary shoeshine and newspaper
Added: $25 each additional guest; 11% tax; $1.50 room tax
Payment: Major credit cards
Children: Welcome, under 17 free
Pets: Check with manager
Smoking: 2 nonsmoking guest floors
Open: All year

The Sheraton Carlton is one of those classic buildings that has been a quiet, consistent fixture of elegance for years—like the

Junior League or the country club. Two blocks from the White House, the Carlton hotel was built in 1926 to resemble an Italian Renaissance palace, eight stone stories high. It has been the flagship property of the Sheraton Corporation since the 1950s. Just recently, between 1988 and 1990, $20 million was invested in the Sheraton Carlton's restoration and renovation.

Guests enter a semicircular drive to a gilded carport. Domed awnings cover the Palladian windows that span the first floor. Inside, the grand lobby is the hotel's treasure, the backdrop for afternoon tea, set to the music of a harpist. Classic and intimate parlor settings cluster over an expansive Oriental carpet. Most breathtaking is the open-beamed, dark wood ceiling, magnificently carved, lit softly by two crystal chandeliers. Four mullioned arched windows stretch to the ceiling, framed by heavy drapery.

Some grand architectural details are echoed in Allegro, the Carlton's restaurant around the corner from the lobby, featuring fine Italian food. The dark beamed ceilings are done in similar deep wood, with less ornate carving, complementing the mahogany bar. The original sconces and free-standing lamps are wonderful art deco specimens, their smoky glass shades in the shape of flower petals. The Palladian windows continue around the perimeter, made into mirrors on the back wall.

The guest rooms, benefiting from the recent renovation, are unusually elegant. In addition to stocked mini-bars, in-room safes, terry bathrobes on satin hangers, and televisions hidden in armoires, the rooms have been decorated with a caring hand in several different schemes. While the guest rooms are quite lovely, the suites are especially nice, decorated to fit the original period of the hotel in neutral and pale blue shades. All the baths have marble walls and floors, makeup mirrors, hair dryers, and television speakers.

Special guest touches make the Sheraton Carlton a kind place to stay. Exercise equipment will be delivered to a guest room if one doesn't wish to make the trudge to the Exercise Room. This city hotel is one of the few with a special welcoming service to its younger guests, who are free (under 17) when they stay with parents in existing bedding. In the Carlton Kids program, children are greeted with a variety of toys and games, including Nintendo, Trivial Pursuit, and board games. Nightly turndown consists of milk and cookies. Infants receive a basket of Pampers and a stuffed animal. The lower level of the hotel houses a salon, and also a celebrity of sorts: resident barber

Milton Pitts has been cutting hair for presidents, except Carter, since 1969.

The Willard Inter-Continental Hotel
1401 Pennsylvania Avenue, N.W.
Washington, D.C. 20004
202-628-9100
800-327-0200

Proprietor: Willard Associates and the Oliver Carr Company
General Manager: Graham K. L. Jeffrey and Inter-
  Continental Hotels
Accommodations: 365 rooms, including 65 suites
Rates:
  Weekdays: Rooms, $265–$355; suites, from $500
  Weekends and winter: $145–$165
Added: $25 each additional guest; 11% tax; $1.50 room tax
Payment: Major credit cards
Children: Welcome
Pets: Not allowed
Smoking: Nonsmoking rooms available
Open: All year

The Willard is basking in the relatively new limelight of its third incarnation. After sitting vacant and boarded up since 1968, the Willard received $74 million worth of attention and was reintroduced to Washington society in 1986 with great fanfare.

The site on which the glorified Willard now sits, catercorner from the White House, has served as a hostelry since 1816. In 1850, the land was bought by Henry Willard, who transformed the property into a 100-room hotel with the help of his brothers Edwin and Joseph. The Willard sat at the focal point of political activity. After receiving death threats, Abraham Lincoln lived secretly at the Willard from February 23 until his inauguration on March 4, 1861. The same year, Julia Ward Howe wrote the "Battle Hymn of the Republic" in her Willard guest room.

When the Willards decided to expand their accommodations, they hired famed architect Henry Janeway Hardenbergh, who had designed such treasures as the Waldorf-Astoria, the Plaza, and the Dakota apartments in New York. Completed in 1904, the Willard was one of the city's first skyscrapers, 12 stories of lavish French Second Empire beaux-arts architecture, reinforced in steel. The hotel prospered, though gradual decline came after the Second World War, when the Willard family sold the property for $5 million. Under new ownership, the hotel survived until 1968. Just several months before the hotel closed its doors, Martin Luther King wrote his "I Have a Dream" speech in his guest room.

In 1976, the Pennsylvania Avenue Development Corporation paid $8 million for the decrepit Willard, inviting bidders in 1978 to propose a fitting restoration. The project was begun in 1981 by the Oliver Carr Company, and in 1983 Inter-Continental Hotels was asked to oversee hotel operations. Since it had been abandoned for 15 years, nearly all of the interior work had to be reconstructed, and five of the original public spaces were painstakingly restored during three years of intensive and academic research, completed in 1986.

The restored public spaces included the lobby, the 189-foot Peacock Alley, the Willard dining room, the F Street Lobby, and the Crystal Room. Originally, the 7,000 square feet of flooring in the lobby and Peacock Alley had been hand-set with marbled mosaic tiles, three-quarters of an inch wide. These were reproduced after several trips to Italy to locate the original marble and hand-set once again. Altogether 35 different marbles were excavated from six countries. Layers of paint were scientifically matched to contemporary hues. Archival photos of the interior were used as documentation to replace millwork, marble flooring, chandeliers, plaster molding, as well as the grand lobby carpet. The intricate craft of scagiola, an elaborate faux marbling, was restored and matched in the columns of the lobby and the Willard dining room. Replicas of the 12 original chandeliers were handmade by the grandson of the original craftsman.

Eclectic antiques carefully decorate the Willard's lobby, but the true treasure lies overhead, in the 48 state seals adorning the coffered ceiling. Hawaii and Alaska have since been added. Other public spaces are the Round Robin Bar, a clubby, masculine space with green fabric walls lined with more than a dozen portraits of well-known guests, like Charles Dickens, Warren Harding, Walt Whitman, Nathaniel Hawthorne, John Philip Sousa, Calvin Coolidge, and Alice Roosevelt Longworth, daughter of Teddy, who created a stir by smoking publicly in the dining room. Above was, at one time, the ladies' lounge, now the Nest, where high tea is served daily.

Guest rooms hover above on 11 floors. Compared to the lavish public areas, the accommodations are subdued, in a muted brown scheme and a more attractive blue. The suites, done in Federal simplicity, are quite nice and worth an upgrade if possible. All rooms have a marble-top mini-bar, a bath with a telephone, hair dryer, and television speaker.

The Willard is a most exquisite dining room, overseen by executive chef Peter Schaffrath. For afternoon fare in a pretty setting, the hotel has the European-style Café Espresso. The service at the Willard is quiet and formal, and the location, of course, is ideal.

Maryland

Peabody Court
612 Cathedral Street
Baltimore, Maryland 21201
410-727-7107
800-732-5301

Proprietors: Grand Heritage Metropolitan
General Manger: Russell Conoglio
Accommodations: 104 rooms, including 20 suites
Rates: Rooms, $132–$152; suites, from $158
Added: $20 each additional guest; 12% tax
Payment: Major credit cards
Children: Welcome
Pets: Not allowed
Smoking: 1 of 12 floors nonsmoking
Open: All year

The clear choice in Baltimore for Old World elegance is the Peabody Court in the historic Mt. Vernon district. The neighborhood, marked by a 178-foot monument to George Washington, was established in 1827 and reigned as the city's most fashionable for years, evidenced today by the charming rows of restored townhouses, the world-renowned Peabody Conservatory of Music, and the Walters Art Gallery.

The hotel is Baltimore's second oldest, built in 1927–1929. It served as an apartment house for years before it was reintroduced as a grand hotel in 1985. The highly polished marble floors and elevators, the six-foot, 500-pound Baccarat crystal chandelier, and the valuable French antiques and hand-loomed carpets throughout the public spaces suggest the intimate luxury of a European boutique hotel. In addition, the Conservatory, with its top-floor, panoramic city view, offers some of Baltimore's finer food and has one of the loveliest dining rooms in this book.

The first four stories of this 13-story brick edifice are brightened with light stone and maroon awnings. The inset two-story entrance is supported by four grand pillars, and guests are welcomed to a small, darkly lit lobby, plush with antiques, art-work, and tapestries. Two marbled elevators whisk guests to rooms or to the Conservatory, or guests might glide up a curved set of marble stairs to the clubby Bistro, with green marble walls, darkly stained wood paneling and exposed floors, elabo-rate crown molding, and forest green leather tooled chairs.

The guest rooms are decorated with European and Empire reproduction furnishings in strong masculine tones of modest, neutral colors and patterns. Structured drapes fall from the ceiling, matching the bedskirt pattern. Remote cable televi-sions are hidden in dark wood armoires, and all rooms have stocked mini-bars. Though the suites have separate parlors, even the standard guest rooms have plush sitting areas. Im-ported lamps on marble-top bedstands were hand-painted to complement the room's hues. All guest rooms are blessed with great bathrooms, marble floors and walls, towel warmers, hair dryers, and separate vanities with makeup mirrors.

Thirteen stories above the city, the Conservatory is a glass-enclosed atrium that has the feeling of a Victorian greenhouse. Swirling low nap Victorian carpeting muffles one's steps past green faux marble pillars, lit by winged brass gasoliers. Black wrought-iron supports curve gracefully along the ceiling like an ivy-filled trellis, echoing the lines of the live plants lining the sills and filling corners. Sweeping drapes are ingeniously gath-ered up the curving glass depending on the time of day, filling the room with light or enclosing it in the warmth of evening. Heavy velvet and tasseled drapes soften the passageways. The food is elegant French, with dinner entrées from $26 to $30. A $32 prix fixe menu is available weekdays.

When the service is not invisibly discreet, it is friendly and softspoken. Guests at the Peabody Court have complimentary passes to the Downtown Athletic Club.

New York

The Algonquin
59 West 44th Street
New York, New York 10036
212-840-6800
800-548-0345

Proprietors: Caesar Park Hotel America, Inc., Aoki
    Corporation
General Manager: Bodo Lemke

Accommodations: 165 rooms, including 23 suites
Rates: Rooms, $170–$180; suites, $300; lower rates on weekends
Included: Weekend parking; welcome drink
Added: $25 each additional guest; 19.25% tax
Payment: Major credit cards
Children: Welcome
Pets: Not allowed
Smoking: 1 nonsmoking floor
Open: All year

In August 1991 the Algonquin completed a several-year $20 million restoration, its most thorough effort since it was built in 1902. The history of this famed institution and the Round Table for which it is most famous did not commence until several years after the scalloped red brick and limestone building was open, when Frank Case, a former employee, bought the hotel in 1907. (It was actually during his years as an employee that Case suggested changing the hotel's name from Puritan to Algonquin to denote strength and pioneerism.)

Case extended his hospitality and credit to his favorite patrons, writers and actors including Douglas Fairbanks, Sr., and H. L. Mencken. The group grew, and Case accommodated them at a round table found originally in the Oak Room, providing celery and popovers as fodder to fuel the intellectual fires. By the mid-1920s, the Round Tablers comprised a group of about 30 literati, including such nobles as Dorothy Parker, George S. Kaufman, Edna Ferber, Ring Lardner, Robert Benchley, and Harold Ross, who went on to use the fruits of the Round Table discussions as editor of *The New Yorker*. Evidence of these halcyon days is found in Al Hirschfeld's drawings throughout the hotel and copies of *The New Yorker* supplied in every guest room.

The reverence displayed by Ben and Mary Bodne during their 30 years of ownership was respected by the new owners during the recent renovation, begun in 1987. The original oak woodwork of the Edwardian lobby, including the arched doorways, supporting beams, and Corinthian capitals, has been restored to its former luster, as have the plaster dentil moldings, the painted glass sconces, and even the furnishings. Today the lobby is a favorite place for afternoon tea, cocktails, and entertainment. The Rose Room, the feminine alternative for afternoon and evening dining, features rose-colored damask walls and banquettes, all under an Austrian crystal chandelier. Last, the Oak Room, with its clubby masculine feel, traditional lamp sconces, and dark paneled walls, is the bastion of New York City cabaret life, matched only at the Carlyle.

The 12 floors of rooms are intimately configured, decorated with original art depicting old New York, Round Tablers, and Algonquin legends. Because of the hotel's landmark status, it was allowed to retain the original open staircase that ascends the center of the building, of white wrought iron and marble. Accommodations are fresh and immaculate. While the standard rooms are quite small, and the smaller rooms cramped, the suites are a nice size and well worth the investment. Or try the standard center rooms with window seats below curved bay windows. Most of the Algonquin's original Edwardian furnishings have been either refinished or reproduced, set into schemes of peachy rose, mint green, or light blue, with solid colored walls, very high ceilings, and floral spreads matching structured drapes. The suites have striped paper in the bedrooms accenting the chintz. The baths are gleaming white, with prints of flowers, and offer Caswell and Massey amenities, a sewing kit, and a hair dryer.

The Carlyle

Madison Avenue at 76th Street
New York, New York 10021
212-744-1600
800-227-5737
Fax: 212-717-4682

Proprietor: Carlyle Management Company
General Manager: Daniel Camp
Accommodations: 190 guest rooms and suites
Rates: Rooms, $275–$350; suites, $500–$1,200
Added: $25 each additional guest; 19.25% tax
Payment: Major credit cards
Children: Welcome
Pets: Allowed
Smoking: Allowed
Open: All year

The Carlyle has consistently offered the highest level of overnight accommodations longer than any other New York City hotel. It was completed in 1931 by architects Bien & Prince, a square building culminating in a tall blanched-brick 35-story tower with a recognizable gilded crown, recipient of the Mobil Five Star award for more than twenty consecutive years. As established as it is in history, the Carlyle has kept up nicely with its modern competitors, with a newly built and gorgeous state-of-the-art fitness center, as well as constant refurbishment which redecorates the rooms every three years.

The Carlyle is just a block from Central Park and Museum Mile and Madison Avenue's finest galleries and boutiques. Inside, it is a world unto itself. One of its most wonderful features is Bemelmans Bar, a gallery of murals painted by Austrian artist Ludwig Bemelmans, author and illustrator of the Madeline books that have charmed generations of children. When he and his wife, Madeline, lived in the Carlyle in 1946–47, Bemelmans painted the murals, derived from his whimsical characters and memories of the monkeys in the Central Park Zoo.

Bemelmans spills into the Gallery, an intimate space like a genie's bottle, a plush re-creation of the Turkish Topkapi Palace where guests have tea and champagne suppers. The Café Carlyle is the forum for the much-loved music of Bobby Short, who has charmed audiences here for 26 years, as well as other cabaret entertainers, a lavish environment for the mural of French artist Vertes. The Carlyle Restaurant is a wondrously beautiful setting for its highly rated food. Banquettes, oil paintings, and a centerpiece five-foot floral arrangement contribute to the salon feel. In addition to renowned dining, the Carlyle wine cellar has an astounding 25,000 bottles.

Guests enter at 76th Street and descend to a lobby rich with Gobelin tapestries, black and white marble flooring, whose magnificent Aubusson antique carpets are lifted for a lighter look in warmer months. Discreet elevator operators politely take guests to their floor. The rooms are all unique in configuration and design. Dorothy Draper was the hotel's original decorator, and today Mark Hampton and his team follow in her footsteps. Uniquely, some rooms have original exposed wood flooring, covered with needlepoint and Oriental carpets. Audubon prints, architectural Piranesi engravings, hunt pictures, and English country scenes decorate the walls. The rooms have quite different looks: some in traditional chintz, others in bold oranges or hunter greens. The beds might have wood or upholstered headboards, the dressers may have antique marble tops supporting Chinese porcelain lamps—all extremely classic in the vein of the Carlyle's residential neighbors. All rooms have televisions, VCRs, stereos, and CD players. The marble baths include phones, and all have whirlpool tubs. As well, every room is equipped with its own fax.

The Carlyle's new fitness center is intimate, private, and beautifully appointed, with Lalique crystal doors, an atrium skylight, serene Canadian maple walls, French limestone, and English green slate tiles. In addition to cardiovascular equipment, there are saunas and steam rooms as well as private massage.

Despite its stature as perhaps the city's most famous grand old hotel, the Carlyle is a welcoming, nonstuffy place. Service is impeccable but approachable, understated without being cold, elegant but not pretentious.

Westbury Hotel

69th Street at Madison Avenue
New York, New York 10021
212-535-2000
800-321-1569
Fax: 212-535-5058

Proprietor: Forte Hotels
General Manager: Stefan Simcovics
Accommodations: 180 rooms, including 51 suites
Rates: Rooms, $270–$290; suites, $2,000–$2,200
Added: $30 each additional guest; 19.25% tax
Payment: Major credit cards
Children: Welcome
Pets: Allowed
Smoking: 1 of 16 floors nonsmoking
Open: All year

The Westbury was built in the Gatsbyesque days of 1926 by the family of an American polo player. It has been a hotel since, run today in the same privileged fashion by the gentle hand of the Forte Group since 1978. It represents a bastion of quiet Old World elegance, housing the Polo Restaurant in a gallery of Ralph Lauren paisleys and equestrian prints amid intimate banquettes along street-front windows. With its Madison Avenue location, the Westbury, along with its relative, the Plaza Athénée, is in the heart of the country's finest and most exclusive boutiques.

The limestone entrance is on 69th Street between Fifth and Madison avenues, marked by an elaborate art nouveau portico and a modest set of highly polished brass revolving doors and trademark red awning valances on upper windows. As with most elite New York properties, the entrance is small, like a mansion's foyer, leading to a modest-sized double-height lobby overlooked by a second-floor balcony. A red-carpeted stairway leads to meeting space. The reception area is richly appointed with hanging tapestries, floral arrangements, and Oriental carpets on a marble floor. The elevators and the entrance to the Polo Lounge rest to the right of the diminutive reception desk.

The guest rooms rest above through 16 floors along a long, straight hall which parallels Madison Avenue. Though most rooms have a view of Madison Avenue, some have a quiet but blunt view of the back of another building. The rooms are extremely warm, having been recently redecorated in wonderful, busy schemes of boldly striped wallcovering and large-print chintz window treatments matching linens and throw pillow. The successful feeling is that of an English country home, with high ceilings and welcoming interior space. An upholstered bench rests at the end of the Chippendale Drexel reproduction headboard. Rooms or suites have several extremely comfortable club chairs or sofas with tasseled dust ruffles separated by tables with delft-type ginger jars or plants. Lovely prints and architectural drawings grace the walls, and Oriental scatter rugs enhance the low nap carpet. All rooms have televisions and VCRs and umbrellas for guest use; the suites have CD players. The pristine baths are clean, lined with marble and equipped with Caswell and Massey amenities; those in the smaller rooms are fit into cozy nooks, those in larger rooms have separate vanity areas.

The third-floor Fitness Center was a new addition in 1991, with views of Madison Avenue and ample cardiovascular equipment in a gray-carpeted room, with separate sauna and steam facilities.

The staff is letter-perfect at this long-standing property, gracious and softspoken.

The Mayfair Hotel
610 Park Avenue at 65th Street
New York, New York 10021
212-288-0800
800-223-0542
Fax: 212-737-0538

Managing Director: Dario Mariotto
Accommodations: 201 rooms, including 105 suites
Rates: Rooms, $275–$410; suites, $440–$1,700
Added: $30 each additional guest; 19.25% tax
Payment: Major credit cards
Children: Welcome
Pets: Allowed
Smoking: Allowed
Open: All year

The Mayfair is one of the few city hotels with working wood-burning fireplaces, with 28 throughout the hotel, mostly in suites. It has been the home of Le Cirque restaurant since 1974, a culinary treasure. Other unique touches include the Mayfair's

Pillow Bank, offering guests twelve kinds of pillows in addition to the four down pillows in each room—neck rolls, water pillows, facial pillows, reading wedges, and so on; free local telephone calls; complimentary chicken soup to guests with colds; and a putting green in the new fitness center. Aside from these unusual offerings, the Mayfair is a picture of a traditional, classic hotel, a fine representative of its tony Park Avenue locale.

The Mayfair House opened in 1925 and evolved into a residential hotel over the years, until 1978, when Regent International Hotels assumed management. A $30 million renovation was completed in 1990, at which time the public and guest rooms were redecorated, and the stunning elevators were entirely restored—though still hand-operated by attendants.

Guests enter from 65th Street between Park and Madison avenues. The reception area is thoroughly elegant with a hint of Tudor influences, arched thresholds, Palladian windows, and mirrors under painted coffered wood ceilings. The Lobby Lounge is one of the better-known aspects of the Mayfair. It was a convivial gathering spot when the hotel opened, and this tradition continues today. Guests stroll the exterior or descend several steps to the sunken inner area with tufted couches, sitting areas, floral arrangements, in lemony, sunny colors, lifted by a series of arches and colonnades.

The rooms have very traditional decor in ecrus and pastels, quite plain, with reproduction Queen Anne furnishings, and some interesting prints on the walls. While the decor is not particularly inspired, the rooms are generously sized and bright, with VCRs and televisions. The baths are very pretty, with Neutrogena, Crabtree and Evelyn, and Vitabath amenities; among the usual features of robes, dryers, and phones are linen hand towels and fresh flowers. Umbrellas are placed in every room for guest use.

The two rooms of the fitness center have bright views of Park Avenue, cardiovascular equipment, and even a professionally designed putting green. Service at the Mayfair is friendly and eager, under the watchful gaze of active director Dario Mariotti. The staff is happy and helpful and easily approachable.

The Pierre
Fifth Avenue at 61st Street
New York, New York 10021
212-838-8000
800-332-3442

Proprietor: Four Seasons Hotels Limited
General Manager: Herbert Pliessnig
Accommodations: 205 rooms, including 46 suites
Rates: Rooms, $310–$420; boudoir, $575; suites, $575–$900
Added: 19.25% tax
Payment: Major credit cards
Children: Welcome
Pets: Small pets allowed
Smoking: 10 nonsmoking floors
Open: All year

In April 1992, the Pierre completed a two-year renovation effort, resulting in the beautification of all its guest rooms and public spaces. The result is simply lovely, not an embellishment of an earlier Pierre, but an affirmation of how we have always thought of it—as one of New York's few and finest grandes dames, located on the southeast corner of Central Park.

Charles Pierre, raised by a European hotelier, was invited into the fashionable set when he arrived in New York in 1904. After several years, he was able to open his own restaurant. By the 1920s, Pierre's Park Avenue was one of Manhattan's chic eateries. Through a venture with Wall Street magnates like Otto Kahn, E. F. Hutton, and Walter Chrysler, Pierre embarked on a dream of a grand hotel on Fifth Avenue. For $15 million, architects Schultze and Wener built a palatial Georgian monolith, its forty stories topped in copper. The Pierre Hotel took a year to build and opened in October 1930; but after only two years, the Depression took hold of the hotel, Pierre filed for bankruptcy, and he tragically died in disappointment in 1934. The Four Seasons Hotels signed on to manage the Pierre in 1981, and the hotel has since reclaimed its upstanding place in New York's high society.

The perfection of the Pierre starts with its location. On 61st Street and Fifth Avenue, the Pierre has all the glamour and scenery of Central Park South without the tourism and horses. Guests enter from Fifth Avenue via a scenic and rather famous hallway, which playfully and elegantly toys with window shopping as art: well-known, upscale boutiques show off displays behind glass. Or guests can enter from the subtle 61st Street side, which brings them immediately to the reception area to the left, with a restful sitting area half a tier removed from the public space. The decor is formal and classic, with Edwardian antiques and glorious floral arrangements.

At ground level, to the immediate right of the 61st Street entrance is the Café Pierre, a quiet, rather undiscovered formal dining spot decorated in neoclassic grays and golds. Eventually, this route will lead to the magnificent Rotunda, a glorious feminine spot for afternoon tea and cocktails, a lounge underneath a French garden of murals. This is one of the Pierre's finest attributes, in an oval space of regal splendor. Intimate tables cluster on a brightly patterned carpet. Two wings of an ornately carved marble staircase ascend to a second floor, under the floor-to-ceiling murals with clouds painted overhead.

Upstairs, the guest rooms are wonderfully redone. In the blessed style of old hotels, the rooms at the Pierre often have surprising configurations and large closets. While the furnishings are nice but uninspired Chippendale or Queen Anne reproductions, the fabrics are lovely. In several schemes, the rooms are redecorated with bold colors and an unusual marriage of patterns. One room might be octagonal, with drapery and bedding in an oversized chintz on a bright yellow background, with a plaid bedskirt. Another room might have twin two-poster beds with fabulous blue toile spreads and drapery. Such unpredictability is refreshing in a large, traditional Old World hotel. The baths are glorious, some with wonderful wide old-fashioned sinks, others with plain pedestal sinks, all with terry towels and robes as well as linen towels. The walls and floors are black and white marble, and all have hair dryers, phones, and interesting amenities like Q-Tips and cotton balls in porcelain jars.

The staff seem extremely pleased in their updated classic environment. While professional and helpful, the Pierre staff don't go overboard with solicitousness—quite confident with their Old World stature.

Radisson Empire Hotel
44 West 63rd Street
New York, New York 10023
212-265-7400
800-333-3333
Fax: 212-315-0349

Proprietor: Radisson Hotel International
General Manager: Christopher Gardner
Accommodations: 375 rooms and suites
Rates: Rooms, $120–$180; suites, $210
Included: Continental breakfast in suites
Added: 19.25% tax
Payment: Major credit cards
Children: Welcome

Pets: Not allowed
Smoking: Nonsmoking floor
Open: All year

The Empire is a fabulous value in a city of inflated hotel rates. Guests here sacrifice space as a result, but this brings them closer to the way native New Yorkers live—or so say the optimists. A stay at the Empire is highly recommended for value and location—it sits opposite Lincoln Center—as long as guests don't have a lot of luggage and as long as they confirm that they don't have the smallest line of Empire rooms.

Though the existing building was erected in 1923, the original Empire Hotel was built in the 19th century. The decor reflects its Old World origins, thanks to a two-year, $30 million renovation completed in 1990. This landmark building has a recognizable red neon sign high above the eleventh floor, its brightly lit art deco copper entrance on 63rd Street. The building sits on the oblique corner between Broadway and Columbus Avenue, its odd site making for intriguing room configurations.

Guests enter a low breezeway that leads to reception and quite a grand double-story lobby, overlooked by a second-floor balcony. The room derives from English Tudor influences, with somber dark wood chairs upholstered in royal red and heavy wrought-iron sconces matching a chandelier. A dark red Oriental rug rests on the marble floor, under a center table dressed with flowers. A lavish tapestry hangs from the wall of the staircase, carpeted in red. The creamy colors of the stone walls and plaster pediments lighten the room, quite a pleasant space.

The elevators whisk guests to the rooms above. Try to get a room overlooking one of the major streets, preferably Broadway, with its dramatic views. The Empire is configured like a misshapen *E*, and about half of the interior rooms look onto a courtyard and one another. The furnishings are traditional Chippendale reproductions, on a dark low nap rug, with yellow-hued walls and bright chintz comforters, drapes, and bedskirts. Rooms have VCRs and CD players. The best features are the baths, small but neat as a pin, with green or blue inset into snappy white ceramic tile. The fixtures are nice and old, and the generous amenities include cotton swabs, a shoe mitt, phones, hair dryers, and even a loofah sponge.

Three meals daily can be taken at the Empire Grill, with an upscale coffee shop atmosphere. Guests have access to the high-tech New York Sports Club in the neighboring building.

The staff are refreshingly kind and approachable.

The Waldorf Towers
100 East 50th Street
New York, New York 10022
212-872-4635
800-HILTONS
Fax: 212-872-4799

Executive Director: Peter O. Wirth
Accommodations: 191 units, including 106 one- to four-
  bedroom suites
Rates: Rooms, $350–$375; suites, $500–$4,000

The Waldorf-Astoria
50th Street and Park Avenue
New York, New York 10022
212-355-3000
800-HILTONS
Fax: 212-421-8103

General Manager: Per Hellmann
Accommodations: 1,410 rooms, including 150 suites
Rates: $250–$325; suites, $375–$800
Added: $25 each additional guest; 19.25% tax
Payment: Major credit cards
Children: Welcome
Pets: Check with manager
Smoking: Nonsmoking floors in main hotel, not in Towers
Open: All year

There are two distinct properties within the massive walls of
this New York landmark. The Waldorf-Astoria is an enormous
hotel occupying floors 1–27; and the Towers are the intimate,
luxury element, with a separate entrance and concierge, on
floors 28–42. Certainly the more luxurious property is the
Towers, offering perhaps the most elegant accommodations in
the city. Yet, if you can't afford to stay there, you most certainly
ought to try a stay at the Waldorf-Astoria, which has its own
charm.

There is an excitement about The Waldorf that encapsulates
being in New York: the large, expansive common areas bustling
with people, some of whom are probably famous; the grand old
art deco architecture that so well represents much of the city;
the feeling that something is going on that you're not a part of
(certainly likely with the Waldorf's 25 meeting rooms); and that
vague, exciting feeling of being lost, which often accompanies a
visit to New York.

The Waldorf-Astoria and the Towers opened in 1931. Conrad Hilton acquired the management rights to the legendary hotel in 1947, and then the Hilton Corporation bought the hotel in 1977. An incredible $180 million renovation was completed in the late 1980s, which revived the mosaics, the bronze doors and elevators, the guest rooms, and all public spaces to their current awe-inspiring splendor.

Staying at the Waldorf Towers is like visiting a palace and staying in the king's quarters—in fact, it's likely that a king from some country or another will be a fellow guest. Guests have access to the public spaces and restaurants of the Waldorf-Astoria and can retreat to their privileged sanctuary where every possible wish is anticipated. Guests enter through the private side of the hotel, on 50th Street, to an impeccably restored lobby, with an intimate sitting area. They are escorted to their rooms on the original bronze and burlwood elevators, which have been brought up to futuristic standards. Every room is different and individually decorated in impeccable, classic taste. Every detail is flawless, from the antiques, to the beautiful and precious fabrics and linens, to the amenity-filled baths, with marble floor, linens and plush terry towels, and fresh flowers.

While the Towers are hushed and discreet, the Waldorf-Astoria is busy and grand-scale—though the magnitude should not imply lackluster service. The Waldorf-Astoria staff is savvy and professional, an attentive army matching guests on a one-to-one basis. In an ongoing refurbishment plan, 300 rooms are redecorated each year at the Waldorf, so be sure to ask for as new a room as possible. These will be assuredly nice, with lots of chintz, some pretty pieces like marble-top dressers, and quite nice baths: either gracefully Old World, similar to those in the Towers, with brown and black parquet in a large square room with arched molding and wide, old sinks and fixtures; or new and marbleized.

A wonderful new feature of the Waldorf-Astoria is the Plus-One Fitness Center, which opened in the spring of 1991, complimentary to Tower guests, available to regular guests for $15 (much less than the usual $25 for outside club use at city hotels). With terrific views looking north on Park Avenue, the club has an airy feel, appointed in beautiful light sycamore. Several staffers are available at once for fitness evaluations and personal training. Cardiovascular equipment is quite extensive, and treadmills and bikes are equipped with headphones and televisions. Five types of massage are available by appointment.

The lavish public spaces include all-day dining at Peacock Alley, with floral, feminine decor; clubby, elegant fare at the Bull & Bear; Oscar's coffee shop; and Inagiku, the country's first outpost of Japan's best restaurant, for lunch and dinner. After-dinner drinks can be had in a safari setting at Harry's Bar and Restaurant or at Cocktail Terrace overlooking the Park Avenue art deco lobby—also a perfect setting for afternoon tea.

Pennsylvania

Hotel Atop the Bellevue
1415 Chancellor Court
Philadelphia, Pennsylvania 19102
215-893-1776
215-732-8518
800-221-0833

Proprietors: Cunard Hotels and Resorts
Managing Director: Chris Van Der Baars
General Manager: Ruedi Bertschinger
Accommodations: 173 rooms, including 28 deluxe and 50 junior suites
Rates: Rooms, $210–$250; suites, $275–$400; presidential suites, from $850
Included: Daily newspaper, shoeshine
Added: $20 each additional guest; 12% tax
Payment: Major credit cards
Children: Welcome
Pets: Not allowed
Smoking: Nonsmoking rooms available
Open: All year

The Bellevue rivals the finest property in any American city. This architectural landmark, just three blocks from City Hall, was reworked during three years for more than $100 million and opened to its current grandeur in March 1989.

The original Bellevue Hotel was owned by George Boldt in 1881 and sat across Walnut Street from its present locale. Boldt's reputation as an unsurpassed hotelier prompted the Astor family to request his presence at their New York hotel in 1898. Four years later, in 1902, Boldt returned to Philadelphia and built the Bellevue-Stratford with $8 million. The massive French Renaissance edifice opened in 1904, with unimaginable grandeur, immense curved stairways, lavish plaster crown moldings, and lighting fixtures designed by Thomas Alva Edison. Each of the 529 guest rooms was heated with its own fireplace. A rose garden was planted on the rooftop, transformed by flooding into a skating rink in winter.

While heeling faithfully to the original grande dame, the recent renovation effort proved quite interesting, especially in the hotel's configuration: the first 11 floors contain independent offices and luxury shops including Polo/Ralph Lauren, Gucci, Dunhill of London, Pierre Deux, and Tiffany. The guest rooms hover above, on floors 12–17, surrounding a seven-story indoor atrium and the informal Conservatory Restaurant.

In 1986, the interior design firm of Tom Lee, Ltd., headed by Sarah Tomerlin Lee, was hired to mastermind the decor. Since little remained of the original hotel but the Edison fixtures,

Mrs. Lee created an imaginary period landscape. The decor of the nineteenth floor and reception areas is described as late Victorian, verging on Edwardian with Belle Époque playfulness. The guest rooms are done in American Empire. The side street entrance and lobby were inspired by the London Ritz.

The Conservatory atrium is an incredibly serene space, overlooked by half the guest rooms. The 3,600-square-foot piazza, in creamy white tones, feels warm in winter and cool in summer. The light wicker furniture, lush plantings, mummified twenty-foot palm trees, green and white tiled floor, fountains, and glowing lanterns all rest under a 75-foot mural of clouds, supported by two pairs of columns.

The elevation of the Bellevue reveals two domes atop the building—the Barrymore Lounge and Founders Restaurant, with a small library tucked between. The Barrymore Lounge, introduced by a portrait of the eponymous actress, is the setting for afternoon high tea, evening cocktails, and hors d'oeuvres. The room looks like an inverted Wedgwood teacup, with seven shades of pale blue offset by white plaster molding, culminating in a ceiling mural 17 feet high, painted with coral, tassels, and swags on a background of stars—the theme echoed in the upholstery and the carpet.

Across the hall, Founders is the mirror image in masculine decor. The dining areas look more like parlor sets, observed by four cast-iron statues of influential Philadelphians from each corner of the room. American regional and Continental cuisine is served to the music of a trio, a preamble to Friday and Saturday night dancing. The Philadelphia Library Lounge rests between, where guests enjoy a fireside drink while browsing through a thousand books by or about Philadelphians.

The guest quarters are unusually large at the Bellevue, averaging 460 square feet, decorated with reproduction and antique American Empire furnishings and period wall coverings and borders. The highly sumptuous decor is done in a celery and rust theme or in several shades of blue. All have stocked minibars, rich cherry armoires with televisions, videocassette players, and stereos, executive desks, and three telephones. The marbled baths are extensively luxurious, with a separate vanity area, hair dryer, makeup mirror, bidet, scale, Cunard amenities, a telephone and television, terry robes, and slippers. Upon full turndown, a kind reminder of tomorrow's weather is propped next to chocolates.

It is rare for a city hotel to have a fitness center, and near to impossible to have one like the Bellevue's. In the connecting building, accessible by fly bridge or a ten-foot walk from the concierge desk, is the Philadelphia Sporting Club. Though it has an outside membership, Bellevue guests have unlimited use of this 95,000-square-foot facility, which fills several floors in the height of utilitarian, neoclassic elegance. Among its features are 125 Nautilus machines, a jogging track, a five-lane junior Olympic indoor pool, and racquetball, handball, squash, and basketball courts. In addition are Jacuzzis, saunas, and steam rooms, a sports medicine center with cardiovascular conditioning, massage therapy, and health bar and café.

For pampering after exercise, the luxurious Pierre and Carlo European Spa Salon is in the Bellevue Shops. Its experts are trained in complex hydrotherapy, application of mineralized body masks, facials including aromatherapy, body scrub, algae hand and foot treatments and reflexology, as well as thorough massage.

Service is to the Bellevue as beauty is to its setting: integral, quiet, classic, and elegant.

Westin William Penn
530 William Penn Place
Pittsburgh, Pennsylvania 15219
412-281-7100
800-228-3000

Proprietors: Servico, managed by Westin Hotels and Resorts
General Manager: Wayne Bodington
Accommodations: 595 rooms, including 47 suites
Rates: Weekends, $99–$115; weekdays, $150–$200; suites, from $275
Included: Continental breakfast, tea, valet parking on weekends
Minimum stay: None
Added: $20 each additional person; 11% tax
Payment: Major credit cards
Children: Welcome
Pets: Not allowed
Smoking: 1 of 9 floors nonsmoking
Open: All year

The Westin William Penn just celebrated its seventy-fifth anniversary. The Pittsburgh matriarch was built as a 1,000-room hotel for $6 million in 1916, a later work of the renowned architect Henry Clay Frick. Soaring a majestic 23 stories above the city's center, the E-shaped brick, terra cotta, and limestone building was most recently renovated in 1984 for $34 million. It lived through Pittsburgh prosperity and poverty, the Depression and Prohibition, hosted 12 U.S. presidents, and the recent restoration efforts have deemed the Westin William Penn a National Historic Landmark.

The hotel was shockingly modern when it was built: every one of the thousand overnight rooms had a private bath with hot and cold running water; the private telephones required the attention of 30 hotel operators; and with the addition of an electric clock in every room, the William Penn contained the largest collection of timepieces in the world. Thirty miles of carpet lined the walnut paneled and green marbled corridors, done in Italian Renaissance style. The smallest room sold for $2.50 a night, and the fifteenth floor was reserved for bachelors. When the Grant Street annex added 600 more rooms in 1929, the William Penn became the second largest in the world after the Chicago Conrad Hilton.

During its 1984 restoration, archives were consulted to find accurate period moldings, wall coverings, fixtures, and carpeting. The only original pieces were the brass doorknobs. Many of the grand common rooms recall the three-quarter-century history. Visitors are awed by the Fontainebleu ceiling of the Georgian lobby. The grand piano belonged to André Previn while he led the Pittsburgh Symphony Orchestra, bought in the mid-1980s for $29,000. While having tea in the Palm Court under the coffered medallion ceiling, guests look through a panorama of elaborately carved two-story arches to an outer court. The Urban Room was designed in 1927 by Ziegfeld Follies Theater set designer Joseph Urban, a great example of art deco style with walls of black Carrara glass beneath a gold Tree of Life ceiling mural. On the top two floors of the hotel, the Grand Ballroom shows off three crystal chandeliers more than one hundred years old, purchased from a Cannes casino, crafted from 7,000 Baccarat crystals. The Terrace Room, walled in rich walnut paneling, is decorated with a mural of George Washington at Fort Pitt.

The suites are decorated in two basic styles of Colonial Williamsburg and Italian neoclassic. Standard guest rooms have classic mahogany furnishings, two-poster beds, striped bedding that complements drapes, a desk and wing chair, all done in light or rosy hues. The marble baths are clean and modern. Managed by the ever-efficient Westin Hotels and Resorts, the hotel manifests no hint of the chaos that might accompany a 600-room property.

Virginia

Commonwealth Park Suites Hotel
Ninth and Bank Streets, Box 455
Richmond, Virginia 23203
804-343-7300
800-343-7302

Proprietors: Jonathan Ruben and Marvin Bush
General Manager: Wendy Swain
Accommodations: 59 rooms, including 56 suites
Rates: $150–$250
Added: $15 each additional guest; 9.5% tax
Payment: Major credit cards
Children: Welcome
Pets: Not allowed
Smoking: Nonsmoking rooms available
Open: All year

Two qualities of the Commonwealth Park Suites beckon the traveler: its location, at the foot of dogwood-flecked Capitol Square, designed by Thomas Jefferson after the Maison Carrée in Nîmes, France; and the highly regarded Assembly restaurant, with a romantic setting and much-appreciated cuisine.

Originally, this historic site was owned by Robert E. Lee's brother Charles. In 1845, he sold the land to the Ruegers family, who erected a hotel in their name that was eventually burned, with much of Richmond, at the hands of Union troops (although the Capitol, farther upwind, escaped without blemish). The present structure went up in 1912, a conservative limestone exterior onto which an eleventh floor was added in 1956. What was then the Raleigh became the Mark Raleigh, and finally, by 1983, the Commonwealth Park Suites came into its own after two years of renovations. All but the marble floors were gutted, and the exterior was restored. In early 1991, the hotel was bought by Jonathan Ruben and his partner Marvin Bush, son of the president.

At one time, the Raleigh Hotel offered 130 guest accommodations. Today, this same space is shared by 56 suites and 3 rooms, with only five or six suites per floor. The result is the privilege of having one's own apartment at one of Richmond's finest addresses, under a trademark wine-colored awning at the foot of the Capitol. The guest rooms are furnished in 18th-century mahogany reproductions, decorated in a rather predictable luxury-hotel style, with thick pile carpeting, blond walls, and rosy chintz spreads matching curtains. The suites have stocked mini-bars, and the elegant baths have terry robes, towel warmers, marble floors, heat lamps, bidets, and oversize tubs. The hotel has a very small exercise room and a whirlpool tub that may be reserved with prior notice. Given the high level of luxury elsewhere, the spare condition of the elevators is rather surprising.

Despite the lack of public space, the dining rooms are quite lovely. Maxine's is a wonderful garden of an interior, which looks through huge windows onto Capitol Square. Caned chairs and chintz cushions lighten the room, along with the sunny yellow walls and marbled floor. Downstairs dining is quite formal at the Assembly, a plush room limited to 48 patrons. The setting is sumptuous with red silk wallcoverings, and red upholstered booths and chairs. The food of chef Doug Brown has been raved about by local reviewers. Entrées, from $16 to $25, might include twin filets Felix, topped with artichoke bottoms filled with crabmeat and sauce béarnaise, or roasted rack of Wyoming lamb served with minted fresh fruit chutney, finished with a Grand Marnier soufflé.

Service is purposefully invisible at the Commonwealth Park Suites, which has the feeling of a Fifth Avenue apartment building in New York City.

The Jefferson Sheraton
Franklin and Adams Streets
Richmond, Virginia 23220
804-788-8000
800-424-8014

Proprietor: Grand Heritage Hotels
General Manager: Prem Devedas
Accommodations: 274 rooms, including 26 suites
Rates: Rooms, $150–$170; suites, $200–$825
Included: Morning newspaper, nightly turndown
Minimum stay: None
Added: 9.5% tax
Payment: Major credit cards
Children: Welcome
Pets: Not allowed
Smoking: Nonsmoking rooms available
Open: All year

The Jefferson Sheraton has a history as rich and grand as the Old South that it so well represents. The hotel was masterminded by Major Lewis Ginter, a mogul who made his fortune as a fabrics merchant and again as a tobacco tycoon in the late 19th century. Having traveled across the Atlantic thirty times and circumnavigated the globe on several occasions, Ginter wanted his hometown of Richmond to have a world-class hotel. His extensive knowledge of art and architecture prompted him to seek out the New York architectural firm of Carrere and Hastings in 1892. Having produced such marvels as the Henry Frick House and the New York Public Library, the architects designed a classic beaux-arts monolith, with Renaissance elements and classic Greek aspects of the Doric and Corinthian order, at times reminiscent of the Villa Medici and 18th-century French châteaux.

After three years and $2 million, the hotel opened on Halloween 1895 in a social extravaganza. Ginter named the property for the prototypical American Renaissance man, Thomas Jefferson. He went to great lengths to obtain a statue of the president from the University of Virginia that proudly greets guests today in the Palm Court. Six years later, half of the hotel was destroyed by fire. By 1907 and with another $1.5 million in improvements, the hotel reopened with some elaborate rococo additions. The Jefferson survived over the decades until 1980, when a gradual downslide in business forced it into closing.

The hotel remained vulnerable for three years until Richmond developer George Ross and investors bought the property and invested $34 million in its resurrection. Under the management of the Sheraton Corporation, the hotel opened to accolades in May 1986. The restoration process was exhaustive. Original art, fixtures, furnishings, and sconces were found in storage; layers of paint and plaster revealed mahogany paneling in the Flemish Room; the plaster moldings and carvings were cleaned; nine of the twelve original Tiffany stained glass windows of the domed ceiling of the Palm Court and Rotunda were restored and replaced; and the faux marbling of the columns and capitals in the Rotunda was restored.

Today, guests stroll through the vast common spaces of the Jefferson in awe. The two-story Palm Court has a magnificent stained glass domed ceiling 35 feet in diameter, under which are fan-shaped stained glass arches hovering above gilded capitals on columns supporting the airy ceiling. Jefferson stands in the middle, flanked by replicas of two reflecting pools containing bronze alligators, calmer descendants of live residents from the hotel's heyday. To the left, not expecting the grandeur which lies ahead, guests descend 36 steps of the red-carpeted staircase, which is said to be the model for that in *Gone With the Wind*. At the bottom, visitors gape 70 feet heavenward to the Rotunda, which soars three stories above, lavishly painted and topped with a stained glass skylight. There are two stories of yellow faux marbling, ornate with gilded capitals, running the perimeter of the rectangular space. Wrought-iron railings make balconies out of the spaces, privatized by plantings, intimate sitting areas of Martha Washington chairs and tufted leather couches.

The guest rooms are generously sized and brightly decorated in rose and green hues, with creamy thick pile carpeting. The custom-made furniture is traditional of dark wood, with bright bed and window treatments, three telephones, including one in the bath. Televisions are hidden in cabinets, the mini-bars are stocked, and rooms with sitting areas have classic wing chairs and couches. A majority of the suites have fireplaces, whirlpool baths, and wet bars.

There are three restaurants at the Jefferson Sheraton: an ice cream parlor in the Terrace Café, informal dining at T.J.'s, and formal new Virginia cuisine in a series of seven rooms at Lemaire, named for the maitre d'hôtel during Jefferson's presidency. The rooms in Lemaire are extraordinarily beautiful, one of which is the Library, with a solid African mahogany fireplace and original tomes from Jefferson's own library.

Service is happy, friendly, replete with southern charm and pride. A tour of the hotel is highly recommended, especially if led by Mary Stuart Cruickshank, who has an encyclopedic knowledge of the hotel's rich history.

West Virginia

Blennerhassett Hotel
Fourth and Market Streets
Parkersburg, West Virginia 26101
304-422-3131
800-262-2536

Proprietor: Bill Isaacs
General Manager: Larry Demme
Accommodations: 104 rooms, including 3 suites
Rates: Rooms, $69; suites, $140–$160
Payment: Major credit cards
Children: Welcome
Pets: Not allowed

Smoking: Nonsmoking rooms available
Open: All year

The fortresslike five-story, turreted brick mansion is the grandest building in Parkersburg, named for Harman Blennerhassett, a folk hero during his West Virginia tenure in the early 19th century. The hotel was built over a period of six years for the influx of Ohio oil magnates to the area and opened in 1889. Almost a century later, the hotel was entirely renovated and expanded during a year's labor, reopening in 1986. The red brick of the lavish Richardson Romanesque facade was cleaned and brightened, the enormous dentil trim painted a gleaming white, and the arched windows refitted. An addition was tacked invisibly onto the back, adding twice as many guest accommodations.

Guests enter under a green awning to the reception area to the left and Harman's restaurant to the right. The latter is a convivial place, with paneled walls and high ceilings, dimly lit, with the feel of a 1920s tavern. Chef Richard Alabaugh has a loyal local following, his entrées reasonably priced from $10 to $20. His beef is shipped in from a Chicago purveyor, featured in specialty dishes like prime rib, served with Yorkshire pudding and fresh horseradish, or filet mignon Aida, served on a bordelaise sauce, topped with shrimp scampi and béarnaise sauce. The Grand Buffet Sunday Brunch is an exhaustive fare that attracts a good crowd.

A bit more than half the rooms rest in the newer part of the hotel, decorated in four historic color schemes of red, green, blue, and maroon trim and upholstery. The furniture is reproduction Chippendale, and English and American Aubudon prints hang on the walls. While the rooms are not luxurious, they are pleasant and comfortable, the beds covered with floral quilts, and desks, sitting chairs, and modern baths with the bonus of Krups coffee makers. The newer rooms are built around the perimeter of a three-story atrium/courtyard with a stone floor, which has a nice patio feel. Most preferable are the three turret rooms, built into the curved corner of the hotel.

The staff are outgoing and warm, and the common areas at the Blennerhassett are delightful, with antique furnishings and dark Victorian decor. Among the many activities surrounding Parkersburg are a visit to the Middleton Doll Company in Ohio and the Fenton Art Glass Company a short drive away. Most exciting is a visit to Blennerhassett Island and the reconstructed 1789 estate of the same name, reputed to be one of the finest mansions in its day.

Revivals and New City Hotels

District of Columbia

Four Seasons Hotel
2800 Pennsylvania Avenue, N.W.
Washington, D.C. 20007
202-342-0444
800-332-3442

Proprietor: Four Seasons Hotels
General Manager: Stan Bromley
Accommodations: 197 rooms, including 30 suites
Rates: Rooms, $250–$295; suites, from $675; weekend and
    corporate rates available
Included: Shoeshine
Minimum stay: None
Added: $30 each additional guest; 11% tax; $1.50 room tax
Payment: Major credit cards
Children: Welcome
Pets: Allowed
Smoking: 4 of 6 floors nonsmoking
Open: All year

Washington is teeming with elegantly refurbished grand old
hotels that blend in with the embassies and beaux-arts government buildings of this landmark city. For those who have come
to visit the White House—and not stay in it—or for business
travelers who appreciate contemporary comforts more than
crown moldings, there is the Four Seasons. This chunky brick
building nestles up to the edge of Georgetown, just over the
C&O Canal and Rock Creek Park. It features one of the finest
fitness facilities of any Washington hotel.
    The Four Seasons lobby is a majestic contemporary space,
paneled with light wood, carpeted with a thick pile extending

down the wide hall in neutral geometric patterns. Geometry is a large part of the Four Seasons, with spaces feeling wider than they are tall, making the rooms expansive and relaxing.

Facing the woodsy C&O Canal at the end of the main corridor are several restaurants, including the Four Seasons formal Aux Beaux Champs, which serves classic modern French cuisine. A waiter is responsible for only one table during the five-course meal. The Garden Terrace is a sunny, tiered area with myriad cozy sitting areas divided by lush plants, where guests enjoy light fare, cocktails, and afternoon high tea accompanied by piano music; the Plaza Café courtyard is yet another option. Downstairs, the Desiree nightclub is a twelve-year Washington veteran of nighttime entertaining, with banquettes and living room seating.

The Fitness Club is a recent addition to the Four Seasons, as of May 1990. It features state-of-the-art equipment as well as business facilities including a fax, computer station, and messenger service. The three levels have sweeping views of the canal and its foliage through large picture windows. Among the facilities are a heated skylit lap pool, whirlpool, sauna and steam baths, massage, aqua aerobics, personal trainers, and fitness evaluations. The exercise bikes and stairmasters are equipped with VCRs and stereo cassette recorders, for which the hotel has a full library. Guests receive complimentary laundry of workout attire and next-day dry cleaning. A nice alternative to treadmill workouts is the towpath to the C&O Canal, which has a jogging path.

Along very wide, carpeted hallways, the guest rooms are furnished in unsurprising luxury hotel themes with floral carpeting and bedding, with three possible views of Rock Creek, the M Street Canal, and the courtyard. Baths feature nice amenities like Q-Tips, a telephone, and a scale. Rooms are serviced twice daily and are given a full turndown. With children's packages, kids are loaned Nintendo games for their stay. The rates reflect not the unusual aspects of the guest rooms but the emphasis on the impeccable service.

Park Hyatt
24th and M Streets, N.W.
Washington, D.C. 20037
202-789-1234
800-922-7275

Proprietor: Hyatt Regency Corporation
General Manager: Paul Limbert

Accommodations: 224 rooms, including 130 suites
Rates: Rooms, $285–$310; suites, from $405; weekends, $159 and $199
Added: $30 each additional guest; 11% tax; $1.50 room tax
Payment: Major credit cards
Children: Welcome
Pets: Allowed
Smoking: Nonsmoking floors available
Open: All year

While 16th Street is the bastion of grand old Washington hotels, a cluster of grand new hotels has opened on the corner of 24th and M streets. Its finest offering is the Park Hyatt, which opened in 1986, designed by Skidmore, Owings, and Merrill. Its first two stories of stone and plentiful glass house the public spaces and Melrose restaurant. The ten higher stories for guest rooms rise above in stone, culminating in a green copper roof.

Guests enter a massive double-height lobby, with floors in two-toned herringbone marble, walls in softer beige and brown marble decorated with contemporary paintings from the Washington Color School and Oriental sculpture, and several precious works by Pablo Picasso and Frank Stella. Glimmering brass, rose and mauve-toned wool carpets, and furnishings upholstered in velvet, silk, and mohair create a grand contemporary space, enjoyed best during afternoon high tea where visitors listen to piano music and muse over French pastries, finger sandwiches, and individual pots of tea over candle warmers. A palm reader circulates Wednesdays and Thursdays—her most certain prediction being that evening caviar and champagne will be served in this setting several hours hence.

On the ground floor, in two stories of enclosed glass, is the Melrose restaurant. Chef Kenneth Juran prepares contemporary American cuisine, in a $34 prix fixe or and à la carte menu, which could include appetizer of angel hair pasta with fresh Maine lobster, mascarpone cheese, tomato, and herbs; or an entrée of Lake Superior whitefish with olive paste and wild mushroom risotto. Melrose overlooks the outdoor café, where guests may enjoy light fare to the sounds of the fountain and scents of surrounding flowers—as late as 3 A.M. on weekends.

The rooms at the Park Hyatt were designed larger than the average, with a majority of suites to which all guests will be upgraded on availability. Contemporarily furnished with light pecan wood, in a pasteled decor of rose, seafoam green, and peach walls and beige and peach carpeting, all rooms have at least a separate dressing area as well as a sitting area and full writing desks. The baths are quite luxurious, done in full marble, with brass and chrome fittings, a phone and television, hair dryer, terry robes, and Crabtree & Evelyn amenities with the bonus of toothbrushes and paste. In addition to evening turn-down, guests receive a morning newspaper. Among other amenities are complimentary shoeshine and foreign currency exchange.

Guests have full use of the Health Club, with Nautilus weights, sun roof pool and Jacuzzi, and massage, steam, and sauna rooms. As well as massages, manicures, and pedicures, the Rendez-Vous in the Park Salon is well recommended by First Lady Barbara Bush, who has her hair done here. In addition, the mezzanine level of the Park Hyatt has a full business center, the Write Choice.

Maryland

The Harbor Court Hotel
550 Light Street
Baltimore, Maryland 21202
410-234-0550
800-824-0076

Proprietors: David H. Murdock
General Manager: Werner R. Kunz
Accommodations: 203 rooms, including 25 suites
Rates: Rooms, $165–$210; suites, from $325
Added: $15 each additional guest; 12% tax
Payment: Major credit cards
Children: Welcome
Pets: Not allowed
Smoking: 1 of 8 floors nonsmoking
Open: All year

Since the summer of 1985, Baltimore's premier hotel has been the Harbor Court. It was built shortly after owner David Mur-dock completed the restoration of the gorgeous Hay-Adams Hotel in Washington, DC. His wife, Gabriele, fresh from her work designing the capital hotel, conceived of the Harbor Court's interior design. Not only is this hotel stunningly ap-pointed with unusual Old World antiques and beautiful ac-commodations, but the Harbor Court is magnificently located. The hotel shares its Inner Harbor waterfront location with the Baltimore Science Center, shop-filled Harborplace, and the National Aquarium, within a short walk of the business district and the Baltimore Convention Center.

The seven-story brick building has a dignified, postmodern exterior, its second floor an array of floor-to-ceiling arched windows, under which billowing flags mark the entrance. Cars drive into a courtyard, centered around a fountain. Through the entrance is the sweeping lobby, its marble floor inlaid with red and green geometric marble. The marble used extensively throughout the hotel was excavated from eleven countries. Circular tables and urns are adorned with floral arrangements, between overstuffed armchairs.

Two stories above, a brass chandelier hangs from a round mural of ivy, reached by a grand red-carpeted circular staircase. Follow this to the second-floor Explorer's Lounge and the Harbor Court's luxurious restaurant, Hampton's. The Explorer's Lounge decor was inspired by safari and African themes. Huge murals of an elephant and monkeys grace the walls. Architectural drawings and African sculpture catch one's eye. Above the crown molding is the brightly painted ceiling. Omnipresent plants suggest the feel of the tropics, though the overwhelming elegance rests in the classic furnishings.

Taking great advantage of the floor-to-ceiling arched windows trimmed in combed wood, Hampton's restaurant provides postcard views of the Inner Harbor. Columns, exposed ceiling beams, and crown molding are done in rich wood. Rust-colored damask silk wallcoverings complement the heavy drapes which frame the windows. Guests dine in modified wing chairs in a room that feels overwhelmingly English. Also the setting for a brunch that has been touted as Baltimore's best, Hampton's is renowned for its fine dinners. Entrées range expensively from $18 to $37, for exotica like Cajun seared and spiced blackened buffalo served with mushroom and shallot marmalade or grilled breast of pheasant with Michigan dried cherries and bourbon sauce. Upwards of two hundred wines are available from Hampton's extensive cellar.

Neighboring, for lighter fare and afternoon high tea, is an exceptionally cheerful garden room called Brighton's, which shares the arched window view of the Inner Harbor, with a crystal chandelier and sunny yellow walls adorned with floral prints.

Gabriele Murdock's design for the guest rooms is beautiful, reminiscent of an English country home with creative touches. Those rooms blessed with a harbor view have enchanting floor-to-ceiling windows in a keyhole shape, offering nonpareil views, masked by either chintz or gold drapes. The furnishings are classic Chippendale reproduction. Most beds are king-size, some with a beautiful Chinese pattern of yellow and beige with splashes of colors, others in a chintz on a gray backdrop, with structured canopy beds. Rooms have televisions in armoires and green marble-top mini-bars. The lovely baths are the height of luxury, with marble vanities, Neutrogena amenities including a sewing kit, telephones and televisions, and five-foot bathtubs. Fluffy robes are presented on satin hangers.

Configured like an open square, with guest rooms around the perimeter, the Harbor Court has a third-floor atrium garden atop the two-story lobby. Four floors up, on the seventh-floor rooftop, the Harbor Court Fitness Center has a heated indoor swimming pool and saunas, whirlpool, racquetball, and a tennis court. Boat cruises on the *Lady Baltimore* and the sailboat *Clipper City* leave from the dock in front of the hotel daily.

Service is outstanding at this rare, glamorous property. A stay at this sophisticated hotel is quite worth a trip in itself, simply to experience such full-service elegance.

New Jersey

Hilton at Short Hills

41 John F. Kennedy Parkway
Short Hills, New Jersey 07078
201-379-0100
800-HILTONS

Proprietors: Hilton Hotel Group
General Manager: Eric Long
Accommodations: 300 rooms, including 37 suites
Rates:
  Rooms: $185–$205; weekends, $125
  Suites: $215–$425
Included: Tower rooms have extra amenities; breakfast on
  weekends
Added: $20 each additional guest; 7% tax
Payment: All credit cards
Children: Welcome
Pets: Not allowed
Smoking: 3 of 7 floors nonsmoking
Open: All year

That the Hilton at Short Hills is New Jersey's first five-diamond property, awarded by AAA, merits some congratulations—and some awe, since it opened only in February 1988. Despite its interior beauty, this bastion of elegance seems rather misplaced, anchored in a concrete landscape of the Short Hills mall—like a swan in a parking lot.

Once through the squat red brick exterior, a guest experiences a sense of calm enveloping the lobby. The rich wood walls are hung with oil paintings. Overstuffed gray couches match classic chairs in similar shades. A geometric carpet lies underfoot on blond marble, and a brass chandelier hangs above. The ubiquitous floral arrangements are designed for the hotel by Emiko Marouka.

The acclaimed dining room, to the right of the lobby, offers highly reputed American cuisine under the direction of chef Joseph Verde. Offerings off the seasonal menu might include an appetizer of scallop seviche and smoked salmon with couscous and lime, followed by an entrée of lobster and sweetbreads parmentier with haricot vert and ginger cardamom sauce. The prix fixe menus are $48 and $58 for three or four courses, enjoyed in this classic setting of mahogany paneling, china-filled breakfronts, art deco chairs, with strains of the harp in the background.

Informal Terrace dining is in the garden area, with pine chairs and trelliswork, leading to banquettes and chairs in another section under a painted dome ceiling. Adjacent is the living room Retreat, featuring piano and harp music during high tea. Later, guests might venture to the rather groovy Club Short Hills, with a sunken dance floor.

The guest rooms are impressively decorated, with formal, masculine furnishings specially made for the hotel. The two-poster beds, side tables, writing desks, and chairs are designed in a lovely burlwood, with black accents. The thick pile carpets are in jade or rose, accenting chintz colors in the drapery. The baths have marble-top sinks, extensive amenities including mouthwash, a hair dryer, a green marble vanity area, as well as cachepots with cotton balls, and two terry robes. French doors divide the two rooms in the suites. The 70 rooms on the top two floors of the Towers have a concierge and a private lounge and receive complimentary Continental breakfast, afternoon tea, and evening cocktails with hors d'oeuvres. These rooms also have scales and pants pressers.

In a sublime setting under a vaulted ceiling, the ground-floor Spa has a three-lane 50-foot lap pool, with a Jacuzzi at its feet, Keiser weight machines, rowing machines, stairmasters, wind racers, aerobics classes, and a full-time trainer. Its European salon offers herbal wraps and mud treatments, facials, hair care, and beauty treatments, as well as Swedish and shiatsu massage.

A business center provides copying, a fax machine, secretaries, transcription, word processing, and personal computers, as well as a personal shopper.

New York

Essex House
160 Central Park South
New York, New York 10019
212-247-0300
800-645-5687

Proprietor: Nikko Hotels International
General Manager: Wolf Walther, Vice President
Accommodations: 591 rooms, including 61 suites
Rates:
  Rooms: $265–$315; weekends, $185–$235
  Suites: $285–$850
Added: $25 each additional guest; 19.25% tax
Payment: Major credit cards
Children: Welcome, under 18 free
Pets: Not allowed
Smoking: Nonsmoking floors
Open: All year

Originally built in 1931 as the city's largest and tallest hotel, Sayville Towers, as the Essex House was called, opened with 1,286 rooms and such luxurious, modern amenities as a radio and private bath in every room. Over the years, the Essex sadly declined. Nikko Hotels bought the dowager in 1989 and undertook a $75 million renovation, completed in September 1991.

The Essex House was redesigned to evoke a nostalgia for the New York City of the roaring thirties: the days of black and white balls, big bands, glamorous movie stars, and art deco extravaganza. Even the location conjures up images of old New York, as the shoppers and hansom cabs whisk by on Central Park South.

There is a great deal of gilt at the Essex House: on the exterior and inside. Guests enter to a grand-scale lobby of brown and white parquet floors and coffered ceilings supported by heavy black pillars. To the left is Café Botanica, serving three meals and light California fare. The wonderful room has a terrace area facing Central Park South through floor-to-ceiling Palladian windows, with wicker and rattan chairs, chintz cushions, and verdigris sconces. Ben Kay offers fabulous traditional Japanese breakfasts. Journeys is the Old World bar with the feel of an English club.

The high point of the public spaces is Les Célébrités, showcase for the French cuisine (with Japanese influences) of chef Christian Delouvrier and a gallery for the artwork of well-known celebrities like Pierce Brosnan, James Dean, Gene Hackman, Elke Sommer, and Billy Dee Williams, among others. The paintings are proudly displayed on the walls, viewed from tapestried banquettes and comfortable chairs in a plush, patterned environment.

Guests proceed up to rooms on 41 floors via original etched brass elevator doors, which open to reveal a painted foyer on each floor. The decor is as traditional as the hotel is art deco, though the colors are bright and fresh, if predictable. Fine features are extremely large closets, pristine gray marble baths with large soaking tubs, phones, scales, eyelet curtains and tassel tiebacks. Chintz and stripes and bold carpets brighten the rooms, against a backdrop of traditional Chippendale furniture.

Nikko thought of its guests at work and at play. They designed a full business center, including computers and even a Japanese word processor. For play, the private health club and spa features a good amount of cardiovascular equipment and two types of massage overseen by a full staff.

The staff are extremely enthusiastic about their new place in New York and solicitous and respectful of the Japanese roots of the Nikko influence.

The Garden City Hotel
Garden City
Long Island, New York 11530
516-747-3000
800-547-0400 out of state
Fax: 516-747-1414

General Manager: Vinod Malhotra
Accommodations: 260 rooms, including 13 suites, 3 with fireplace
Rates: Rooms, $220; suites, from $400; weekends, $169 (with breakfast)
Added: $20 each additional guest; 13.5% tax
Payment: Major credit cards
Children: Welcome
Pets: Allowed

Smoking: Nonsmoking rooms available
Open: All year

About 35 minutes east of Manhattan, in its own corporate community, the Garden City Hotel reopened in May 1983 as Long Island's finest full-service hotel. It stands on the site of the former and classic Garden City Hotel, a great Georgian structure which reigned on the island from 1874 to 1971 and hosted such notables as the Vanderbilts, the Astors, the Cushings, the Morgans, and Charles Lindbergh on the eve of his historic flight to Paris.

The building is quite a lovely modernization of its former Georgian self, nine stories of brick and scalloped bay windows, centered on a traditional bell tower topped by a gilded cupola. Guests drive under the double-height carport to the lobby appointed with some stunning French antiques, including a Louis XIII marble-top bombe under a gilded mirror and French provincial reproduction furnishings and bergères. The polished Italian marble floors and rich mahogany walls gleam under the light of the chandeliers and brass sconces. Guests may proceed to the lower lobby to the café, Health Club, and shops.

The guest rooms are on floors 2–9, with moderate to penthouse rooms which ascend in rate as they do by floor. Superior rooms are on floors 4, 5, and 6; deluxe rooms on 7 and 8; and the 15 penthouse rooms on the ninth floor all have patios. They rooms are very traditionally decorated in Drexel reproduction furnishings, bright chintz or floral Schumacher fabrics on the beds matching structured drapes and sometimes crown canopies. Creamy marble baths all have telephones.

At the G. C. Spa, guests enjoy a 32-foot swimming pool as well as whirlpool, sauna and steam rooms, cardiovascular equipment, and massage therapy and facials.

The Polo Grill serves three meals daily in American contemporary cuisine; in addition, guests may venture to the Market Street Grill for seafood specialties at dinner. The Polo Lounge offers tea, cocktails, and hors d'oeuvres; and the G Club is for dancing and socializing.

The staff is friendly and professional at this busy, well-run hotel, which has a curious market of weekend shoppers and weekday corporates.

The Helmsley Palace
455 Madison Avenue
New York, New York 10022
212-888-7000
800-221-4982
Fax: 212-355-0820

Proprietor: The Helmsley Corporation
General Manager: Kevin Malloy
Accommodations: 1,060 rooms, including 160 suites
Rates: Rooms, $255–$325; suites, $395–$2,500
Added: $40 each additional guest; 19.25% tax
Payment: Major credit cards
Children: Welcome
Pets: Not allowed
Smoking: 3 of 53 floors nonsmoking
Open: All year

The Helmsley Palace is best known for its recognizable matriarch. However, there are quite wonderful aspects of the hotel that are relatively unappreciated. A marriage of old and new, the hotel houses one of New York's finest Old World mansions along with an efficient glass and aluminum skyscraper. A block-long carpeted corridor connects the 50th and 51st Street entrances; or guests may also enter from Madison Avenue, behind St. Patrick's Cathedral, through wrought-iron gates, past the inlaid courtyard embraced by the palatial U-shaped five-story Villard mansion.

In 1882, financier Henry Villard commissioned the architectural firm McKim, Mead, and White to design a mansion for his family; the mansion was completed three years later in the manner of the Palazzo della Cancelleria in Rome. Bought by the Helmsleys, the Villard Mansion was magnificently restored over several years, starting in 1979 while the Tower was being built. Today it houses some of the city's loveliest public spaces: the Gold Room, for afternoon tea; the Madison Room, for hors d'oeuvres and cocktails, designed by Stanford White; and the Hunt Bar. With their marble pillars and fireplaces, gold leaf, hand-painted murals, inlaid flooring, mosaic groin vaulting, and marble pocket doors, these rooms defy description. Rather, guests ought to make plans for a tour with historian Rupert Rodriguez; or request the Treasures of the Palace walking tour.

The rose marble foyer of the Villard Mansion is flanked by two staircases going up to the highly reputed Trianon Restaurant and the Hunt Room or descending to the block-long corridor. This marks the new hotel, designed by Emery Roth & Sons architects and, on the interior, by Tom Lee Ltd. Much effort has been made to replicate the wood, moldings, and marble of the Villard mansion in the new building. Harry's Bar is part of the new space, near the 51st Street entrance and several upscale shops.

The majority of guest rooms are in the main part of the hotel on floors 5–39. The Tower rooms and suites, above to the fifty-fourth floor, have their own private concierge, check-in, and extra amenities and services. All floors have a regal red and gold carpet and gold-painted millwork on the doors. The room design features the trademark gilded and upholstered headboards, matching spreads and drapery in a framed window, with Louis XV reproduction bergères, benches, desks, and marble-top dressers. The marble baths have terry and linen towels, scales, quite complete amenities including a sewing kit, and a stool by the oversized bath vanity. The suites have additional antiques, as well as bright yellow couches and some stocked kitchens. Compared with those in older hotels, the guest rooms are missing high ceilings and crown moldings— traded for 24-hour room service, full amenities, and triple-padded carpets in a soundproofed building.

The staff is letter-perfect in etiquette and service, and guests will surely forget that they are in a thousand-room hotel.

Hôtel Plaza Athénée

37 East 64th Street
New York, New York 10021
212-734-9100
800-223-5843
Fax: 212-772-0958

Proprietor: Forte Hotels
General Manager: Bernard Lackner
Accommodations: 160 rooms, including 30 suites
Rates: Rooms, $310–$350; suites, $590–$900; single rates $35 less
Added: $30 each additional guest; 19.25% tax
Payment: Major credit cards
Children: Welcome
Pets: Not allowed
Smoking: 1 of 16 floors nonsmoking
Open: All year

With its bright red awnings flagging every window, the New York Hôtel Plaza Athénée pledges allegiance to its Paris inspiration, one of the world's finest hotels since it was built over a century ago. Despite its Old World appearance, the New York Plaza Athénée opened in September 1984, a transformation of the former 1927 Alrae Hotel with a redesign by architect John Carl Warnecke. It is surely the ritziest of the Madison Avenue boutique hotels and caters to an elegant European crowd.

Guests enter on 64th Street between Madison and Park avenues, under a portico draped with French and American flags, through polished brass doors, to a foyerlike lobby, with white marble inset with black squares, appointed in Italian marble and luxurious French antiques. Registration is at an 18th-century desk by the concierge, in a room of green silk-covered walls and antiques. Visitors may proceed down several steps at the center of the lobby to the restaurant Le Régence. The restaurant serves Continental food with a French flair by the hand of chef Jean Robert de Cavel in a very French setting, an ornate room with gold millwork, green walls, leather chairs, and crystal sconces and chandeliers under a cloud mural. The neighboring piano lounge is a clubby, intimate place for drinks and cocktails, under Brazilian mahogany millwork, with walls covered in dark green fabric and oil paintings.

The elevator banks in the lower lobby are surrounded by three walls of a lavish hand-painted mural of classical pastoral scenes. Guest rooms occupy 17 floors on intimate, hushed hallways appointed with Old World moldings. Irish Navan carpets quiet the step. Headboards are upholstered velvet. Two schemes of decor are a serene palette of muted aquas and beiges and a romantic setting of rusts. There is no chintz or clutter here, but classic silk and velvet in complementary colors or paisleys in handsome tones, with stretched valances above the windows. The furnishings were handmade for the hotel, from the Directoire night tables to the desks and television cabinets in dark wood. The bathrooms are beautiful, with stunning Portuguese Aurora Rose marble on the floors and walls. Lanvin amenities and Italian Frette terry robes add to the elegance. Eight suites have terraces or solariums. The rooms do not have mini-bars since the hotel places such emphasis on its full service.

The staff is reserved and solicitous, emphasizing the aura of formality that pervades the Plaza Athénée.

The Lowell
28 East 63rd Street
New York, New York 10021
212-838-1400
800-221-4444
Fax 212-319-4230

General Manager: Martin Hale
Accommodations: 61 rooms, including 48 suites
Rates: Roos, $320; suites, $420–$1,500
Minimum stay: None
Added: $20 each additional guest; 19.25% tax; $2 occupancy tax
Payment: Major credit cards

Children: Allowed
Pets: Check with manager
Smoking: Allowed
Open: All year

Though it was built in 1928 as a residence hotel, the Lowell was purchased by its present owners in 1984. They recently invested $25 million into its renovation, returning it to the glory days when Scott and Zelda Fitzgerald, Dorothy Parker, Eugene O'Neill, and Noel Coward were regular guests.

Extremely intimate, the Lowell is the only full-service New York City hotel with fewer than 100 rooms, other than Sotto's new Hotel Mercer. Unusually, it has 33 working fireplaces in its suites. While others scramble to establish unique identities, the Lowell sits comfortably in its exclusivity. As a member of the elite Relais et Châteaux, the hotel is necessarily privately owned, since 1984. A recent $25 million renovation on this boutique property established it as an elite Manhattan hideaway.

The 17-story art deco landmark in patterned brick sits on 63rd Street between Madison and Park avenues, its exterior so understated as to be mistaken for a private apartment building. Guests, laden with packages from Givenchy and Ungaro around the corner, enter the very formal lobby, with faux marbling and Empire parlor sets accented by Scalamadre window treatments and upholstery in regal gold silk. The concierge sits attentively behind his Edgar Brandt desk, adjacent to the modestly sized reception desk. Behind is a pediment-shaped bookcase, which is actually a faux door to offices. A neoclassic mural enlivens the setting.

Guests are escorted up black lacquer elevators to their rooms, a wide assortment of layouts and variety, though assuredly appointed in the height of good taste. Thirty-three suites have working wood-burning fireplaces, and 56 accommodations have kitchens stocked with china and silver. Ten suites have private terraces. In addition, the Gym Suite has a private exercise room with a treadmill, stairmaster, weights, and even a ballet bar with a wonderful view of the Upper East Side.

The rooms are as elegant as they are understated, with an overall relaxing feel amid precious antiques and furnishings. Appointed more in the vein of a Park Avenue pied-à-terre than a standard upscale hotel, the rooms are decorated with French and Oriental furnishings, leather chairs, ormolu mirrors, 18th- and 19th-century prints, and Chinese porcelain. The original mantels and fireplaces have been restored. Some spreads are heavy woven tapestries, others are done in quilted or in muted colors. Every room has its own library with leatherbound books. Umbrellas are provided for guest use. The baths are done in rich brown Italian marble with brass fixtures and exclusive Saks Fifth Avenue amenities including a loofah, terry robes, and fresh flowers. All rooms have mini-bars, televisions, and VCRs.

Service at the Lowell is hushed, discreet, and extremely personable, as if the staff is working for the guests rather than for the hotel.

The Mark

Madison Avenue at East 77th Street
New York, New York 10021
212-744-4300
800-843-6275
Fax: 212-744-2749

Proprietors: The Rafael Group, Georg Rafael and E. William Judson
General Manager: Raymond N. Bickson
Accommodations: 180 rooms, including 60 suites
Rates: Rooms, $265–$295; suites, $450–$1,800
Minimum stay: None
Added: $20 each additional guest; 19.25% tax
Payment: Major credit cards
Children: Welcome
Pets: Check with manager
Smoking: Allowed
Open: All year

The Mark is a welcome addition to the traditional row of elite Upper East Side hotels, with unique neoclassic decor and a highly regarded restaurant. Built in 1926 and known over the years as the Hyde Park Residence and the Madison Avenue Hotel, the building was bought by the Rafael Group, transformed for about $35 million, and opened in April 1989. The Mark stands proudly as the American flagship property of the Rafael Group, launched by hotelier Georg Rafael, who spent a decade mastering the trade with Regent International Hotels.

The entrance sits on 77th Street, between Madison and Fifth avenues. While the building is a classic Upper East Side brick monolith, the brightly lit glass and brass doors at the Mark promise something new. The intimate black and white marble lobby is a transitional space with Beidermier furnishings, beckoning to a visitor to relax in the library setting of Mark's Bar or to have tea or a lavish meal at the Mark's Restaurant.

The Restaurant is a wonderful gallery of tufted circular banquettes, gossipy sets of chairs around low tables under a backlit greenhouse ceiling, separated from an upper dining tier by tapestried screens and a wrought-iron rail under a faux skylight, in tones of teal, burgundy, and rose. The artistry of Normandy native Philippe Boulot is described as French-inspired cuisine moderne and has been widely praised.

Architects Pennoyer Turino P. C. and designer Mimi Russell are responsible for the neoclassic and Italian Renaissance elements of the interior spaces. Among the pieces that set the tone are original Piranesi prints, Gundolt wool carpeting, and plentiful and neutral tones of Italian marble. The hallways are serene spaces with classic molding, in muted grays and whites, with classic sconces. The standard guest rooms have an odd, modernish scheme of rose lacquer, though all have mini-bars, VCRs, and televisions. The suites are highly worth the upgrade, unique in decor and configuration, with handsome furnishings in muted tones, and lovely neo-classic art on the walls. All rooms feature Frette top sheets and Belgian cotton linens and down pillows.

Most attractive at the Mark are the bathrooms, which accounted for about a quarter of the restoration's budget. Either done in geometric black and white ceramic tile or in several tones of Italian marble, they are quite deluxe, with Kohler soaking tubs and free-standing showers, crystal bath grains, Molton Brown amenities, fresh flowers, and potpourri. The suites feature several rooms with a marble bath, most with bidets.

With the Carlyle across the street, the Mark tries valiantly and gracefully to rise to its competition—an exciting and tasteful addition to the new New York hotels.

Paramount
235 West 46th Street
New York, New York 10019
212-764-5500
800-225-7474
Fax: 212-354-5237

Proprietors: Ian Shrager, Philip Pilevsky, and Arthur Cohen
General Manager: David Miskit, managed by Morgans Hotel
  Company
Accommodations: 610 rooms, including 13 suites
Rates: $110–$170
Added: $20 each additional guest; 19.25% tax
Payment: Major credit cards

Children: Welcome
Pets: Not allowed
Smoking: 2 of 17 floors nonsmoking
Open: All year

In the heart of the theater district, Paramount is the stage and its guests are the players. This showcase of daring design was reborn in August 1990 after a three-year, $75 million investment. Predicting the recession in his latest venture, noting the abundance of unaffordable hotels in New York, owner Ian Shrager invented stylish overnighting on a shoestring.

The Century Paramount Hotel was designed by Thomas Lamb in 1927, architectural author of the Ziegfeld and the Pierre, which fell into dowdiness over the years until Ian Shrager and partners bought it in 1986. While Mr. Shrager's Royalton is an example of the high art of hotel design, the Paramount is performance art with a sense of humor, designed by Philippe Starck.

The formidable exterior looks like the grandest of grand old hotels, its Carrara marble facade restored by Rockwell Newman, fresh from restoring Carnegie Hall and the Statue of Liberty. A marble breezeway is the transition where the fun begins. Like guests at a potluck dinner, Europe's best designers showcase their signature pieces: odd couches, a silver chair, weird lamps, under a ceiling inspired by Joan Miró, on a backdrop floor of gray Italian slate. Guests gaze up at framed duets of diners at the Mezzanine restaurant, which wraps entirely around the perimeter. From their second-floor balcony, they observe the lobby players, reached by a platinum leaf staircase.

Much is conceptual at the Paramount. The 18 floors of guest rooms are reached by elevators lit in primary colors. A wide weather mirror posts the day's climatic events on a stark wall along white hallways lined with rope rails, reminiscent of the ocean liners of the twenties and thirties.

All rooms have a black and white parquet low nap rug, a stark, Brancusi-style light/chandelier, clean-lined white cabinets for televisions and VCRs, and a brightly colored Starck armchair. Headboards in the single rooms are oversized replicas of Vermeer's masterpiece *Lacemaker*, with a maternal figure hovering over the bed, a restful platform smooth and white, with a long cylindrical pillow tied at both ends. The immaculate baths retain their Old World tiling with New Age charm, with Philippe Starck's trademark stainless steel sink and personalized amenities. Though the public spaces are playful galleries of design, the rooms were designed to be restful and welcoming.

Among the public spaces are a room derivative of PeeWee's Playhouse, done by the selfsame designer Gary Panter; a 24-hour exercise club; a sunny breakfast room off the Mezzanine; a Dean & DeLuca espresso/pastry bar; and an incredibly chic supper club that draws lines most evenings. If you can't stay overnight, a visit to the lobby restrooms will convey the playful, postmodern creativity of the Paramount.

Despite the overwhelming chicness of the Paramount, it is a very down-to-earth, friendly, accessible, affordable place. The theatrical staff literally auditioned for their respective roles as bellmen and concierges.

Parc Fifty-One

152 West 51st Street
New York, New York 10019
212-765-1900
800-338-1338

Proprietor: Park Lane Hotels International
General Manager: Cary Turecamo
Accommodations: 178 rooms, including 52 suites
Rates: Rooms, $255–$325; suites, from $395
Included: Continental breakfast, morning newspaper
Added: $25 each additional guest; 19.25% tax
Payment: Major credit cards
Children: Welcome
Pets: Not allowed
Smoking: 1 of 7 floors nonsmoking
Open: All year

This elegant theater district hotel has the tony feel of an Upper East Side property, with one of the prettiest lobbies in Midtown Manhattan. Built in 1926 as the Taft Hotel, it enjoyed for nearly forty years a tradition of a bohemian, eclectic theater crowd. The property was closed for four years as it underwent a $100 million renovation, reopening to rave reviews in October 1987 as the Grand Bay Hotel at Equitable Center. The property transferred to the hands of Park Lane Hotels in 1990.

Guests enter on 51st Street on the corner of Seventh Avenue, a block from Radio City Music Hall, through a well-lit portico. By the time they reach the reception desk at the lobby's far end, they have forgotten the blaring horns and madding crowds of this neighborhood. The marbled setting is lovely and serene, with rosy and cocoa brown floors. Oil paintings hang above the French antiques and bergères and gilded coffee tables. The main lobby reaches two stories upward, culminating in a gilded, pressed tin ceiling from which hangs a crystal chandelier. Huge floral arrangements dress polished antique tables. The original brass elevator doors were restored from the roaring twenties days of the Taft.

Throughout five floors of guest rooms, the hallways are lined with plush neutral carpeting in gray, beige, and taupe, made residential by right-angled turns, antiques, and original art. Rooms have light-colored marble foyers and are unusually large with an average of 500 square feet. The doubles are done with geometric pastels and solids and traditional wood furniture with black and gold accents; the suites are done in French country and art deco. The French country rooms have beautiful pine furnishings, a king-size sleigh bed, and a large Empire sofa. Dividing the living from the sleeping room is a floor-to-ceiling armoire containing a swiveling television, stereo, and bookshelves (unusually, all rooms have several classic novels and books). The duvets, carpeting, and upholstery are done in neutral solids. The art deco rooms are surprisingly different, furnished in black lacquer and mauve accents. A unifying theme is the bottled mineral water offered in every room next to trademark green marble ice buckets.

All rooms, regardless of size, have magnificent baths, including five-foot tubs, cotton bath sheets, towels, and robes, hair dryers, televisions, and phones, amenities by Crabtree and Evelyn, and Neutrogena soaps. The floors and walls are done in blond marble, and the separate sinks and vanities are finished in green marble.

The Lobby Lounge near the reception area is a living room setting of muted tapestried chairs and plush down-filled sofas, featuring piano music and finger food in the afternoon and evening. Guests are served complimentary Continental breakfast in the hotel's restaurant, Bellini by Cipriani, an affiliate of the famous Harry's Bar in Venice, the hotel restaurant. Northern Italian lunch and dinner are served to the public in this light setting of leather chairs and verdigris sconces.

The Peninsula
700 Fifth Avenue at 55th Street
New York, New York 10019
212-247-2200
800-262-9467
Fax: 212-903-3949

Proprietor: The Peninsula Group
General Manager: Manfred Timmel

Accommodations: 250 rooms, including 30 suites
Rates: Rooms, $275–$395; suites, $550–$1,100
Added: $20 each additional guest; 19.25% sales tax
Payment: Major credit cards; no personal checks
Children: Welcome
Pets: Not allowed
Smoking: 4 of 17 floors nonsmoking
Open: All year

This grand old property is actually quite a new property, the Peninsula Group's first American hotel. Built as the Gotham Hotel in 1905 by Hiss and Weekes for $2.25 million, the hotel was designed to complement its neighbor, the University Club. It sits across Fifth Avenue from the masterpiece St. Regis, completing quite an astounding trio of beaux-arts Italian Renaissance architecture just below 57th Street.

The 23-story limestone structure lived a long life before a renovation was undertaken in 1979. However, plans were disrupted and the hotel sat boarded up for seven years. The property was bought in 1986 by the Pratt Corporation, renovated to its present grandeur, and opened in the spring of 1988 under the aegis of Maxim's de Paris. The Peninsula Group bought the hotel in October 1988 for $127 million.

While renovations have become as common as pillow mints in New York hotels, the Peninsula has two outstanding features that separate it from its cousins: a 35,000-square-foot state-of-the-art health club and spa and the wonderful PenTop Bar & Terrace, each with panoramic city views and wrap terraces peering over the copper cornice.

Guests enter from 55th Street to a transitional lobby with double-height ceilings, flanked by cozy parlors furnished with art nouveau antiques. A sweeping staircase of Italian classico marble ascends five steps and divides in either direction to Adrienne restaurant and Le Bistro d'Adrienne to the left and to the reception area and the Gotham Lounge for high tea and cocktails to the right. Immediately, a visitor is awestruck by the ornate plaster ceiling and faux pink marble under Corinthian capitals. The armoire on the landing was featured at the 1904 Exposition des Beaux-Arts in Paris. Other original pieces throughout the public spaces, including bergères, tables, and a sofa, were designed by art nouveau master Louis Marjorelle. The Palm Court features the astounding legerdemain of Ben Strauss, who painted the faux limestone walls.

The guest rooms are furnished with original art nouveau antiques and lighting fixtures, custom-designed furnishings, in masculine understated decor. The futuristic telephone consoles control temperature, lighting, and the television and offer assistance in seven languages. The baths have dignified brass fixtures, bidets, phones, and Lanvin amenities. Compared with the lavish public space, however, the rooms are muted, and a number have poor views of the interior air shaft.

The fabulous trilevel Spa hovers above the hotel on top floors, a blessed contribution of the Peninsula Group in April 1991. Guests enjoy the Cybex circuits and extensive cardiovascular machines in several windowed rooms with city views. Under an atrium roof is a 17-by-42-foot pool and whirlpool. The salon offers massages, facials, and beauty services. Guests enjoy a carpeted wraparound sundeck.

Chef Adam Odegard is a wonderful contribution to Adrienne, and his fine European cuisine is complimented in the restaurant's pretty salmon-colored setting. All is softspoken and understated at the Peninsula — the guests as well as the staff elegant and hushed in these grand-scale public spaces.

Rihga Royal Hotel

151 West 54th Street
New York, New York 10019
212-307-5000
800-937-5454

Proprietors: Rihga International U.S.A.
General Manager: Frank Arthur Banks
Accommodations: 476 one- and two-bedroom suites,
    including 6 Grand Royal Suites
Rates: $260–$390; Grand Royal Suites from $425
Added: $25 each additional guest; 19.25% tax
Payment: Major credit cards
Children: Welcome
Pets: Not allowed
Smoking: 5 of 52 floors nonsmoking
Open: All year

Having opened in November 1990, the Rihga Royal initiated a challenge to all business-oriented New York City hotels. It runs like a clock and was planned very well by its Japanese-owned company. There are only 10 or 12 rooms per floor, creating an unusual amount of privacy and quiet for a 500-room property. The rooms are exceptionally large, averaging 572 square feet, with at least one bedroom set apart from a living room. The fitness facilities are extensive and brand new. The hotel offers a nice business center to guests, with a fax, a copier, a computer, and typewriter. And half the guest rooms have fairly good views of Central Park, others with views of the Hudson or East River.

The city's second tallest hotel—the tallest is Wall Street's new 58-story Millenium—stands 54 stories, designed by Frank Williams and Associates in the classic form of the soaring skyscrapers of the 1920s and 1930s. A tower of rose-beige brick and granite, the Rihga Royal teeters above 54th Street, narrowing toward its top. Porters flock to the revolving doors. The lobby is quite small for such a large hotel, decorated in two tones of polished marble two stories high. The elevator banks rest behind the lobby, extremely quick and efficient.

Guest rooms line the intimate hallways on either side, and again a visitor will be thankful for the tower structure, which permits more floors and fewer rooms per floor. Either one or two bedrooms, they are decorated similarly with white painted woodwork, in a peach or an aqua-teal color scheme. All guest rooms have sofabeds and bay windows in the living rooms, with remote cable televisions built into corner cupboards. Mirrored French doors close or open to the bedroom, most with a king-size bed. A bit lacking in warmth, the rooms are immaculate, colorful, and very utilitarian—some with wondrous views. The mini-bars have ice makers, the rooms have safes, and there are two televisions, one with a VCR. The baths are small but quite nice, with marble floors, a separate bath and shower, a telephone, amenities including Crabtree and Evelyn, a hair dryer, a lint brush, and a scale.

The Fitness Center, open 24 hours and staffed with a daytime personal trainer, has brand-new equipment in a large setting, including treadmills, Lifecycles, universal weights, and two saunas, with views to a small garden outdoors.

On the ground floor, to the right of the lobby is Halcyon, the Rihga's restaurant. The decor is quite classic, with forest green banquettes and Empire chairs under a lovely Italian mural. The sommelier is proud of the 140-wine list. Visitors have drinks and enjoy piano music in the living room setting of the Halcyon Lounge, open for light fare until 2 A.M. Halcyon also services the guests with 24-hour room service.

The Ritz-Carlton New York
112 Central Park South
New York, New York 10019
212-757-1900
800-241-3333
Fax: 212-757-9620

Proprietor: The Ritz-Carlton Hotel Company
General Manager: Edward A. Mady
Accommodations: 228 rooms, including 23 suites and 5
   junior suites
Rates: Rooms, $230–$380; suites, from $475
Included: Morning newspaper, morning limousine to Wall
   Street
Added: $30 each additional guest; 19.25% tax
Payment: Major credit cards
Children: Welcome
Pets: Not allowed
Smoking: Nonsmoking rooms available
Open: All year

The Navarro Hotel was built in 1928, and the Ritz-Carlton
Hotel moved into its shell in 1982. This New York property
embodies all the aspects of a Ritz-Carlton to a tee: the Old
World flavor of its Central Park South address and regal brick
facade convince a passerby or even a long-term guest that this is
one of New York's grand old hotels—especially in the understated elegance displayed by the solicitous staff and at the wonderful Jockey Club.

Guests enter from Central Park South through revolving
doors, descend several steps, and reach the parlorlike lobby.
The knotty pine paneling and oil paintings lend a living room
feel. Elevator banks rest beyond the lobby, and the Jockey Club
is through a threshold to the left. This is quite an institution, a
wonderful room lifted off the shores of Great Britain. The pine
walls are filled with oil paintings of equestrian and hunt themes
illuminated by lantern sconces, accented by corner shell cabinets, red leather banquettes adorned with brass. The room feels
like an English men's club, treated to the work of chef Tom Parlo
and an extensive wine list of about 175 bottles. After dinner,
guests will enjoy a nightcap at the Jockey Club Bar, presided
over by the internationally known bartender Norman Bu-
kofzer.

The guest rooms are gradually being transformed throughout 1992. While the older rooms have the gracious modest
elegance of a Park Avenue apartment, the new schemes are
highly decorated, with heavy drapery in Wedgwood blue laced
with gold thread, matching linens, and classic sofas. Televisions
and mini-bars are fixed in lovely custom-designed armoires,
wood with brass accents. While the rooms undergo redecoration, the baths are all in pristine condition, of light marble on
the walls and floors, with classic fixtures, hair dryers, vanity
mirrors, scales, phones, two robes, and an eyelet shower cur-

tain, with extensive amenities. A nice touch is a Ritz-Carlton umbrella provided for guest use in every room. Be sure to request a park view.

Reliably, the service at The Ritz-Carlton is faultless, discreet, and extremely understated—a quiet refuge in the midst of Manhattan glitz.

The Royalton
44 West 44th Street
New York, New York 10036
212-869-4400
800-635-9013

Proprietor: Ian Shrager
General Manager: Terry Ford
Accommodations: 168 rooms, including 28 suites, 40 rooms
with fireplace
Rates: Rooms, $235–$350; suites, $370
Added: $25 each additional guest; 19.25% tax
Payment: Major credit cards
Children: Welcome
Pets: Not allowed
Smoking: Allowed
Open: All year

The Royalton is first a phenomenon, then a hotel. It looks like an art deco retrospective during the twenty-first century, like Alice in Wonderland in corporate America, as if the Algonquin's Round Table suddenly went elliptical under the hands of a space-suited Dorothy Parker.

Although it was built in 1898 as the Hotel Royalton, only the name remains remotely the same since its reintroduction to the New York chic elite in 1988 by the late Steve Rubell and Ian Shrager—a Hollywood-type producer of sophisticated Manhattan hotels. There is nothing to introduce the hotel from the street—no signs or flying flags—but the name modestly carved in stone on the pediment of the Greek Revival portico and the unearthly glow of the polished mahogany doors that signify importance.

Mr. Shrager and Mr. Rubell had this in mind: what nightclubs were to the seventies and restaurants were to the eighties, hotel lobbies will be to the nineties. The interior design of Philippe Starck immediately transports a guest into the Royalton world. A cobalt blue carpet, bordered on one side with a line of white dancing ghosts, stretches nearly the block-long distance of the hotel's granite floor. A gleaming bank of highly varnished mahogany doors lines one side of the corridor, topped by wall sconces with a peculiar horn shape repeated throughout the hotel. Lining the other side of the carpet are cylindrical gray pillars and dramatically lit spare furnishings. Asymmetrical white muslin–covered chairs with broad backs of yellow, purple, green, or peach velvet contrast with generic white-slipcovered wing chairs, with dangerous-looking stainless steel legs.

Down several steps are dining and sociable tables, and decorating the walls are such oddities as four large glass bowls inhabited by fighting fish, a huge rectangular beveled mirror hung with two purple tassels, and exaggerated vases stuck with primary-colored tulips. Occasional lines of bright color emerge from the neutral backdrop of gray slate, stone, and carpet.

Visitors must be sure to visit the Round Bar for a drink. Its entirely round celery-colored tufted velvet walls give the feeling of being in a genie's bottle. Traditional black and white parquet floors are distorted in a dizzying round design. Like all things at the Royalton, the Round Bar has classic origins, designed after Ernest Hemingway's favorite bar, that of the Paris Ritz.

Whisked up in small mahogany elevators to one of 16 floors of guest rooms, a visitor is left off in a hallway as if dropped at sea at midnight. The halls are painted the same cobalt blue of the familiar specter carpet. The round room numbers glow eerily from the mahogany doors like portals from a ship's hull. The halls feel claustrophobic, and once inside the guest rooms, one feels an immediate sense of calm.

The palette is a simple one of slate gray, stainless steel, and white light from the lamps and bedding, the glow of mahogany, with the exception of a midnight blue velvet easy chair. Cool Vermont slate floors are covered in a thick-pile gray carpet. The low bedding is an oasis of creamy white brushed cotton down comforter with seven down pillows perfectly arranged. The upholstered headboard is covered in stretched cotton. Nightstands are inset portals cut into the mahogany wall on either side of the bed, with one fresh flower, a notepad, and a pencil. Tiny round stainless steel tables are placed just so. A candle is replaced at nightly turndown. Many of the rooms feature working fireplaces.

The spacious baths are the highest of high tech, a panoply of slate, steel, glass, and mirrors, warmed slightly by the plush white terry robes and towels. A stainless steel basin rests on one wall and a vanity mirror on another, with an amenity tray including potpourri, a fresh flower, and Royalton soap, shampoo, and cotton buds. The room may have either a five-foot-diameter tub or a tub with glassed-in shower, each with bath salts and a loofah sponge.

The rooms all contain mini-bars without liquor, pastries made by Dean and DeLuca in black lacquer boxes designed for the hotel. As well, all rooms are outfitted with a television, a VCR and stereo cassette, with volumes of tapes available at the front desk which will be delivered to one's room with a bowl of warm popcorn.

The black-suited model types at reception also serve as concierges, ever efficient and highly trained. Among other things, they will make reservations at the highly reputed 44, which serves a nouvelle Continental cuisine. Odd-hour diners will be glad for the Sushi Bar Without the Sushi, which serves light fare around the clock.

The St. Regis

Two East 55th Street at Fifth Avenue
New York, New York 10022
212-753-4500
800-759-7550

Proprietor: The ITT Sheraton Corporation
Managing Director: Peter W. Tischmann
Accommodations: 359, including 49 suites
Rates: Roosm, $350–$450; suites, $550–$3,000
Added: 19.25% tax
Payment: Major credit cards
Children: Welcome
Pets: Not allowed
Smoking: 4 of 19 floors nonsmoking
Open: All year

When it was completed in 1905, the St. Regis was New York's tallest building. While it no longer holds that honor, it does bring to mind other superlatives as the city's newest, most expensive, and most upscale new hotel. After three years and $100 million of restoration and renovation, the St. Regis reopened in September 1991 to a glorious reception.

The 18-story building was constructed as a hotel for $5.5 million by Colonel John Jacob Astor IV, between 1902 and 1905, designed by Trowbridge and Livingston, who also designed the Hayden Planetarium and B. Altman's. The beaux-arts masterpiece was intended to be the world's finest hotel, with crystal chandeliers, antique tapestries, Oriental rugs, and antique Louis XV furnishings. While today's hotels boast of large video libraries for guest use, the original St. Regis had a 3,000-volume gold-tooled library of books for guests to check out. The restoration project was intended to replicate that turn-of-the-century majesty. Throughout the hotel are 600 crystal chandeliers, handmade in Czechoslovakia. Nearly 200 miles of wood molding and 23 miles of plaster molding were installed. The restoration involved the second largest gold leafing project ever undertaken in this country.

When Colonel Astor died on the *Titanic* in 1912, the St. Regis went to his busy son Vincent, who was forced to sell to the Duke family in 1927. One of the hotel's most noted treasures is the Maxfield Parrish mural *King Cole*, which was installed in the hotel in 1932. Three years later, Vincent Astor reclaimed the grande dame, and the hotel became the center of New York social life. When it opened in 1938, the Iridium Room was an immediate success for dining and dancing, with a skating rink that pulled out from under the stage. It was renamed the King Cole Grille in 1948 when the Parrish mural was hung here. The hotel was bought in 1966 by the Sheraton Corporation, which undertook the restoration in 1988.

The guest rooms on the upper floors were greatly enlarged during the renovation, their number reduced from 557 to 359, all with 12-foot ceilings and crown moldings. While furnished similarly, there are nearly 70 different room configurations given the old floor plan of the hotel. Decorated with reproduction Louis XV furnishings, the rooms are exquisitely done in soothing gray silks and damasks. These match stretched valances and heavy drapery, as well as chairs and sitting areas. The beds have upholstered headboards and featherbeds. The beautiful wood armoires with brass fittings were custom-designed to house the television and mini-bar, and the contents of the latter are complimentary to guests. The large baths are exquisite, with linen and terry towels, robes, Bijan amenities, in white marble, with large tubs and free-standing showers. Every floor has its own butler.

For mind and body, there is a full-service business center, as well as a fitness center on the lower level with ample cardiovascular equipment and saunas in a neoclassic setting.

Guests will certainly want to enjoy high tea in the Astor Court, with its hand-painted murals in a French, feminine setting. For a more masculine experience behind the Astor Court, the King Cole bar is a smoky, woody room featuring the romantic landscape of Maxfield Parrish. Lespinasse is the setting for formal French cuisine. Executive chef Michael Carrer and chef Gary Kunz received three stars from the *New York Times* shortly after the hotel opened. The china and flatware were designed specially for the St. Regis by Tiffany.

Expect solicitous service at every turn. The staff is exceptionally attentive at the St. Regis, as the hotel tries to live up to all the expectations prompted by the renovation.

Strathallan
550 East Avenue
Rochester, New York 14607
716-461-5010
800-678-7284

General Manager: Barbara Ruocco
Accommodations: 151 studio, 1-bedroom, and 2-bedroom suites
Rates: $115–$205; weekend rates $10 less
Included: Weekend breakfast buffet; weekday Continental
  breakfast on two-floor Executive Level
Minimum stay: None
Added: 11%; 16% over $100
Payment: Major credit cards
Children: Welcome
Pets: Not allowed
Smoking: 1 of 8 floors nonsmoking
Open: All year

Rochester is sadly lacking in accommodations, and Strathallan is its finest offering. Unfortunately, its worst feature is its facade, an uninspired eight-story rectangular chunk of balconies and concrete. Rest assured, things get better inside. While not glamorous and gleaming with marble, the Strathallan is a comfortable refuge in quite a lovely neighborhood on Rochester's Museum Trail. Within walking distance are dozens of charming Victorian homes and a park; the Memorial Art Gallery with ancient and European art; the Rochester Museum and Science Center, with one of the world's best collections of Iroquois Indian artifacts; the International Museum of Photography in the former mansion of Kodak founder George Eastman; and the toy-filled Strong Museum, with one of the world's most extensive doll collections.

The Strathallan was built in the 1970s as an apartment building but sat empty for four years as the project went bankrupt. Bought by ambitious owners, the Strathallan was remodeled and turned into a hotel in 1980.

The guest rooms are decorated with traditional—if predictable—cherry or mahogany reproduction furnishings, in bright color schemes that reflect nicely on the recent 1989 remodeling effort. The majority of accommodations are one-bedroom suites, an occasional two-bedroom suite, and roomy standard rooms with large sitting areas. All rooms have televisions in armoires, refrigerators, and coffee makers, and most have balconies. Guests pay an additional $20 for Executive Level privileges such as complimentary breakfast, newspaper, robes, hair dryers, two balconies per room, and use of the private lounge with sweeping views of the city.

Sabrinas restaurant, to the right of the living room lobby, serves three meals daily in a businesslike setting, leaning toward French food later in the day. The uppermost floor has a nice cocktail lounge called Hatties with a fabulous view of the Rochester skyline, enlivened by weekend jazz. In addition, the hotel has fitness facilities, with a sauna, Lifecycles, and exercise equipment in a solarium setting.

The staff is understated and happy, seemingly glad to be in this relaxing and interesting neighborhood.

U.N. Plaza–Park Hyatt

One United Nations Plaza
New York, New York 10017-3575
212-355-3400
800-233-1234
Fax: 212-702-5051

Proprietors: Park Hyatt Corporation
General Manager: John F. Power
Accommodations: 428 rooms, including 110 with kitchenette and 45 suites
Rates: Rooms, $235–$255; suites, $325–$1,100
Added: $20 each additional guest; 19.25% tax
Payment: Major credit cards
Children: Welcome
Pets: Not allowed
Smoking: 2 nonsmoking floors
Open: All year

One of a small handful of New York City hotels with a pool, and the only one with a tennis court, the U.N. Plaza also has the bonus of wonderful views from most of its rooms. This gleaming glass tower across First Avenue from the United Nations is a change of pace from the beaux-arts revivals in Midtown Manhattan.

The interior of the building is a bold, contemporary play between deep green marble and smoky mirrors. The hotel comprises two separate towers flanking an octagonal, brightly lit double-height lobby. In addition to the lobby lounge, with leather and muted tapestry contemporary parlor sets, the Wisteria lounge off the reception area is an intimate space with trellised walls and gilded arches where guests take breakfast and afternoon high tea. Most exceptional is the hotel's interesting and lovely art collection displayed throughout the public spaces: framed textiles representing United Nations countries, such as batik, tapas, tapestries, silks, and embroidery.

Rooms begin on the twenty-eighth and twenty-ninth floors of either tower and soar to 40 stories, providing wonderful views of the East River and three city views. While the original East Tower of the hotel was built in the mid-1970s and the West Tower five years later, all public spaces and rooms recently underwent an extensive redecoration. Compared to the swank public spaces, the guest floor halls are rather muted, in maroons and mauves, with East Tower doors done in burlwood. Because of the irregular-shaped exterior, the rooms have interesting angles and exceptional views through oversized windows. Sensitive to these dramatic details, the rooms are simple, bright, contemporary, in pastels or warm, lemony color schemes, with nice bright marble baths. Unusual are the suites, each decorated entirely differently: some contemporary, others lavishly feminine.

The Ambassador Grill is an intriguing setting of green and white parquet marble, red carpets, and banquettes, with an atrium-type ceiling created by mirrors. Three meals daily are served here, including a traditional Japanese breakfast, and a Sunday seafood and lobster brunch. American grill entrées are about $25.

The twenty-ninth floor of the East Tower houses a fitness room, with Cybex and cardiovascular equipment, which looks onto the East River and north over the open space of the United Nations park. Each pink-marbled locker room has its own sauna and teak lockers. The swimming pool also has two views of the East River and downtown through floor-to-ceiling windows. The ceiling is draped in a reflective cloth, so the room is flooded with sunlight. The regulation tennis court, on the top floor, is staffed with a full-time pro.

Among the usual amenities of morning newspaper and complimentary shoeshine, guests are treated to daily limousine service to Wall Street and the garment district and evenings to the theater district. The staff speaks nearly fifty languages and is extremely accommodating as a result of their international exposure and setting.

Pennsylvania

Four Seasons Hotel
One Logan Square
Philadelphia, Pennsylvania 19103
215-963-1500
800-332-3442

Proprietor: Urban Investment Development Corporation
General Manager: John Indrieri
Accommodations: 371 rooms, including 92 executive suites
    and 7 full suites
Rates: Rooms, $145–$195 weekends, $235–$285 weekdays;
    suites, $195–$285
Included: Complimentary shoeshine and morning paper
Added: $30 each additional guest; 12% tax
Payment: Major credit cards
Children: Welcome
Pets: Allowed
Smoking: 7 of 8 floors nonsmoking
Open: All year

Although the Four Seasons Philadelphia has quite a contemporary facade, it is one of the city's senior properties. Philadelphia's hotel boom occurred in the mid-1980s, foreshadowed by the opening of the Four Seasons in 1983. Most notably, the majority of its guest rooms and the public spaces have a superb, rather historic view of Logan Square's Swann Memorial Fountain, recently restored as a result of a $2 million fundraising effort, fashioned by Alexander Stirling Calder and installed in 1924. The fountain, also referred to as Three Rivers, represents the Delaware, Schuylkill, and Wissahickon rivers.

This eight-story gray granite structure, taking up an entire city block, opened in July 1983, designed by Eugene Kohn. Guests enter at the well-trafficked corner of Ben Franklin Parkway and Race and 18th streets, at a wide carport. The trademark Four Seasons wide hallways are finished in polished rose marble, the walls a light anegre wood.

The finest aspects of this Four Seasons hotel are found in its guest rooms, in furniture copied by Henredon from original Philadelphia Federal pieces in the city's Museum of Art, within view of most rooms. There are two color schemes to the rooms, historically appropriate, in blue-cocoa and ivory-rust. The researched wallpapers are unusually patterned. While all rooms have stocked mini-bars, some have interesting pieces like an English wing chair in a toile print or perhaps an armoire with delicate inlay. The baths are fine, furnished with a terry robe, a scale, a phone, and hair dryer.

The popular Fountain Restaurant is a formal setting with tapestried chairs and blue, brown, and beige geometric carpeting, offering three meals under the supervision of chef Jean-Marie Lacroix. The Swann Lounge is the cushy, plush setting for afternoon tea, intimate conversations, and a Viennese dessert buffet on evening weekends, accompanied by the Tom Lawton jazz trio. The outdoor Courtyard Café, on the non–Logan Square side of the hotel, is a lovely alternative in warmer months, where visitors enjoy light-fare dining under umbrellas to the music of a cascading fountain on a backdrop of flowers and greenery.

The thorough Health Spa offers an indoor swimming pool, a Jacuzzi, a sauna, fitness classes, and an exercise room with universal equipment. Swedish, shiatsu, and sport massages are available.

Families are happy at the Four Seasons. Children are treated to milk and cookies upon arrival, child-sized terry robes in rooms, special menus, Nintendo and children's movies, as well as the Swann Lounge brunch, with stuffed animals, toys, and a train and edibles like Jell-O squares, M&M cookies, chicken fingers, mini-pizzas, and bite-sized hot dogs.

The Rittenhouse

210 West Rittenhouse Square
Philadelphia, Pennsylvania 19103
215-546-9000
800-635-1042

Proprietors: Amerimar Realty Co., General Electric Pension Trust
General Manager: Paul E. Seligson

Accommodations: 98 rooms, including 12 suites
Rates: Rooms, $235–$260 weekdays, $130–$150, weekends;
   suites, $300–$350
Added: $25 each additional guest; 12% tax
Payment: Major credit cards
Children: Welcome
Pets: Small pets allowed
Smoking: Every other floor nonsmoking
Open: All year

Philadelphia is blessed with two entirely different, consummate luxury properties: the Hotel Atop the Bellevue and the Rittenhouse, which received its first five-diamond award from AAA in 1992. This elegant and very full-service property opened in June 1989 as a result of a $120 million effort, masterminded by developer David Marshall. In addition to housing 98 beautiful guest rooms on floors 5–9, the Rittenhouse has a deluxe Health Club and Spa, two highly rated restaurants, nonpareil views of Rittenhouse Square, and the exclusive Nan Duskin women's boutique.

The Rittenhouse sits on the west side of the square that inspired its name, one of five of William Penn's original city squares. The 6.5-acre park is named for David Rittenhouse, born in Germantown in 1732, said to have invented America's first telescope, who served as Pennsylvania state treasurer from 1777 to 1789 and as first director of the United States Mint in Philadelphia in 1792.

Despite its surrounding history, the Rittenhouse is a modern piece of architecture, a glass trapezoid that looks like a very wide staircase standing on its side. Interestingly, the Rittenhouse foundation was laid in 1973, but because the original developer went bankrupt, the 30-story shell stood empty for eighteen years before Mr. Marshall took the helm in 1987.

The lobby is a beautiful array of olive, taupe, teal, and cream, featuring ash wood molding and millwork, pine Louis XIV bergères, smooth round columns supporting a coffered ceiling with massive glowing ceiling sconces, and polished golden marble underfoot. The Cassatt Tea Room and Lounge rests beyond the columns, named for the family whose mansion graced this site. Son Alexander was the president of the Pennsylvania Railroad who married the niece of President James Buchanan, and daughter Mary was the famous American Impressionist, whose work graces some of the hotel's public spaces. The lounge is the setting for afternoon tea, cocktails, and piano music amid tapestried French chairs and huge potted trees. In warmer months, the arched French doorways open to a copper-green trellised garden café.

Rittenhouse accommodations are oversized and beautiful, reputed to have Philadelphia's finest baths. As a result of the building's jagged exterior, half of the guest rooms have not only wonderful views of Rittenhouse Square but interesting interiors with 90-degree alcoves. The staterooms are decorated in country French themes, with masculine navy blues and camels, with striped bergères, Queen Anne chairs and writing desks, and border paper matching the striped drapes. Each room has three phones (one in the bath), a VCR and two televisions (one in the bath), and a mini-bar. The feminine suites are done in Laura Ashley pink chintz, with an upholstered king-size headboard under a gathered crown canopy. The beige and light brown marble baths have Neutrogena amenities, a hair dryer, and terry robes. Even the hallways are graced with original art, among which are paintings by Joe Barker, who was discovered selling his work outdoors by Mr. Marshall.

Award-winning Restaurant 210 offers contemporary cuisine during lunch and dinner in a high-tech elegant setting overlooking the square. Neoclassic mahogany chairs and millwork, black and beige upholstery, black silk banquettes, and silver linen on the walls and columns—all make a muted backdrop for colorful abstract art. Executive chef Gary Coyle came from New York's La Côte Basque and prepares entrées, all above $20, like grilled magret of duck with smoked apple and jimaca torte and green peppercorn sauce; preceded perhaps by a tian of Maine lobster medallions with tarragon roe quinoa and lobster dressing; or Savoy, leek, and oyster pot pie with California chardonnay and mixed herb seasoning.

TreeTops is a floor below, a pleasant café decorated with rattan chairs, pastel yellow walls, and terra cotta floors, which shares the view of Rittenhouse Square. The jumbo lump crabcakes have been praised loudly around town. The woody Boathouse Row Bar is home to the *Liz Ann* scull which John B. Kelly, father of Grace, rowed toward a gold medal in the 1920 Olympics.

A grand feature of the Rittenhouse is Toppers Spa and Fitness Center, which opened in August 1990. The fitness facilities offer a pool, sauna, steam room, rowing and cycling machines, stairmasters, and Cybex exercise equipment. The Esthetique Spa features massage, aromatherapy facials, seaweed body wraps, body scrubbing and polishing, and hydrotherapy baths. The staff extends itself markedly; as well, management has provided a full business center for guest use.

The Ritz-Carlton

17th and Chestnut Streets at Liberty Place
Philadelphia, Pennsyvlania 19103
215-563-1600
800-241-3333

Proprietors: Liberty Place Hotel Associates
General Manager: Jim Beley, under The Ritz-Carlton Hotel
    Company
Accommodations: 290 rooms, including 16 suites
Rates: Rooms, $195–$265; suites, from $425
Included: Five complimentary meal presentations on the
    Club level
Minimum stay: None
Added: $35 each addditional guest; 12% tax
Payment: Major credit cards
Children: Welcome
Pets: Not allowed
Smoking: Nonsmoking rooms available
Open: All year

While the majority of its properties are of entirely new construction, Ritz-Carlton hotels represent the finest in sophisticated Old World hospitality, inspired by the Ritz of London. With rich wood paneling, classic moldings, extensive art collections, lavish antiques, handwoven carpets, marble floors, and elegant and comfortably furnished public spaces, the Ritz-Carlton properties emulate stately mansions and English country manors.

The Philadelphia Ritz opened in November 1990. To get here, look for the city's version of the Chrysler Building. Liberty Place is two twin glass skyscrapers, one of which pierces the sky with its needle tip. A squat 15-story adjunct rests between them: the Shops at Liberty Place, with about 70 boutiques and specialty stores, and the Ritz-Carlton Philadelphia.

Guests enter a foyer at ground level from the busy street front and take an elevator to reception, a floor above. Such is the Ritz-Carlton way, ridding the lobby and reception area from the street's bustle, creating an elite approach or a well-guarded secret. When the elevators open, all is as it should be: the trademark Italian marble floors gleam, handwoven carpets muffle one's step, 18th- and 19th-century oils are kind to the eye, and the softspoken staff is eager to assist.

The common spaces on the reception floor are lovely and civilized. The Dining Room serves formal French cuisine under the direction of starred Michelin chef Philippe Reininger. In this American Federal room with light paint and bright white molding, guests dine under crystal chandeliers on bone china and the Ritz-Carlton trademark cobalt blue glasses, with Waterford crystal oil lamps on each table. The Grill and the Grill Bar serve all-day dining and lighter fare in a dark, clubby atmosphere, with rich wood molding and ceilings. The walls are covered in green damask, lit by a wood-burning French fireplace, flickering off the green marble bar. The Lobby Lounge serves morning coffee, afternoon high tea, and cocktails in the evening, with a relaxing backdrop of live classical music or a jazz trio.

The guest rooms are reliably lovely. The wallcoverings are damask gray behind the traditional furnishings. The baths are entirely marble, with two terry robes and ample Ritz-Carlton amenities, including a sewing kit and shower cap. The two top floors of guest rooms are under the tutelage of the Ritz-Carlton Club, with their own concierge and lounge and five complimentary meals. The beautiful red Oriental hall carpet is modeled after the original London Ritz.

The fourth-floor Fitness Center has a Nautilus and a rowing machine, two bikes, a dry sauna, Jacuzzi, and massage therapy upon request, all in a pristine marble setting.

Virginia

The Berkeley Hotel
Twelfth and Cary Streets, Box 1259
Richmond, Virginia 23210
804-780-1300

Proprietors: Summitt Enterprises
General Manager: Mr. Voorhees
Accommodations: 55 rooms, some with terraces, including 23 suites and Governor's Suite
Rates: $118–$128; Governor's Suite, $350
Added: $10 each additional guest; 9.5% tax
Payment: Major credit cards
Children: Welcome
Pets: Not allowed
Smoking: Nonsmoking rooms on all floors
Open: All year

The Berkeley is an extremely handsome postmodern structure built in 1988 in the heart of Richmond's restored Shockoe Slip neighborhood. When Richmond was burned by Confederate troops in the Civil War, the tobacco warehouses of Shockoe Slip were the first to be destroyed, and the first again to be rebuilt. Today they stand, preserved in time, on either side of cobblestoned streets, housing charming shops and businesses. The Berkeley Hotel is a sensitive addition to the area, incorporating the facade of an old townhouse in part of its exterior whose historic lines are echoed throughout the newer structure.

Sitting on the corner of Twelfth and Cary streets, the center portion of the Berkeley Hotel culminates in a six-story brick and mortar tower, flanked on either side by similar four-story townhouses, with its three-story inspiration tacked on near the Cary Street entrance. The substantive part of the hotel rests just behind the brick facade, unseen from the street, terraced back on each floor providing balconies for about a third of the guest rooms.

Under the green awning, guests enter an antique-filled foyer, with dark wood molding, traditional wing chairs, and a lovely swirling-patterned deep Victorian carpet underfoot. The cozy Berkeley Restaurant has received four diamonds from AAA and fine local reviews. Three meals are served here daily in a dressy, intimate setting with lacy Roman shades, cherry paneled walls illuminated by tiny brass sconces, and dark wood-beamed ceilings. Nightingales Lounge borders on the restaurant space.

Mr. Voorhees's interest in cartography is evidenced throughout the public spaces. Across from the elegant elevator banks on each of six floors are prints of old maps detailing the progress of the Civil War from Cornwallis's campaign to the surrender in Yorktown. The guest rooms are nicely decorated in traditional luxury hotel themes, with chintz bedding matching floor-to-ceiling drapes and complementary tones in sitting areas. If televisions aren't hidden in armoires, they are mounted on stands. Most of the beds are king-size, and robes are available upon request. The baths have coffee makers and telephones. Rooms are serviced twice daily, including European turndown. Some rooms have terraces.

New hotels not sponsored by a major chain are exciting properties in the hotel industry—especially when done as professionally and beautifully as the Berkeley. With only 55 rooms and the stunning Governor's Suite with its thirty-foot vaulted ceiling, the Berkeley is small enough to offer personal service with the feeling of a large, luxury hotel.

The Ritz-Carlton Pentagon City

1250 South Hayes Street
Arlington, Virginia 22202
703-415-5000
800-241-3333

Proprietor: The Melvin Simon Company
General Manager: Robert Warmon and the Ritz-Carlton Hotel Company
Accommodations: 345 rooms, including 41 suites
Rates: Rooms, $170–$210; Ritz-Carlton Club, $240; suites, from $400
Included: Five meal presentations at Club level
Added: $15 each additional guest; 9.75% tax
Payment: Major credit cards
Children: Welcome
Pets: Not allowed

Smoking: 13 of 17 floors nonsmoking
Open: All year

The Ritz-Carlton Pentagon City opened in May 1990, just across the Potomac from Washington, D.C. Among its other virtues, the hotel is quite proud of its two-star Michelin chef, Gérard Pangaud, who oversees the intimate Restaurant.

Pentagon City is a surreal place, with a spare landscape and clusters of gleaming postmodern skyscrapers. On South Hayes Street, an 18-story light stone monolith puts its narrow face forward, like a brick placed sideways, between a vaultlike Nordstroms, which looks like the National Gallery, and the expansive Pentagon City Fashion Centre, with 140 shops. Upon entry are all the telltale signs of the Ritz-Carlton: large parquet marble floors, vast Oriental carpets, rich 19th-century oil paintings and portraits hanging on lush wood paneling, dentil crown molding, and beautifully upholstered classic parlor sets.

Aside from the public spaces, two restaurants and a lounge are on the ground level. The Grill is the setting for three daily meals, with lovely tapestried chairs. The large 18th-century fireplace mantel framed in carved wood and green marble was found in a French château. Visitors gather in the Lounge for the civilized occasion of afternoon tea, evening cocktails, and piano entertainment.

The Restaurant is the sublime setting for an intimate dinner, which holds about 75 guests within its silk-covered walls. Dinners are served on Rosenthal china, accompanied by the Ritz-Carlton signature cobalt blue goblets. Two-star Michelin chef de cuisine Gérard Pangaud might offer turnip ravioli with duck confit; black radish cake with sweetbreads, truffle, wild mushrooms, and fava beans; and from the entrées one might select a cold salmon soufflé with wine sauce or poached lobster in ginger lime sauce. The prix fixe menu for four courses is $62, for five courses, $75. Sommelier David Howard is from the Inn at Little Washington (see Gourmet Getaways).

The traditionally decorated guest rooms are emblematic of any Ritz-Carlton. In addition to damask chairs and sofas, stocked honor bars, televisions hidden in armoires, and floral bedding matching drapes, guests can expect marble baths with vanity mirrors, hair dryers, and terry robes. The Club Floor offers all these amenities in addition to a lounge, concierge, and five meal presentations throughout the day, from a Continental breakfast to chocolate and cordials after dinner.

While city properties scramble to find fitness facilities, the Pentagon City location has a large Fitness Center on the third floor, with a lap pool, universal equipment, Bio Cycle, Bio Climber, and Life Rower, and steam, Jacuzzi, and sauna rooms. A Fitness Center Bar features juices, fruits, and vegetables.

This Ritz-Carlton has a unique feature in a pamphlet that leads interested guests on a self-guided tour of the $2 million art collection at Pentagon City.

The Ritz-Carlton Tysons Corner
1700 Tysons Boulevard
McLean, Virginia 22102
703-506-4300
800-241-3333
Fax: 703-506-4305

Proprietor: The Ritz-Carlton Hotel Company
General Manager: Peter Faraone
Accommodations: 399 rooms, including 33 suites
Rates: Rooms, $125–$195; suites, $325–$900
Included: Five meal presentations at Club level
Added: $30 each additional guest; 6.5% tax
Payment: Major credit cards
Children: Welcome
Pets: Not allowed
Smoking: Nonsmoking rooms available
Open: All year

Halfway between Dulles and National airports, the extensive new Ritz-Carlton at Tysons Corner has an urban convenience to the capital, 14 miles east, and easy access to rural and historic Virginia. Already with a prime representative on DuPont Circle in Washington, D.C., and a new property in Pentagon City, it seems odd that the Ritz-Carlton Company would open yet another satellite hotel outside of the capital—especially one with 400 rooms. However, the deluxe Tysons Corner Ritz-Carlton debuted in November 1991, built for Washingtonians who want to get away for romance, Virginia sightseeing, and especially for shopping.

The hotel sits adjacent to the Tysons II Galleria, with 125 shops, restaurants, and boutiques, like Neiman Marcus, Saks Fifth Avenue, and Macy's; close by is the Fairfax Square Mall, with Fendi, Hermes, and Louis Vuitton; and Tysons Corner Center, with more than 300 shops.

Much of the amenities and virtues of this hotel mirror those at the Pentagon City property. Guest can expect formal dining at the Restaurant, all-day dining at the Grill, and cocktails and high tea in the Lounge. Guest rooms are similarly decorated to those at Pentagon City, in 18th-century reproduction furnishings, with lots of damask, mahogany molding, chintz drapery, and original art. The uppermost floors feature the upscale Ritz-Carlton Club with its own concierge, lounge, and five complimentary food presentations daily. As well, there is a state-of-the-art fitness center, with a 40-foot lap pool, cardiovascular equipment, and steam and sauna rooms.

The staff is on its toes, solicitous, and courteous. While Washington hotels might be weary with competition, the Tysons Corner Ritz-Carlton sits confidently in the relative countryside. Mt. Vernon Plantation is a short drive, as is the Wolf Trap Farm for the Performing Arts.

Grand Old Resorts

New York

Gideon Putnam Hotel
Box 476
Saratoga Springs, New York 12866
518-584-3000
800-732-1560

Proprietors: TW Recreation Services, Inc.
General Manager: Ken Boyles
Accommodations: 132 rooms, including 18 parlor and porch
   suites
Rates:
   November–April: $75–$135 EP; $121–$227 AP
   August: $229–$405 EP; $270–$487 AP
   Rest of year: $94–$152 EP; $140–$244 AP
Included: Up to three meals depending on rate
Minimum stay: None
Added: Additional person, $12–$30 EP, $58–$71 AP; 11% tax;
   16% tax over $100
Payment: Major credit cards
Children: Welcome
Pets: Not allowed
Smoking: Nonsmoking rooms available
Open: All year

Only in Saratoga Springs can a state park represent the height
of luxury. The Gideon Putnam Hotel sits in the middle of the
1,500-acre Saratoga Spa State Park. Hotel guests are welcome to
use all the park facilities, including a PGA 18-hole golf course,
a 9-hole par 3 course, three outdoor swimming pools, eight
tennis courts, ice skating, and cross-country skiing. Sharing the
grounds is the Saratoga Performing Arts Center, summer home
of the New York City Ballet, and the Roosevelt Mineral Baths in
their original turn-of-the-century setting.

   Built in 1934, the classic red brick hotel is trimmed in white in high Georgian style. A three-story portico supported by eight pillars shades the long inset veranda, topped by a balcony across the fourth floor, balanced on either side by symmetrical five-story wings. A circular drive is carved into the sweeping front lawn of the Gideon Putnam. Guests enter the grand reception hall under a green and white striped awning covering bright flowers in window boxes.

The hotel was bought in 1988 by TW Services, which undertook a two-year redecorating project. The result is a toned-down version of the Williamsburg Inn: Old World elegance and hospitality, formal sitting areas with floral arrangements atop side tables, cream-colored walls, classic moldings, high and wide archways, and Palladian windows opening out to patios and gardened walkways. While the Williamsburg Inn was done in exacting, formal Regency style, the grand Georgian nature of the Gideon Putnam stops short of museum-perfect elegance.

Guests dine in several rooms: the walls of the Georgian Room were gloriously painted with landscape murals in 1935 by an Irish artist; the Garden Room has lighter murals interrupting an unusual wall textured with plaster vines; and the smaller Estate Room is classic, with a working marble fireplace. The Saratoga Room bar is enlivened by a black and white mural depicting Saratoga scenes; and the Arches Room offers jazz in the summer, in a great setting of sunlit archways. The Victoria pool is quite lovely, set in a palazzo of Georgian architecture with covered brick archways.

While the common areas are extremely elegant, the guest rooms, throughout the five floors of the hotel, are rather predictable. Decorated traditionally in reproduction Queen Anne furniture, they are comfortable and spacious with televisions and phones, though the colors and patterns are uninspired. Preferable are the six porch rooms that take advantage of the lovely scenery surrounding the hotel.

Service at the hotel is friendly and prompt, though assuredly hectic during the summer high season. The remarkable park setting and lovely Georgian architecture are quite worth the trip, especially in the off-season.

Mohonk Mountain House
Lake Mohonk
New Paltz, New York 12561
914-255-1000
Reservations: 914-255-4500, 800-772-6646

Proprietors: Albert and Alfred Smiley
Accommodations: 276 rooms, most with private bath, many with fireplace
Rates: $171–$369 per couple AP (seasonally)
Included: Three meals a day and afternoon tea
Minimum stay: 2 nights on weekends, 3 nights on holidays
Added: $60 each additional guest over age 12 AP; $50 each additional guest age 4–12 AP; 15% service charge; 7% state tax; 2.5% occupancy tax; $1 county tax
Payment: Visa, MasterCard, American Express
Children: Welcome
Pets: Not allowed
Smoking: Allowed
Open: All year

One of this book's most magical places was discovered during a picnic in 1869 when Alfred H. Smiley was captivated by the beauty of Lake Mohonk in the Shawangunk Mountains. He spent the night in a ten-room tavern on the property and soon began discussions with its owner to buy the surrounding 300 acres. He and his identical twin, Albert, had long hoped to own a country house and they saw this as an early and ideal opportunity.

Such were the modest beginnings of the Mohonk Mountain House, which grew from 10 to 276 rooms, from 300 acres to 7,500. The brothers built this dream together, extending their Quaker beliefs to unite nature and people in harmony. Mohonk remains in the Smiley family today and looks most certainly as it did at the turn of the century, focused around "the lake in the sky."

Though it's only 90 miles from New York City just barely off the Hudson, Mohonk is as secluded on its acreage as anything else in this book. The setting, several miles up a mountain drive, floating on an azure lake, seems truly out of a fairy tale. The freshwater Lake Mohonk is a half mile long and 60 feet deep. Conjuring up images of European castles, the Mohonk Mountain House is an elegant collage of Romanesque, Richardson, and Adirondack architecture. In 1870, the House was expanded to accommodate 40 guests. The large Central Building was built in the late 1880s, followed by the seven-story Stone Building in 1899 and 1902. Through the hallowed doors, across the wooden transoms conducting ever-present breezes, guests come to the wide, rocker-filled veranda overlooking the lovely lake itself which so inspired the Smiley brothers. The eye floats across the mirrorlike lake to the craggy heights of Sky Top and its stone tower. Such a scene is painted in the minds of those who have been to Mohonk, remembered with an ageless smile.

There's an Old World sociability here from the days when people vacationed for months at a time, content with company and natural surroundings. Throughout the house are 151 working fireplaces, 200 balconies, six parlors, and three verandas. Almost all the guest rooms have porches, and all porches have caned rockers, a good deal of which are original to the old house.

The rooms themselves are all different, some quite luxurious like a Ritz-Carlton-gone-Gothic; and some are nearly ascetic, with a sink in the corner or closet. All have antiques, old dressers, ceiling fans, with Crabtree and Evelyn amenities.

The rooms, however, are a minuscule part of the Mohonk experience. Quite telling of the times gone by are the abundance and variety of the public places which somehow remain so private: little libraries with well-worn leatherbound classics, a nook in a wraparound porch untrespassed for hours. The dining room, for example, is one of the glories of the place: a wonder of open space which carries one's eye across the pined wainscoting to the large picture windows which look across the mountains—here the sunsets are the most delectable part of the meal, viewed in a panorama of 30 feet of window.

Throughout the 2,000 acres of the Mohonk Mountain House and 5,500 acres of the Mohonk Preserve, guests have a choice of more organized activities than any of the five presidents who visited would ever have had in a daily schedule. Romantics enjoy a picnic in one of the 115 Adirondack gazebos that dot the landscape; kids yearn for the daily cookouts at the Granary. An astounding 85 miles of hiking trails are groomed. There is a 9-hole rambling Scottish-style golf course, a putting green on the front Lawn, a bowling green, croquet, six tennis courts (four clay and two Har-Tru), horses for western and English and pony riding, rowboats, paddleboats, canoes, carriage and sleigh rides, cross-country skiing, fishing, ice skating, horseshoes, platform tennis, shuffleboard, snow tubing, softball, volleyball—and countless other activities, including storytelling, a grand tradition at Mohonk. In addition, Mohonk offers an extensive children's program during the weekends, holidays, and summers for kids age 2–17.

Like the founding fathers of Mohonk, generations of guests have vacationed over the years, returning for the beauty and serenity of this unique setting.

The Otesaga Hotel
Cooper Inn
Cooperstown, New York 13326
607-547-9931
607-547-2567

General Manager: Robert Holliday
Accommodations: 125 rooms, plus 20 rooms in Cooper Inn
Rates: $202–$282 per couple MAP in Hotel; $104–$114 in the
  Inn
Included: Breakfast and dinner in Hotel, Continental
  breakfast in Inn
Minimum stay: None
Added: $60–$65 each additional adult MAP; $22–$30 each
  child age 2–11 MAP; $9 per person per day gratuity
Payment: Major credit cards
Children: Welcome
Pets: Not allowed
Smoking: Allowed
Open: May–October; Cooper Inn all year

A great way to see America's greatest sport is to stay at the
Otesaga Hotel while visiting the Baseball Hall of Fame in Cooperstown. The town itself is a picture-perfect vision of Americana, with small 19th-century brick buildings on quaint
straight and narrow streets. Founded in 1786 by William Cooper, father of the author James Fenimore, the town is better
known as the laboratory in which Abner Doubleday invented
the game of baseball in 1839. The southern shores of Lake Otsego are just a block or two from town, its lazy waves falling in
the lap of the Otesaga Hotel, whose front lawn is a charming
lakefront blue.

The Otesaga was built in 1909, a fine Georgian structure of
solid brick that is highly reminiscent of the Gideon Putnam in
Saratoga. Shaped like a flattish *H*, the Otesaga has a grand
Greek Revival three-story portico in the center at the front
entrance supported by four columns; behind is the trademark
curved veranda overlooking the lake. Flanking the center portion are two four-story wings. The common rooms are grand
and regal, with original moldings, soft-hued plaster walls, classic and elegant furnishings, and chintz curtains framing bright
views of the lake. Less magnificent are the guest rooms: clean,
standard, traditional, unsurprising, with televisions and reproduction furnishings.

The 18-hole Leatherstocking par 72 championship golf
course is within a short walk of the Otesaga. On the property

are two tennis courts and an outdoor heated swimming pool. The adventurous or the romantic might want to embark on a boat cruise on the lake.

Guests who prefer more intimate accommodations might try the Cooper Inn around the corner, also owned by the Otesaga. Built in 1816 by Henry Phinney as Willowbrook, the gracious Italianate house became the Cooper Inn in 1936. Guests here are treated to Continental breakfast and use of the facilities at its sister property. Some of the furnishings are nice antiques, and several guest rooms have black marble fireplaces and the original plaster ceiling medallions and moldings.

The hotel is rather bustling when open, often the choice for groups. While the guest rooms are uninspired, they are clean and comfortable. The elegant common spaces, glorious lake views, and fine dining certainly provide for an exciting stay in Cooperstown.

The Sagamore — An Omni Classic Resort
On Lake George
Bolton Landing, New York 12814
518-644-9400
800-358-3585

Proprietor: Green Island Associates
General Manager: Stephen Rosenstock of Omni Hotels
Accommodations: 340 rooms (100 rooms in Hotel, 240 in new Lodge units, including 120 suites with fireplaces)
Rates: Hotel, $147–$215 MAP; Lodge, $115–$199 MAP
Included: Breakfast and dinner
Minimum stay: None
Added: $66 each additional person; $30 each child age 3–12 MAP; $52 each child age 13–17 MAP; $11 per person service charge; 7% tax; 12% tax over $100
Payment: Major credit cards
Children: Welcome
Pets: Not allowed
Smoking: Allowed
Open: All year

The Sagamore has one of the most breathtaking resort settings in the East. It sits on a 70-acre island in the middle of azure Lake George, across a causeway from the village of Bolton Landing. There have been several incarnations of the graceful Sagamore resort on Lake George, though all recall an Old World magnificence from the days of Pullman cars and sojourns lasting months. The first was built in the English Tudor style in 1881–

82, accommodated approximately 300 guests, including *New York Times* publisher Adolph Ochs and photographer Alfred Stieglitz. When it burned to the ground only a decade later, the Sagamore was quickly replaced with a modern structure, outfitted with electricity, Western Union wires, steam elevators, and private baths. This time, the hotel managed to elude destruction by fire for 20 years, until Easter Sunday 1914.

In 1922, the present structure was erected, a 100-room clubhouse. The stock market crash delayed expansion until 1930 when the hotel reopened along with a new golf course built by Donald Ross atop Federal Hill, about two miles up the mountain from Lake George. The Brandt family owned the Sagamore from the mid-1940s until 1981. The hotel underwent a major expansion process over four years and $75 million with the financial backing of Norman Wolgin and Kennington Properties of California.

The classic 1930 white clapboard building looks as it always did, facing downlake from its perch on a tiered grassy hill, shaped like a bow tie. The three stories of white clapboard are trimmed in black, with several lower levels trenched into the hill. One hundred guest rooms remain in the refurbished 1930 hotel, and 240 new units were added in seven contemporary lodges along the tree-lined shore behind the hotel. An exciting addition was the transformation of the nightclub into extensive spa facilities in 1991.

The common areas at the Sagamore are just beautiful, offering up views of the lake through an endless number of windows from different angles. The reception area opens out to a two-story portico onto the tiered south lawn. The appointments are classic and traditional, and every cornice, chair rail, and archway seems to be gleaming with a fresh coat of paint. There are six restaurants: from the pool and golf eateries, to Mister Brown's pub setting, to the large Sagamore Dining Room and the ladylike Veranda for high tea and early evening hors d'oeuvres, to the elegant Trillium.

Above the main hallway and in the four-story wings, the guest rooms in the hotel are done in two schemes: classic and Adirondack rooms, the latter fewer but more interesting. The rooms are quite smart and new-looking, with a touch of Omni-ubiquitous decor which is thankfully enlivened by the magnificent views. Families and groups may prefer the Lodge units, done in contemporary or Adirondack decor, half with living rooms, wet bars, wood-burning fireplaces, and terraces.

At the new Spa and Fitness Center, guests look out over the lake while working out on the ten-station Keiser Training Circuit, stairmasters, lifecycles, windracers, rowers, and treadmills. The heated indoor-outdoor pool is open year-round. The spa offers many therapeutic treatments including Moortherapy, a mud wrap used in full-body, masks, and scalp treatments. Other offerings include European facials, salt-glo and loofah scrub, herbal wraps, seaweed body mask, foot reflexology, hydrotherapy, and salon services. Therapists offer four types of massage; saunas, Turkish steam rooms, whirlpools, hot and cold plunge pools complete the facilities.

Several miles from the Sagamore is the par 70 Donald Ross golf course, 18 holes on 188 acres overlooking the Lake. By the Lodge units, the Tennis Club has two indoor and five outdoor courts of Har-Tru or hard surface and a racquetball court. Winter activities abound: cross-country skiing, ice skating, ice fishing, sledding, and daily shuttle service to Gore and West mountains. For a fee, guests enjoy water skiing, surfing, sailing, and parasailing. As well, a thorough summer children's program provides a plethora of activity for kids in two age groups: 3–5 and 6–13.

Pennsylvania

The Hotel Hershey
Box 400
Hershey, Pennsylvania 17033
717-533-2171
800-533-3131
800-HERSHEY
800-437-7439

General Manager and Vice President: Patrick J. Kerwin
Accommodations: 243 rooms and suites, plus VIP guest cottage
Rates:
   April–November: From $252 per couple MAP and AP
   Rest of year: From $198 per couple MAP and AP
Included: Breakfast and dinner MAP; three meals a day AP;
   full use of Hershey Country Club
Minimum stay: Flexible 3 nights on holidays
Added: $54–$69 each additional adult; $24–$30 each child
   4–9 years; $39–$49 each child 9–18 years; 6% tax; gratuities
Payment: Major credit cards
Children: Welcome, under 4 free
Pets: Not allowed
Smoking: Nonsmoking rooms available
Open: All year

The Hotel Hershey is a grand resort of intriguing contradictions: a living part of a make-believe world; a luxury hotel adjacent to amusement parks, a zoo, and streetlights shaped like kisses; in a town which makes world-famous chocolate set in rural Pennsylvania Dutch farmland; a sophisticated refuge for adults and a wondrous place for children. Over a million and a half people visit Chocolate World every year, but the Hotel Hershey accommodates overnight guests in a gracious, unhurried manner.

Many years after Milton Hershey's company had gotten off the ground (to say the least) and the reputation of the world's greatest chocolate bar was well established, Hershey decided to build a world-class hotel. In 1930, he showed his architect plans for the Heliopolis Hotel in Cairo, which he and his wife Kitty had greatly admired, but the endeavor proved too great. Instead, plans for the hotel were drawn from a postcard of a similar Mediterranean property.

The Depression-era structure gave employment to 800 workers and was finally completed in 1933. The five-story brick building has an extensive veranda, which opens like outstretched arms. Its cream-colored brick is lined with Spanish arches, under a green tiled roof and twin bell towers. Its grand lobby displays the essential Mediterranean influence with tiled floors and a fountain etched with mosaics. European reflecting pools sit astride sculpted gardens behind the original structure, seen through the stained glass windows of the circular dining room.

The guest rooms are furnished traditionally, with reproduction furniture and classic fabrics and all the expected amenities of a luxury property. The feeling is that of a country club, where guests dress for dinner and enjoy an indoor and outdoor swimming pool, fitness facilities, lawn bowling, shuffleboard, four tennis courts, and putting greens. There are no surprises inside the hotel, since all the surprises rest in the 76 acres of family entertainment at Hershey.

The vast holdings include HersheyPark, with 45 amusement rides; Chocolate World; 10 acres of ZooAmerica; the Hershey Museum of American Life, founded by Mr. Hershey in 1933; and 23 acres of flora and fauna at the lavish Hershey Gardens.

Hershey offers more holes of golf per square foot than any other resort in the world. Of all the nonchocolate activities in town, golf is perhaps the most attractive, with 72 holes in the vicinity. Three championship 18-hole courses are at the Country Club and Parkview, and the Hotel Hershey Golf Course and Spring Creek add another 18 holes.

While many grand old resorts have somewhat of a formal nature, the Hotel Hershey is an overwhelmingly friendly place. Milton Hershey's love for chocolate, children, community, and business is continued in every facet of his property.

Skytop Lodge

Skytop, Pennsylvania 18357
717-595-7401
800-422-7SKY in Pennsylvania
800-345-7SKY outside Pennsylvania

General Manager: William Malleson
Resident Manager: Eugene B. Yacuboski
Accommodations: 183 rooms in main lodge, including 12 mini-suites, 3 VIP suites, and 9 four-bedroom cottages
Rates: Rooms, $208–$278; suites, $240–$315; cottages, $215–$285, all AP; special family plans available
Included: Three meals a day, use of all facilities
Minimum stay: None
Added: $70 each additional guest; $12 each additional child; 15% gratuities; 6% tax
Payment: Visa, MasterCard, American Express, Diners Club
Children: Welcome
Pets: Not allowed
Smoking: Nonsmoking rooms available
Open: All year

Skytop was christened in the mid-1920s, with a name borrowed from the highest peak at the Mohonk Mountain House in New Paltz, New York—which tells a visitor a great deal about this mountaintop haven. That Skytop is the least known of the grand old resorts is either a grave oversight or a blessing. Nonetheless, the fact remains that a traveler is unprepared for the Old World magnificence of this four-story stone lodge that sits three miles north of Canadensis atop a 5,500-acre mountain plateau in an untouched area of the Poconos. While the exterior looks a bit like an English stone castle, the high-ceilinged great hall and elegant dining room invoke the feeling of Gatsby-era wealth.

The turn off rural Route 390 brings a visitor across a causeway that stretches over 74-acre Skytop Lake. The road winds gracefully, revealing the four-story mansion across groomed grounds and plantings. The lodge was successfully designed to look as if it rose out of the mountain, which is made up mostly of red shale and sandstone. The stone has the blanched, weathered look of exposure to many a hardy winter, the small-paned windows and dormers designed to hold in as much heat as possible. While the enclosed North Porch has an elevation of 1,576 feet, the property reaches above 2,000 feet on West Mountain. Everything in sight, around eight square miles, belongs to Skytop.

The great reception hall is the Pine Room, with rich paneled walls and exposed floors warmed by an enormous fireplace, classically furnished with comfortable reading chairs and gregarious sitting areas with traditional living room suites, lit by large windows hung with crewel drapes. In a clubby setting off the Pine Room is the Library, where guests read books at fireside. In the west wing, guests dine in a formal setting looking through Palladian paned windows; and in the east wing are the fitness area and indoor pool. The guest rooms rest upstairs and in the two wings. These are done in a classic pine suite with four-poster pineapple beds, wing chairs, a television tucked into an armoire, and bright, interesting window treatments that differ from room to room.

One of Skytop's finest and rarest features is its naturalist program. In 1983, Patrick Fasano became Skytop's first on-staff naturalist and wrote an excellent primer of the land available at the Lodge, called *The Nature of Skytop*. He has since been replaced by wondrous John Serrao, who cultivates and maintains the acreage, the nine miles of hiking trails, the forestation, Leavitts and Indian Ladder waterfalls, five miles of streams, and the 265 species of wildflowers.

So as to have the links ready for guests, Robert White designed the golf course in 1926, a year before ground was broken for the lodge. The 18-hole 6,220 yard course offers beautiful scenery on an enjoyable route that suffers little from the mountainous terrain. Twenty bluebird houses are strategically stationed throughout the links.

In addition to golf, guests enjoy trout fishing along a mile and a half of private stream; paddle tennis and tennis on seven courts; as well as lawn bowling, miniature golf, shuffleboard, nightly deer spotting, and other activities. There is downhill skiing and instruction on West Mountain with two poma lifts, as well as cross-country skiing. Skating is offered indoors in the Pavilion or on the lake, which was at one time staffed with a skating waiter carrying coffee and hot chocolate. The health club and fitness room has exercise equipment, a sauna and whirlpool, and an indoor pool in a lovely atrium setting. An outdoor pool rests below the lodge. For everyone's enjoyment,

Skytop offers a special Children's Camp-in-the-Clouds during the summer months.

The staff at Skytop is unpretentious, gracious, and unusually pleased that visitors had the insight to find the place. Just 100 miles from New York City and Philadelphia, with intimate service and resort amenities, Skytop feels like a blue-blooded family secret.

Virginia

The Homestead
Hot Springs, Virginia 24445
703-839-5500
800-336-5771
800-542-5734 in Virginia

Proprietors: The Ingalls family and Virginia Hot Springs Inc.
General Manager and Vice President: Charles F. Ingalsbee, Jr.
Accommodations: 521 rooms, including 75 parlor suites
Rates:
   High season: $215–$295 per couple; $50 extra per person
      MAP
   Off-season: $150–$220 per couple; $50 extra per person
      MAP
   Suites: $90 extra
Minimum stay: None
Added: $25 each additional guest; $75 each additional guest
   MAP; $7.50 daily housekeeping; 4.5% tax
Payment: Major credit cards
Children: Allowed, 12 and under free
Pets: Not allowed
Smoking: Nonsmoking rooms available
Open: All year

A quintessential grand old resort, the Homestead is a gracious property steeped in tradition, 2,500 feet up in the Allegheny Mountains of western Virginia. Since Chesapeake and Ohio Railroad president M. E. Ingalls bought the property with a group of associates in 1891, the resort has been run by his family for four generations. Certainly because of this influence, the Homestead retains a small-town warmth highly unusual in a 500-room resort. In fact, it looks rather touchingly like an enormous—albeit luxurious—schoolhouse.

Hot Springs was settled in 1721. By mid-century, the curative nature of its mineral waters were well known. George Washington visited in 1761, five years before the land was sold to Thomas Bullitt, who built the first Homestead. A modern building was erected in 1846, expanded in the 1890s when the resort opened formally. The Casino, the Cottages, the Bathhouse, and the first tee of the Homestead golf course were laid out in 1892. It wasn't until 1901 that the recognizable Georgian exterior was built of red Kentucky brick, expanded to the west in 1903, and again to the east in 1914 when the Ingalls family bought a controlling interest in the property. The trademark Homestead Tower, completed in 1929, was recently placed on the National Register of Historic Places.

A visitor won't believe that such an extensive property is nestled so inconspicuously into the hills. On its 1,500 acres are three championship golf courses, 19 tennis courts (4 all-weather), a spa and an indoor pool naturally heated by mineral waters, two outdoor pools, four skeet and two trap fields, rifle and archery ranges, trout fishing in Cascades Stream, 100 miles of trails cut for hiking and horseback riding, some of Virginia's best trout fishing, an Olympic skating rink and eight ski slopes, two lawn bowling greens that date to colonial times, an eight-lane bowling alley, croquet, badminton, horseshoes, and putting greens.

Guests enter the long veranda to the 200-foot-long Great Hall, supported by 16 magnificent Corinthian columns, the afternoon setting for tea and a classical concert. The common rooms are elegantly appointed with antiques and lavish floral arrangements, and guest rooms fill the wings that radiate from the Great Hall. The rooms, redecorated in a recent multimillion-dollar effort, are traditionally furnished in dark wood reproductions in several schemes, all extremely classic and understated.

Swiss-born executive chef Albert Schnarwyler has been at the Homestead since 1962, his legendary skills admired in the elegant and formal main dining room. Guests have a number of other less formal dining options, including Sam Snead's Tavern in the village. Upscale shops line one of the main wings. The Cottages below the Homestead, rebuilt in the 1920s to resemble the original 1890s structures, house boutiques and the Café Albert.

The original bathhouse, built in 1892, is an architectural marvel and a vision from the past. As well as the naturally heated indoor pool, built in 1903, guests enjoy two outdoor pools, full spa amenities, and hydrotherapy in mineral waters that range from 102.5 to 106 degrees.

The three golf courses at the Homestead are among the East Coast's finest. The original tee of the Homestead course, built in 1892, is the oldest in the country in continuous use. Three miles south is the Cascades course, designed by William S. Flynn in 1923, said to be one of the country's better mountain courses. Robert Trent Jones designed the Lower Cascades Course in 1963, the resort's longest. Sam Snead, a member of the Homestead staff since 1975, grew up a mile and a half from the resort and caddied here as youngster.

Guests who opt for a more golf-oriented or value-oriented stay might want to inquire about the 50-room Cascades Inn three miles away near the Homestead and Lower Cascades Courses, a low white clapboard building with a country club look.

Skiing has been a Homestead feature since 1959, with three trails and eight slopes. With a base elevation of 2,500 feet and a vertical drop of 700 feet, it's a great place to learn how to ski. For those few who might disagree, the Olympic-size outdoor ice rink offers figure skating instruction.

Younger guests at the Homestead have an indoor and outdoor playground. Summers offer even more to 7–10-year-olds, who can receive instruction in golf, tennis, fishing, swimming, hiking, and target archery.

While the atmosphere is the same formal one which greeted the country's wealthiest moguls and eight presidents over three centuries, there is a genuine friendliness from the generations of staff who make the Homestead a grand family resort.

Williamsburg Inn
Post Office Box 1776
Williamsburg, Virginia 23187-1776
1-800-HISTORY

Proprietors: Colonial Williamsburg Foundation
General Manager: John H. Hallowell
Accommodations: 232 rooms (102 in main house, 43 in
  Providence Hall, 87 in Colonial Houses [see Historic Stops])
Rates: $205–$335 (seasonally); special packages available for
  meal plans
Minimum stay: None
Added: $12 for rollaways
Payment: Major credit cards
Children: Welcome
Pets: Not allowed
Smoking: Nonsmoking rooms available
Open: All year

In 1926, John D. Rockefeller, Jr. undertook a $79 million effort to bring colonial America to the 20th century. The result is one of the country's most popular tourist attractions, the living museum of Colonial Williamsburg, set on 173 acres in southeastern Virginia. Plans for the Williamsburg Inn were set forth in the mid-1930s with much discussion between Rockefeller and architects who decided that the town needed a European-style luxury hotel.

It was agreed that the inn would not compete architecturally with the colonial themes that were done so authentically.

Rather, the grand scale of the West Virginia resort "springs" hotels was adopted, all built in the formal Georgian, Federal, and Regency styles of the early 1800s. Rockefeller and his architects agreed that the Regency style was most fitting, with its lighter colors, whitewashed brick, bright flat plaster walls, Greek Revival pediments, arches, and columns. The ground floor is a grand colonnade, above which floats a two-story portico supported by four Ionic columns and a classic pediment.

Guest wings hover above and in the East Wing. The inn was furnished in symmetrical simplicity. The East Wing was added in 1950, and in 1972 the Regency Dining Room was built as well as two contemporary Providence Hall wings a short walk from the inn. Much like a southern plantation, everything in Colonial Williamsburg is made by local artisans. Carpenters, upholsterers, and designers must maintain historical accuracy—in the colonial style as well as in the Regency style of the inn.

The rooms are furnished in exacting authenticity, redecorated in a continual process which turns the rooms around every five years. Each is different, but all the rooms in the main inn are furnished in formal Regency style, sometimes with pastel walls and complementary window treatments that match the bedding, sometimes with a bold surprise in brightly colored wallpaper border simulating swags that matches the bedding or a wing chair.

So thorough is the design of the Williamsburg Inn that even the surrounding grounds are interesting, an incredibly diverse and thorough horticultural display. Those who come twice yearly will notice different furnishings in the grand reception hall, which has a new decor for winter and summer. The Regency Dining Room is the setting for formal dining, opening to the gardens behind the inn.

Second to the outdoor museum of Colonial Williamsburg, guests are apt to concentrate on golf, which is quite formidable at the Williamsburg Inn. The original championship Golden Horseshoe Course was designed by Robert Trent Jones in the 1963, as was the 9-hole Spotswood. In October 1991, Jones's son Rees introduced the Green Course, with a new clubhouse.

Fitness facilities are found at the neighboring Williamsburg Lodge in the Tazewell Club Fitness Center. In addition, there are eight tennis courts, four of them Har-Tru surfaces, lawn bowling, croquet, shuffleboard, and two swimming pools.

Colonial Williamsburg is a busy place. The service is extremely professional, as is every aspect of the organization.

West Virginia

The Greenbrier
White Sulphur Springs, West Virginia 24986
304-536-1110
800-624-6070

Proprietors: CSX Corporation
President and Managing Director: Ted J. Kleisner
General Manager: Gil Patrick
Accommodations: 650 guest rooms, including 51 suites and
 69 cottages
Rates:
 Rooms: $114–$208 per person MAP; other packages avail-
  able
 Suites: From $200 per person (up to 14 guests) MAP
 Cottages: $155–$278 per person (4–8 guests) MAP
Included: Breakfast and dinner in most facilities
Minimum stay: 2 nights on weekends
Added: 6% tax; $12.25 service per person per day
Payment: Major credit cards
Children: Welcome
Pets: Not allowed
Smoking: Nonsmoking rooms available
Open: All year

The magnificence of the Greenbrier is simply overwhelming.
To appreciate the scale and the 200 plus years of history at the
Greenbrier, a visitor ought to take a tour of the grounds conducted daily by the on-staff historian, Dr. Bob Conte. As old
and historic as the Greenbrier is, it is also one of the most
consistently updated properties in this book.

As recently as 1987, $7 million was invested in the glorious spa
and mineral baths. The rooms and public space are constantly
being redecorated by Carleton Varney, president of the Dorothy
Draper Company of New York. The 6,500 acres of groomed
grounds provide more activities than one visitor can possibly
imagine, from the usual fun on three golf courses, 20 tennis
courts, and Olympic swimming pools, to trap and skeet shooting, bowling, horseback riding, sleigh rides, and croquet.

As early as 1778, afflicted souls began coming to White Sulphur Springs for its curative mineral waters. In 1808, a tavern
holding 60 guests was built on the site, which now serves as a
croquet lawn. The first cottages were built as early as 1810. By
1858, the Grand Central Hotel was erected, referred to fondly as

Old White because of its whitewashed brick. From 1861 to 1865, the resort was tugged between Union and Confederate troops, the former winning out as West Virginia seceded from Confederate rule in 1863.

After the Civil War, Old White became one of the country's most elite gathering spots. It was bought by the Chesapeake & Ohio Railroad in 1910 for $150,000; and architect Frederick Junius Sterner was commissioned to design a fireproof addition, resulting in the herculean Greenbrier. A Roman bath–inspired indoor pool was added in 1912, the largest in the world at the time, measuring 100 by 42 feet. In 1913, Charles Blair McDonald designed the Old White golf course, though by 1922 the building for which it was named was dismantled. During World War II, the Greenbrier became the Ashford General Hospital, closing for two years before it reopened as a splendid resort once again in 1948. Various wings were added in 1930, 1954, and 1962, and further renovations included the Greenbrier's first tap room in 1970 in the Old White Club. In 1977, the Greenbrier golf course was added to the grounds under the supervision of Jack Niklaus.

The long, formal driveway ends in a loop under a colonnade at the front entrance. The grand hallways, exaggeratedly large squares of the black and white marble parquet floor, lead to the 30 lobbies and public spaces, outfitted with extensive floral arrangements, opening to terraces and sculpted gardens hosting afternoon tea concerts and, at one entrance, to the oft-photographed 80,000-bulb tulip garden.

The mastery of the Greenbrier's aesthetics is the product of legendary Dorothy Draper, who first decorated the resort in 1946. Her vision lives on today through Carleton Varney. While the furniture is always traditional, from wing chairs to Queen Anne settees and mahogany tables, the fabrics, from the upholstery to the bedding and drapes, are boldly colored in swatches of red, yellow, blue, or green or dramatically patterned in floral and chintz, recalling the Greenbrier theme of the rhododendron, West Virginia's state flower.

The guest rooms, the majority of which are twin-bedded, might have a wide-striped pink and white wallpaper, with royal blue pile carpeting, red club chairs, and pink chintz drapes; or perhaps canary yellow drapes, bright red carpeting, blue club chairs, and wild floral bouquets papering the walls. The variety and audacity is highly successful.

In addition to the hundreds of guest rooms in the main building, the ten rows of cottages are a unique option in accommodations. Running the perimeter of the groomed Greenbrier commons, most are historic and original, some have fireplaces, and all have porches and private patios, and stocked kitchens.

The new Spa wing is not only functional as it houses the new coffee shop and salon, pool and Spa, but simply beautiful, with its green and pink inlaid marble floor, pastel walls and white trimmed archways leading to the Spa and the original 1912 pool. The latter is a most tranquil setting, the walls tiled in an intricate mosaic, the pool flanked by colonnades, resting under a softly canopied ceiling. Among facilities using mineral waters are soak tubs, whirlpools, Swiss showers, Scotch sprays, and saunas. Beauty treatments and therapy massage are also performed.

The food is one of the highlights at the Greenbrier, prepared by a team of chefs trained in its own Culinary Apprentice Program. The six-course formal dinner is served in the three-room dining salon. Amateurs might inquire about week-long cooking school packages, conducted by Ann Willan of La Varenne in Paris.

For a complete experience in luxury, Greenbrier guests may arrive and depart as they did a century prior, in a plushly appointed private passenger train. The Greenbrier Limited is the first privately operated sleeper car since the Broadway Limited, which discontinued service in 1967. The stunningly beautiful route from Chicago to New York City makes stops at major cities. Guests dine on silver, crystal, and linens in a car of Honduran mahogany; and sleep amid lavish French fabrics.

Grand New Resorts

New Jersey

Marriott's Seaview Golf Resort
US Route 9, Absecon
Galloway Township, New Jersey 08201
609-652-1800
800-228-9290

Proprietor: Marriott Corporation
Accommodations: 299 rooms, including 37 suites
Rates: $198; $169 on weekends; special golf packages available
Included: Up to four people per room
Minimum stay: None
Added: 7% tax
Payment: Major credit cards
Children: Welcome
Pets: Not allowed
Smoking: Allowed
Open: All year

Marriott's Seaview Resort is a premier spot for golfers. Its Bay Course was planned by utility mogul Clarence H. Geist, who vowed to build his own course as he waited in frustration to tee off during a leisurely day on the links in 1912. He did just that, in 1914, with the help of Scottish designer Donald Ross.

The course begged for a country club, which soon followed, a graceful three-story manor house, later decorated by a generous porte-cochere and a circular dining room to one side of the building. The Pines Course was added in the 1940s, designed by William Flynn and Howard Toomey and rated as one of New Jersey's best. The property remained a private country club until Marriott came along in 1983 with the intent of creating a premier golf resort. The corporation bought the property, added a wing toward the back of the original building, redecorated the rooms in 1986, introduced the John Jacobs' Practical Golf School in 1989, and a new fitness center in 1990.

The 670-acre property sits on Reeds Bay, six miles northwest of Atlantic City. While the Seaview still has the feel of a tony country club, it's a full-scale resort, with indoor and outdoor pools, two Har-Tru and six all-weather tennis courts, two paddle tennis courts, a marked jogging trail on the golf courses, sauna and steam baths, hydrotherapy pool, and exercise facilities.

The new wing was built when Marriott acquired the property in 1983, with 150 rooms throughout four floors; the original wing has about the same number of rooms on three floors. They are decorated unsurprisingly, with traditional reproduction furniture, luxury hotel style, with two phones, remote cable televisions, and king-size beds with triple sheeting and nightly turndown.

The formal oval main dining room with its rotunda ceiling looks out over the putting green with panoramic views. The Grill Room has the woody air of an English men's club. On the other side of the reception area is the pro shop, on the way outdoors to the pool, gazebo, and gardens.

The John Jacobs' Practical Golf Schools were established in 1971 and are represented in about twenty resorts across the country. Its largest facility is here at the Seaview, on 22 acres with a state-of-the-art Golf Learning Center, with putting, chipping, and teeing greens, a driving range, and one instructor for at least every five students.

The Seaview still feels like a country club, a refreshing change of pace from the hype of Atlantic City, and a great place to concentrate on golf. The staff is respectful, understated, and solicitous. Though the glitz of Atlantic City is a safe distance away, it is close enough for an evening's fun.

New York

Tarrytown House
East Sunnyside Lane
Tarrytown, New York 10591
914-591-8200
800-553-8118

Proprietors: Jones Lang Wootton Reatly Advisors, Frank S. Fisher
Management: Fisher Hotel Group

Accommodations: 148 rooms, including 12 rooms in historic
   King House
Rates: $125 Sunday–Thursday; $99 weekends
Included: Breakfast
Minimum stay: None
Added: $30 each additional guest; 11.75% tax
Payment: Major credit cards
Children: Welcome, under 12 free
Pets: Not allowed
Smoking: Nonsmoking rooms available
Open: All year

Although best known as a conference center—in fact, pur-
ported to be the country's first, opened in 1963—Tarrytown
House is putting a new face forward to welcome overnight
guests as well. The property was bought in 1986 and completed
a $7 million renovation during the subsequent four years. It sits
like a treasure unveiled, waiting patiently to be discovered. The
property is beautiful and unique, set on a 26-acre estate outside
of Tarrytown facing the dramatic banks of the Hudson River,
an incongruous 24 miles north of Manhattan.

Tarrytown House comprises seven buildings, connected by
a series of immaculate paved roads winding around gardens,
shrubs, and foliage. Two of these are pristine restorations of
historic mansions. The King House was built in 1840, a
museum-quality Greek Revival named for a wealthy businessman. The house accommodates 12 guests in sumptuous accommodations. As well, the magnificent public rooms, with
rich-paneled walls, exposed floors, and Oriental carpets, make
for regal meeting space or reading space, depending on one's
orientation. The King House restaurant has Continental cuisine, with entrées around $20.

The Biddle House is the first structure one sees upon arrival.
The majestic granite mansion was built in 1895 for one of the
country's wealthiest women, Mary Duke Biddle, who made the
castle a Gatsbyesque retreat in the 1920s for guests yachting into
Tarrytown. Mullioned and picture windows stretch across the
vast facade of the granite mansion, overlooking the sloping
lawns, spilling out to patios and terraces. The dining spaces
reach around two views to peek at the Hudson. All is appointed
lavishly in marble, brass, wood paneling, and faux grained
mantels. While the Biddle House has no guest rooms, it does
feature a bowling alley, billiards tables, several restaurants, and
the Sleepy Hollow Pub.

The great majority of the guest rooms are in the new Fair-
field, Rockland, and Westchester Houses, between King and

Biddle. Decorated with a tasteful masculine black and white plaid silk comforter over a king-size or two double beds, with upholstered headboards, the rooms are traditional but unique.

The Recreation House was transformed from the Biddle's former poolhouse, with an indoor and outdoor swimming pool, tennis, racquetball, an exercise room with stairmasters, ski machines, weights, and whirlpool and sauna facilities.

An example of the unusual way of Tarrytown House is the film weekends held here annually, hosted by film critic Judith Crist for more than twenty years. Call for special packages like this—the resort has a creative, flexible staff which is actively seeking transient travelers.

Pennsylvania

Hidden Valley
1 Craighead Drive
Somerset, Pennsylvania 15501
814-443-6454
800-458-0175

Proprietors: Kettler Brothers, Inc.
Managing Director: James Coulter
General Manager: John Scanlan
Accommodations: 230 one- to three-bedroom units, most with fireplace
Rates: $120–$180 per couple; special ski packages available
Minimum stay: None
Added: $15–25 each additional guest; 6% tax
Payment: Major credit cards
Children: Allowed, 12 and under free
Pets: Not allowed
Smoking: Nonsmoking rooms available
Open: All year

Where singles and younger people buy passes at Seven Sisters Ski Resort, families flock to Hidden Valley in the Laurel Mountains of southwestern Pennsylvania, 60 miles east of Pittsburgh. The 2,000 acres of Hidden Valley neighbor three state parks, which provide access to more than 30,000 acres of Pennsylvania forest.

While skiing is a major draw, with 17 Alpine slopes and trails with a 610-foot vertical drop, Hidden Valley has myriad other activities for all seasons and ages: a par 72 championship golf course completed in 1988; 30 miles of groomed and patrolled cross-country ski trails; 12 tennis courts, some lit for night play; 8 restaurants; a Racquet Club with extensive fitness equipment, 4 courts, steamroom and sauna, and suntanning; two lakes for fishing and boating of all kinds; and an unusual under-21 club called Club Soda with a state-of-the-art lighting and sound system.

Hidden Valley developed around a stone farmhouse built in the 1850s. A century later, George and Helen Parke bought 106 acres, which included the farmhouse in the Laurel Mountains, as a weekend escape from their Pittsburgh home—all for $12,500. They began welcoming guests in 1953 and by 1958 had added three ski slopes. In 1977, the Parkes joined family friends the Kettler Brothers Inc. in a venture that brought townhouses to Hidden Valley. By 1983, the Kettler Brothers owned the entire facility, adding tens of millions of dollars in improvements in road, ski, and snow making facilities, as well as in accommodations.

Overnight guests have access to hotel accommodations in Four Seasons or in the Summit, Vista, and Fairway condominiums along the mountain. The decor is contemporary and extremely tidy; most units have fireplaces, some have stocked kitchens. Guests are given many dining options, including formal fare in the chestnut-walled Hearthside, where Helen Parke served her first country cooking in 1953, and California cuisine in the new cathedral-ceilinged Clock Tower. Several lounges feature nightlife for adults, while kids escape to Club Soda, with its two stereo systems, fog machines, and strobe lights.

Carved into the 3,000-foot summit of Laurel Mountain, Hidden Valley's golf course offers beautiful views from more than 6,000 yards of greens. The 85 acres of skiable terrain receive an average of 150 inches of snow each year, supplemented with extensive snow making. The ski school offers children's and adult programs.

Throughout, Hidden Valley is an informal, active, friendly place. Though contemporary in design, the buildings are thoughtfully spread around the acreage so as not to seem overwhelming or disruptive.

Nemacolin Woodlands Resort

Box 188
Farmington, Pennsylvania 15437
412-329-8555
800-422-2736 in Pennsylvania

Proprietor: Joe Hardy
President: Maggie Hardy
General Manager: Jim Miller
Accommodations: 96 rooms in the main inn, 1- and 2-bedroom accommodations in three condominium units
Rates:
  Rooms: Winter, $70–$185 (except New Year's); April–October, $96–$250
  Condominiums: Winter, $90–$120 (except New Year's); April–October, $117–$175
Included: Use of all facilities except greens fees
Minimum stay: None
Added: 6% tax
Payment: MasterCard, Visa, American Express, Diners Club
Children: Welcome in condominiums
Pets: Not allowed
Smoking: Allowed
Open: All year

The rural town of Farmington, 12 miles southeast of Uniontown, is near the reckoning spot between its own state, Pennsylvania, and Maryland and West Virginia. This remote spot is home to Pennsylvania's most luxurious new resort. Named for a Delaware Indian guide, Nemacolin Woodlands is an exclusive property on 550 acres of the lush Laurel Mountains, renowned for its top spa facilities and award-winning golf academy. The contemporary Tudor architecture throughout the resort was designed by Craig Johnson and is quite winning. Flags fly from gabled rooftops of the main buildings, their Tudor themes echoed in varied structures which dot the vast landscape like outbuildings on a plantation.

The property was first occupied in 1959 as a hunting preserve for the Rockwell family. Joe Hardy of 84 Lumber bought the land in 1987 and after stunning embellishments—including a copper roof on the Woodlands Spa and a 4,000-foot airstrip—opened Nemacolin Woodlands in 1988. The inn stretches its open arms around a circular drive and groomed commons. Inside, visitors will find a surprisingly cosmopolitan interior designed by Amy Storrs in the height of luxury: varied and colorful marble underfoot and classic archways and moldings done in rich mahogany. The Hardys worked hard to amass their eclectic collection of painting and sculpture, and the traditional furnishings are covered in richly patterned materials. The Inn Manor houses accommodations as well as an upper and lower lobby, group facilities, a library, the Club Room, Joseph's, Café

Woodlands, the Rose Garden, Fables Lounge, the large wine cellar, and acclaimed dining in Allures and the Golden Trout.

The guest rooms on four floors are exceptionally lovely, with an intriguing European influence. All rooms, from resort doubles to deluxe penthouse suites, are decorated differently with brass or canopy beds or rich wooden headboards, plush club chairs, and original art. The classic architecture rendered interesting interior spaces set under eaves, with oblique angles and unusual configurations from the scalloped exterior. The furnishings are traditional reproductions in dark wood, with colorful wallpaper and borders, and rich patterned bed and window treatments in dark greens, rusts, and classic patterns. Some rooms have balconies overlooking the mountains and whirlpools, and all have mini-bars.

At the base of the circular drive, facing the inn, is the three-story Woodlands Spa, reputed to be one of the country's more luxurious. Gloriously appointed in several marbles and rich inlaid wood, the spa has three large, varied floors. The ground level has an indoor pool (temperature 90 degrees), aerobics studios, and a Keiser weight room. The main level has whirlpools, lockers, a boutique and a lounge and juice bar. The upper level houses the beauty salon and facial treatment and massage facilities. While the groomed grassy croquet court rests to one side of the spa, a plethora of activities is adjacent: tennis, badminton, and shuffleboard courts, the outdoor swimming pool, the Woodlands Activities Center, and Misty Gardens, the greenhouse with an on-staff botanist who provides the wonderful fresh arrangements seen throughout the rooms and property. On the slope below the spa are the Woodlands Zoo, the Mews Family Recreational Center, the Playground, and the Maples Condominiums.

The par 71 golf course is 6,643 yards, and from the Gazebo Snack Shop golfers have views of Maryland and West Virginia. PGA pros teach at the Golf Academy with state-of-the-art equipment and on a specially designed short game at the super range. Playing the links on the Nemacolin course is a great way to tour the property. The fairways run past Lakes Louise, Dottie, and Carol, named for the women in the Hardy family, and past the condos at the Links and Fairway Villas line. Outer fairways run past the riding stables.

The staff has been thoroughly trained in a team effort that prompts professional, efficient, and friendly service. Guests venturing outside the groomed grounds of Nemacolin will want to go whitewater rafting at the neighboring Ohiopyle State Park or visit Frank Lloyd Wright's Fallingwater or the Laurel Caverns.

Virginia

The Boar's Head Inn & Sports Club
200 Ednam Drive, Box 5307
Charlottesville, Virginia 22905
804-296-2181
800-476-1988

Proprietors: Universtiy of Virginia Real Estate Foundation
General Manager: Sandie Greenwood
Accommodations: 174 rooms, including 14 suites, 10 rooms
   with fireplace
Rates: $110–$200
Minimum stay: Graduation weekend only
Added: $10 each additional guest; pets $15 per night; 6.5% tax
Payment: Major credit cards
Children: Welcome, under 18 free
Pets: Allowed
Smoking: Nonsmoking rooms available
Open: All year

A recent $4 million renovation, completed in August 1991, has revitalized the Boar's Head Inn, best known for its extensive

tennis and racquet facilities. This clubby, surprisingly traditional resort sits in the Ednam Woods two miles west of Charlottesville, a fitting retreat for the elite families visiting the
University of Virginia. Despite its size and recent additions, the
Boar's Head feels intimate and old school. The property centers
around a 19th-century gristmill, around which classic pitched-
roof wings were gradually added.

The Boar's Head opened in 1965, though its interesting history dates to 1834 when the gristmill was built on the banks of
the Hardware River near Monticello. The mill survived the
years, including a torching during the Civil War, squelched by a
rainstorm. In the early 1960s, John B. Rogan bought the gristmill and took it apart piece by piece to transport it to its present
site where it was rebuilt. The dining room flaunts the features
of the old mill: the large hearth was built from the mill's fieldstone foundation, and present are the 40-foot heart pine beams,
warm planked walls, and original scarred flooring. One common room sits in the old mill—the rest is all new. A downstairs
Tavern offers nightly entertainment.

The 53 acres of the Boar's Head are well groomed, with a
manmade lake, adjacent to the 18-hole par 72 championship
Birdwood golf course, owned by the university. The old mill
stretches toward the lake, fronted with a new garden room, for
special functions and dinners, with wrought-iron furniture and
trellis wallpaper. Behind the dining room, the reception area
retains the clubby feel of the 19th-century property, with deep
wood walls, hunting pictures, and forest green rugs.

Several floors of guest rooms are above the reception area,
though the majority rest in two new wings between the parking
area and the lake toward the Sports Club. They were redecorated in 1991 with bright pile carpeting, chintz spreads and window treatments, upholstered benches at the foot of king-size or
double beds in traditional dark wood—with the added feature
of coffee makers. All rooms have balconies, most of which face
the lake. The Hunt Club rooms on the other side of the mill are
the newest and most deluxe, with king-size beds (or two doubles), hair dryers and telephones in the bath, and fluffy terry
robes. Original art includes hunt and equestrian themes. These
rooms overlook the outdoor pool and sundeck.

The Sports Club has 17 tennis courts: 3 indoor Grasstex
courts, 10 clay courts, 4 all-weather Grasstex courts, as well as 2
platform tennis and 4 squash courts. Additional exercise facilities include a large fitness center, two outdoor swimming pools,
and saunas.

Kingsmill Resort and Conference Center
1010 Kingsmill Road
Williamsburg, Virginia 23185
804-253-1703
800-832-5665

Proprietor: Busch Properties, Inc.
General Manager: Charles E. Dickerman
Accommodations: 388 units, including one- to three-bedroom suites
Rates: $140–507; Riverside Villas, $173–$599
Included: Par 3 golf
Minimum stay: None
Added: $12 each additional guest; 4.5% state tax
Payment: Major credit cards
Children: Welcome, under 18 free
Pets: Not allowed
Smoking: Allowed
Open: All year

A short drive south from Colonial Williamsburg to the contemporary Kingsmill Resort reveals three miles of unadulterated James River coast. Kingsmill is part of the huge enterprise of Anheuser-Busch, with its base and Busch Gardens a short drive away on private, patrolled roads. The property is best known as a conference center, but Kingsmill attracts a goodly number of golfers who play on the two 18-hole championship and par 3 golf courses.

Named for English colonist Richard Kingsmill, who settled here in 1736, the resort has nearly 3,000 acres of protected forest and wildlife. Anheuser-Busch bought the property in 1974 to develop private homes and opened the resort a decade later. The groomed grounds, radar-patrolled roads, and similar contemporary architecture give Kingsmill Resort the feeling of a private country club.

Although conferences are a huge part of Kingsmill's market, transient guests will not feel overwhelmed because the accommodations are rather independent. Guests stay in one of 32 villas clustered in four groups around the conference center. There are two sets of Riverside Villas overlooking the James River and two sets of Sports Villas set on the golf courses, one added as recently as 1991. A villa contains about ten rooms on three floors, from guest rooms to three-bedroom units, some with fireplaces and kitchens and all with balconies. The rooms are bright and traditionally furnished with light wood, chintz fabrics, and modern comforts.

The championship golf courses include the River Course, which hosts the PGA annually, with continuous water views, and the Plantation Course, designed by Arnold Palmer. The Bray Links par 3 course was completed in 1990. The Riverview Dining Room at the Golf Club has a lovely water view and formal dining.

In addition to golf, Kingsmill has 15 tennis courts—2 all-weather, and 2 lit for night play. The Sports Club was completed in May 1988, a particularly airy building with a wall of sliding glass doors surrounding the indoor pool, under a cathedral ceiling, with racquetball courts, Nautilus, aerobics, saunas, and whirlpools.

During the summer months, children may participate in the Kingsmill Kampers program, a supervised day camp with organized activities, sports, and arts and crafts.

Though the resort is contemporary, the architecture has classic influences with gabled roofs, green rooftops, and white-washed brick. The many activities are within easy reach, and historic activities are just around the corner.

The Tides Inn
King Carter Drive
Irvington, Virginia 22480
804-438-5000
800-TIDES INN

Proprietors: The Stephens Family
Resident Manager: Randy Stephens
Accommodations: 110 rooms
Rates (per person, AP): Rooms, $120–$130; suites, $137–$143;
    weekends, $155 (lower rates with three-night weekend stay)
Included: Three meals per day
Minimum stay: None
Added: $40–$60 each additional guest; gratuities; 4.5% state tax
Payment: Major credit cards
Children: Allowed, under 4 free
Pets: Small pets (not more than 50 pounds)
Smoking: Allowed
Open: Mid-March to early January

The Tides Inn is quite an anomaly in a business of hungry corporations whizzing with marketing strategies. Reputed to be one of the East Coast's tonier resorts, the Tides has been family-run since 1947. E. A. Stephens felled the cypress for the Dining and View rooms from a nearby swamp and salvaged the tile roof from the army's Langley Field; and as soon as he put up the building, Mrs. Stephens decorated with a traditional eye. The property, much expanded but entirely faithful, is now run by a younger generation of Stephenses. The refined southern hospitality of the Stephens family resort remains like a relic from the past: cherished, rare, and timeless.

The Tides Inn floats on the southern reaches of Virginia's marshlike Northern Neck, where the two-mile-wide Rappahannock River meets the Chesapeake Bay. Carter's Creek dissolves off the Rappahannock, surrounding at one point a subtle 25-acre peninsula that serves as the home of the Tides Inn. Water burrows in and out of the flat lowland fields, as the coastline is lost at every turn.

The architecture is traditional and classic: three stories of white clapboard and whitewashed brick, topped with a red tiled roof. The Main House undulates along the shoreline, housing two common rooms, the Chesapeake Club, and the Dining Room—with water views which evoke the feeling of a houseboat. In the Main House, the East Wing guest quarters are the only ones without outdoor spaces. With porches, the Garden House follows the line of the Main House. Steps across a path from the Main House, with views of the other side of Carter's Creek, are the Windsor House, consisting of deluxe suites and porches, and the Lancaster House, built in the mid-1950s, with balconies.

All guest rooms are decorated very traditionally, with long drapes matching bedding, complementing colors in the wallpaper, lampshades, and club chairs. As with any formal resort, televisions and telephones are easily within sight. Though some of the rooms are a bit on the small side, even these have dressing areas outside the bath. Guests with early tee times will appreciate the coffeemakers in each room.

Carter's Creek is a formidable 25 to 30 feet deep in most places, explored by the classic *Miss Ann*, which embarks on daily cruises, and the *High Tide II*, which offers smaller luncheon cruises.

The staff is extremely solicitous at the Tides. Employees not only are kind and helpful, but seem quite proud, having been at the Tides Inn for generations. The Tides Inn has unusually representative southern cooking, and Sunday seafood brunches are legendary.

The Summer House has one of the two outdoor pools at the inn, this filled with saltwater. In addition to swimming, the inn has four tennis courts, and a 9-hole par 3 golf course. The Tartan

Course and the Golden Eagle Course are within several minutes' drive, the latter one of Virginia's finest.

The Tides Lodge
Irvington, Virginia 22480
804-438-6000
800-248-4337

Proprietor: E.A. Stephens
Accommodations: 60 rooms in three wings
Rates (per person, MAP): Fall, $103–$182; summer, $99–$174; rest of year, $72–$120; EP rates also available
Included: Breakfast and dinner MAP
Minimum stay: None
Added: $45 each additional guest; small pets $8; gratuities; 4.5% tax
Payment: Major credit cards
Children: Free under 4 and all ages on weekdays
Pets: Small pets allowed
Smoking: Smoking and nonsmoking rooms
Open: Mid-March through December

The Tides Inn and Tides Lodge are entirely different properties, each run by a Stephens brother. The choice for Old World southern elegance is the Tides Inn; the informal choice with immediate access to golf is the Tides Lodge. While the Tides Inn is decorated in the manner of a formal parlor, the Lodge is done in the manner of a casual family room.

Across Carter's Creek from its brother property, the Lodge is run by E. A. Stephens, son of E.A. the elder who constructed the Tides Inn in 1947. The younger E.A. built the Tides Lodge in 1969, a geometric series of two-story flat-topped buildings of weathered shingle and wood, with contemporary results.

Lodge guests will quickly notice the Scottish theme at the Tides Lodge, a tribute to Sir Guy Campbell, the architect and designer of the first nine holes on the Tartan Course, which begins at the front door. Campbell died while building the course, and the lodge makes its tribute to Campbell and his people for their golfing tradition. Tartans are everywhere: from the rugs to drapes running through the public and dining areas.

All the rooms have private balconies and are decorated more casually than at the Tides Inn in an unsurprising hotel manner. A 60-foot yacht takes daily cruises around Carter's Creek and, in addition, the Lodge has a 41-slip marina. There are two swimming pools (one saltwater) and three tennis courts. While the Tartan Course begins at the Lodge steps, the Golden Eagle Course is a shuttle away but as one of Virginia's top courses, certainly worth the trip. Families might prefer the informality of the lodge and also its supervised children's summer programs.

West Virginia

Oglebay Resort
Wheeling, West Virginia 26003
304-243-4000
800-624-6988

Proprietor: Wheeling Park Commission
General Manager: Randy Worls
Accommodations: 180 rooms in main building, 24 rooms in 3 chalets, 37 cabins
Rates: Wilson Lodge, $59–$109, $85–$125 with living room; 2-, 4-, and 6-bedroom Family Cabins, from $550 weekly
Minimum stay: 2 nights on weekends
Added: $5 for rollaway; 9% tax
Payment: Major credit cards
Children: Welcome
Pets: Not allowed
Smoking: Allowed
Open: All year

In the narrow northern neck of West Virginia, wedged between Pennsylvania and Ohio, Wheeling offers a wonderful family resort and park called Oglebay. In 1926, philanthropist and industrialist Colonel Earl W. Oglebay willed his summer estate, Waddington Farm, to the citizens of Wheeling to be used for recreation and education. The 1,500 acres are maintained by a private board, the only self-sustaining municipal park in the country. As a result, accommodations and activities are a bit more reasonably priced than at a private organization. Oglebay's identity is more a nature sanctuary than a full-service resort, though it does enjoy two wonderful golf courses, 14 tennis courts, an indoor and outdoor pool, and full fitness facilities.

Accommodations for Oglebay guests are in three contemporary wings of the main Wilson Lodge set high above the acreage, three satellite chalets, as well as 37 family cabins scattered throughout the lower reaches of the park. The three wings in the Lodge are Kline, built in 1966 with rustic paneled walls;

Allen, the original wing built of knotty pine; and Byrd, the favorite because of its breathtaking mountain views. The rooms are furnished identically in the comfortable style of a moderate hotel, with remote television and private phones, balconies, coffee makers, and some fireplaces. The chalets are a bit more luxurious and private. The cabins all have fireplaces and stocked kitchens.

However pleasant, the guest rooms are a small part of life at Oglebay. At the entrance to the park is the Mansion Museum, Colonel Oglebay's former residence, a majestic piece of Greek Revival architecture with a two-story portico supported by six columns, which looks very much like the White House. The museum contains a substantial glass collection and changing exhibits, furnished in faithful Federal formality.

The Good Children's Zoo rests in the valley just below the Wilson Lodge, a 65-acre natural habitat home to bison, elk, and the endangered red wolf. Visitors take a mile-and-a-half adventure ride on a vintage 1863 miniature Huntington train which runs the perimeter of the zoo, through the bison range, and over a waterfall. The Benedum Science Theater shows films and seasonal laser shows. A miniature golf course prepares kids for a bright future on the Oglebay links.

Naturalists appreciate the vast horticultural efforts of the Oglebay group. The Brooks Nature Center offers lectures, guided walks, and workshops. The Wheeling Civic Garden Center and Oglebay Greenhouse rest at the entrance to the park by the mansion. The Wigginton Arboretum offers miles of paths throughout some of Oglebay's most breathtaking scenery. The park's most recent project is the Waddington Gardens, a $1.25 million restoration project which opened in 1992.

Perhaps Oglebay's greatest attraction are the two public golf courses set into the scenic hills, offering magnificent views. The Crispin Course rests at the foot of Wilson Lodge; and the tougher Speidel Course, designed by Robert Trent Jones, is ten-year home of the West Virginia LPGA. The driving range and the 40-acre par 3 course are lit for night golfers, the latter becoming a ski center from December through March, complete with snow making, poma lift, and rentals.

Guests dine in the tiered Ihlenfeld dining room, expanded in 1990 to encompass wonderful western views through picture windows of Schenck Lake and the hills beyond. The Continental cuisine is quite reasonably priced, with special family and fitness menus.

Three-acre Schenck Lake is stocked with trout, catfish, and bass; and nonfishermen will enjoy the paddleboating.

Itineraries

District of Columbia

The 67 square miles of the nation's capital are bordered on the southwest by Virginia and the Potomac River and otherwise surrounded by Maryland. Ten square miles of the nation's seat were planned by Pierre Charles L'Enfant, a French engineer who had accompanied Lafayette to the United States. In 1790, Washington ordered that land in Virginia be sold for $66 an acre to serve as the capital, and in September 1793 the cornerstone of the White House was set.

While 600,000 call Washington home (about half of whom work for the federal government), more than 20 million visitors arrive annually. Since the bicentennial in 1976, about fifty new hotels have been added to this city, which has one of the highest concentrations of hotel rooms in the world.

Although the city is arranged in quadrants, a better orientation is by neighborhood: the Capitol Hill area and the Smithsonian Mall; the White House and the business district around Lafayette, Farragut, and McPherson squares; DuPont Circle and Embassy Row; and Georgetown and Foggy Bottom. Notable sites will keep a visitor occupied for weeks; and the Visitor's Center publication called *Attractions* is a helpful guide. Among the high points are a tour of the Capitol and the Smithsonian Institution's 14 discrete museums, including the National Zoo. Art museums abound in Washington, and in addition to the Washington Monument are the Lincoln, Jefferson, and Vietnam Veterans memorials.

Day trips to Mt. Vernon and Old Town Alexandria are great ideas, especially when the summer crowds get oppressive.

For information, call the Washington, D.C., Conventions and Visitors Bureau, 202-789-7000, or visit their offices at 1455 Pennsylvania Avenue, N.W.

Delaware

The first of the original 13 states to ratify the Constitution in 1787. Delaware is also the second smallest state, with an area of 1,982 square miles. Just under 600,000 people live in Delaware. Wilmington and the northern part of the state hook under Pennsylvania's Brandywine Valley, separated from New Jersey by the Delaware River, which flows into the Delaware Bay. On its west and south, Delaware is bordered by eastern Maryland. From 3 to 35 miles in width, Delaware stretches 96 miles long, with 28 miles of beautiful Atlantic coastline beginning at Cape Henlopen State Park and shooting down to Fenwick Island State Park.

The Delaware Bay was first explored by Henry Hudson in 1609. It was named a year later for Sir Thomas West III, Lord de la Warr, Governor of Virginia. Delaware's history was a tug-of-war between the Dutch and Swedish, who succumbed finally to English rule. The Dutch first landed in Delaware in 1631 near Lewes and were quite trampled by the Lenni Lenape Indians. The country's first Swedish settlers alit on Wilmington shores in 1638, followed closely by a second band of Dutch who founded New Castle in 1651 and conquered their Swedish neighbors in 1655. The British ended the dispute by capturing all settlements in 1664.

Wilmington was crafted by a Frenchman named Eleuthère Irénée DuPont, who landed in 1802 and whose black powder mill eventualy emerged as one of the country's largest chemical plants. While the magnificent landmark Hotel DuPont is under renovation until mid-1993, there is a great deal to do in Wilmington's environs. The Brandywine River Museum houses three generations of paintings from the Andrew Wyeth family, as well as other well-known artists like Maxfield Parrish; the Delaware Art Museum has the country's largest public display of English pre-Raphaelite painting and decorative arts. The Chaddsford Winery is a bit north, as are the famous Longwood Gardens and Winterthur Museum, on 200 acres, famous for its collection of decorative arts between 1640 and 1840. The Nemours Mansion and Gardens, on 300 acres, was the Louis XVI–style palace of Alfred I. DuPont, and also quite worth a tour.

Historic **New Castle**, 7 miles south of Wilmington, just below the Delaware Memorial Bridge, is one of the better preserved 18th-century communities in the Mid-Atlantic, with more than fifty 18th- and 19th-century historic buildings and a wonderful cobblestoned waterfront park called the Strand.

On the drive south to **Lewes** and Delaware's beaches, try to plan an overnight in **Milford** at the **Towers Bed and Breakfast**, with a meal at the Banking House Inn. The next day, leave plenty of time to enjoy Lewes, an unspoiled, preserved piece of history, several miles off the very beaten path of busy Route 1. The town is charming and picturesque, best appreciated with a stay at the **New Devon Inn**. There are a handful of historic museums, commemorating the Dutch settlers, and Lewes's strategic involvement in several wars. At Front Street, the Lewes and Rehoboth Canal bisects the town, separating the historic section from modern development.

Across the canal is spit of land that serves as breakwater for the Delaware Bay, the landing spot for the ferry from Cape May, and, to the east, 3,400 acres of protected Cape Henlopen State Park, which juts into the water like a brave hook. Its three miles of beaches are entirely windswept and protected, as untouched as they were when the first settlers arrived in the 17th century. There is hiking, camping, a 9-hole Frisbee golf course, and the Seaside Nature Center. Make sure to tour Shipcarpenter Square, a residential preservation project that saves and re-stores Delaware's historic homes. Closer to town is a similar civic project called the Complex, a two-acre site of colonial and 19th-century buildings open for guided and self-guided tours.

Below Cape Henlopen State Park are the Delaware Seashore State Park, a spit between the Atlantic and Rehoboth Bay, and Fenwick Island State Park at Delaware's base. Be sure to take the ferry to Cape May, across the Delaware Bay.

For Delaware travel information, call 800-441-8846 out of state, 800-282-8667 in Delaware.

Maryland

The seventh of the 13 original states to ratify the Constitution, in 1788, Maryland was settled a century and a half earlier, in 1634, by Lord Baltimore's brother Leonard Calvert. He sailed into the mouth of the Potomac River and proclaimed the southermost stretch of land St. Mary's City, after Henrietta Maria, wife of King Charles I. In 1694, the capital was moved to Annapolis and remains there today.

Maryland is an incredibly beautiful, diverse state, with a Rorschach ink blot shape. The top of Maryland borders entirely on Pennsylvania and the Allegheny Mountains; and the rest is a ragged-edged land mass which creeps into the Virginias, wraps around Washington, D.C., and ends at Delaware. Maryland really comprises four areas: western Maryland, a narrow peninsula that hosts the main vein of Route 40, America's first National Pike, to West Virginia; the main chunk of the state including Frederick, landlocked between Washington and Baltimore; the western shore including Annapolis, which undulates between the Chesapeake Bay and the Potomac River on the south; and the tony eastern shore of the Chesapeake, which also sees a bit of the Atlantic Ocean around Ocean City and Assateague Island National Seashore. Maryland has more than four million inhabitants, and of its 9,838 square miles of land, it has more than 3,000 square miles of tidal shoreline.

Baltimore and Western Maryland

One out of every four Marylanders lives in **Baltimore**, an exciting, revitalized city whose Inner Harbor is not only a major tourist attraction, but one of the country's busier working ports. Harborplace was built in 1981, with a panoply of shops and restaurants on the docks of Inner Harbor. The National Aquarium shares its waterfront locale, as does the Baltimore Maritime Museum and the Maryland Science Center and Davis Planetarium. For cultural diversion, visit the Edgar Allan Poe House and the Baltimore & Ohio Railroad Museum, an imporant site as Baltimore was the launching spot for America's first passenger train.

An hour's drive west of Baltimore takes a traveler to lovely farmland and horse country, to **Frederick** and **New Market**, a haven for antiques lovers. In the distance are the Catoctin Mountains and Camp David, and Hagerstown, Harper's Ferry, and Cumberland beyond.

Annapolis

Less than an hour's drive south of Baltimore brings a visitor to the state capital. **Annapolis** has 1,500 period buildings within the city, an ideal place for walkers. In 1990, the town's electricity was partially wired underground, so sidewalks are illuminated by warm-glowing lanterns at night. Annapolis is very much a planned town, organized by British Governor Francis Nicholson in 1695. The focal point is the state capitol building and its State Circle, which winds around groomed lawns, and the lesser Church Circle to the west. Around these two hubs, narrow streets radiate like spokes on a wheel, pointing toward the water, home to the 17th-century British settlers. The U.S. Naval Academy, founded in 1846, rests expansively on the waterfront to the east of town, and the venerable St. John's College, from 1697, sits contemplatively to the northeast.

The Eastern Shore

The Bay Bridge is an introduction to another world of Maryland. The pace slackens, the land spreads out in a leisurely stretch. The eastern shore is Maryland's retreat, and while there is a good deal of farming and fishing, much of this land is used for private recreation, for boating, swimming, and pleasantries. Flat, green, and low, this landscape is fed by the Chesapeake Bay. On a map, this portion of Maryland looks like an incomplete puzzle, as the water reaches into the land from all sides. North of the Bay Bridge are charming small towns. **Chestertown**, on the Chester River, is an adorable historic village that features some of the eastern shore's finest dining at the **Imperial Hotel**.

South of the Bay Bridge, toward Virginia's eastern shore, a pleasurable day trip will take one to bustling **St. Michaels**, the Chesapeake Maritime Museum, and the exclusive **Inn at Perry Cabin,** in elite Talbot County. The landscape becomes rural and windswept as one continues toward Tilghman Island, a quiet, moorlike refuge. Route 50 leads to southernmost Crisfield, the launch point for the ferry to Tangier Island. The land is wonderfully remote here, populated by fishing communities off the main roads.

The short exposure to the Atlantic Ocean is introduced at **Ocean City,** a Miami Beach of the north that may host as many as 200,000 beachgoers on a busy summer day. Its 10 miles of populous beach are between the havens of Delaware's Fenwick Island State Park and Assateague National Seashore. Should guests insist on an Ocean Beach pilgrimage, stay at one of the two **Fager's Island** properties, **Coconut Malorie** or the **Lighthouse Club,** or at the **Atlantic Hotel** in Berlin, eight miles away. Assateague is worth the trip in itself, south of Ocean City, providing at least a full day's activities in hiking, birding, and watching the packs of wild ponies who live here.

For Maryland tourist information, call 800-543-1036. The state sales tax is 5%.

New Jersey

Surprisingly, New Jersey is the most concentrated Mid-Atlantic state, with about 1,000 people per square mile and a population of nearly 8 million. Despite these figures and its reputation as an industrial highway, New Jersey has forty state parks and eleven state forests, eleven wineries, a huge amusement park, several racetracks, and 127 miles of coastline, making it a recreational haven in the Mid-Atlantic. The state stretches 166 miles, from the New York border to Cape May and the Delaware Bay, and is 32 miles wide.

There are two scenic avenues to New Jersey: on its vast, straight Atlantic coastline, ranging from ticky-tacky to quaint to elegant; and the western Delaware River side and the New Jersey Highlands north of the Delaware Water Gap.

The fifty beach communities along the Atlantic coastline stretch from Sandy Hook National Park to Cape May. There are terrific books detailing the different towns, culture, and history. Briefly, the breakdown is as follows: from Sandy Hook to Asbury Park; from elegant **Spring Lake** and Belmar to Long Beach Island, including Island Beach State Park; Atlantic City; Ocean City down to the Wildwoods; and Victorian Cape May.

Cape May is a most wonderful Victorian enclave on the southernmost tip of New Jersey, truly a world unto itself. When here, be sure to visit the Emlen Physick House and the Cape May Point Lighthouse, among other places. Ferry service goes daily to Lewes, Delaware, across the bay.

Above Trenton on New Jersey's western border are Mercer and Hunterdon counties, which sit across the Delaware River from the cultural enclave of Bucks County, Pennsylvania. Some may prefer the New Jersey side, which is often calmer, with wonderfully historic towns of **Lambertville, Stockton, French-town,** and **Milford**. A short jaunt east brings a shopper to Flemington, an outlet mecca for bargain-hungry shoppers.

The Delaware Water Gap introduces more than 30 miles of lovely and wild landscape which culminates at High Point State Park.

The New Jersey Tourism Authority's number is 1-800-JERSEY-7.

New York

The country's second most populous state has nearly 18 million people, spread over 47,400 square miles; yet more than half its occupants live in several square miles around New York Harbor at the base of the Hudson, explored by Giovanni da Verrazano in 1524. In 1609, Henry Hudson discovered his river and Samuel de Champlain discovered his lake. The Dutch followed, settling Albany in 1614 and Manhattan in 1626. New York offers the best of all the Mid-Atlantic states in one state: the largest city and several great smaller ones; the longest stretch of the finest beaches; the Adirondacks and Catskills mountains, which rival others in wilderness beauty; vineyards in the Finger Lakes as well as in Long Island as fine and varied as those in Virginia; and more lakes than any other Mid-Atlantic state.

New York City

The best way to see **New York City** is on foot, and several recommended books will give a visitor wonderful routes. A Manhattan walk can take one through ethnic neighborhoods of Little Italy, Chinatown, Delancey Street, or Yorkville; shopping tours of Madison or Fifth Avenue or SoHo's West Broadway; around the theater district; past the bulls and bears of Wall Street; several days' work along Museum Mile of Upper Fifth Avenue; jazz clubs of the West Village; or architectural archives of the avenues.

Though it's quite touristy, the Circle Line Tours, operating since 1945, are a great way to get a sense of the island, its architecture, history, and configuration, during a three-and-a-half-hour tour. The guides are well trained and knowledgeable, and amid the one-liners and puns a passenger will glean some good stories.

Long Island

Like Mercury, Long Island has two faces: one watches the rough surf of the Atlantic, and the other looks at the quiet, lapping Long Island Sound. These two sides of the Island are entirely different. The south shore starts out as Long Beach and Jones Beach. The miraculous refuge of Robert Moses Beach and the Fire Island National Seashore follows, about 30 miles of protected beachfront, with about 20 tiny communities that do without cars in the summer, accessible by various ferries from the mainland.

The exclusive beaches of the Hamptons pick up where Fire Island's long sandy stretch ends. If you're extremely lucky, you have a house in the Hamptons; if you're lucky, you know someone with a house in the Hamptons; if you're average, you tan in Central Park—but everyone ought to make the trek to the Long Island beaches at some hot and sticky point in the summer. Westhampton Beach comes first; then **Quogue**, then **Southampton**, the first English colony established in its state. **East Hampton** follows, then Amagansett, and **Montauk**.

Compared with its western neighbors, Montauk remains curiously undiscovered, three hours east of New York City on Long Island's exposed southern fork. The surf of the Atlantic beats down on wide expansive beaches that remain sparely populated. The crowds, in fact, stop just west of here at East Hampton and Amagansett, before Hither Hills State Park where the south fork abruptly thins into a 15-mile peninsula ending at Montauk. Easternmost Route 27 is the only main road out to the peninsula, though it digresses at a certain point as the scenic Old Montauk Highway, laid out in the 1700s. The landscape is quite unusual here: scrubby, windswept dunes, rough undulating rock with stubborn, thick shrubbery growing low to the ground—in fact, the name *Montauk*, dubbed by Indian settlers, means "hilly country."

Backtracking a bit, an explorer goes back to East Hampton and heads north on Route 114 to the charming and quite subdued town of **Sag Harbor**. From this fishing village—which is actually one of the island's most exclusive escape towns—take a five-minute ferry to **Shelter Island**, perfectly wedged between the north and south forks of Long Island alee of the Sound and the Atlantic. New England Quakers sought refuge here from persecuting Puritans in 1652. There is no surf, but there is water everywhere, introduced by sandy and rocky beaches. Unlike the other Long Island shore towns, Shelter Island remains relatively unvisited, and its generations of blue-blooded summering families prefer it this way. Shelter Island is a wonderful refuge, with about a quarter of its land protected as the Mashomack Preserve, alee of the Atlantic in Gardiner's Bay.

A ferry to Greenport brings a visitor to the north shore. **Port Jefferson** and **Stony Brook** are worth a visit on one's return. Among the sites and estates to see on the Gatsby side of the Island are the Museums at Stony Brook, the Vanderbilt Museum Eagles Nest in Centerport, the Guggenheim estates at Sands Point Preserve, Cold Spring's Whaling Museum, Planting Fields Arboretum and Teddy Roosevelt's summer house Sagamore Hill in Oyster Bay, Old Westbury Gardens and its Georgian Revival mansion, and the antebellum restoration of Old Bethpage Village.

The Hudson Valley

A good distance to cover is between Cold Spring and Rhinebeck. Valley visitors will need to consult a guidebook to plan their city exodus. They may want to take the Henry Hudson Parkway on the river's east banks, or the refuge of the Palisades Parkway and cross the Hudson at **Tarrytown,** or proceed up to West Point for a visit and cross the Hudson at the Bear Mountain Bridge. **Cold Spring** is the first wonderful refuge of note, and after a long day's antiquing and romancing along the picturesque banks of the Hudson, a hungry traveler has two good choices for dinners at the Bird and Bottle Inn or at Plumbush. Just past **Poughkeepsie** are the sites for which the Hudson Valley is best known: Hyde Park and a 16-mile historic district which lines the Hudson's eastern shore. Before anything—in fact several months before—make reservations at the Culinary Institute of America for an evening's dinner. A trio of activities for a busy day includes the Vanderbilt Mansion National Historic Site, the Franklin D. Roosevelt Library Museum, Val-Kill, Eleanor Roosevelt's one-time retreat, and the Mills Mansion.

On to **Rhinebeck**, summer and early fall visitors may watch the air shows at the Rhinebeck Aerodrome or spend time antiquing in this historic village.

It is a must, when in this area, to make a special trip to the **Mohonk Mountain House**, a world unto itself in the Shawangunk Preserve. A Mohonk visit is embellished with a dinner at the DePuy Canal House in High Falls, an eclectic colonial tavern. The Hudson Valley Wine Company in Highland is a great diversion on the way back to New York City.

The Catskills

While best known for the boisterous family resorts of the 1950s and the bad comics who worked them, the Catskills are actually a beautiful, protected landscape which inspired painters like Thomas Cole and George Inness with its rough beauty.

Despite the reputation of the old resorts, the Catskills are quite remote and unspoiled, and the protected Forest Preserve, about 100 miles from New York City, measures 50 miles across at its widest. Aside from its finest ski resort, Hunter Mountain, with 17 lifts and a 1,600-foot vertical drop, the Catskills are home to gentle mountains, lovely scenery, as well as the artistic enclave of Woodstock, which hosted a concert and a generation more than twenty years ago. A scenic drive across the preserve will bring a fly-fisherman back to his roots, to **Beaverkill Valley** in **Lewbeach,** and the inn which bears its name, birthplace of American fly-fishing.

The Capital, Saratoga Springs, and Cooperstown

Albany is a tiny city, the state's government seat which received some much-needed revitalization in the past several years around the tricentennial in 1986. The downtown capital district is very walkable, best viewed from the forty-second story of Corning Tower at the Empire State Plaza, near the visitors center. From here, visit the New York State Museum on the Empire Plaza's south end. After a tour of the capitol, one can visit the Albany Institute of History and Art several blocks behind.

Less than an hour's drive north of Albany is the state's premier Victorian and Roaring Twenties resort town, **Saratoga Springs**. People think of horse racing when they think of the extraordinary wealth and frivolity of Saratoga—its season is about six weeks long around August—though its true attraction was its natural mineral springs, still very much a part of this privileged community. The town is simply beautiful, home to Skidmore College. One mile south of charming Victorian downtown is the Saratoga Spa State Park, a culturally enriched setting on 1,500 acres of groomed grounds. In addition to housing the Saratoga Performing Arts Center and the Roosevelt Mineral Baths, the park is home to the **Gideon Putnam Hotel,** which has full use of the park's generous array of activities.

As well as providing the stage for fine theater, the Saratoga Performing Arts Center is home to the New York City Ballet and Opera and the Philadelphia Orchestra during its August season. The Roosevelt Baths offer mineral baths, massages, and hot packs in an original turn-of-the-century setting. Also within the park's acreage are a PGA 18-hole golf course, a 9-hole par 3 course, three outdoor swimming pools, eight tennis courts, ice skating, and cross-country skiing.

Among the sights to see in Saratoga are the National Museum of Racing and Hall of Fame, the artistic retreat Yaddo, and the National Musem of Dance.

A seventy-mile drive west of Albany is mecca for any fan of America's pasttime, on the southern banks of Lake Otsego.

Cooperstown is home to the Baseball Hall of Fame where, in 1839, Abner Doubleday is said to have invented the game. William Cooper founded the charming town in 1786 and also sired a son named James Fenimore Cooper, one of the more endemic American novelists. Do take a cruise on this lake, which is wonderfully picturesque, and complete the day with tea on the porch of the Otesaga Hotel.

The Adirondacks

The Adirondacks are the state's most precious and uninvaded refuge, six million acres of wilderness with more than 2,000 lakes and 45 mountains measuring more than 4,000 feet. Even the people here seem like pioneers, bearing little relation to their downstate neighbors. In addition to the unfathomable beauty of its forests, the Adirondacks are home to one of the state's finest museums, the Adirondack Museum in **Blue Mountain Lake.** The Adirondacks begin at Glens Falls, stretch up to Plattsburgh to the north, and are introduced by Old Forge in the west, famous for its Hardware Store, a cultural enclave in the wilderness.

The azure waters of Lake George begin shortly after Glens Falls, reaching about 40 miles to Fort Ticonderoga and its restored 18th-century military complex, which sit on the lower waters of Lake Champlain. Lake George Village is quite touristy, but several miles north, grace returns in **Bolton Landing** at the famous **Sagamore Resort.** The drive along the lake is magnificent to Fort Ticonderoga, where the drive north continues with gorgeous scenery, all the way to **Westport.** Here, a trek westward plunges immediately from water to mountains, past **Keene** to **Lake Placid** and abundant winter and water sports.

Lake Placid introduces a traveler to the Great Camps along Route 30, which bends west and then south. At the turn-of-the-century, with the increased leisure and wealth provided by the enlightened industrial age, New York City financiers and magnates conquered the northern wilderness. They built, with lavish abandon, the rustic, highly crafted Adirondack Great Camps, playgrounds of the opulent, where the pampered would rough it in a most civilized manner. Route 30 is the best avenue from which to see some of these estates, most of which are private—though the architecture is abundant, recognizable, beautiful, and entirely specific to the area. The drive takes one from Lake Placid Lower and **Upper Saranac Lakes,** past Tupper Lake, down to **Blue Mountain Lake** and the Adirondack Museum, west to **Raquette Lake** and **Sagamore Lodge,** the great camp of the Vanderbilts. West of Racquette Lake is Old Forge, the western gateway to the Adirondacks.

Quite a distance, though well worth the trip, is a visit to the Thousand Islands, at Alexandria Bay, dotting the St. Lawrence River across from Canada. Aside from fishing, there are some wonderful activities in the area. Boldt Castle, on Heart Island in the bay, was already partially built by magnate George C. Boldt when his wife died in 1904. He was too heartbroken to complete the mansion, and it remains today a sad tribute to unrequited love. About a half hour's drive south is the Frederic Remington Museum in his hometown of Ogdensburg.

The Finger Lakes, Rochester, and Corning

The western stretch of the state below Lake Ontario is reached via dull Route 80, from Utica to Buffalo. A tenable and very scenic patch along this route is from Syracuse to **Rochester,** the northernmost border of the Finger Lakes. The parallel access road to the Finger Lakes is Route 20, often quite busy and traffic-ridden. The lakes bleed south from Route 20, truly like fingers on an outstretched hand, ranging from several miles in length to more than 40 miles: Skaneateles, Owasco, Cayuga, Seneca, Keuka, and Canandaigua, and some smaller ones. The area was conquered with horrific force in 1779 by General John Sullivan, who ravaged the many outposts of Iroqouis Indians. There are so many activities here, from museums to wineries and historic sites, that consultation with a favored book is the best tack. Each lake has its focal point town: **Ithaca,** for example, at the southernmost point of Lake Cayuga, **Hammondsport** at the base of Lake Keuka, and car racing hub Watkins Glen at the base of Seneca Lake.

Corning sits below the Finger Lakes nearing Pennsylvania, one of the state's largest tourist attractions. The Corning Museum of Glass, which welcomes millions of visitors yearly, is divided into three different sections: historical aspects of glass through changing exhibits, glass in the making at the Steuben Glass Factory, and displays with an eye to the future at the Hall of Science and Industry. In addition to the Corning Museum of Glass, the town is also home to the highly acclaimed Rockwell Museum, located in the 1893 restored city hall, which offers one of the country's most comprehensive exhibits of American western art and Indian artifacts. A town replete with history, its boom began in 1868, when the Flint Glass Company moved from Brooklyn to Corning, a sleepy railroad depot about forty years old. The main venue, Market Street, was restored and put on the National Register of Historic Places in the 1970s, lined with brick sidewalks and many Victorian facades from the town's heydey.

Rochester is removed from Lake Ontario by several miles of the Genesee River. There is a great deal to this small city: Susan B. Anthony was arrested here en route to the ballot box, and Frederick Douglas's bold periodical *The North Star* was printed here. Rochester is still a formidable corporate hub, the largest resident of which is Eastman Kodak. The International Museum of Photography is a fascinating site in the former mansion of Kodak founder George Eastman, and for a ready-made tour, visit Kodak Park. Other museums include the Memorial Art Gallery, with ancient and European art; the Rochester Museum & Science Center, with one of the world's best collections of Iroquois Indian artifacts; and the Strong Museum, with one of the world's most extensive doll collections, upwards of 20,000, and domestic artifacts. Try to slate a visit during May for the annual Festival of Lilacs at Highland Park.

Niagara Falls, Buffalo, the Erie Coast

Aside from visiting the falls, there is little to do in this tourist town, though a visit to the Canadian side is quite recommended. Be sure to have a meal at the Red Coach Inn, a Tudor house on the rapids, one of the town's oldest buildings, erected in the 1920s.

Generous travelers will be glad to spend extra time in Buffalo. It's interesting to cruise the waters of Lake Erie, filled by the waters from Niagara and its river. Among the notable sights are the Buffalo Museum of Science and the Buffalo and Erie County Historical Society, which features archaeological history of the Niagara frontier, Indians, and the Erie Canal. The Albright-Knox Art Gallery has some great contemporary art. Be sure to stop at the Buffalo Zoo, laid out by Frederick Law Olmsted more than a century ago.

A drive south along sightless Route 90 takes a traveler eventually to **Chautauqua,** a sleepy Victorian haven on a lake which shares its name. During nine summer weeks, the town comes to life as the famed Chautauqua Institution, gifted with an infusion of art, dance, music, and academic performances. The abundance of adorable Victorian architecture is a testament to the Institution's beginnings—in 1874, a band of Methodist Sunday School teachers came here as a cultural and intellectual refuge.

For New York travel information, 800-CALLNYS, or 518-474-4116.

Pennsylvania

Pennsylvania is the country's fifth largest state, with more than 12 million people living in 45,000 square miles of a good deal of forestland. This vast rectangular state, 180 miles wide and 310 miles long, is traversed by the 470-mile-long Pennsylvania Turnpike, with 44,000 miles of state highways, and nearly 70,000 miles of other roads. The state was settled first by the Swedish in 1643 but became an official place of religious tolerance when William Penn established his Quaker state here in 1682. It was here that the Declaration of Independence was signed, and the Constitution was drafted.

Philadelphia

There was a great deal of excitement and refurbishment in **Philadelphia** for the two-hundredth anniversary of the Constitution, and the city still shows its pride. Having served almost continuously as the nation's capital from 1774 to 1800, the city still retains a great sense of importance to historic America. Bordered to the east by the Delaware River and to the west by the Schuylkill River, Philadelphia was designed by William Penn to be a "greene countrie town," with five pastoral commons, which today are known as Penn, Washington, Franklin, Rittenhouse, and Logan squares (though Logan has since become a circle). Independence National Historic Park sits on the eastern part of the city, filled with a week's worth of activity. Betsy Ross, Edgar Allan Poe, and Norman Rockwell have histories tied to Philadelphia and respective museums open to the public. The Rodin Museum has the largest collection of the artist's work outside France; the Franklin Institute Science Museum and Planetarium is an interactive museum; and, of course, the Philadelpia Museum of Art is internationally renowned. The 8,700-acre Fairmount Park is the world's largest landscaped city park, with 100 miles of jogging paths as well as bountiful historic sights and sculpture, and America's first zoo, from 1874.

Pennsylvania Dutch Country, the Capital, and Hershey

This area is replete with history and culture, much endemic to the area for generations, home most famously to the Amish and Mennonites, who are very much in evidence. Wheatland is here, home of President James Buchanan, as are the Hans Herr House, one of the country's oldest Mennonite meeting houses, and the **Ephrata Cloister,** an eerie, intriguing 18th-century German monastic settlement.

For a sojourn for outlets and bargains, take a side trip to **Reading,** which has one of the lovelier bed-and-breakfasts in this book, at Centre Park.

On the vast banks of the Susquehanna River, Harrisburg has been the state's capital for nearly two hundred years, featuring the wonderful State Museum of Pennsylvania since 1905.

Twelve miles east is **Hershey.** By 1900, a young entrepreneur named Milton Hershey was carting his singular chocolate recipe around Lancaster County by means of horseless electric carriage. Hershey built his chocolate factory from 1903 to 1905 and built a town around it which soon adopted its founder's name.

HersheyPark has 45 amusement park rides including three roller coasters; Carousel Circle, one of the oldest such carousels in use in the country, built in 1919, hand-carved by Italian craftsman; a 17th-century village called Tudor Square; an 18th-century village called Pennsylvania Dutch Place with crafts and foods; Kid Stuff, with activities and games for children; and Rhine Land, an 18th-century German village.

In addition to touring Chocolate World, there are countless activities in the Hershey complex including 10 acres of ZooAmerica. The Hershey Museum of American Life was opened by Milton Hershey in 1933 to enrich knowledge of Native Americans, Eskimos, and Pennsylvania Germans.

The Hershey Gardens are quite extensive. Milton Hershey introduced a rose garden in 1936 on 3.5 acres, in which 12,500 roses in 112 varieties were planted. Today the gardens sprawl over 23 acres with 700 varieties of roses, 30,000 tulips, and altogether 120,000 plants, shrubs, and trees.

York and **Gettysburg** are a short jaunt south, including the 3,500-acre Gettysburg National Military Park and a history book's worth of Civil War activities.

Pittsburgh

About an hour's drive to Wheeling, West Virginia, and also to Youngstown Ohio, **Pittsburgh** sits in the southwest part of its state at the confluence of the Ohio, Monongahela, and Allegheny rivers—the Golden Triangle. George Washington surveyed the land, named Fort Pitt in 1758, the history of which is detailed at Fort Pitt Museum. Just east of the Golden Triangle is Three Rivers Stadium in Oakland, also home to the Carnegie, which houses the Museum of Art and the Museum of Natural

History, and the Frick Art Museum, with lavish Italian and French decorative arts.

Erie sits 100 miles north of Pittsburgh, the only bit of "coast" in the state, on the Great Lake of its name. Visitors will see, at the city's center, the Old Customs House and the Erie Art Museum within this Greek Revival monument. On the city's outskirts is a wonderful recreational facility in Presque Isle State Park, a peninsular spit of beach and greenery.

Central and Northern Pennsylvania

The vast wilderness of the state is best realized with a drive across its center, to the Cook Forest in **Cooksburg** and the Clarion River, below the Allegheny Forest to **State College,** and up to **Williamsport**, on the northern stretches of the Susquehanna River. Williamsport, once home to millionaire lumber barons, has the popular attraction of the Peter J. McGovern Little League Baseball Museum.

The Poconos

Derived from the Indian word *pocohonne*, this area is named for the stream between the mountains—between the New Jersey Highlands and the low, old mountain of Pennsylvania's northeast corner. It's the most popular vacation spot in the state and has the rather unfortunate reputation (occasionally well deserved) of heart-shaped tubs and nightclub-hotels. Aside from low-level skiing, the area hosts wonderful outdoor activities; the Delaware Water Gap, with spectacular hiking along its 35 miles of resources; 13-mile-long manmade Lake Wallenpaupack at **Hawley**, with 52 miles of shore, the state's largest recreational lake; and **Jim Thorpe**, a cozy town which served as the country's railroad capital during the late 19th century.

Bucks County

Named for the shire from which William Penn came, Bucks (from Buckingham) County is a wonderfully beautiful stretch of land shouldering the Delaware River northeast of Philadelphia. **New Hope** and **Doylestown** are the focal points of this county, featuring the Bucks County Vineyards, the Moravian Pottery and Tile Works, and the Mercer Museum, which displays the artistry of more than 60 crafts and 40,000 tools, named for the master craftsman who made his home and trade here at the turn of the century. His home, Fonthill Museum, is also open to the public.

A thoroughly scenic drive, interrupted by rickety narrow bridges across the Delaware to New Jersey, is along 60 miles of River Road, which follows the winding path of the Delaware from New Hope to Bethlehem. During the 1920s and 1930s, Bucks County was an artistic haven, a kind of Greenwich Village weekend retreat. The country's most brilliant intellectuals, artists, writers, and musicians vacationed here, and there is a great deal of lore at every turn.

For visitor information, call 800-VISIT-PA.

Virginia

Virginia is most assuredly a southern state. More than 6 million people live in 41,000 square miles of incredibly varied landscape: from mountains which peak over 4,000 feet, to sandy beaches, to river-soaked marshland, to fairly cosmopolitan cities. To know Virginia history is to know American history, and it has more than 1,500 historic sites on the state's 35,000 miles of paved roads. The English enclave of Jamestown was the country's first settlement in 1607, and the state was divided formally from West Virginia in 1863.

Fredericksburg and the Northern Neck

Fredericksburg, 50 miles south of Washington, D.C., shoulders the Rappahannock River on its south shore. One of the town's finest sights is the estate Kenmore, built by George Washington's sister Betty. From here, travelers may explore the flat, marshy plantation land of the Northern Neck, a watrous peninsula which has the Rappahannock on the south and the Potomac to the north, ending at the Chesapeake Bay. The 538-acre George Washington Birthplace National Monument is here. North of **Irvington**, at the end of the neck, take a ferry to Tangier Island and farther to the eastern shore; or to Smith Island and Crisfield, Maryland.

The Eastern Shore

The ferry to Crisfield takes a traveler to the Delaware-Maryland peninsula and the southern-pointing peninsula of Virginia's eastern shore. Just below the Virginia border is **New Church**. A drive east will bring one to the eastern shore's busiest town, **Chincoteague**, which sits in its own bay alee of the Assateague Island National Seashore. This protected park stretches up to Maryland, a 37-mile thin vertical strip of protected beach on the Atlantic Ocean which is best known as the home to a herd of wild ponies, a wonderful attraction for this part of the Delmarva peninsula.

The peninsula, never more than several miles wide, stretches for about 60 miles from Chincoteague down to Cape Charles, linked to Virginia Beach by a 20-mile scenic highway. As well as having wonderful beaches on the Atlantic, the eastern shore has a great deal of history, with 17th-century communities and Victorian enclaves, as well as quaint Tangier Island, which prohibits cars. From here, the drive south down the peninsula on its main vein Route 13 takes one past lovely Onancock, 18th-century Eastville, and 19th-century Cape Charles.

Williamsburg and Plantation Country

The base of the eastern shore connects to Tidewater Virginia via the 17-mile-long Chesapeake Bay Bridge-Tunnel. Here, bustling Virginia Beach, Norfolk, and Hampton cluster around beaches at the confluence of the James, Elizabeth, and Nansemond rivers.

Upriver from Newport News is the state's most popular tourist attraction, **Colonial Williamsburg**. The first history of Williamsburg began in the late 1600s, when the town called Middle Plantation took over from Jamestown to serve as the capital of the British crown colony of Virginia until 1780. A second, more recent history of Colonial Williamsburg commenced in 1926 when W.A.R. Goodwin and John D. Rockefeller, Jr., undertook a $79 million effort to resurrect an authentic colonial town in the 20th century. Within 3,000 acres of protected land along the James River in Virginia's southwestern corner, Colonial Williamsburg is a 173-acre window to the past, one mile long and five blocks wide, home to 88 original 18th- and early-19th-century buildings, with another 50 resurrected buildings, and more than 90 acres of authentic period gardens.

In addition to the historic buildings and streets, there are 20 studios of craftspeople working at the art of colonial survival: binders, yarnmakers, milliners, coopers, and blacksmiths, among others. For sightseeing, the National Park Service maintains the scenic Colonial Parkway to Jamestown and Yorktown.

Today, more than a million visitors each year travel to this magical place and peruse the 800 acres of history.

Richmond, Charlottesville, and the Piedmont

En route to Richmond from Williamsburg, visit Petersburg, a major railroad hub and stronghold of the Confederacy. Seventy-five miles up the James River from the state's first settlement, **Richmond** was settled more than a century after, in the 1730s. The buildings of the capital were designed by the governor at the time in 1785, near the house where he and Mrs. Jefferson lived. It's quite fun to tour the James River by boat. As well, be sure to visit St. John's Church, where Patrick Henry made his "Give Me Liberty" speech in 1775. Additional sights in the area are the Edgar Allan Poe Museum, the Lewis Ginter Botanical Gardens at Bloemendaal Farm, the largest collection of Confederate memorabilia at the Museum and White House of the Confederacy, home to Jefferson Davis during the Civil War, and the world's largest film projector at the Science Museum of Virginia. Of the many plantations of the area, Berkeley Plantation is perhaps the best known, the setting for the first Thanksgiving in 1619, a year before the Pilgrims gave thanks in Massachusetts.

Charlottesville rests 71 miles northwest of Richmond and about 30 miles east of Waynesboro. After meticulously constructing the masterpiece of his home, Monticello, from 1769 to 1804, Thomas Jefferson founded the University of Virginia down the hill in Charlottesville in 1819. Other sights in this lovely town are Ash Lawn, modest home to James Monroe, and historic Michie Tavern. Several wineries are within a half hour's drive, and in September and April the area is home to the Foxfield steeplechase.

A short jaunt northeast of Charlottesville takes a visitor to **Orange** and another presidential territory, that of James Madison and Montpelier.

The Shenandoah Valley

The Shenandoah National Park is 80 miles long, composed of 200,000 acres, and averages between 2 and 13 miles in width between Front Royal and Waynesboro. It averages 2,000 feet above sea level, with spectacular views from the **Skyline Drive**. South of Waynesboro, the Skyline Drive becomes the Blue Ridge Parkway, 470 miles long with 217 miles of drive in Virginia.

Along the way are wonderful towns, nestled in the valley between the Shenandoah National Park and the one million acres of the George Washington National Forest, which forms a natural border with West Virginia. On the road south are dozens of wonderful activities. Luray Caverns might be a good first stop. **Harrisonburg** is a bustling town, home to James Madison University and Mennonite College. **Staunton** is a San Francisco of the Mid-Atlantic, with flashy Victorian architecture amid steep hills. Though settled as early as 1731, the city was chartered in 1870 in the heyday of Victoriana and became a large intersection of the Chesapeake-Western and the Chesapeake and Ohio railroads. It is home to Mary Baldwin College and the Woodrow Wilson Birthplace and has a great resource in the Museum of American Frontier Culture. The next college town after Staunton is **Lexington**, home to the Virginia Military Institute and Washington and Lee University, as well as the Virginia Horse Center.

Farther west a traveler will arrive at **Hot Springs,** home of the **Homestead Resort** and some of the state's finest golf and skiing. The virtues of this resort are found in natural mineral springs discovered in the 18th century which attracted followers over the centuries. Five miles north of the Homestead are the original Warm Springs Pools, heated naturally by underground springs to a steady 96 degrees year-round. The men's pool, built in 1761, is said to have been designed by Thomas Jefferson; the women's pool was added in 1836.

The Blue Ridge Parkway begins here. Below Lexington about 15 miles is a wondrous sight in Natural Bridge, a limestone arch 215 feet high and 90 feet long, supporting U.S. 11. Roanoke is the gateway to Virginia's southwest, a hardworking town strong in fine arts. **Smith Mountain Lake**, an endless recreation area, is about 20 miles southeast of Roanoke, within close proximity to Booker T. Washington National Monument. Just north is the wonderful estate of Poplar Forest, the summer retreat of Thomas Jefferson between 1806 and 1813, an octagonal Palladian tribute.

With tickets in hand to an event at the Barter Theater, visitors will find a side trip to **Abingdon** quite rewarding. The theater was named because barter was accepted as payment for tickets when it opened in 1932.

Nortern Virginia Horse Country and Old Town Alexandria

Between Front Royal, the head of the Skyline Drive, and Washington, D.C., is horse country. Along Route 50 is lovely scenery, antiquing in **Strasburg**, and great overnighting in **White Post, Millwood, Paris,** and **Middleburg**. Mount Vernon, George

Washington's home, is only 16 miles south of Washington, D.C., one of the country's most visited sights. Three miles away is the house Washington built for his nephew, called Woodlawn, designed by William Thornton, who built the Capitol. Another several miles south is Gunston Hall, home of George Mason, who is best known for having refused to sign the Constitution because it did not prohibit slavery. A wonderful place for an overnight from here is **Alexandria**, established in 1749, a great village for walking and perusing dozens of historic 18th-century homes.

For Virginia travel information, call 800-VISIT-VA.

West Virginia

With a population just under 2 million spread over 24,000 square miles, West Virginia has a lot of room for visitors, more than any other Mid-Atlantic state. While New Jersey has about 1,000 people per square mile, West Virginia has 77. With eight ski resorts, 36 state recreation areas, and the vast Monongahela National Forest, West Virginia is a naturalist's paradise. Early explorers of the largely ignored half of Virginia were Daniel Boone and George Washington, the latter visiting the restorative springs in the southeastern part of the state. This vast tract of mountains and forests became autonomous during the tussle of the War Between the States, finally named West Virginia in 1863.

The eastern panhandle is the part of the state that looks most like the other states in the Mid-Atlantic, with rolling hills along the banks of the Chesapeake and Ohio Canal and the Potomac River. Several charming towns rest in the easternmost hook of the state. Harper's Ferry National Historical Park rests at the confluence of the Potomac and Shenandoah rivers, in the Blue Ridge Mountains. Its town, which earned its wealth from water power, was the site of the nation's first armory, ordered at the behest of President Washington in 1790. It thrived well into the mid-1800s with the C&O Canal presence and the B&O Railroad, though the Civil War destroyed any industrial potential it had.

Charles Town is an adorable village nearby, on the way to **Martinsburg** and **Shepherdstown**. The latter is just across the border from western Maryland's Antietam Battlefield, on the bluffs above the Potomac, the state's oldest settlement, originally named Mecklenburg, dating to 1762. It bills itself as the birthplace of the steamboat at the hands of West Virginian John

Rumsey. Last, **Berkeley Springs** attracted wealthy Victorians with its curative mineral springs. Berkeley Castle was built during this era, in 1875, an incongruous stone edifice cut into the hill above town, and worth a special visit. The town's state park features warm, bubbling mineral springs all year, and nearby Cacapon State Park features an 18-hole golf course designed by Robert Trent Jones, among other outdoor activities.

The drive from the eastern panhandle to **Parkersburg** bordering Ohio is quite dramatic. There is a good deal to do in this small town, which once hosted the country's oil, lumber, and gas moguls. It was for them that the **Blennerhassett Hotel** was built in 1889. The property was named for Harman Blennerhassett, a West Virginian folk hero of sorts. He was born in Ireland and after marrying his niece, Margaret Agnew, was rather ostracized from his family. They moved to America and bought an island in the middle of the Ohio River, about two miles below Parkersburg. In 1798, the couple built a mansion which they called Eden, a 7,000-square-foot regal retreat of white clapboard, which was burned in 1811.

Before this, however, Blennerhassett's life was touched by tragedy when Aaron Burr visited him on his island and solicited support to fund his conspiracy. Blennerhassett was twice arrested for his part in the Burr affair and remained imprisoned until after Burr's release. His life never returned to normal, and he finally returned to Ireland where he died in 1831. There is a happy ending of sorts to the Blennerhassett tragedy; in 1980, the West Virginia legislature formed the Historic Blennerhassett Commission, which reconstructed the mansion. The Blennerhassett Island Historical State Park is a wonderful site to visit after a short riverboat ride. The Middleton Doll Company in Ohio and the Fenton Art Glass Company are interesting jaunts, each a short drive away.

From the capital, Charleston, to White Sulpher Springs is a magnificent drive on unbelievably mountainous and remote roads, with a stop in breathtaking **Beckley** for a visit to **Pence Springs Resort,** once a pilgrimage destination for the wealthy who flocked here on the railroads that stopped a dozen times daily during the Roaring Twenties. While here, be sure to visit the Exhibition Coal Mine and the Riverside Inn for wonderful food.

Concluding a West Virginia visit is a trip to its finest attraction, the **Greenbrier** resort in **White Sulphur Springs**.

For West Virginia tourist information, call the Tourism Authority at 800-CALL-WVA.

Recommended Reading

For help in compiling this reading list, the Travellers Bookstore proved invaluable, a resource in travel books since 1982. Owners Candy Olmsted and Jane Grossman also offer a mail order catalog with close to 800 practical and eclectic listings, available for $2 by calling 212-664-0995 or by writing 22 West 52nd Street (75 Rockefeller Plaza), New York, New York 10019.

General Travel and Mid-Atlantic

Smithsonian Guide to Historic America *(Stewart, Tabori, and Chang). $17.95.*

Three pertinent volumes include New York, New Jersey, Pennsylvania; Virginia, The Capitol Region; The Carolinas and Appalachian States, West Virginia. Thoroughly researched, wonderfully written history and cultural almanacs, including original maps, photographs and prints, and architectural notes.

The Discerning Traveler's Guide to the Middle-Atlantic. *David and Linda Glickstein (St. Martin's). $16.95.*

Personally researched and tenderly written guide with ten regional itineraries on where to go, stay, dine, and what to do.

Romantic Weekend Getaways, Mid-Atlantic. *Larry Fox and Barbara Radin Fox (Wiley). $12.95.*

Creative, manageable itineraries for amorous couples.

Getaways for Gourmets. *Nancy Webster and Richard Woodworth (Wood Pond). $14.95.*

Well-researched, thorough itineraries for culinary-minded travelers.

Travel with Your Pet USA (Artco). $9.95.
A must-have almanac for those intending to vacation with a furry family member.

Away for the Weekend. Eleanor Berman *(Clarkson Potter).* *$12.95.*
Thoughtful, trusted itineraries within 250 miles of Mid-Atlantic cities.

Daytrips, Getaway Weekends, and Vacations in the Mid-Atlantic States. Patricia and Robert Foulke *(Globe Pequot).* *$13.95.*
Easy, varied itineraries around six states.

Civil War Sourcebook. Chuck Lawliss *(Harmony). $18.*
A detailed history of the War within the context of travel. Sightseeing tours of Virginia and points north, including historic, battlefields, and monument sites.

The Complete Guide to Music Festivals in America. Carol Price Rabin *(Berkshire Traveler Press). $10.95.*
Over 250 listings and descriptions of classical, opera, jazz, ragtime, dixie, pops, folk, Cajun, bluegrass, and country music festivals.

The Amusement Park Guide. Tim O'Brien *(Globe Pequot Press).* *$12.95.*
Comprehensive listing, description, and interesting histories of amusement parks, first popularized in Coney Island and Pennsylvania.

National Park Guide. Michael Frome *(Prentice Hall). $14.95.*
Listing and descriptions of national, Washington, D.C., area, archaeological, historic, and natural/recreational parks.

Pat Dickerman's Adventure Travel North America. Pat Dickerman *(Adventure Guides Inc.). $15.95.*
Detailed information on hiking, mountaineering, canoeing, ballooning, sailing, cycling trips.

Family Sports Adventures. Megan Stine *(Time Life Inc.).*
From *Sports Illustrated for Kids,* geared for parents and children to plan together.

Wine Routes of America. Jan Aaron (E. P. Dutton). $15.95.
   A wonderful reference guide for beginners or advanced, in a thick volume detailing vineyards and wineries, as well as terminology and cultural activities in the area.

Great Vacations with Your Kids. Dorothy Jordon and Marjorie Adoff Cohen (E. P. Dutton). $12.95.
   An expert guide with itineraries in cities, resorts, skiing, farming, skiing, with advice on modes of travel, babysitting, and surprising other topics.

Where the Old Roads Go: Driving the First Federal Highways of the North East. George Cantor (Harper & Row). $10.95.
   An interesting history and guide to U.S. routes, such as the 319-mile stretch of U.S. 11 between Champlain and Binghamton, or U.S. 20 between Cardiff and Ripley, New York—in the vein of *On the Road.*

Waterside Escapes: Great Getaways by Lake, River, and Sea. Betsy Wittemann and Nancy Webster (Wood Pond Press). $13.95.
   Detailed waterside itineraries in the Mid-Atlantic states.

Delaware

Canoeing the Delaware. Gary Letcher (Rutgers University Press). $25.
   A timeless, long-standing book written by an expert.

District of Columbia

Washington, D.C. Access. (HarperCollins). $12.95.
   Impeccably organized, detailed all-in-one guide for architecture, history, culture, events. Wonderful maps.

Gault-Millau Washington D.C. $16.95.
   Stocked with information and opinion about every aspect of the capital.

Zagat Restaurant Survey. (Zagat Publishing). $12.95.
   A highly respected insider's guide to restaurants, with considerate cross-referencing in a handy size.

Michelin Green Guide to Washington, D.C. $14.95.
The reliable standby, a must for loyal Micheliners.

Fodors: Washington, D.C. (Random House). $11.
Thorough handbook on every aspect of everyday travel in the capital—with a handy alternative in *Pocket Washington, D.C.,* for $8. Features detailed maps.

Places to Go with Children in Washington D.C. Judy Colbert (Chronicle Books). $9.95.
Good, sensible advice and plans for parents for the activity-filled capital.

Kidding Around, Washington D.C. Anne Pedersen (John Muir). $9.95.
A children's guide to the city written for young readers.

Maryland

Maryland: Off the Beaten Path. (Globe Peqout). $8.95.
One in a series of thin, down-to-earth books filled with creative suggestions, written in a friendly fashion.

Zagat Restaurant Survey: Baltimore. (Zagat). $9.95.
A highly respected insider's guide to restaurants, with considerate cross-referencing in a handy size.

New Jersey

New Jersey: Off the Beaten Path. (Globe Pequot). $8.95.
One in a series of thin, down-to-earth books filled with creative suggestions, written in a friendly fashion.

Guide to the Jersey Shore: From Sandy Hook to Cape May. Robert Santelli (Globe Pequot). $11.95.
Detailed eclectic guide to activities along the shore, including boating, fishing, antiquing, concerts, horse racing, casinos, and Victorian, tulip, and film festivals in Cape May.

25 Bicycle Tours in New Jersey. Arline and Joel Zatz (Backcountry Publishing). $9.95.
Details more than 900 miles of tours around the state.

New Jersey Day Trips. Barbara Hudgins (Woodmont Press). $10.95.
Short outings in New Jersey and neighboring states.

Fodors: Atlantic City and New Jersey Shore. (Random House). $8.95.
A thin, useful guide to the gambling mecca and beach attractions, with detailed maps.

Fodors: Vacations on the Jersey Shore. (Random House). $11.
A great, detailed primer for the state's great sites, with terrific maps.

New York City

Access New York City. Richard Saul Wurman (HarperCollins). $16.95.
Impeccably organized, detailed all-in-one guide for architecture, history, culture, events for the five boroughs.

Blue Guide New York. Carol von Pressentin Wright (Norton). $19.95.
Cultural landscape of New York City rich on history and good writing.

Gault-Millau New York. (Prentice Hall). $16.95.
Stocked with information and opinion about every aspect of a traveler's New York.

New York, Cadogan City Guides. Vanessa Letts (Globe Pequot). $14.95.
A tour of the city via eight neighborhood walks, with information on history, art, cafés, dining, shopping, and day trips.

American Express Pocket Guide: New York. Herbert Bailey Livesey (Prentice Hall). $10.95.
A handy at-your-fingertips book.

Michelin Green Guide to New York City. $14.95.
The reliable standby, a must for loyal Micheliners.

AIA Guide to New York City. Elliot Willensky and Norval White (Harcourt Brace Jovanovitch). $21.95.
Encyclopedic listing and description of important architectural landmarks in five boroughs by neighborhood.

Fodors: New York City. (Random House). $13.
Highly detailed maps and thorough research make this a great all-around guide; includes 25 walking tours.

Museums in New York. Fred W. McDarrah (St. Martin's). $13.95.
A long-standing, much needed reference guide to the city's art world.

Born to Shop. Suzy Gershman and Judith Thomas (Bantam Books). $8.95.
A budget hunter's almanac.

Shopping Manhattan. Corky Pollan (Penguin). $12.95.
New York magazine's Best Bets columnist reveals where to find anything in New York.

Art Walks in New York. Marina Harrison and Lucy D. Rosenfeld (Michael Kensend). $14.95.
Guide to public art and gardens in and around Manhattan.

The Complete Guide to Ethnic New York. Zelda Stern (St. Martin's). $8.95.
An interesting breakdown of the original melting pot.

Zagat Restaurant Survey New York. (Zagat Publishing). $12.95.
A highly respected insider's guide to restaurants, with considerate cross-referencing.

Kidding Around, New York. Sarah Lovett (John Muir). $9.95.
A children's guide to the city written for young readers.

New York State

New York Walk Book. The New York, New Jersey Trail Conference (Doubleday). $15.95.
Professionally prepared field guide for serious walkers.

Zagat Restaurant Survey, Suburban New York City. (Zagat Publishing). $12.95.
A highly respected insider's guide to restaurants, with considerate cross-referencing in a handy size.

The Hudson River Valley. Tim Mulligan (Random House). $12.
  Highly recommended, well-written guide to this varied area.

Guide to Adirondack Trails: Highland Parks Region. Edited by
Tony Goodwin (Adirondack Mountain Club).
  A thorough, technical guide with extensive maps.

New York: Off the Beaten Path. (Globe Pequot). $8.95.
  One in a series of thin, down-to-earth books filled with creative suggestions, written in a friendly fashion.

One Day Adventures by Car: Daytrips from New York City.
Lida Newberry, updated by Joy Johannessen (Hastings House).
$12.95.
  A manageable guide to getting away.

Country Walks near New York. William G. Scheller (Appalachian Mountain Club). $8.95.
  Handy pocket book detailing 20 rural walks.

Short Nature Walks on Long Island. Rodney and Priscilla Al-
bright (Globe Pequot). $8.95.
  Twenty-five walks on beaches, in towns, in woods, and on
great estates.

Short Bicycle Rides on Long Island. Phil Angelillo (Globe Pequot). $8.95.
  Thirty well-mapped, conversantly described rides in a down-
to-earth format.

Fodors: Vacations in New York State. (Random House). $14.95.
  An everything-in-one, personally researched book with history, culture, practical advice, and wonderful maps.

Great Camps of the Adirondacks. Harvey H. Kaiser (David
Godine). $50 hardcover, $35 paperback.
  Fascinating, wonderfully written cultural and architectural
history of the playgrounds of the wealthy at the turn of the
century, with great maps and more than 200 pictures.

Pennsylvania

Guide's Guide to Philadelphia. Julie P. Curson (Curson House).
$11.95.
  A professional takes you touring

Pennsylvania: Off the Beaten Path. *(Globe Pequot).* *$8.95.*
One in a series of thin, down-to-earth books filled with creative suggestions, written in a friendly fashion.

Zagat Restaurant Survey Philadelphia. *(Zagat Publishing).* *$12.95.*
A highly respected insider's guide to restaurants, with considerate cross-referencing in a handy size.

Virginia

Virginia: A History and Guide. *Tim Mulligan.* *$10.95.*
A rich history and culture of the state and its major cities.

Sierra Club Guides to the National Parks: East and Middle West. *(Stewart, Tabori, and Chang).* *$14.95.*
An invaluable, insightful, and well-written book from authoritative environmentalists.

Virginia: Off the Beaten Path. *(Globe Pequot).* *$8.95.*
One in a series of thin, down-to-earth books filled with creative suggestions, written in a friendly fashion.

Hiking the Old Dominion. *Allen DeHart (Sierra Club).* *$12.95.*
Commendably researched by a writer who loves his subject.

West Virginia

Hiking the Mountain State and Trails of West Virginia. *Allen DeHart (AMC Books).* *$14.95.*
A much-needed book by a caring environmentalist.

Appendixes

Good Places for Families

Good Value

Suitable for Groups

Swimming Pool

Tennis

Horseback Riding

Golf

Fishing

Cross-Country Skiing

Fitness Facility

State or National Park Nearby

Pets Welcome

DC	Four Seasons Hotel 375
	Hotel Washington 342
	Jefferson 343
	Mayflower Hotel 358
	Park Hyatt 376
	Sheraton Carlton 348
	Watergate Hotel 255
MD	Inn at the Colonnade 295
NJ	Peacock Inn 299
NY	Athenaeum Hotel 142
	Box Tree 323
	Carlyle 355
	Garden City Hotel 383
	Inn at Quogue 262
	Lincklaen House 112
	Lowell 387
	Mansion Hill Inn 326
	Mayfair Hotel 358
	Old Drovers Inn 144
	Pierre 359
	Point 264
	Ram's Head Inn 32
	Rosewood Inn 76
	Sherwood Inn 119
	Waldorf-Astoria and Towers 363
	Westbury Hotel 357
PA	Duling-Kurtz House 40
	Four Seasons Hotel 405
	Gateway Lodge and Cabins 290
	Historic Smithton 237
	Inn at Turkey Hill 304
	Lincklaen House 112
	Rittenhouse 406
	Sherwood Inn 119
	Sweetwater Farm 240
VA	Boar's Head Inn and Sports Club 442
	Conyers House 24
	Hotel Strasburg 132
	Tides Inn 445
	Tides Lodge 447
	Willow Grove Plantation 55
WV	Pence Springs Hotel 56

No Smoking

DE	Towers 212
MD	Ann Street Bed and Breakfast 318
	Celie's Waterfront Bed & Breakfast 319
	Inn at Henderson's Wharf 322
	Wades Point Inn on the Bay 2
NJ	Abbey 158
	Captain Mey's Bed and Breakfast Inn 160
	Chestnut Hill on the Delaware 66
	Chimney Hill Farm 4
	Colvmns by the Sea 218
	Conover's Bay Head Inn Bed and Breakfast 163
	Henry Ludlam Inn 181
	John Wesley Inn 167
	Mainstay Inn 220
	Old Hunterdon House 68
	Queen Victoria 170
	Sea Crest by the Sea 172
	Whistling Swan Inn 70
NY	Asa Ransom House 103
	Bark Eater 280
	Blushing Rosé 182
	Centennial House 73
	Chequit Inn 111
	J. P. Morgan House Bed and Breakfast Inn 7
	J. P. Sill House 228
	Pig Hill Bed and Breakfast 75
	Plumbush 8
	Sagamore Lodge 145
	Sarah's Dream 78
	Rose Inn 231
	Taughannock Farms Inn 35
	Toad Hall 10
	Village Victorian Inn at Rhinebeck 81
	William Seward Inn 11
PA	Clearview Farm Bed and Breakfast 16
	Historic Smithton 237
	Inn at Centre Park 330
	Inn at Fordhook Farm 19
	Inn at Turkey Hill 304
	Sweetwater Farm 240
	Wedgwood Collection of Historic Inns 86
VA	Bailiwick Inn 243

Index

Best Places Report

We appreciate any information you can supply about the quality of the lodging. Detailed information about the building, furniture, service, food, and setting is most important. Describe as many rooms as you can, including living rooms, dining rooms, other common rooms, and of course bedrooms. A note about activities and nearby sights would be helpful. Tell us what category you think the place belongs in and why. Finally, how did you hear about the place, and how long have you been going there?

We will be happy to send you a free copy of the next edition of the book if we use your suggestion.

To: Chris Paddock
      Best Places to Stay in the Mid-Atlantic
      The Harvard Common Press
      535 Albany Street
      Boston, Massachusetts 02118

Name of hotel _____

Telephone _____

Address _____

_____ Zip _____

_____

Description _____

_____

_____

_____

_____

_____

_____

Your Name _____

Telephone _____

Address _____

_____ Zip _____

_____

Best Places Report

We appreciate any information you can supply about the quality of the lodging. Detailed information about the building, furniture, service, food, and setting is most important. Describe as many rooms as you can, including living rooms, dining rooms, other common rooms, and of course bedrooms. A note about activities and nearby sights would be helpful. Tell us what category you think the place belongs in and why. Finally, how did you hear about the place, and how long have you been going there?

We will be happy to send you a free copy of the next edition of the book if we use your suggestion.

To: Chris Paddock
     Best Places to Stay in the Mid-Atlantic
     The Harvard Common Press
     535 Albany Street
     Boston, Massachusetts 02118

Name of hotel _____

Telephone _____

Address _____

_____ Zip _____

_____

Description _____

_____

_____

_____

_____

_____

_____

Your Name _____

Telephone _____

Address _____

_____ Zip _____

_____

Best Places Report

We appreciate any information you can supply about the quality of the lodging. Detailed information about the building, furniture, service, food, and setting is most important. Describe as many rooms as you can, including living rooms, dining rooms, other common rooms, and of course bedrooms. A note about activities and nearby sights would be helpful. Tell us what category you think the place belongs in and why. Finally, how did you hear about the place, and how long have you been going there?

We will be happy to send you a free copy of the next edition of the book if we use your suggestion.

To: Chris Paddock
     Best Places to Stay in the Mid-Atlantic
     The Harvard Common Press
     535 Albany Street
     Boston, Massachusetts 02118

Name of hotel _____

Telephone _____

Address _____

_____ Zip _____

_____

Description _____

_____

_____

_____

_____

_____

Your Name _____

Telephone _____

Address _____

_____ Zip _____

_____

Best Places Report

We appreciate any information you can supply about the quality of the lodging. Detailed information about the building, furniture, service, food, and setting is most important. Describe as many rooms as you can, including living rooms, dining rooms, other common rooms, and of course bedrooms. A note about activities and nearby sights would be helpful. Tell us what category you think the place belongs in and why. Finally, how did you hear about the place, and how long have you been going there?

We will be happy to send you a free copy of the next edition of the book if we use your suggestion.

To: Chris Paddock
Best Places to Stay in the Mid-Atlantic
The Harvard Common Press
535 Albany Street
Boston, Massachusetts 02118

Name of hotel _____

Telephone _____

Address _____

_____ Zip _____

_____

Description _____

_____

_____

_____

_____

_____

_____

Your Name _____

Telephone _____

Address _____

_____ Zip _____

_____

Best Places Report

We appreciate any information you can supply about the quality of the lodging. Detailed information about the building, furniture, service, food, and setting is most important. Describe as many rooms as you can, including living rooms, dining rooms, other common rooms, and of course bedrooms. A note about activities and nearby sights would be helpful. Tell us what category you think the place belongs in and why. Finally, how did you hear about the place, and how long have you been going there?

We will be happy to send you a free copy of the next edition of the book if we use your suggestion.

To: Chris Paddock
     Best Places to Stay in the Mid-Atlantic
     The Harvard Common Press
     535 Albany Street
     Boston, Massachusetts 02118

Name of hotel _____

Telephone _____

Address _____

_____ Zip _____

_____

Description _____

_____

_____

_____

_____

_____

Your Name _____

Telephone _____

Address _____

_____ Zip _____

_____

Best Places Report

We appreciate any information you can supply about the quality of the lodging. Detailed information about the building, furniture, service, food, and setting is most important. Describe as many rooms as you can, including living rooms, dining rooms, other common rooms, and of course bedrooms. A note about activities and nearby sights would be helpful. Tell us what category you think the place belongs in and why. Finally, how did you hear about the place, and how long have you been going there?

We will be happy to send you a free copy of the next edition of the book if we use your suggestion.

To: Chris Paddock
      Best Places to Stay in the Mid-Atlantic
      The Harvard Common Press
      535 Albany Street
      Boston, Massachusetts 02118

Name of hotel _____

Telephone _____

Address _____

_____ Zip _____

Description _____

_____

_____

_____

_____

_____

_____

_____

Your Name _____

Telephone _____

Address _____

_____ Zip _____